3 Ways to Master the Accounting Cycle for Course Success.

Practice: An open-access online practice environment enables you to master chapter material. Selected end-of-chapter problems (marked with an icon) are available for all learning objectives in Chapters 1-3. The problems: (a) are algorithmic, giving you a chance to practice until you have mastered the material, (b) provide immediate feedback, giving you a chance to see how well you are doing and/or where you need practice, and (c) mirror those in the book, giving you a chance to practice before doing "the real thing."

Remember: A unique **Accounting Cycle Pocket Guide** is included in the textbook following Chapter 2. It is a tear-out, 4-color, 3-fold guide that illustrates the key steps in the accounting cycle. You can use it as a reference as you work through the remainder of the course.

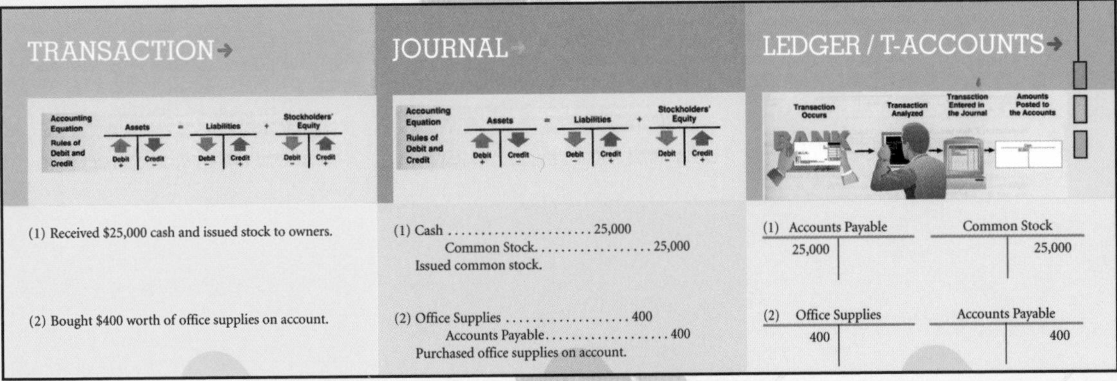

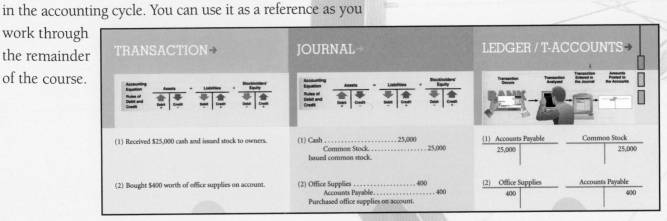

Where to find resources: www.prenhall.com/harrison

Financial
Accounting

Financial Accounting

SIXTH EDITION

Walter T. Harrison Jr.

Baylor University

Charles T. Horngren

Stanford University

Upper Saddle River, NJ 07458

Library of Congress Cataloging-in-Publication Data

Harrison, Walter T.

Financial accounting/Walter T. Harrison, Jr., Charles T. Horngren. — 6th ed.

p. cm.

Includes bibliographical references and index.

ISBN 0-13-149945-9

1. Accounting. I. Horngren, Charles T. II. Title.

HF5635.H333 2005

657—dc22 2004065978

Senior Acquisitions Editor: Wendy Craven
VP/Editorial Director: Jeff Shelstad
VP/Director of Development: Steve Deitmer
Developmental Editor: Jeannine Ciliotta
Project Manager (Editorial): Kerri Tomasso
Editorial Assistant: Joanna Doxey
Media Project Manager: Caroline Kasterine
Marketing Assistant: Tina Panagiotou
Managing Editor (Production): Cynthia Regan
Production Editor: Carol Samet
Permissions Supervisor: Charles Morris
Production Manager: Arnold Vila
Design Manager: Maria Lange
Art Director: Kevin Kall
Interior Design: MLM design/ BLACK DIAMOND GRAPHICS
Cover Design: Kevin Kall/Carol Samet
Cover Illustration/Photo: IndexStock
Illustrator (Interior): GGS Book Services, Atlantic Highlands
Director, Image Resource Center: Melinda Reo
Manager, Rights and Permissions: Zina Arabia
Manager: Visual Research: Beth Brenzel
Manager, Cover Visual Research & Permissions: Karen Sanatar
Image Permission Coordinator: Craig A. Jones
Manager, Multimedia Production: Christy Mahon
Composition/Full-Service Project Management: GGS Book Services, Atlantic Highlands
Printer/Binder: RRDonnelley-Willard
Typeface: 11/13.5 Berkeley Book

Credits and acknowledgments borrowed from other sources and reproduced, with permission, in this textbook appear on appropriate page within text. Chapter 1: © 2004 Digital Vision, 3; PhotoEdit, 7; Chapter 2: © 2004 Digital Vision, 49; Getty Images Inc./PhotoDisc, 53; Chapter 3: EyeWire Collection/Getty Images/Photodisc, 105; PhotoEdit, 107; Chapter 4: Getty Images, Inc/Liaison, 181; Chapter 5: ©Photodisc/ Getty Images, 218; Photolibrary.Com, 232; Chapter 6: © 2004 Digital Vision, 262; UNOVA, Inc., 282; Chapter 7: © 2004 Digital Vision, 315; AP Wide World Photos, 320; Chapter 8: © 2004 Digital Vision, 363; Getty Images, Inc/Liaison, 370; Chapter 9: Charles Miller/AP Wide World Photos, 417; AP Wide World Photos, 426; Chapter 10: Permanent Now/Digital Vision Ltd., 469; AP Wide World Photos, 475; Chapter 11: Photolibrary.Com, 511; eBay Inc., 519; Chapter 12: © 2004 Digital Vision, 547; Getty Images Inc./Image Bank, 549; Chapter 13: AP Wide World Photos, 607; Getty Images, Inc./Photodisc, 628.

Pearson Education LTD.
Pearson Education Singapore, Pte. Ltd
Pearson Education, Canada, Ltd
Pearson Education–Japan
Pearson Education Australia PTY, Limited
Pearson Education North Asia Ltd
Pearson Educación de Mexico, S.A. de C.V.
Pearson Education Malaysia, Pte. Ltd

10 9 8 7 6 5 4 3 2
ISBN 0-13-149945-9

For our wives,

Nancy and Joan

Brief Contents

Contents

Chapter 7

Chapter 8

Chapter 9

Chapter 10

Preface

The Accounting Cycle: Key To Success

Note to the Instructor: This financial accounting course builds on the first three chapters, which focus on accounting fundamentals and the accounting cycle. You've told us that mastering these chapters will guarantee your students' success as they move through the course. For this reason, *Financial Accounting, 6th edition* is focused on students' success in learning accounting basics and mastering the mechanics so that they are motivated to excel throughout the course.

Review the inside front cover to see exactly what we are offering your students.

New In-Chapter Learning Tools

- *Accounting Alerts!* Boxes in each chapter focus on issues that can affect accounting decisions or on pitfalls to watch out for.
- *Taking Action:* Immediately after they learn a concept, students are asked to make a business decision. Their ability to make this decision with the information provided gives them an immediate application of the concept and allows them to check their understanding of the material.
- *Making Managerial Decisions:* This feature presents a specific situation that needs a decision, along with the accounting guidelines to use in making the decision, in an easy-to-use table format.
- *Focus on Financials: YUM! Brands.* Yum! Brands, Inc. financial statements are used in case exercises at the end of each chapter. Selected excerpts from YUM! statements also appear throughout the text where appropriate to assist learning. The full statements appear in Appendix A.
- *Focus on Analysis: Pier 1 Imports.* Pier 1 Imports financial statements are used in an additional case exercise focused on analysis that appears at the end of each chapter. The full statements appear in Appendix B.

Learning Approach: Focus On Practice and Performance

Student success and "practice, practice, practice," go hand in hand. That's why we increased quizzing opportunities for you and self-guided practice for your students.

In-Text Practice Material

- **Chapter Review Quiz:** At the end of chapter, these multiple-choice questions include answers for quick self-assessment.
- **Practice Quiz:** Multiple-choice questions in the end-of-chapter assignments section have answers in the Check Figures appendix at the end of the book.

Practice Quiz

Test your understanding of the financial statements by answering the following questions. Select the best choice from among the possible answers given.

PQ1-1 The *primary* objective of financial reporting is to provide information

a. To the federal government.
b. About the profitability of the enterprise.
c. On the cash flows of the company.
d. Useful for making investment and credit decisions.

PQ1-2 Which type of business organization provides the least amount of protection for bankers and other creditors of the company?

a. Corporation
b. Partnership
c. Proprietorship
d. Both b and c

PQ1-3 Assets are usually reported at their

a. Appraised value
b. Historical cost
c. Current market value
d. None of the above

Online Practice and Homework Material

- **Practice Material:** An open-access online practice environment enables students to master chapter material. Selected end-of-chapter problems are available for all learning objectives in Chapters 1-3. The problems (a) are algorithmic, giving students a chance to practice until they have mastery; (b) provide immediate feedback, giving students a chance to see how well they are doing right away; (c) mirror those in the book, giving students a chance to practice before doing "the real thing."
- **Homework and Quiz Material: Prentice Hall Grade Assist (PHGA)**

PHGA is an online homework and quizzing environment that allows instructors to completely customize homework and quiz options for their classes.

Selected end-of-chapter (even-numbered) exercises and (A) problems from the text are available. Instructors can post assignments and receive grades. All questions are algorithmically generated so each student session offers different problems and answers while providing immediate feedback and scoring for instructors and their students.

Special Section for Current Users

Thank you for your continued use of Harrison Financial Accounting in your classroom. To ease your transition, here are highlights of chapter changes for the 6th edition.

Chapter 1. The Financial Statements

New feature company for the book, YUM! Brands
New Accounting Alert: We Need an Audit to Validate the Financial Statements
Accounting Cycle Tutorial

Chapter 2. Transaction Analysis

New chapter opener about Apple Computer
New Accounting Alert: Single-Entry Accounting Doesn't Cut It
New section on Transaction Analysis
New formatting of exhibits for better pedagogy
Streamlined coverage of journalizing transactions
Accounting Cycle Tutorial

Chapter 3. Using Accrual Accounting to Measure Income

New chapter opener on Callaway Golf Company
New Accounting Alert: Cash Basis Accounting Doesn't Cut It, Either
New exhibit on How Transactions Affect the Ratios
Accounting Cycle Tutorial

Chapter 4. Internal Control & Cash

New chapter opener on Merrill Lynch & Co.
New section on the Sarbanes-Oxley Act
New Accounting Alert: Are Outside Auditors Really Independent?
New Accounting Alert: Three Faces of Internal Control
Streamlined coverage and new exhibit for Internal Control over Cash Receipts
Streamlined coverage and new exhibit for Internal Control over Cash Payments

Chapter 5. Short-Term Investments & Receivables

New chapter opener on Ford Motor Company
New "road-map" exhibit for classifying investments
Expanded coverage of realized gain on sale of investments
Revamped section on Accounting for Uncollectible Receivables
New Accounting Alert: Is That Investment Really a Current Asset?
New Accounting Alert: Shifting Sales into the Current Period

Chapter 6. Merchandise Inventory & Cost of Goods Sold

New chapter opener on Pier 1 Imports
Revamped chapter: Clearer distinction between sale price and cost of a unit of inventory
Cost of Goods Sold Model moved to the end of the chapter
New coverage of Perpetual Inventory System
New diagrams to illustrate cost flows under FIFO, LIFO, and Average Costing
New coverage of FIFO, LIFO, and Average Costing using T-accounts to replace old Exhibit 6-6
Deleted section on Materiality
New illustration of inventory write-down under lower of cost or market
New exhibit comparing Pier 1 Imports, May Co. Department Stores, and Wal-Mart
New Accounting Alert: Cooking the Books to Increase Reported Income

Chapter 7. Plant Assets, Natural Resources & Intangibles

New chapter opener on eBay and United Parcel Service (UPS)
New Accounting Alert: Is That Cost Really an Asset?

Chapter 8. Current & Long-Term Liabilities

New chapter opener comparing AMR (American Airlines) and UAL (United Airlines)
New coverage of unearned revenue
New Accounting Alert: Are All Your Liabilities Reported on the Balance Sheet?

Chapter 9. Stockholders' Equity
New chapter opener on IHOP (International House of Pancakes)
New summary of the components of stockholders' equity on the balance sheet
New Accounting Alert: Stock Issuance for Other Than Cash

Chapter 10. Long-Term Investments & International Operations
New chapter opener on General Electric
New exhibit summarizing the accounting rules for long-term investments
New Accounting Alert: When Should We Sell That Investment in HP (Hewlett Packard) Stock?

Chapter 11. Income Statement & Statement of Stockholders' Equity
New chapter opener on Best Buy
New Accounting Alert: Watch Out for Voluntary Accounting Changes that Increase Reported Income
New Accounting Alert: Beware of Pro Forma Earnings
Deleted sections: Using the P/E Ratio and Restrictions on Retained Earnings

Chapter 12. Statement of Cash Flows
New Accounting Alert: Telltale Signs of Financial Difficulty

Chapter 13. Financial Statement Analysis
Return to feature company, YUM! Brands, for evaluation and analysis
New Stop & Think section focused on YUM! Brands
Streamlined Common Size Statements section
Streamlined Benchmarking section
New Accounting Alert: The Limitations of Ratio Analysis
New Accounting Alert: Red Flags in Financial Statement Analysis

Teaching And Learning Support

For Instructors

At a Glance Supplements Grid

	Instructor's Manual	Test Item File	Instructor Solutions Manual	Interactive Solution PowerPoints	PH Accounting Excel Tips	PH Grade Assist	One Key	Companion Website	Accounting Cycle Tutorial
Print	√	√	√		√				
Online	√	√	√	√	√	√	√	√	X
IRCD	√	√	√	√					

Instructor's Resource Center www.prenhall.com/accounting This password-protected site is accessible from the catalog page for *Financial Accounting, 6e* and hosts the following resources:

- **New! Interactive Solution PowerPoints**, by Robert Bauman: These Powerpoints provide instructors with tools for presenting one worked-out electronic solution for an end-of-chapter exercise based on each chapter learning objective. They simplify classroom preparation by providing teaching and learning tips.
- Instructor's Manual
- Test Item File

- TestGen EQ for PC
- Image Library: Access to most of the images and illustrations featured in the text.
- Peachtree and QuickBooks Computer Workshops (Software NOT included): These Workshops (beginning at the end of Chapter 2) enable instructors to integrate the latest release of Peachtree and/or QuickBooks Software in order to solve specific accounting problems in a real-world company setting.
- General Ledger and Excel Spreadsheet Templates: Use these templates to complete homework assignments. These problems are designated by an icon in the text.
- Excel Application Problems: These problems show when, why, and how people use the accounting guidelines in order to make business decisions. Students can apply the Making Managerial Decisions guidelines to a realistic situation and use the power of Excel to determine a solution.
- Essentials of Excel, by Drs. L. Murphy Smith and Katherine T. Smith: This section introduces students to the fundamental tools and techniques available in Microsoft Excel. Students will learn through experience by following directions and creating the example worksheets shown.
- **Solutions Manual**, by Tom Harrison (ISBN: 0-13-149969-6): This manual contains the fully worked-out and accuracy-checked solutions for every question, exercise, and problem in the text.

Instructor's Manual by Angela Sandberg, Jacksonville State University (ISBN: 0-13-149959-9): Each chapter of this comprehensive resource consists of a list of the student learning objectives, a narrative overview of main topics, an outline with teaching tips, a suggested assignment grid for all end-of-chapter questions, problems, and exercises, and an integration grid that contains the list of exercises and problems available in PH Grade Assist, Microsoft Excel, and General Ledger.

Test Item File by Anne Wessley, St. Louis Community College (ISBN: 0-13-149960-2): This section features over 1,800 questions written specifically for the 6th edition. Multiple-choice, true/false, conceptual and quantitative questions, critical thinking problems, and exercises are organized by level of difficulty and include the corresponding learning objective number.

Instructor's Resource CD (ISBN 0-13-149961-0): This CD-ROM now has a new interface and searchable database. It contains all the supplements that are hosted on our online Instructor's Resource Center, including all the book line art. The CD-ROM also provides the **NEW** interactive Solution PowerPoints that provide an instructor with one worked-out electronic solution for an end-of-chapter exercise based on each chapter learning objective for in-class discussion and student learning and comprehension.

Solutions Transparencies (ISBN: 0-13-149962-9): Every page of the solutions manual has been reproduced in acetate form for use on an overhead projector.

PH Accounting Excel Tips (ISBN: 0-13-149965): A laminated resource useful for every B-School course, these tips cover basic tasks, navigation keys, shortcuts, productivity tips, and new features of Microsoft Excel 2003. Ask your local representative about FREE Value Pack options.

PHGA-Instructor Access Card (ISBN: 0-13-149951-3): This card is available for instructors to set up PH Grade Assist, an online homework assessment system available through our OneKey.

OneKey CourseCompass, WebCT and BlackBoard for Financial Accounting Prentice Hall's OneKey site is all that instructors and students need for anytime online access to interactive materials that enhance this text.

OneKey WebCT, Financial Accounting by Walter T. Harrison © 2006 (ISBN: 0-13-149966-1), Electronic Book, Estimated Publication 07/01/2005: Prentice Hall's OneKey site is all instructors and students need for anytime online access to interactive materials that enhance this text. Premium Resources that are hosted on OneKey include: PH Grade Assist and Interactive Solution PowerPoints.

OneKey BlackBoard, Financial Accounting by Walter T. Harrison © 2006 (ISBN 0-13-149967-X), Electronic Book, Estimated Publication 07/01/2005: Prentice Hall's OneKey site is all instructors and students need for anytime online access to interactive materials that enhance this text. Premium Resources that are hosted on OneKey include: PH Grade Assist and Interactive Solution PowerPoints.

For Students

MASTERING THE ACCOUNTING CYCLE

http://www.prenhall.com/harrison

Open Access (no registration or password needed) Companion Website that provides you with:

- Accounting Cycle Tutorial: For practice on material from Chapters 1–3
- Online Practice Environment with algorithmic questions for Chapters 1–3
- Accounting Cycle Pocket Guide: Reference tool that walks you through each step of the accounting cycle
- Interactive study guide for all chapters of the book

OneKey CourseCompass, Student Access Kit, Financial Accounting
ISBN: 0-13-149955-6

OneKey WebCT, Student Access Kit, Financial Accounting
ISBN: 0-13-149957-2

OneKey BlackBoard, Student Access Kit, Financial Accounting
ISBN: 0-13-149958-0

PHGA-Student Access Card
ISBN: 0-13-149952-1

Note: All Mastering the Accounting Cycle material can be found within OneKey courses previously listed.

PRINT STUDY AIDS

Study Guide by Alan Campbell, Saint Leo University Center for Online Learning (ISBN: 0-13-149953-X): This chapter-by-chapter learning aid helps you learn financial accounting and get the maximum benefit from study time. Each chapter contains a Chapter Overview and Review, a Featured Exercise that covers all of the most important chapter material, and Review Questions and Exercises with Solutions that test your understanding of the material.

Working Papers by L. Murphy Smith, Texas A&M University and Katherine T. Smith (ISBN: 0-13-149950-5): Available in traditional printed format and also online (in OneKey) as downloadable Excel files.

Acknowledgments

In revising this edition of *Financial Accounting*, we had the help of instructors from across the country who have participated in online surveys, chapter reviews, and focus groups. Their comments and suggestions for both the text and the supplements have been a great help in planning and carrying out the revision, and we thank them for their contributions.

Online Reviewers

Lucille Berry, Webster University, MO
Patrick Bouker, North Seattle Community College
Michael Broihahn, Barry University, FL
Kam Chan, Pace University
Hong Chen, Northeastern Illinois University
Charles Coate, St. Bonaventure University, NY
Bryan Church, Georgia Tech at Atlanta
Terrie Gehman, Elizabethtown College, PA
Brian Green, University of Michigan at Dearborn
Chao-Shin Liu, Notre Dame
Herb Martin, Hope College, MI
Bruce Maule, College of San Mateo
Michelle McEacharn, University of Louisiana at Monroe
Bettye Rogers-Desselle, Prairie View A&M University, TX
Norlin Rueschhoff, Notre Dame
William Schmul, Notre Dame
Arnie Schnieder, Georgia Tech at Atlanta
J. B. Stroud, Nicholls State Univesity, LA
Bruce Wampler, Louisiana State University, Shreveport
Myung Yoon, Northeastern Illinois University
Lin Zeng, Northeastern Illinois University

Focus Group Participants

Ellen D. Cook, University of Louisiana at Lafayette
Theodore D. Morrison III, Wingate University, NC
Alvin Gerald Smith, University of Northern Iowa
Carolyn R. Stokes, Frances Marion University, SC
Suzanne Ward, University of Louisiana at Lafayette

Chapter Reviewers

Kim Anderson, Indiana University of Pennsylvania
Peg Beresewski, Robert Morris College, IL
Helen Brubeck, San Jose State University, CA

Mark Camma, Atlantic Cape Community College, NJ
Freddy Choo, San Francisco State University, CA
Laurie Dahlin, Worcester State College, MA
Ronald Guidry, University of Louisiana at Monroe
Ellen Landgraf, Loyola University, Chicago
Nick McGaughey, San Jose State University, CA
Mark Miller, University of San Francisco, CA
Craig Reeder, Florida A&M University
Brian Stanko, Loyola University, Chicago
Marcia Veit, University of Central Florida
Ronald Woan, Indiana University of Pennsylvania

Online Supplement Reviewers

Shawn Abbott, College of the Siskiyous, CA
Sol Ahiarah, SUNY College at Buffalo (Buffalo State)
M. J. Albin, University of Southern Mississippi
Gary Ames, Brigham Young University, Idaho
Walter Austin, Mercer University, Macon GA
Brad Badertscher, University of Iowa
Sandra Bailey, Oregon Institute of Technology
Barbara A. Beltrand, Metropolitan State University, MN
Jerry Bennett, University of South Carolina-Spartanburg
John Bildersee, New York University, Stern School
Candace Blankenship, Belmont University, TN
Charlie Bokemeier, Michigan State University
Scott Boylan, Washington and Lee University, VA
Robert Braun, Southeastern Louisiana University
Linda Bressler, University of Houston Downtown
Carol Brown, Oregon State University
Marcus Butler, University of Rochester, NY
Kay Carnes, Gonzaga University, WA
Brian Carpenter, University of Scranton, PA
Sandra Cereola, James Madison University, VA
Hong Chen, Northeastern Illinois University
Shifei Chung, Rowan University, NJ
Bryan Church, Georgia Tech
Charles Christy, Delaware Tech and Community College, Stanton Campus
Corolyn Clark, Saint Joseph's University, PA
Dianne Conry, University of California State College Extension-Cupertino
John Coulter, Western New England College
Donald Curfman, McHenry County College, IL
Alan Czyzewski, Indiana State University
Bonita Daly, University of Southern Maine
Patricia Derrick, George Washington University
Charles Dick, Miami University
Barbara Doughty, New Hampshire Community Technical College
Carol Dutton, South Florida Community College
James Emig, Villanova University, PA
Ellen Engel, University of Chicago
Alan Falcon, Loyola Marymount University, CA

Janet Farler, Pima Community College, AZ
Andrew Felo, Penn State Great Valley
Ken Ferris, Thunderbird College, AZ
Lou Fowler, Missouri Western State College
Lucille Genduso, Nova Southeastern University, FL
Frank Gersich, Monmouth College, IL
Bradley Gillespie, Saddleback College, CA
Brian Green, University of Michigan-Dearborn
Konrad Gunderson, Missouri Western State College
William Hahn, Southeastern College, FL
Jack Hall, Western Kentucky University
Gloria Halpern, Montgomery College, MD
Kenneth Hart, Brigham Young University, Idaho
Al Hartgraves, Emory University
Thomas Hayes, University of North Texas
Larry Hegstad, Pacific Lutheran University, WA
Candy Heino, Anoka-Ramsey Community College, MN
Anit Hope, Tarrant County College, TX
Thomas Huse, Boston College
Fred R. Jex, Macomb Community College, MI
Beth Kern, Indiana University, South Bend
Hans E. Klein, Babson College, MA
Willem Koole, North Carolina State University
Emil Koren, Hillsborough Community College, FL
Dennis Kovach, Community College of Allegheny County—North Campus
Ellen Landgraf, Loyola University Chicago
Howard Lawrence, Christian Brothers University, TN
Barry Leffkov, Regis College, MA
Chao Liu, Notre Dame University
Barbara Lougee, University of California, Irvine
Heidemarie Lundblad, California State University, Northridge
Anna Lusher, West Liberty State College, WV
Harriet Maccracken, Arizona State University
Carol Mannino, Milwaukee School of Engineering
Aziz Martinez, Harvard University, Harvard Business School
Cathleen Miller, University of Michigan–Flint
Frank Mioni, Madonna University, MI
Bruce L. Oliver, Rochester Institute of Technology
Charles Pedersen, Quinsigamond Community College, MA
George Plesko, Massachusetts Institute of Technology
David Plumlee, University of Utah
Gregory Prescott, University of South Alabama
Craig Reeder, Florida A&M University
Darren Roulstone, University of Chicago
Angela Sandberg, Jacksonville State University, AL
George Sanders, Western Washington University, WA
Betty Saunders, University of North Florida
Arnie Schneider, Georgia Tech
Gim Seow, University of Connecticut
Itzhak Sharav, CUNY-Lehman Graduate School of Business

Gerald Smith, University of Northern Iowa
James Smith, Community College of Philadelphia
Beverly Soriano, Framingham State College, MA
J. B. Stroud, Nicholls State University, LA
Al Taccone, Cuyamaca College, CA
Diane Tanner, University of North Florida
Howard Toole, San Diego State University
Bruce Wampler, Louisiana State University, Shreveport
Frederick Weis, Claremont McKenna College, CA
Frederick Weiss, Virginia Wesleyan College
Allen Wright, Hillsborough Community College, FL
Tony Zordan, University of St. Francis, IL

Supplement Authors and Preparers

Excel templates: Al Fisher, Community College of Southern Nevada
General Ledger templates: Lanny Nelms, The Landor Group
Instructor's Manual: Angela Sandberg, Jacksonville State University
Interactive Powerpoints: Robert Bauman, Emeritus Professor of Accounting; Allan Hancock Joint Community College
PHGA: Larry Kallio, University of Minnesota at Mankato
Solutions Manual preparer: Diane Colwyn
Study Guide: Alan Campbell, Saint Leo University Center for Online Learning
Test Item File: Anne Wessley, St. Louis Community College
Working Papers, Essentials of Excel: Dr. L. Murphy Smith, Texas A&M University; Dr. Katherine T. Smith
Videos: Beverly Amer, Northern Arizona University; Lanny Nelms, The Landor Group

Prologue

ACCOUNTING CAREERS: MUCH MORE THAN COUNTING THINGS

What kind of career can you have in accounting? Almost any kind you want. A career in accounting lets you use your analytic skills in a variety of ways, and it brings both monetary and personal rewards. According to the 2002 Jobs Rated Almanac, "accountant" was the fifth best job in terms of low stress, high compensation, lots of autonomy, and tremendous hiring demand.[1]

Look at what these accountants do:

- Jeffrey S. Sallet is a CPA at the FBI who investigates the financial side of criminal activities. He conducts interviews, surveillance, and crime scene investigations as well as reviewing financial documents and testifying in court. "I have conducted numerous organized crime, public corruption and terrorism investigations," Sallet says. "While conducting these investigations I have applied traditional investigative techniques and forensic accounting. My efforts have resulted in the conviction of members and associates of Organized Crime and Union Officials."[2]
- Alan Friedman loves music. He plays guitar in a band and knows the industry inside and out. As a CPA, he helps music store retailers, musicians, and independent recording labels with accounting and tax services. "My clients appreciate the fact that we are intimately familiar with the product they sell, the suppliers they deal with and the ever-changing condition of the music retailing marketplace," Friedman says. There are 9,000 music retailers in the United States, and while most of them already have a CPA, chances are that they do not have one who's an expert in the music business. Friedman found his niche by combining his hobby with his work.[3]
- Jane Cozzarelli, CPA, is vice president of internal audit at Batelle Memorial Institute, a $1 billion research and development enterprise. She helps Battelle evaluate the risks of multi-million-dollar deals such as joint ventures and acquisitions. "By measuring your risks, you can direct capital to them more efficiently. You also are better able to understand the upside and downside of undertaking a risk," Jane says.[4]
- Regine Metellus, CPA, is the CFO for the Germantown Settlement, a charity that empowers over 195,000 elderly and low-to-moderate income residents in Philadelphia. "Germantown needed someone to organize their records and put in place policies and procedures and help improve the financial reporting," Regine says. By making the charity's financial operations more efficient, she helps Germantown Settlement put more money back into the community and truly "make a difference."[5]
- After doing auditing work at KPMG and serving as a controller for a venture-capital-backed firm, David Kupferman started his own CPA practice. He specializes in serving high-net-worth individuals and businesses looking for sound

advice along with technology ventures. Day to day, Kupferman provides taxation advice, litigation support, business valuation, complex business modeling, and CFO-like financial consulting for early stage companies. He has a particular interest in bringing foreign technology companies to the United States and works with clients from Australia, Spain, Hungary, England, France, Byelorussia, Singapore, and Japan.[6]

- Mark Denton, an accountant at NASA's Marshall Space Flight Center, is helping to implement NASA's Core Financial Project. The project is an agencywide effort to provide timely, consistent, and reliable financial information to managers making program budget decisions. "This project will be a good thing, enabling NASA to operate more like a business," Denton says. "I love working with money," he adds, "but, more importantly, I love working with people."[7]

And then there is the opportunity for flexible work arrangements:

"I'm probably one of the first people who stayed in public accounting because of quality-of-life advantages," says Eileen Garvey, an audit partner at Ernst & Young in New York. Garvey works a 3-day-a-week schedule. The mother of two, she made partner as a part-timer. Flexibility works for men, too: Carl Moilienkamp, a manager with a firm in Chicago, took a summer leave to pursue his other career as a chef.

Where Accountants Work

Where can you work as an accountant? There are four kinds of employers.

Public Practice

You can work for a public accounting firm, which could be a large international firm such as one of the Big Four where Eileen Garvey works, or a small CPA firm such as Alan Friedman's. Within the CPA firm, you can specialize in areas such as tax, audit, or consulting. In this capacity, you'll be serving as an external accountant to many different clients. Most CPAs start their career at a large CPA firm. From there, they can find themselves in a variety of situations:

- Josh Young's first consulting engagement found him on the site of the Northridge earthquake outside Los Angeles. One of his clients was a supermarket chain with 150 damaged stores. Young needed to visit the actual site to determine how much damage had occurred to help prepare the insurance claims.

- Jennifer Tufer is a Deloitte & Touche senior manager on assignment in Moscow. As she looks through her incoming mail, she finds a request from a U.S. manufacturer interested in expanding into Russia. "The company wants to know how they would be taxed," she says.

The highest career level in a CPA firm is partner—becoming a part owner of the firm. Only 2% to 3% of accountants in a Big Four CPA firm make partner.[8]

Deloitte & Touche	Employees: 29,000	Offices: 97
Ernst & Young	Employees: 103,000	Offices: 670
KPMG	Employees: 100,000	Offices: 103
PricewaterhouseCoopers	Employees: 122,000	Countries Served: 139

Managerial Accounting

Instead of working for a wide variety of clients, you can work within one corporation or nonprofit enterprise. Your role within the organization is to analyze financial information and communicate that information to managers, who use it to plot strategy and make decisions. You may be called upon to make recommendations on how best to allocate corporate resources or improve financial performance. For example, you might do a cost-benefit analysis to help management decide whether to acquire a company or build a factory; or you might describe the financial implications of choosing one strategy over another. You might work in areas such as internal auditing, financial management, financial reporting, treasury management, and tax planning. The highest position in management accounting is the CFO position, with some CFOs rising all the way to the top to become CEOs.

Phil Knight, CEO of Nike, and Arthur Blank, cofounder of Home Depot, are CPAs.

Government

You can also work as an accountant for the government, be it at the federal, state, or local level. Like your counterparts in public accounting and business, your role as an accountant in government includes responsibilities in the areas of auditing, financial reporting, and management accounting. You'll evaluate how government agencies are being run and advise decision makers in allocating resources to promote efficiency. You might find yourself working for the IRS, the Securities and Exchange Commission, the Department of Treasury, or even the White House.

WORKING FOR THE GAO

Government Accountability Office (GAO)—formerly called the General Accounting Office—is an agency that works for Congress and the American people. Congress asks GAO to study federal government programs and expenditures. GAO studies how the federal government spends taxpayer dollars and advises Congress and the heads of executive agencies (such as the Environmental Protection Agency, Department of Defense, and Health and Human Services) about ways to make government more effective and responsive. GAO evaluates federal programs, audits federal expenditures, and issues legal opinions.

Within the GAO, you can work in an area such as health care. Much of this work focuses on the ability of these federal programs to provide access to quality care while paying appropriately for that care. Accountants in health care also examine the activities of federal public health agencies, including the National Institutes of Health, the Food and Drug Administration, and the Centers for Disease Control and Prevention. They examine not only the achievement of program goals but also the management, information systems, human capital, and financial operations of these agencies.

Education

Finally, you can work at a college or university or a professional school of accountancy, advancing the thought and theory of accounting and teaching future generations of new accountants. On the research side of education, you might study how companies use or misuse accounting to further their goals, or you might develop new ways of categorizing financial flows, or study accounting practices in different countries. You then publish your ideas in journal articles and books and present them to your colleagues at meetings around the world. On the education side, you can help others learn about accounting and give them the tools they need to be their best.

Did you know that 15% of FBI new hires in 2004 were CPAs?[9] In fact, 1,400 of the FBI's special agents are accountants, and the number 3 man at the FBI, Assistant Director Thomas Pickard, is a CPA.[10]

CPA: THREE LETTERS THAT SPEAK VOLUMES

When employers see the CPA designation, they know what to expect about your education, knowledge, abilities, and personal attributes. They value your analytic skills and extensive training. Your CPA credential gives you a distinct advantage in the job market and instant credibility and respect in the workplace. It's a plus when dealing with other professionals such as bankers, attorneys, auditors, and federal regulators. In addition, your colleagues in private industry tend to defer to you when dealing with complex business matters, particularly those involving financial management.[11]

The Hottest Growth Areas in Accounting

Recent legislation, such as the Sarbanes-Oxley Act of 2002, has brought rising demand for accountants of all kinds. In addition to strong overall demand, certain areas of accounting are especially hot.[12]

Sustainability Reporting

Sustainability reporting involves reporting on an organization's performance with respect to health, safety, and environmental (HSE) issues. As businesses take a greater interest in environmental issues, CPAs are getting involved in reporting on such matters as employee health, on-the-job accident rates, emissions of certain pollutants, spills, volumes of waste generated, and initiatives to reduce and minimize such incidents and releases. Utilities, manufacturers, and chemical companies are particularly affected by environmental issues. As a result, they turn to CPAs to set up a preventive system to ensure compliance and avoid future claims or disputes or to provide assistance once legal implications have arisen.

Corporate social responsibility reporting is similar to HSE reporting but with a broadened emphasis on social matters such as ethical labor practices, training, education, and diversity of workforce and corporate philanthropic initiatives. Here's a sampling of companies across industries that provide corporate social responsibility reports:

Company	Primary Industry
Anheuser-Busch	Beverages, theme parks
AT&T	Telecommunications
Bristol-Myers Squibb	Pharmaceuticals
Chiquita Brands	Agribusiness
Conoco	Energy
Dow Chemical	Chemicals
General Motors	Vehicle manufacture
Intel	Microprocessors
Johnson & Johnson	Health-care products and services
McDonald's	Restaurants
Mead	Forest products
Nike	Apparel
PepsiCo	Consumer products
Procter & Gamble	Consumer products
University of Florida	Academic institution

Source: AICPA

Assurance Services

Assurance services are services provided by a CPA that improve the quality of information, or its context, for decision makers. Such information can be financial or nonfinancial; it can be about past events or about ongoing processes or systems. This broad concept includes audit and attestation services and is distinct from consulting because it focuses primarily on improving information rather than on providing advice or installing systems. You can use your analytical and information-processing expertise by providing assurance services in areas ranging from electronic commerce to elder care, comprehensive risk assessment, business valuations, entity performance measurement, and information systems quality assessment.

Information Technology Services

Companies can't compete effectively if their information technology systems don't have the power or flexibility to perform essential functions. Companies need accountants with strong computer skills who can design and implement advanced systems to fit a company's specific needs and to find ways to protect and insulate data. CPAs skilled in software research and development (including multimedia technology) are also highly valued.

International Accounting

Globalization means that cross-border transactions are becoming commonplace. Countries in Eastern Europe and Latin America, which previously had closed economies, are opening up and doing business with new trading partners. The passage of the North American Free Trade Agreement (NAFTA) and the General Agreement on Tariffs and Trade (GATT) facilitates trade, and the economic growth in areas such as the Pacific Rim further brings greater volumes of trade and financial flows. Organizations need accountants who understand international trade rules, accords, and laws; cross-border merger and acquisition issues; and foreign business customs, languages, cultures, and procedures.

Forensic Accounting

Forensic accounting is in growing demand after scandals such as the collapse of Enron. Forensic accountants look at a company's financial records for evidence of criminal activity. This could be anything from securities fraud to overvaluation of inventory to money laundering and improper capitalization of expenses. Their work is becoming so well known that forensic accountants are appearing in mainstream novels. In *The Devil's Banker* by best-selling author Christopher Reich, a spy teams up with a forensic accountant to chase down a terrorist ring.

So, whether you seek

- a steady career or a life of international adventure
- a home in a single organization or exposure to the needs of an ever-changing mix of clients
- the personal satisfaction of work for a nonprofit or the financial success in a hot new company

Accounting has a career for you. Every organization, from the smallest mom-and-pop music retailer to the biggest government in the world, needs accountants to help manage its resources. Global trade demands accountability, and ever-more complex tax laws mean an ever-increasing need for the skills and services of accountants.

Endnotes

[1]Alba, Jason, and Manisha Bathija. *Vault Career Guide to Accounting.* (New York: Vault, 2002).
[2]CPA Track. Sponsored by Massachusetts Society of Certified Public Accountants, Inc. http://www.cpatrack.com/cool_cpas/.
[3]http://www.startheregoplaces.com.
[4]Banham, Russ. "Enterprising Views of Risk Management," *Journal of Accountancy*, 197, no. 6 (June 2004): 65–72.
[5]http://www.startheregoplaces.com.
[6]Kahan, Stuart. "Capitalizing on CFO Experiences," *The Practical Accountant*, 37, no. 2 (February 2004): 42–44.
[7]"NASA Accountant," *Paraplegia News*, 58, no. 1 (January 2004): 19(1).
[8]www.careers-in-accounting.com.
[9]*CPA Letter*, January 2004.
[10]Alba, Jason, and Manisha Bathija. *Vault Career Guide to Accounting* (New York: Vault, 2002).
[11]http://www.startheregoplaces.com/news/news_half5.asp.
[12]AICPA, the American Institute of Certified Public Accountants, www.aicpa.org.

Financial Accounting

spotlight

YUM! BRANDS

YUM! Brands, Inc.
Consolidated Statements of Income (Adapted)
Years Ended December 31, 2003, and 2002

(In millions)	2003	2002
Revenues		
1 Company sales	$7,441	$6,891
2 Franchise and license fees	939	866
3 Total revenues	8,380	7,757
Expenses		
Company restaurants		
4 Food and paper (Cost of goods sold)	2,300	2,109
5 Payroll and employee benefits expense	2,024	1,875
6 Occupancy and other operating expenses	2,013	1,806
	6,337	5,790
7 General and administrative expenses	945	913
8 Franchise and license expenses	28	49
9 Other operating expenses (income)	11	(25)
10 Total expenses	7,321	6,727
11 Operating profit	1,059	1,030
12 Interest expense	173	172
13 Income before income taxes	886	858
14 Income tax expense	269	275
15 Net income	$ 617	$ 583

It's late, and you have an exam tomorrow morning. There's no food in the fridge. Where do you go for a quick bite? You may enjoy a pizza at Pizza Hut, a "Taco Supreme" at Taco Bell, a frosty mug of root beer at A&W, a bucket of fried chicken at KFC, or a "Shrimp Cruiser" at Long John Silver's. One thing you won't get at any of these restaurants is Coke; they sell only Pepsi. That's because PepsiCo used to own all these companies. Now YUM! Brands owns and operates them.

The bottom line of business operations is either a profit or a loss. Profitable companies survive; losers go out of business. YUM! Brands reports that it's a winner. But did the company really sell that many pizzas, tacos, drumsticks, and root beer? Were profits really $617 million? The information in the financial statements is verified in an audit by independent accountants.

1

The Financial Statements

LEARNING OBJECTIVES

1 **Use** accounting vocabulary for decision making

2 **Apply** accounting concepts and principles

3 **Use** the accounting equation to describe an organization

4 **Evaluate** operating performance, financial position, and cash flows

5 **Explain** the relationships among the financial statements

Each chapter of this book begins with an actual financial statement. In this chapter, it's the income statement of YUM! Brands, Inc. This chapter lays the foundation. The core of the chapter—and indeed of the course—is the basic financial statements:

- Income statement (the statement of operations)
- Statement of retained earnings
- Balance sheet (the statement of financial position)
- Statement of cash flows

In this chapter we explain all the items that appear in each statement and how the statements relate to give you a clear view of where you are headed. Examine YUM! Brands' income statement. During 2003 YUM earned revenues of $8,380 million (line 3) and bottom-line net income of $617 million (line 15). After completing this chapter, you'll understand what these terms mean.

This course will also help you develop the skills to address real questions. To learn accounting, focus on the decisions people make to accomplish their goals. Decisions require information, which accounting provides.

You take actions every day that require accounting information. The following diagram illustrates a decision many college students make each year in March.

For this student, the decision to go to the beach depends on whether he can afford it. The same is true for big businesses like PepsiCo and YUM! Brands. They must weigh what they want to accomplish against what they can afford to do.

We begin with an overview of the business environment of accounting and some of the principles that govern the way accounting is practiced.

For more practice and review of accounting cycle concepts, use ACT, the Accounting Cycle Tutorial, online at www.prenhall.com/harrison. Margin logos like this one, directing you to the appropriate ACT section and material, appear throughout Chapters 1, 2, and 3. When you enter the tutorial, you'll find three buttons on the opening page of each chapter module. Here's what the buttons mean: Tutorial gives you a review of the major concepts, Application gives you practice exercises, and Glossary reviews important terms.

FOCUS ON F

Business Decisions

YUM! Brands managers make lots of decisions. Which fast foods are selling best? Is pizza bringing in profits? Should YUM! Brands expand into Japan? Accounting helps managers make these decisions.

Take a look at YUM! Brands' income statement on page 2. Focus on net income (line 15). Net income is profit, the excess of revenues over expenses. You can see that YUM! Brands earned a $617 million profit in 2003. That's good news because it means that YUM had $617 million more revenue than expenses for the year.

YUM's income statement conveys more good news. Net income for 2003 exceeded the net income for 2002. Companies want net income to grow because increasing profits signal that the company is growing, and investors buy the stocks of growing companies.

Suppose you have $9,000 to invest. What information would you need before investing in YUM! Brands? Let's see how accounting works.

✔ Check Point 1-1

Accounting: The Language of Business

OBJECTIVE

1 **Use** accounting vocabulary for decision making

Accounting is an information system. It measures business activities, processes data into reports, and communicates results to people. Accounting is "the language of business." The better you understand the language, the better you can manage your own finances. Financial planning, auto loans, and income taxes all depend on accounting information.

Accounting
The information system that measures business activities, processes that information into reports and financial statements, and communicates the results to decision makers.

Accounting produces **financial statements**, which report information about a business entity. The financial statements measure performance and tell where a business stands in financial terms. In this chapter we focus on YUM! Brands. After completing this chapter, you will be familiar with the financial statements YUM and other companies use to represent themselves to the public.

Financial statements
Business documents that report financial information about a business entity to decision makers.

Don't confuse bookkeeping and accounting. Accounting is broader, and bookkeeping is only a part of accounting, just as arithmetic is a part of mathematics. Exhibit 1-1 illustrates accounting's role in business. The process starts and ends with people making decisions.

✔ Check Point 1-2

■ **EXHIBIT 1-1** The Flow of Accounting Information

1. People make decisions.

2. Business transactions occur.

3. Companies report their operating results.

NDAMENTALS

Who Uses Accounting Information?

Decision makers need information. A banker decides who gets a loan. YUM! Brands decides where to locate the next Pizza Hut. An investor decides whether to buy YUM! Brands stock. Let's see how some other people use accounting information.

- *Individuals.* People like you manage bank accounts and decide whether to rent an apartment or buy a house. Accounting provides the information you need.
- *Investors and Creditors.* Investors and creditors provide the money to finance YUM! Brands. To decide whether to invest in any company, people want to know how much income they can expect to earn on their investment. This requires accounting data.
- *Taxing Authorities.* There are all kinds of taxes. Pizza Hut pays property tax on its assets and income tax on its profits. Taco Bell collects sales tax from you and forwards the tax to the state. Taxes are based on accounting data.
- *Nonprofit Organizations.* Nonprofit organizations—churches, hospitals, and charities such as Habitat for Humanity and the Red Cross—pay rent and use computers the same way profit-oriented businesses do. They base many of their decisions on accounting data.

Two Kinds of Accounting: Financial Accounting and Management Accounting

There are both *external users* and *internal users* of accounting information. We therefore help classify accounting into financial accounting and management accounting.

Financial accounting provides information for people outside the firm, such as Wall Street investors and bankers. Government agencies and the public are other external users. Financial accounting information must meet certain standards of relevance and reliability.

Financial accounting The branch of accounting that provides information to people outside the firm.

Management accounting generates inside information for internal decision makers, such as the managers of YUM! Brands. Management information is tailored to serve the company's specific needs and thus does not have to meet external standards of reliability.

Management accounting The branch of accounting that generates information for the internal decision makers of a business, such as top executives.

Ethics in Accounting: Standards of Professional Conduct

Ethical considerations pervade accounting. Companies need money to operate. To attract outside money, they must provide relevant and reliable information to the public. Without that information, people won't invest. The United States has laws that require companies to report relevant and reliable information to outsiders. Relevant means "able to affect a decision." Reliable means "verifiable and free of error and bias." The infographic on page 7 diagrams this process.

The top managers of a company such as YUM! Brands know a lot more about the company than anyone else. As they report on company operations, they are tempted to make the company look good—even if times are hard. The legal requirement for relevant and reliable information creates an ethical challenge. Most managers meet this challenge by providing full and fair information.

Occasionally, a company will report biased information. It may overstate profits or understate its debts. In recent years, several well-known companies reported

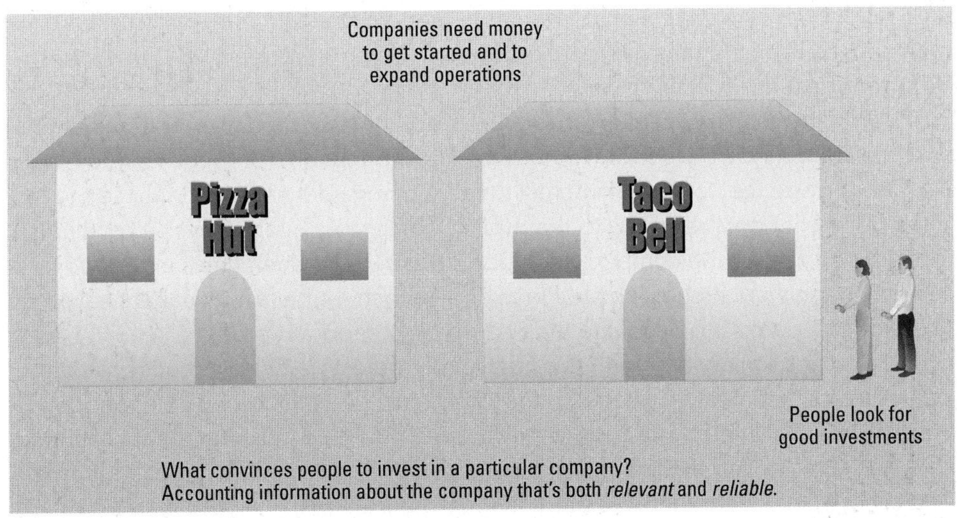
Companies need money to get started and to expand operations
Pizza Hut
Taco Bell
People look for good investments
What convinces people to invest in a particular company? Accounting information about the company that's both *relevant* and *reliable*.

misleading information. Enron Corporation, once one of the largest companies in the United States, admitted understating its debts. Tyco, WorldCom, and Qwest were accused of overstating profits. These companies' data were unreliable, and their information thus failed the test of good ethics. The results? People invested in them, lost money, and filed lawsuits to recover their losses. Reporting relevant, reliable information to the public is the ethical course of action.

What are the criteria for ethical judgments in accounting? The *American Institute of Certified Public Accountants (AICPA)*, other professional organizations, and most companies have codes of conduct that require ethical conduct. The AICPA is the country's largest organization of accountants, similar to the American Medical Association for physicians and the American Bar Association for attorneys.

The Code of Professional Conduct of the AICPA provides guidance in performing professional duties: "[A] certified public accountant assumes an obligation of self-discipline above and beyond the requirements of laws and regulations . . . [and] an unswerving commitment to honorable behavior, even at the sacrifice of personal advantage." Recent events have underscored the need for good ethics among accountants. The accounting firm of Arthur Andersen was the auditor of Enron, Tyco, WorldCom, and Qwest, when these companies' financial reports proved to be unreliable. The damage to Arthur Andersen's reputation was so great that the firm had to close its doors.

Check Point 1-3

ACCOUNTING ALERT

We Need an Audit to Validate the Financial Statements

Each chapter of this book begins with an actual financial statement—Chapter 1 has the income statement of YUM! Brands, Inc. Throughout this book we use actual examples to show how accounting relates to your daily activities. For example, where do you stop for a quick bite? You may enjoy a pizza at Pizza Hut, a taco at Taco Bell, fried chicken at KFC, or a root beer at A&W. All of these companies are part of YUM! Brands.

TACO BELL

NDAMENTALS

YUM! Brands reports that it's profitable. But did the company really sell that many pizzas, tacos, drumsticks, and root beer? Were profits really $617 million? Who reports these figures?

YUM's top management is responsible both for (a) company operations—how well the company *really* performs—and (b) the information YUM *reports* to the public. Can you see the conflict of interest here? A company's *real* performance may differ from what gets *reported* to the public. Company management has a built-in motivation to make the company look good—especially when times are tough. Most managers are high-principled men and women, but a few managers have "cooked the books" to overstate their companies' *reported* profits.

How does society deal with this conflict of interest? U.S. law requires all companies that sell their stock to the public to have an annual audit by independent accountants. Audits are intended to protect the public by ensuring that accounting data are relevant and reliable. It turns out that YUM! Brands passed the audit test. The accounting firm of KPMG stated, among other things,

> "We have audited the [financial statements] of YUM! Brands, Inc. . . . "
> "In our opinion, the . . . financial statements . . . present fairly . . . the . . . financial position of YUM, . . . and the results of its operations and its cash flows. . . . "

The take-away lesson form this accounting alert is this:

> Avoid a company if its auditor does not state that the company's financial statements "present fairly . . ."

Organizing a Business

A business can take one of three forms and you need to understand the differences among the three types: proprietorships, partnerships, and corporations. Exhibit 1-2 compares the three ways to organize a business.

■ EXHIBIT 1-2
The Three Forms of Business Organization

	Proprietorship	Partnership	Corporation
1. *Owner(s)*	Proprietor—one owner	Partners—two or more owners	Stockholders—generally many owners
2. *Personal liability of owner(s) for business debts*	Proprietor is personally liable	Partners are personally liable	Stockholders are not personally liable

Proprietorship
A business with a single owner.

Proprietorships. A **proprietorship** has a single owner, called the proprietor. Dell Computer started out in the dorm room of Michael Dell, the owner. Proprietorships tend to be small retail stores or a professional service—a physician, an attorney, or an accountant. Legally, the business *is* the proprietor, and the proprietor is personally liable for all the business's debts. But for accounting, a proprietorship is distinct from its proprietor. Thus, the business records do not include the proprietor's personal finances.

Partnership
An association of two or more persons who co-own a business for profit.

Partnerships. A **partnership** has two or more persons as co-owners, and each owner is a partner. Many retail establishments and some professional organizations are partnerships. Most partnerships are small or medium-sized, but some are gigan-

FOCUS ON F

tic, with 2,000 or more partners. Like proprietorships, the law views a partnership as the partners. The business is its owners. For this reason, each partner is personally liable for all the partnership's debts. Partnerships are quite risky. In a recent example, the accounting firm of Arthur Andersen was found guilty of obstructing justice. A few Andersen partners virtually killed the entire firm. Accounting views the partnership as entirely separate from the partners.

Corporations. A **corporation** is a business owned by the **stockholders**, also called **shareholders**. These people own **stock**, which represents shares of ownership in a corporation. Corporations dominate business activity even though proprietorships and partnerships are more numerous. Corporations transact much more business and are larger in terms of assets, income, and number of employees. Most well-known companies, such as YUM! Brands, PepsiCo, General Motors, and Dell Computer, are corporations. Their full names include *Corporation* or *Incorporated* (abbreviated *Corp.* and *Inc.*) to indicate that they are corporations—for example, YUM! Brands, Inc., and General Motors Corporation. Some bear the name "Company," such as Ford Motor Company.

Corporation
A business owned by stockholders. A corporation is a legal entity, an "artificial person" in the eyes of the law.

Stockholder
A person who owns stock in a corporation. Also called a *shareholder*.

A corporation is formed under state law. Unlike proprietorships and partnerships, a corporation is legally distinct from its owners. The corporation is like an artificial person and possesses many of the rights that a person has. For example, a corporation may buy, own, and sell property in its own name. A corporation may enter into contracts, sue, and be sued. Unlike proprietors and partners, stockholders have no personal obligation for the corporation's debts.

Shareholder
Another name for *stockholder*.

Stock
Shares into which the owners' equity of a corporation is divided.

A corporation's ownership is divided into shares of stock. One becomes a stockholder by purchasing the corporation's stock. YUM! Brands, for example, has issued 292 million shares of stock. An investor with no personal relationship to YUM! Brands can become a stockholder by buying 1, 30, 5,000, or any number of shares of YUM stock through the New York Stock Exchange.

Ultimate control of a corporation rests with the stockholders, who get one vote for each share of stock they own. Stockholders elect the **board of directors**, which sets policy and appoints officers. The board elects a chairperson, who holds the most power in the corporation and often carries the title chief executive officer (CEO). The board also appoints the president as head of day-to-day operations. Corporations have vice presidents in charge of sales, accounting and finance, and other key areas.

Board of directors
Group elected by the stockholders to set policy for a corporation and to appoint its officers.

Accounting's Foundation: Principles and Concepts

OBJECTIVE

2 Apply accounting concepts and principles

Accountants follow professional guidelines called **GAAP**, which stands for **generally accepted accounting principles**. In the United States, the *Financial Accounting Standards Board (FASB)* formulates GAAP.

Exhibit 1-3 gives an overview of the conceptual framework of accounting. GAAP, at the bottom, follows from the conceptual framework. To be useful, information must be relevant, reliable, comparable, and consistent. This course will expose you to generally accepted accounting; we cover the methods relevant to each topic. We also summarize them in Appendix E. We begin with the basic concepts that underlie accounting practice.

Generally accepted accounting principles (GAAP)
Accounting guidelines, formulated by the Financial Accounting Standards Board, that govern how accounting is practical.

■ **EXHIBIT 1-3**

Conceptual Foundation of Accounting

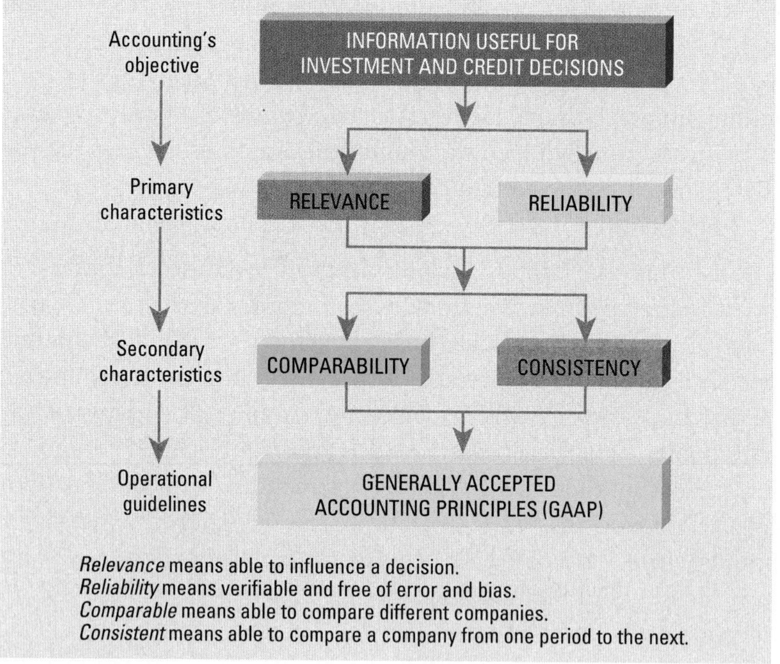
Accounting's objective
INFORMATION USEFUL FOR INVESTMENT AND CREDIT DECISIONS
Primary characteristics
RELEVANCE
RELIABILITY
Secondary characteristics
COMPARABILITY
CONSISTENCY
Operational guidelines
GENERALLY ACCEPTED ACCOUNTING PRINCIPLES (GAAP)
Relevance means able to influence a decision.
Reliability means verifiable and free of error and bias.
Comparable means able to compare different companies.
Consistent means able to compare a company from one period to the next.

The Entity Concept

Entity
An organization or a section of an organization that, for accounting purposes, stands apart from other organizations and individuals as a separate economic unit.

The most basic accounting concept is the **entity**, which is any organization that stands apart as a separate economic unit. Sharp boundaries are drawn around each entity so as not to confuse its affairs with those of others.

Consider David C. Novak, Chairman of the Board of YUM! Brands, Inc. Mr. Novak owns a home and several automobiles. He may owe money on some personal loans. All these assets and liabilities belong to David Novak and have nothing to do with YUM! Brands. Likewise, YUM's cash, computers, and food inventories belong to the company and not to Novak. Why? Because the entity concept draws a sharp boundary around each entity; in this case YUM! Brands is one entity, and David Novak is a separate entity.

Let's consider the various restaurant chains that make up YUM! Brands. Top managers evaluate Pizza Hut separately from Taco Bell, A&W, and KFC. If pizza sales are dropping, YUM can identify the reason. But if sales figures from all the restaurant chains are combined in a single total, managers can't tell how many pizzas and how many tacos the company is selling. To correct the problem, managers need data for each division of the company. Each restaurant chain keeps its own records in order to be evaluated separately.

Check Point 1-4

The Reliability Principle

Reliability principle
The accounting principle that ensures that accounting records and statements are based on the most reliable data available. Also called the *objectivity principle*.

To ensure relevance and reliability, accounting records are based on the most objective data available. This is the **reliability principle**, also called the **objectivity principle**. Ideally, accounting records are based on information supported by objective evidence. For example, a $9 purchase of a pizza is supported by a paid receipt, which gives objective evidence of the cost of the pizza. Without the reliability principle, accounting records would be based on opinions and subject to dispute.

Suppose you open a Taco Bell/Pizza Hut store, and you're buying a building. You believe the building is worth $185,000. Two real estate professionals appraise the building at $210,000. The owner of the building demands $200,000. Suppose you pay $190,000. Your belief about the building's value and the real-estate appraisals are merely opinions. The accounting value of the building is $190,000 because that amount is supported by a completed transaction. The business should therefore record the building at its cost of $190,000.

The Cost Principle

The **cost principle** states that assets and services should be recorded at their actual *historical cost*. Suppose your Taco Bell/Pizza Hut purchases kitchen equipment from a Domino's Pizza that is moving. Assume that you get a good deal on this purchase and pay only $50,000 for equipment that would have cost you $70,000 elsewhere. The cost principle requires you to record this equipment at its actual cost of $50,000, not the $70,000 that you believe it's worth.

Cost principle
Principle that states that assets and services should be recorded at their actual cost.

The cost principle also holds that accounting records should maintain historical costs for as long as the business holds the asset. Why? Because cost is a reliable measure. Suppose your store holds the equipment for 6 months. Prices increase and the equipment can be sold for $60,000. Should its accounting value be the actual cost of $50,000 or the current market value of $60,000? According to the cost principle, the equipment remains on the books at a cost of $50,000.

The Going-Concern Concept

The **going-concern concept** assumes that the entity will remain in operation long enough to use existing assets—land, buildings, supplies—for their intended purpose. Consider the alternative to the going-concern concept: going out of business.

Going-concern concept
Holds that the entity will remain in operation for the foreseeable future.

A store that is going out of business sells all its assets. In that case, the relevant measure of the assets is their current market value. But going out of business is the exception rather than the rule, and so accounting lists a going concern's assets at their historical cost.

The Stable-Monetary-Unit Concept

In the United States, we record transactions in dollars because that is our medium of exchange. British accountants record transactions in pounds sterling, Japanese in yen, and Europeans in euros.

Unlike a liter or a mile, the value of a dollar changes over time. A rise in the general price level is called *inflation*. During inflation, a dollar will purchase less food, less toothpaste, and less of other goods and services. When prices are stable—there is little inflation—a dollar's purchasing power is also stable.

Under the **stable-monetary-unit concept**, accountants assume that the dollar's purchasing power is stable. We ignore inflation, and this allows us to add and subtract dollar amounts as though each dollar has the same purchasing power.

Stable-monetary-unit concept
The basis for ignoring the effect of inflation in the accounting records, based on the assumption that the dollar's purchasing power is relatively stable.

stop AND think. . .

You are considering the purchase of land for future expansion. The seller is asking $500,000 for land that cost him $300,000. An appraisal shows a value of $450,000. You first offer $400,000, the seller makes a counteroffer of $480,000, and you pay $460,000. What dollar value is reported for the land on your financial statements?

Answer:
Report the land at $460,000, which is its historical cost.

OBJECTIVE

3 Use the accounting equation to describe an organization

The Accounting Equation

YUM! Brands' financial statements tell us how the business is performing and where it stands. The statements are the final product of financial accounting. But how do we arrive at the financial statements?

Accounting equation
The most basic tool of accounting: Assets = Liabilities + Owners' Equity.

Asset
An economic resource that is expected to be of benefit in the future.

Liability
An economic obligation (a debt) payable to an individual or an organization outside the business.

Owners' equity
The claim of the owners of a business to the assets of the business. Also called *capital, stockholders' equity,* or *net assets.*

Capital
Another name for the *owners' equity* of a business.

Assets and Liabilities

The financial statements are based on the **accounting equation**. This equation presents the resources of a company and the claims to those resources.

- **Assets** are economic resources that are expected to produce a benefit in the future. YUM! Brands' cash, office supplies, food inventory, furniture, land, and buildings are examples of assets.

Claims on assets come from two sources:

- **Liabilities** are "outsider claims." They are debts that are payable to outsiders, called *creditors*. For example, a creditor who has loaned money to YUM! Brands has a claim—a legal right—to a part of YUM's assets until YUM repays the debt.
- **Owners' equity** (also called **capital**) represents the "insider claims" of a business. Equity means ownership, so YUM's stockholders' equity is their interest in the assets of the corporation.

The accounting equation shows the relationship among assets, liabilities, and owners' equity. Assets appear on the left side and liabilities and owners' equity on the right. As Exhibit 1-4 shows, the two sides must be equal:

Assets = Liabilities + Owners' Equity

■ **EXHIBIT 1-4**
The Accounting Equation

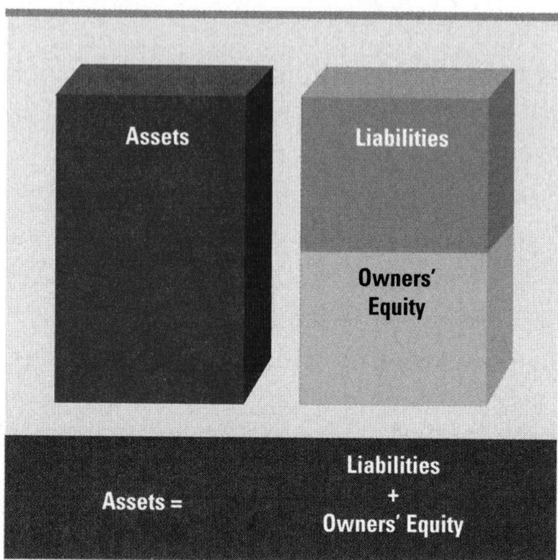

Cash
Money and any medium of exchange that a bank accepts at face value.

Merchandise inventory
The merchandise that a company sells to customers.

Property, plant, and equipment
Long-lived assets, such as land, buildings, and equipment, used in the operation of the business. Also called *plant assets* or *fixed assets*.

What are some of YUM! Brands' assets? The first asset is **cash**, the liquid asset that is the medium of exchange. Another important asset is **merchandise inventory** (often called Inventories)—the food and paper items—that YUM's restaurants sell. YUM also has assets in the form of property, plant, and equipment. These are the long-lived assets the company uses to do business—kitchen equipment, buildings, computers, and so on. Land, buildings, and equipment are called **property, plant, and equipment** (often abbreviated as PPE), **plant assets**, or **fixed assets**.

YUM! Brands' liabilities include a number of payables, such as accounts payable and notes payable. The word *payable* always signifies a liability. An **account payable** is a liability for goods or services purchased on credit and supported only by the credit standing of the purchaser. A **note payable** is a written promise to pay on a certain date. **Long-term debt** is a liability that's payable beyond 1 year from the date of the financial statements.

Account payable
A liability backed by the general reputation and credit standing of the debtor.

Note payable
A liability evidenced by a written promise to make a future payment.

Long-term debt
A liability that falls due beyond one year from the date of the financial statements.

Owners' Equity

The owners' equity of any business is its assets minus its liabilities. This applies both to individuals and large corporations such as YUM! Brands. We can write the accounting equation to show that owners' equity is what's left over when we subtract liabilities from assets.

Assets − Liabilities = Owners' Equity

A corporation's equity—called **stockholders' equity**—has two main subparts, paid-in capital and retained earnings. The accounting equation can be written as

Stockholders' equity
The stockholders' ownership interest in the assets of a corporation.

Check Point 1-5

Assets = Liabilities + Stockholders' Equity

Assets = Liabilities + Paid-in Capital + Retained Earnings

Paid-in capital is the amount invested in the corporation by the stockholders. The basic component of paid-in capital is **common stock**, which the corporation issues as evidence of ownership.

Retained earnings is the amount earned by income-producing activities and kept for use in the business. Two types of transactions affect retained earnings:

Paid-in capital
The amount of stockholders' equity that stockholders have contributed to the corporation. Also called *contributed capital.*

Common stock
The most basic form of capital stock.

Retained earnings
The amount of stockholders' equity that the corporation has earned through profitable operation and has not given back to stockholders.

- **Revenues** increase retained earnings by delivering goods or services to customers. For example, Pizza Hut's receipt of cash from the sale of a cheese pizza brings in revenue and increases YUM! Brands' retained earnings.
- **Expenses** decrease retained earnings due to operations. For example, the wages that Pizza Hut pays employees are an expense and decrease retained earnings. Expenses are the cost of doing business; they are the opposite of revenues. Expenses include building rent, salaries, and utility payments. Expenses also include the depreciation of computers and other equipment.

Check Point 1-6

Check Point 1-7

Revenue
Increase in retained earnings from delivering goods or services to customers or clients.

Businesses strive for profits. When total revenues exceed total expenses, the result is called **net income**, **net earnings**, or **net profit**. When expenses exceed revenues, the result is a **net loss**. Net income or net loss is the "bottom line" on an income statement. YUM! Brands' bottom line reports net income of $617 million on page 2 (line 15).

A successful business may pay dividends. **Dividends** are distributions to stockholders of assets (usually cash) generated by net income. Remember: **Dividends are not expenses. Dividends never affect net income.** Exhibit 1-5 shows the relationships among

- Retained earnings
- Revenues − expenses = net income (or net loss)
- Dividends

Expense
Decrease in retained earnings that results from operations; the cost of doing business; opposite of revenues.

Net income
Excess of total revenues over total expenses. Also called *net earnings* or *net profit.*

■ **EXHIBIT 1-5** Components of Retained Earnings

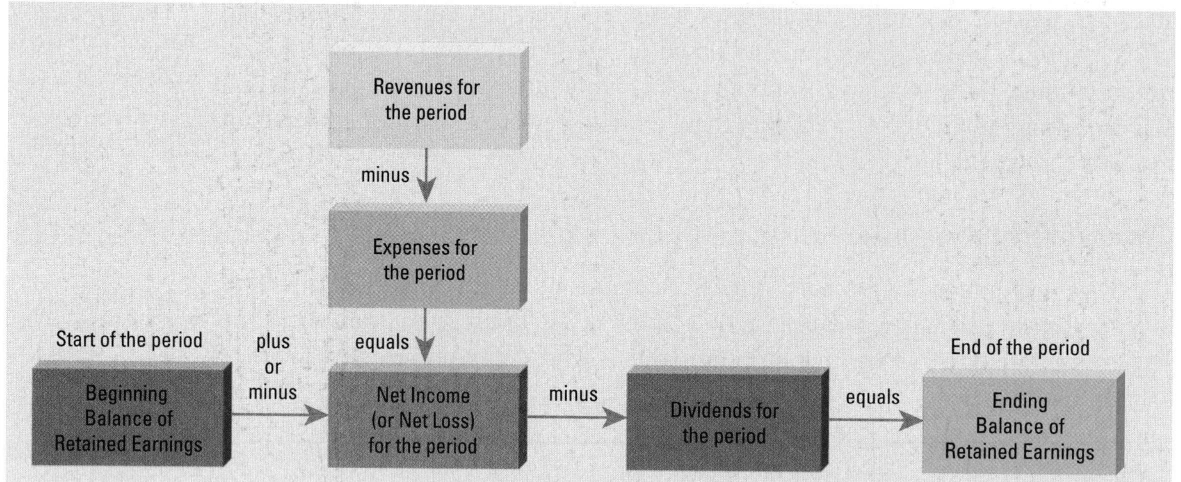

Net loss
Excess of total expenses over total revenues.

Dividends
Distributions (usually cash) by a corporation to its stockholders.

The owners' equity of proprietorships and partnerships is different. Proprietorships and partnerships don't identify paid-in capital and retained earnings. Instead, they use a single heading—Capital—for example, Randall Walker, Capital, for a proprietorship and Pratt, Capital, and Salazar, Capital for a partnership.

stop AND think. . .

1. If the assets of a business are $174,000 and the liabilities are $82,000, how much is the owners' equity?
2. If the owners' equity in a business is $22,000 and the liabilities are $36,000, how much are the assets?
3. A company reported monthly revenues of $77,000 and expenses of $81,000. What is the result of operations for the month?

Answers:

1. $92,000 ($174,000 – $82,000)
2. $58,000 ($22,000 + $36,000)
3. Net loss of $4,000 ($77,000 – $81,000); expenses minus revenues

The Financial Statements

The financial statements depict a company in financial terms. Each financial statement relates to a specific date or time period. What would managers and investors want to know about YUM! Brands, Inc., at the end of December? Exhibit 1-6 summarizes four questions decision makers may ask. Each answer comes from one of the financial statements.

FOCUS ON F

■ **EXHIBIT 1-6**

Information Reported in the Financial Statements

Question	Answer	Financial Statement
1. How well did the company perform during December?	Revenues – Expenses Net income (or Net loss)	Income statement (also called the Statement of operations)
2. Why did the company's retained earnings change during the year?	Beginning retained earnings + Net income (or – Net loss) – Dividends Ending retained earnings	Statement of retained earnings
3. What is the company's financial position at December 31?	Assets = Liabilities + Owners' Equity	Balance sheet (also called the Statement of financial position)
4. How much cash did the company generate and spend during the year?	Operating cash flows ± Investing cash flows ± Financing cash flows Increase (decrease) in cash	Statement of cash flows

OBJECTIVE

4 **Evaluate** operating performance, financial position, and cash flows

To learn how to use financial statements, let's work through YUM! Brands' statements for the year ended December 31, 2003. The following diagram shows how the data flow from one financial statement to the next.

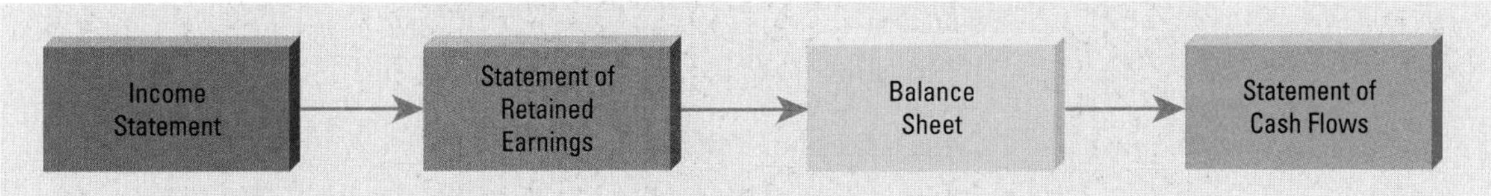

We begin with the income statement in Exhibit 1-7.

■ **EXHIBIT 1-7**

Income Statement (Adapted)

YUM! Brands, Inc.
Consolidated Statements of Income (Adapted)
Years Ended December 31, 2003 and 2002

(In millions)	2003	2002
Revenues		
1 Company sales	$7,441	$6,891
2 Franchise and license fees	939	866
3 Total revenues	8,380	7,757
Expenses		
Company restaurants		
4 Food and paper (Cost of goods sold)	2,300	2,109
5 Payroll and employee benefits expense	2,024	1,875
6 Occupancy and other operating expenses	2,013	1,806
	6,337	5,790
7 General and administrative expenses	945	913
8 Franchise and license expenses	28	49
9 Other operating expenses (income)	11	(25)
10 Total expenses	7,321	6,727
11 Operating profit	1,059	1,030
12 Interest expense	173	172
13 Income before income taxes	886	858
14 Income tax expense	269	275
15 Net income	$ 617	$ 583

The Income Statement: Measuring Operating Performance

Income statement
A financial statement listing an entity's revenues, expenses, and net income or net loss for a specific period. Also called the *statement of operations*.

The **income statement** or **statement of operations** reports revenues, expenses, and net income or net loss for the period. At the top of Exhibit 1-7 is the company's name, YUM! Brands Inc. YUM! Brands, the parent company, owns other companies that are its subsidiaries. To include all the resources that YUM! Brands controls, the company's financial statements report consolidated figures for YUM plus all its subsidiaries. Most large companies' financial statements include the word *consolidated* in the title.

The date of YUM's income statement is "Years Ended December 31, 2003, and 2002." YUM uses the calendar period as its accounting year, as do around 60% of large companies.[1] Some use a fiscal year, which ends on a date other than December 31. For example, Pier 1 Imports, Wal-Mart, and most other retailers end their accounting year on or around January 31. FedEx's year end falls on May 31. Companies adopt an accounting year that ends on the low point of their operations.

YUM! Brands' income statement in Exhibit 1-7 reports operating results for 2 years, 2003 and 2002. The income statement includes more than 1 year of data to show trends for revenues, expenses, and net income. To avoid clutter, YUM reports in millions of dollars. During 2003, YUM increased total revenues (line 3) from $7,757 million to $8,380 million. Net income rose from $583 million to $617 million (line 15). YUM! Brands restaurants sold more pizzas, tacos, and fried chicken in 2003, and that boosted profits.

The income statement reports two main categories:

- Revenues and gains
- Expenses and losses

Revenues and expenses measure net income as follows:

Net Income = Total Revenues and Gains − Total Expenses and Losses

In accounting, the word "net" refers to an amount after a subtraction. *Net* income is the profit left over after subtracting expenses and losses from revenues and gains.

Revenues. Revenues do not always carry the term *revenue* in their titles. For example, net sales revenue is often abbreviated as *net sales*. *Net* sales means sales revenue after subtracting all the goods customers have returned to the company. Wal-Mart, Best Buy, and Gap get some goods back from customers due to product defects. YUM! Brands and other restauranteurs don't have much in the way of sales returns.

YUM! Brands has two sources of revenue: company sales (line 1) and fees that YUM earns by licensing its products to others (line 2).

Expenses. Not all expenses have the word *expense* in their title. For example, YUM! Brands' largest expense is for Food and paper (line 4). Another title of this expense is Cost of goods sold. *Cost of goods sold* (also called *cost of sales*, line 4) represents the cost to YUM of the food it sold to customers. For example, suppose it costs Pizza Hut $3 to make a pepperoni pizza. Assume Pizza Hut sells the pizza for $8. Sales revenue is $8, and cost of goods sold is $3. Cost of goods sold is the major expense of merchandising entities such as Best Buy, Wal-Mart, and Safeway (the grocery store chain).

[1]YUM actually reports for the fiscal year that ends on the Saturday nearest December 31. For practical purposes we treat this as the calendar year.

YUM has a number of other expenses.

- Payroll and employee benefits expense (line 5) is for the salaries and wages paid to company employees.
- Occupancy and other operating expenses (line 6) include building rent, utilities, advertising, and depreciation on computers and kitchen equipment.
- General and administrative expenses (line 7) are executive salaries and other home-office expenses.
- Franchise and license expenses (line 8) result from YUM's letting others sell its products. A *franchise* grants a right to another party to operate a Pizza Hut or a Taco Bell.
- Other operating expenses (line 9) is a catchall label for expenses that don't fit another category. During 2003, YUM had other operating expenses of $11 million. In 2002, YUM had other operating income. Parentheses around the $25 million mean that this amount's category runs opposite the others in its column.
- Interest expense (line 12) was $173 million for 2003. This is YUM's cost of borrowing money.
- Income tax expense (line 14) is the expense levied on YUM! Brands by the government.

Check Point 1-8

Check Point 1-9

YUM! Brands reports both Operating Profit (line 11) and Net Income (line 15). Some investors use operating profit to measure operating performance. Others use the "bottom-line" net income.

Now let's move on to the statement of retained earnings in Exhibit 1-8.

Accounting Cycle Tutorial
Income Statement Accounts

The Statement of Retained Earnings

Retained earnings means exactly what the term implies: that portion of net income the company has retained. Net income flows from the income statement to the **statement of retained earnings** (line 2 in Exhibit 1-8). Net income increases retained earnings.

Statement of retained earnings Summary of the changes in the retained earnings of a corporation during a specific period.

■ EXHIBIT 1-8

Statement of Retained Earnings (Adapted)

YUM! Brands, Inc.
Consolidated Statement of Retained Earnings (Adapted)
Years Ended December 31,

(In millions)	2003	2002
Retained earnings:		
1 Balance, beginning of year	$(203)	$(786)
2 Net income	617	583
3 Less: Cash dividends declared	(0)	(0)
4 Balance, end of year	$ 414	$(203)

YUM's statement of retained earnings needs explanation. Focus on 2003. Prior to 2003, YUM! Brands had some years with big net losses, and Retained Earnings had a negative balance. The parentheses in Exhibit 1-8 mean negative numbers.

In 2003, YUM's retained earnings turned the corner and finally achieved a positive balance, which is normal. A negative balance in retained earnings (called a *Deficit*) is rare.

After a company earns net income, the board of directors decides whether to pay a dividend to the stockholders. In 2003, YUM! Brands declared no dividends (line 3). But if dividends existed, they would decrease retained earnings (the parentheses indicate a subtraction). YUM ended 2003 with retained earnings of $414 million (line 4). Trace retained earnings to the balance sheet in Exhibit 1-9 (line 29). Ending retained earnings carries over and becomes the beginning balance of 2004.

Check Point 1-10

■ **EXHIBIT 1-9**

Balance Sheet (Adapted)

YUM! Brands, Inc.
Consolidated Balance Sheets (Adapted)
December 31, 2003 and 2002

(In millions)		2003		2002
1 ASSETS				
2 **Current Assets**				
3 Cash and cash equivalents		$ 192		$ 130
4 Short-term investments		15		27
5 Accounts and notes receivable		169		168
6 Inventories		67		63
7 Prepaid expenses and other current assets		363		342
8 **Total Current Assets**		806		730
9 Property, plant and equipment, at cost	$5,606		$5,201	
10 Less: Accumulated depreciation	(2,326)		(2,164)	
11 Property, plant and equipment, net		3,280		3,037
12 Intangible assets		878		849
13 Investments		184		229
14 Other assets		472		555
15 **Total Assets**		$5,620		$5,400
16 LIABILITIES				
17 **Current Liabilities**				
18 Accounts payable		$ 439		$ 417
19 Income taxes payable		238		208
20 Short-term borrowings		10		146
21 Salaries and wages payable		257		258
22 Other current liabilities		517		491
23 **Total Current Liabilities**		1,461		1,520
24 Long-term debt		2,056		2,299
25 Other long-term liabilities		983		987
26 **Total Liabilities**		4,500		4,806
27 SHAREHOLDERS' EQUITY				
28 Common stock		916		1,046
29 Retained earnings (Deficit)		414		(203)
30 Other equity		(210)		(249)
31 **Total Shareholders' Equity**		1,120		594
32 **Total Liabilities and Shareholders' Equity**		$5,620		$5,400

Balance sheet
List of an entity's assets, liabilities, and owners' equity as of a specific date. Also called the *statement of financial position.*

A company's **balance sheet**, also called the **statement of financial position**, reports three items: assets, liabilities, and stockholders' equity (which YUM! Brands calls *shareholders' equity*). See lines 1, 16, and 27.

Current asset
An asset that is expected to be converted to cash, sold, or consumed during the next 12 months, or within the business's normal operating cycle if longer than a year.

Assets. Assets have two main categories, current and long-term. **Current assets** are expected to be converted to cash, sold, or consumed during the next 12 months or within the business's operating cycle if longer than a year. Current assets consist of Cash, Short-term investments, Accounts and notes receivable, Merchandise inventory, and Prepaid expenses (lines 3 to 7). YUM's current assets at December 31, 2003, total $806 million (line 8).

YUM! Brands has $192 million in cash and cash equivalents. Cash is the liquid asset that's the medium of exchange, and cash equivalents include money-market accounts that are the same as cash. Short-term investments include stocks and bonds that YUM intends to sell within the next year. Accounts receivable are amounts the company expects to collect from customers. Notes receivable are amounts YUM expects to collect from a party who has signed a promissory note to YUM. These notes receivable come from people to whom YUM has lent money. Cash, short-term investments, and current receivables are the most liquid assets, in that order.

Merchandise inventory (line 6) is the company's most important asset even though it totals only $67 million. *Inventory* is a common abbreviation for *Merchandise inventory*, and the two names are used interchangeably. Prepaid expenses represent prepayments for advertisements, rent, insurance, and supplies. Prepaid expenses are assets because YUM Brands will benefit from these expenditures in the future. **An asset always represents a future benefit.**

The main categories of *long-term assets* are Property, plant, and equipment (lines 9–11), Intangibles, and Investments. Intangibles are assets with no physical form, such as patents and trademarks. Investments (line 13), with no other words attached, are *long-term* because YUM does not expect to sell them within the next year.

Property, plant, and equipment (PPE) includes YUM! Brands' land, buildings, computers, store fixtures, and kitchen equipment. YUM reports PPE on three lines. Line 9 shows the company's cost of PPE, which is $5,606 million through December 31, 2003. Cost means the acquisition price to YUM. It does not mean that YUM could sell its PPE for $5,606 million. After all, the company may have acquired the assets several years ago.

Line 10 shows how much accumulated depreciation YUM has recorded on its PPE. (*Depreciation* is the process of allocating an asset's cost to expense; we discuss depreciation in later chapters.) Accumulated depreciation is the total amount of depreciation recorded on PPE from acquisition through the end of the year. It represents the used-up portion of the asset. We subtract accumulated depreciation from the cost of PPE to determine its book value ($3,280 million on line 11).

Other assets (line 14) is a catchall category for items difficult to classify. Overall, YUM! Brands reports total assets of $5,620 million at December 31, 2003 (line 15).

Liabilities. Liabilities are also divided into current and long-term categories. **Current liabilities** (lines 17–23) are debts payable within 1 year or within YUM's operating cycle if longer than a year. Chief among the current liabilities are Accounts payable, Income taxes payable, Short-term borrowing (same as short-term notes payable), and Salaries and wages payable. *Long-term liabilities* are payable after 1 year.

Current liability
A debt due to be paid within one year or within the entity's operating cycle if the cycle is longer than a year.

Accounts payable (line 18) represents amounts owed for food and paper inventory. Income taxes payable are owed to the government. Short-term borrowings (line 20) are notes payable that YUM has promised to pay back within 1 year or less. Salaries and wages payable (line 21) are amounts owed to employees.

The company's last current liability is Other current liabilities. Included in the other category are interest payable on borrowed money, utility payables, and expenses that YUM has not yet paid. At December 31, 2003, YUM's current liabilities total $1,461 million. YUM also owes $2,056 million in long-term debt (line 24). These liabilities include notes payable due after 1 year. At the end of 2003, total liabilities are $4,500 million (line 26). This is high relative to total assets (line 15), and that indicates a not-so-strong financial position.

stop AND think. . .

Examine YUM! Brands' balance sheet in Exhibit 1-9. Look at total assets on line 15 and total liabilities on line 26. Which total increased? Which decreased? Did shareholders' equity increase or decrease?

Answer:

Total assets increased, and total liabilities decreased. As a result, shareholders' equity increased.

Owners' Equity. The accounting equation states that

Assets − Liabilities = Owners' Equity

The assets (resources) and the liabilities (debts) of YUM! Brands are fairly easy to understand. Owners' equity is harder to pin down. Owners' equity is simple to calculate, but what does it *mean*?

YUM! Brands, Inc. call its owners' equity *shareholders' equity* (line 27), and this title is descriptive. Remember that a company's owners' equity represents the shareholders' ownership of business assets. YUM's equity consists of common stock, represented by millions of shares issued to stockholders for $916 million through December 31, 2003 (line 28).

Accounting Cycle Tutorial Balance Sheet Accounts

Retained earnings at December 31, 2003, is $404 million (line 29). A year earlier YUM! Brands had a retained earnings deficit. We saw these figures on the statement of retained earnings in Exhibit 1-8 (line 4). Retained earnings links the income statement to the balance sheet.

YUM! Brands' equity holds another item, Other equity, which is a collection of miscellaneous items. For now, focus on the two main components of stockholders' equity: common stock and retained earnings.

At December 31, 2003, YUM! Brands has Total shareholders' equity of $1,120 million (line 31). We can now prove that YUM's total assets equal total liabilities and equity (amounts in millions):

Operating activities
Activities that create revenue or expense in the entity's major line of business; a section of the statement of cash flows. Operating activities affect the income statement.

Investing activities
Activities that increase or decrease the long-term assets available to the business; a section of the statement of cash flows.

Total assets (line 15)	$5,620	←
Total liabilities (line 26)	$4,500	Must equal
+ Total shareholders' equity (line 31)	1,120	
Total liabilities and equity (line 32)	$5,620	←

Check Point 1-11

The statement of cash flows is the fourth required financial statement.

Financing activities
Activities that obtain from investors and creditors the cash needed to launch and sustain the business; a section of the statement of cash flows.

The Statement of Cash Flows: Measuring Cash Receipts and Payments

Organizations engage in three basic types of activities:

1. **Operating activities** 2. **Investing activities** 3. **Financing activities**

FOCUS ON F

The **statement of cash flows** reports cash flows under these three categories. Think about the cash flows (receipts and payments) in each category:

- ***Companies operate by selling goods and services to customers.*** Operating activities result in net income or net loss and either increase or decrease cash. The income statement tells whether the company is profitable. The cash-flow statement reports whether operations increased cash. Operating activities are most important, and cash flow from operations should always be positive. Negative cash flow from operations can mean bankruptcy.
- ***Companies invest in long-term assets.*** YUM! Brands buys buildings and equipment, and when these assets wear out, the company sells them. Both purchases and sales of long-term assets are investing cash flows. Investing cash flows are next most important after operations.
- ***Companies need money for financing.*** Financing includes both issuing stock and borrowing. YUM issues stock to its shareholders and borrows from banks. These are cash receipts. The company pays off loans. Many companies pay dividends. These payments are financing cash flows.

Statement of cash flows
Reports cash receipts and cash payments classified according to the entity's major activities: operating, investing, and financing.

Overview. Each category of cash flows—operating, investing, and financing—either increases or decreases cash. In Exhibit 1-10, YUM! Brands' operating activities provided cash of $1,053 million in 2003 (line 4). This signals strong cash flow from operations. 2003's investing activities used cash of $519 million (line 9). That signals expansion. Financing activities used $472 million (line 14). YUM paid off a lot of debt. On a statement of cash flows, cash receipts appear as positive amounts. Cash payments are negative and enclosed by parentheses.

■ **EXHIBIT 1-10**

Statement of Cash Flows (Adapted)

YUM! Brands, Inc.
Consolidated Statements of Cash Flows (Adapted)
Years Ended December 31, 2003 and 2002

(In millions)	2003	2002
1 **Cash Flows—Operating Activities**		
2 Net income	$ 617	$ 583
3. Adjustments to reconcile net income to net cash provided by operating activities	436	505
4 **Net Cash Provided by Operating Activities**	1,053	1,088
5 **Cash Flows—Investing Activities**		
6 Purchases of property, plant, and equipment	(663)	(760)
7 Sales of property, plant, and equipment	46	58
8 Other, net	98	(183)
9 **Net Cash Used in Investing Activities**	(519)	(885)
10 **Cash Flows—Financing Activities**		
11 Issuance of common stock	110	125
12 Payment of short-term and long-term debt	(307)	(467)
13 Other, net	(275)	159
14 **Net Cash Used in Financing Activities**	(472)	(183)
15 **Net Increase in Cash and Cash Equivalents**	62	20
16 **Cash and Cash Equivalents—Beginning of Year**	130	110
17 **Cash and Cash Equivalents—End of Year**	$ 192	$ 130

See accompanying Notes to Consolidated Financial Statements.

Overall, YUM's cash increased by $62 million during 2003 (line 15) and ended the year at $192 million (line 17). Trace ending cash back to the balance sheet in Exhibit 1-9 (line 3). Cash links the statement of cash flows to the balance sheet.

Check Point 1-12

Let's now summarize the relationships that link the financial statements.

Relationships Among the Financial Statements

OBJECTIVE

5 **Explain** the relationships among the financial statements

Exhibit 1-11 summarizes the relationships among the financial statements of ABC Company. Study the exhibit carefully because these relationships apply to all organizations. Specifically, note the following:

1. The income statement for the year ended December 31, 2006
   a. Reports revenues and expenses of the year. Revenues and expenses are reported *only* on the income statement.
   b. Reports net income if total revenues exceed total expenses. If expenses exceed revenues, there is a net loss.
2. The statement of retained earnings for the year ended December 31, 2006
   a. Opens with the beginning retained earnings balance.
   b. Adds net income (or subtracts net loss). Net income comes directly from the income statement (arrow ① in Exhibit 1-11).
   c. Subtracts dividends.
   d. Reports the retained earnings balance at the end of the year.
3. The balance sheet at December 31, 2006, end of the accounting year
   a. Reports assets, liabilities, and stockholders' equity at the end of the year. Only the balance sheet reports assets and liabilities.
   b. Reports that assets equal the sum of liabilities plus stockholders' equity. This balancing feature follows the accounting equation and gives the balance sheet its name.
   c. Reports retained earnings, which comes from the statement of retained earnings (arrow ② in Exhibit 1-11).
4. The statement of cash flows for the year ended December 31, 2006
   a. Reports cash flows from operating, investing, and financing. Each category results in net cash provided (an increase) or used (a decrease).
   b. Reports whether cash increased (or decreased) during the year. The statement shows the ending cash balance, as reported on the balance sheet (arrow ③ in Exhibit 1-11).

Accounting Cycle Tutorial Glossary

Accounting Cycle Tutorial Glossary Quiz

Check Point 1-13

FOCUS ON F

■ **EXHIBIT 1-11**

Relationships Among the Financial Statements (These statements are summarized, with all amounts assumed for the illustration)

ABC Company
Income Statement
Year Ended December 31, 2006

Revenues	$700,000
Expenses	670,000
Net income	$ 30,000

①

ABC Company
Statement of Retained Earnings
Year Ended December 31, 2006

Beginning retained earnings	$180,000
Net income	30,000
Cash dividends	(10,000)
Ending retained earnings	$200,000

②

ABC Company
Balance Sheet
December 31, 2006

Assets	
Cash	$ 25,000
All other assets	275,000
Total assets	$300,000
Liabilities	
Total liabilities	$120,000
Stockholders' Equity	
Common stock	40,000
Retained earnings	200,000
Other equity	(60,000)
Total liabilities and stockholders' equity	$300,000

③

Accounting Cycle Tutorial Applications Cottage Kitchen

ABC Company
Statement of Cash Flows
Year Ended December 31, 2006

Net cash provided by operating activities	$ 90,000
Net cash used for investing activities	(110,000)
Net cash provided by financing activities	40,000
Net increase in cash	20,000
Beginning cash balance	5,000
Ending cash balance	$25,000

Accounting Cycle Tutorial Applications Marwood Homes

MAKING MANAGERIAL DECISIONS

IN EVALUATING A COMPANY, WHAT DO DECISION MAKERS LOOK FOR?

Making Managerial Decisions illustrates how managers, investors, and lenders use financial statements. Making Managerial Decisions appears throughout the book to show how accounting information aids decision making.

Suppose you are considering an investment in YUM! Brands stock. How do you proceed? Where do you get the information you need? What do you look for?

Question/Decision	What to Look for
1. Can the company sell its products?	1. Sales revenue on the income statement. Are sales growing or falling?
2. What are the main income measures to watch for trends?	2. a. Gross profit (sales – cost of goods sold) b. Operating income (gross profit – operating expenses) c. Net income (bottom line of the income statement) All three income measures should be increasing over time.
3. What percentage of sales revenue ends up as profit?	3. Divide net income by sales revenue. Examine the trend of the net income percentage from year to year.
4. Can the company collect its receivables?	4. From the balance sheet, compare the percentage increase in accounts receivable to the percentage increase in sales. If receivables are growing much faster than sales, collections may be too slow, and a cash shortage may result.
5. Can the company pay its a. Current liabilities? b. Current and long-term liabilities?	5. From the balance sheet, compare a. Current assets to current liabilities. Current assets should be somewhat greater than current liabilities. b. Total assets to total liabilities. Total assets must be quite a bit greater than total liabilities.
6. Where is the company's cash coming from? How is cash being used?	6. On the cash-flow statement, operating activities should provide the bulk of the company's cash during most years. Otherwise, the business will fail. Examine investing cash flows to see if the company is purchasing long-term assets—property, plant, and equipment and intangibles (this signals growth). Examine financing cash flows for heavy borrowing (a bad sign) or issuance of stock (less risky).

Summary Problem

END-OF-CHAPTER

Air & Sea Travel, Inc., a travel agency, began operations on April 1, 20X6. During April, the business provided travel services for clients. It is now April 30, and investors wonder how well Air & Sea Travel performed during its first month. They also want to know the company's financial position at the end of April and its cash flows during the month.

The following data are listed in alphabetical order. Prepare the Air & Sea Travel financial statements at the end of April 20X6.

Accounts payable	$ 100	Land	$18,000
Accounts receivable	2,000	Office supplies	500
Adjustments to reconcile net income to net cash provided by operating activities	(2,400)	Payments of cash:	
		Acquisition of land	40,000
		Dividends	2,100
Cash balance at beginning of April	0	Rent expense	1,100
Cash balance at end of April	33,300	Retained earnings at beginning of April	0
Cash receipts:			
Issuance (sale) of stock to owners	50,000	Retained earnings at end of April	?
Sale of land	22,000	Salary expense	1,200
Common stock	50,000	Service revenue	8,500
Dividends	2,100	Utilities expense	400

Required

1. Prepare the income statement, the statement of retained earnings, and the statement of cash flows for the month ended April 30, 20X6, and the balance sheet at April 30, 20X6. Draw arrows linking the statements.
2. Answer the following questions:
   a. How well did Air & Sea Travel perform during its first month of operations?
   b. Where does Air & Sea Travel stand financially at the end of April?
3. If you were a banker, would you loan money to Air & Sea Travel, Inc.?

Answers

Requirement 1

Financial Statements of Air & Sea Travel, Inc.

Air & Sea Travel, Inc.
Income Statement
Month Ended April 30, 20X6

Revenue:		
Service revenue		$8,500
Expenses:		
Salary expense	$1,200	
Rent expense	1,100	
Utilities expense	400	
Total expenses		2,700
Net income		$5,800

NDAMENTALS

Air & Sea Travel, Inc.
Statement of Retained Earnings
Month Ended April 30, 20X6

①

Retained earnings, March 31, 20X6	$ 0
Add: Net income for the month	5,800
	5,800
Less: Dividends	(2,100)
Retained earnings, April 30, 20X6	$3,700

Air & Sea Travel, Inc.
Balance Sheet
April 30, 20X6

②

Assets		*Liabilities*	
Cash	$33,300	Accounts payable	$ 100
Accounts receivable	2,000		
Office supplies	500	*Stockholders' Equity*	
Land	18,000	Common stock	50,000
		Retained earnings	3,700
		Total stockholders' equity	53,700
		Total liabilities and	
Total assets	$53,800	stockholders' equity	$53,800

Air & Sea Travel, Inc.
Statement of Cash Flows
Month Ended April 30, 20X6

③

Cash flows from operating activities:		
Net income		$ 5,800
Adjustments to reconcile net income to net cash provided by operating activities		(2,400)
Net cash provided by operating activities		3,400
Cash flows from investing activities:		
Acquisition of land	$(40,000)	
Sale of land	22,000	
Net cash used for investing activities		(18,000)
Cash flows from financing activities:		
Issuance (sale) of stock	$ 50,000	
Payment of dividends	(2,100)	
Net cash provided by financing activities		47,900
Net increase in cash		$33,300
Cash balance, March 31, 20X5		0
Cash balance, April 30, 20X6		$33,300

Requirements 2 and 3

2. a. The company performed rather well in April. Net income was $5,800—very good in relation to service revenue of $8,500. The company was able to pay cash dividends of $2,100.
   b. The business ended April with cash of $33,300. Total assets of $53,800 far exceed total liabilities of $100. Stockholders' equity of $53,700 provides a good cushion for borrowing. The business's financial position at April 30, 20X6, is strong.
3. The company has plenty of cash, and assets far exceed liabilities. Operating activities generated positive cash flow in the first month of operations. Lenders like to see these features before making a loan. Most bankers would be willing to lend to Air & Sea Travel at this time.

FOCUS ON F

REVIEW THE FINANCIAL STATEMENTS

Chapter Review Quiz

1. All of the following statements are true except one. Which statement is false?
   a. Bookkeeping is only a part of accounting.
   b. The organization that formulates generally accepted accounting principles is the Financial Accounting Standards Board.
   c. Professional accountants are held to a high standard of ethical conduct.
   d. A proprietorship is a business with several owners.

2. The valuation of assets on the balance sheet is generally based on:
   a. What it would cost to replace the asset
   b. Historical cost
   c. Current fair market value as established by independent appraisers
   d. Selling price

3. The accounting equation can be expressed as:
   a. Assets + Liabilities = Owners' Equity
   b. Assets = Liabilities – Owners' Equity
   c. Assets – Liabilities = Owners' Equity
   d. Owners' Equity – Assets = Liabilities

4. The nature of an asset is best described as:
   a. Something with physical form that's valued at cost in the accounting records.
   b. An economic resource that's expected to benefit future operations.
   c. An economic resource representing cash or the right to receive cash in the near future.
   d. Something owned by a business that has a ready market value.

5. Which financial statement covers a period of time?
   a. Income statement
   b. Balance sheet
   c. Statement of cash flows
   d. Both A and C

6. How would net income be most likely to affect the accounting equation?
   a. Increase assets and increase liabilities
   b. Increase liabilities and decrease stockholders' equity
   c. Increase assets and increase stockholders' equity
   d. Decrease assets and decrease liabilities

7. During the year, Semper Investments has $60,000 in revenues, $40,000 in expenses, $10,000 in issuance of stock, $3,000 in dividend payments, and $15,000 in payments on accounts payable. Stockholders' equity changed by:
   a. +$27,000
   b. +$42,000
   c. +$12,000
   d. –$8,000
   e. None of the above

8. Semper Investments in question 7 had net income (or net loss) of
   a. Net income of $2,000
   b. Net income of $27,000
   c. Net income of $20,000
   d. Net loss of $40,000

9. Robin Corporation holds cash of $5,000 and owes $25,000 on accounts payable. Robin has accounts receivable of $30,000, inventory of $20,000, and land cost $50,000. How much are Robin's total assets and owners' equity?

	Total assets	*Owners' equity*
a.	$105,000	$25,000
b.	$105,000	$80,000
c.	$80,000	$55,000
d.	$80,000	105,000
e.	$105,000	Cannot be determined from the data given

10. Which item(s) are reported on the balance sheet?
    a. Retained earnings
    b. Cost of goods sold
    c. Franchise fee revenue
    d. All of the above

11. During the year, Dobson Company's stockholders' equity increased from $30,000 to $38,000. Dobson earned net income of $5,000 and paid dividends of $3,000. How much did the owners invest in the business during the year?
    a. $6,000
    b. $-0-
    c. $3,000
    d. $5,000

12. Benson Company had total assets of $300,000 and total stockholders' equity of $100,000 at the beginning of the year. During the year assets increased by $50,000 and liabilities decreased by $40,000. Stockholders' equity at the end of the year is:
    a. $90,000
    b. $110,000
    c. $140,000
    d. $150,000
    e. $190,000

Answers

1. d
2. b
3. c
4. b
5. d
6. c
7. a ($60,000 – $40,000 + $10,000 – $3,000 = $27,000)
8. c ($60,000 – $40,000 = $20,000)
9. b Total assets = $105,000 ($5,000 + $30,000 + $20,000 + $50,000)
   Total equity = $80,000 ($105,000 – $25,000)
10. a
11. a ($30,000 + Investments by owners (x) + Net income ($5,000) – Dividends ($3,000) = $38,000; x = $6,000)
12. e

	ASSETS	=	LIABILITIES	+	EQUITY
Begin.	$300,000	=	$200,000*	+	$100,000
Increase (Decrease)	50,000	=	– 40,000	+	90,000*
Ending	$350,000*	=	$160,000*	+	$190,000*

*Must solve for these amounts.

Accounting Vocabulary

Accounting, like many other subjects, has a special vocabulary. It is important that you understand the following terms. They are defined in the chapter and also in the glossary at the end of the book.

account payable (p. 13)
accounting (p. 5)
accounting equation (p. 12)
assets (p. 12)
balance sheet (p. 18)
board of directors (p. 9)
capital (p. 12)
cash (p. 12)
common stock (p. 13)
corporation (p. 9)
cost principle (p. 11)
current assets (p. 18)
current liabilities (p. 19)
dividends (p. 14)
entity (p. 10)
expenses (p. 13)
financial accounting (p. 6)
financial statements (p. 5)
financing activities (p. 20)
fixed assets (p. 12)
generally accepted accounting principles (GAAP) (p. 9)
going-concern concept (p. 11)
income statement (p. 16)
investing activities (p. 20)
liabilities (p. 12)
long-term debt (p. 13)

FOCUS ON F

management accounting (p. 6)
merchandise inventory (p. 12)
net earnings (p. 13)
net income (p. 13)
net loss (p. 14)
net profit (p. 13)
note payable (p. 13)
objectivity principle (p. 10)
operating activities (p. 20)
owners' equity (p. 12)
paid-in capital (p. 13)
partnership (p. 8)
plant assets (p. 12)
property, plant, and equipment (p. 12)
proprietorship (p. 8)
reliability principle (p. 10)
retained earnings (p. 13)
revenues (p. 13)
shareholders (p. 9)
stable-monetary-unit concept (p. 11)
statement of cash flows (p. 21)
statement of financial position (p. 18)
statement of operations (p. 16)
statement of retained earnings (p. 17)
stock (p. 9)
stockholders (p. 9)
stockholders' equity (p. 13)

ASSESS YOUR PROGRESS

Check Points

Making management and investor decisions (Obj. 1)

CP1-1 (p. 5) Suppose you manage a Taco Bell restaurant. Identify three decisions you must make, and state how accounting will aid your decisions. Answer in your own words.

Now suppose you are considering the purchase of YUM! Brands stock as an investment. Study YUM's income statement at the beginning of the chapter and identify certain items that will help you decide whether to make this investment.

Distinguishing accounting from bookkeeping (Obj. 1)

CP1-2 (p. 5) Briefly discuss the difference between accounting and bookkeeping. How does bookkeeping fit into accounting?

Making ethical judgments (Obj. 1)

CP1-3 (p. 7) Accountants follow ethical guidelines in the conduct of their work. What are these standards of professional conduct designed to produce? Why is this goal important? Assume that there are no ethical guidelines for accountants and that managers could report to the public whatever they wish about their companies. What would be a likely result?

Applying accounting concepts (Obj. 2)

CP1-4 (p. 10) Return to the discussion of David Novak, Chairman of the Board of YUM! Brands, Inc., on page 10. Suppose Mr. Novak has just founded YUM! Brands, and assume that he treats his home and other personal assets as part of YUM! Brands. Answer these questions about the evaluation of YUM! Brands, Inc.

1. What can Novak be misled into believing?
2. Which accounting concept governs this situation?
3. How can the proper application of this accounting concept give Novak and others a realistic view of YUM! Brands, Inc.? Explain in detail.

Using the accounting equation (Obj. 3)

CP1-5 (p. 13) Review the accounting equation on page 12.

1. Show how to determine the amount of eBay's or Coca-Cola's owners' equity. How would your answer change if you were analyzing your own household or a Pizza Hut restaurant?
2. If you know the assets and the owners' equity of a business, how can you measure its liabilities? Give the equation.
3. Can you compute total assets with the knowledge of total owners' equity and total liabilities? If so, show how. If not, explain why it is impossible.

Defining key accounting terms (Obj. 1)

CP1-6 (p. 13) Accounting definitions are precise, and you must understand the vocabulary to properly use accounting. Sharpen your understanding of key terms by answering the following questions:

1. How do the *assets* and *owners' equity* of YUM! Brands, Inc. differ from each other? Which one (assets or owners' equity) must be at least as large as the other? Which one can be smaller than the other?
2. How are YUM! Brands' *liabilities* and *owners' equity* similar? Different?

Classifying assets, liabilities, and owners' equity (Obj. 1)

CP1-7 (p. 13) Consider Microsoft Corporation, the world's largest software company. Classify the following items as an Asset (A), a Liability (L), or an Owners' Equity (E) for Microsoft:

____	**a.** Accounts receivable	____	**g.** Accounts payable
____	**b.** Long-term debt	____	**h.** Common stock
____	**c.** Merchandise inventory	____	**i.** Supplies
____	**d.** Notes payable	____	**j.** Retained earnings
____	**e.** Expenses payable	____	**k.** Land
____	**f.** Equipment	____	**l.** Prepaid expenses

Using the income statement (Obj. 4)

CP1-8 (p. 17) Use YUM! Brands' income statement in Exhibit 1-7 (page 15) to answer the following questions about the company's operations during the year ended December 31, 2003:

1. Identify the two basic categories of items on YUM's income statement.
2. What do we call the bottom line of the income statement?
3. YUM's total assets are $5,620 million, as reported on the company's balance sheet (page 18). How are total assets used to measure net income? Explain your answer.

Preparing an income statement (Obj. 4)

CP1-9 (p. 17) Return to YUM! Brands' income statement in Exhibit 1-7 (page 15). Compute the percentage of cost of goods sold to company sales for 2003 and 2002. Is the trend in this percentage favorable or unfavorable for YUM? Give the reason for your answer.

Preparing a statement of retained earnings (Obj. 4)

CP1-10 (p. 18) IHOP Corp., famous for pancakes, began 2003 with retained earnings of $274 million. Revenues during the year were $405 million and expenses totaled $368 million. IHOP declared dividends of $16 million. What was the company's ending balance of retained earnings? To answer this question, prepare IHOP's statement of retained earnings for the year ended December 31, 2003, complete with its proper heading.

Preparing a balance sheet (Obj. 4)

CP1-11 (p. 20) At December 31, 2008, Toby Landscaping Services has cash of $13,000, receivables of $2,000, and inventory of $40,000. The company's equipment totals $85,000, and other assets amount to $10,000. Toby owes accounts payable of $8,000, short-term notes payable of $12,000, and long-term debt of $80,000.

Common stock is $15,000. The general manage of Toby Landscaping is unsure about the amount of the company's retained earnings.

Prepare Toby's balance sheet at December 31, 2008, complete with its proper heading.

Preparing a statement of cash flows (Obj. 4)

CP1-12 (p. 22) Clearsource Cable, Inc. ended 2005 with cash of $24,000. During 2006, Clearsource earned net income of $88,000 and had adjustments to reconcile net income to net cash provided by operations totaling $20,000 (this is a negative amount).

Clearsource paid $300,000 for equipment during 2006 and had to borrow half of this amount. During the year, the company paid dividends of $10,000 and sold old equipment for $90,000.

Prepare Clearsource's statement of cash flows for the year ended December 31, 2006, complete with its proper heading. Follow the format in the summary problem on page 26.

Identifying items with the appropriate financial statement (Obj. 5)

CP1-13 (p. 22) Suppose you are analyzing the financial statements of Wendy's International, Inc. Identify each item with its appropriate financial statement, using the following abbreviations: Income statement (IS), Statement of retained earnings (SRE), Balance sheet (BS), and Statement of cash flows (SCF). Three items appear on two financial statements, and one item shows up on three statements.

____	**1.** Cash	____	**8.** Dividends
____	**2.** Net cash used for financing activities	____	**9.** Salary expense
		____	**10.** Inventory
____	**3.** Accounts payable	____	**11.** Sales revenue
____	**4.** Common stock	____	**12.** Retained earnings
____	**5.** Interest revenue	____	**13.** Net cash provided by operating activities
____	**6.** Long-term debt		
____	**7.** Increase or decrease in cash	____	**14.** Net income (or net loss)

Exercises

PH Grade Assist

Most of the even-numbered exercises can be found within Prentice Hall Grade Assist (PHGA), an online homework and practice environment. Your instructor may ask you to complete these exercises using PHGA.

Organizing a business (Obj. 1)

writing assignment ■

E1-1 Web Services Inc. develops Web sites for other companies. Web Services needs funds, and Hugo Nurnberg, the president, has asked you to consider investing in the business. Answer the following questions about the different ways that Nurnberg might organize the business. Explain each answer.

a. What form of business organization will give Nurnberg the most freedom to manage the business as he wishes?
b. What form of organization will give creditors the maximum protection in the event that Web Services fails and cannot pay its debts?
c. What form of organization will enable the owners of Web Services to limit their risk of loss to the amount they have invested in the business?
d. What form of organization will probably enable Web Services to raise the most money from owners' equity over the life of the business?

If you were Nurnberg and could organize the business as you wish, what form of organization would you choose for Web Services? Explain your reasoning.

Explaining the income statement and the balance sheet (Obj. 1)

writing assignment ■

E1-2 Mina Carlotti wants to open an Italian restaurant in St. Louis. In need of cash, she asks Missouri Bank & Trust for a loan. The bank requires financial statements to show likely results of operations for the year and the expected financial position at year end. With little knowledge of accounting, Carlotti doesn't know how to proceed. Explain to her the information provided by the income statement and the balance sheet. Indicate why a lender would require this information.

Applying accounting concepts and principles (Obj. 2)

E1-3

a. YUM! Brands has several restaurant divisions. Managers of each division are evaluated on their division's profit performance. Which concept or principle helps YUM design an accounting system to identify the division managers who are most profitable?
b. Suppose Xerox Corporation decides to get out of the magnetic-imaging business and offers its magnetic-imaging division for sale. Xerox reports the assets of the magnetic-imaging division at their current market value. Which accounting concept or principle helps Xerox report its magnetic-imaging division differently from its main operations?
c. General Motors must pay for the materials, labor, and overhead that go into its automobiles. After assembly, a Chevy is much more valuable than the sum of the inputs. Which accounting concept or principle tells how to account for the materials, labor and overhead?
d. Lands' End began in Gary Comer's garage at home. Suppose Comer kept a single checkbook to account for both his personal affairs and all his company's transactions. Would Comer be able to determine the success or failure of Lands' End? Which accounting concept or principle is applicable to this situation?
e. PepsiCo owns real estate in Purchase, New York. Suppose PepsiCo purchased land for $5 million in 2002, and its value has risen. The business is offering the land for sale. One appraiser says the land is worth $10 million; another values the land at $15 million. Should PepsiCo record a gain on the value of the land, or wait to record the gain after selling the land? Which accounting concept or principle controls this situation?

Accounting equation (Obj. 3)

E1-4 Compute the missing amount in the accounting equation for each company (amounts in billions):

	Assets	Liabilities	Owners' Equity
Dell	$?	$ 13	$ 6
Pier 1 Imports	0.9	?	0.6
Boeing	53	45	?

Which company appears to have the strongest financial position? Explain your reasoning.

Accounting equation (Obj. 3, 4)

E1-5 Krispy Kreme Doughnuts has current assets of $141 million; property, plant, and equipment of $202 million; and other assets totaling $67 million. Current liabilities are $60 million and long-term liabilities total $77 million.

Required

1. Use these data to write Krispy Kreme Doughnuts' accounting equation.
2. How much in resources does Krispy Kreme have to work with?
3. How much does Krispy Kreme owe creditors?
4. How much of the company's assets do the Krispy Kreme stockholders actually own?
5. Does Krispy Kreme appear able to pay its current liabilities? Its total liabilities? How can you tell?

Accounting equation (Obj. 3)

E1-6 The Home Depot's comparative balance sheet nearest January 31, 2004, and 2003, reports (in billions):

	2004	2003
Total assets	$34	$30
Total liabilities	12	10

Required

Three assumed situations about Home Depot's issuance of stock and payment of dividends during the year ended January 31, 2004, follow. For each situation, compute the amount of Home Depot's net income or net loss during the year ended January 31, 2004.

1. Home Depot issued $1 billion of stock and paid no dividends.
2. Home Depot issued no stock but paid dividends of $2 billion.
3. Home Depot issued $5 billion of stock and paid dividends of $1 billion.

Which situation indicates the strongest operating results for Home Depot? Which situation indicates the weakest operating results? Give your reason for each answer.

Accounting equation (Obj. 3, 4)

E1-7 Answer these questions about two actual companies.

1. Fossil, Inc., famous for wristwatches and leather goods, began the year with total liabilities of $142 million and total stockholders' equity of $341 million. During the year, total assets increased by 21.7%. How much are total assets at the end of the year?
2. Bed Bath & Beyond began the year with total assets of $2.2 billion and total liabilities of $0.7 billion. Net income for the year was $0.4 billion, and dividends were zero. How much is stockholders' equity at the end of the year?

Identifying financial statement information (Obj. 4)

E1-8 Assume top managers at The Coca-Cola Company are expanding bottling operations in Japan. They must decide where to locate the plant, how much to spend on the building, and how to finance construction. Identify the financial statement where these decision makers can find the following information about Coca-Cola Company. (In some cases, more than one statement will report the needed data.)

a. Long-term debt
b. Revenue
c. Common stock
d. Income tax payable
e. Dividends
f. Income tax expense
g. Ending balance of retained earnings
h. Cost of goods sold
i. Total assets
j. Cash spent to acquire the building
k. Selling, general, and administrative expenses
l. Adjustments to reconcile net income to net cash provided by operations
m. Ending cash balance
n. Liabilities that must be paid next year
o. Net income

E1-9 Amounts of the assets and liabilities of Wells Fargo & Company, the banking chain, as of December 31, 2003, are adapted as follows. Also included are revenue and expense figures for the year ended on that date (amounts in billions):

Business organization, balance sheet (Obj. 2, 5)

■ **spreadsheet**

Total revenue	$ 32	Property and equipment, net	$ 4
Receivables	253	Investment assets	72
Current liabilities	290	Long-term liabilities	64
Common stock	12	Other expenses	14
Interest expense	3	Cash	16
Salary and other employee expenses	9	Retained earnings, beginning	19
Other assets	43	Retained earnings, ending	?

Required

Prepare the balance sheet of Wells Fargo & Company at December 31, 2003.

E1-10 This exercise should be used with Exercise 1-9. Refer to the data of Wells Fargo & Company in Exercise 1-9.

Income statement (Obj. 2, 5)

■ **spreadsheet**

Required

1. Prepare the income statement of Wells Fargo & Company, for the year ended December 31, 2003.
2. What amount of dividends did Wells Fargo declare during the year ended December 31, 2003?

E1-11 ADP, Inc. began the year 2004 with $145 million in cash. During 2004, ADP earned net income of $395 million, and adjustments to reconcile net income to net cash provided by operations totaled $2,330 million, a positive amount. Investing activities used cash of $3,140 million, and financing activities provided cash of $420 million. ADP ended 2004 with total assets of $15,195 million and total liabilities of $10,550 million.

Statement of cash flows (Obj. 2, 4, 5)

Required

Prepare ADP, Inc.'s statement of cash flows for the year ended December 31, 2004. Identify the data items given that do not appear on the statement of cash flows. Also identify the financial statement that reports the unused items.

E1-12 Assume a Kinko's store ended the month of July 20X6, with these data:

Preparing an income statement and a statement of retained earnings (Obj. 5)

Cash balance at beginning of July	$ 0	Payments of cash:	
Cash balance at end of July	6,500	Acquisition of equipment	$36,000
Cash receipts:		Dividends	2,000
Issuance (sale) of stock to owners	35,000	Retained earnings at the end of June	0
Rent expense	700	Retained earnings at the end of July	?
Common stock	35,000	Utilities expense	200
Equipment	36,000	Adjustments to reconcile net income to cash provided by operations	2,000
Office supplies	1,200	Salary expense	4,000
Accounts payable	3,200		
Service revenue	12,400		

Required

Prepare the income statement and the statement of retained earnings of Kinko's for the month ended July 31, 20X6.

E1-13 Refer to the data in the preceding exercise. Prepare the balance sheet of Kinko's at July 31, 20X6.

Preparing a balance sheet (Obj. 5)

Preparing a statement of cash flows (Obj. 5)

E1-14 Refer to the data in Exercise 1-12. Prepare the statement of cash flows of Kinko's for the month ended July 31, 20X6. Draw arrows linking the statements you prepared for Exercises 1-12 through 1-14.

Advising a business (Obj. 4, 5)

writing assignment ■

E1-15 This exercise should be used in conjunction with Exercises 1-12 through 1-14.

The owner of the Kinko's store now seeks your advice as to whether he should cease operations or continue the business. Write a report giving him your opinion of operating results, dividends, financial position, and cash flows during his first month of operations. Cite specifics from the financial statements to support your opinion. Conclude your memo with advice on whether to stay in business or cease operations.

Applying accounting concepts to explain business activity (Obj. 2, 5)

writing assignment ■

E1-16 Apply your understanding of the relationships among the financial statements to answer these questions.

a. If you could pick a single source of cash for your business, what would it be? Why?
b. How can a business lose money several years in a row and still have plenty of cash?
c. How can a business earn large profits but have a small balance of retained earnings?
d. Give two reasons why a business can have a steady stream of net income over a 5-year period and still experience a cash shortage.
e. Suppose your business must pay $100,000 of current liabilities within the next 3 months. Your current assets total only $70,000, and your sales and collections from customers are slow. Identify two ways to finance the extra $30,000 needed to pay your current liabilities.

Practice Quiz

Test your understanding of the financial statements by answering the following questions. Select the best choice from among the possible answers given.

PQ1-1 The *primary* objective of financial reporting is to provide information

a. To the federal government.
b. About the profitability of the enterprise.
c. On the cash flows of the company.
d. Useful for making investment and credit decisions.

PQ1-2 Which type of business organization provides the least amount of protection for bankers and other creditors of the company?

a. Corporation
b. Partnership
c. Proprietorship
d. Both b and c

PQ1-3 Assets are usually reported at their

a. Appraised value
b. Historical cost
c. Current market value
d. None of the above (fill in the blank)

PQ1-4 During January, assets increased by $20,000 and liabilities decreased by $4,000. Stockholders' equity must have

a. Increased by $16,000.
b. Increased by $24,000.
c. Decreased by $24,000.
d. Decreased by $16,000.

PQ1-5 The amount a company expects to collect from customers appears on the

a. Income statement in the expenses section.
b. Income statement in the revenues section.
c. Balance sheet in the stockholders' equity section.
d. Balance sheet in the current assets section.

PQ1-6 All of the following are current assets except

a. Furniture
b. Accounts Receivable
c. Inventory
d. Cash

PQ1-7 Revenues are

a. Increases in paid-in capital resulting from the owners investing in the business.
b. Increases in retained earnings resulting from selling products or performing services.
c. Decreases in liabilities resulting from paying off loans.
d. All of the above.

PQ1-8 The financial statement that reports revenues and expenses is called the

a. Statement of retained earnings.
b. Statement of cash flows.
c. Income statement.
d. Balance sheet.

PQ1-9 Another name for the balance sheet is the

a. Statement of operations.
b. Statement of earnings.
c. Statement of profit and loss.
d. Statement of financial position.

PQ1-10 Robinson Corporation began the year with cash of $35,000 and a computer that cost $20,000. During the year Robinson earned sales revenue of $140,000 and had the following expenses: salaries, $22,000; rent, $8,000; and utilities, $3,000. At year end Robinson's cash balance was down to $16,000. How much net income (or net loss) did Robinson experience for the year?

a. ($19,000)
b. $39,000
c. $107,000
d. $140,000

PQ1-11 Quartz Instruments had retained earnings of $110,000 at December 31, 20X1. Net income for 20X2 totaled $95,000, and dividends for 20X2 were $30,000. How much retained earnings should Quartz report at December 31, 20X2?

a. $205,000
b. $235,000
c. $140,000
d. $175,000

PQ1-12 Net income appears on which financial statement(s)?

a. Income statement
b. Statement of retained earnings
c. Statement of cash flows
d. All of the above
e. Balance sheet

PQ1-13 Cash paid to pay off a loan appears on the statement of cash flows among the

a. Operating activities.
b. Financing activities.
c. Investing activities.
d. Extracurricular activities.

PQ1-14 The stockholders' equity of Serta Company at the beginning and end of 20X0 totaled $15,000 and $18,000, respectively. Assets at the beginning of 20X0 were $25,000. If the liabilities of Serta Company decreased by $8,000 in 20X0, how much were total assets at the end of 20X0?

a. $20,000
b. $16,000
c. $2,000
d. Some other amount (fill in the blank)

PQ1-15 CuJo Company had the following on the dates indicated:

	12/31/X3	12/31/X2
Total assets	$750,000	$520,000
Total liabilities	300,000	200,000

CuJo had no stock transactions in 20X3 and thus the change in stockholders' equity for 20X3 was due to net income and dividends. If dividends were $30,000, how much was CuJo's net income for 20X3?

a. $100,000
b. $130,000
c. $160,000
d. Some other amount (fill in the blank)

Problems
(Group A)

Most of these A problems can be found within Prentice Hall Grade Assist (PHGA), an online homework and practice environment. Your instructor may ask you to complete these problems using PHGA.

Analyzing a loan request (Obj. 1, 5)

writing assignment ■

P1-1A Assume **Prudential Financial Services** is considering an investment in Genome Science Corporation. It is your job to write recommendations to the firm's investment committee. Genome Science has submitted these summary data to support its request for Prudential to purchase $100,000 of the company's stock.

	2005	2004	2003
Statement of Cash Flow Data			
Net cash flow from operations	$190,000	$170,000	$170,000
Net cash flow from investing	(180,000)	(180,000)	(50,000)
Net cash flow from financing	30,000	20,000	(110,000)
Increase (decrease) in cash	$ 40,000	$ 10,000	$ 10,000
Income Statement Data			
Total revenues	$950,000	$820,000	$720,000
Total expenses	640,000	570,000	540,000
Net income	$310,000	$250,000	$180,000
Statement of Retained Earnings Data			
Dividends	$160,000	$140,000	$120,000
Balance Sheet Data			
Total assets	$990,000	$720,000	$590,000
Total liabilities	$440,000	$320,000	$300,000
Total stockholders' equity	550,000	400,000	290,000
Total liabilities and stockholders' equity	$990,000	$720,000	$590,000

Required

Analyze these financial statement data to decide whether the firm should purchase Genome stock. Write a one-paragraph recommendation to the investment committee.

Applying accounting concepts and principles to the income statement (Obj. 2, 4, 5)

writing assignment ■

P1-2A Assume that **General Electric (GE)** experienced the following transactions during the year ended December 31, 20X5:

a. GE sold products for $53 billion. Company management believes the value of these products is approximately $80 billion. Other revenues totaled $73 billion.
b. It cost GE $36 billion to manufacture the products it sold. If GE had purchased the products instead of manufacturing them, GE's cost would have been $42 billion.
c. All other expenses, excluding income taxes, totaled $70 billion for the year. Income tax expense was 30% of income before tax.
d. GE has several operating divisions including aircraft engines, appliances, and NBC, the television network. Each division is accounted for separately to show how well each division is performing. At year end, GE combines the statements of all the divisions to report on the company as a whole.
e. Inflation affects GE's cost to manufacture goods. To show the effects of inflation, the company's net income would drop by $0.7 billion.
f. If GE were to go out of business, the sale of its assets may bring in over $500 billion in cash.

FOCUS ON F

Required

1. Prepare GE Company's income statement for the year ended December 31, 20X5.
2. For items a through f, identify the accounting concept or principle that tells how to account for the item described. State how you have applied the concept or principle in preparing GE's income statement.

Using the accounting equation (Obj. 3)

P1-3A Compute the missing amount (?) for each company (adapted and in billions).

	FedEx Corporation	Coca-Cola Company	Ford Corporation
Beginning			
Assets	$12	$17	$279
Liabilities	7	10	228
Ending			
Assets	$13	$19	$?
Liabilities	7	11	204
Owners' Equity			
Issuance of stock	$?	$ 0	$ 1
Dividends	1	3	9
Income Statement			
Revenues	$20	$19	$119
Expenses	19	?	97

At the end of the year, which company has the

- Lowest percentage of liabilities to assets?
- Highest percentage of net income to revenues?

On these two measures, which company looks strongest? Why?

Balance sheet (Obj. 2, 5)

P1-4A The manager of ICON, Inc. prepared the balance sheet of the company while the accountant was ill. The balance sheet contains numerous errors. In particular, the manager knew that the balance sheet should balance, so he plugged in the stockholders' equity amount needed to achieve this balance. The stockholders' equity amount, however, is *not* correct. All other amounts are accurate.

ICON, Inc.
Balance Sheet
Month Ended July 31, 20X7

Assets		**Liabilities**	
Cash	$15,000	Accounts receivable	$12,000
Office furniture	10,000	Service revenue	50,000
Note payable	16,000	Property tax expense	800
Rent expense	4,000	Accounts payable	9,000
Office supplies	1,000	Total	71,800
Land	44,000	**Stockholders' Equity**	
Advertising expense	2,500	Stockholder's equity	20,700
Total assets	$92,500	Total liabilities	$92,500

Required

1. Prepare the correct balance sheet and date it properly. Compute total assets, total liabilities, and stockholders' equity.
2. Is ICON, Inc. actually in better (or worse) financial position than the erroneous balance sheet reports? Give the reason for your answer.

(continued)

3. Identify the preceding accounts that should *not* be reported on the balance sheet. State why you excluded them from the correct balance sheet you prepared for Requirement 1. Which financial statement should these accounts appear on?

Balance sheet, entity concept (Obj. 2, 5)

P1-5A Marjorie Caballero is a realtor. Caballero organized her business as a corporation on November 24, 2004. The business received $50,000 from Caballero and issued common stock. Consider these facts as of November 30, 2004:

a. Caballero has $10,000 in her personal bank account and $6,000 in the business bank account.
b. Caballero owes $1,800 on a personal charge account with **Nordstrom** department store.
c. The business bought furniture for $17,000 on November 25. Of this amount, the business owes $6,000 on accounts payable at November 30.
d. Office supplies on hand at the real estate office total $1,000.
e. The business owes $40,000 on a note payable for some land acquired for a total price of $120,000.
f. The business spent $20,000 for a **Century 21** real estate franchise, which entitles Caballero to represent herself as a Century 21 agent. Century 21 is a national affiliation of independent real estate agents. This franchise is a business asset.
g. Caballero owes $100,000 on a personal mortgage on her personal residence, which she acquired in 2001 for a total price of $160,000.

Required

1. Prepare the balance sheet of the real estate business of Marjorie Caballero, Realtor, Inc., at November 30, 2004.
2. Does it appear that Caballero's realty business can pay its debts? How can you tell?
3. Identify the personal items given in the preceding facts that should not be reported on the balance sheet of the business.

Income statement, statement of retained earnings, balance sheet (Obj. 5)

spreadsheet

P1-6A The assets and liabilities of Hercules, Inc., as of December 31, 20X8, and revenues and expenses for the year ended on that date follow.

Land	$ 98,000	Property tax expense	$ 4,000
Note payable	185,000	Accounts receivable	12,000
Accounts payable	19,000	Advertising expense	13,000
Rent expense	23,000	Building	150,000
Cash	10,000	Salary expense	63,000
Common stock	40,000	Salary payable	1,000
Furniture	20,000	Service revenue	220,000
Interest expense	9,000	Supplies	3,000

Beginning retained earnings were $10,000, and dividends totaled $70,000 for the year.

Required

1. Prepare the income statement of Hercules, Inc., for the year ended December 31, 20X8.
2. Prepare Hercules' statement of retained earnings for the year.
3. Prepare Hercules' balance sheet at December 31, 20X8.
4. Analyze Hercules, Inc., by answering these questions:
   a. Was Hercules profitable during 20X8? By how much?
   b. Did retained earnings increase or decrease? By how much?
   c. Which is greater, total liabilities or total equity? Who owns more of Hercules' assets, creditors or the Hercules stockholders?

Preparing a statement of cash flows (Obj. 4)

P1-7A The following data are adapted from the financial statements of **Nike, Inc.**, at the end of a recent year (in millions).

FOCUS ON F

Required

Revenues	$9,187	Sales of property, plant, and equipment	$ 24
Cash, beginning of year	262	Adjustments to reconcile net income to net cash provided by operating activities	(473)
end of year	445	Cost of goods sold	5,503
Purchases of property, plant, and equipment	510	Other investing cash receipts	33
Long-term debt	296	Accounts receivable	1,754
Net income	796	Borrowing	388
Payment of dividends	101		
Common stock	2,858		
Issuance of common stock	26		
Retained earnings	2,974		

1. Prepare Nike, Inc.'s statement of cash flows for the year ended May 31, 20X4. Follow the solution of the summary problem on page 26. Not all the items given appear on the statement of cash flows.
2. Which activities provided the bulk of Nike's cash? Is this a sign of financial strength or weakness?

P1-8A StrideRite, Inc. operates discount shoe stores. Condensed versions of the company's financial statements, with certain items omitted, follow for two recent years.

Analyzing a company's financial statements (Obj. 4, 5)

	20X6	20X5
Statement of Income	(Thousands)	
Revenues	$ k	$88,412
Cost of goods sold	74,564	a
Other expenses	15,839	13,564
Income before income taxes	4,346	9,262
Income taxes (36.95% in 20X6)	l	1,581
Net income	$ m	$ b
Statement of Retained Earnings		
Beginning balance	$ n	$ 9,987
Net income	o	c
Dividends	(559)	(455)
Ending balance	$ p	$ d
Balance Sheet		
Assets:		
Cash	$ q	$ e
Property, plant, and equipment	23,894	20,874
Other assets	r	16,900
Total assets	$ s	$37,819
Liabilities:		
Current liabilities	$ t	$ 9,973
Long-term debt and other liabilities	11,331	10,120
Total liabilities	22,785	f
Shareholders' Equity:		
Common stock	$ 229	$ 230
Retained earnings	u	g
Other shareholders' equity	133	283
Total shareholders' equity	v	17,726
Total liabilities and shareholders' equity	$ w	$ h
Statement of Cash Flows		
Net cash provided by operating activities	$ x	$ 2,906
Net cash used for investing activities	(3,332)	(3,792)
Net cash provided by financing activities	987	911
Increase (decrease) in cash	38	i
Cash at beginning of year	y	20
Cash at end of year	$ z	$ j

Required

1. Determine the missing amounts denoted by the letters.
2. Use StrideRite's financial statements to answer these questions about the company. Explain each of your answers.
   a. Did operations improve or deteriorate during 20X6?
   b. What is the company doing with most of its income—retaining it for use in the business or using it for dividends?
   c. How much in total resources does the company have to work with as it moves into 20X7?
   d. At the end of 20X5, how much did the company owe outsiders? At the end of 20X6, how much did the company owe?
   e. What is the company's major source of cash? What is your opinion of the company's ability to generate cash? How is the company using most of its cash? Is the company growing or shrinking?

(Group B)

Some of these B problems can be found online at www.prenhall.com/harrison. These problems are algorithmically generated, allowing you endless practice. You'll receive immediate assessment and feedback as you complete each problem.

Analyzing a loan request (Obj. 1, 5)

writing assignment ■

P1-1B As an analyst for Edward Jones Company, it is your job to write recommendations to the firm's loan committee. Kaiser Corporation, a pharmaceutical company, has submitted these summary data to support Kaiser's request for a $50 million loan.

	All amounts in millions		
	2007	2006	2005
Statement of Cash Flow Data			
Net cash flow from operations	$ 70	$ 90	$110
Net cash flow from investing	(40)	(100)	60
Net cash flow from financing	$ (80)	(40)	(190)
Increase (decrease) in cash	$ (50)	$(50)	$(20)
Income Statement Data			
Total revenues	$790	$830	$820
Total expenses	640	570	540
Net income	$150	$260	$280
Statement of Retained Earnings Data			
Dividends	$200	$280	$270
Balance Sheet Data			
Total assets	$730	$700	$660
Total liabilities	$390	$320	$260
Total stockholders' equity	330	380	400
Total liabilities and stockholders' equity	$720	$700	$660

Required

Analyze these financial statement data to determine whether the firm should lend $50 million to Kaiser. Write a one-paragraph recommendation to the loan committee.

Applying accounting concepts and principles to the income statement (Obj. 2, 4, 5)

P1-2B Assume that the **Chrysler Division of DaimlerChrysler Corporation** experienced the following transactions during the year ended December 31, 20X5:

a. Suppose Chrysler sold its automobiles and other products for the discounted price of $69.4 billion. In past years Chrysler would have sold these products for $73 billion. Other revenues totaled $5.8 billion.
b. It cost Chrysler $59.0 billion to manufacture the products it sold. If Chrysler had purchased the products instead of manufacturing them, the cost would have been $61.6 billion.

FOCUS ON F

c. Selling and administrative expenses were $3.7 billion. All other expenses, excluding income taxes, totaled $4.5 billion for the year. Income tax expense was 35% of income before tax. Round to the nearest 1/10 billion (for example, $3.2 billion).

d. Chrysler has several operating subdivisions: Dodge, Chrysler, Jeep, and Eagle. Each subdivision is accounted for separately to indicate how well each is performing. At year end, Chrysler combines the statements of all subdivisions to show results for the Chrysler Division as a whole.

e. Inflation affects the amounts that Chrysler must pay for auto parts. To show the effects of inflation, net income would drop by $0.4 billion.

f. If Chrysler were to go out of business, the sale of its assets would bring in $90 billion in cash.

Required

1. Prepare the Chrysler Division's income statement for the year ended December 31, 20X5.
2. For items a through f, identify the accounting concept or principle that provides guidance in accounting for the item. State how you have applied the concept or principle in preparing Chrysler's income statement.

Using the accounting equation (Obj. 3)

P1-3B Compute the missing amount (?) for each company (adapted and in billions).

	Best Buy	Pier 1	Wal-Mart
Beginning			
Assets	$ 3.0	$0.7	$ 78
Liabilities	1.9	0.2	47
Ending			
Assets	$ 4.8	$0.9	$?
Liabilities	3.0	0.3	48
Owners' Equity			
Issuance of stock	$?	$ 0	$ 0
Dividends	0	0	3
Income Statement			
Revenues	$15.3	$1.5	$218
Expenses	14.9	?	211

At the end of the year, which company has the

- Lowest percentage of liabilities to assets?
- Highest percentage of net income to revenues?

On these two measures, which company looks strongest? Why?

Balance sheet (Obj. 2, 5)

P1-4B Greg Ogden, the manager of **Shipp Belting, Inc.**, which manufactures conveyor belts, prepared the company's balance sheet while the accountant was ill. The balance sheet contains some errors. In particular, Ogden knew that the balance sheet should balance, so he plugged in the stockholders' equity amount needed to achieve this balance. The stockholders' equity amount is *not* correct. All other amounts are accurate.

Shipp Belting, Inc.
Balance Sheet
Month Ended October 31, 20X8

Assets		**Liabilities**	
Cash	$ 15,400	Notes receivable	$ 14,000
Equipment	36,700	Interest expense	2,000
Accounts payable	3,000	Office supplies	800
Utilities expense	2,100	Accounts receivable	2,600
Advertising expense	300	Note payable	50,000
Land	80,500	Total	69,400
Salary expense	3,300	**Stockholders' Equity**	
		Stockholders' equity	71,900
Total assets	$141,300	Total liabilities	$141,300

NDAMENTALS

Required

1. Prepare the correct balance sheet and date it properly. Compute total assets, total liabilities, and stockholders' equity.
2. Is Shipp Belting actually in better (or worse) financial position than the erroneous balance sheet reports? Give the reason for your answer.
3. Identify the accounts listed on the incorrect balance sheet that should not be reported on the balance sheet. State why you excluded them from the correct balance sheet you prepared for Requirement 1. On which financial statement should these accounts appear?

Balance sheet, entity concept (Obj. 2, 5)

P1-5B Mike Cassell is a realtor. He organized his business as a corporation on March 10, 2008. The business received $75,000 cash from Cassell and issued common stock. Consider the following facts as of March 31, 2008:

a. Cassell has $9,000 in his personal bank account and $16,000 in the business bank account.
b. Office supplies on hand at the real estate office total $1,000.
c. Cassell's business spent $35,000 for a **Century 21** franchise, which entitles him to represent himself as an agent. Century 21 is a national affiliation of independent real estate agents. This franchise is a business asset.
d. Cassell's business owes $33,000 on a note payable for some land acquired for a total price of $100,000.
e. Cassell owes $65,000 on a personal mortgage on his personal residence, which he acquired in 2002 for a total price of $190,000.
f. Cassell owes $300 on a personal charge account with **Sears**.
g. Cassell acquired business furniture for $12,000 on March 26. Of this amount, Cassell's business owes $6,000 on accounts payable at March 31.

Required

1. Prepare the balance sheet of the real estate business of Mike Cassell Realtor, Inc., at March 31, 2008.
2. Does it appear that Cassell's realty business can pay its debts? How can you tell?
3. Identify the personal items given in the preceding facts that should not be reported on the balance sheet of the business.

Income statement, statement of retained earnings, balance sheet (Obj. 5)

spreadsheet

P1-6B The assets and liabilities of Kellogg Services, Inc., as of December 31, 20X7, and revenues and expenses for the year ended on that date are listed here.

Equipment	$ 31,000	Land	$ 8,000
Interest expense	4,000	Note payable	31,000
Interest payable	1,000	Property tax expense	2,000
Accounts payable	12,000	Rent expense	14,000
Salary expense	34,000	Accounts receivable	10,000
Building	126,000	Service revenue	115,000
Cash	4,000	Supplies	2,000
Common stock	10,000	Utilities expense	3,000

Beginning retained earnings was $111,000, and dividends totaled $42,000 for the year.

Required

1. Prepare the income statement of Kellogg Services, Inc. for the year ended December 31, 20X7.
2. Prepare the company's statement of retained earnings for the year.
3. Prepare the company's balance sheet at December 31, 20X7.
4. Analyze Kellogg Services by answering these questions:
   a. Was Kellogg profitable during 20X7? By how much?
   b. Did retained earnings increase or decrease? By how much?
   c. Which is greater, total liabilities or total equity? Who owns more of Kellogg's assets, creditors or the Kellogg stockholders?

P1-7B The following data are adapted from the financial statements of **The Home Depot, Inc.**, at the end of a recent year (in millions):

Preparing a statement of cash flows (Obj. 4)

Purchases of property, plant, and equipment	$ 3,393	Other investing cash payments	$ 263
Long-term debt	1,250	Accounts receivable	920
Net income	3,044	Borrowing	532
Adjustments to reconcile net income to cash provided by operations	2,919	Payment of dividends	396
Revenues	53,553	Common stock	5,529
Cash, beginning of year	167	Issuance of common stock	445
end of year	2,477	Sales of property, plant, and equipment	176
Cost of goods sold	37,406	Retained earnings	12,799
		Payment of long-term debt	754

Required

1. Prepare Home Depot's statement of cash flows for the year ended January 31, 20X3. Follow the format of the summary problem on pages 25 to 26.
2. What was Home Depot's largest source of cash? Is this a sign of financial strength or weakness?

P1-8B McConnell Corporation manufactures recreational aircraft. Summarized versions of the company's financial statements are given for two recent years.

Analyzing a company's financial statements (Obj. 4, 5)

	20X5	20X4
Statement of Income	(In thousands)	
Revenues	$ k	$15,487
Cost of goods sold	11,026	a
Other expenses	1,230	1,169
Income before income taxes	920	1,496
Income taxes (35% in 20X5)	l	100
Net income	$ m	$ b
Statement of Retained Earnings		
Beginning balance	$ n	$ 2,702
Net income	o	c
Dividends	(65)	(55)
Ending balance	$ p	$ d
Balance Sheet		
Assets:		
Cash	$ q	$ e
Property, plant, and equipment	1,597	1,750
Other assets	r	10,190
Total assets	$ s	$13,026
Liabilities:		
Current liabilities	$ t	$ 5,403
Notes payable and long-term debt	2,569	3,138
Other liabilities	69	72
Total liabilities	$ 8,344	$ f
Shareholders' Equity:		
Common stock	$ 117	$ 118
Retained earnings	u	g
Other shareholders' equity	179	252
Total shareholders' equity	v	4,413
Total liabilities and shareholders' equity	$ w	$ h

(continued)

Statement of Cash Flows	20X5	20X4
	(In thousands)	
Net cash provided by operating activities	$ x	$ 575
Net cash provided by investing activities	58	474
Net cash used for financing activities	(709)	(1,045)
Increase (decrease) in cash	335	i
Cash at beginning of year	y	1,082
Cash at end of year	$ z	$ j

Required

1. Determine the missing amounts denoted by the letters.
2. Use McConnell's financial statements to answer these questions about the company. Explain each of your answers.
   a. Did operations improve or deteriorate during 20X5?
   b. What is the company doing with most of its income—retaining it for use in the business or using it for dividends?
   c. How much in total resources does the company have to work with as it moves into the year 20X6?
   d. At the end of 20X4, how much did the company owe outsiders? At the end of 20X5, how much did the company owe? Is this trend good or bad in comparison to the trend in assets?
   e. What is the company's major source of cash? Is cash increasing or decreasing? What is your opinion of the company's ability to generate cash?

Apply Your Knowledge

Decision Cases

Analyzing a company as an investment (Obj. 2, 4, 5)

Case 1. After a year out of college, you now have $5,000 to invest. You visit the Web sites of **eBay**, **AOL Time Warner**, and **Yahoo!**, but their stocks seem overpriced. A friend has started Data Services Corp., and she asks you to invest in her company. You obtain the company's financial statements, which are summarized at the end of the first year as follows:

Data Services Corp.
Income Statement
Year Ended Dec. 31, 2004

Revenues	$80,000
Expenses	60,000
Net income	$20,000

Data Services Corp.
Balance Sheet
Dec. 31, 2004

Cash	$ 3,000	Liabilities	$30,000
Other assets	67,000	Equity	40,000
		Total liabilities	
Total assets	$70,000	and equity	$70,000

Visits with your friend turn up the following facts:

a. Revenues and receivables of $10,000 were overlooked and omitted.

b. Software costs of $25,000 were recorded as assets. These costs should have been expenses. Data Services paid cash for these expenses and recorded the cash payment correctly.

c. The company owes an additional $5,000 for advertising expense in December.

Required

1. What is Data Services' most pressing need?
2. Prepare corrected financial statements.
3. Use your corrected statements to evaluate Data Services' results of operations and financial position.
4. Will you invest in Data Services Corp.? Give your reason.

Using financial statements to evaluate a loan request (Obj. 1, 2)

Case 2. Two businesses, MLK, Inc. and JFK Corporation, have sought business loans from you. To decide whether to make the loans, you have requested their balance sheets.

JFK Corporation
Balance Sheet
August 31, 2005

Assets		Liabilities	
Cash	$ 11,000	Accounts payable	$ 3,000
Accounts receivable	4,000	Notes payable	388,000
Supplies	1,000	Total liabilities	391,000
Furniture	36,000		
Land	79,000	**Owners' Equity**	
Equipment	300,000	Owners' equity	40,000
		Total liabilities and	
Total assets	$431,000	owners' equity	$431,000

MLK, Inc.
Balance Sheet
August 31, 2005

Assets		Liabilities	
Cash	$ 9,000	Accounts payable	$ 12,000
Accounts receivable	14,000	Note payable	18,000
Merchandise inventory	85,000	Total liabilities	30,000
Supplies	500		
Furniture and fixtures	9,000		
Building	82,000	**Stockholders' Equity**	
Land	14,000	Stockholders' equity	183,500
		Total liabilities and	
Total assets	$213,500	stockholders' equity	$213,500

Required

Solely on the basis of these balance sheets, to which entity would you be more comfortable lending money? Explain fully, citing specific items and amounts from the respective balance sheets.

Ethical Issue

During 2002, **Enron Corporation** admitted hiding large liabilities from its balance sheet. **WorldCom** confessed to recording expenses as assets. Both companies needed to improve their appearance as reported in their financial statements.

Required

1. What is the fundamental ethical issue in these situations?
2. Use the accounting equation to show how Enron abused good accounting. Use a separate accounting equation to demonstrate WorldCom's error.
3. What can happen when companies report financial data that are untrue?

Focus on Financials: ■ YUM! Brands

Identifying items from a company's financial statements (Obj. 4)

This and similar cases in succeeding chapters are based on the financial statements of YUM! Brands, Inc. As you work with YUM! Brands throughout this course, you will develop the ability to use actual financial statements.

Required

Refer to the YUM! Brands' financial statements in Appendix A at the end of the book.

1. Suppose you own stock in YUM. If you could pick one item on the company's income statement to increase year after year, what would it be? Why is this item so important? Did this item increase or decrease during 2003? Is this good news or bad news for the company?
2. What was YUM's largest expense each year? In your own words, explain the meaning of this item. Give specific examples of items that make up this expense. Why is this expense less than sales revenue? The chapter gives another title for this expense. What is it?
3. Use the balance sheet of YUM in Appendix A to answer these questions: At the end of 2003, how much in total resources did YUM have to work with? How much did the company owe? How much of its assets did the company's stockholders actually own? Use these amounts to write YUM's accounting equation at December 27, 2003.
4. Use YUM's statement of cash flows in Appendix A at the back of the book to answer these questions: Where does YUM get most of its cash? How much cash did YUM have at the beginning of the most recent year? How much cash did YUM have at the end of the year?

Focus on Analysis: ■ Pier 1 Imports

Evaluating a leading company (Obj. 3, 4)

This and similar cases in each chapter are based on the financial statements of Pier 1 Imports, Inc., given in Appendix B at the end of this book. As you work with Pier 1, you will develop the ability to analyze the financial statements of actual companies.

Required

1. Write Pier 1's accounting equation at the end of 2004 (express all items in millions and round to the nearest $1 million). Does Pier 1's financial condition look strong or weak? How can you tell?
2. Examine accounts payable on the blaance sheet. What caused accounts payable to increase so much during 2004?
3. Which part of shareholders' equity increased the most during 2004? What caused this item to increase?
4. Which statement reports cash as part of Pier 1's financial position? Which statement tells *why* cash increased (or decreased) during the year? What two items caused Pier 1's cash to decrease the most during 2004?
5. What was the result of Pier 1's operations during 2004? Identify both the name and the dollar amount of the result of operations for 2004, and indicate whether it increased or decreased during the year. Does an increase (decrease) signal good news or bad news for the company and its stockholders?

Group Projects

Project 1. As instructed by your professor, obtain the annual report of a well-known company.

Required

1. Take the role of a loan committee of Charter Bank, a large banking company headquartered in Charlotte, North Carolina. Assume the company has requested a loan from

Charter Bank. Analyze the company's financial statements and any other information you need to reach a decision regarding the largest amount of money you would be willing to lend. Go as deeply into the analysis and the related decision as you can. Specify the following:

a. The length of the loan period—that is, over what period will you allow the company to pay you back?
b. The interest rate you will charge on the loan. Will you charge the prevailing interest rate, a lower rate, or a higher rate? Why?
c. Any restrictions you will impose on the borrower as a condition for making the loan.

Note: The long-term debt note to the financial statements gives details of the company's existing liabilities.

2. Write your group decision in a report addressed to the bank's board of directors. Limit your report to two double-spaced word-processed pages.
3. If your professor directs, present your decision and your analysis to the class. Limit your presentation to 10 to 15 minutes.

Project 2. You are the owner of a company that is about to "go public"—that is, issue its stock to outside investors. You wish to make your company look as attractive as possible to raise $1 million of cash to expand the business. At the same time, you want to give potential investors a realistic picture of your company.

Required

1. Design a booklet to portray your company in a way that will enable outsiders to reach an informed decision as to whether to buy some of your stock. The booklet should include the following:
   a. Name and location of your company.
   b. Nature of the company's business (be as detailed as possible).
   c. How you plan to spend the money you raise.
   d. The company's comparative income statement, statement of retained earnings, balance sheet, and statement of cash flows for 2 years: the current year and the preceding year. Make the data as realistic as possible with the intent of receiving $1 million.
2. Word-process your booklet, not to exceed five pages.
3. If directed by your professor, make a copy for each member of your class. Distribute copies to the class and present your case with the intent of interesting your classmates in investing in the company. Limit your presentation to 10 to 15 minutes.

spotlight

APPLE COMPUTER, INC.

Apple Computer, Inc.
Consolidated Statements of Operations (Adapted)
Fiscal Years Ended September 27, 2003, and 2002

(In millions)	2003	2002
Net sales	$6,207	$5,742
Cost of sales	4,499	4,139
Gross margin	1,708	1,603
Operating expenses:		
Research and development	471	446
Selling, general, and administrative	1,212	1,109
Restructuring costs and other operating expenses	26	31
Total operating expenses	1,709	1,586
Operating income (loss)	(1)	17
Other income and expense, net	93	70
Income before income taxes	92	87
Income tax expense	24	22
Income before accounting changes	68	65
Cumulative effects of accounting changes, net of income taxes	1	—
Net income (loss)	$ 69	$ 65

How do you create and manage your digital music library? Where do you go for free Internet radio stations? Do you burn your custom playlists of songs to CDs and DVDs? If so, you may be using iTunes®, the digital music management application of Apple Computer, Inc. Apple has both Mac and Windows versions of iTunes®.

Apple's Music Store features 500,000 tracks, including all five major labels—for 99¢ each. Music fans have purchased and downloaded over 100 million songs from the iTunes Music Store. Apple also features iMovie®, a digital video editing application for creating home movies.

How does Apple Computer, Inc., keep track of the cost of developing iTunes®, iMovie®, and its other software? How does Apple determine the amount of its revenues, expenses, and net income? Like all other companies, Apple Computer has a comprehensive accounting system that follows generally accepted accounting principles (GAAP). Apple's income statement (statement of operations) is given at the start of this chapter. The income statement shows that during fiscal year 2003, Apple made over $6 billion of sales and earned net income of $69 million. Where did those figures come from? In this chapter, we'll show you.

Chapter 1 introduced the financial statements and showed the end product of an accounting system—the income statement, the balance sheet, and the statement of cash flows. Chapter 2 will show you how companies actually record the transactions that eventually become part of the financial statements.

2

Transaction Analysis

LEARNING OBJECTIVES

1. **Analyze** business transactions
2. **Understand** how accounting works
3. **Record** business transactions
4. **Use** a trial balance
5. **Analyze** transactions for quick decisions

For more practice and review of accounting cycle concepts, use ACT, the Accounting Cycle Tutorial, online at **www.prenhall.com/harrison**. Margin logos like this one, directing you to the appropriate ACT section and material, appear throughout Chapters 1, 2, and 3. When you enter the tutorial, you'll find three buttons on the opening page of each chapter module. Here's what the buttons mean: Tutorial gives you a review of the major concepts, Application gives you practice exercises, and Glossary reviews important terms.

Transactions

Transaction
Any event that has a financial impact on the business and can be measured reliably.

Business activity is all about transactions. A **transaction** is any event that has a financial impact on the business and can be measured reliably. For example, Apple Computer pays programmers to create iTunes® software. The payment of employee salaries is a business transaction. Apple sells computers, and that is another transaction. Apple borrows money—a third transaction—and repays the loan—a fourth transaction. Accountants record the effects of transactions on Apple Computer, Inc.

But not all events that affect Apple Computer qualify as transactions. iTunes® may be featured in *Showtime Magazine* and motivate you to consider buying an Apple computer. The magazine article may create lots of new business for Apple. But no transaction occurs until someone actually buys an Apple product. A transaction must occur before Apple records anything.

Transactions provide objective information about the financial impacts on Apple Computer. Every transaction has two sides:

- You give something, and
- You receive something

Remember: You must be able to measure the financial impact of the event on the business before recording it as a transaction. You must assign a dollar amount to the transaction in order to record it on the books.

What is so special about the value arising from a transaction? Suppose you are buying software from a Best Buy store. You are determined to pay the lowest price possible. The sales clerk, on the other hand, is trying to sell you the software at the list price. When you and Best Buy agree upon a price and strike a deal, the dollar amount of the transaction provides objective evidence of its true value. Until the transaction is completed, the value of the merchandise is subject to dispute.

Accounting also uses accounts, which are the basic summary device of accounting. An account is the record of all the changes in a particular asset, liability, or stockholders' equity during a period. Before launching into transaction analysis, let's briefly review the accounts that companies use to measure their progress.

The Account

Account
The record of the changes that have occurred in a particular asset, liability, or stockholders' equity during a period. The basic summary device of accounting.

As we saw in Chapter 1, the accounting equation is the basic tool of accounting. It measures the assets of the business and the claims to those assets. We use a record called an **account** for every asset, liability, and stockholders' equity of the business. Accounts are of three broad types, following the accounting equation:

Assets = Liabilities + Stockholders' (or Owners') Equity

FOCUS ON F

Assets

Assets are economic resources that provide a future benefit for a business. Most firms use the following asset accounts:

Cash. **Cash** means money and any medium of exchange including bank account balances, paper currency, coins, certificates of deposit, and checks. Most business failures result from a shortage of cash.

Cash
Money and any medium of exchange that a bank accepts at face value.

Accounts Receivable. Apple Computer, like most other companies, sells its goods and services and receives a promise for future collection of cash. The Accounts Receivable account holds these amounts.

Notes Receivable. A business may sell its goods or services for a note receivable called a *promissory note*. A note receivable is similar to an account receivable, but a note receivable is more binding on the customer. Also, notes receivable usually specify an interest rate.

Inventory. Apple Computer's most important asset is its inventory—the hardware and software Apple sells to customers. Other titles for this account include *Merchandise* and *Merchandise Inventory.*

Prepaid Expenses. Apple Computer pays certain expenses in advance, such as insurance and rent. A **prepaid expense** is an asset because the payment provides a *future* benefit for the business. Prepaid Rent, Prepaid Insurance, and Office Supplies are prepaid expenses.

Prepaid expense
A category of miscellaneous assets that typically expire or get used up in the near future. Examples include prepaid rent, prepaid insurance, and supplies.

Land. The Land account is a record of the cost of land the business uses in its operations.

Buildings. The costs of Apple's office building, manufacturing plant, and the like appear in the Buildings account.

Equipment, Furniture, and Fixtures. Apple Computer has a separate asset account for each type of equipment, for example, Manufacturing Equipment and Office Equipment. The Furniture and Fixtures account shows the cost of these assets, which are similar to equipment.

Liabilities

Recall that a *liability* is a debt. A payable is always a liability. The most common types of liabilities include:

Notes Payable. A note payable is the opposite of a note receivable. The Notes Payable account includes the amounts Apple must *pay* because it signed promissory notes that require a future payment. Notes payable, like notes receivable, also carry interest.

Accounts Payable. The Accounts Payable account is the direct opposite of Accounts Receivable. Apple's promise to pay a debt arising from a credit purchase of an item of inventory appears in the Accounts Payable account.

Accrued liability
A liability for an expense that has not yet been paid by the company. Another name for *accrued expense*.

Accrued Liabilities. An **accrued liability** is a liability for an expense that has not yet been paid. Interest Payable and Salary Payable are accrued liability accounts for most companies. Income Tax Payable is also an accrued liability.

Stockholders' (Owners') Equity

The owners' claims to the assets of a corporation are called *stockholders' equity, shareholders' equity*, or simply *owners' equity*. In a proprietorship, there is a single capital account. For a partnership, each partner has a separate owner equity account. A corporation such as Apple Computer uses Common Stock, Retained Earnings, and Dividends accounts to record changes in stockholders' equity.

Common Stock. The Common Stock account shows the owners' investment in the corporation. Apple Computer receives cash and issues common stock to its stockholders. A stock certificate lists the stockholder's name as proof of ownership.

Retained Earnings. Apple Computer must earn a profit (net income) to survive. The Retained Earnings account shows the cumulative net income earned by Apple over its lifetime, minus cumulative net losses and dividends.

Dividends. The owners of a corporation demand a return on their investment. Many stockholders want cash dividends. After profitable operations, the board of directors of Apple Computer may (or may not) declare and pay a cash dividend. Dividends are optional and decided by the board of directors. The corporation may keep a separate account titled *Dividends*, which indicates a decrease in Retained Earnings.

Revenues. The increase in stockholders' equity from delivering goods or services to customers is called *revenue*. The company uses as many revenue accounts as needed. Apple Computer uses a Sales Revenue account for revenue earned by selling its products to customers. A lawyer provides legal services for clients and uses a Service Revenue account. A business that loans money to an outsider needs an Interest Revenue account. If the business rents a building to a tenant, it needs a Rent Revenue account.

Expenses. The cost of operating a business is called *expense*. Expenses *decrease* stockholders' equity, the opposite of revenues. A business needs a separate account for each type of expense, such as Cost of Sales, Salary Expense, Rent Expense, Advertising Expense, and Utilities Expense. Businesses strive to minimize expenses and thereby maximize net income.

stop AND think. . .

Name two things that (1) increase Apple Computer's stockholders' equity and (2) decrease Apple's stockholders' equity.

Answer:

(1) Sale of stock and net income (revenue greater than expenses). (2) Dividends and net loss (expenses greater than revenue).

FOCUS ON F

ACCOUNTING ALERT

Single-Entry Accounting Doesn't Cut It

If you're like most people, you keep a checkbook that looks something like this:

Date	Payee	✓	Check	Deposit	Balance
May 1					$1,400
1	Cash		$ 50		1,350
1	Bentwood Apartments		250		1,100
3	Ralph Jones			$ 40	1,140
6	Best Buy		60		1,080
11	Kroger		40		1,040
15	Paycheck			600	1,640
16	Cash (ATM)		140		1,500
21	Texas Utilities		80		1,420
24	VISA		160		1,260
27	Interest on bank balance			2	1,262
31	Paycheck			600	1,862

This checkbook may work for you, but a company like Apple Computer couldn't get by with only this information. The data are incomplete. For example, the May 6 check doesn't tell what you bought at Best Buy. The May 3 deposit from Ralph Jones doesn't tell why Ralph gave us $40.

The checkbook is an example of a single-entry accounting, with each transaction described by only one piece of information. Single-entry works well if you're only keeping track of your cash. For example, the checkbook tells us

- where cash *went* (May 1—we cashed a check)
- where cash *came from* (May 15—our paycheck)
- our *balance* (we ended the month of May with cash of $1,862)

The May 1 check lists only Bentwood Apartments. Was this check for monthly rent? Single-entry shows only the payee of the check, so the income statement shows no rent expense. The May 15 cash receipt doesn't record the revenue you've earned.

In the business world, accounting is practiced with double-entry accounting. Double-entry is based on the fact that every transaction has two sides and **double-entry** records both the giving side and the receiving side of each transaction. With double-entry accounting,

- The *income statement* reports revenues and expenses.
- The *balance sheet* reports assets, liabilities, and owners' equity.
- The *statement of cash flows* reports the sources and uses of cash.

The take-away lessons from this acounting alert are this:

- Avoid single-entry accounting for a business enterprise.
- Use double-entry for a business, because only double-entry gives you the data for the financial statements.

Now let's see how to record business transactions.

Accounting for Business Transactions

Example: Air and Sea Travel, Inc.

OBJECTIVE

1 **Analyze** business transactions

To illustrate accounting for business transactions, let's return to Air & Sea Travel, Inc. In Chapter 1's End-of-Chapter Problem, Gary and Monica Lyon opened a travel agency in April 20X6, incorporated as Air & Sea Travel, Inc. We consider 11 events and analyze each in terms of its effect on Air & Sea Travel. We use the accounting equation.

Transaction 1. The Lyons invest $50,000 to begin the business, and Air & Sea Travel issues common stock to Gary and Monica Lyon. The effect of this transaction on the accounting equation of the business entity Air & Sea Travel, Inc. is a receipt of cash and issuance of common stock, as follows:

ASSETS		LIABILITIES +	STOCKHOLDERS' EQUITY	TYPE OF STOCKHOLDERS' EQUITY TRANSACTION
Cash	=		**Common Stock**	
(1) + 50,000			+ 50,000	Issued stock

Every transaction's net amount on the left side of the equation must equal the net amount on the right side. The first transaction increases both the cash and the common stock of the travel agency. To the right of the transaction we write "Issued stock" to record the reason for the increase in stockholders' equity.

Every transaction affects the financial statements of the business, and we can prepare the statements after one, two, or any number of transactions. For example, Air & Sea Travel, Inc., could report the company's balance sheet after its first transaction, shown here.

Air & Sea Travel, Inc.
Balance Sheet
April 1, 20X6

Assets		**Liabilities**	
Cash	$50,000	None	
		Stockholders' Equity	
		Common stock	$50,000
		Total stockholders' equity	50,000
Total assets	$50,000	Total liabilities and stockholders' equity	$50,000

This balance sheet shows that Air & Sea Travel holds cash of $50,000 and owes no liabilities. The company's equity (ownership) is denoted as *Common stock* on the balance sheet. A bank would look favorably on the Air & Sea Travel balance sheet because the business has $50,000 cash and no debt—a strong financial position.

As a practical matter, most entities report their financial statements at the end of the accounting period—not after each transaction. But an accounting system can produce statements whenever managers need to know where the business stands.

FOCUS ON F

Transaction 2. Air & Sea Travel purchases land for an office location and pays cash of $40,000. The effect of this transaction on the accounting equation is:

	ASSETS				LIABILITIES	+ STOCKHOLDERS' EQUITY	TYPE OF STOCKHOLDERS' EQUITY TRANSACTION
	Cash	+	Land	=		Common Stock	
(1)	50,000					50,000	Issued stock
(2)	−40,000	+	40,000				
Bal.	10,000		40,000			50,000	
	50,000					50,000	

The purchase increases one asset (Land) and decreases another asset (Cash) by the same amount. After the transaction is completed, Air & Sea Travel has cash of $10,000, land of $40,000 and no liabilities. Stockholders' equity is unchanged at $50,000. Note that total assets must always equal total liabilities and equity.

Check Point 2-1

Transaction 3. The business buys office supplies on account, agreeing to pay $500 within 30 days. This transaction increases both the assets and the liabilities of the business. Its effect on the accounting equation follows.

	ASSETS						LIABILITIES	+	STOCKHOLDERS' EQUITY
	Cash	+	Office Supplies	+	Land		Accounts Payable	+	Common Stock
Bal.	10,000				40,000	=			50,000
(3)			+500				+500		
Bal.	10,000		500		40,000		500		50,000
			50,500					50,500	

The new asset is Office Supplies, and the liability is an Account Payable. Air & Sea Travel signs no formal promissory note, so the liability is an account payable, not a note payable.

Transaction 4. Air & Sea Travel earns $5,500 of service revenue by providing travel services for clients. Assume the business collects the cash up front. The effect on the accounting equation is an increase in the asset Cash and an increase in Retained Earnings, as follows:

	ASSETS				LIABILITIES +	STOCKHOLDERS' EQUITY		TYPES OF STOCKHOLDERS' EQUITY TRANSACTION
	Cash +	Office Supplies +	Land		Accounts Payable +	Common Stock +	Retained Earnings	
Bal.	10,000	500	40,000	=	500	50,000		
(4)	+ 5,500						+5,500	Service revenue
Bal.	15,500	500	40,000		500	50,000	5,500	
		56,000				56,000		

To the right we record "Service revenue" to keep track of where the $5,500 of increase in Retained Earnings came from.

Transaction 5. Air & Sea Travel also performs services on account, that is, for customers who do not pay immediately. Air & Sea arranges travel for a customer and is promised $3,000 within 1 month. This promise is an account receivable of Air & Sea Travel. Performing a service for a customer earns revenue, regardless of whether we receive cash now or collect it later. The transaction record follows.

	ASSETS					LIABILITIES +	STOCKHOLDERS' EQUITY		TYPE OF STOCKHOLDERS' EQUITY TRANSACTION
	Cash +	Accounts Receivable +	Office Supplies +	Land		Accounts Payable +	Common Stock	+ Retained Earnings	
Bal.	15,500		500	40,000	=	500	50,000	5,500	
(5)		+3,000						+3,000	Service revenue
Bal.	15,500	3,000	500	40,000		500	50,000	8,500	
	59,000					59,000			

Again, we record "Service revenue" to denote the reason for the increase in Retained Earnings.

Transaction 6. During the month, Air & Sea Travel pays $2,700 for the following expenses: office rent, $1,100; employee salary, $1,200; and utilities, $400. The effect on the accounting equation is:

Check Point 2-2

	ASSETS					LIABILITIES +	STOCKHOLDERS' EQUITY		TYPE OF STOCKHOLDERS' EQUITY TRANSACTION
	Cash +	Accounts Receivable +	Office Supplies +	Land		Accounts Payable +	Common Stock	+ Retained Earnings	
Bal.	15,500	3,000	500	40,000		500	50,000	8,500	
(6)	−1,100				=			−1,100	Rent expense
	−1,200							−1,200	Salary expense
	− 400							− 400	Utilities expense
Bal.	12,800	3,000	500	40,000		500	50,000	5,800	
	56,300					56,300			

The expenses decrease the asset Cash and the owners' equity account, Retained Earnings. List each expense to keep track of its amount.

Transaction 7. Air & Sea Travel pays $400 on account—to the store from which it purchased office supplies in Transaction 3. The transaction decreases Cash and also decreases Accounts Payable as follows:

FOCUS ON F

	ASSETS					LIABILITIES +	STOCKHOLDERS' EQUITY	
	Cash +	Accounts Receivable +	Office Supplies +	Land		Accounts Payable +	Common Stock +	Retained Earnings
Bal.	12,800	3,000	500	40,000	=	500	50,000	5,800
(7)	− 400					−400		
Bal.	12,400	3,000	500	40,000		100	50,000	5,800
		55,900					55,900	

Air & Sea Travel is paying off a liability, so the payment on account does not affect Office Supplies or any expense account.

Transaction 8. The Lyons paid $30,000 to remodel their home. This event is a personal transaction of the Lyon family. It is not recorded by the Air & Sea Travel business. We focus solely on the business entity, and this event does not affect it. This transaction illustrates the entity concept from Chapter 1.

Transaction 9. In Transaction 5, Air & Sea Travel performed services for customers on account. The business now collects $1,000 from the customer. We say that Air & Sea Travel ***collects the cash on account***. Air & Sea will record an increase in Cash and a decrease in Accounts Receivable. This is not service revenue because Air & Sea already recorded the revenue in Transaction 5. Performing the service, not collecting the cash, earns the revenue. The effect of collecting cash on account is:

	ASSETS					LIABILITIES +	STOCKHOLDERS' EQUITY	
	Cash +	Accounts Receivable +	Office Supplies +	Land		Accounts Payable +	Common Stock +	Retained Earnings
Bal.	12,400	3,000	500	40,000	=	100	50,000	5,800
(9)	+1,000	−1,000						
Bal.	13,400	2,000	500	40,000		100	50,000	5,800
		55,900					55,900	

Transaction 10. Air & Sea Travel sells land for $22,000, which is the same amount it paid for the land. Air & Sea receives $22,000 cash, and the effect on the accounting equation is:

	ASSETS					LIABILITIES + STOCKHOLDERS' EQUITY		
	Cash +	Accounts Receivable +	Office Supplies +	Land		Accounts Payable +	Common Stock +	Retained Earnings
Bal.	13,400	2,000	500	40,000	=	100	50,000	5,800
(10)	+22,000			−22,000				
Bal.	35,400	2,000	500	18,000		100	50,000	5,800
	55,900					55,900		

Note that the company did not sell all its land; it still owns $18,000 worth of land.

Transaction 11. Air & Sea Travel declares a dividend and pays Gary and Monica Lyon $2,100 cash. The effect on the accounting equation is:

	ASSETS					LIABILITIES +	STOCKHOLDERS' EQUITY		TYPE OF STOCKHOLDERS' EQUITY TRANSACTION
	Cash +	Accounts Receivable +	Office Supplies +	Land		Accounts Payable +	Common Stock +	Retained Earnings	
Bal.	35,400	2,000	500	18,000	=	100	50,000	5,800	
(11)	− 2,100							− 2,100	Dividends
Bal.	33,300	2,000	500	18,000		100	50,000	3,700	
	53,800					53,800			

The dividend decreases both the asset Cash and the retained earnings of the business. *But dividends are not an expense.*

Transactions and Financial Statements

Exhibit 2-1 summarizes the 11 preceding transactions. Panel A gives the details of the transactions, and Panel B shows the transaction analysis. As you study the exhibit, note that every transaction maintains the equality:

Assets = Liabilities + Stockholders' Equity

Exhibit 2-1 provides the data for Air & Sea Travel's financial statements:

- *Income statement* data appear as revenues and expenses under Retained Earnings. The revenues increase retained earnings; the expenses decrease retained earnings.
- The *balance sheet* data are composed of the ending balances of the assets, liabilities, and stockholders' equities shown at the bottom of the exhibit. The accounting equation shows that total assets ($53,800) equal total liabilities plus stockholders' equity ($53,800).
- The *statement of retained earnings* repeats net income (or net loss) from the income statement. Dvidends are subtracted. Ending retained earnings is the final result.
- Data for the *statement of cash flows* are aligned under the Cash account. Cash receipts increase cash, and cash payments decrease cash.

FOCUS ON F

■ EXHIBIT 2-1 Transaction Analysis: Air & Sea Travel, Inc.

PANEL A—Transaction Details

(1) Received $50,000 cash and issued stock to the owners
(2) Paid $40,000 cash for land
(3) Bought $500 of office supplies on account
(4) Received $5,500 cash from customers for service revenue earned
(5) Performed services for customers on account, $3,000
(6) Paid cash expenses: rent, $1,100; employee salary, $1,200; utilities, $400
(7) Paid $400 on the account payable created in Transaction 3
(8) Owners paid personal funds to remodel home, *not* a transaction of the business
(9) Received $1,000 on account
(10) Sold land for cash at its cost of $22,000
(11) Declared and paid a dividend of $2,100 to the stockholders

PANEL B—Transaction Analysis

	ASSETS				=	LIABILITIES +	STOCKHOLDERS' EQUITY		TYPE OF STOCKHOLDERS' EQUITY TRANSACTION
	Cash +	Accounts Receivable +	Office Supplies +	Land		Accounts Payable +	Common Stock +	Retained Earnings	
(1)	+50,000						+50,000		Issued stock
(2)	−40,000			+40,000					
(3)			+500			+500			
(4)	+5,500							+5,500	Service revenue
(5)		+3,000						+3,000	Service revenue
(6)	−1,100							−1,100	Rent expense
	−1,200							−1,200	Salary expense
	− 400							− 400	Utilities expense
(7)	− 400					−400			
(8)	Not a transaction of the business								
(9)	+1,000	−1,000							
(10)	+22,000			−22,000					
(11)	−2,100							−2,100	Dividends
Bal.	33,300	2,000	500	18,000		100	50,000	3,700	
	53,800					53,800			

Statement of Cash Flows Data (Cash column)

Income Statement Data (transactions 4–6)

Statement of Retained Earnings Data (transaction 11)

Balance Sheet Data

Exhibit 2-2 shows the Air & Sea Travel financial statements at the end of April, the company's first month of operations. You can recognize the statements from the solution to the summary problem at the end of Chapter 1. We repeat the statements here. Follow the flow of data to observe the following:

1. The income statement reports revenues, expenses, and either a net income or a net loss for the period. During April, Air & Sea earned net income of $5,800. Compare the Air & Sea Travel income statement with that of Apple Computer at the beginning of the chapter. The income statement includes only two types of accounts: revenues and expenses.

When analyzing a transaction, first pinpoint its effects (if any) on cash. Did cash increase or decrease? Typically, it is easiest to identify cash effects. Then identify the effects on other accounts. In the discussions that follow, we temporarily ignore the date of each transaction to focus on the accounts and their dollar amounts.

Copying Information (Posting) from Journal to Ledger

Ledger
The book of accounts and their balances.

The journal is a chronological record of all company transactions listed by date. But the journal does not indicate how much cash is left over for the business to use. The **ledger** is a grouping of all the T-accounts, with their balances. For example, the balance of the Cash T-account indicates how much cash the business has. The balance of Accounts Receivable shows the amount due from customers. Accounts Payable tells how much the business owes suppliers on open account, and so on.

In the phrase "keeping the books," ***books*** refers to the accounts in the ledger. In most accounting systems, the ledger is computerized. Exhibit 2-8 shows how the asset, liability, and stockholders' equity accounts are grouped in the ledger.

■ **EXHIBIT 2-8**

The Ledger (Asset, Liability, and Stockholders' Equity Accounts)

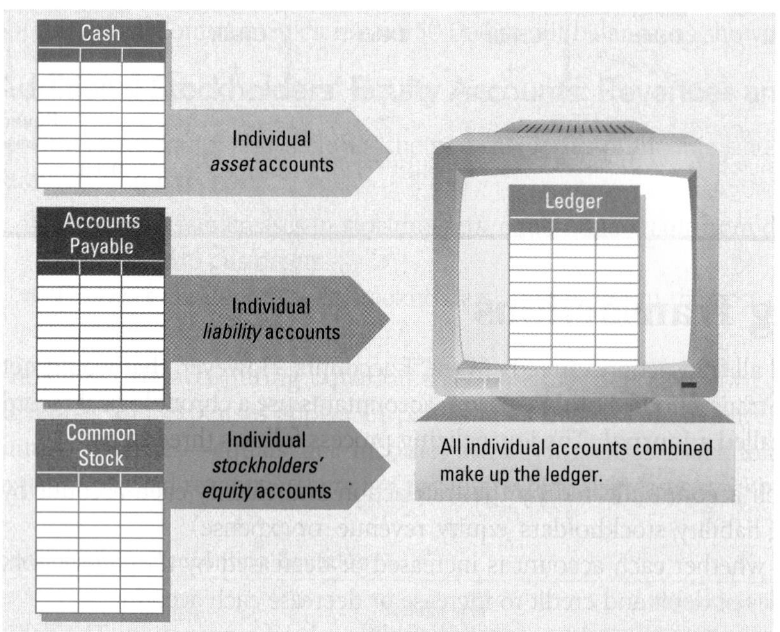

Posting
Copying amounts from the journal to the ledger.

Entering a transaction in the journal does not get the data into the ledger. Data must be copied to the ledger—a process called **posting**. Debits in the journal are posted as debits in the accounts, and likewise for credits. Exhibit 2-9 shows how Air & Sea Travel's stock issuance transaction is posted to the accounts.

■ **EXHIBIT 2-9**

Journal Entry and Posting to the Accounts

PANEL A—Journal Entry

ACCOUNTS AND EXPLANATION	DEBIT	CREDIT
Cash	50,000	
Common Stock		50,000
Issued common stock		

PANEL B—Posting to the Accounts

Cash	
50,000	

Common Stock	
	50,000

FOCUS ON F

The Flow of Accounting Data

Exhibit 2-10 summarizes the flow of accounting data from the business transaction to the ledger. Let's continue the example of Air & Sea Travel, Inc., and account for the same 11 transactions we illustrated earlier. Here we use the journal and the accounts.

■ EXHIBIT 2-10 Flow of Accounting Data

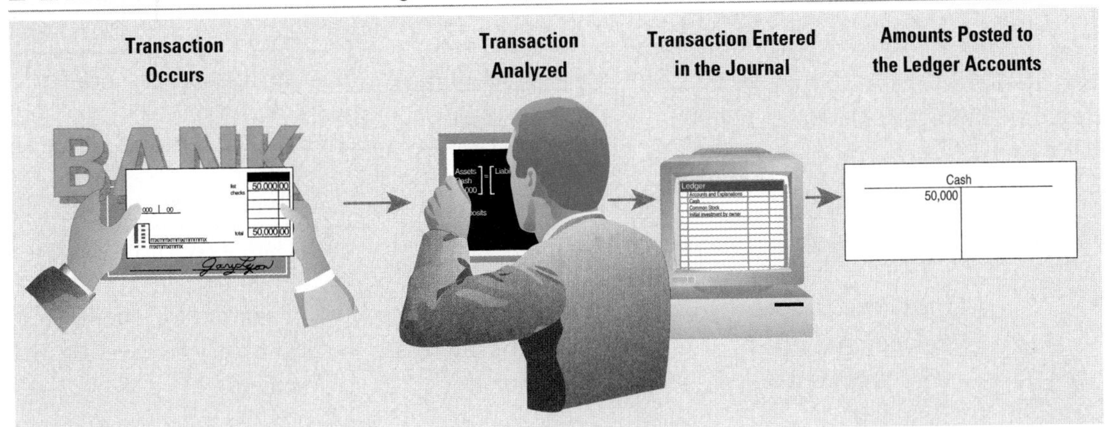

Each journal entry posted to the accounts is keyed by date or by transaction number. This linking allows you to locate any information you may need.

Transaction 1 Analysis. Air & Sea Travel, Inc., received $50,000 cash from the Lyons and in turn issued common stock to them. The journal entry, accounting equation, and ledger accounts follow.

Journal entry

Cash	50,000	
Common Stock		50,000
Issued common stock.		

Accounting equation

ASSETS	=	LIABILITIES	+	STOCKHOLDERS' EQUITY
50,000	=	0	+	50,000

The ledger accounts

Cash			
(1)	50,000		

Common Stock			
		(1)	50,000

Transaction 2 Analysis. The business paid $40,000 cash for land. The purchase decreased cash; therefore, credit Cash. The purchase increased the asset land; to record this increase, debit Land.

Journal entry

Land	40,000	
Cash		40,000
Paid cash for land.		

Accounting equation

ASSETS	=	LIABILITIES	+	STOCKHOLDERS' EQUITY
+40,000	=	0	+	0
−40,000				

The accounts

Cash			
(1)	50,000	(2)	40,000

Land			
(2)	40,000		

NDAMENTALS

Transaction 3 Analysis. The business purchased office supplies for $500 on account payable. The purchase increased office supplies, an asset, and Accounts Payable, a liability.

Journal entry

	Debit	Credit
Office Supplies	500	
Accounts Payable		500
Purchased office supplies on account.		

Accounting equation

ASSETS	=	LIABILITIES	+	STOCKHOLDERS' EQUITY
+500	=	+500	+	0

The ledger accounts

Office Supplies			
(3)	500		

Accounts Payable			
		(3)	500

Transaction 4 Analysis. The business performed travel service for clients and received cash of $5,500. The transaction increased cash and service revenue. To record the revenue, credit Service Revenue.

Journal entry

	Debit	Credit
Cash	5,500	
Service Revenue		5,500
Performed services for cash.		

Accounting equation

ASSETS	=	LIABILITIES	+	STOCKHOLDERS' EQUITY	+	REVENUES
+5,500	=	0	+		+	5,500

The ledger accounts

Cash			
(1)	50,000	(2)	40,000
(4)	5,500		

Service Revenue			
		(4)	5,500

Transaction 5 Analysis. Air & Sea Travel performed services for clients on account. They did not pay immediately, so Air & Sea billed the clients for $3,000. The transaction increased accounts receivable; therefore, debit Accounts Receivable. Service revenue also increased, so credit the revenue account.

Journal entry

	Debit	Credit
Accounts Receivable	3,000	
Service Revenue		3,000
Performed services on account.		

Accounting equation

ASSETS	=	LIABILITIES	+	STOCKHOLDERS' EQUITY	+	REVENUES
+3,000	=	0	+		+	3,000

The ledger accounts

Accounts Receivable			
(5)	3,000		

Service Revenue			
		(4)	5,500
		(5)	3,000

Transaction 6 Analysis. The business paid $2,700 for the following expenses: office rent, $1,100; employee salary, $1,200; and utilities, $400. Credit Cash for the sum of the expense amounts. The expenses increased, so debit each expense account.

Journal entry

Rent Expense	1,100	
Salary Expense	1,200	
Utilities Expense	400	
Cash		2,700
Paid expenses.		

✔Check Point 2-3
✔Check Point 2-4
✔Check Point 2-5

Accounting equation

ASSETS	=	LIABILITIES	+	STOCKHOLDERS' EQUITY	–	EXPENSES
−2,700	=	0	+		–	2,700

The ledger accounts

Cash

(1)	50,000	(2)	40,000
(4)	5,500	(6)	2,700

Rent Expense

(6)	1,100		

Salary Expense

(6)	1,200		

Utilities Expense

(6)	400		

Transaction 7 Analysis. The business paid $400 on the account payable created in Transaction 3. Credit Cash for the payment. The payment decreased a liability, so debit Accounts Payable.

Journal entry

Accounts Payable	400	
Cash		400
Paid cash on account.		

✔Check Point 2-6

Accounting equation

ASSETS	=	LIABILITIES	+	STOCKHOLDERS' EQUITY
−400	=	−400	+	0

The ledger accounts

Cash

(1)	50,000	(2)	40,000
(4)	5,500	(6)	2,700
		(7)	400

Accounts Payable

(7)	400	(3)	500

Transaction 8 Analysis. The Lyons remodeled their personal residence. This is not a transaction of the travel agency, so the business does not record the transaction.

Transaction 9 Analysis. The business collected $1,000 cash on account from the clients in Transaction 5. Cash increased so debit Cash. The asset accounts receivable decreased; therefore, credit Accounts Receivable.

Journal entry

Cash	1,000	
Accounts Receivable		1,000
Collected cash on account.		

✔Check Point 2-7

Accounting equation

ASSETS	=	LIABILITIES	+	STOCKHOLDERS' EQUITY
+1,000	=	0	+	0
−1,000				

The ledger accounts

Cash

(1)	50,000	(2)	40,000
(4)	5,500	(6)	2,700
(9)	1,000	(7)	400

Accounts Receivable

(5)	3,000	(9)	1,000

Transaction 10 Analysis. The business sold land for its cost of $22,000, receiving cash. The asset cash increased; debit Cash. The asset land decreased; credit Land.

Journal entry

	Debit	Credit
Cash	22,000	
Land		22,000
Sold land.		

Accounting equation

ASSETS	=	LIABILITIES	+	STOCKHOLDERS' EQUITY
+22,000	=	0	+	0
−22,000				

The ledger accounts

Cash

(1)	50,000	(2)	40,000
(4)	5,500	(6)	2,700
(9)	1,000	(7)	400
(10)	22,000		

Land

(2)	40,000	(10)	22,000

Transaction 11 Analysis. Air & Sea Travel, Inc., paid the Lyons cash dividends of $2,100. Credit Cash for the payment. The transaction also decreased stockholders' equity and requires a debit to an equity account. Therefore, debit Dividends.

Journal entry

	Debit	Credit
Dividends	2,100	
Cash		2,100
Declared and paid dividends.		

Accounting equation

ASSETS	=	LIABILITIES	+	STOCKHOLDERS' EQUITY	−	DIVIDENDS
−2,100	=	0	+		−	2,100

The ledger accounts

Cash

(1)	50,000	(2)	40,000
(4)	5,500	(6)	2,700
(9)	1,000	(7)	400
(10)	22,000	(11)	2,100

Dividends

(11)	2,100		

Accounts after Posting to the Ledger

Accounting Cycle Tutorial Application 1—Xpert Driving School

Accounting Cycle Tutorial Application 2—Small Business Services

Exhibit 2-11 shows the accounts after all transactions have been posted to the ledger. Group the accounts under assets, liabilities, and equity.

Each account has a balance, denoted as Bal., which is the difference between the account's total debits and its total credits. For example, the Accounts Payable's balance of $100 is the difference between the credit ($500) and the debit ($400). Cash has a debit balance of $33,300.

A horizontal line separates the transaction amounts from the account balance. If an account's debits exceed its total credits, that account has a debit balance, as for Cash. If the sum of the credits is greater, the account has a credit balance, as for Accounts Payable.

FOCUS ON F

■ **EXHIBIT 2-11** Air & Sea Travel's Ledger Accounts after Posting

ASSETS = LIABILITIES + STOCKHOLDERS' EQUITY

ASSETS

Cash

	Debit		Credit
(1)	50,000	(2)	40,000
(4)	5,500	(6)	2,700
(9)	1,000	(7)	400
(10)	22,000	(11)	2,100
Bal.	33,300		

Accounts Receivable

	Debit		Credit
(5)	3,000	(9)	1,000
Bal.	2,000		

Office Supplies

	Debit		Credit
(3)	500		
Bal.	500		

Land

	Debit		Credit
(2)	40,000	(10)	22,000
Bal.	18,000		

LIABILITIES

Accounts Payable

	Debit		Credit
(7)	400	(3)	500
		Bal.	100

STOCKHOLDERS' EQUITY

Common Stock

	Debit		Credit
		(1)	50,000
		Bal.	50,000

Dividends

	Debit		Credit
(11)	2,100		
Bal.	2,100		

REVENUE

Service Revenue

	Debit		Credit
		(4)	5,500
		(5)	3,000
		Bal.	8,500

EXPENSES

Rent Expense

	Debit		Credit
(6)	1,100		
Bal.	1,100		

Salary Expense

	Debit		Credit
(6)	1,200		
Bal.	1,200		

Utilities Expense

	Debit		Credit
(6)	400		
Bal.	400		

The Trial Balance

A **trial balance** lists all accounts with their balances—assets first, then liabilities and stockholders' equity. The trial balance summarizes all the account balances for the financial statements and shows whether total debits equal total credits. A trial balance may be taken at any time, but the most common time is at the end of the period. Exhibit 2-12 is the trial balance of Air & Sea Travel, Inc., after all transactions have been journalized and posted.

OBJECTIVE

4 Use a trial balance

Trial balance
A list of all the ledger accounts with their balances.

■ **EXHIBIT 2-12**
Trial Balance

Air & Sea Travel, Inc.
Trial Balance
April 30, 20X3

Account Title	Balance Debit	Balance Credit
Cash	$33,300	
Accounts receivable	2,000	
Office supplies	500	
Land	18,000	
Accounts payable		$ 100
Common stock		50,000
Dividends	2,100	
Service revenue		8,500
Rent expense	1,100	
Salary expense	1,200	
Utilities expense	400	
Total	$58,600	$58,600

Check Point 2-8

Check Point 2-9

Accounting Cycle Tutorial Glossary

Accounting Cycle Tutorial Glossary Quiz

stop AND think. . .

Air & Sea Travel Needs a Loan

Suppose you are Monica Lyon, one of the owners. Your accountant is out of town, and the only accounting record available to you is the trial balance. Your banker requests some information. Use the trial balance in Exhibit 2-12 to answer the following questions:

1. How much are Air & Sea Travel's total assets? [*Answer:* $53,800 = $33,300 + $2,000 + $500 + $18,000.]
2. Does the business already have any loans payable to other banks? [*Answer:* No the trial balance lists no notes payable.]
3. How much does the business owe in total? [*Answer:* $100 for accounts payable.]
4. What was the business's net income or net loss for the month of April? [*Answer:* Net income was $5,800 [Revenues of $8,500 – Expenses of $2,700 ($1,100 + $1,200 + $400)].]

Correcting Accounting Errors

Accounting errors can occur even in computerized systems. Input data may be wrong, or they may be entered twice or not at all. A debit may be entered as a credit, and vice versa. You can detect the reason or reasons behind many out-of-balance conditions by computing the difference between total debits and total credits. Then perform one or more of the following actions:

1. Search the records for a missing account. Trace each account back and forth from the journal to the ledger. A $200 transaction may have been recorded incorrectly in the journal or posted incorrectly to the ledger. Search the journal for a $200 transaction.
2. Divide the out-of-balance amount by 2. A debit treated as a credit, or vice versa, doubles the amount of error. Suppose Air & Sea Travel added $300 to Cash instead of subtracting $300. The out-of-balance amount is $600, and dividing by 2 identifies $300 as the amount of the transaction. Search the journal for the $300 transaction and trace to the account affected.
3. Divide the out-of-balance amount by 9. If the result is evenly divisible by 9, the error may be a ***slide*** (writing $61 as $610) or a ***transposition*** (entering $61 as $16). Suppose Air & Sea Travel listed the $100 Accounts Payable balance as $1,000. The accounts would be out of balance by $900 ($1,000 – $100 = $900). Dividing $900 by 9 yields $100, the correct amount of the accounts payable. Trace this amount through the journal and then to the Accounts Payable account.

Check Point 2-10

Chart of Accounts

As you know, the ledger contains the business accounts grouped under these headings:

1. **Balance sheet accounts: Assets, Liabilities, and Stockholders' Equity**
2. **Income statement accounts: Revenues and Expenses**

Chart of accounts
List of all a company's accounts and their account numbers.

Organizations use a **chart of accounts** to list all their accounts and account numbers. Account numbers usually have two or more digits. Asset account numbers may begin with 1, liabilities with 2, stockholders' equity with 3, revenues with 4, and expenses with 5. The second, third, and higher digits in an account number indicate the posi-

FOCUS ON F

tion of the individual account within the category. For example, Cash may be account number 101, which is the first asset account. Accounts Payable may be number 201, the first liability. All accounts are numbered by using this system.

Organizations with many accounts use lengthy account numbers. For example, the chart of accounts of **Johnson & Johnson**, famous for Band-Aids and other health products, may use five-digit account numbers. The chart of accounts for Air & Sea Travel, Inc., appears in Exhibit 2-13. The gap between account numbers 111 and 141 leaves room to add another category of receivables, for example, Notes Receivable, which may be numbered 121.

■ **EXHIBIT 2-13**

Chart of Accounts—Air & Sea Travel, Inc.

Balance Sheet Accounts

Assets	Liabilities	Stockholders' Equity
101 Cash	201 Accounts Payable	301 Common Stock
111 Accounts Receivable	231 Notes Payable	311 Dividends
141 Office Supplies		312 Retained Earnings
151 Office Furniture		
191 Land		

Income Statement Accounts (Part of Stockholders' Equity)

Revenues	Expenses
401 Service Revenue	501 Rent Expense
	502 Salary Expense
	503 Utilities Expense

Appendix D to this book gives two expanded charts of accounts that you will find helpful as you work through this course. The first chart lists the typical accounts that a *service* corporation, such as Air & Sea Travel, would have after a period of growth. The second chart is for a *merchandising* corporation, one that sells a product instead of a service.

The Normal Balance of an Account

An account's *normal balance* falls on the side of the account—debit or credit—where increases are recorded. The normal balance of assets is on the debit side, so assets are *debit-balance accounts*. Conversely, liabilities and stockholders' equity usually have a credit balance, so they are *credit-balance accounts*. Exhibit 2-14 illustrates the normal balances of all the assets, liabilities, and stockholders' equities, including revenues and expenses.

■ **EXHIBIT 2-14**

Normal Balances of the Accounts

Assets	Debit	
Liabilities		Credit
Stockholders' Equity—overall		Credit
Common stock		Credit
Retained earnings		Credit
Dividends	Debit	
Revenues		Credit
Expenses	Debit	

Check Point 2-11

As explained earlier, stockholders' equity usually contains several accounts. In total, the equity accounts show a normal credit balance. But there are exceptions. Dividends and expenses carry debit balances because they represent decreases in stockholders' equity.

Account Formats

Accounting Cycle Tutorial
The Journal, the Ledger, and the Trial Balance

So far we have illustrated accounts in a two-column T-account format, with the debit column on the left and the credit column on the right. Another format has four *amount* columns, as illustrated for the Cash account in Exhibit 2-15. The first pair of amount columns are for the debit and credit amounts of individual transactions. The last two columns are for the account balance. This four-column format keeps a running balance in the two right columns.

■ **EXHIBIT 2-15**
Account in Four-Column Format

Account: Cash — **Account No. 101**

Date	Item	Debit	Credit	Balance	
				Debit	Credit
20X3					
Apr. 2		50,000		50,000	
3			40,000	10,000	

OBJECTIVE

5 **Analyze** transactions for quick decisions

Quick Decision Making with T-Accounts

Businesspeople must often make decisions without the benefit of a complete accounting system. For example, the managers of Apple Computer may consider buying equipment that costs $100,000. Apple will borrow the money. To see how the two transactions affect Apple, the manager can go directly to T-accounts, as follows:

Transaction *A*
Borrow $100,000

T-accounts:

Cash	
(a) 100,000	

Note Payable	
	(a) 100,000

Transaction *B*
Purchase equipment and pay cash

T-accounts:

Cash	
(a) 100,000	(b) 100,000

Equipment	
(b) 100,000	

Note Payable	
	(a) 100,000

This informal analysis shows immediately that Apple will add $100,000 of equipment and a $100,000 note payable. Assuming that Apple began with zero balances, the equipment and note payable transactions would result in the following balance sheet (date assumed for illustration only):

FOCUS ON F

Apple Computer, Inc.
Balance Sheet
September 12, 20X3

Assets		Liabilities	
Cash	$ 0	Note payable	$100,000
Equipment	100,000	Total liabilities	100,000
		Stockholders' Equity	0
Total assets	$100,000	Total liabilities and stockholders' equity	$100,000

Check Point 2-12

Accounting Cycle Tutorial Application Constanza Architect

Companies do not actually keep records in this shortcut fashion, but a decision maker who needs information immediately does not have time to journalize transactions, post to the accounts, take a trial balance, and prepare the financial statements. By knowing the accounting, the manager can analyze the transaction quickly and make the decision in full view of the facts.

This chapter covers a lot of material on the processing of accounting information. The Making Managerial Decisions feature "How to Measure Results of Operations and Financial Position," will help you focus on the essential elements covered in the chapter. As we proceed through this book, we emphasize the use of the information for decision making. The more accounting you learn, the better equipped you are to make decisions in your organization.

MAKING MANAGERIAL DECISIONS

HOW TO MEASURE RESULTS OF OPERATIONS AND FINANCIAL POSITION

Any entrepreneur must determine whether the venture is profitable. To do this, he or she needs to know its results of operations and financial position. If Steve Jobs, who founded Apple Computer, Inc., wanted to know whether the business was making money, the Guidelines that follow would help him.

Decision	Guidelines
Has a transaction occurred?	If the event affects the entity's financial position and can be reliably recorded—Yes. If either condition is absent—No.
Where to record the transaction?	In the *journal*, the chronological record of transactions
How to record an increase or decrease in the following accounts?	Rules of *debit* and *credit*: **Increase / Decrease** Asset . . . . . Debit / Credit Liability . . . . . Credit / Debit Stockholders' equity . . . . . Credit / Debit Revenue . . . . . Credit / Debit Expense . . . . . Debit / Credit
Where to store all the information for each account?	In the *ledger*, the book of accounts
Where to list all the accounts and their balances?	In the *trial* balance
Where to report the:	
Results of operations?	In the *income* statement (revenues – expenses = net income or net loss)
Financial position?	In the *balance sheet* (assets = liabilities + stockholders' equity)

FOCUS ON F

Summary Problem

END-OF-CHAPTER

The trial balance of Calderon Service Center, Inc., on March 1, 20X3, lists the entity's assets, liabilities, and stockholders' equity on that date.

	Balance	
Account Title	**Debit**	**Credit**
Cash	$26,000	
Accounts receivable	4,500	
Accounts payable		$ 2,000
Common stock		10,000
Retained earnings		18,500
Total	$30,500	$30,500

During March, the business completed the following transactions:

a. Borrowed $45,000 from the bank, with Calderon signing a note payable in the name of the business.
b. Paid cash of $40,000 to a real estate company to acquire land.
c. Performed service for a customer and received cash of $5,000.
d. Purchased supplies on credit, $300.
e. Performed customer service and earned revenue on account, $2,600.
f. Paid $1,200 on account.
g. Paid the following cash expenses: salaries, $3,000; rent, $1,500; and interest, $400.
h. Received $3,100 on account.
i. Received a $200 utility bill that will be paid next week.
j. Declared and paid dividend of $1,800.

Required

1. Open the following accounts, with the balances indicated, in the ledger of Calderon Service Center, Inc. Use the T-account format.
   - Assets—Cash, $26,000; Accounts Receivable, $4,500; Supplies, no balance; Land, no balance
   - Liabilities—Accounts Payable, $2,000; Note Payable, no balance
   - Stockholders' Equity—Common Stock, $10,000; Retained Earnings, $18,500; Dividends, no balance
   - Revenues—Service Revenue, no balance
   - Expenses—(none have balances) Salary Expense, Rent Expense, Interest Expense, Utilities Expense
2. Journalize the preceding transactions. Key journal entries by transaction letter.
3. Post to the ledger and show the balance in each account after all the transactions have been posted.
4. Prepare the trial balance of Calderon Service Center, Inc., at March 31, 20X3.
5. To determine the net income or net loss of the entity during the month of March, prepare the income statement for the month ended March 31, 20X3. List expenses in order from the largest to the smallest.
6. Suppose the organizers of Calderon Service Center ask you to invest $5,000 in the company stock. Cite specifics from the income statement and the trial balance to support your decision.

Answers

Requirement 1

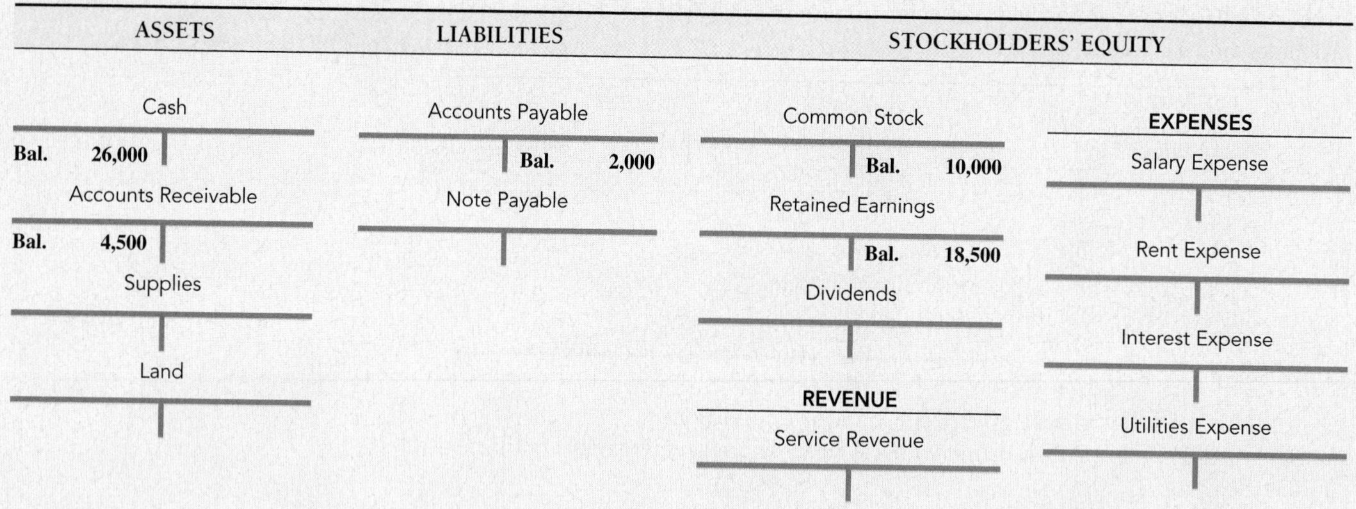

Requirement 2

Accounts and Explanation	Debit	Credit
a. Cash	45,000	
Note Payable		45,000
Borrowed cash on note payable.		
b. Land	40,000	
Cash		40,000
Purchased land for cash.		
c. Cash	5,000	
Service Revenue		5,000
Performed service and received cash.		
d. Supplies	300	
Accounts Payable		300
Purchased supplies on account.		
e. Accounts Receivable	2,600	
Service Revenue		2,600
Performed service on account.		
f. Accounts Payable	1,200	
Cash		1,200
Paid on account.		

Accounts and Explanation	Debit	Credit
g. Salary Expense	3,000	
Rent Expense	1,500	
Interest Expense	400	
Cash		4,900
Paid cash expenses.		
h. Cash	3,100	
Accounts Receivable		3,100
Received on account.		
i. Utilities Expense	200	
Accounts Payable		200
Received utility bill.		
j. Dividends	1,800	
Cash		1,800
Declared and paid dividends.		

Requirement 3

ASSETS

Cash

Bal.	26,000	(b)	40,000
(a)	45,000	(f)	1,200
(c)	5,000	(g)	4,900
(h)	3,100	(j)	1,800
Bal.	31,200		

Accounts Receivable

Bal.	4,500	(h)	3,100
(e)	2,600		
Bal.	4,000		

Supplies

(d)	300		
Bal.	300		

Land

(b)	40,000		
Bal.	40,000		

LIABILITIES

Accounts Payable

(f)	1,200	Bal.	2,000
		(d)	300
		(i)	200
		Bal.	1,300

Note Payable

		(a)	45,000
		Bal.	45,000

STOCKHOLDERS' EQUITY

Common Stock

		Bal.	10,000

Retained Earnings

		Bal.	18,500

Dividends

(j)	1,800		
Bal.	1,800		

REVENUE

Service Revenue

		(c)	5,000
		(e)	2,600
		Bal.	7,600

EXPENSES

Salary Expense

(g)	3,000		
Bal.	3,000		

Rent Expense

(g)	1,500		
Bal.	1,500		

Interest Expense

(g)	400		
Bal.	400		

Utilities Expense

(i)	200		
Bal.	200		

Requirement 4

Calderon Service Center, Inc.
Trial Balance
March 31, 20X3

	Balance	
Account Title	Debit	Credit
Cash	$31,200	
Accounts receivable	4,000	
Supplies	300	
Land	40,000	
Accounts payable		$ 1,300
Note payable		45,000
Common stock		10,000
Retained earnings		18,500
Dividends	1,800	
Service revenue		7,600
Salary expense	3,000	
Rent expense	1,500	
Interest expense	400	
Utilities expense	200	
Total	$82,400	$82,400

Requirement 5

Calderon Service Center, Inc. Income Statement Month Ended March 31, 20X3		
Revenue		
Service revenue		$7,600
Expenses		
Salary expense	$3,000	
Rent expense	1,500	
Interest expense	400	
Utilities expense	200	
Total expenses		5,100
Net income		$2,500

Requirement 6

A $5,000 investment in Calderon appears to be warranted because

a. The company earned net income of $2,500, so the business appears profitable.
b. Total assets of $75,500 ($31,200 + $4,000 + $300 + $40,000) far exceed total liabilities of $46,300 ($45,000 + $1,300), which suggests that Calderon can pay its debts and remain in business.
c. Calderon is paying a dividend, so an investment in the stock may yield a quick return in the form of dividends.

REVIEW · TRANSACTION ANALYSIS

Chapter Review Quiz

1. A debit entry to an account:
   a. increases liabilities
   b. increases assets
   c. increases stockholders' equity
   d. both a and c

2. Which of the following account types does not normally have a credit balance?
   a. liabilities
   b. revenues
   c. expenses
   d. stockholders' equity

3. An architect performs services of $800 for a client and receives $200 cash with the rest on account. The journal entry for this transaction would be:
   a. debit Cash, debit Accounts Receivable, credit Service Revenue
   b. debit Cash, credit Accounts Receivable, credit Service Revenue
   c. debit Cash, credit Service Revenue
   d. debit Cash, debit Service Revenue, credit Accounts Receivable

4. Accounts Payable had a normal beginning balance of $1,000. During the period, there were debit postings of $600 and credit postings of $400. What was the ending balance?
   a. $800 debit
   b. $800 credit
   c. $1,200 debit
   d. $1,200 credit

5. The list of all accounts with their balances is the:
   a. account
   b. ledger
   c. journal
   d. trial balance

FOCUS ON F

6. The basic summary device used in accounting is the:
   a. account
   b. ledger
   c. journal
   d. trial balance

7. The beginning Cash balance was $5,000. At the end of the period, the balance was $6,200. If total cash paid out during the period was $24,600, the amount of cash receipts was:
   a. $23,400
   b. $13,400
   c. $25,800
   d. $35,800

8. In a double-entry accounting system
   a. a debit entry is recorded on the left side of a T-account.
   b. all the accounts have a normal credit balance.
   c. liabilities, owners' equity, and revenue accounts all have normal debit balances.
   d. both a and d are correct.

9. Which accounts appear on which financial statement?

	Balance sheet	*Income statement*
a.	Cash, revenues, land	Expenses, payables
b.	Receivables, land, payables	Revenues, supplies
c.	Expenses, payables, cash	Revenues, receivables, land
d.	Cash, receivables, payables	Revenues, expenses

10. A doctor purchases medical supplies of $670 and pays $200 cash with the rest on account. The journal entry for this transaction would be:

    a. Supplies
    Accounts Payable
    Cash

    b. Supplies
    Cash
        Accounts Payable

    c. Supplies
        Cash

    d. Supplies
    Accounts Receivable
        Cash

    e. Supplies
        Accounts Payable
        Cash

11. Which is the correct sequence of accounting procedures?
    a. Ledger, trial balance, journal, financial statements
    b. Journal, ledger, trial balance, financial statements
    c. Financial statements, trial balance, ledger, journal
    d. Ledger, journal, trial balance, financial statements

12. Which of the following errors can cause the trial balance to be out of balance?
    a. A debit entry is entered in the wrong debit account.
    b. An entire transaction is entered in the general journal as $96 instead of $69.
    c. The balance of an account is incorrectly computed.
    d. An entire transaction is not recorded in the journal.
    e. An entire journal entry is not posted to the ledger.

Answers:

1. b	3. a	5. d	7. c	9. d	11. b
2. c	4. b	6. a	8. a	10. e	12. c

Accounting Vocabulary

account (p. 50)
accrued liability (p. 52)
cash (p. 51)
chart of accounts (p. 72)
credit (p. 63)
debit (p. 63)
journal (p. 65)
ledger (p. 66)
posting (p. 66)
prepaid expense (p. 51)
transaction (p. 50)
trial balance (p. 71)

ASSESS YOUR PROGRESS

Check Points

Explaining an asset versus an expense (Obj. 1)

CP2-1 (p. 55) Brad Hickman opened a software consulting firm that immediately paid $9,000 for a computer. Was Hickman's payment an expense of the business? If not, explain.

Analyzing the effects of transactions (Obj. 1)

CP2-2 (p. 56) Review transactions 4, 5, and 6 of Air & Sea Travel on page 55 and 56. Suppose Air & Sea Travel is applying for a business loan, and the bank requires the following financial information (after transaction 6 is completed):

a. How much cash does the business have?
b. How much cash does the business hope to collect from clients?
c. How much in total assets does the business have?
d. How much does Air & Sea Travel owe?
e. Thus far, how much net income has the business earned?

Answer these questions.

Analyzing transactions (Obj. 1)

CP2-3 (p. 69) Meg Garland, M.D., opened a medical practice in Columbus, Ohio. The business completed the following transactions:

May 1	Garland invested $30,000 cash to start her medical practice. The business issued stock to Garland.
1	Purchased medical supplies on account totaling $9,000.
2	Paid monthly office rent of $4,000.
3	Recorded $8,000 revenue for service rendered to patients, received cash of $2,000, and sent bills to patients for the remainder.

After these transactions, how much cash and how much in accounts receivable does the business have to work with? Use T-accounts to show your answer.

Analyzing transactions (Obj. 1)

CP2-4 (p. 69) Refer to Check Point 2-3. Which of the transactions of Meg Garland, M.D., increased the total assets of the business? Which transactions increased total liabilities? Which transaction decreased total assets? For each transaction, identify the asset or liability that was increased or decreased.

Recording transactions (Obj. 2, 3)

CP2-5 (p. 69) After operating for several months, attorney Bruce Raney completed the following transactions during the latter part of April:

April 15	Borrowed $50,000 from the bank, signing a note payable.
22	Performed service for clients on account totaling $9,000.
28	Received $6,000 cash on account from clients.
29	Received a utility bill of $600, which will be paid during May.
30	Paid monthly salary of $3,000 to assistant.
30	Paid interest expense of $300 on the bank loan.

Journalize the transactions of Bruce Raney, Attorney. Include an explanation with each journal entry.

Journalizing transactions; posting (Obj. 2, 3)

CP2-6 (p. 69) Architect Sonia Biaggi purchased supplies on account for $2,000. Later Biaggi paid $500 on account.

1. Journalize the two transactions on the books of Sonia Biaggi, Architect. Include an explanation for each transaction.

FOCUS ON F

2. Open a T-account for Accounts Payable and post to Accounts Payable. Compute the balance and denote it as Bal.
3. How much does Biaggi's business owe after both transactions? In which account does this amount appear?

Journalizing transactions; posting (Obj. 2, 3)

CP2-7 (p. 69) Childhood Development Center (The Center) performed service for a client who could not pay immediately. The Center expected to collect the $1,200 the following month. A month later, The Center received $500 cash from the client.

1. Record the two transactions on the books of Childhood Development Center. Include an explanation for each transaction.
2. Open these T-accounts: Cash, Accounts Receivable, and Service Revenue. Post to all three accounts. Compute each account balance and denote as Bal.
3. Answer these questions based on your analysis:
   a. How much did The Center earn? Which account shows this amount?
   b. How much in total assets did The Center acquire as a result of the two transactions? Show the amount of each asset.

Preparing and using a trial balance (Obj. 4)

CP2-8 (p. 71) Assume that **Old Navy**, a division of **Gap, Inc.**, reported the following summarized data at December 31, 20X8. Accounts appear in no particular order; dollar amounts are in millions.

Revenues	$30	Other liabilities	$ 2
Other assets	9	Cash	2
Accounts payable	1	Expenses	24
Stockholders' equity	2		

Prepare the trial balance of Old Navy at December 31, 20X8. List the accounts in their proper order, as on page 71. How much was Old Navy's net income or net loss?

Using a trial balance (Obj. 4)

CP2-9 (p. 71) Refer to Air & Sea Travel's trial balance on page 71. Compute these amounts for the business:

1. Total assets
2. Total liabilities
3. Total stockholders' equity
4. Net income or net loss during April

Using a trial balance (Obj. 4)

CP2-10 (p. 72) Refer to Air & Sea Travel's trial balance on page 71. The purpose of this check point is to help you learn how to correct three common errors in accounting:

Error 1. Transposition: Assume the trial balance lists Land as $81,000 instead of $18,000. Recompute column totals, take the difference, and divide by 9. The result is an integer (no decimals), which suggests that the error is either a transposition or a slide.

Error 2. Slide. Assume the trial balance lists Accounts receivable as $20,000 instead of $2,000. Recompute column totals, take the difference, and divide by 9. You get back to the original amount of Accounts receivable, $2,000.

Error 3. Mislabelling an item: Assume that Air & Sea Travel accidentally listed Accounts receivable as a credit balance instead of a debit. Recompute the trial balance totals for debits and credits. Then take the difference between total debits and total credits, and divide the difference by 2. You get back to the original amount of Accounts receivable.

Using key accounting terms (Obj. 2)

CP2-11 (p. 74) Accounting has its own vocabulary and basic relationships. Match the accounting terms at left with the corresponding definition or meaning at right.

____	1. Journal	A. Using up assets in the course of operating a business
____	2. Receivable	B. Always a liability
____	3. Owners' equity	C. Revenues – expenses

____	4. Debit	D.	Grouping of accounts
____	5. Expense	E.	Assets – liabilities
____	6. Net income	F.	Record of transactions
____	7. Ledger	G.	Always an asset
____	8. Posting	H.	Left side of an account
____	9. Normal balance	I.	Side of an account where increases are recorded
____	10. Payable	J.	Copying data from the journal to the ledger

Analyzing transactions without a journal (Obj. 5)

CP2-12 (p. 75) Carolina First Bank began by issuing common stock for cash of $250,000. The bank immediately purchased computer equipment on account for $100,000.

1. Set up the following T-accounts of Carolina First Bank: Cash, Computer Equipment, Accounts Payable, Common Stock.
2. Record the first two transactions of Carolina First Bank directly in the T-accounts without using a journal.
3. Compute the balance in each account and show that total debits equal total credits.

Exercises

Most of the even-numbered exercises can be found within Prentice Hall Grade Assist (PHGA), an online homework and practice environment. Your instructor may ask you to complete these exercises using PHGA.

Reporting on business activities (Obj. 1)

writing assignment ■

E2-1 Assume **Kinko's** has opened a store in Oklahoma City. Starting with cash and stockholders' equity (common stock) of $40,000, Keith Farris, the store manager, borrowed $320,000 by signing a note payable in the name of the store. Prior to opening the store, Farris purchased land for $90,000 and a building for $120,000. He also paid $60,000 for copy equipment and $10,000 for supplies to use in the business.

Suppose the home office of Kinko's requires a weekly report from store managers. Write Farris's memo to the home office to report on his borrowing and purchases. Include the store's balance sheet as the final part of your memo.

Business transactions and the accounting equation (Obj. 1)

E2-2 **Wanda Fannin Limited** specializes in imported clothing. During April, Fannin completed a series of transactions. For each of the following items, give an example of a business transaction that has the described effect on the accounting equation of Wanda Fannin Limited.

a. Increase an asset and increase owners' equity.
b. Increase an asset and increase a liability.
c. Increase one asset and decrease another asset.
d. Decrease an asset and decrease owners' equity.
e. Decrease an asset and decrease a liability.

Transaction analysis (Obj. 1)

E2-3 The following selected events were experienced by either Diamondback's Restaurant, a corporation, or Peter Fleming, the major stockholder. State whether each event (1) increased, (2) decreased, or (3) had no effect on the total assets of the business. Identify any specific asset affected.

a. Borrowed $50,000 from the bank.
b. Made cash purchase of land for a building site, $85,000.
c. Received $20,000 cash and issued stock to a stockholder.
d. Paid $60,000 cash on accounts payable.
e. Purchased equipment and signed a $100,000 promissory note in payment.
f. Purchased merchandise inventory on account for $15,000.
g. The business paid Fleming a cash dividend of $4,000.

(continued)

h. Received $9,000 cash from customers on account.
i. Fleming used personal funds to purchase a swimming pool for his home.
j. Sold land and received cash of $60,000 (the land was carried on the company's books at $60,000).

Transaction analysis; accounting equation (Obj. 1)

E2-4 William Beard opens a medical practice specializing in pediatrics. During the first month of operation (October), the business, titled William Beard, Professional Corporation (P.C.), experienced the following events:

October	6	Beard invested $40,000 in the business, which in turn issued its common stock to him.
	9	The business paid cash for land costing $30,000. Beard plans to build an office building on the land.
	12	The business purchased medical supplies for $2,000 on account.
	15	William Beard, P.C., officially opened for business.
	15–31	During the rest of the month, Beard treated patients and earned service revenue of $8,000, receiving cash for half the revenue earned.
	15–31	The business paid cash expenses: employee salaries, $1,400; office rent, $1,000; utilities, $300.
	31	The business sold supplies to another physician for cost of $500.
	31	The business borrowed $10,000, signing a note payable to the bank.
	31	The business paid $1,500 on account.

Required

1. Analyze the effects of these events on the accounting equation of the medical practice of William Beard, P.C. Use a format similar to that of Exhibit 2-1, Panel B, with headings for Cash, Accounts Receivable, Medical Supplies, Land, Accounts Payable, Note Payable, Common Stock, and Retained Earnings.
2. After completing the analysis, answer these questions about the business.
   a. How much are total assets?
   b. How much does the business expect to collect from patients?
   c. How much does the business owe in total?
   d. How much of the business's assets does Beard really own?
   e. How much net income or net loss did the business experience during its first month of operations?

Journalizing transactions (Obj. 2, 3)

E2-5 Refer to Exercise 2-4. Record the transactions in the journal of William Beard, P.C. List the transactions by date and give an explanation for each transaction.

■ general ledger

Analyzing transactions (Obj. 1)

E2-6 **Time Warner Cable** provides cable TV and Internet services to various areas of the United States. Assume that Time Warner Cable began business in 20X8 by issuing common stock for $100 million and completed the following transactions. The company paid $70 million to purchase satellite and other communication equipment. During the remainder of the year, Time Warner bought supplies and other equipment on account for $60 million. Before year end the company paid $55 million on account. Time Warner borrowed $35 million on a note payable. Revenues for the year totaled $26 million, and expenses were $22 million. All revenues were collected in cash, and $21 million of the expenses were paid during the year. Time Warner has a liability for the remaining expenses.

The top managers of the company are evaluating Time Warner at December 31, 20X8, and they wish to know where the company stands financially. They ask you the following questions:

1. How much are the company's total assets?
2. How much does the company owe?
3. What was the net income or net loss for the year?

Journalizing transactions (Obj. 2, 3)

■ spreadsheet

■ general ledger

E2-7 Coaxial Electronic Systems, Inc., completed the following transactions during August 20X6, its first month of operations:

Aug	1	Received $19,500 and issued common stock.
	2	Purchased $800 of office supplies on account.
	4	Paid $14,000 cash for land to use as a building site.
	6	Performed service for customers and received cash of $2,000.
	9	Paid $100 on accounts payable.
	17	Performed service for **IBM** on account totaling $1,200.
	23	Collected $900 from IBM on account.
	31	Paid the following expenses: salary, $1,000; rent, $500.

Required

1. Record the transactions in the journal of Coaxial Electronic Systems, Inc. Key transactions by date and include an explanation for each entry, as illustrated in the chapter.
2. After these transactions, how much cash does Coaxial have to work with?
   How much does Coaxial expect to collect from customers on account?
   How much are total liabilities?
   Did Coaxial have a profit or a loss and how much?

Posting to the ledger and preparing and using a trial balance (Obj. 3, 4)

■ general ledger

E2-8 Refer to Exercise 2-7.

Required

1. After journalizing the transactions of Exercise 2-7, post the entries to the ledger, using T-accounts. Key transactions by date. Date the ending balance of each account August 31.
2. Prepare the trial balance of Coaxial Electronic Systems, Inc., at August 31, 20X6.
3. How much are total assets, total liabilities, and total stockholders' equity on August 31?

Journalizing transactions (Obj. 2, 3)

E2-9 The first seven transactions of Quail Hollow RV Park have been posted to the company's accounts as follows:

Cash

	Debit		Credit
(1)	10,000	(3)	8,000
(2)	7,000	(6)	6,000
(5)	100	(7)	300

Supplies

	Debit		Credit
(4)	600	(5)	100

Equipment

	Debit		Credit
(6)	6,000		

Land

	Debit		Credit
(3)	31,000		

Accounts Payable

	Debit		Credit
(7)	300	(4)	600

Note Payable

	Debit		Credit
		(2)	7,000
		(3)	23,000

Common Stock

	Debit		Credit
		(1)	10,000

Required

Prepare the journal entries that served as the sources for the seven transactions. Include an explanation for each entry. As Quail Hollow moves into the next period, how much cash does the business have? How much does Quail Hollow owe?

Preparing and using a trial balance (Obj. 4)

■ spreadsheet

E2-10 The accounts of Whirlpool Appliance Service follow with their normal balances at June 30, 20X6. The accounts are listed in no particular order.

Account	Balance	Account	Balance
Common stock	$48,800	Building	$40,250
Accounts payable	4,300	Dividends	6,000
Service revenue	22,000	Utilities expense ...	1,400
Land	29,000	Accounts receivable .	15,500
Note payable	13,000	Delivery expense ...	300
Cash	9,000	Retained earnings ..	?
Salary expense	8,000		

Required

1. Prepare the company's trial balance at June 30, 20X6, listing accounts in proper sequence, as illustrated in the chapter. For example, Supplies comes before Building and Land. List the expense with the largest balance first, the expense with the next largest balance second, and so on.
2. Prepare the financial statement for the month ended June 30, 20X6, that will tell the company's top managers the results of operations for the month.

Correcting errors in a trial balance (Obj. 4)

E2-11 The trial balance of Car Connection, Inc., at December 31, 20X3, does not balance:

Account	Debit	Credit
Cash	$ 4,200	
Accounts receivable	13,000	
Inventory	17,000	
Supplies	600	
Land	55,000	
Accounts payable		$ 12,000
Common stock		47,900
Sales revenue		35,700
Salary expense	1,700	
Rent expense	800	
Utilities expense	700	
Total	$84,000	$86,600

The accounting records hold the following errors:

a. Recorded a $400 cash revenue transaction by debiting Accounts Receivable. The credit entry was correct.
b. Posted a $1,000 credit to Accounts Payable as $100.
c. Did not record utilities expense or the related account payable in the amount of $200.
d. Understated Common Stock by $400.
e. Omitted Cost of Goods Sold, an expense of $3,900, from the trial balance.

Required

Prepare the correct trial balance at December 31, 20X3, complete with a heading. Journal entries are not required.

Recording transactions without a journal (Obj. 5)

E2-12 Set up the following T-accounts: Cash, Accounts Receivable, Office Supplies, Office Furniture, Accounts Payable, Common Stock, Dividends, Service Revenue, Salary Expense, and Rent Expense.

Record the following transactions directly in the T-accounts without using a journal. Use the letters to identify the transactions.

a. LaVell Oxford opened a law firm by investing $12,500 cash and office furniture valued at $9,000. Organized as a professional corporation, the business issued common stock to Oxford.
b. Paid monthly rent of $1,500.
c. Purchased office supplies on account, $800.
d. Paid employees' salaries of $1,800.
e. Paid $400 of the account payable created in Transaction c.
f. Performed legal service on account, $8,300.
g. Declared and paid dividends of $2,000.

Preparing and using a trial balance (Obj. 4)

E2-13 Refer to Exercise 2-12.

1. After recording the transactions in Exercise 2-12, prepare the trial balance of LaVell Oxford, Attorney, at July 31, 20X8.
2. How well did the business perform during its first month? Give the basis for your answer.

writing assignment ■

Serial Exercise

Exercise 2-14 begins an accounting cycle that is completed in Chapter 3.

Recording transactions and preparing a trial balance (Obj. 2, 3, 4)

general ledger

E2-14 Matthew Rogers, Certified Public Accountant, Professional Corporation (P.C.), completed these transactions during the first part of December:

Dec.	2	Received $7,000 cash from Rogers, and issued common stock to him.
	2	Paid monthly office rent, $500.
	3	Paid cash for a Dell computer, $3,000, with the computer expected to remain in service for 5 years.
	4	Purchased office furniture on account, $3,600, with the furniture projected to last for 5 years.
	5	Purchased supplies on account, $300.
	9	Performed tax service for a client and received cash for the full amount of $800.
	12	Paid utility expenses, $200.
	18	Performed consulting service for a client on account, $1,700.

Required

1. Set up T-accounts for Cash, Accounts Receivable, Supplies, Equipment, Furniture, Accounts Payable, Common Stock, Dividends, Service Revenue, Rent Expense, Utilities Expense, and Salary Expense.
2. Journalize the transactions. Explanations are not required.
3. Post to the T-accounts. Key all items by date and denote an account balance on December 18 as Bal.
4. Prepare a trial balance at December 18. In the Serial Exercise of Chapter 3, we add transactions for the remainder of December and will require a trial balance at December 31.

Challenge Exercises

Computing financial statement amounts (Obj. 5)

E2-15 The owner of Victoriana Gifts is a fashion designer with little understanding of accounting. She needs to compute the following summary information from the accounting records:

a. Net income for the month of March
b. Total cash paid during March
c. Cash collections from customers during March
d. Cash paid on a note payable during March

The quickest way to compute these amounts is to analyze the following accounts:

Account	Balance Feb. 28	Balance Mar. 31	Additional Information for the Month of March
1. Retained Earnings	$ 7,000	$10,500	Dividends, $15,800
2. Cash	11,600	5,000	Cash receipts, $81,200
3. Accounts Receivable	24,300	26,700	Sales on account, $49,400
4. Note Payable	13,900	21,400	New borrowing, $25,000

The net income for March can be computed as follows:

Retained Earnings

		Feb. 28 Bal.	XX
March dividends	XX	**March net income**	X = ?
		March 31 Bal.	XX

Use a similar approach to compute the other three items.

FOCUS ON F

Analyzing transactions; using a trial balance (Obj. 1, 4)

E2-16 The trial balance of Road Runner, Inc., at December 31, 20X5, does not balance.

Cash	$ 4,200	Common stock	$20,000
Accounts receivable	7,200	Retained earnings	7,300
Supplies	800	Service revenue	9,100
Land	34,000	Salary expense	3,400
Accounts payable	5,800	Advertising expense	900
Note payable	5,000		

Required

1. How much out of balance is the trial balance? Determine the out-of-balance amount. The error lies in the Accounts Receivable account. Add the out-of-balance amount to, or subtract it from, Accounts Receivable to determine the correct balance of Accounts Receivable.
2. Road Runner also failed to record the following transactions during December:
   a. Purchased additional land for $80,000 by signing a note payable.
   b. Earned service revenue on account, $7,000.
   c. Paid salary expense of $400.
   d. Purchased a television advertisement for $2,000 on account. This account will be paid during January.

   Add these amounts to, or subtract them from, the appropriate accounts to properly include the effects of these transactions. Then prepare the corrected trial balance of Road Runner, Inc.
3. After correcting the accounts, advise the top management of Road Runner, Inc. on (a) the amount of the company's total assets and (b) whether the business was profitable during December.

Analyzing transactions (Obj. 1)

E2-17 This question concerns the items and the amounts that two entities, City of San Francisco (San Francisco), and Bay Area Health Organization, Inc. (Bay Area) should report in their financial statements.

During June, Bay Area provided City of San Francisco with medical exams for city employees and sent a bill for $40,000. On July 7 San Francisco sent a check to Bay Area for $32,000. San Francisco began June with a cash balance of $55,000; Bay Area began with cash of $0.

Required

For this situation, show everything that both San Francisco and Bay Area will report on their June and July income statements and on their balance sheets at June 30 and July 31. Use the following format for your answer:

San Francisco:		
Income statement	June	July
Balance sheet	June 30	July 31
Bay Area:		
Income statement	June	July
Balance sheet	June 30	July 31

After showing what each company should report, briefly explain how San Francisco and the Bay Area data relate to each other. Be specific.

Practice Quiz

Test your understanding of transaction analysis by answering the following questions. Select the best choice from among the possible answers.

PQ2-1 An investment of cash into the business will

a. Increase total assets.
b. Decrease total liabilities.
c. Decrease stockholders' equity.
d. Have no effect on total assets.

PQ2-2 Purchasing office equipment on account will

a. Increase total assets.
b. Increase total liabilities.
c. Have no effect on stockholders' equity.
d. All of the above.

PQ2-3 Performing a service on account will

a. Increase total assets.
b. Increase stockholders' equity.
c. Decrease total liabilities.
d. Both a and b.

PQ2-4 Receiving cash from a customer on account will

a. Increase total assets.
b. Have no effect on total assets.
c. Decrease liabilities.
d. Increase stockholders equity.

PQ2-5 Purchasing computer equipment for cash will

a. Increase both total assets and total liabilities.
b. Decrease both total assets and stockholders' equity.
c. Have no effect on total assets, total liabilities, or stockholders' equity.
d. Decrease both total liabilities and stockholders' equity.

PQ2-6 Purchasing a building for $100,000 by paying cash of $20,000 and signing a note payable for $80,000 will

a. Increase both total assets and total liabilities by $100,000.
b. Increase both total assets and total liabilities by $80,000.
c. Decrease total assets and increase total liabilities by $20,000.
d. Decrease both total assets and total liabilities by $20,000.

PQ2-7 What is the effect on total assets and stockholders' equity of paying the electric bill as soon as it is received each month?

	Total assets	Stockholders' equity
a.	Decrease	Decrease
b.	No effect	No effect
c.	Decrease	No effect
d.	No effect	Decrease

PQ2-8 Which of the following transactions will increase an asset and increase a liability?

a. Payment of an account payable.
b. Purchasing office equipment for cash.
c. Issuing stock.
d. Borrowing money from a bank.

PQ2-9 Which of the following transactions will increase an asset and increase stockholders' equity?

a. Performing a service on account for a customer.
b. Collecting cash from a customer on an account receivable.
c. Borrowing money from a bank.
d. Purchasing supplies on account.

PQ2-10 Where do we first record a transaction?

a. Ledger
b. Trial balance
c. Journal
d. Account

PQ2-11 Which of the following is not a *temporary* retained earnings account?

a. Common Stock
b. Salary Expense
c. Service Revenue
d. Dividends

FOCUS ON F

PQ2-12 Which statement is false?

a. Dividends are increased by credits.
b. Assets are increased by debits.
c. Revenues are increased by credits.
d. Liabilities are decreased by debits.

PQ2-13 The journal entry to record an owner investment of land and a building into the business

a. Debits Land and credits Building.
b. Debits Land and credits Common Stock.
c. Debits Common Stock and credits Building.
d. Debits Building and also debits Common Stock.

PQ2-14 The journal entry to record the purchase of supplies on account

a. Debits Supplies and credits Accounts Payable.
b. Credits Supplies and debits Cash.
c. Debits Supplies Expense and credits Supplies
d. Credits Supplies and debits Accounts Payable

PQ2-15 If the debit to record the purchase of supplies on account is not posted,

a. Liabilities will be understated.
b. Expenses will be overstated.
c. Assets will be understated.
d. Stockholders' equity will be understated.

PQ2-16 The journal entry to record a payment on account will

a. Debit Accounts Payable and credit Retained Earnings.
b. Debit Cash and credit Expenses.
c. Debit Accounts Payable and credit Cash.
d. Debit Expenses and credit Cash.

PQ2-17 If the credit to record the payment of an account payable is not posted,

a. Liabilities will be understated.
b. Expenses will be understated.
c. Stockholders' equity will be overstated.
d. Assets will be overstated.

PQ2-18 Which statement is false?

a. A trial balance lists all the accounts with their current balances.
b. A trial balance is the same as a balance sheet.
c. A trial balance can verify the equality of debits and credits.
d. A trial balance may be taken at any time.

PQ2-19 An owner's investment of a $100,000 building, with an $85,000 mortgage payable, into the business will

a. Increase assets by $15,000.
b. Increase stockholders' equity by $15,000.
c. Increase assets by $85,000.
d. Increase stockholders' equity by $100,000.

PQ2-20 Martex, a new company, completed these transactions. What will Martex's total assets equal?

(1) Owner invested $50,000 cash and inventory worth $25,000.
(2) Sales on account, $12,500; collections from customers, $10,600.
(3) Purchase supplies on account, $5,400; payments to vendors on account, $2,300.
(4) Payment of dividends, $1,200.

a. $79,300
b. $89,400
c. $91,100
d. $100,500

NDAMENTALS

Problems
(Group A)

Most of these A problems can be found within Prentice Hall Grade Assist (PHGA), an online homework and practice environment. Your instructor may ask you to complete these problems using PHGA.

Analyzing a trial balance (Obj. 1)

writing assignment ■

P2-1A The owners of Salon Adeva, Inc. a small chain of hair-design salons, are selling the business. They offer the following trial balance to prospective buyers.

Your best friend is considering buying Salon Adeva. She seeks your advice in interpreting this information. Specifically, she asks whether this trial balance is the same as a balance sheet and an income statement. She also wonders whether Salon Adeva is a sound company. After all, the accounts are in balance.

Salon Adeva, Inc. Trial Balance December 31, 20X5		
Cash	$ 12,000	
Accounts receivable	47,000	
Prepaid expenses	4,000	
Equipment	231,000	
Accounts payable		$105,000
Note payable		92,000
Common stock		30,000
Retained earnings		50,000
Dividends	18,000	
Service revenue		134,000
Salary expense	63,000	
Rent expense	26,000	
Supplies expense	7,000	
Advertising expense	3,000	
Total	$411,000	$411,000

Required

Write a memo to answer your friend's questions. To aid her decision, state how she can use the information on the trial balance to compute the Salon Adeva net income or net loss for the current period. State the amount of net income or net loss in your note.

Analyzing transactions with the accounting equation and preparing the financial statements (Obj. 1)

P2-2A Lisa Lane operates and is the major stockholder of an interior design studio called Lane Designers, Inc. The following amounts summarize the financial position of the business on April 30, 20X5:

	ASSETS							=	LIABILITIES	+	STOCKHOLDERS' EQUITY		
	CASH	+	ACCOUNTS RECEIVABLE	+	SUPPLIES	+	LAND	=	ACCOUNTS PAYABLE	+	COMMON STOCK	+	RETAINED EARNINGS
Bal.	1,720		2,240				24,100		5,400		10,000		12,660

During May 20X5, the business completed these transactions:

a. Lane received $42,000 as a gift and deposited the cash in the business bank account. The business issued common stock to Lane.

b. Paid $1,400 on accounts payable.

c. Performed services for a client and received cash of $4,100.

d. Collected cash from a customer on account, $750.

FOCUS ON F

e. Purchased supplies on account, $720.
f. Consulted on the interior design of a major office building and billed the client for services rendered, $5,000.
g. Received cash of $1,700 and issued common stock to Lane.
h. Recorded the following expenses for the month: (1) paid office rent—$1,200; (2) paid advertising—$660.
i. Declared and paid a cash dividend of $2,400.

Required

1. Analyze the effects of the preceding transactions on the accounting equation of Lane Designers, Inc. Adapt the format of Exhibit 2-1, Panel B.
2. Prepare the income statement of Lane Designers, Inc., for the month ended May 31, 20X5. List expenses in decreasing order by amount.
3. Prepare the statement of retained earnings of Lane Designers, Inc., for the month ended May 31, 20X5.
4. Prepare the balance sheet of Lane Designers, Inc., at May 31, 20X5.

Recording transactions, posting (Obj. 2, 3)

general ledger

P2-3A This problem can be used in conjunction with Problem 2-2A. Refer to Problem 2-2A.

Required

1. Journalize the transactions of Lane Designers, Inc. Explanations are not required.
2. Set up the following T-accounts: Cash, Accounts Receivable, Supplies, Land, Accounts Payable, Common Stock, Retained Earnings, Dividends, Service Revenue, Rent Expense, and Advertising Expense. Insert in each account its balance as given (example: Cash $1,720). Post to the accounts.
3. Compute the balance in each account. For each asset account, each liability account, and for Common Stock, compare its balance to the ending balance you obtained in Problem 2-2A. Are the amounts the same or different? (In Chapter 3, we complete the accounting process. There you will learn how the Retained Earnings, Dividends, Revenue, and Expense accounts work together in the processing of accounting information.)

Analyzing transactions with the accounting equation (Obj. 1, 2)

P2-4A Charles Ming practiced law with a large firm, a partnership, for 10 years after graduating from law school. Recently, he resigned his position to open his own law office, which he operates as a professional corporation. The name of the new entity is Charles Ming, Attorney and Counselor, Professional Corporation (P.C.). Ming experienced the following events during the organizing phase of his new business and its first month of operations. Some of the events were personal and did not affect the law practice. Others were business transactions and should be accounted for by the business.

July	1	Ming sold 1,000 shares of **Eastman Kodak** stock, which he had owned for several years, and received $88,000 cash from his stockbroker.
	2	Ming deposited in his personal bank account the $88,000 cash from sale of the Eastman Kodak stock.
	3	Ming received $150,000 cash from his former partners in the law firm from which he resigned.
	5	Ming deposited $30,000 cash in a new business bank account titled Charles Ming, Attorney and Counselor, P.C. The business issued common stock to Ming.
	6	A representative of a large company telephoned Ming and told him of the company's intention to transfer $15,000 of legal business to Ming.
	7	The business paid $550 cash for letterhead stationery for the law office.

(continued)

July	9	The business purchased office furniture. Ming paid cash of $10,000 and agreed to pay the account payable for the remainder, $9,500, within 3 months.
	23	Ming finished court hearings on behalf of a client and submitted his bill for legal services, $3,000. He expected to collect from this client within 1 month.
	29	The business paid $5,000 of its account payable on the furniture purchased on July 9.
	30	The business paid office rent of $1,900.
	31	The business declared and paid a cash dividend of $500.

Required

1. Classify each of the preceding events as one of the following:
   a. A business transaction to be recorded by the business of Charles Ming, Attorney and Counselor, P.C.
   b. A business-related event but not a transaction to be recorded by the business of Charles Ming, Attorney and Counselor, P.C.
   c. A personal transaction not to be recorded by the business of Charles Ming, Attorney and Counselor, P.C.
2. Analyze the effects of the preceding events on the accounting equation of the business of Charles Ming, Attorney and Counselor, P.C. Use a format similar to Exhibit 2-1, Panel B.
3. At the end of the first month of operations, Ming has a number of questions about the financial standing of the business. Explain the following to him:
   a. How the business can have more cash than retained earnings.
   b. How much in total resources the business has, how much it owes, and what Ming's ownership interest is in the assets of the business.
4. Record the transactions of the business in its journal. Include an explanation for each entry.

Analyzing and recording transactions (Obj. 2, 3)

■ general ledger

P2-5A Schwartz, Inc. owns movie theaters in the shopping malls of a major metropolitan area. The business completed the following transactions:

Feb.	1	Received cash of $30,000 and issued common stock to the investor.
	2	Paid $20,000 cash and signed a $30,000 note payable to purchase land for a theater site.
	5	Borrowed $100,000 from the bank to finance part of the construction of the new theater and signed a note payable to the bank.
	7	Received $15,000 cash from ticket sales and deposited that amount in the bank (labeling the revenue as Sales Revenue).
	10	Purchased theater supplies on account, $1,700.
	15	Paid employees' salaries, $2,800, and rent on a theater building, $1,800.
	15	Paid property tax expense, $1,200.
	16	Paid $800 on account.
	17	Declared and paid a cash dividend of $3,000.

Schwartz, Inc. uses the following accounts: Cash, Supplies, Land, Accounts Payable, Notes Payable, Common Stock, Dividends, Sales Revenue, Salary Expense, Rent Expense, and Property Tax Expense.

Required

1. Journalize each transaction. Explanations are not required.
2. After these transactions, how much cash does the business have? How much does it owe in total?

P2-6A Tomás Lopez opened a law office on September 3 of the current year. During the first month of operations, the business completed the following transactions:

Journalizing transactions, posting, and preparing and using a trial balance (Obj. 2, 3, 4)

■ **general ledger**

Sept.	3	Transferred $25,000 cash from the Lopez personal bank account to a business account titled Tomás Lopez, Attorney, Professional Corporation (P.C.). The corporation issued common stock to Lopez.
	4	Purchased supplies, $200, and furniture, $1,800, on account.
	6	Performed legal services for a client and received $1,000 cash.
	7	Paid $15,000 cash to acquire land for an office site.
	10	Defended a client in court, billed the client, and received his promise to pay the $600 within 1 week.
	14	Paid for the furniture purchased September 4 on account.
	16	Paid the telephone bill, $120.
	17	Received partial payment from client on account, $500.
	24	Paid the water and electricity bills, $110.
	28	Received $1,500 cash for helping a client sell real estate.
	30	Paid secretary's salary, $1,200.
	30	Declared and paid dividends of $2,400.

Required

Set up the following T-accounts: Cash, Accounts Receivable, Supplies, Furniture, Land, Accounts Payable, Common Stock, Dividends, Service Revenue, Salary Expense, and Utilities Expense.

1. Record each transaction in the journal, using the account titles given. Key each transaction by date. Explanations are not required.
2. Post the transactions to the T-accounts, using transaction dates as posting references. Label the ending balance of each account Bal., as shown in the chapter.
3. Prepare the trial balance of Tomás Lopez, Attorney, P.C., at September 30 of the current year.
4. Lopez asks you how much in total resources the business has to work with, how much it owes, and whether September was profitable (and by how much).

P2-7A Britt Hendrix obtained a corporate charter from the state of Connecticut and started a computer graphics firm. During the first month of operations (June 20X3), the business completed the following selected transactions:

Recording transactions directly in T-accounts; preparing and using a trial balance (Obj. 3, 4)

a. Began the business with an investment of $11,000 cash and a building valued at $60,000. The corporation issued common stock to Hendrix.
b. Borrowed $90,000 from the bank; signed a note payable.
c. Purchased office supplies on account for $1,300.
d. Paid $88,000 for computer equipment.
e. Paid employees' salaries totaling $2,200.
f. Performed computer graphic service on account for a client, $2,100.
g. Paid $800 of the account payable created in Transaction c.
h. Received a $600 bill for advertising expense that will be paid in the near future.
i. Performed service for clients and received $1,100 in cash.
j. Received $1,200 cash on account.
k. Paid the following cash expenses: (1) rent, $700; (2) utilities, $400.
l. Declared and paid dividends of $500.

Required

1. Set up the following T-accounts: Cash, Accounts Receivable, Office Supplies, Computer Equipment, Building, Accounts Payable, Note Payable, Common Stock, Dividends, Service Revenue, Salary Expense, Advertising Expense, Rent Expense, and Utilities Expense.

2. Record each transaction directly in the T-accounts without using a journal. Use the letters to identify the transactions.
3. Prepare the trial balance of Hendrix Computer Graphics Service, Inc., at June 30, 20X3.
4. Hendrix is afraid the business's total liabilities exceed its total assets. He also fears that the business suffered a net loss during June. Compute the amounts needed to answer his questions.

(Group B)

Some of these B problems can be found online at www.prenhall.com/harrison. These problems are algorithmically generated, allowing you endless practice. You'll receive immediate assessment and feedback as you complete each problem.

Analyzing a trial balance (Obj. 1)

writing assignment ■

P2-1B The owners of Mach-1, Inc., a credit-counseling service, are selling the business. They offer the following trial balance to prospective buyers:

Mach-1, Inc.
Trial Balance
December 31, 20X6

Cash	$ 16,000	
Accounts receivable	11,000	
Prepaid expenses	4,000	
Equipment	171,000	
Building	100,000	
Accounts payable		$ 31,000
Note payable		120,000
Common stock		103,000
Retained earnings		40,000
Dividends	21,000	
Service revenue		86,000
Rent expense	14,000	
Advertising expense	3,000	
Wage expense	33,000	
Supplies expense	7,000	
Total	$380,000	$380,000

Clay Cornelius, your best friend, is considering buying Mach-1, Inc. He seeks your advice in interpreting this information. Specifically, he asks whether this trial balance is the same as a balance sheet and an income statement. He also wonders whether Mach-1, Inc. is a sound company. After all, the accounts are in balance.

Required

Write a short note to answer Cornelius's questions. To aid his decision, state how he can use the information on the trial balance to compute the Mach-1 net income or net loss for the current period. State the amount of net income or net loss in your note.

Analyzing transactions with the accounting equation and preparing the financial statements (Obj. 1)

P2-2B Dudley Haas operates and is the major stockholder of an interior design studio called Haas Interiors, Inc. The following amounts summarize the financial position of the business on August 31, 20X8:

	ASSETS							=	LIABILITIES	+	STOCKHOLDERS' EQUITY		
	CASH	+	ACCOUNTS RECEIVABLE	+	SUPPLIES	+	LAND	=	ACCOUNTS PAYABLE	+	COMMON STOCK	+	RETAINED EARNINGS
Bal.	1,250		1,500				12,000		8,000		4,000		2,750

FOCUS ON F

During September 20X8, the business completed these transactions:

a. Haas inherited $9,000 and deposited the cash in the business bank account. The business issued common stock to Haas.
b. Performed services for a client and received cash of $6,700.
c. Paid $5,000 on accounts payable.
d. Purchased supplies on account, $1,000.
e. Collected cash from a customer on account, $500.
f. Received cash of $1,000 and issued common stock to Haas.
g. Consulted on the interior design of a major office building and billed the client for services rendered, $2,400.
h. Recorded the following business expenses for the month: (1) paid office rent—$900; (2) paid advertising—$300.
i. Declared and paid a cash dividend of $1,800.

Required

1. Analyze the effects of the preceding transactions on the accounting equation of Haas Interiors, Inc. Adapt the format of Exhibit 2-1, Panel B.
2. Prepare the income statement of Haas Interiors, Inc., for the month ended September 30, 20X8. List expenses in decreasing order by amount.
3. Prepare the entity's statement of retained earnings for the month ended September 30, 20X8.
4. Prepare the balance sheet of Haas Interiors, Inc., at September 30, 20X8.

Recording transactions, posting (Obj. 2, 3)

■ general ledger

P2-3B This problem can be used in conjunction with Problem 2-2B. Refer to Problem 2-2B.

Required

1. Journalize the transactions of Haas Interiors, Inc. Explanations are not required.
2. Set up the following T-accounts: Cash, Accounts Receivable, Supplies, Land, Accounts Payable, Common Stock, Retained Earnings, Dividends, Service Revenue, Rent Expense, and Advertising Expense. Insert in each account its balance as given (example: Cash $1,250). Post the transactions to the accounts.
3. Compute the balance in each account. For each asset account, each liability account, and for Common Stock, compare its balance to the ending balance you obtained in Problem 2-2A. Are the amounts the same or different? (In Chapter 3, we complete the accounting process. There you will learn how the Retained Earnings, Dividends, Revenue, and Expense accounts work together in the processing of accounting information.)

Analyzing transactions with the accounting equation (Obj. 1, 2)

P2-4B Don Gerbing practiced law with a large firm, a partnership, for 5 years after graduating from law school. Recently, he resigned his position to open his own office, which he operates as a professional corporation. The name of the new entity is Don Gerbing, Attorney, Professional Corporation (P.C.). Gerbing experienced the following events during the organizing phase of his new business and its first month of operations. Some of the events were personal and did not affect his law practice. Others were business transactions and should be accounted for by the business.

Feb.	4	Gerbing received $65,000 cash from his former partners in the law firm from which he resigned.
	5	Gerbing deposited $22,000 cash in a new business bank account titled Don Gerbing, Attorney, P.C. The business issued common stock to Gerbing.
	6	The business paid $300 cash for letterhead stationery for the new law office.
	7	The business purchased office furniture. The company paid cash of $10,000 and agreed to pay the account payable for the remainder, $7,000, within 3 months.

(continued)

Feb.	10	Gerbing sold IBM stock, which he had owned for several years, receiving $75,000 cash from his stockbroker.
	11	Gerbing deposited the $75,000 cash from sale of the IBM stock in his personal bank account.
	12	A representative of a large company telephoned Gerbing and told him of the company's intention to transfer $10,000 of legal business to Gerbing.
	18	Gerbing finished court hearings on behalf of a client and submitted his bill for legal services, $4,000. Gerbing expected to collect from this client within 2 weeks.
	21	The business paid half its account payable for the furniture purchased on February 7.
	25	The business paid office rent of $1,000.
	28	The business declared and paid a cash dividend of $2,000.

Required

1. Classify each of the preceding events as one of the following:
   a. A business transaction to be recorded by the business of Don Gerbing, Attorney, P.C.
   b. A business-related event but not a transaction to be recorded by the business of Don Gerbing, Attorney, P.C.
   c. A personal transaction not to be recorded by the business of Don Gerbing, Attorney, P.C.
2. Analyze the effects of the preceding events on the accounting equation of the business of Don Gerbing, Attorney, P.C. Use a format similar to that in Exhibit 2-1, Panel B.
3. At the end of the first month of operations, Gerbing has a number of questions about the financial standing of the business. Explain to him
   a. How the business can have more cash than retained earnings.
   b. How much in total resources the business has, how much it owes, and what Gerbing's ownership interest is in the assets of the business.
4. Record the transactions of the business in its journal. Include an explanation for each entry.

Analyzing and recording transactions (Obj. 2, 3)

■ **general ledger**

P2-5B Patricia Libby practices medicine under the business title Patricia Libby, M.D., Professional Corporation (P.C.). During May, Libby's medical practice completed the following transactions:

May	1	Libby deposited $9,000 cash in the business bank account. The business issued common stock to her.
	5	Paid monthly rent, $700.
	9	Paid $1,000 cash and signed a $25,000 note payable to purchase land for an office site.
	10	Purchased supplies on account, $1,200.
	19	Paid $1,000 on account.
	22	Borrowed $20,000 from the bank for business use. Libby signed a note payable to the bank in the name of the business.
	31	Revenues earned during the month included $6,000 cash and $5,000 on account.
	31	Paid employees' salaries ($2,400), office rent ($1,500), and utilities ($400).
	31	Declared and paid a cash dividend of $4,000.

Libby's business uses the following accounts: Cash, Accounts Receivable, Supplies, Land, Accounts Payable, Notes Payable, Common Stock, Dividends, Service Revenue, Salary Expense, Rent Expense, and Utilities Expense.

Required

1. Journalize each transaction of Patricia Libby, M.D., P.C. Explanations are not required.
2. After these transactions, how much cash does the business have? How much in total does it owe?

FOCUS ON F

P2-6B Pat O'Dell opened a law office on January 2 of the current year. During the first month of operations, the business completed the following transactions:

Journalizing transactions, posting, and preparing and using a trial balance (Obj. 2, 3, 4)

■ general ledger

Jan	2	O'Dell deposited $33,000 cash in the business bank account Pat O'Dell, Attorney, Professional Corporation (P.C.). The corporation issued common stock to O'Dell.
	3	Purchased supplies, $500, and furniture, $2,600, on account.
	4	Performed legal service for a client and received cash, $1,500.
	7	Paid cash to acquire land for an office site, $22,000.
	11	Defended a client in court and billed the client $800.
	16	Paid for the furniture purchased January 3 on account.
	17	Paid the telephone bill, $110.
	18	Received partial payment from client on account, $400.
	22	Paid the water and electricity bills, $130.
	29	Received $1,800 cash for helping a client sell real estate.
	31	Paid secretary's salary, $1,300.
	31	Declared and paid dividends of $2,200.

Required

Set up the following T-accounts: Cash, Accounts Receivable, Supplies, Furniture, Land, Accounts Payable, Common Stock, Dividends, Service Revenue, Salary Expense, and Utilities Expense.

1. Record each transaction in the journal, using the account titles given. Key each transaction by date. Explanations are not required.
2. Post the transactions to the T-accounts, using transaction dates as posting references. Label the ending balance of each account Bal., as shown in the chapter.
3. Prepare the trial balance of Pat O'Dell, Attorney, P.C., at January 31 of the current year.
4. O'Dell asks you how much in total resources the business has to work with, how much it owes, and whether January was profitable (and by how much).

P2-7B Betty Doss obtained a corporate charter from the state of Michigan and started CableVision, Inc. During the first month of operations (January 20X7), the business completed the following selected transactions:

Recording transactions directly in T-accounts; preparing and using a trial balance (Obj. 3, 4)

■ general ledger

a. Doss began the business with an investment of $10,000 cash and a building valued at $50,000. The corporation issued common stock to Doss.
b. Borrowed $20,000 from the bank; signed a note payable.
c. Paid $22,000 for transmitting equipment.
d. Purchased office supplies on account, $400.
e. Paid employees' salaries, $1,300.
f. Received $500 for cable TV service performed for customers.
g. Sold cable service to customers on account, $1,800.
h. Paid $100 of the account payable created in Transaction d.
i. Received a $600 bill for utility expense that will be paid in the near future.
j. Received cash on account, $1,100.
k. Paid the following cash expenses: (1) rent, $1,000; (2) advertising, $800.
l. Declared and paid dividends of $2,600.

Required

1. Set up the following T-accounts: Cash, Accounts Receivable, Office Supplies, Transmitting Equipment, Building, Accounts Payable, Note Payable, Common Stock, Dividends, Service Revenue, Salary Expense, Rent Expense, Advertising Expense, and Utilities Expense.
2. Record the foregoing transactions directly in the T-accounts without using a journal. Use the letters to identify the transactions.

(continued)

3. Prepare the trial balance of CableVision, Inc., at January 31, 20X7.
4. Doss is afraid that the total liabilities of the business exceed the total assets. She also fears that the business suffered a net loss during January. Compute the amounts needed to answer her questions.

APPLY YOUR KNOWLEDGE

Decision Cases

Correcting financial statements; deciding whether to expand a business (Obj. 2)

Case 1. Carlo Ponti opened an Italian restaurant in Boston. Business has been good, and Ponti is considering expanding the restaurant. A cousin has produced the following financial statements at December 31, 20X5, end of the first three months of operations:

Carlo Ponti Fine Foods, Inc.
Income Statement
Quarter Ended December 31, 20X5

Sales revenue	$50,000
Common stock	38,000
Total revenue	88,000
Accounts payable	8,000
Advertising expense	5,000
Rent expense	6,000
Total expenses	19,000
Net income	$69,000

Carlo Ponti Fine Foods, Inc.
Balance Sheet
December 31, 20X5

Assets	
Cash	$14,000
Cost of goods sold (expense)	19,000
Food inventory	5,000
Furniture	47,000
Total assets	$85,000
Liabilities	
None	
Owners' Equity	$85,000

In these financial statements all *amounts* are correct, except for Owners' Equity. Ponti's cousin heard that total assets should equal total liabilities plus owners' equity, so he plugged in the amount of owners' equity at $85,000 to make the balance sheet come out even.

Required

Carlo Ponti has asked whether he should expand the restaurant. His banker says Ponti may be wise to expand if (a) net income for the first quarter reaches $20,000 and (b) total assets are at least $60,000. It appears that the business has reached these milestones, but Ponti doubts his cousin's understanding of accounting. Ponti needs your help in making this decision. Prepare a corrected income statement and balance sheet. (Remember that Retained Earnings, which was omitted from the balance sheet, should equal net income for the first year; there were no dividends.) After preparing the statements, give Carlo Ponti your recommendation as to whether he should expand the restaurant.

Recording transactions directly in T-accounts, preparing a trial balance, and measuring net income or loss (Obj. 4, 5)

Case 2. A friend named Charlene Budd has asked what effect certain transactions will have on her company. Time is short, so you cannot apply the detailed procedures of journalizing and posting. Instead, you must analyze the transactions without the use of a journal. Budd will continue the business only if she can expect to earn monthly net income of $10,000. The following transactions occurred this month:

a. Budd deposited $25,000 cash in a business bank account, and the corporation issued common stock to Budd.

b. Borrowed $4,000 cash from the bank and signed a note payable due within 1 year.

c. Paid $300 cash for supplies.

d. Purchased advertising in the local newspaper for cash, $800.

(continued)

e. Purchased office furniture on account, $4,400.

f. Paid the following cash expenses for 1 month: secretary's salary, $1,750; office rent, $600.

g. Earned revenue on account, $9,650.

h. Earned revenue and received $2,500 cash.

i. Collected cash from customers on account, $1,200.

j. Paid on account, $1,000.

k. Declared and paid dividends of $900.

Required

1. Set up the following T-accounts: Cash, Accounts Receivable, Supplies, Furniture, Accounts Payable, Notes Payable, Common Stock, Dividends, Service Revenue, Salary Expense, Advertising Expense, and Rent Expense.
2. Record the transactions directly in the accounts without using a journal. Key each transaction by letter.
3. Prepare a trial balance at the current date. List expenses with the largest amount first, the next largest amount second, and so on. The business name will be Budd Network Consulting, Inc.
4. Compute the amount of net income or net loss for this first month of operations. Why or why not would you recommend that Budd continue in business?

Ethical Issues

Issue 1. Blaine McCormick is the president and principal stockholder of McCormick's Restaurant, Inc. During 20X4, the company earned total revenue of $800,000 and incurred expenses of $450,000. The resulting net income is $350,000, which is quite good. To expand, the business is applying for a $250,000 bank loan, and the bank requires the company to have owners' equity of at least as much as the loan. The present balance sheet of McCormick's Restaurant, Inc. reports total assets of $300,000 and liabilities of $200,000. To get the loan, McCormick is considering two options for beefing up the owners' equity of the business:

Option 1. Issue common stock for cash. A friend has been wanting to invest in the company. This may be the right time to extend the offer.

Option 2. Transfer land to the business, and issue common stock to McCormick. Then, after obtaining the loan, he can transfer the land back to himself and zero out the common stock.

Journalize the transactions required by each option. Which plan is ethical? Which is unethical and why?

Issue 2. Human Habitat, a charitable organization in Taos, New Mexico, has a standing agreement with Taos State Bank. The agreement allows Habitat to overdraw its cash balance at the bank when donations are running low. In the past, Habitat managed funds wisely and rarely used this privilege. Douglas Byrd has been named president of Habitat. To expand operations, he is acquiring office equipment and spending a lot for fund-raising. During Byrd's presidency, Habitat has maintained a negative bank balance of about $3,000.

Required

What is the ethical issue in this situation? Do you approve or disapprove of Byrd's management of Habitat's and Taos State Bank's funds? Why?

Focus on Financials: ■ YUM! Brands

Recording transactions and computing net income (Obj. 3, 4)

Refer to YUM! Brands' financial statements in Appendix A at the end of the book. Assume that YUM completed the following selected transactions during 2003.

a. Made company sales and collected cash of $7,441 million.

b. Earned franchise and license fee revenue on account, $939 million.

c. Purchased inventories, paying cash of $2,304 million.

d. Incurred food and paper expense of $2,300 million. Credit the Inventories account.

e. Paid operating and other expenses of $5,463 million.

f. Collected cash on accounts receivable, $938 million.

g. Paid cash for other assets, $550 million.

Required

1. Set up T-accounts for: Cash (debit balance of $130 million); Accounts Receivable (debit balance of $168 million); Inventories (debit balance of $63 million); Other Assets ($0 balance); Company Sales ($0 balance); Franchise and License Fee Revenue ($0 balance); Food and Paper Expense ($0 balance); Operating and Other Expenses ($0 balance).
2. Journalize YUM's transactions a–g. Explanations are not required.
3. Post to the T-accounts, and compute the balance for each account. Key posting by transaction letters a–g.
4. For each of the following accounts, compare your computed balance to YUM's actual balance as shown on YUM's 2003 income statement or balance sheet in Appendix A. All your amounts should agree to the actual figures.
   a. Cash
   b. Accounts Receivable
   c. Inventories
   d. Company Sales
   e. Franchise and License Fee Revenue
   f. Food and Paper Expense
5. Use the relevant accounts from requirement 4 to prepare a summary income statement for YUM! Brands, Inc., for 2003. Compare the net income you computed to YUM's actual net income. The two amounts should be equal.

Focus on Analysis: ■ Pier 1 Imports

Analyzing a leading company's financial statements (Obj. 1, 2)

Refer to the **Pier 1 Imports** financial statements in Appendix B at the end of the book. Suppose you are an investor considering buying Pier 1 stock. The following questions are important: Show amounts in millions and round to the nearest $1 million.

1. Explain whether Pier 1 had more sales revenue, or collected more cash from customers, during 2004. Combine Pier 1's two receivable accounts, and then analyze total receivables to answer this question.
2. A major concern of lenders, such as banks, is the amount of "long-term debt" a company owes. How much long-term debt does Pier 1 owe at the end of 2004? at the end of 2003? What must have happened to Pier 1's long-term debt during 2004?
3. Investors are vitally interested in a company's sales and profits, and its trends of sales and profits over time. Consider Pier 1's net sales and net income during the period from 2002 through 2004. Compute the percentage increases in net sales and also in net income from 2002 to 2004. Which item grew faster during this period, net sales or net income? (For convenience, show dollar amounts in millions.) Which would you prefer to grow faster, net sales or net income? Give the reason for your answer.

Group Projects

Project 1. Contact a local business and arrange with the owner to learn what accounts the business uses.

Required

1. Obtain a copy of the business's chart of accounts.
2. Prepare the company's financial statements for the most recent month, quarter, or year. You may use either made-up account balances or balances supplied by the owner.

If the business has a large number of accounts within a category, combine related accounts and report a single amount on the financial statements. For example, the company

may have several cash accounts. Combine all cash amounts and report a single Cash amount on the balance sheet.

You will probably encounter numerous accounts that you have not yet learned. Deal with these as best you can. The charts of accounts given in the appendix at the end of the book can be helpful.

Project 2. You are promoting a rock concert in your area. Your purpose is to earn a profit, so you need to establish the formal structure of a business entity. Assume you organize as a corporation.

Required

1. Make a detailed list of 10 factors you must consider as you establish the business.
2. Describe 10 of the items your business must arrange to promote and stage the rock concert.
3. Identify the transactions that your business can undertake to organize, promote, and stage the concert. Journalize the transactions, and post to the relevant T-accounts. Set up the accounts you need for your business ledger. Refer to the appendix at the end of book if needed.
4. Prepare the income statement, statement of retained earnings, and balance sheet immediately after the rock concert, that is, before you have had time to pay all the business bills and to collect all receivables.
5. Assume that you will continue to promote rock concerts if the venture is successful. If it is unsuccessful, you will terminate the business within 3 months after the concert. Discuss how to evaluate the success of your venture and how to decide whether to continue in business.

spotlight

CALLAWAY GOLF COMPANY

Callaway Golf Company
Income Statement (Adapted)
Year Ended December 31, 2003

	Millions
Revenues:	
Net sales	$814
Other income, net	2
Total revenues	$816
Expenses:	
Cost of goods sold	$445
Selling expenses	208
General and administrative expenses	65
Research and development expense	30
Income tax expense	22
Total expenses	770
Net income for the year	$ 46

Callaway Golf Company
Statement of Cash Flows (Adapted)
Year Ended December 31, 2003

	Millions
Operating activities:	
Net cash provided by operations	$119
Investing activities:	
Net cash used for investing	(168)
Financing activities:	
Net cash used for financing	(12)
Net increase (decrease) in cash for the year	$(61)

Says Eli Callaway: "Just make a better product and tell the truth about it." This credo has served Callaway Golf Company well. Even if you don't play golf, you've no doubt heard of Callaway Big Bertha golf clubs. Annika Sorenstam, the world's number one woman golfer, hits with Callaway clubs, as do many other pros.

Callaway revolutionized golf with oversize clubs. What is the advantage of an oversize club? It is *forgiving*. That means you don't have to hit the ball on the club's sweet spot to make a decent shot. Each year the company refines its woods, irons, and putters to keep making "a better product." That is why Callaway spends millions each year on research and development (see the company income statement above).

Using Accrual Accounting to Measure Income

LEARNING OBJECTIVES

1 **Relate** accrual accounting and cash flows

2 **Apply** the revenue and matching principles

3 **Update** the financial statements by adjusting the accounts

4 **Prepare** the financial statements

5 **Close** the books

6 **Use** the current ratio and the debt ratio to evaluate a business

Suppose you are Ronald Drapeau or Patrice Hutin, two of Callaway Golf's top executives. You are looking back over the past year, and you want to evaluate Callaway's performance. Where do you look? This chapter begins with adapted versions of Callaway's most recent income statement and statement of cash flows.

The Callaway income statement reports revenues, expenses, and net income of $46 million for the year. The company's statement of cash flows shows that cash decreased by $61 million during the year. Which statement should Drapeau and Hutin analyze to measure operating performance? Is it net income or is it cash flow? Both net income and cash flow are critically important for Callaway and for every other company.

How does Callaway Golf Company know whether it is profitable? By analyzing the financial statements. Which financial statement reports profits and losses? The income statement. Cash flow plays very little role in measuring profits and losses because (using illustrative figures):

Total revenues	**$1,000**
– Total expenses	**850**
= Net income	**$ 150**

Revenues and expenses measure profits and losses, regardless of whether Callaway Golf receives or pays cash now or later.

This chapter rounds out coverage of the accounting cycle. It completes the basics of what you need before moving on to the details of individual topics such as receivables, inventory, and cash flows.

For more practice and review of accounting cycle concepts, use ACT, the accounting Cycle Tutorial, online at www.prenhall.com/harrison. Margin logos like this one, directing you to the appropriate ACT section and material, appear throughout Chapters 1, 2, and 3. When you enter the tutorial, you'll find three buttons on the opening page of each chapter module. Here's what the buttons mean: Tutorial gives you a review of the major concepts, Application gives you practice exercises, and Glossary reviews important terms.

Accrual Accounting Versus Cash-Basis Accounting

Investors search for corporations whose stock price will increase. Banks seek borrowers who will pay their debts. Managers want to lead their companies into profitable business ventures. Accounting provides the information these people use for decision making. Accounting can be based on the accrual basis or the cash basis.

Accrual accounting
Accounting that records the impact of a business event as it occurs, regardless of whether the transaction affected cash.

Cash-basis accounting
Accounting that records only transactions in which cash is received or paid.

In **accrual accounting**, an accountant records the impact of a business transaction as it occurs. When the business performs a service, makes a sale, or incurs an expense, the accountant records the transaction even if it receives or pays no cash. In **cash-basis accounting**, the accountant records a transaction only when it receives or pays cash. Cash receipts are treated as revenues, and cash payments are handled as expenses.

Generally accepted accounting principles (GAAP) require that businesses use accrual accounting. This means that the business records revenues as they are *earned* and expenses as they are *incurred*—not necessarily when cash changes hands.

FOCUS ON F

ACCOUNTING ALERT

Cash-Basis Accounting Doesn't Cut It Either

The Accounting Alert for Chapter 2 shows how single-entry accounting records only one side of a transaction. As a result, single entry fails to capture all the effects on a company. Single-entry accounting doesn't cut it.

For the vast majority of companies, cash-basis accounting doesn't cut it either. There are two basic ways to do accounting:

- Cash basis
- Accrual basis

The cash basis of accounting records only *cash* transactions—cash receipts, cash payments, and the balance of cash on hand. By contrast, the accrual basis records *all* transactions and their effects on a company. In this book we use the accrual basis of accounting.

The basic defect of cash-basis accounting is that the cash basis ignores important information. That makes the financial statements incomplete. The result? People using the statements make bad decisions. For example, investors may be led to believe a company is better than it really is; they buy the stock and lose their money. Managers make wrong predictions about the results of their actions.

The following diagram frames this Accounting Alert:

Defective Accounting Method		Appropriate Accounting Method
Single-entry	——→	Double-entry
Cash basis	——→	Accrual basis

Suppose your business makes a sale on account. The cash basis does not record the sale because you received no cash. You may be thinking, "We need not record the sale because we haven't gotten any cash yet. Let's wait until we collect cash and then record the sale. After all, we pay the bills with cash, so ignore transactions that don't affect cash."

What's wrong with this argument? Consider the financial statements—the balance sheet and the income statement. Not recording a sale on account—waiting until we receive cash—is bad accounting for both the balance sheet and the income statement.

Balance-Sheet Defect If we fail to record a sale on account, the balance sheet reports no account receivable. Why is this so bad? The receivable is a real asset, and it should appear on the balance sheet. Without this information, investors cannot value the business realistically.

Income-Statement Defect A sale on account provides revenue that increases the company's wealth. Ignoring the sale robs investors of the information about the revenue. As a result, investors cannot value the business realistically.

The take-away lessons from this accounting alert are:

- Watch out for companies that use the cash basis of accounting. Their financial statements omit important information.
- All but the smallest businesses use the accrual basis of accounting.

Accrual Accounting and Cash Flows

OBJECTIVE

1 **Relate** accrual accounting and cash flows

Accrual accounting is more complex—and more complete—than cash-basis accounting. Accrual accounting records *cash* transactions, including

- Collecting from customers
- Receiving cash from interest earned
- Paying salaries, rent, and other expenses
- Borrowing money
- Paying off loans
- Issuing stock

Accrual accounting also records *noncash* transactions, such as

- Purchases of inventory on account
- Sales on account
- Accrual of expenses incurred but not yet paid
- Depreciation expense
- Usage of prepaid rent, insurance, and supplies

Check Point 3-1

Check Point 3-2

This chapter shows how accrual accounting completes the process leading up to the financial statements.

Accrual accounting is based on a framework of concepts and principles. We turn now to the time-period concept, the revenue principle, and the matching principle.

The Time-Period Concept

The only way for a business to know for certain how well it performed is to shut down, sell the assets, pay the liabilities, and return any leftover cash to the owners. This process, called *liquidation*, means going out of business. Ongoing businesses cannot measure income this way. Instead, they need regular progress reports. Accountants, therefore, prepare financial statements for specific periods. The **time-period concept** ensures that accounting information is reported at regular intervals.

Time-period concept
Ensures that accounting information is reported at regular intervals.

The basic accounting period is 1 year, and virtually all businesses prepare annual financial statements. Around 60% of large companies—including Callaway Golf—use the calendar year from January 1 through December 31.

A *fiscal year* ends on a date other than December 31. Most retailers, including JCPenney Company, use a fiscal year that ends on January 31 because the low point in their business activity falls during January, after Christmas sales. JCPenney does more than 30% of its yearly sales during November and December but only 5% in January.

Managers and investors cannot wait until the end of the year to gauge a company's progress. Companies prepare financial statements for interim periods of less than a year, such as a month, a quarter (3 months), or a semiannual period (6 months). Most of the discussions in this text are based on an annual accounting period.

The Revenue Principle

OBJECTIVE

2 **Apply** the revenue and matching principles

The **revenue principle** governs two things:

1. *When* to record revenue (make a journal entry)
2. The *amount* of revenue to record

When should you record revenue? After it has been earned—and not before. In most cases, revenue is earned when the business has delivered a good or service to a customer. It has done everything required to earn the revenue by transferring the good or service to the customer.

Revenue principle
The basis for recording revenues; tells accountants when to record revenue and the amount of revenue to record.

Exhibit 3-1 shows two situations that provide guidance on when to record revenue. Situation 1 illustrates when *not* to record revenue: No transaction has occurred, so Callaway Golf records nothing. Situation 2 illustrates when revenue *should* be recorded—after a transaction has occurred.

The *amount* of revenue to record is the cash value of the goods transferred to the customer. Suppose that in order to gain Anika Sorenstam's business, Callaway Golf sells

■ **EXHIBIT 3-1** When to Record Revenue

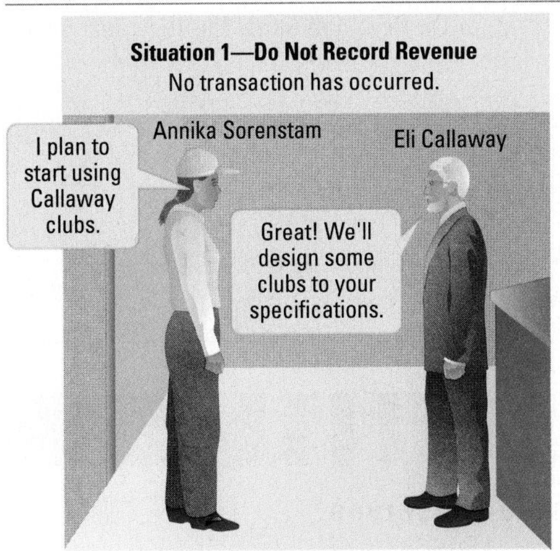

the clubs for the discount price of $500. Ordinarily, Callaway would charge $2,000 for these clubs. How much revenue should Callaway record? The answer is $500—the cash value of the transaction. The amount of the sale, $500, is the amount of revenue earned.

The Matching Principle

The **matching principle** is the basis for recording expenses. *Expenses* are the costs of assets used up, and of liabilities created, in the earning of revenue. Expenses have no future benefit to the company. The matching principle includes two steps:

Matching principle
The basis for recording expenses. Directs accountants to identify all expenses incurred during the period, to measure the expenses, and to match them against the revenues earned during that same period.

1. Identify all the expenses incurred during the accounting period.
2. Measure the expenses, and match expenses against the revenues earned.

To *match* expenses against revenues means to subtract expenses from revenues to compute net income or net loss. Exhibit 3-2 illustrates the matching principle.

Some expenses are paid in cash. Other expenses arise from using up an asset such as supplies. Still other expenses occur when a company creates a liability. For

■ **EXHIBIT 3-2**
The Matching Principle

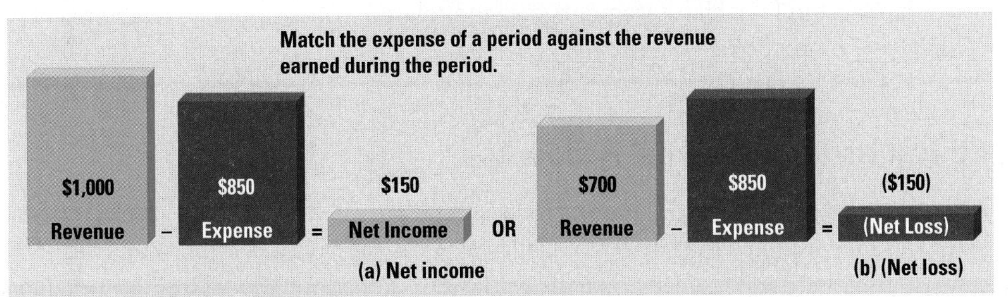

NDAMENTALS

Check Point 3-3

example, Callaway Golf's salary expense occurs when employees work for the company. Callaway may pay the salary expense immediately, or it may record a liability for the expense. In either case, Callaway has salary expense. The critical event for recording an expense is the occurrence of the expense, not the payment of cash.

stop AND think...

1. A customer pays Callaway Golf $900 on March 15 for golf clubs to be delivered in April. Has Callaway earned revenue on March 15? When will Callaway earn the revenue?
2. Callaway pays $4,500 on July 31 for office rent for the next 3 months. Has the company incurred an expense on July 31?

Answers:

1. No. Callaway has received the cash but will not deliver the merchandise until later. Callaway earns the revenue when it gives the goods to the customer. Until that time, Callaway has a liability to the customer.
2. No. Callaway has paid cash for rent in advance. This prepaid rent is an asset because Callaway has the use of an office in the future.

ACCOUNTING ALERT

Earnings Management and Cookie-Jar Reserves

Companies strive to meet or beat Wall Street forecasts. Companies that report higher-than-expected profits are rewarded with rising stock prices. And companies that fail to meet their earnings forecasts are punished severely. Therefore, managers try not to surprise the market with bad news. How can a company keep earnings trending upward and stay within GAAP? The best way is to follow Eli Callaway's advice to "make a better product and tell the truth." Regrettably, some companies try to "manage their earnings," a practice frowned on by the Securities and Exchange Commission (SEC).

One way to abuse the adjusting process is by creating "cookie-jar reserves." An example of a cookie-jar reserve is a liability created when a company overstates an expense that will be paid next year. Companies may overstate an expense when profits are high because they can afford to take the hit to income. Then later, when profits are low, the company debits the liability (the reserve) rather than an expense. The result is a "smoothing" of net income, with net income still trending upward. Analysts may be tricked into recommending the company's stock, and everyone is happy until the truth comes out.

The take-away lessons from this accounting alert are:

- Watch out for companies that always beat their targets for net income. Very few companies are that successful.
- Examine the financial statements and the related notes carefully. The notes may reveal some cookie-jar reserves.

Ethical Issues in Accrual Accounting

Accrual accounting provides some ethical challenges that cash accounting avoids. For example, suppose that in 2006, Callaway Golf prepays a $3 million advertising campaign to be conducted by Saatchi & Saatchi, a leading advertising agency. The

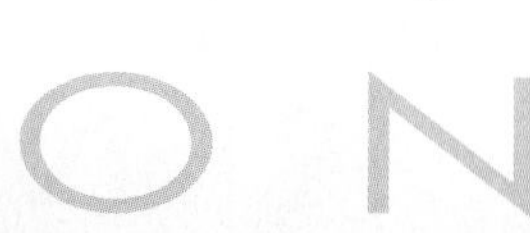

advertisements are scheduled to run during December, January, and February. Callaway is buying an asset, a prepaid expense. Suppose Callaway pays for the advertisements on December 1 and the ads start running immediately. Callaway should record one-third of the expense ($1 million) during the year ended December 31, 2006, and two-thirds ($2 million) during 2007.

Suppose 2006 is a great year for Callaway—net income is better than expected. Callaway's top managers believe that 2007 will not be as profitable. In this case, the company has a strong incentive to expense the full $3 million during 2006 in order to report all the expense in the 2006 income statement. This unethical action would keep $2 million of advertising expense off the 2007 income statement and make 2007's net income look better.

Updating the Accounts: The Adjustment Process

OBJECTIVE

3 Update the financial statements by adjusting the accounts

At the end of the period, the business reports its financial statements. This process begins with the trial balance from Chapter 2. We refer to this trial balance as *unadjusted* because the accounts are not yet ready for the financial statements. In most cases the label *trial balance* means "unadjusted."

Which Accounts Need to Be Updated (Adjusted)?

Gary and Monica Lyon, the stockholders, need to know how well Air & Sea Travel performed during April. The financial statements report this information, and all accounts must be up-to-date. That means some accounts must be adjusted. Exhibit 3-3 gives the trial balance of Air & Sea Travel, Inc., at April 30, 20X3.

■ **EXHIBIT 3-3**

Unadjusted Trial Balance

Air & Sea Travel, Inc.
Unadjusted Trial Balance
April 30, 20X3

Cash	$24,800	
Accounts receivable	2,250	
Supplies	700	
Prepaid rent	3,000	
Furniture	16,500	
Accounts payable		$13,100
Unearned service revenue		450
Common stock		20,000
Retained earnings		11,250
Dividends	3,200	
Service revenue		7,000
Salary expense	950	
Utilities expense	400	
Total	$51,800	$51,800

Scan the trial balance in Exhibit 3-3. Can you identify the accounts with balances that are already up-to-date? Those accounts are ready for the balance sheet. Start with Cash. Cash, Furniture, Accounts Payable, Common Stock, and Dividends are up-to-date and need no further adjustment. Why? Because the day-to-day transactions of the period provide the data for these accounts.

Accounts Receivable, Supplies, Prepaid Rent, and the other accounts are another story. These accounts are not yet up-to-date on April 30. Why? Because certain transactions have not yet been recorded. Take Supplies. During April, Air & Sea Travel used stationery and other supplies to serve clients. But Air & Sea Travel did not make a journal entry every time it printed a travel plan for a client. That would waste time and money. Instead, Air & Sea Travel waits until the end of the period and then records the supplies used up during the month.

The cost of supplies used up is an expense. An adjusting entry at the end of April updates both Supplies (an asset) and Supplies Expense. Once adjusted, these accounts are ready for the April financial statements. We must adjust all accounts whose balances are not yet up-to-date.

Categories of Adjusting Entries

Accounting adjustments fall into three basic categories: *deferrals, depreciation*, and *accruals*.

Deferral
An adjustment for which the business paid or received cash in advance. Examples include prepaid rent, prepaid insurance, and supplies.

Deferrals. A **deferral** is an adjustment for which the business paid or received cash in advance. Callaway Golf purchases supplies for use in its operations. During the period, some supplies (assets) are used up and thus become expenses. At the end of the period, an adjustment is needed to decrease the Supplies account for the supplies used up. This is Supplies Expense. Prepaid rent, prepaid insurance, and all other prepaid expenses require deferral adjustments.

There are also deferral adjustments for liabilities. Companies such as Callaway Golf collect cash in advance of earning the revenue. When Callaway receives cash up front, the company has a liability to provide golf equipment for the customer. This liability is called Unearned Sales Revenue. Then, when Callaway delivers the goods to the customer, it earns Sales Revenue. This earning process requires an adjustment at the end of each accounting period. The adjustment decreases the liability and increases the revenue for the amount of revenue earned. Publishers such as Time, Inc. and your local newspaper sell subscriptions and collect cash in advance. Their accounting parallels that of Callaway Golf Company.

Depreciation
Expense associated with spreading (allocating) the cost of a plant asset over its useful life.

Depreciation. **Depreciation** is the allocation of the cost of a plant asset to expense over the asset's useful life. Depreciation is the most common long-term deferral. The business buys long-term plant assets, such as buildings, equipment, and furniture. As the company uses the assets, it records depreciation for their wear-and-tear and obsolescence. The accounting adjustment records Depreciation Expense, which decreases the book value of the asset over its life. The process is identical to a deferral-type adjustment; the only difference is the type of asset involved.

Accrual
An expense or a revenue that occurs before the business pays or receives cash. An accrual is the opposite of a deferral.

Accruals. An **accrual** is the opposite of a deferral. For an accrued expense, the business records an expense before paying cash. For an accrued revenue, it records the revenue before collecting cash.

Salary Expense can create an accrual adjustment. As employees work for Callaway Golf, the company's salary expense accrues with the passage of time. At December 31, 2003, Callaway owed employees $25.5 million, to be paid next year. At December 31, Callaway recorded Salary Expense and Salary Payable for the $25.5 million. Other examples of expense accruals include interest expense and income tax expense.

An accrued revenue is a revenue that the business will collect the next year. At December 31, it must accrue the revenue. The adjustment debits a receivable and credits a revenue. For example, accrual of interest revenue debits Interest Receivable and credits Interest Revenue.

FOCUS ON F

Let's see how the adjusting process actually works. We begin with prepaid expenses. Recall that prepaid expenses are assets, not expenses.

Prepaid Expenses

A **prepaid expense** is an expense paid in advance. The prepayment will be used up in the near future. Therefore, prepaid expenses are assets, because they provide a future benefit for the owner. Let's do the adjustments for prepaid rent and supplies.

Prepaid expense
A category of miscellaneous assets that typically expire or get used up in the near future. Examples include prepaid rent, prepaid insurance, and supplies.

Prepaid Rent. Companies pay rent in advance. This prepayment creates an asset for the renter, who can then use the rented item in the future. Suppose Air & Sea Travel prepays 3 months' office rent ($3,000) on April 1, 20X3. The entry for the prepayment of 3 months' rent debits Prepaid Rent as follows:

Apr. 1	Prepaid Rent ($1,000 × 3)	3,000	
	Cash		3,000
	Paid 3 months' rent in advance.		

The accounting equation shows that one asset increases and another decreases. Total assets are unchanged.

ASSETS	=	LIABILITIES	+	STOCKHOLDERS' EQUITY
3,000	=	0	+	0
−3,000				

After posting, the Prepaid Rent account appears as follows:

Prepaid Rent			
Apr. 1	3,000		

Throughout April, the Prepaid Rent account carries this beginning balance, as shown in Exhibit 3-3 (p. 111). At April 30, Prepaid Rent must be adjusted. Rent expense is 1 month of the prepayment ($3,000 × 1/3 = $1,000). The adjustment transfers $1,000 from Prepaid Rent to Rent Expense as follows:*

Apr. 30	Rent Expense ($3,000 × 1/3)	1,000	*Adjusting entry a*
	Prepaid Rent		1,000
	To record rent expense.		

Both assets and stockholders' equity decrease.

ASSETS	=	LIABILITIES	+	STOCKHOLDERS' EQUITY	−	EXPENSES
−1,000	=	0			−	1,000

After posting, Prepaid Rent and Rent Expense appear as follows:

Prepaid Rent			
Apr. 1	3,000	Apr. 30	1,000
Bal.	2,000		

Rent Expense			
Apr. 30	1,000		
Bal.	1,000		

This expense illustrates the matching principle. We record an expense in order to measure net income.

*See Exhibit 3-8, page 122, for a summary of adjustments a–g.

Supplies. Supplies are another type of prepaid expense. On April 2, Air & Sea Travel paid cash of $700 for office supplies:

Apr. 2	Supplies	700	
	Cash		700
	Paid cash for supplies.		

ASSETS	=	LIABILITIES	+	STOCKHOLDERS' EQUITY
700	=	0	+	0
−700				

The cost of the supplies Air & Sea Travel used is *supplies expense* for April. To measure supplies expense, the business counts the supplies on hand at the end of the month. The count shows that $400 of supplies remain. Subtracting the $400 of supplies on hand from the supplies available ($700) measures supplies expense for the month ($300):

ASSET AVAILABLE DURING THE PERIOD	−	ASSET ON HAND AT THE END OF THE PERIOD	=	ASSET USED (EXPENSE) DURING THE PERIOD
$700	−	$400	=	$300

The April 30 adjusting entry debits the expense and credits the asset, as follows:

Apr. 30	Supplies Expense ($700 – $400)	300		Adjusting entry b
	Supplies		300	
	To record supplies expense.			

ASSETS	=	LIABILITIES	+	STOCKHOLDERS' EQUITY	−	EXPENSES
−300	=	0			−	300

After posting, the Supplies and Supplies Expense accounts appear as follows. The adjustment is highlighted for emphasis.

Supplies

Apr. 2	700	Apr. 30	300
Bal.	400		

Supplies Expense

Apr. 30	300		
Bal.	300		

Check Point 3-4

Supplies then enters the month of May with a $400 balance, and the adjustment process is repeated each month.

stop AND think...

At the beginning of the month, supplies were $5,000. During the month, $7,800 of supplies were purchased. At month's end, $3,600 of supplies were still on hand. What are the adjusting entry and the ending balance in the Supplies account?

Answer:

Supplies Expense ($5,000 + $7,800 – $3,600)	9,200	
Supplies		9,200

Ending balance of supplies = $3,600 (the supplies still on hand)

FOCUS ON F

Depreciation of Plant Assets

Plant assets Long-lived assets, such as land, buildings, and equipment, used in the operation of the business. Also called *fixed assets*.

Plant assets are long-lived tangible assets, such as land, buildings, furniture, machinery, and equipment. All plant assets but land decline in usefulness as they age, and this decline is an *expense*. Accountants spread the cost of each plant asset, except land, over its useful life. This process of allocating cost to expense is called *depreciation*.

To illustrate depreciation, consider Air & Sea Travel. Suppose that on April 3 the business purchased furniture on account for $16,500:

Apr. 3	Furniture	16,500	
	Accounts Payable		16,500
	Purchased office furniture on account.		

ASSETS	=	LIABILITIES	+	STOCKHOLDERS' EQUITY
16,500	=	16,500	+	0

After posting, the Furniture account appears as follows:

Furniture		
Apr. 3	16,500	

Air & Sea Travel records an asset when it purchases furniture. Then, as the asset is used, a portion of the asset's cost is transferred to Depreciation Expense. Accounting matches the expense against revenue—this is the matching principle. In computerized systems, the depreciation entry is programmed for each month of the asset's life.

Air & Sea Travel's office furniture will remain useful for 5 years and then be worthless. One way to compute the amount of depreciation for each year is to divide the cost of the asset ($16,500 in our example) by its expected useful life (5 years). This procedure—called the *straight-line method*—gives annual depreciation of $3,300. The depreciation amount is an *estimate*. (Chapter 7 covers plant assets and depreciation in more detail.)

Depreciation = $16,500/5 years = $3,300 per year

Depreciation for April is $275

Depreciation = $3,300/12 months = $275 per month

The Accumulated Depreciation Account. Depreciation expense for April is recorded as follows:

Apr. 30	Depreciation Expense—Furniture	275		Adjusting entry c
	Accumulated Depreciation—Furniture		275	
	To record depreciation on furniture.			

Total assets decrease by the amount of the expense:

ASSETS	=	LIABILITIES	+	STOCKHOLDERS' EQUITY	−	EXPENSES
−275	=	0			−	275

NDAMENTALS

The Accumulated Depreciation account (not Furniture) is credited to preserve the original cost of the furniture in the Furniture account. Managers can then refer to the Furniture account if they need to know how much the asset cost.

Accumulated depreciation The cumulative sum of all depreciation expense from the date of acquiring a plant asset.

The **Accumulated Depreciation** account shows the sum of all depreciation expense from using the asset. Therefore, the balance in the Accumulated Depreciation account increases over the asset's life.

Accumulated Depreciation is a *contra asset* account—an asset account with a normal credit balance. A **contra account** has two distinguishing characteristics:

Contra account An account that always has a companion account and whose normal balance is opposite that of the companion account.

1. It always has a companion account.
2. Its normal balance is opposite that of the companion account.

In this case, Accumulated Depreciation is the contra account to Furniture, so Accumulated Depreciation appears directly after Furniture on the balance sheet. A business carries an accumulated depreciation account for each depreciable asset, for example, Accumulated Depreciation—Building and Accumulated Depreciation—Machinery.

After posting, the plant asset accounts of Air & Sea Travel are as follows—with the adjustment highlighted:

Furniture		Accumulated Depreciation—Furniture		Depreciation Expense—Furniture	
Apr. 3 16,500			Apr. 30 275	Apr. 30 275	
Bal. 16,500			Bal. 275	Bal. 275	

Book value (of a plant asset) The asset's cost minus accumulated depreciation.

Book Value. The net amount of a plant asset (cost minus accumulated depreciation) is called that asset's **book value** or *carrying amount*. Exhibit 3-4 shows how Air & Sea Travel would report the book value of its furniture and building at April 30.

■ **EXHIBIT 3-4**

Plant Assets on the Balance Sheet of Air & Sea Travel

Air & Sea Travel Plant Assets at April 30

Furniture	$16,500	
Less Accumulated Depreciation	(275)	$16,225
Building	$48,000	
Less Accumulated Depreciation	(200)	47,800
Book value of plant assets		$64,025

At April 30, the book value of furniture is $16,225; the book value of the building is $47,800.

Check Point 3-5

stop AND think...

1. What is the book value of Air & Sea Travel's furniture at the end of May?
2. Is book value what the furniture could be sold for?

Answers:

1. $16,500 – $275 – $275 = $15,950.
2. Not necessarily. Book value represents the part of the asset's cost that has not yet been depreciated. Book value is not necessarily related to the amount that an asset can be sold for.

FOCUS ON F

Exhibit 3-5 shows how Callaway Golf Company reports property, plant, and equipment in its annual report. Lines 1 to 6 list specific assets and their cost. Line 7 shows the cost of all Callaway plant assets. Line 8 gives the amount of accumulated depreciation, and line 9 shows the assets' book value of $165 million.

■ **EXHIBIT 3-5**

Callaway Golf's Reporting of Property, Plant, and Equipment (Adapted, in millions)

1	Land	$ 13
2	Buildings and improvements	91
3	Machinery and equipment	129
4	Furniture, computers, and equipment	91
5	Production molds	27
6	Construction in process	3
7	Property, plant, and equipment, at cost	354
8	Less: Accumulated depreciation	(189)
9	Property, plant, and equipment, net	$165

Accrued Expenses

Businesses incur expenses before they pay cash. Consider an employee's salary. The employer's expense and payable grow as the employee works, so the liability is said to accrue. Another example is interest expense on a note payable. Interest accrues as the clock ticks. The term **accrued expense** refers to a liability that arises from an expense that has not yet been paid.

Accrued expense
An expense incurred but not yet paid in cash.

Companies don't accrue expenses daily or weekly. Instead, they wait until the end of the period and use an adjusting entry to update each expense (and related liability) for the financial statements. Let's look at salary expense.

Most companies pay their employees at set times. Suppose Air & Sea Travel pays its employee a monthly salary of $1,900, half on the 15th and half on the last day of the month. The following calendar for April has the paydays circled:

April

Sun.	Mon.	Tue.	Wed.	Thur.	Fri.	Sat
					1	2
3	4	5	6	7	8	9
10	11	12	13	14	(15)	16
17	18	19	20	21	22	23
24	25	26	27	28	29	(30)

Assume that if a payday falls on the weekend, Air & Sea Travel pays the employee on the following Monday. During April, the agency paid its employee's first half-month salary of $950 and made the following entry:

Apr. 15	Salary Expense	950	
	Cash		950
	To pay salary.		

ASSETS	=	LIABILITIES	+	STOCKHOLDERS' EQUITY	–	EXPENSES
–950	=	0			–	950

NDAMENTALS

After posting, the Salary Expense account is

Salary Expense	
Apr. 15 950	

The trial balance at April 30 (Exhibit 3-3, p. 111) includes Salary Expense, with its debit balance of $950. Because April 30, the second payday of the month, falls on a Saturday, the second half-month amount of $950 will be paid on Monday, May 2. At April 30, therefore, Air & Sea adjusts for additional *salary expense* and *salary payable* of $950 as follows:

Apr. 30	Salary Expense........................	950		*Adjusting entry d*
	Salary Payable		950	
	To accrue salary expense.			

An accrued expense increases liabilities and decreases stockholders' equity:

ASSETS	=	LIABILITIES	+	STOCKHOLDERS' EQUITY	–	EXPENSES
0	=	950			–	950

After posting, the Salary Payable and Salary Expense accounts appear as follows (adjustment highlighted):

Salary Payable	
	Apr. 30 950
	Bal. 950

Salary Expense	
Apr. 15 950	
Apr. 30 950	
Bal. 1,900	

Check Point 3-6

Check Point 3-7

The accounts now hold all of April's salary information. Salary Expense has a full month's salary, and Salary Payable shows the amount owed at April 30. All accrued expenses are recorded this way—debit the expense and credit the liability.

Computerized systems contain a payroll module. Accrued salaries are automatically journalized and posted at the end of each period.

stop AND think...

What is the adjusting entry at April 30 for the following situation? Weekly salaries for a 5-day work week total $3,500, payable on Friday; April 30 falls on a Tuesday.

Answer:

$3,500 × 2/5 = $1,400. The adjusting entry is

Salary Expense	1,400	
Salary Payable....................		1,400
To accrue salary expense.		

FOCUS ON F

Accrued Revenues

Businesses often earn revenue before they receive the cash. A revenue that has been earned but not yet collected is called an **accrued revenue**.

Accrued revenue
A revenue that has been earned but not yet received in cash.

Bank One employees must travel in their work. Assume that Bank One hires Air & Sea Travel on April 15 to arrange travel services on a monthly basis. Suppose Bank One will pay the travel agency $500 monthly, with the first payment on May 15. During April, Air & Sea will earn half a month's fee, $250, for work done April 15 through April 30. On April 30, Air & Sea Travel makes the following adjusting entry:

Apr. 30	Accounts Receivable ($500 × 1/2)..........	250	Adjusting entry e
	Service Revenue.....................		250
	To accrue service revenue.		

Revenue increases both total assets and stockholders' equity:

ASSETS	=	LIABILITIES	+	STOCKHOLDERS' EQUITY	+	REVENUES
250	=	0			+	250

Recall that Accounts Receivable has an unadjusted balance of $2,250, and Service Revenue's unadjusted balance is $7,000 (Exhibit 3-3, p. 111). This April 30 adjusting entry has the following effects (adjustment highlighted):

Accounts Receivable

	Debit	Credit
	2,250	
Apr. 30	250	
Bal.	**2,500**	

Service Revenue

Debit		Credit
		7,000
	Apr. 30	250
	Bal.	**7,250**

All accrued revenues are accounted for similarly—debit a receivable and credit a revenue.

Check Point 3-8

stop AND think...

Suppose Air & Sea Travel holds a note receivable from a client. At the end of April, $125 of interest revenue has been earned. Journalize the adjustment at April 30.

Answer:

Interest Receivable	125	
Interest Revenue		125
To accrue interest revenue.		

Unearned Revenues

Unearned revenue
A liability created when a business collects cash from customers in advance of earning the revenue. The obligation is to provide a product or a service in the future.

Some businesses collect cash from customers before earning the revenue. This creates a liability called **unearned revenue**. Only when the job is completed does the business earn the revenue. Suppose **Plantation Foods**, a major producer of turkey food products, engages Air & Sea Travel, agreeing to pay the travel agency $450 monthly, beginning immediately. If Air & Sea collects the first amount on April 20, it records this transaction as follows:

Apr. 20	Cash	450	
	Unearned Service Revenue		450
	Received cash for revenue in advance.		

ASSETS	=	LIABILITIES	+	STOCKHOLDERS' EQUITY
450	=	450	+	0

After posting, the liability account appears as follows:

Unearned Service Revenue			
		Apr. 20	450

Unearned Service Revenue is a liability because Air & Sea is obligated to perform services for the client. The April 30 unadjusted trial balance (Exhibit 3-3, p. 111) lists Unearned Service Revenue with a $450 credit balance. During the last 10 days of the month, the travel agency will *earn* one-third of the $450, or $150. On April 30, the accountant makes the following adjustment:

Apr. 30	Unearned Service Revenue ($450 × 1/3)	150		*Adjusting entry f*
	Service Revenue.		150	
	To record unearned service revenue that has been earned.			

ASSETS	=	LIABILITIES	+	STOCKHOLDERS' EQUITY	+	REVENUES
0	=	−150			+	150

This adjusting entry shifts $150 of the total amount received ($450) from liability to revenue. After posting, Unearned Service Revenue is reduced to $300, and Service Revenue is increased by $150, as follows (adjustment highlighted):

Unearned Service Revenue			
Apr. 30	150	Apr. 20	450
		Bal.	300

Service Revenue			
			7,000
		Apr. 30	250
		Apr. 30	150
		Bal.	7,400

Check Point 3-9

All revenues collected in advance are accounted for this way. *An unearned revenue is a liability, not a revenue.*

One company's prepaid expense is unearned revenue to the other company. For example, Plantation Foods' prepaid expense is Air & Sea Travel's liability for unearned revenue.

Exhibit 3-6 diagrams the distinctive timing of prepaids and accruals. Study prepaid expenses all the way across. Then study unearned revenues, and so on.

FOCUS ON F

■ **EXHIBIT 3-6**
Prepaid and Accrual Adjustments

PREPAIDS—The Cash Transaction Occurs First

	First			Later		
Prepaid expenses	Pay cash and record an asset:			Record an expense and decrease the asset:		
	Prepaid Expense . . .	XXX		Expense	XXX	
	Cash		XXX	Prepaid Expense		XXX
Unearned revenues	Receive cash and record unearned revenue:			Record revenue and decrease unearned revenue:		
	Cash	XXX		Unearned Revenue	XXX	
	Unearned Revenue		XXX	Revenue		XXX

ACCRUALS—The Cash Transaction Occurs Later

	First			Later		
Accrued expenses	Accrue expense and a payable:			Pay cash and decrease the payable:		
	Expense	XXX		Payable	XXX	
	Payable		XXX	Cash		XXX
Accrued revenues	Accrue revenue and a receivable:			Receive cash and decrease the receivable:		
	Receivable	XXX		Cash	XXX	
	Revenue		XXX	Receivable		XXX

The authors thank Darrel Davis and Alfonso Oddo for suggesting this exhibit.

Summary of the Adjusting Process

Two purposes of the adjusting process are to

- Measure income
- Update the balance sheet

Therefore, every adjusting entry affects at least one

- Revenue or expense—to measure income
- Asset or liability—to update the balance sheet

Exhibit 3-7 summarizes the standard adjustments.

■ **EXHIBIT 3-7**
Summary of Adjusting Entries

	Type of Account	
Category of Adjusting Entry	**Debit**	**Credit**
Prepaid expense	Expense	Asset
Depreciation	Expense	Contra asset
Accrued expense	Expense	Liability
Accrued revenue	Asset	Revenue
Unearned revenue	Liability	Revenue

Adapted from material provided by Beverly Terry.

Exhibit 3-8 on page 122 summarizes the adjustments of Air & Sea Travel, Inc., at April 30—the adjusting entries we've examined over the past few pages.

- Panel A repeats the data for each adjustment.
- Panel B gives the adjusting entries.
- Panel C shows the accounts after posting the adjusting entries. The adjustments are keyed by letter.

■ **EXHIBIT 3-8** The Adjusting Process of Air & Sea Travel, Inc.

PANEL A—Information for Adjustments at April 30, 20X3	PANEL B—Adjusting Entries		
(a) Prepaid rent expired, $1,000.	(a) Rent Expense	1,000	
	Prepaid Rent		1,000
	To record rent expense.		
(b) Supplies used, $300.	(b) Supplies Expense	300	
	Supplies		300
	To record supplies used.		
(c) Depreciation on furniture, $275.	(c) Depreciation Expense—Furniture	275	
	Accumulated Depreciation—Furniture		275
	To record depreciation on furniture.		
(d) Accrued salary expense, $950.	(d) Salary Expense	950	
	Salary Payable		950
	To accrue salary expense.		
(e) Accrued service revenue, $250.	(e) Accounts Receivable	250	
	Service Revenue		250
	To accrue service revenue.		
(f) Amount of unearned service revenue that has been earned, $150.	(f) Unearned Service Revenue	150	
	Service Revenue		150
	To record unearned revenue that has been earned.		
(g) Accrued income tax expense, $540.	(g) Income Tax Expense	540	
	Income Tax Payable		540
	To accrue income tax expense.		

PANEL C—Ledger Accounts

ASSETS

Cash

Debit	Credit
Bal. 24,800	

Accounts Receivable

Debit	Credit
2,250	
(e) 250	
Bal. 2,500	

Supplies

Debit	Credit
700	(b) 300
Bal. 400	

Prepaid Rent

Debit	Credit
3,000	(a) 1,000
Bal. 2,000	

Furniture

Debit	Credit
Bal. 16,500	

Accumulated Depreciation—Furniture

Debit	Credit
	(c) 275
	Bal. 275

LIABILITIES

Accounts Payable

Debit	Credit
	Bal. 13,100

Salary Payable

Debit	Credit
	(d) 950
	Bal. 950

Unearned Service Revenue

Debit	Credit
(f) 150	450
	Bal. 300

Income Tax Payable

Debit	Credit
	(g) 540
	Bal. 540

STOCKHOLDERS' EQUITY

Common Stock

Debit	Credit
	Bal. 20,000

Retained Earnings

Debit	Credit
	Bal. 11,250

Dividends

Debit	Credit
Bal. 3,200	

Revenue

Service Revenue

Debit	Credit
	7,000
	(e) 250
	(f) 150
	Bal. 7,400

Expenses

Rent Expense

Debit	Credit
(a) 1,000	
Bal. 1,000	

Salary Expense

Debit	Credit
950	
(d) 950	
Bal. 1,900	

Supplies Expense

Debit	Credit
(b) 300	
Bal. 300	

Depreciation Expense—Furniture

Debit	Credit
(c) 275	
Bal. 275	

Utilities Expense

Debit	Credit
Bal. 400	

Income Tax Expense

Debit	Credit
(g) 540	
Bal. 540	

Exhibit 3-8 includes an additional adjusting entry that we have not yet discussed—the accrual of income tax expense. Like individual taxpayers, corporations are subject to income tax. They typically accrue income tax expense and the related income tax payable as the final adjusting entry of the period. Air & Sea Travel, Inc. accrues income tax expense with adjusting entry g, as follows:

Apr. 30	Income Tax Expense	540		*Adjusting entry g*
	Income Tax Payable		540	
	To accrue income tax expense.			

The income tax accrual follows the pattern for accrued expenses.

The Adjusted Trial Balance

This chapter began with the unadjusted trial balance (see Exhibit 3-3, p. 111). After the adjustments are journalized and posted, the accounts appear as shown in Exhibit 3-8, Panel C. A useful step in preparing the financial statements is to list the accounts, along with their adjusted balances, on an **adjusted trial balance**. This document lists all the accounts and their final balances in a single place. Exhibit 3-9 shows the adjusted trial balance of Air & Sea Travel.

Adjusted trial balance
A list of all the ledger accounts with their adjusted balances.

✓ Check Point 3-10

✓ Check Point 3-11

✓ Check Point 3-12

■ Exhibit 3-9 Adjusted Trial Balance

Air & Sea Travel, Inc.
Preparation of Adjusted Trial Balance
April 30, 20X3

	Trial Balance		Adjustments		Adjusted Trial Balance		
Account Title	**Debit**	**Credit**	**Debit**	**Credit**	**Debit**	**Credit**	
Cash	24,800				24,800		
Accounts Receivable	2,250		(e) 250		2,500		
Supplies	700			(b) 300	400		
Prepaid rent	3,000			(a) 1,000	2,000		
Furniture	16,500				16,500		
Accumulated depreciation—furniture				(c) 275		275	**Balance Sheet**
Accounts payable		13,100				13,100	(*Exhibit 3-12*)
Salary payable				(d) 950		950	
Unearned service revenue		450	(f) 150			300	
Income tax payable				(g) 540		540	
Common stock		20,000				20,000	
Retained earnings		11,250				11,250	**Statement of Retained**
Dividends	3,200				3,200		**Earnings** (*Exhibit 3-11*)
Service revenue		7,000		(e) 250		7,400	
				(f) 150			
Rent expense			(a) 1,000		1,000		
Salary expense	950		(d) 950		1,900		**Income Statement**
Supplies expense			(b) 300		300		(*Exhibit 3-10*)
Depreciation expense			(c) 275		275		
Utilities expense	400				400		
Income tax expense			(g) 540		540		
	51,800	51,800	3,465	3,465	53,815	53,815	

Which Accounts Need to Be Closed?

It is now April 30, the end of the month. Gary and Monica Lyon can use Air & Sea Travel's income statement and balance sheet to evaluate company progress. The income statement lets them know the profit for April, and the balance sheet reports financial position.

OBJECTIVE

5 **Close** the books

Closing the books
The process of preparing the accounts to begin recording the next period's transactions. Closing the accounts consists of journalizing and posting the closing entries to set the balances of the revenue, expense, and dividends accounts to zero. Also called *closing the accounts*.

Closing entries
Entries that transfer the revenue, expense, and dividends balances from these respective accounts to the Retained Earnings account.

Temporary account
The revenue and expense accounts that relate to a limited period and are closed at the end of the period are temporary accounts. For a corporation, the Dividends account is also temporary.

Permanent account
Asset, liability, and stockholders' equity accounts that are not closed at the end of the period.

The Lyons will continue operating the travel agency into May, June, and beyond. But wait—the revenue and the expense accounts still hold amounts for April. At the end of each accounting period, it is necessary to close the books.

Closing the books means to prepare the accounts for the next period's transactions. The **closing entries** set the revenue and expense balances back to zero at the end of the period. The idea is the same as setting the scoreboard back to zero after a game.

Closing is easily handled by computers. Recall that the income statement reports only one period's income. For example, net income for Callaway Golf or Air & Sea Travel for 2006 relates exclusively to 2006. At each year end, Callaway accountants close the company's revenues and expenses for that year. Because revenues and expenses relate to a limited period, they are called **temporary accounts**. The Dividends account is also temporary. The closing process applies only to temporary accounts (revenues, expenses, and dividends).

Let's contrast the temporary accounts with the **permanent accounts**: assets, liabilities, and stockholders' equity. The permanent accounts are not closed at the end of the period because they carry over to the next period. Consider Cash, Receivables, Buildings, Accounts Payable, Common Stock, and Retained Earnings. Their ending balances at the end of one period become the beginning balances of the next period.

Closing entries transfer the revenue, expense, and dividends balances to Retained Earnings. Here are the steps to close the books of a corporation such as Callaway Golf or Air & Sea Travel:

① Debit each revenue account for the amount of its credit balance. Credit Retained Earnings for the sum of the revenues. Now the sum of the revenues is in Retained Earnings.

② Credit each expense account for the amount of its debit balance. Debit Retained Earnings for the sum of the expenses. The sum of the expenses is now in Retained Earnings.

③ Credit the Dividends account for the amount of its debit balance. Debit Retained Earnings. This entry places the dividends amount in the debit side of Retained Earnings. *Remember that dividends are not expenses. Dividends do not affect net income.*

After closing the books, the Retained Earnings account of Air & Sea Travel appears as follows:

Retained Earnings

		Beginning balance	**11,250**
Expenses	**4,415**	**Revenues**	**7,400**
Dividends	**3,200**		
		Ending balance	**11,035**

Assume that Air & Sea Travel closes the books at the end of April. Exhibit 3-13 presents the complete closing process for the business. Panel A gives the closing journal entries, and Panel B shows the accounts after closing.

FOCUS ON F

■ EXHIBIT 3-13

Journalizing and Posting the Closing Entries

PANEL A—Journalizing the Closing Entries Page 5

Closing Entries

	Date	Accounts	Debit	Credit
①	Apr. 30	Service Revenue	7,400	
		Retained Earnings		7,400
②	30	Retained Earnings	4,415	
		Rent Expense		1,000
		Salary Expense		1,900
		Supplies Expense		300
		Depreciation Expense		275
		Utilities Expense		400
		Income Tax Expense		540
③	30	Retained Earnings	3,200	
		Dividends		3,200

✓Check Point 3-13

PANEL B—Posting to the Accounts

Rent Expense

Adj.	**1,000**		
Bal.	**1,000**	**Clo.**	**1,000**

Salary Expense

	950		
Adj.	**950**		
Bal.	**1,900**	**Clo.**	**1,900**

Supplies Expense

Adj.	**300**		
Bal.	**300**	**Clo.**	**300**

Depreciation Expense

Adj.	**275**		
Bal.	**275**	**Clo.**	**275**

Utilities Expense

	400		
Bal.	**400**	**Clo.**	**400**

Income Tax Expense

Adj.	**540**		
Bal.	**540**	**Clo.**	**540**

② (expense closing amounts → Retained Earnings)

Service Revenue

			7,000
		Adj.	**250**
		Adj.	**150**
Clo.	**7,400**	**Bal.**	**7,400**

① (Service Revenue → Retained Earnings)

Retained Earnings

Clo.	**4,415**		**11,250**
Clo.	**3,200**	**Clo.**	**7,400**
		Bal.	**11,035**

Dividends

Bal.	**3,200**	**Clo.**	**3,200**

③ (Dividends → Retained Earnings)

Adj. = Amount posted from an industry entry
Clo. = Amount posted from a closing entry
Bal. = Balance
As arrow ② in Panel B shows, it is not necessary to make a separate closing entry for each expense. In one closing entry, we record one debit to Retained Earnings and a separate credit to each expense account.

Accounting Cycle Tutorial
Adjusting & Closing the Books

Accounting Cycle Tutorial
Application—Cottage Kitchen

Accounting Cycle Tutorial
Application—Cottage Kitchen 2

Classifying Assets and Liabilities Based on Their Liquidity

Liquidity
Measure of how quickly an item can be converted to cash.

On the balance sheet, assets and liabilities are classified as *current* or *long term* to indicate their relative liquidity. **Liquidity** measures how quickly an item can be converted to cash. Cash is the most liquid asset. Accounts receivable are relatively liquid because cash collections usually follow quickly. Inventory is less liquid than accounts receivable because the company must first sell the goods. Furniture and buildings are even less liquid because these assets are held for use and not for sale.

Users of financial statements are interested in liquidity because financial problems arise from a shortage of cash. How quickly can the business convert an asset to cash and pay a debt? How soon must a liability be paid? These are questions of liquidity. A balance sheet lists assets and liabilities in the order of relative liquidity.

Current asset
An asset that is expected to be converted to cash, sold, or consumed during the next 12 months, or within the business's normal operating cycle if longer than a year.

Operating cycle
Time span during which cash is paid for goods and services that are sold to customers who pay the business in cash.

Current Assets. As we saw in Chapter 1, **current assets** are the most liquid assets. They will be converted to cash, sold, or consumed during the next 12 months or within the business's normal operating cycle if longer than a year. The **operating cycle** is the time span during which (1) cash is paid for goods and services and (2) these goods and services are sold to bring in cash. For most businesses, the operating cycle is a few months. Cash, Accounts Receivable, Merchandise Inventory, and Prepaid Expenses are current assets of Callaway Golf Company. Service entities such as America Online (AOL) and Air & Sea Travel do not hold inventory.

Long-term asset
An asset that is not a current asset.

Long-Term Assets. **Long-term assets** are all assets not classified as current assets. One category of long-term assets is plant assets, often labeled Property, Plant, and Equipment. Land, Buildings, Furniture and Fixtures, and Equipment are plant assets. Of these, Air & Sea Travel has only Furniture. Long-Term Investments, Intangible Assets, and Other Assets (a catchall category for assets that are not classified more precisely) are also long term.

Bankers and other lenders are interested in the due dates of an entity's liabilities. The sooner a liability must be paid, the more pressure it creates for the company. Therefore, the balance sheet lists liabilities in the order in which they must be paid. Balance sheets usually report two liability classifications, *current liabilities* and *long-term liabilities*.

Current liability
A debt due to be paid within one year or within the entity's operating cycle if the cycle is longer than a year.

Current Liabilities. As we saw in Chapter 1, **current liabilities** are debts that must be paid within 1 year or within the entity's operating cycle if longer than a year. Accounts Payable, Notes Payable due within 1 year, Salary Payable, Unearned Revenue, Interest Payable, and Income Tax Payable are current liabilities.

Long-term liability
A liability that is not a current liability.

Check Point 3-14

Long-Term Liabilities. All liabilities that are not current are classified as **long-term liabilities**. Many notes payable are long term. Some notes payable are paid in installments, with the first installment due within 1 year, the second installment due the second year, and so on. The first installment is a current liability and the remainder is long term.

Let's see how a real company reports these asset and liability categories on its balance sheet.

Reporting Assets and Liabilities: Callaway Golf Company

Classified balance sheet
A balance sheet that shows current assets separate from long-term assets, and current liabilities separate from long-term liabilities.

Exhibit 3-14 shows the actual classified balance sheet of Callaway Golf Company. A **classified balance sheet** separates current assets from long-term assets and current liabilities from long-term liabilities. You should be familiar with most of Callaway's accounts. Study the Callaway balance sheet all the way through—line by line.

FOCUS ON F

Callaway Golf Company
Balance Sheet (Adapted)
December 31, 2003 and 2002

■ **EXHIBIT 3-14**

Classified Balance Sheet of Callaway Golf Company (Adapted, in millions)

(millions) **Assets**	2003	2002
Current assets:		
Cash and cash equivalents	$ 47	$108
Accounts receivable	101	64
Inventories	185	152
Prepaid expenses and other current assets	50	45
Total current assets	383	369
Property, plant, and equipment, net	165	167
Intangible assets	170	121
Other assets	31	23
Total assets	$749	$680
Liabilities and Shareholders' Equity		
Current liabilities:		
Accounts payable and accrued expenses payable	$ 80	$ 62
Accrued employee compensation and benefits payable	25	23
Accrued warranty payable	13	13
Note payable, current portion	—	3
Income taxes payable	12	8
Total current liabilities	130	109
Long-term liabilities:		
Deferred compensation payable	9	7
Other long-term liabilities	20	20
Shareholders' equity:		
Common stock	402	373
Retained earnings	466	439
Other equity	(278)	(268)
Total shareholders' equity	590	544
Total liabilities and shareholders' equity	$749	$680

Formats for the Financial Statements

Companies can format their financial statements in different ways. Both the balance sheet and the income statement can be formatted in two basic ways.

Report format
A balance-sheet format that lists assets at the top, followed by liabilities and stockholders' equity below.

Balance Sheet Formats

The **report format** lists the assets at the top, followed by the liabilities and stockholders' equity below. The balance sheet of Callaway Golf Company in Exhibit 3-14 illustrates the report format. Either format is acceptable. The report format is more popular, with approximately 60% of large companies using it.

Account format
A balance-sheet format that lists assets on the left and liabilities and stockholders' equity on the right.

The **account format** lists the assets on the left and the liabilities and stockholders' equity on the right in the same way that a T-account appears, with assets (debits) on the left and liabilities and equity (credits) on the right. Exhibit 3-12 (page 125) shows an account-format balance sheet.

Single-step income statement
An income statement that lists all the revenues together under a heading such as Revenues or Revenues and Gains. Expenses appear in a separate category called Expenses or perhaps Expenses and Losses.

Income Statement Formats

A **single-step income statement** lists all the revenues together under a heading such as Revenues or Revenues and Gains. The expenses are listed together in a single category titled Expenses, or Expenses and Losses. There is only one step, the subtraction of Expenses and Losses from the sum of Revenues and Gains, in arriving at net income. Callaway Golf's income statement (page 134) appears in single-step format.

Multi-step income statement An income statement that contains subtotals to highlight important relationships between revenues and expenses.

A **multi-step income statement** reports a number of subtotals to highlight important relationships between revenues and expenses. Exhibit 3-15 shows Callaway Golf Company's income statement in multi-step format. Gross profit, income from operations, income before tax, and net income are highlighted for emphasis.

■ **EXHIBIT 3-15**

Callaway Golf Company Income Statement in Multi-Step Format

Callaway Golf Company
Income Statement (Adapted)
Year Ended December 31, 2003

	Millions
Net sales revenue	$814
Cost of goods sold	445
Gross profit	369
Selling expenses	208
General and administrative expenses	65
Research and development expense	30
Income from operations	66
Other income, net	2
Income before income tax	68
Income tax expense	22
Net income	$ 46

In particular, income from operations ($66 million) is separated from "Other income," which Callaway did not earn by selling golf equipment. The other income was mainly interest revenue earned on investments. Most companies consider it important to report their operating income separately from nonoperating sources such as interest and dividends.

Most companies' income statements do not conform to either a pure single-step format or a pure multi-step format. Business operations are too complex for all companies to conform to rigid reporting formats.

Using Accounting Ratios

OBJECTIVE

6 **Use** the current ratio and the debt ratio to evaluate a business

As we've seen, accounting provides information for decision making. A bank considering lending money must predict whether the borrower can repay the loan. If the borrower already has a lot of debt, the probability of repayment may be low. If the borrower owes little, the loan may go through. To analyze a company's financial position, decision makers use ratios computed from various items in the financial statements. Let's see how this process works.

Current Ratio

Current ratio Current assets divided by current liabilities. Measures a company's ability to pay current liabilities with current assets.

One of the most widely used financial ratios is the **current ratio**, which divides total current assets by total current liabilities, taken from the balance sheet.

$$\text{Current ratio} = \frac{\text{Total current assets}}{\text{Total current liabilities}}$$

FOCUS ON F

For Callaway Golf (amounts in millions for 2003):

$$\frac{\$383}{\$130} = 2.95$$

The current ratio measures the company's ability to pay current liabilities with current assets. A company prefers a high current ratio, which means that the business has plenty of current assets to pay current liabilities. An increasing current ratio from period to period indicates improvement in financial position.

As a rule of thumb, a strong current ratio is 1.50, which indicates that the company has $1.50 in current assets for every $1.00 in current liabilities. A company with a current ratio of 1.50 would probably have little trouble paying its current liabilities. Most successful businesses operate with current ratios between 1.20 and 1.50. A current ratio of 1.00 is considered quite low. Callaway Golf's current ratio of 2.95 is very high and indicates an extremely strong current position.

Debt Ratio

A second aid to decision making is the **debt ratio**, which is the ratio of total liabilities to total assets:

Debt ratio
Ratio of total liabilities to total assets. States the proportion of a company's assets that is financed with debt.

$$\text{Debt ratio} = \frac{\text{Total liabilities}}{\text{Total assets}}$$

For Callaway Golf (amounts in thousands for 2003),

$$\frac{\$130 + \$9 + \$20}{\$749} = \frac{\$159}{\$749} = .21$$

The debt ratio indicates the proportion of a company's assets that is financed with debt. This ratio measures a business's ability to pay both current and long-term debts (total liabilities).

A low debt ratio is safer than a high debt ratio. Why? Because a company with few liabilities has low required debt payments. This company is unlikely to get into financial difficulty. By contrast, a business with a high debt ratio may have trouble paying its liabilities, especially when sales are low and cash is scarce. Callaway Golf's debt ratio of 21% (0.21) is low compared to most companies in the United States. The norm for the debt ratio ranges from 60% to 70%.

When a company fails to pay its debts, creditors can take the company away from its owners. All bankruptcies result from high debt ratios.

Check Point 3-15

How Do Transactions Affect the Ratios?

Companies such as Callaway Golf are keenly aware of how transactions affect their ratios. Lending agreements often require that a company's current ratio not fall below a certain level. Another loan requirement is that the company's debt ratio may not rise above a threshold, such as 0.70. When a company fails to meet one of these conditions, it is said to *violate its lending agreements*. The penalty can be severe: The lender can require immediate payment of the loan. Callaway Golf has so little debt that Callaway is in no such danger. But many companies are.

Let's use Callaway Golf Company to examine the effects of some transactions on the company's current ratio and debt ratio. As shown in the preceding section, Callaway's ratios are as follows (dollar amounts in millions):

$$\text{Current ratio} = \frac{\$383}{\$130} = 2.946 \qquad \text{Debt ratio} = \frac{\$159}{\$749} = 0.212$$

The managers of any company would be concerned about how inventory purchases, payments on account, expense accruals, and depreciation would affect its ratios. Let's see how Callaway would be affected by some typical transactions. For each transaction, the journal entry helps identify the effects on the company.

a. Issued stock and received cash of $20 million.

Journal entry:			
	Cash	20	
	Common Stock		20

Cash, a current asset, affects both the current ratio and the debt ratio as follows:

$$\text{Current ratio} = \frac{\$383 + \$20}{\$130} = 3.10 \qquad \text{Debt ratio} = \frac{\$159}{\$749 + \$20} = 0.207$$

The issuance of stock improves both ratios.

b. Purchased a building for $5 million.

Journal entry:			
	Building	5	
	Cash		5

Cash, a current asset, decreases, but total assets stay the same.

$$\text{Current ratio} = \frac{\$383 - \$5}{\$130} = 2.908 \qquad \text{Debt ratio} = \frac{\$159}{\$749 + \$5 - \$5} = 0.212;\ \text{no change}$$

A cash purchase of a building hurts the current ratio.

c. Made a $30 million sale on account.

Journal entry:			
	Accounts Receivable	30	
	Sales Revenue		30

The increase in Accounts Receivable increases current assets and total assets, as follows:

$$\text{Current ratio} = \frac{\$383 + \$30}{\$130} = 3.177 \qquad \text{Debt ratio} = \frac{\$159}{\$749 + \$30} = 0.204$$

A sale on account improves both ratios.

d. Collected the account receivable, $30 million.

Journal entry:			
	Cash	30	
	Accounts Receivable		30

This transaction has no effect on total current assets or on total assets. Both ratios are unaffected.

FOCUS ON F

e. Accrued salary expense at year end, $1 million.

Journal entry:	Salary Expense	1	
	Salary Payable		1

Salary Payable, a current liability, increases, and that affects both ratios.

$$\text{Current ratio} = \frac{\$383}{\$130 + \$1} = 2.924 \qquad \text{Debt ratio} = \frac{\$159 + \$1}{\$749} = 0.214$$

An expense always hurts both ratios.

f. Recorded depreciation, $2 million.

Journal entry:	Depreciation Expense	2	
	Accumulated Depreciation . .		2

No current accounts are part of a depreciation transaction, so only debt ratio is affected.

$$\text{Current ratio} = \frac{\$383}{\$130} = 2.946 \qquad \text{Debt ratio} = \frac{\$159}{\$749 - \$2} = 0.213$$

Depreciation decreases total assets and therefore hurts the debt ratio.

g. Recorded supplies expense, $2.5 million.

Journal entry:	Supplies Expense	2.5	
	Supplies		2.5

Supplies, a current asset, decreases.

$$\text{Current ratio} = \frac{\$383 - \$2.5}{\$130} = 2.927 \qquad \text{Debt ratio} = \frac{\$159}{\$749 - \$2.5} = 0.213$$

An expense always hurts the current ratio and the debt ratio.

h. Earned interest revenue and collected cash, $4 million.

Journal entry:	Cash	4	
	Interest Revenue		4

Cash, a current asset, affects both the current ratio and the debt ratio as follows:

$$\text{Current ratio} = \frac{\$383 + \$4}{\$130} = 2.977 \qquad \text{Debt ratio} = \frac{\$159}{\$749 + \$4} = 0.211$$

A revenue improves both ratios.

Now, let's wrap up the chapter by seeing how to use the current ratio and the debt ratio for decision making. The Making Managerial Decisions feature offers some clues.

c. On July 1, when we collected $6,000 rent in advance, we debited Cash and credited Unearned Rent Revenue. The tenant was paying for 2 years' rent.
d. Salary expense is $1,000 per day—Monday through Friday—and the business pays employees each Friday. This year, December 31 falls on a Thursday.
e. The unadjusted balance of the Supplies account is $3,100. The total cost of supplies on hand is $800.
f. Equipment was purchased at the beginning of this year at a cost of $60,000. The equipment's useful life is 5 years. Record depreciation for this year and then determine the equipment's book value.
g. On September 1, we prepaid $1,200 for a 1-year insurance policy.

Separating accrual accounting and cash flows (Obj. 1, 3)

E3-10 Use the data in Exercise 3-9 to answer these questions. Each letter links to the same lettered item in Exercise 3-9.

a. Refer to item f in Exercise 3-9. Show what Home Depot will report on its
   1. Balance sheet (show all the data items needed to report the asset's book value)
   2. Income statement
b. Refer to item g in Exercise 3-9. Show what Home Depot will report on the following financial statements:
   1. Income statement of the current year.
   2. Balance sheet at end of the current year.
   3. Income statement of the following year.
   4. Balance sheet at end of the following year.

Making adjustments in T-accounts (Obj. 3)

E3-11 The accounting records of **Studio Art Gallery** include the following unadjusted balances at May 31: Accounts Receivable, $1,100; Supplies, $900; Salary Payable, $0; Unearned Service Revenue, $800; Service Revenue, $4,700; Salary Expense, $1,200; Supplies Expense, $0. Studio Art Gallery's accountant develops the following data for the May 31 adjusting entries:

a. Supplies on hand, $500.
b. Salary owed to employee, $700.
c. Service revenue accrued, $600.
d. Unearned service revenue that has been earned, $550.

Open the foregoing T-accounts with their beginning balances. Then record the adjustments directly in the accounts, keying each adjustment amount by letter. Show each account's adjusted balance. Journal entries are not required.

Preparing the financial statements (Obj. 4)

E3-12 The adjusted trial balance of Upper 10 Cola Company (adapted) follows.

Upper 10 Cola Company
Adjusted Trial Balance
December 31, 20X6

(Millions)	Adjusted Trial Balance	
	Debit	**Credit**
Cash	900	
Accounts receivable	1,800	
Inventories	1,100	
Prepaid expenses	1,900	
Property, plant, equipment	6,600	
Accumulated depreciation		2,400
Other assets	9,900	
Accounts payable		7,700
Income tax payable		600
Other liabilities		2,200

(continued)

	Adjusted Trial Balance	
	Debit	Credit
Common stock		4,900
Retained earnings (beginning, December 31, 20X5)		4,500
Dividends	1,700	
Sales revenue		20,500
Cost of goods sold	6,200	
Selling, administrative, and general expense	9,700	
Income tax expense	3,000	
Total	42,800	42,800

Required

Prepare Upper 10 Cola Company's income statement and statement of retained earnings for the year ended December 31, 20X6, and its balance sheet on that date. Draw the arrows linking the three statements.

Measuring financial statement amounts (Obj. 3)

E3-13 The adjusted trial balances of **Best Buy Co., Inc.**, at March 1, 2003, and March 2, 2002, include these amounts (adapted and in millions):

	2003	2002
Receivables	$312	$221
Prepaid expenses (rent, insurance)	188	116
Accrued liabilities (for other operating expenses)	729	613

Assume Best Buy completed these transactions during the year ended March 1, 2003.

Collections from customers	$20,855
Payment of prepaid expenses	407
Cash payments for other operating expenses	4,110

Compute the amount of sales revenue, rent and insurance expense (a combined total), and other operating expenses to report on the income statement for the year ended March 1, 2003.

Reporting on the financial statements (Obj. 4)

E3-14 This question deals with the items and the amounts that two entities, Hillcrest Health Maintenance Organization, Inc. (Hillcrest) and City of Denver (Denver) should report in their financial statements.

Required

1. On July 31, 20X5, Hillcrest collected $6,000 in advance from Denver, a client. Under the contract Hillcrest is obligated to perform medical exams for City of Denver employees evenly during the year ended July 31, 20X6. Assume you are Hillcrest. Hillcrest's income statement for the year ended December 31, 20X5, will report ____ of $____.
   Hillcrest's balance sheet at December 31, 20X5, will report ____ of $____.
2. Assume now that you are City of Denver (Denver). What will Denver report on its balance sheet at December 31, 20X5, and on its income statement for the year ended December 31, 20X5?
   Denver's income statement for the year ended December 31, 20X5, will report ____ of $____.
   Denver's balance sheet at December 31, 20X5, will report ____ of $____.

Linking deferrals and cash flows (Obj. 1, 3)

E3-15 This exercise builds from a simple situation to a slightly more complex situation. **Vodafone**, the British wireless phone service provider, collects cash in advance from customers. All amounts are in millions.

Assume Vodafone collected £440 in advance during 20X5 and at year end still owed customers phone service worth £90.

Required

1. Show what Vodafone will report for 20X5 on its
   - Income statement
   - Balance sheet
2. Use the same facts for Vodafone as in item 1. Further, assume Vodafone reported unearned service revenue of £70 back at the end of 20X4.

   Show what Vodafone will report for 20X5 on the same financial statements. Explain why your answer here differs from your answer to item 1.

Closing the accounts (Obj. 5)

writing assignment ■

E3-16 Prepare the closing entries from the following accounts adapted from the records of **Sprint Corporation** at December 31, 20X2 (amounts in millions):

Service revenue	$23,613	Unearned revenues	$ 607
Notes payable	17,514	Cost of services sold	11,620
Depreciation expense	4,144	Accumulated depreciation	17,799
Other revenue	675	Selling, general, and administrative expense	6,919
Dividends	476	Other expense	396
Income tax expense	126	Retained earnings, December 31, 20X1	1,961
Interest expense	990		
Income tax payable	440		

How much net income did Sprint earn during 20X2? Prepare a T-account for Retained Earnings to show the December 31, 20X2, balance of Retained Earnings. What caused Retained Earnings to decrease during 20X2?

Identifying and recording adjusting and closing entries (Obj. 3, 5)

E3-17 The unadjusted trial balance and income statement amounts from the March adjusted trial balance of Wall Street Workout Company follow. Wall Street Workout is a turnaround specialist.

Required

Journalize the adjusting and closing entries of Wall Street Workout Company at March 31. There was only one adjustment to Service Revenue.

Wall Street Workout Company

Account Title	Unadjusted Trial Balance		From the Adjusted Trial Balance	
Cash	10,200			
Supplies	2,400			
Prepaid rent	1,100			
Equipment	32,100			
Accumulated depreciation		6,200		
Accounts payable		4,600		
Salary payable				
Unearned service revenue		8,400		
Income tax payable				
Common stock		8,700		
Retained earnings		10,300		
Dividends	1,000			
Service revenue		12,800		17,900
Salary expense	3,000		3,800	
Rent expense	1,200		1,400	
Depreciation expense			300	
Supplies expense			400	
Income tax expense			1,600	
	51,000	51,000	7,500	17,900
Net income			10,400	
			17,900	17,900

FOCUS ON F

Preparing a classified balance sheet and using the ratios (Obj. 4, 6)

E3-18 Refer to Exercise 3-17.

Required

1. After solving Exercise 3-17, use the data in that exercise to prepare Wall Street Workout Company's classified balance sheet at March 31 of the current year. Use the report format.
2. Compute Wall Street Workout's current ratio and debt ratio at March 31. A year ago, the current ratio was 1.30 and the debt ratio was 0.29. Indicate whether the company's ability to pay its debts improved or deteriorated during the current year.

Measuring the effects of transactions on the ratios (Obj. 6)

E3-19 **Johnson & Johnson**, the health-care products company, reported these ratios at December 31, 2003 (dollar amounts in billions):

$$\text{Current ratio} = \frac{\$23}{\$13} = 1.77 \qquad \text{Debt ratio} = \frac{\$21}{\$48} = 0.44$$

Assume that Johnson & Johnson completed these transactions during 2004:

a. Purchased equipment on account, $4.
b. Paid long-term debt, $5.
c. Collected cash from customers in advance, $2.
d. Accrued interest expense, $1.
e. Made cash sales, $6.

Determine whether each transaction improved or hurt Johnson & Johnson's current ratio and debt ratio. Round all ratios to two decimal places.

Serial Exercise

Exercise 3-20 continues the Matthew Rogers, Certified Public Accountant, P.C., situation begun in Exercise 2-14 of Chapter 2 (p. 88).

Adjusting the accounts, preparing the financial statements, closing the accounts, and evaluating the business (Obj. 3, 4, 5, 6)

■ general ledger

E3-20 Refer to Exercise 2-14 of Chapter 2. Start from the trial balance and the posted T-accounts that Matthew Rogers, Certified Public Accountant, Professional Corporation (P.C.), prepared for his accounting practice at December 18. A professional corporation is not subject to income tax. Later in December, the business completed these transactions:

Dec. 21	Received $900 in advance for tax work to be performed evenly over the next 30 days.
21	Hired a secretary to be paid $1,500 on the 20th day of each month.
26	Paid for the supplies purchased on December 5.
28	Collected $600 from the consulting client on December 18.
30	Declared and paid dividends of $1,600.

Required

1. Open these T-accounts: Accumulated Depreciation—Equipment, Accumulated Depreciation—Furniture, Salary Payable, Unearned Service Revenue, Retained Earnings, Depreciation Expense—Equipment, Depreciation Expense—Furniture, and Supplies Expense. Also, use the T-accounts opened for Exercise 2-14.
2. Journalize the transactions of December 21 through 30.
3. Post the December 21 to 30 transactions to the T-accounts, keying all items by date.
4. Prepare a trial balance at December 31. Also set up columns for the adjustments and for the adjusted trial balance, as illustrated in Exhibit 3-9, page 123.
5. At December 31, Rogers gathers the following information for the adjusting entries:
   a. Accrued service revenue, $400.
   b. Earned a portion of the service revenue collected in advance on December 21.

(continued)

c. Supplies on hand, $100.
d. Depreciation expense—equipment, $50; furniture, $60.
e. Accrued expense for secretary's salary. Use a 30-day month to simplify the computation.
Make these adjustments directly in the adjustments columns and complete the adjusted trial balance at December 31.

6. Journalize and post the adjusting entries. Denote each adjusting amount as Adj. and an account balance as Bal.
7. Prepare the income statement and statement of retained earnings of Matthew Rogers, Certified Public Accountant, P.C. for the month ended December 31 and the classified balance sheet at that date. Draw arrows to link the financial statements.
8. Journalize and post the closing entries at December 31. Denote each closing amount as Clo. and an account balance as Bal.
9. Compute the current ratio and the debt ratio of Rogers' accounting practice and evaluate these ratio values as indicative of a strong or weak financial position.

Challenge Exercises

Evaluating the current ratio (Obj. 6)

E3-21 **AOL Time Warner Inc.** provides Internet service, publishing, and entertainment. At December 31, 2002, AOL Time Warner reported the following current accounts (adapted, and in millions):

Inventory	$1,896
Accounts payable	2,459
Prepaid expenses	1,862
Cash	1,730
Unearned revenues	1,209
Accrued expenses payable	9,727
Receivables	5,667

Assume that during 2003, AOL Time Warner completed these transactions:

- Sold services on account, $8,555.
- Depreciation expense, $444.
- Paid for expenses, $7,186, which includes prepaid expenses of $150.
- Collected from customers on account, $7,586.
- Accrued expenses, $256.
- Purchased services on account, $477.
- Paid on account, $453.
- Used up prepaid expenses, $141.
- Collected cash from customers in advance, $270.
- Paid accrued expenses payable, $399.

Compute AOL Time Warner's current ratio at December 31, 2002, and again at December 31, 2003. Did the current ratio improve or deteriorate during 2003? Comment on the level of the company's current ratio.

Computing financial statement amounts (Obj. 3, 4)

E3-22 The accounts of Turnberry Hotel Company, prior to the year-end adjustments, follow on the next page.

Adjusting data at the end of the year include:

a. Unearned service revenue that has been earned, $1,900.
b. Accrued rent revenue, $1,200.
c. Accrued property tax expense, $900.

(continued)

d. Accrued service revenue, $1,700.
e. Supplies used in operations, $600.
f. Accrued salary expense, $1,400.
g. Insurance expense, $1,800.
h. Depreciation expense—furniture, $800; building, $2,100.
i. Accrued interest expense, $500.

Cash	$ 4,200	Note payable, long-term	$ 6,000
Accounts receivable	7,200	Common stock	10,000
Rent receivable		Retained earnings	50,100
Supplies	1,100	Dividends	16,200
Prepaid insurance	2,200	Service revenue	4,100
Furniture	15,700	Rent revenue	151,000
Accumulated depreciation—furniture	1,300	Salary expense	32,700
Building	107,800	Depreciation expense—furniture	
Accumulated depreciation—building	14,900	Depreciation expense—building	
Land	51,200	Supplies expense	
Accounts payable	6,100	Insurance expense	
Salary payable		Interest expense	
Interest payable		Advertising expense	7,800
Property tax payable		Property tax expense	
Unearned service revenue	5,300	Utilities expense	2,700

Faye O'Reilly, the principal stockholder, has received an offer to sell Turnberry Hotel Company. She needs to know the following information within 1 hour:

a. Net income for the year covered by these data.
b. Total assets.
c. Total liabilities.
d. Total stockholders' equity.
e. Proof that total assets = total liabilities + total stockholders' equity after all items are updated

Required

Without opening any accounts, making any journal entries, or using a work sheet, provide Ms. O'Reilly with the requested information. The business is not subject to income tax. Show all computations.

Practice Quiz

Test your understanding of Accrual Accounting by answering the following questions. Select the best choice from among the possible answers given.

The first three questions are based on the following facts:

Remmy Brandt began a painting business in July 20X4. Brandt prepares monthly financial statements and uses the accrual basis of accounting. The following transactions are Brandt Company's only activities during July through October:

July 14	Bought paint on account for $10, with payment to the supplier due in 90 days.
Aug. 3	Did a paint job on account for Lisa Mona for $25, collectible from Ms. Mona in 30 days. Used up all the paint.
Sept. 16	Collected the $25 receivable.
Oct. 22	Paid the $10 owed to the supplier from the July transaction.

PQ3-1 Based on the foregoing facts, in which month should Brandt Company report the $25 revenue on its income statement?

a. July
b. August
c. September
d. October

PQ3-2 In which month should Brandt record the cost of the paint as an expense?

a. July
b. August
c. September
d. October

PQ3-3 If Brandt Company uses the cash basis of accounting instead of the accrual basis, in what month will Brandt report revenue and in what month will it report expense?

	Revenue	Expense
a.	July	July
b.	September	July
c.	August	October
d.	September	October

PQ3-4 On January 1 of the current year, Aladdin Company paid $600 rent to cover six months (January–June). Aladdin recorded this transactions as follows:

Prepaid Rent.	600	
Cash		600

Aladdin adjusts the accounts at the end of each month. Based on these facts, the adjusting entry at the end of January should include

a. a credit to Prepaid Rent for $500.
b. a debit to Prepaid Rent for $500.
c. a credit to Prepaid Rent for $100.
d. a debit to Prepaid Rent for $100.

PQ3-5 Assume the same facts as in the previous problem. Aladdin's adjusting entry at the end of February should include a debit to Rent Expense in the amount of

a. $100
b. $200
c. $400
d. $500

PQ3-6 If the adjusting entry in question 5 is not recorded, net income for February will be

a. understated
b. overstated
c. unaffected
d. none of the above

PQ3-7 Solar Company has a one-month accounting period. On March 31, an adjusting entry recorded March salary expense that will be paid in April. Which statement best describes the effect of this adjusting entry on Solar's accounting equation?

a. Assets are not affected, liabilities are increased, and stockholders' equity is increased.
b. Assets are decreased, liabilities are increased, and stockholders' equity is decreased.
c. Assets are not affected, liabilities are increased, and stockholders' equity is decreased.
d. Assets are decreased, liabilities are not affected, and stockholders' equity is decreased.

PQ3-8 On April 1, 20X1, Metro Insurance Company sold a one-year insurance policy covering the year ended April 1, 20X2. The customer paid the full $960 on April 1, 20X1. Metro made the following journal entry:

Cash	960	
Unearned Revenue		960

Nine months have passed, and Metro has made no adjusting entries pertaining to this policy because Metro prepares annual financial statements rather than monthly statements. Based on these facts, the adjusting entry needed by Metro at December 31, 20X1, is

a.	Unearned Revenue	720	
	Insurance Revenue		720

FOCUS ON F

b. Insurance Revenue	240	
Unearned Revenue		240
c. Unearned Revenue	240	
Insurance Revenue		240
d. Insurance Revenue	720	
Unearned Revenue		720

PQ3-9 The Unearned Revenue account of Jack Company began 20X5 with a normal balance of $5,700 and ended 20X5 with a normal balance of $12,500. During 20X5, the Unearned Revenue account was debited for $19,900 due to revenue that became earned in 20X5. Based on these facts, how much cash was received and credited to Unearned Revenue in 20X5?

a. $19,900
b. $44,900
c. $33,500
d. $26,700

PQ3-10 What is the effect on the financial statements of *recording* depreciation on plant assets?

a. Net income, assets, and stockholders' equity are all decreased.
b. Assets are decreased, but net income and stockholders' equity are not affected.
c. Net income and assets are decreased, but stockholders' equity is not affected.
d. Net income is not affected, but assets and stockholders' equity are decreased.

PQ3-11 For 20X3, Cameron Company had revenues in excess of expenses. Which statement describes Cameron's closing entries at the end of 20X3?

a. Revenues will be debited, expenses will be credited, and retained earnings will be debited.
b. Revenues will be debited, expenses will be credited, and retained earnings will be credited.
c. Revenues will be credited, expenses will be debited, and retained earnings will be debited.
d. Revenues will be credited, expenses will be debited, and retained earnings will be credited.

PQ3-12 Which of the following accounts would *not* be included in the closing entries?

a. Depreciation Expense
b. Taxi Fare Revenue
c. Accumulated Depreciation
d. Retained Earnings

PQ3-13 A major purpose of preparing closing entries is to

a. zero out the liability accounts.
b. update the retained earnings account.
c. adjust the asset accounts to their correct current balances.
d. all of the above.

PQ3-14 Selected data for the Jangle Company follow:

Current assets	$50,000	Current liabilities	$25,000
Long-term assets	70,000	Long-term liabilities	35,000
Total revenues	30,000	Total expenses	20,000

Based on these facts, what is Jangle's current ratio and debt ratio?

Current ratio	**Debt ratio**
a. 2 to 1	.5 to 1
b. .83 to 1	.5 to 1
c. 2 to 1	1.2 to 1
d. 1.87 to 1	5.33 to 1

NDAMENTALS

PQ3-15 In which month should revenue be recorded?

a. In the month that goods are ordered by the customer.
b. In the month that goods are shipped to the customer.
c. In the month that the invoice is mailed to the customer.
d. In the month that cash is collected from the customer.

PQ3-16 Unadjusted net income equals $5,900. After the following adjustments, net income will be (fill in the blank) $____

(1) Salaries payable to employees, $500.
(2) Interest due on note payable at the bank, $100.
(3) Interest receivable on note from customer, $50.
(4) Unearned revenue that has been earned, $600.
(5) Supplies used, $200.

PQ3-17 Salary Payable at the beginning of the month totals $24,000. During the month, $125,000 of cash is paid for salaries. If ending Salary Payable is $18,000, what amount of Salary Expense was recorded during the month? (Hint: Draw a T-account.)

a. $119,000
b. $124,000
c. $125,000
d. $131,000

Problems

(Group A)

PH Grade Assist

Most of these A problems can be found within Prentice Hall Grade Assist (PHGA), an online homework and practice environment. Your instructor may ask you to complete these problems using PHGA.

Linking accrual accounting and cash flows (Obj. 1)

P3-1A During 20X1, **Nike, Inc.**, earned revenues of $9.5 billion from the sale of shoes and clothing. Nike ended the year with net income of $0.6 billion. Nike collected cash of $9.4 billion from customers and paid cash for all 20X1 expenses plus an additional $0.3 billion for 20X0 expenses that were accrued at the end of 20X0. Answer these questions about Nike's operating results, financial position, and cash flows during 20X1:

1. How much were Nike's total expenses? Show your work.
2. Identify all the items that Nike will report on its income statement for 20X1. Show each amount.
3. How much cash did Nike pay for expenses and accrued liabilities during 20X1?
4. Nike began 20X1 with receivables of $1.6 billion. What was Nike's receivables balance at the end of 20X1? Identify the appropriate financial statement and show how Nike will report its ending receivables balance in the company's 20X1 annual report.
5. Nike began 20X1 owing accounts payable and accrued expenses payable totaling $1.2 billion. How much in accounts payable and accrued expenses payable did Nike owe at the end of 20X1? Identify the appropriate financial statement and show how Nike will report these two items in its 20X1 annual report. (For this requirement combine accounts payable and accrued expenses payable into a single amount.)

Cash basis versus accrual basis (Obj. 1)

P3-2A **Buzzard Billy's Restaurant** had the following selected transactions during May:

May 1	Received $800 in advance for a banquet to be served later.
5	Paid electricity expenses, $700.
9	Received cash for the day's sales, $1,400.
14	Purchased two video games, $1,800 (ignore depreciation).
23	Served a banquet, receiving a note receivable, $1,900.
31	Accrued salary expense, $900.
31	Prepaid building rent for June, July, and August, $3,000.

Required

1. Show how each transaction would be handled using the cash basis and the accrual basis. Under each column, give the amount of revenue or expense for May. Journal entries are not required. Use the following format for your answer, and show your computations:

Buzzard Billy's Amount of Revenue (Expense) for May		
Date	Cash Basis	Accrual Basis

2. Compute income (loss) before tax for May under the two accounting methods.
3. Which method better measures income and assets? Use the last transaction to explain.

Applying accounting principles (Obj. 1, 2)

writing assignment ■

P3-3A As the controller of Maribeaux Plastics, you have hired a new employee, whom you must train. He objects to making an adjusting entry for accrued salaries at the end of the period. He reasons, "We will pay the salaries soon. Why not wait until payment to record the expense? In the end, the result will be the same." Write a reply to explain to the employee why the adjusting entry is needed for accrued salary expense.

Making accounting adjustments (Obj. 3)

P3-4A Journalize the adjusting entry needed on December 31, the end of the current accounting period, for each of the following independent cases affecting Bulova Engineering, Inc. (BEI):

a. Each Friday, BEI pays employees for the current week's work. The amount of the payroll is $2,500 for a 5-day work week. The current accounting period ends on Monday.

b. BEI has received notes receivable from some clients for professional services. During the current year, BEI has earned accrued interest revenue of $2,640, which will be received next year.

c. The beginning balance of Engineering Supplies was $1,800. During the year, the entity purchased supplies costing $12,530, and at December 31 the inventory of supplies on hand is $2,970.

d. BEI is conducting tests of the strength of the steel to be used in a large building, and the client paid BEI $36,000 at the start of the project. BEI recorded this amount as Unearned Engineering Revenue. The tests will take several months to complete. BEI executives estimate that the company has earned three-fourths of the total fee during the current year.

e. Depreciation for the current year includes Office Furniture, $5,500; Engineering Equipment, $6,360; and Building, $3,790. Make a compound entry.

f. Details of Prepaid Insurance are shown in the account:

Prepaid Insurance

Jan. 1	Bal.	600		
Apr. 30		2,400		

BEI pays the annual insurance premium (the payment for insurance coverage is called a *premium*) on April 30 each year.

Analyzing and recording adjustments (Obj. 3)

■ **general ledger**

P3-5A DuPont Realty Company's unadjusted and adjusted trial balances at December 31, 20X7, are given on the next page.

Required

1. Make the adjusting entries that account for the difference between the two trial balances. DuPont Realty is not subject to income tax.
2. Compute DuPont's total assets, total liabilities, total equity, and net income.

Preparing the financial statements and using the debt ratio (Obj. 4, 6)

■ **spreadsheet**

P3-6A The adjusted trial balance of Thrifty Nickel Advertising, Inc., at December 31, 20X1, follows.

Required

1. Prepare Thrifty Nickel's 20X1 income statement, statement of retained earnings, and balance sheet. List expenses in decreasing order on the income statement and show total liabilities on the balance sheet. Draw arrows linking the three financial statements.
2. Thrifty Nickel's lenders require that the company maintain a debt ratio no higher than 0.60. Compute Thrifty Nickel's debt ratio at December 31, 20X1, to determine whether the company is in compliance with this debt restriction. If not, suggest a way that Thrifty Nickel could have avoided this difficult situation.

P3-5A

DuPont Realty Company
Adjusted Trial Balance
December 31, 20X7

Account Title	Trial Balance Debit	Trial Balance Credit	Adjusted Trial Balance Debit	Adjusted Trial Balance Credit
Cash	4,120		4,120	
Accounts receivable	11,260		12,090	
Supplies	1,090		780	
Prepaid insurance	2,600		910	
Office furniture	21,630		21,630	
Accumulated depreciation		8,220		9,360
Accounts payable		6,310		6,310
Salary payable				960
Interest payable				480
Note payable		12,000		12,000
Unearned commission revenue		1,840		1,160
Common stock		10,000		10,000
Retained earnings		3,510		3,510
Dividends	29,370		29,370	
Commission revenue		72,890		74,400
Depreciation expense			1,140	
Supplies expense			310	
Utilities expense	4,960		4,960	
Salary expense	26,660		27,620	
Rent expense	12,200		12,200	
Interest expense	880		1,360	
Insurance expense			1,690	
	114,770	114,770	118,180	118,180

P3-6A

Thrifty Nickel Advertising Inc.
Adjusted Trial Balance
December 31, 20X1

Cash	$ 11,640	
Accounts receivable	41,490	
Prepaid rent	1,350	
Equipment	75,690	
Accumulated depreciation		$ 22,240
Accounts payable		13,600
Unearned service revenue		4,520
Interest payable		2,130
Salary payable		930
Income tax payable		8,800
Note payable		36,200
Common stock		12,000
Retained earnings		20,380
Dividends	48,000	
Service revenue		187,670

(continued)

Depreciation expense	11,300	
Salary expense	94,000	
Rent expense	12,000	
Interest expense	4,200	
Income tax expense	8,800	
Total	$308,470	$308,470

P3-7A Consider the unadjusted trial balance of Alpha Beta Internet Connections at October 31, 20X2, and the related month-end adjustment data.

Preparing an adjusted trial balance and the financial statements; using the current ratio to evaluate the business (Obj. 3, 4, 6)

Alpha Beta Internet Connections
Trial Balance
October 31, 20X2

Cash	$ 5,300	
Accounts receivable	7,000	
Prepaid rent	4,000	
Supplies	600	
Furniture	36,000	
Accumulated depreciation		$ 3,000
Accounts payable		8,800
Salary payable		
Common stock		15,000
Retained earnings		21,000
Dividends	4,600	
Advertising revenue		14,400
Salary expense	4,400	
Rent expense		
Utilities expense	300	
Depreciation expense		
Supplies expense		
Total	$62,200	$62,200

Adjustment data:

a. Accrued advertising revenue at October 31, $2,900.
b. Prepaid rent expired during the month. The unadjusted prepaid balance of $4,000 relates to the period October 20X2 through January 20X3.
c. Supplies used during October, $200.
d. Depreciation on furniture for the month. The furniture's expected useful life is 5 years.
e. Accrued salary expense at October 31 for Tuesday through Friday; the 5-day weekly payroll is $2,000.

Required

1. Using Exhibit 3-9, page 123, as an example, prepare the adjusted trial balance of Alpha Beta at October 31, 20X2. Key each adjusting entry by letter.
2. Prepare the income statement, the statement of retained earnings, and the classified balance sheet. Draw arrows linking the three financial statements.
3. a. Compare Alpha Beta's net income for October to the amount of dividends paid to the owners. Suppose this trend continues into 20X3. What will be the effect on the business's financial position, as shown by its accounting equation?
   b. Will the trend make it easier or more difficult for Alpha Beta to borrow money if the business gets in a bind and needs cash? Why?
   c. Does either the current ratio or the cash position suggest the need for immediate borrowing? Explain.

Preparing a classified balance sheet and using the ratios to evaluate the business (Obj. 4, 6)

P3-8A The accounts of Gay Gillen eTravel, Inc., at December 31, 20X5, are listed here in alphabetical order.

Accounts payable	$ 5,100	Insurance expense	$ 800
Accounts receivable	6,600	Note payable, long-term	10,600
Accumulated depreciation—furniture	11,600	Note receivable, long-term	4,000
Advertising expense	2,200	Other assets	3,600
Cash	7,300	Prepaid expenses	7,700
Commission revenue	93,500	Retained earnings, December 31, 20X4	5,300
Common stock	15,000	Salary expense	24,600
Current portion of note payable	2,200	Salary payable	3,900
Depreciation expense	1,300	Supplies expense	5,700
Dividends	47,400	Unearned commission revenue	5,400
Furniture	41,400		

Required

1. All adjustments have been journalized and posted, but the closing entries have not yet been made. Prepare the company's classified balance sheet in report format at December 31, 20X5. Label total assets, total liabilities, and total liabilities and stockholders' equity. The travel agency is not subject to income tax.
2. Compute Gillen's current ratio and debt ratio at December 31, 20X5. At December 31, 20X4, the current ratio was 1.52 and the debt ratio was 0.45. Did Gillen's overall ability to pay debts improve or deteriorate during 20X5?

Closing the books and evaluating retained earnings (Obj. 5)

P3-9A Refer back to Problem 3-8A.

1. Use the Gay Gillen eTravel data in Problem 3-8A to journalize Gillen's closing entries at December 31, 20X5.
2. Set up a T-account for Retained Earnings and post to that account. What is the ending balance of Retained Earnings?
3. Did Retained Earnings increase or decrease during the year? What caused the increase or decrease?

Analyzing financial ratios (Obj. 6)

P3-10A This problem demonstrates the effects of transactions on the current ratio and the debt ratio of a well-known company. **Sony Corporation** is famous for its electronics products. Sony's condensed balance sheet at March 31, 20X1, is given in yen (¥), the Japanese monetary unit.

	(In trillions)
Total current assets	¥3.0
Properties, net, and other assets	3.8
	¥6.8
Total current liabilities	¥2.2
Total long-term liabilities	2.4
Total stockholders' equity	2.2
	¥6.8

Assume that during the following year, ending March 31, 20X2, Sony completed the following transactions:

a. Paid half the current liabilities.
b. Borrowed ¥3 trillion on long-term debt.
c. Earned revenue of ¥2.5 trillion on account.
d. Paid selling expense of ¥1 trillion.
e. Accrued general expense of ¥0.8 trillion. Credit General Expense Payable, a current liability.
f. Purchased equipment, paying cash of ¥1.4 trillion and signing a long-tern note payable for ¥2.8 trillion.
g. Recorded depreciation expense of ¥0.6 trillion.

Required

1. Compute Sony's current ratio and debt ratio at March 31, 20X1.
2. Compute Sony's current ratio and debt ratio after each transaction during 20X2. Consider each transaction separately.
3. Based on your analysis, you should be able to readily identify the effects of certain transactions on the current ratio and the debt ratio. Test your understanding by completing these statements with either "increase" or "decrease":
   a. Revenues usually ____________ the current ratio.
   b. Revenues usually ____________ the debt ratio.
   c. Expenses usually ____________ the current ratio. (*Note:* Depreciation is an exception to this rule.)
   d. Expenses usually ____________ the debt ratio.
   e. If a company's current ratio is greater than 1.0, as for Sony, paying off a current liability will always ____________ the current ratio.
   f. Borrowing money on long-term debt will always ____________ the current ratio and ____________ the debt ratio.

(Group B)

Some of these B problems can be found online at www.prenhall.com/harrison. These problems are algorithmically generated, allowing you endless practice. You'll receive immediate assessment and feedback as you complete each problem.

Linking accrual accounting and cash flows (Obj. 1)

P3-1B Sara Lee Corporation earned revenues of $17.7 billion during 20X1 and ended the year with net income of $2.3 billion. During 20X1, Sara Lee collected $18.0 billion from customers and paid cash for all of its expenses plus an additional $0.4 billion on 20X0 expenses left over from the preceding year. Answer these questions about Sara Lee's operating results, financial position, and cash flows during 20X1:

Required

1. How much were the company's total expenses? Show your work.
2. Identify all the items that Sara Lee will report on its 20X1 income statement. Show each amount.
3. How much cash did Sara Lee pay for expenses in 20X1?
4. Sara Lee began 20X1 with receivables of $1.8 billion. What was the company's receivables balance at the end of 20X1? Identify the appropriate financial statement, and show how Sara Lee will report ending receivables in the 20X1 annual report.
5. Sara Lee began 20X1 owing accounts payable and accrued expenses payable totaling $2.7 billion. How much in accounts payable and accrued expenses payable did the company owe at the end of the year? Identify the appropriate financial statement and show how Sara Lee will report these two items in its 20X1 annual report. (For this requirement, combine accounts payable and accrued expenses payable into a single amount.)

Cash basis versus accrual basis (Obj. 1)

P3-2B Lexington Image Consultants had the following selected transactions in October:

October 1	Prepaid insurance for October through December, $900.
4	Purchased software for cash, $800 (ignore depreciation).
5	Performed service and received cash, $700.
8	Paid advertising expense,$300.
11	Performed service on account, $2,500.
19	Purchased computer on account, $1,600 (ignore depreciation).
24	Collected for the October 11 service.
26	Paid account payable from October 19.
29	Paid salary expense, $900.
31	Adjusted for October insurance expense (see Oct. 1).
31	Earned revenue of $1,300 that was collected in advance back in September.

Required

1. Show how each transaction would be handled using the cash basis and the accrual basis. Under each column, give the amount of revenue or expense for October. Journal entries are not required. Use the following format for your answer, and show your computations:

Lexington Image Consultants Amount of Revenue (Expense) for October		
Date	Cash Basis	Accrual Basis

2. Compute October income (loss) before tax under each accounting method.
3. Indicate which measure of net income or net loss is preferable. Use the transactions on October 11 and 24 to explain.

Applying accounting principles (Obj. 1, 2)

writing assignment ■

P3-3B Write a memo to explain for a new employee the difference between the cash basis of accounting and the accrual basis. Mention the roles of the revenue principle and the matching principle in accrual accounting.

Making accounting adjustments (Obj. 3)

P3-4B Journalize the adjusting entry needed on December 31, end of the current accounting period, for each of the following independent cases affecting First Bancorp, Inc.

a. Details of Prepaid Insurance are shown in the account:

Prepaid Insurance				
Jan. 1	Bal.	600		
Mar. 31		3,000		

First Bancorp prepays insurance each year on March 31.

b. First Bancorp pays employees each Friday. The amount of the weekly payroll is $6,000 for a 5-day work week, and the daily salary amounts are equal. The current accounting period ends on Thursday.
c. First Bancorp has loaned money, receiving notes receivable. During the current year, the entity has earned accrued interest revenue of $509 that it will receive next year.
d. The beginning balance of supplies was $2,680. During the year, First Bancorp purchased supplies costing $6,180, and at December 31 the cost of supplies on hand is $2,150.
e. First Bancorp is providing financial services for Manatee Investments, and the owner of Manatee paid First Bancorp $12,900 as the annual service fee. First Bancorp recorded this amount as Unearned Service Revenue. First Bancorp estimates that the bank has earned one-fourth of the total fee during the current year.
f. Depreciation for the current year includes Office Furniture, $700; Equipment, $2,730; and Buildings, $10,320. Make a compound entry.

Analyzing and recording adjustments (Obj. 3)

■ general ledger

P3-5B Western Hoteliers, Inc.'s unadjusted and adjusted trial balances at September 30, 20X1, is given on next page:

Required

1. Make the adjusting entries that account for the differences between the two trial balances. Western is not subject to income tax.
2. Compute Western's total assets, total liabilities, total equity, and net income.

Preparing the financial statements and using the debt ratio (Obj. 4, 6)

■ spreadsheet

P3-6B The adjusted trial balance of Oriental Design Studio, Inc., at December 31, 20X6, follows on the next page.

Required

1. Prepare Oriental Design's 20X6 income statement, statement of retained earnings, and balance sheet. List expenses (except for income tax) in decreasing order on the income statement and show total liabilities on the balance sheet. Draw arrows linking the three financial statements.

2. Oriental Design's lenders require that the company maintain a debt ratio no higher than 0.50. Compute Oriental Design's debt ratio at December 31, 20X6, to determine whether the company is in compliance with this debt restriction. If not, suggest a way that Oriental could have avoided this difficult situation.

P3-5B

Western Hoteliers, Inc.
Adjusted Trial Balance
September 30, 20X1

	Trial Balance		Adjusted Trial Balance	
Account Title	**Debit**	**Credit**	**Debit**	**Credit**
Cash	8,180		8,180	
Accounts receivable	6,360		6,840	
Interest receivable			300	
Note receivable	4,100		4,100	
Supplies	980		290	
Prepaid insurance	2,480		720	
Building	66,450		66,450	
Accumulated depreciation		16,010		18,210
Accounts payable		6,920		6,920
Wages payable				170
Unearned rental revenue		670		110
Common stock		18,000		18,000
Retained earnings		42,790		42,790
Dividends	3,600		3,600	
Rental revenue		9,940		10,980
Interest revenue				300
Wage expense	1,600		1,770	
Insurance expense			1,760	
Depreciation expense			2,200	
Property tax expense	370		370	
Supplies expense			690	
Utilities expense	210		210	
	94,330	94,330	97,480	97,480

P3-6B

Oriental Design Studio, Inc.
Adjusted Trial Balance
December 31, 20X6

Cash	$ 1,320	
Accounts receivable	8,920	
Supplies	2,300	
Prepaid rent	1,600	
Equipment	37,180	
Accumulated depreciation		$ 4,350
Accounts payable		3,640
Interest payable		830
Unearned service revenue		620
Income tax payable		2,100
Note payable		18,620
Common stock		5,000
Retained earnings		1,090
Dividends	44,000	

(continued)

Service revenue		127,910
Depreciation expense	1,680	
Salary expense	39,900	
Rent expense	10,300	
Interest expense	3,100	
Insurance expense	3,810	
Supplies expense	2,950	
Income tax expense	7,100	
Total	164,160	164,160

Preparing an adjusted trial balance and the financial statements; using the current ratio to evaluate the business (Obj. 3, 4, 6)

P3-7B The unadjusted trial balance of Colorado Valley Legal Associates at July 31, 20X2, and the related month-end adjustment data follow.

Colorado Valley Legal Associates
Trial Balance
July 31, 20X2

Cash	$ 5,600	
Accounts receivable	11,600	
Prepaid rent	3,600	
Supplies	800	
Furniture	36,000	
Accumulated depreciation		$ 3,500
Accounts payable		10,450
Salary payable		
Common stock		26,200
Retained earnings		13,650
Dividends	4,000	
Legal service revenue		10,750
Salary expense	2,400	
Rent expense		
Utilities expense	550	
Depreciation expense		
Supplies expense		
Total	$64,550	$64,550

Adjustment data:

a. Accrued legal service revenue at July 31, $400.
b. Prepaid rent expired during the month. The unadjusted prepaid balance of $3,600 relates to the period July through October.
c. Supplies used during July, $600.
d. Depreciation on furniture for the month. The estimated useful life of the furniture is 5 years.
e. Accrued salary expense at July 31 for Monday and Tuesday. The 5-day weekly payroll of $1,750 will be paid on Friday, August 2.

Required

1. Using Exhibit 3-9, page 123, as an example, prepare the adjusted trial balance of Colorado Valley Legal Associates, at July 31, 20X2. Key each adjusting entry by letter. The business is not subject to income tax.
2. Prepare the income statement, the statement of retained earnings, and the classified balance sheet. Draw arrows linking the three financial statements.
3. **a.** Compare the business's net income for July to the amount of dividends paid to the owners. Suppose this trend continues each month for the remainder of 20X2. What will be the effect on the business's financial position, as shown by its accounting equation?
   b. Will the trend make it easier or more difficult to borrow money if the business gets in a bind and needs cash? Why?
   c. Does either the current ratio or the cash position suggest the need for immediate borrowing? Explain.

FOCUS ON F

Preparing a classified balance sheet and using the ratios to evaluate the business (Obj. 4, 6)

P3-8B The accounts of Datacom Service Center, Inc., at March 31, 20X3, are listed here in alphabetical order.

Accounts payable	$14,700	Furniture	$43,200
Accounts receivable	11,500	Insurance expense	600
Accumulated depreciation— building	47,300	Note payable, long-term	6,200
		Note receivable, long-term	6,900
Accumulated depreciation— furniture	7,100	Other assets	2,300
		Prepaid expenses	5,300
Advertising expense	900	Retained earnings, March 31, 20X2	30,800
Building	55,900		
Cash	6,400	Salary expense	17,800
Common stock	9,100	Salary payable	2,400
Current portion of note payable	800	Service revenue	71,100
		Supplies	3,800
Depreciation expense	1,900	Supplies expense	4,600
Dividends	31,200	Unearned service revenue	2,800

Required

1. All adjustments have been journalized and posted, but the closing entries have not yet been made. Prepare the company's classified balance sheet at March 31, 20X3. Use captions for total assets, total liabilities, and total liabilities and stockholders' equity. A professional corporation is not subject to income tax.
2. Compute Datacom's current ratio and debt ratio at March 31, 20X3. At March 31, 20X2, the current ratio was 1.28 and the debt ratio was 0.29. Did Datacom's ability to pay debts improve or deteriorate during 20X3? Evaluate Datacom's overall debt position as strong or weak and give your reason.

Closing the books and evaluating retained earnings (Obj. 5)

P3-9B Refer back to Problem 3-8B.

1. Use the Datacom Service Center data in Problem 3-8B to journalize Datacom's closing entries at March 31, 20X3.
2. Set up a T-account for Retained Earnings and post to that account. What is the ending balance of Retained Earnings?
3. Did Retained Earnings increase or decrease during the year? What caused the increase or the decrease?

Analyzing financial ratios (Obj. 6)

P3-10B This problem demonstrates the effects of transactions on the current ratio and the debt ratio of a well-known company. **Johnson & Johnson** produces Band-Aids and other medical products. Johnson & Johnson's condensed and adapted balance sheet at December 31, 20X0, is:

	(In billions)
Total current assets	$15.5
Properties, plant, equipment, and other assets	15.8
	$31.3
Total current liabilities	$ 7.2
Total long-term liabilities	5.3
Total stockholders' equity	18.8
	$31.3

Assume that during the first quarter of the following year, 20X1, Johnson & Johnson completed the following transactions:

a. Paid half the current liabilities.
b. Borrowed $3 billion on long-term debt.

(continued)

c. Earned revenue, $2.5 billion, on account.
d. Paid selling expense of $1 billion.
e. Accrued general expense of $800 million. Credit General Expense Payable, a current liability.
f. Purchased equipment, paying cash of $1.4 billion and signing a long-term note payable for $2.8 billion.
g. Recorded depreciation expense of $600 million.

Required

1. Compute Johnson & Johnson's current ratio and debt ratio at December 31, 20X0.
2. Compute Johnson & Johnson's current ratio and debt ratio after each transaction during 20X1. Consider each transaction separately.
3. Based on your analysis, you should be able to readily identify the effects of certain transactions on the current ratio and the debt ratio. Test your understanding by completing these statements with either "increase" or "decrease":
   a. Revenues usually ____________ the current ratio.
   b. Revenues usually ____________ the debt ratio.
   c. Expenses usually ____________ the current ratio. (*Note:* Depreciation is an exception to this rule.)
   d. Expenses usually ____________ the debt ratio.
   e. If a company's current ratio is greater than 1.0, as it is for Johnson & Johnson, paying off a current liability will always ____________ the current ratio.
   f. Borrowing money on long-term debt will always ____________ the current ratio and ____________ the debt ratio.

Apply Your Knowledge

Decision Cases

Adjusting and correcting the accounts; computing and evaluating the current ratio (Obj. 3, 6)

Case 1. The stockholders need to know the current ratio of Armstrong, Inc. The unadjusted trial balance of Armstrong at February 28, 20X6, does not balance. In addition, the trial balance needs to be adjusted before the financial statements at February 28, 20X6 can be prepared.

Cash	$ 4,200
Accounts receivable	2,200
Supplies	800
Prepaid rent	1,200
Land	41,000
Accounts payable	5,400
Salary payable	0
Unearned service revenue	700
Note payable, due in 3 years	25,400
Common stock	5,000
Retained earnings	7,300
Service revenue	9,100
Salary expense	3,400
Rent expense	0
Advertising expense	900
Supplies expense	0

Required

1. How much *out of balance* is the trial balance?
2. Armstrong needs to make the following adjustments at February 28:
   a. Supplies of $600 were used during February.
   b. The balance of Prepaid Rent was paid on January 1 and covers the whole year 20X6.

FOCUS ON F

c. At February 28, Armstrong owes employees $400.
d. Unearned service revenue of $200 was earned during February.
Prepare a corrected, adjusted trial balance. The error is in the Accounts Receivable account.

3. After the error is corrected and after these adjustments are made, compute the current ratio of Armstrong Inc. If your business had this current ratio, could you sleep at night?

Preparing financial statements; continue or shut down the business? (Obj. 4)

Case 2. On June 1, Bobby Bonds opened Home Run Restaurant, Inc. After the first month of operations, Bonds is at a crossroads. The June financial statements paint a dismal picture of the business, and Bonds has asked you whether he should continue in business or shut down the restaurant. He is sure of one thing: To start the business, he invested $12,000, not the $2,000 amount reported as "Investments by owner" on the income statement. The bookkeeper plugged the $2,000 "Investments by owner" amount as common stock into the balance sheet to make it balance. Bonds shows you the following financial statements that the bookkeeper prepared.

Required

Prepare corrected financial statements for Home Run Restaurant, Inc.: Income Statement, Statement of Retained Earnings, and Balance Sheet. Then, based on your corrected statements, recommend to Mr. Bonds whether he should close the restaurant or continue in business.

Home Run Restaurant, Inc.
Income Statement
Month Ended June 30, 20X4

Revenues:		
Investments by owner	$2,000	
Unearned banquet sales revenue	3,000	
		$ 5,000
Expenses:		
Wages expense	$5,000	
Rent expense	4,000	
Dividends	3,000	
Depreciation expense—fixtures	1,000	
		13,000
Net income (Net loss)		$(8,000)

Home Run Restaurant, Inc.
Balance Sheet
June 30, 20X4

Assets:		**Liabilities:**	
Cash	$ 6,000	Accounts payable	$ 5,000
Prepaid insurance	1,000	Sales revenue	32,000
Insurance expense	1,000	Accumulated depreciation—	
Food inventory	3,000	fixtures	1,000
Cost of goods sold (expense)	14,000		38,000
Fixtures (tables, chairs, etc.)	11,000	**Owners' equity:**	
Dishes and silverware	4,000	Common stock	2,000
	$40,000		$40,000

Valuing a business on the basis of its net income (Obj. 3, 4)

Case 3. Deborah Trotter has owned and operated Trotter Advertising, Inc. since its beginning 10 years ago. Recently, Trotter mentioned that she would consider selling the company for the right price.

Assume that you are interested in buying this business. You obtain its most recent monthly trial balance, which follows. Revenues and expenses vary little from month to month, and April is a typical month. Your investigation reveals that the trial balance does not include the effects of monthly revenues of $3,800 and expenses totaling $1,100. If you were to buy Trotter Advertising, you would hire a manager so you could devote your time to other duties. Assume that your manager would require a monthly salary of $4,000.

Trotter Advertising, Inc.
Trial Balance
April 30, 20XX

Cash	$ 10,000	
Accounts receivable	4,900	
Prepaid expenses	3,200	
Plant assets	221,300	
Accumulated depreciation		$189,600
Land	158,000	
Accounts payable		13,800
Salary payable		
Unearned advertising revenue		56,700
Common stock		50,000
Retained earnings		88,000
Dividends	9,000	
Advertising revenue		12,600
Rent expense		
Salary expense	3,400	
Utilities expense	900	
Depreciation expense		
Supplies expense		
Total	$410,700	$410,700

Required

1. Assume that the most you would pay for the business is 30 times the amount of monthly net income *you could expect to earn* from it. Compute this possible price.
2. Trotter states that the least she will take for the business is 1.5 times its stockholders' equity on April 30. Compute this amount.
3. Under these conditions, how much should you offer Trotter? Give your reason.

Completing the accounting cycle to develop the information for a bank loan (Obj. 3, 5)

Case 4. One year ago, Jack Hewlett and Melanie Packard founded Hewlett-Packard (HP) Service Center, Inc. The business has prospered. Packard, who remembers that you majored in accounting while in college, comes to you for advice. She wishes to know how much net income the business earned during the past year. She also wants to know what the entity's total assets, liabilities, and stockholders' equity are. The accounting records consist of the T-accounts that follow.

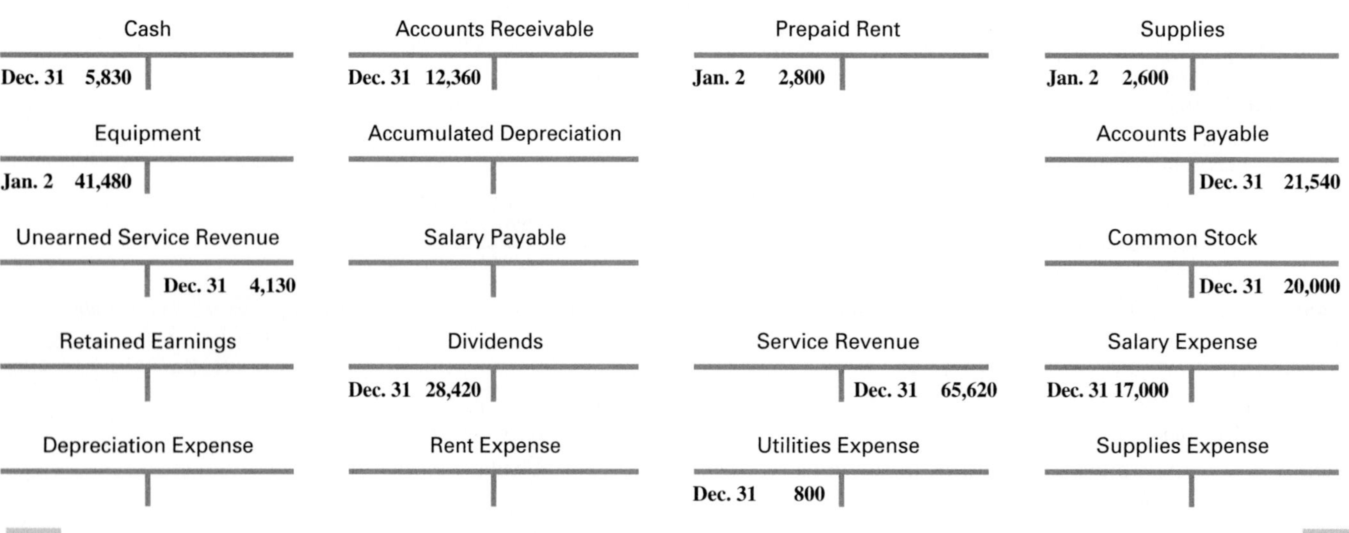

FOCUS ON F

Packard indicates that at the year's end, customers owe the business $1,600 accrued service revenue, which it expects to collect early next year. These revenues have not been recorded. During the year, HP collected $4,130 service revenue in advance from customers, but it earned only $600 of that amount. Rent expense for the year was $2,400, and HP used up $2,100 in supplies. Packard estimates that depreciation on equipment was $5,900 for the year. At December 31, the business owes employees $1,200 accrued salary.

At the conclusion of your meeting, Hewlett and Packard express concern that dividends during the year might have exceeded net income. To get a loan to expand the business, HP must show the bank that total stockholders' equity has grown from its original $20,000 balance. Has it? You, Hewlett, and Packard agree that you will meet again in 1 week. You should perform the analysis and prepare the financial statements to answer Packard's questions.

Ethical Issues

Issue 1. The net income of Mother Earth Provision Company decreased sharply during 2003. Clay Rollins, owner of the store, anticipates the need for a bank loan in 2004. Late in 2003, he instructed the accountant to record a $50,000 sale of recreational gear to the Rollins family, even though the goods will not be shipped from the manufacturer until January 2004. Rollins also told the accountant *not* to make the following December 31, 2003, adjusting entries:

Salaries owed to employees	$1,000
Prepaid insurance that has expired	500

Required

1. Compute the overall effect of these transactions on the store's reported income for 2003. Is income overstated or understated?
2. Why did Rollins take these actions? Are they ethical? Give your reason, identifying the parties helped and the parties harmed by Rollins' action.
3. As a personal friend, what advice would you give the accountant?

Issue 2. BAE, a management consulting firm, is in its third year of operations. The company was initially financed by owners' equity as the two partners each invested $50,000. The first year's slim profits were expected because new businesses often start slowly. During the second year, BAE landed a large contract and referrals from that project brought in more jobs. To expand the business, BAE borrowed $75,000 from the Bank of Kansas City. As a condition for making this loan, the bank required that BAE maintain a current ratio of at least 1.50 and a debt ratio of no more than 0.50.

Business during the third year has been less than expected. Expenses have brought the current ratio down to 1.47 and the debt ratio up to 0.51 at December 15. Stephen Hyde, the general manager, is considering the result of reporting this current ratio to the bank. Hyde is considering recording some revenue on account that BAE will earn next year. The contract for this job has been signed, and BAE will perform the management consulting service during January.

Required

1. Journalize the revenue transaction, and indicate how recording this revenue in December would affect the current ratio and the debt ratio.
2. State whether it is ethical to record the revenue transaction in December. Identify the accounting principle relevant to this situation.
3. Propose for BAE a course of action that is ethical.

Focus on Financials: ■ YUM! Brands

Tracing account balances to the financial statements (Obj. 3, 6)

YUM! Brands, Inc.—like all other businesses—adjusts accounts prior to year end to get correct amounts for the financial statements. Examine YUM's balance sheet in Appendix A, and pay particular attention to (a) Prepaid Expenses and Other Current Assets and (b) Income Taxes Payable.

Required

1. Why aren't Prepaid Expenses "true" expenses? Why does a company have income taxes payable at year end?
2. Open T-accounts for the two accounts listed above. Insert YUM's balances (in millions) at December 28, 2002.
3. Journalize the following for the year ended December 27, 2003. Key entries by letter, and show amounts in millions. Explanations are not required.
   a. Recorded General Expense for expiration of the beginning balance of Prepaid Expenses.
   b. Paid off the beginning balance of Income Taxes Payable.
   c. Paid the ending balance of Prepaid Expenses.
   d. Recorded Income Tax Expense of $268 million, paying $30 million and accruing the remainder.
4. Post these entries and show that the ending balances of Prepaid Expenses and Other Current Assets and of Income Taxes Payable agree with the corresponding amounts reported in the December 27, 2003, balance sheet.
5. Compute the current ratios and debt ratios for YUM! Brands at December 27, 2003, and at December 28, 2002. Did the ratio values improve, deteriorate, or hold steady during 2003? Do the ratio values indicate financial strength or weakness?

Focus on Analysis: ■ Pier 1 Imports

Explaining accruals and deferrals (Obj. 3)

During 2004, **Pier I Imports** had numerous accruals and deferrals. As a new member of Pier 1's accounting staff, it is your job to explain the effects of accruals and deferrals on Pier 1's net income for 2004. The accrual and deferral data follow, along with questions that Pier 1 stockholders have raised (all amounts in millions):

1. Beginning total receivables for 2004 were $52. Ending receivables for 2004 are $59. Which of these amounts did Pier 1 earn in 2003? Which amount did Pier 1 earn in 2004? Which amount is included in Pier 1's net income for 2004?
2. Accumulated depreciation stood at $325 at the end of 2003 and at $363 at year end 2004. Depreciation expense for 2004 was $65. What other event affected accumulated depreciation during 2004? Identify the item, and give its amount.
3. Pier 1 reports an account titled Gift Cards, Gift Certificates, and Merchandise Credits Outstanding. This account carried credit balances of $38 at the end of 2003 and $46 at the end of 2004. What type of account is Gift Cards, Gift Certificates, and Merchandise Credits Outstanding? Make a single journal entry to show how this account could have increased its balance during 2004. Then explain the event in your own words.
4. Certain income-statement accounts are directly linked to specific balance-sheet accounts other than cash. Examine Pier 1's income statement in Appendix B at the end of this book. For each "Operating cost and expense," each "Nonoperating (income) and expense," and Provision for income taxes, identify the related balance sheet account (other than cash). Use standard account titles, not necessarily the titles Pier 1 uses.

Group Project

Doug Andrews formed a lawn service company as a summer job. To start the business on May 1, he deposited $1,000 in a new bank account in the name of the corporation. The $1,000 consisted of a $600 loan from his father and $400 of his own money. The corporation issued 400 shares of common stock to Andrews.

Andrews rented lawn equipment, purchased supplies, and hired high school students to mow and trim his customers' lawns. At the end of each month, Andrews mailed bills to his customers. On August 31, Andrews was ready to dissolve the business and return to Indiana University for the fall semester. Because he had been so busy, he had kept few records other than his checkbook and a list of amounts owed by customers.

At August 31, Andrews' checkbook shows a balance of $1,190, and his customers still owe him $500. During the summer, he collected $4,750 from customers. His checkbook lists payments for supplies totaling $400, and he still has gasoline, weedeater cord, and other supplies that cost a total of $50. He paid his employees $1,900, and he still owes them $200 for the final week of the summer.

Andrews rented some equipment from Ludwig Tool Company. On May 1, he signed a 6-month lease on mowers and paid $600 for the full lease period. Ludwig will refund the unused portion of the prepayment if the equipment is in good shape. To get the refund, Andrews has kept the mowers in excellent condition. In fact, he had to pay $300 to repair a mower that ran over a hidden tree stump.

To transport employees and equipment to jobs, Andrews used a trailer that he bought for $300. He figures that the summer's work used up one-third of the trailer's service potential. The business checkbook lists an expenditure of $460 for dividends paid to Andrews during the summer. Andrews paid his father back during the summer.

Required

1. Prepare the income statement of Andrews Lawn Service, Inc. for the 4 months May through August. The business is not subject to income tax.
2. Prepare the classified balance sheet of Andrews Lawn Service, Inc., at August 31.

spotlight

MERRILL LYNCH TAKES A HIT

Merrill Lynch & Co., Inc.
Balance Sheets (Partial, Adapted)

(Dollars in millions)

Assets	December 31, 2003	December 31, 2002
Cash and cash equivalents	$ 119	$ 939
Cash pledged as collateral	296	375
Investment securities	16,203	7,983
Advances to affiliates	78,282	73,825
Investments in affiliates, at equity	29,332	25,194
Equipment and facilities (net of accumulated depreciation and amortization of $222 in 2003 and $236 in 2002)	66	109
Other receivables and assets	3,996	4,568
Total Assets	$128,294	$112,993

What happens when a company fails to supervise an employee's day-to-day activities? Merrill Lynch answered this question the hard way when Darlyne Lopez stole $565,059 from the company.

Exactly what did Lopez do? Randy Ramey, resident manager of the Merrill Lynch office, explained in court that Lopez, a cashier, stole the money by transferring customers' deposits into her own account. She then covered the missing amounts with deposits made by other customers. The accounts always balanced—until Lopez's car wreck. She missed work, and customers at the end of the "Rob-Peter-to-pay-Paul scheme" noted discrepancies in their accounts. They notified Ramey, and Lopez's cover vanished.

Discovery of the scheme "was one of the most severe shocks I've received in my life," said Ramey. "As big as this thing got, a person [had] to [work] on it and [think] about it every moment of every day. . . . I am frankly surprised at the magnitude of it and the expertise it took to keep it all going." Ramey considered Lopez a dedicated employee because she never took a day off and never took a vacation. Now Ramey knows why: Lopez had to be on the job to cover her tracks. Years earlier Merrill Lynch became suspicious when Lopez's account revealed "unusual activity." And for a $15,000-a-year employee, she wore expensive clothes. But the company didn't follow up adequately.

Lopez's scheme is well known to accountants. It is called *lapping*—similar to laying shingles on a roof. Lapping does take lots of ingenuity and purpose. In fact, guilty employees have been known to come crying to the boss, "Please get me out of this mess! I can't sleep at night. Send me to jail. Do anything. Help!"

Internal Control & Cash

4

LEARNING OBJECTIVES

1 **Set up** an effective system of internal control

2 **Use** a bank reconciliation as a control device

3 **Apply** internal controls to cash receipts and cash payments

4 **Use** a budget to manage cash

5 **Weigh** ethical judgments in business

Merrill Lynch could have avoided the loss by taking a few precautions known as *internal controls*. This chapter covers the basics of internal control. It also shows how to account for cash. These two topics—internal control and cash—go together because cash is the asset that is stolen most often.

The excerpt from the Merrill Lynch balance sheet reports the company's assets. Focus on the top line, Cash and cash equivalents. At December 26, 2003, Merrill Lynch reported cash of $119 million. If Lopez's scheme hadn't been detected, the reported cash balance would have been overstated by a half million dollars. One purpose of internal control is to produce accurate and reliable accounting records. After all, the records produce the amounts that Merrill Lynch reports to the public. Either the company has the full $119 million that it reports, or it does not.

Internal Control

Owners and executives set goals, managers lead the way, and employees carry out the plans. If managers don't control operations, the entity may suffer losses, as Merrill Lynch did.

Internal control
Organizational plan and related measures adopted by an entity to safeguard assets, encourage adherence to company policies, promote operational efficiency, and ensure accurate and reliable accounting records.

Internal control is the organizational plan and related measures that an entity adopts to

1. Safeguard assets
2. Encourage adherence to company policies
3. Promote operational efficiency
4. Ensure accurate and reliable accounting records

Exhibit 4-1 is an excerpt from Merrill Lynch's Management Discussion of Financial Responsibility, taken from the company's 2003 Annual Report. The company's top managers take responsibility for internal controls.

■ **EXHIBIT 4-1**
Merrill Lynch & Co., Inc. Management Discussion of Financial Responsibility (Excerpt)

Management's Discussion of Financial Responsibility

Merrill Lynch regularly reviews its framework of internal controls, which includes policies, procedures and organizational structures, taking into account changing circumstances. Corrective actions are taken to address control deficiencies, if any, and other opportunities for improvement are implemented as appropriate.

Source: Merrill Lynch & Co., Annual Report 2003, p. 45.

The Sarbanes-Oxley Act (SOX)

The Enron and WorldCom accounting scandals rocked the accounting profession. Enron overstated profits and understated expenses and liabilities. The company, once the darling of Wall Street, went out of business almost overnight. WorldCom (now MCI) reported expenses as assets, effectively overstating both profits and assets. The company is reeling from its accounting misdeeds. Sadly, the same accounting firm, Arthur Andersen LLP, had issued clean audit opinions on both companies' financial statements. Arthur Andersen then closed its doors.

As the scandals unfolded, many people asked, "How can these things happen? Where were the auditors?" To address public concern, Congress passed the Sarbanes-Oxley Act, abbreviated as SOX. SOX revamped corporate governance in the United States and also had sweeping effects on the accounting profession. Here are some of the SOX provisions:

1. A newly created body, the Public Company Accounting Oversight Board, oversees the work of auditors of public companies. Public companies are those that sell their stock to the public.
2. Accounting firms may not both audit the financial statements of a public client and also provide certain consulting services for the same client.
3. The same person can serve as the lead auditor on a public client for no more than 7 years. That person can resume prior audit duties only after a 2-year time-out period.
4. Public companies must issue an internal control report, and the outside auditor must evaluate the client's internal controls.
5. Stiff penalties await violators—25 years in prison for securities fraud; 20 years for destroying records; and 20 years for a CEO or a CFO making false sworn statements.

It will take several years to determine how SOX affects financial reporting.

Designing a System of Internal Control

OBJECTIVE

1 **Set up** an effective system of internal control

Whether the business is Merrill Lynch, Coca-Cola, or an Exxon convenience store, an effective system of internal control must have the following characteristics.

Competent, Reliable, and Ethical Personnel. Employees should be *competent*, *reliable*, and *ethical*. Paying good salaries, training employees, and supervising their work build a competent staff. Rotating employees through various jobs makes them more valuable to the organization. If one employee is sick or on vacation, a second employee can step in and do the job.

Assignment of Responsibilities. A business with good internal controls oversees all important duties. Each employee is assigned certain responsibilities. A model *assignment of responsibilities* appears in Exhibit 4-2. Notice that the corporation has a vice president of finance and accounting. Two other officers, the treasurer and the controller, report to that vice president. The treasurer manages cash, and the **controller** is in charge of accounting. The controller may be responsible for approving invoices (bills) for payment, while the treasurer may actually sign the checks.

Controller
The chief accounting officer of a business.

Proper Authorization. An organization needs rules to govern approval procedures. Any deviation from company policy requires *authorization*. For example, managers of retail stores approve customer checks for amounts above the store's usual limit. Department chairs of colleges must authorize juniors to enroll in senior-level courses.

Supervision of Employees. Even the most trusted workers can be tempted to steal or defraud a company if they are not supervised. In the chapter-opening story, the work of Darlyne Lopez was not supervised. The result was a $565,000 loss for Merrill Lynch. All employees, no matter what their position, need supervision.

■ **EXHIBIT 4-2** Organizational Chart of a Corporation

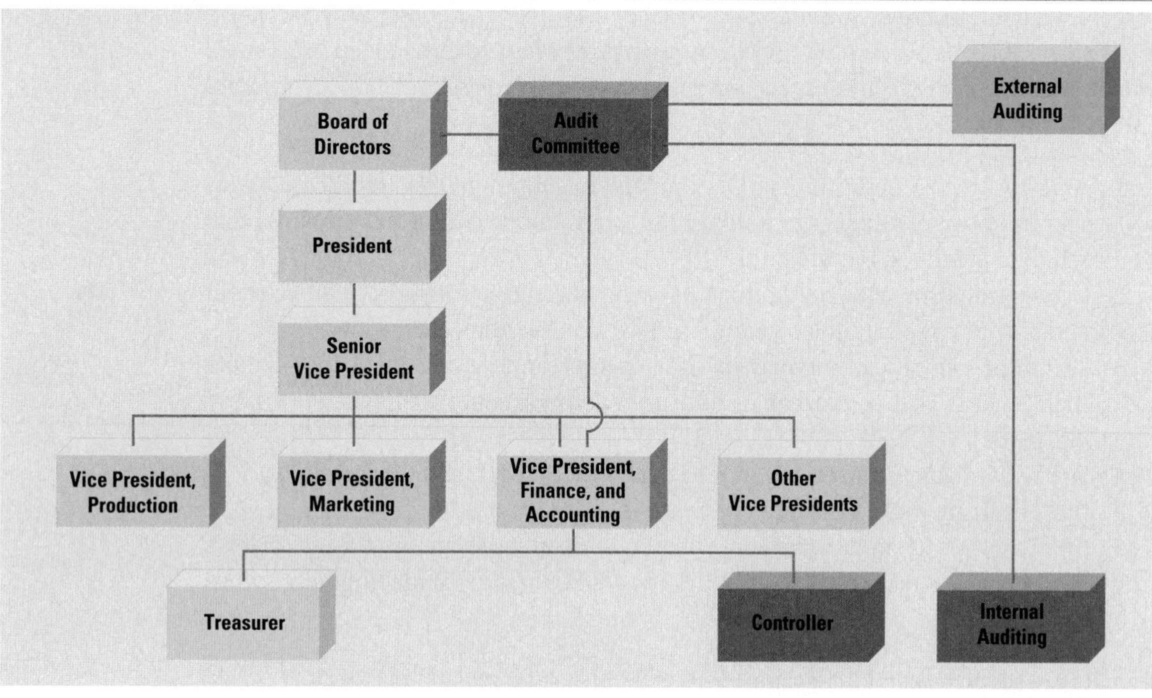

Separation of Duties. Smart managers divide responsibilities for transactions between two or more people. *Separation of duties* limits the chances for fraud and promotes the accuracy of accounting records. Separation of duties, often mentioned as the cornerstone of internal control, can be divided into two parts:

1. *Separation of operations from accounting.* Accounting should be completely separate from operating departments such as manufacturing and sales. For example, computer programmers should not operate a company's computers, because they can program the computer to write checks to themselves.
2. *Separation of the custody of assets from accounting.* Accountants should not be allowed to handle cash, and cashiers should have no access to the accounting records. If one employee has both cash-handling and accounting duties, that person can steal cash and conceal the theft by making a bogus entry on the books. We saw this breakdown of internal control in the chapter-opening story. In Exhibit 4-2, the treasurer has custody of the cash while the controller accounts for the cash. Neither person has both duties.

Check Point 4-1

Audit
A periodic examination of a company's financial statements and the accounting systems, controls, and records that produce them.

Internal and External Audits. An **audit** is an examination by an outside party. In accounting, an auditing firm examines the company's financial statements, accounting system, and internal controls. Auditors must be independent of the operations they examine. Managers immersed in day-to-day operations may overlook their own weaknesses.

Auditors cannot examine all the transactions during a period, so they must rely on the accounting system to produce accurate records. Auditors therefore evaluate the client's system of internal controls.

Audits can be internal or external. Exhibit 4-2 shows *internal auditors* as employees of the business, reporting to the audit committee. Internal auditors examine various segments of the organization to ensure that employees follow company policies.

External auditors are not employees of the companies they audit. They are hired by a company such as Merrill Lynch, Intel, or General Electric to audit the entity as a whole. External auditors are concerned mainly with the financial statements.

ACCOUNTING ALERT

Are the Outside Auditors Really Independent?

The Securities and Exchange Commission (SEC) requires publicly traded companies to have an annual audit by independent accountants. The purpose is to ensure that the information in the company's financial statements is relevant and reliable. Outside auditors are supposed to be completely independent of their clients so they can render unbiased opinions on the financial statements they audit. Recently Congress passed the Sarbanes-Oxley Act (SOX) to ensure the independence of the outside auditors. Consider two cases, and you will see a difference.

Case 1. John Smith was an independent CPA and served for 10 years as the lead auditor for Chi Alpha Enterprises. Recently Chi Alpha hired Smith as CFO. Now Smith will be directing all accounting matters at Chi Alpha. Smith plans to continue having his old CPA firm audit the financial statements of Chi Alpha.

Case 2. Rhonda Masters was an independent CPA and served for 5 years as the lead auditor for Phi Beta, Inc. Recently Phi Beta hired Masters as the CFO. Now Masters will be directing all accounting matters at Phi Beta. Masters plans to hire a new CPA firm to audit the financial statements of Phi Beta.

In which company's financial information would you have more confidence?

Under SOX, Chi Alpha cannot continue using its old audit firm for a period of one year after Smith leaves the firm. Why not? Because last year Smith audited Chi Alpha, and this year Smith is working for Chi Alpha. Smith's former partners in the CPA firm may be unduly influenced by Smith's work on last year's audit, and that may lead them to overlook problems at Chi Alpha.

In Case 2 the outside auditors look more independent because a new audit firm would have no apparent influence from either Masters or her former CPA firm. Under the provisions of SOX, after a one-year "cooling-off period," Masters would be free to hire her old CPA firm to audit Phi Beta. Case 2 is also better for another reason: In Case 1, Smith had audited Chi Alpha for 10 years. In Case 2, Masters had audited Phi Beta for only 5 years. In which case does the auditor look more independent? In Case 2, because over a 10-year period the auditor may tend to take more for granted and overlook client problems. This is why SOX requires the lead auditor to rotate every 7 years—to keep the auditor from growing too chummy with the client.

The take-away lesson from this accounting alert is:

- Ensure that the auditor is independent of the client. Otherwise, the client's financial statements may be biased.

Documents and Records. There are many different business *documents* and *records*. They include invoices (bills), paid checks, and accounting journals.

Documents should be prenumbered. A gap in the numbered sequence points to a missing document. Prenumbering sales receipts discourages theft by cashiers. The receipts can be checked against the actual amount of cash received. If the receipts are not prenumbered, the cashier can destroy a receipt and pocket the cash. With prenumbered receipts, the missing transaction can be identified.

Electronic and Computer Controls. Businesses use electronic devices to safeguard assets. Retailers such as **Target**, **Bradlees**, and **Sears** control inventories by attaching electronic sensors to merchandise. If a customer leaves the store with a sensor attached, an alarm sounds. According to Checkpoint Systems, these electronic sensors reduce theft by as much as 50%.

Computers provide dishonest employees using quirky ways to steal. We are all aware that dollar amounts get rounded to the nearest cent. A dishonest computer programmer had all the discarded third-digit amounts accumulated in a "Suspense" account (for example, $35.504; $.004 is the discarded third digit). He then programmed the computer to write a check to him for each week's total. This fraud was caught when the programmer's supervisors investigated how he could afford a new Lexus on a $38,000 salary.

The receivables department relies on computer operators to post to customer accounts. Proper posting can be ensured by devising customer account numbers so that the last digit is the sum of the previous digits (for example, 1359, where 1 + 3 + 5 = 9). Miskeying a customer account number triggers an error, and the computer won't accept the number.

E-Commerce, *e.fr@ud*, and Internal Controls

In an information economy, information provides access to assets. Companies must protect their assets, so some special internal controls safeguard the information that drives e-commerce.

Most companies, including Gap, Ford Motor Company, and Kinko's, transact business by e-commerce. Security issues are paramount: Companies must protect against hackers and system failures. KPMG, an international accounting firm, finds that hackers pose the greatest threat to system security.

To prevent *e.fr@ud*, experts in information technology, have devised the *onion model* of system security. Exhibit 4-3 shows how this model includes several layers of devices and techniques to protect hardware, software, and data.

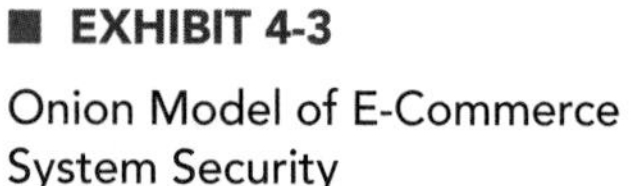

■ **EXHIBIT 4-3**

Onion Model of E-Commerce System Security

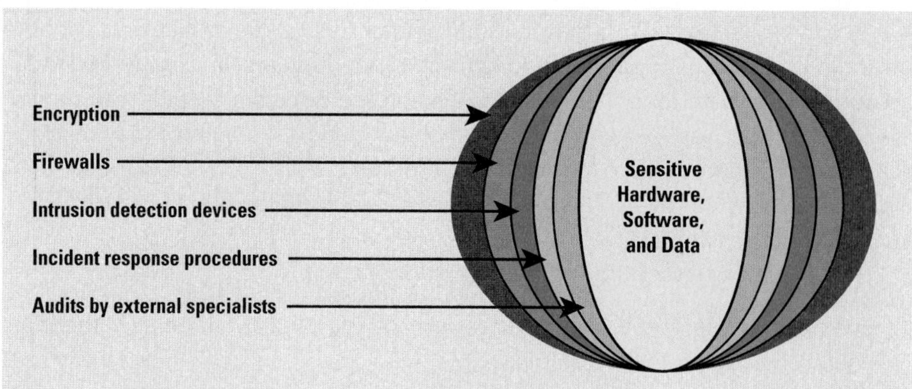

Encryption is the transformation of data by a mathematical process into a form that is unreadable by those without the secret decryption key. For example, Procter and Gamble (P&G) may send encrypted messages to buy chemicals online from DuPont. A hacker who intercepts this buy order would find it difficult to interpret P&G's message without the decryption key. Exhibit 4-4 illustrates the encryption process.

■ **EXHIBIT 4-4**

Encryption

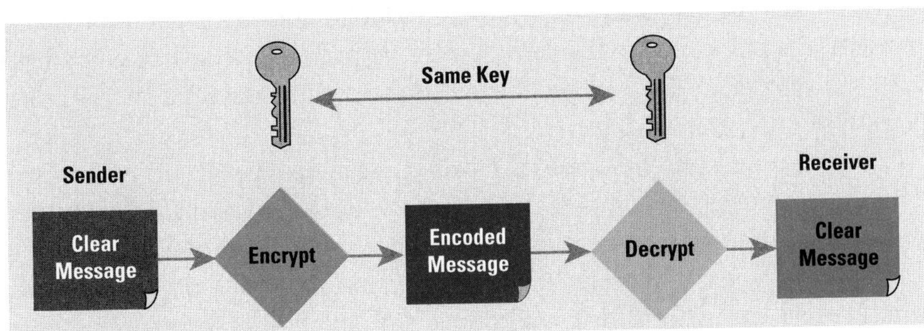

A *firewall* limits access to hardware, software, or data to persons within a network. The challenge with designing firewalls is to allow legitimate users to enter the system while denying access to intruders. Most companies use a series of firewalls, as illustrated in Exhibit 4-5.

■ **EXHIBIT 4-5**

How Firewalls Work

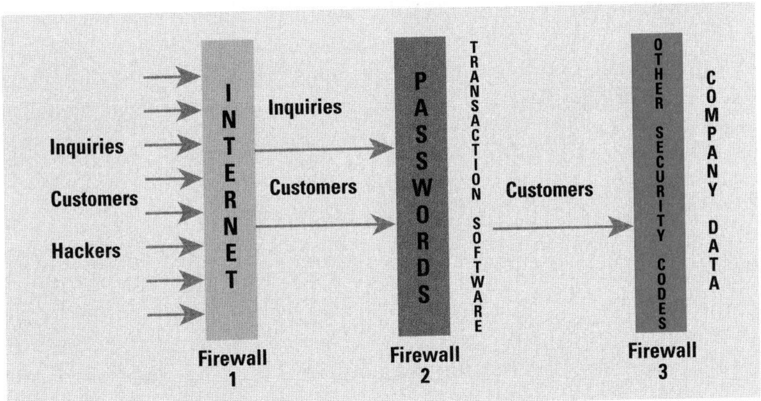

Let's return to the P&G and DuPont transaction. Suppose these two companies use the Internet to conduct e-commerce. P&G may log onto DuPont's Web site at www.dupont.com. Then P&G may go to "Quick Links for Customers and Suppliers" and proceed through the next firewall using a password. This process would continue until P&G sends an encrypted order to DuPont.

Hackers try to burrow into secure Web sites and unfortunately they sometimes succeed. The next layer of the onion model (Exhibit 4-3) consists of *intrusion detection devices*. These electronic monitors identify unauthorized entries to the system. Then incident response procedures kick in to apprehend hackers and remove them from the system. Finally, some companies pay for *audits* by external specialists, such as WebTrust, SysTrust, and CPA firms, to test their e-commerce systems. You may see their logos on e-commerce Web sites that you frequent.

Other Controls

Businesses keep cash and important business documents such as contracts and property titles in *fireproof vaults*. They use *burglar alarms* to protect buildings and other property. Retailers receive most of their cash from customers in their stores. To safeguard cash, they use *point-of-sale terminals* that serve as cash registers and record each transaction in the machine. Retailers deposit cash in the bank quickly—maybe several times a day. The sooner the money gets into the bank, the safer it is.

Credit card and bankcard sales require different controls. With no cash changing hands at the point of sale, the clerk has no chance to steal cash. Companies such as Target encrypt their data and use firewalls to secure the data transmitted electronically to VISA or MasterCard.

Companies can purchase *fidelity bonds* on cashiers. The bond is an insurance policy that reimburses the company for losses due to employee theft. Before issuing a fidelity bond, the insurance company investigates the employee's past. *Mandatory vacations* and *job rotation* require that employees be trained to do a variety of jobs. General Electric, Eastman Kodak, and other large companies move employees from job to job. If Merrill Lynch had forced Darlyne Lopez to take a vacation, it probably would have caught her theft sooner.

stop AND think. . .

Ralph works the late movie at Galaxy Theater. Occasionally, he must both sell the tickets and take them as customers enter the theater. Standard procedure requires Ralph to tear the tickets, give one-half to the customer, and keep the other half. To control cash receipts, the theater manager compares each night's cash receipts with the number of tickets stubs on hand.

What is the internal control weakness in this situation? What might a dishonest employee do to steal cash? What additional steps should the manager take to strengthen the control over cash receipts?

Answer:

The weakness is the lack of separation of duties. Ralph not only receives cash from customers but also controls the tickets. Ralph should handle either cash or the tickets, but not both. If he were dishonest, he could fail to issue a ticket and then keep the customer's cash. To control that behavior, the manager could physically count the people watching a movie and compare that number with the ticket stubs collected. Or, the manager could account for all ticket stubs by serial number. Missing serial numbers raise questions for investigation.

Limitations of Internal Control

Unfortunately, most internal control measures can be overcome. Two or more employees working together—*colluding*—can defraud the firm. One of the most dramatic frauds in U.S. business history was a case of massive collusion. High-level managers of Equity Funding of America, an insurance company, okayed the writing of phony insurance policies. In fact, the Equity Funding employees held "parties" to create the fictitious insurance policies. Whenever top managers are involved in a fraud, or when they fail to supervise employees, internal controls may fail.

A system of internal control that is too complex can strangle the business with red tape. Managers must make sensible judgments. Investments in internal control must be worth more than they cost.

ACCOUNTING ALERT

Three Faces of Internal Control

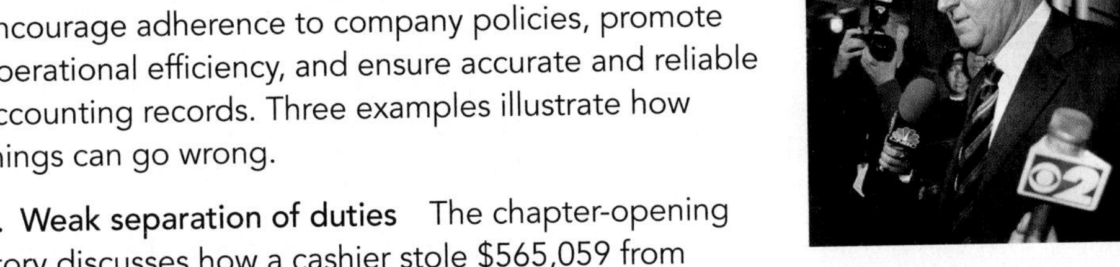

Internal controls are designed to safeguard assets, encourage adherence to company policies, promote operational efficiency, and ensure accurate and reliable accounting records. Three examples illustrate how things can go wrong.

1. Weak separation of duties The chapter-opening story discusses how a cashier stole $565,059 from Merrill Lynch. Darlyne Lopez, the cashier, received incoming deposits from customers. The main duty of a cashier is to *handle* cash—so no problem there. But Lopez also had access to the accounting records. Giving the cashier access to the accounting records offers the opportunity to steal and doctor the records to cover the theft. This is exactly what happened.

The most obvious way to limit this risk is to deny the cashier access to the accounting records. But in many companies, especially small businesses, it isn't feasible to separate all duties. It may have been inefficient to deny the cashier access to the records. To manage its risk, Merrill Lynch could have done several things:

- Require employees to take vacations. That way other employees must review the work of the one on vacation. Discrepancies will probably come to light.
- Routinely check on the cashier's work. For example, another employee can reconcile customer accounts. Discrepancies can then be detected.
- Mail questionnaires to customers, and ask them to confirm their account balances to a responsible official of the company. Investigate all discrepancies.

It appears that Merrill Lynch failed to take these actions.

2. No proper authorization Dennis Kozlowski, former CEO of Tyco International, may have set the world record for squandering company resources. Kozlowski took Tyco from an also-ran to the top tier with a dazzling array of company acquisitions. For a time Kozlowski was hailed as one of the most innovative executives in America. But he got greedy and wound up in court defending against charges of looting Tyco of $600 million. Among other things, Kozlowski threw a lavish party for hundreds of guests on a Mediterranean island to celebrate his wife's birthday—and had the company pick up the tab. How did Kozlowski get away with such outrageous behavior?

It appears that Kozlowski did many deals *without* the approval of Tyco's board of directors. In fact, he did so many deals that it was impossible to keep up with him. Proper authorization broke down at Tyco International. The board of directors forgot to monitor the activities of the CEO. Everyone, even the CEO, must be held accountable.

3. Inaccurate accounting records At one time, MCI (then known as WorldCom) looked poised to take over the world of long-distance telephoning. Then cell phones became popular and siphoned off lots of MCI business. Rather than report declining profits, top executives at MCI started cooking the books. What were they doing?

A strange series of accounting entries on MCI's books caught the eye of a mid-level executive. Numerous entries totaling $10.6 billion debited assets and credited expenses. These entries were very strange indeed. When a company buys assets, it usually credits cash or a payable—not an expense. MCI was intentionally understating expenses in order to overstate assets and profits. MCI's CFO has pleaded guilty of intentional fraud, and the company is trying to recover.

The Bank Account as a Control Device

Cash is the most liquid asset because it is the medium of exchange. Cash is easy to conceal and relatively easy to steal. As a result, most businesses have elaborate controls to safeguard cash.

Keeping cash in a bank account is important because banks safeguard cash and also provide independent records of cash transactions. To take full advantage of these control features, the business should deposit all cash receipts in the bank and make all cash payments through it (except petty cash, which we cover later in this chapter).

Check
Document instructing a bank to pay the designated person or business the specified amount of money.

To draw money from an account, the depositor writes a **check**, the document that instructs the bank to pay a specified amount of money. There are three parties to a check:

- the *maker*, who signs the check
- the *payee*, to whom the check is drawn; and
- the *bank*, on which the check is drawn.

Checks are serially numbered and preprinted with the name and address of the maker and the bank. Exhibit 4-6 shows a check drawn by Business Research, Inc. The *remittance advice* is an optional attachment that gives the reason for the payment. Business Research requires two signatures.

■ **EXHIBIT 4-6**
Check with Remittance Advice

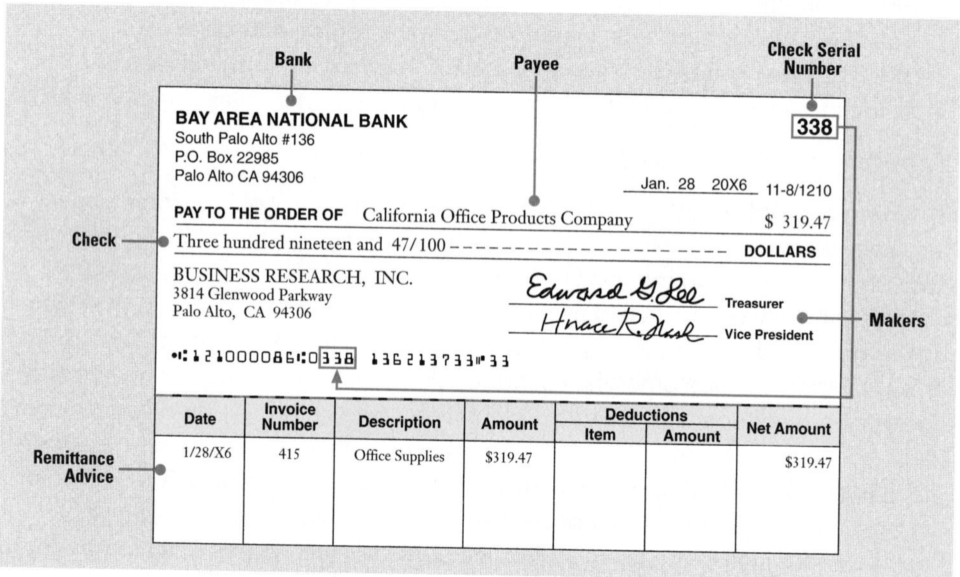

Date	Invoice Number	Description	Amount	Deductions Item	Deductions Amount	Net Amount
1/28/X6	415	Office Supplies	$319.47			$319.47

Bank statement
Document showing the beginning and ending balances of a particular bank account listing the month's transactions that affected the account.

Banks send monthly **bank statements** to their depositors. Exhibit 4-7 is the bank statement of Business Research, Inc. for the month of January. We will use this bank statement to illustrate a bank reconciliation.

Electronic fund transfer (EFT)
System that transfers cash by electronic communication rather than by paper documents.

Electronic fund transfer (EFT) relies on electronic communications—not paper documents—to transfer cash. It is much cheaper to pay employees by EFT (direct deposit) than by issuing payroll checks. Also, many people pay their bills by prior arrangement with the bank and never write checks. The bank statement lists EFT cash receipts and EFT cash payments along with the other transactions. Exhibit 4-7 includes one of each.

■ EXHIBIT 4-7 Bank Statement

ACCOUNT STATEMENT

BAY AREA NATIONAL BANK
SOUTH PALO ALTO #136 P.O. BOX 22985 PALO ALTO, CA 94306

Business Research, Inc.
3814 Glenwood Parkway
Palo Alto, CA 94306

CHECKING ACCOUNT 136–213733

CHECKING ACCOUNT SUMMARY AS OF 01/31/X6

BEGINNING BALANCE	TOTAL DEPOSITS	TOTAL WITHDRAWALS	SERVICE CHARGES	ENDING BALANCE
6,556.12	4,352.64	4,963.00	14.25	5,931.51

CHECKING ACCOUNT TRANSACTIONS

DEPOSITS	DATE	AMOUNT
Deposit	01/04	1,000.00
Deposit	01/04	112.00
Deposit	01/08	194.60
EFT—Collection of rent	01/17	904.03
Bank Collection	01/26	2,114.00
Interest	01/31	28.01

CHARGES	DATE	AMOUNT
Service Charge	01/31	14.25
Checks:		

CHECKS

Number	Date	Amount
332	01/12	3,000.00
656	01/06	100.00
333	01/12	150.00
334	01/10	100.00
335	01/06	100.00
336	01/31	1,100.00

BALANCES

Date	Balance	Date	Balance
12/31	6,556.12	01/17	5,264.75
01/04	7,616.12	01/20	4,903.75
01/06	7,416.12	01/26	7,017.75
01/08	7,610.72	01/31	5,931.51
01/12	4,360.72		

OTHER CHARGES	DATE	AMOUNT
NSF	01/04	52.00
EFT—Insurance	01/20	361.00

MONTHLY SUMMARY

Withdrawals: 8   Minimum Balance: 4,360.00   Average Balance: 6,091.00

The Bank Reconciliation

There are two records of a business's cash:

1. The company's Cash account on its own books.
2. The bank statement, which shows the actual amount of cash in the bank.

The cash balance on the books rarely equals the balance shown on the bank statement. But both the books and the bank may be correct because there is a time lag in recording transactions. When a firm writes a check, it immediately credits the Cash account. The bank, however, will not subtract the check from the business's balance until the bank receives the check and pays it. This step may take a few days. Likewise, the business immediately debits Cash for all cash receipts, but it may take a day or so for the bank to add this amount to the firm's balance.

To ensure accurate financial records, the firm's accountant creates a document called the **bank reconciliation**. The bank reconciliation ensures that the company accounts for all its cash transactions and also that the bank records are correct.

Bank reconciliation
A document explaining the reasons for the difference between a depositor's records and the bank's records about the depositor's cash.

Items for Reconciliation. The items that cause differences between the bank balance and the book balance include

Deposit in transit
A deposit recorded by the company but not yet by its bank.

Outstanding check
A check issued by the company and recorded on its books but not yet paid by its bank.

Bank collection
Collection of money by the bank on behalf of a depositor.

Nonsufficient funds (NSF) check
A "hot" check, one for which the payer's bank account has insufficient money to pay the check. NSF checks are cash receipts that turn out to be worthless.

- ***Items recorded by the company but not yet recorded by the bank.***
  a. **Deposits in transit** (outstanding deposits). The company has recorded these cash receipts, but the bank has not.
  b. **Outstanding checks**. The company has recorded cash payments on its books, but the bank has not yet paid them.
- ***Items recorded by the bank but not yet recorded by the company. We may learn of these items from the bank statement.***
  a. **Bank collections**. Banks collect money on behalf of depositors. Many businesses have their customers pay directly to the company bank account. This practice, called a ***lockbox system***, places the business's cash in circulation immediately.
  b. **Electronic funds transfers**. The bank may receive or pay cash on behalf of the depositor. The bank statement lists the EFTs.
  c. **Service charge and the cost of printed checks.** Banks charge these fees.
  d. **Interest revenue earned on checking account.** Depositors earn interest if they keep a large enough balance of cash in their account.
  e. **Nonsufficient funds (NSF) checks** received from customers. NSF checks are cash receipts that turn out to be worthless. Deduct NSF checks on the book side of the reconciliation. Several other items are treated in the same way as NSF checks. Banks return checks to the payee if (1) the maker's account has closed, (2) the date is stale ("void after 30 days"), (3) the signature is not authorized, or (4) the check has been altered.
- ***Errors by the company or the bank.*** The bank may improperly decrease the bank balance of Business Research, Inc., for a check drawn by another company. Also Business Research may record a check incorrectly. All errors must be corrected, and the corrections will be a part of the bank reconciliation.

OBJECTIVE

2 Use a bank reconciliation as a control device

Bank Reconciliation Illustrated. The bank statement in Exhibit 4-7 indicates that the January 31 bank balance of Business Research, Inc. is $5,931.51. However, the company's Cash account on the books has a balance of $3,294.21 (Exhibit 4-8). The following reconciling items explain the difference:

1. The January 31 deposit of $1,591.63 does not appear on the bank statement. This is a deposit in transit.
2. The bank erroneously charged Business Research, Inc. for $100 —check number 656—written by Research Associates, another company (Exhibit 4-7). This is a bank error and must be corrected on the bank side of the reconciliation.
3. Five company checks issued late in January and recorded by Business Research have not been paid by the bank. These are outstanding checks.

Check No.	Date	Amount
337	Jan. 27	$ 286.00
338	28	319.47
339	28	83.00
340	29	203.14
341	30	458.53
Total		$1,350.14

■ **EXHIBIT 4-8**

Cash Records of Business Research, Inc.

ACCOUNT Cash

Date	Item	Debit	Credit	Balance
20X6				
Jan. 1	Balance			6,556.12
2	Cash receipt	1,112.00		7,668.12
7	Cash receipt	194.60		7,862.72
31	Cash payments		6,160.14	1,702.58
31	Cash receipt	1,591.63		3,294.21

Cash Payments

Check No.	Amount	Check No.	Amount
332	$3,000.00	338	$ 319.47
333	510.00	339	83.00
334	100.00	340	203.14
335	100.00	341	458.53
336	1,100.00		
337	286.00	Total	$6,160.14

Check Point 4-2

4. The bank received $904.03 by EFT on behalf of Business Research, Inc. This EFT is like a bank collection.
5. The bank collected for Business Research a note receivable, $2,114 (including interest revenue of $214). This is another bank collection.
6. The bank statement shows interest revenue of $28.01, which the company has earned on its cash balance.
7. Business Research wrote check number 333 to pay Brown Company $150 on account. But Business Research credited cash for $510. This error created a $360 understatement of the Cash balance on the books. Correct book errors on the book side of the reconciliation.
8. The bank service charge for the month was $14.25.
9. The bank statement shows an NSF check for $52, received from a customer.
10. Business Research pays insurance expense monthly by EFT. The company has not yet recorded this $361 payment.

Exhibit 4-9 is the bank reconciliation based on the preceding data. After the reconciliation, the adjusted bank balance equals the adjusted book balance. This equality checks the accuracy of both the bank and the books.

Here is a summary of how to treat the various reconciling items:

Bank Balance	Book Balance
Add deposits in transit.	*Add* bank collection items, interest revenue, and EFT receipts.
Subtract outstanding checks.	*Subtract* service charges, NSF checks, and EFT payments.
Add or *subtract* corrections of bank errors, as appropriate.	*Add* or *subtract* corrections of book errors, as appropriate.

■ **EXHIBIT 4-9**

Bank Reconciliation

Business Research, Inc.
Bank Reconciliation
January 31, 20X6

Bank			**Books**		
Balance, January 31		$5,931.51	Balance, January 31		$3,294.21
Add:			Add:		
1. Deposit of January 30 in transit		1,591.63	4. EFT receipt of rent revenue		904.03
2. Correction of bank error—Research Associates check 656 erroneously charged against company account		100.00	5. Bank collection of note receivable, including interest revenue of $214		2,114.00
			6. Interest revenue earned on bank balance		28.01
			7. Correction of book error—overstated amount of check no. 333		360.00
		7,623.14			6,700.25
3. Less: Outstanding checks:			Less:		
No. 337	$286.00		8. Service charge	$14.25	
No. 338	319.47		9. NSF check	52.00	
No. 339	83.00		10. EFT payment of insurance expense	361.00	(427.25)
No. 340	203.14				
No. 341	458.53	(1,350.14)			
Adjusted bank balance		$6,273.00	Adjusted book balance		$6,273.00

These amounts should agree

Check Point 4-3

Accounting for Transactions from the Reconciliation. The bank reconciliation does not directly affect the accounts (the books). The reconciliation is entirely separate from the company's books. Based on the reconciliation in Exhibit 4-9, Business Research, Inc., makes the following journal entries. Numbers correspond to the reconciling items described earlier.

(4)	Cash	904.03	
	Rent Revenue		904.03
	Receipt of monthly rent.		
(5)	Cash	2,114.00	
	Notes Receivable		1,900.00
	Interest Revenue		214.00
	Note receivable collected by bank.		
(6)	Cash	28.01	
	Interest Revenue		28.01
	Interest earned on bank balance.		
(7)	Cash	360.00	
	Accounts Payable		360.00
	Correction of check no. 333.		
(8)	Miscellaneous Expense*	14.25	
	Cash		14.25
	Bank service charge.		
(9)	Accounts Receivable	52.00	
	Cash		52.00
	NSF customer check returned by bank.		
(10)	Insurance Expense	361.00	
	Cash		361.00
	Payment of monthly insurance.		

Check Point 4-4

**Note:* Miscellaneous Expense is debited for the bank service charge because the service charge pertains to no particular expense category.

stop AND think. . .

The bank statement balance is $4,500 and shows a service charge of $15, interest earned of $5, and an NSF check for $300. Deposits in transit total $1,200; outstanding checks are $575. The bookkeeper recorded as $152 a check of $125 in payment of an account payable.

1. What is the adjusted bank balance?
2. What was the book balance of cash before the reconciliation?

Answers:

1. $5,125 ($4,500 + $1,200 – $575).
2. $5,408 ($5,125 + $15 – $5 + $300 – $27). The adjusted book and bank balances are the same. The answer can be determined by working backward from the adjusted balance.

Using the Bank Reconciliation to Control Cash

The bank reconciliation is a powerful control device. Randy Vaughn is a CPA in Houston, Texas. He owns several apartment complexes that are managed by his aunt. His aunt signs up tenants, collects the monthly rents, arranges custodial and maintenance work, hires and fires employees, writes the checks, and performs the bank reconciliation. In short, she does it all. This concentration of duties in one person is evidence of weak internal control. Vaughn's aunt could be stealing from him, and as a CPA he is aware of this possibility.

Vaughn trusts his aunt because she is a member of the family. Nevertheless, he exercises some controls over her management of his apartments. Vaughn periodically drops by his properties to see whether the custodial/maintenance staff is keeping the property in good condition. To control cash, Vaughn occasionally examines the bank reconciliation that his aunt has performed. Vaughn would know immediately if his aunt is writing checks to herself. By examining each check, Vaughn establishes control over cash payments.

Vaughn has a simple method for controlling cash receipts. He knows the occupancy level of his apartments. He also knows the monthly rent he charges. He multiplies the number of apartments—say 20—by the monthly rent (which averages $500 per unit) to arrive at expected monthly rent revenue of $10,000. By tracing the $10,000 revenue to the bank statement, Vaughn can tell if all his rent money went into his bank account. To keep his aunt on her toes, Vaughn lets her know that he periodically audits her work.

Check Point 4-5

Check Point 4-6

Control activities such as these are critical. If there are only a few employees, separation of duties may not be feasible. The manager must control operations, or the assets will slip away.

MID-CHAPTER Summary Problem

The Cash account of Curtis Clements, Inc., at February 28, 20X6 follows.

Cash

Feb. 1	Balance	3,995	Feb. 3	400
6		800	12	3,100
15		1,800	19	1,100
23		1,100	25	500
28		2,400	27	900
Feb. 28	Balance	4,095		

Clements deposits all cash receipts in the bank and makes all cash payments by check. Clements receives this bank statement on February 28, 20X6 (as always, negative amounts are in parentheses):

Bank Statement for February 20X6

Beginning balance		$3,995
Deposits:		
Feb. 7	$ 800	
15	1,800	
24	1,100	3,700
Checks (total per day):		
Feb. 8	$ 400	
16	3,100	
23	1,100	(4,600)
Other items:		
Service charge		(10)
NSF check from customer		(700)
Bank collection of note receivable		1,000*
EFT—monthly rent expense		(330)
Interest on account balance		15
Ending balance		$3,070

*Includes interest of $119

Required

1. Prepare the bank reconciliation of Curtis Clements, Inc., at February 28, 20X6.
2. Record the journal entries based on the bank reconciliation.

Answers

Requirement 1

Curtis Clements, Inc.
Bank Reconciliation
February 28, 20X6

Bank:

Balance, February 28, 20X6		$3,070
Add:	Deposit of February 28 in transit	2,400
		5,470
Less:	Outstanding checks issued on Feb. 25 ($500) and Feb. 27 ($900)	(1,400)
Adjusted bank balance, February 28, 20X6		$4,070

Books:

Balance, February 28, 20X6			$4,095
Add:	Bank collection of note receivable, including interest of $119		1,000
	Interest earned on bank balance		15
			5,110
Less:	Service charge	$ 10	
	NSF check	700	
	EFT—Rent expense	330	(1,040)
Adjusted book balance, February 28, 20X6			$4,070

Requirement 2

Date	Account	Debit	Credit
Feb. 28	Cash	1,000	
	Note Receivable ($1,000 – $119)		881
	Interest Revenue		119
	Note receivable collected by bank.		
28	Cash	15	
	Interest Revenue		15
	Interest earned on bank balance.		
28	Miscellaneous Expense	10	
	Cash		10
	Bank service charge.		
Feb. 28	Accounts Receivable	700	
	Cash		700
	NSF check returned by bank.		
28	Rent Expense	330	
	Cash		330
	Monthly rent expense.		

Controlling and Managing Cash

Internal Control: Cash Receipts

OBJECTIVE

3 **Apply** internal controls to cash receipts and cash payments

Internal control over cash receipts is designed to ensure that all cash is deposited in the bank and no collections are lost. Each source of cash receipts—over the counter or through the mail—calls for its own security measures.

Over-the-Counter Receipts. The point-of-sale terminal (cash register) offers control over cash receipts. Consider a Macy's store. Company policy requires issuance of a sales receipt so that each sale gets recorded. The cash drawer opens only when the clerk enters an amount on the keypad, and the machine records each transaction. Exhibit 4-10 diagrams this process.

■ **EXHIBIT 4-10**
Cash Receipts Over the Counter

At the end of the day, a manager compares the cash in the register with the machine's record of the day's sales. The company treasurer then deposits the cash in the bank, and the total amount of the cash receipts goes electronically to the accounting department, which debits Cash.

Mail Receipts. Many companies use a lockbox system for cash receipts by mail. Customers send checks directly to an address that is essentially a bank account, so company personnel do not handle incoming cash. The lockbox system improves efficiency because the cash goes to work for the company immediately.

Check Point 4-7

If the company receives cash by mail, all incoming mail should be opened by a mail room employee. This person should compare the check received with the attached remittance advice. The mail room clerk totals the remittance advices. At the end of the day, this control total is given to a responsible official for verification. Cash receipts go to the treasurer, who prepares the bank deposit.

The mail room employee forwards the remittance advices to the accounting department, which debits Cash and credits customers' accounts receivable. As a final step, the controller compares the three records of the day's cash receipts:

- The control total from the mail room.
- The bank deposit amount from the cashier. The money went into the bank.
- The debit to Cash from the accounting department. The books are updated.

Exhibit 4-11 diagrams the cash receipts by mail process.

■ **EXHIBIT 4-11** Cash Receipts by Mail

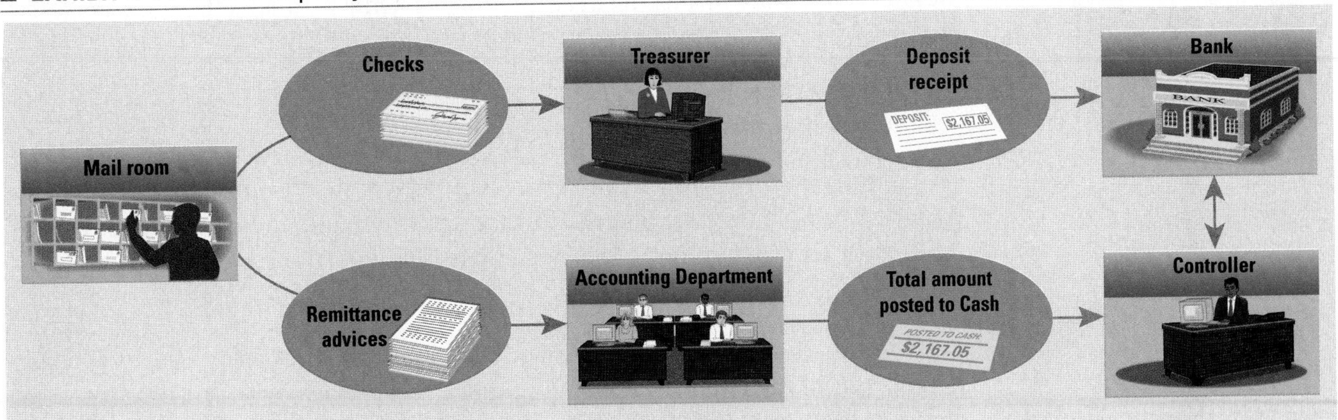

Internal Control: Cash Payments

It is critical for an organization to control cash payments, by both checks and petty cash.

Payment by Check. Payment by check is an important internal control. First, the check provides a record of each payment. Second, to be valid, the check must be signed by an authorized official. Suppose the business is buying inventory for sale to customers. Let's examine the process of paying for inventory.

The purchasing process starts when the company identifies the need for merchandise and prepares a ***purchase request*** (or ***requisition***). The purchasing department specializes in buying and sends a ***purchase order*** to the supplier, the outside company that sells the needed goods. When the supplier ships the goods, the supplier also sends the *invoice*, or bill, which indicates the need to pay. Exhibit 4-12 diagrams the purchasing/paying process.

Check Point 4-8

■ **EXHIBIT 4-12**

The Purchasing/Paying Process

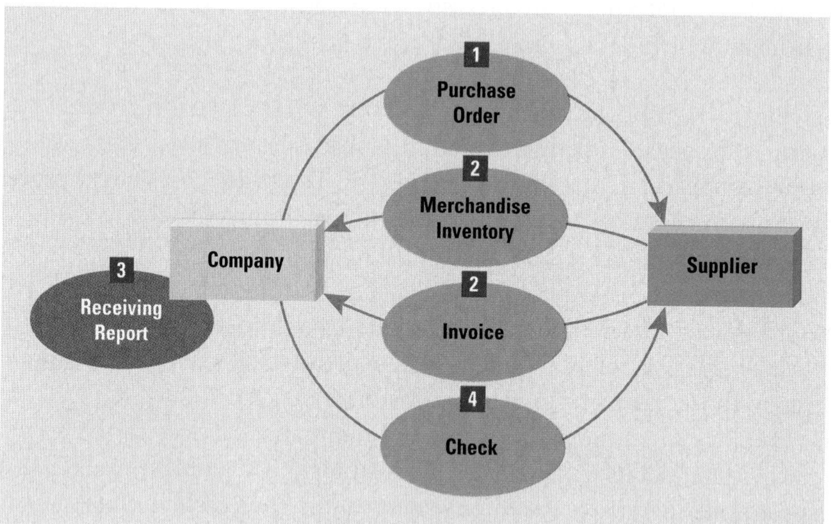

■ **EXHIBIT 4-13**

Payment Packet

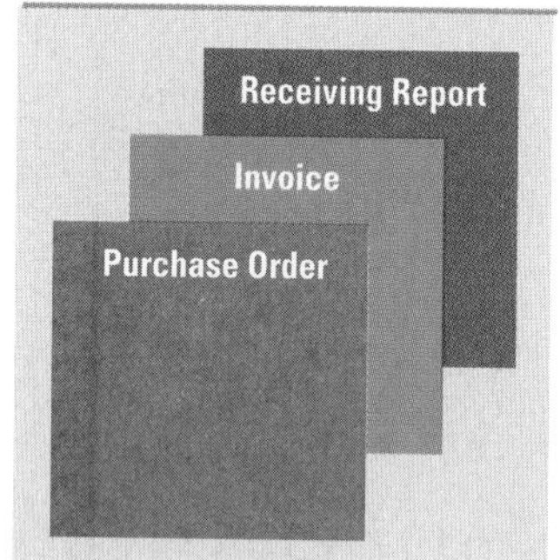

As the goods arrive, the receiving department checks them for damage and lists the merchandise received on a document called the *receiving report*. The accounting department combines all the foregoing documents, checks them for agreement, and forwards this *payment packet* to designated officers for approval and payment. The packet includes the purchase order, invoice, and receiving report, as shown in Exhibit 4-13.

Before approving the payment, the controller or the treasurer should examine the packet to ensure that all the documents agree. Only then does the company know that

1. It received the goods ordered.
2. It pays only for the goods received.

After payment, the check signer can punch a hole through the payment packet. This hole denotes that the invoice has been paid and discourages dishonest employees from running the documents through the system for a duplicate payment.

Petty cash
Fund containing a small amount of cash that is used to pay minor amounts.

Petty Cash. It would be wasteful to write separate checks for an executive's taxi fare, floppy disks needed right away, or delivery of a package across town. Therefore, companies keep a **petty cash** fund on hand to pay such minor amounts.

The petty cash fund is opened with a particular amount of cash. A check for that amount is then issued to Petty Cash. Assume that on February 28, **Cisco Systems**, the worldwide leader in networks for the Internet, establishes a petty cash fund of $500 in a sales department. The custodian of the petty cash fund cashes the check and places $500 in the fund, which may be a cash box or other device.

For each petty cash payment, the custodian prepares a *petty cash ticket* to list the item purchased. The sum of the cash in the petty cash fund plus the total of the ticket amounts should equal the opening balance at all times—in this case, $500. The Petty Cash account keeps its $500 balance at all times. Maintaining the Petty Cash account at this balance, supported by the fund (cash plus tickets), is how an **imprest system** works. The control feature is that it clearly identifies the amount for which the custodian is responsible.

Imprest system
A way to account for petty cash by maintaining a constant balance in the petty cash account, supported by the fund (cash plus payment tickets) totaling the same amount.

Using a Budget to Manage Cash

OBJECTIVE

4 **Use** a budget to manage cash

Managers control operations with a budget. A **budget** is a financial plan that helps coordinate business activities. Cash is budgeted most often.

Budget
A quantitative expression of a plan that helps managers coordinate the entity's activities.

How for example does Merrill Lynch decide when to invest in new wireless technology? How will Merrill Lynch decide how much to spend? Will borrowing be needed, or can Merrill Lynch finance the purchase with internally generated cash? Similarly, by what process do you decide how much to spend on your education? On an automobile? On a house? All these decisions depend to some degree on the information that a cash budget provides.

A cash budget helps a company or an individual manage cash by planning receipts and payments during a future period. The company must determine how much cash it will need and then decide whether or not operations will bring in the needed cash. Managers proceed as follows:

1. Start with the entity's cash balance at the beginning of the period, the amount left over from the preceding period.
2. Add the budgeted cash receipts and subtract the budgeted cash payments.
3. The beginning balance plus receipts and minus payments equals the expected cash balance at the end of the period.
4. Compare the ending cash balance to the budgeted cash balance at the end of the period. Managers know the minimum amount of cash they need (the budgeted balance). If the budget shows excess cash, they can invest the excess. But if the expected cash balance falls below the budgeted balance, the company will need to obtain additional financing. The budget is a valuable tool for helping the company plan for the future.

The budget period can span any length of time—a day, a week, a month, or a year. Exhibit 4-14 shows a cash budget for **Gap, Inc.**, for the year ended January 31, 20X6. Study it carefully, because at some point you will use a cash budget.

Gap's hypothetical cash budget in Exhibit 4-14 begins with $202.6 million of cash (line 1). Then add budgeted cash receipts and subtract budgeted payments. In this case, Gap expects to end the year with a *negative* cash balance of $213.9 million (line 11). Assume that Gap managers wish to maintain a cash balance of at least $200 million (line 12). They need to arrange $413.9 million of financing (line 13). Add lines 11 and 12 to arrive at the amount of new financing needed.

✓Check Point 4-9

✓Check Point 4-10

The cash budget helps managers arrange any new financing in an orderly manner. With enough cash, Gap can expand its stores and search out new products that keep customers coming back.

■ **EXHIBIT 4-14**
Cash Budget

Gap, Inc.
Cash Budget (Hypothetical)
For the Year Ended January 31, 20X6

			(In millions)
(1)	Cash balance, January 31, 20X5		$ 202.6
	Budgeted cash receipts:		
(2)	Collections from customers		2,858.3
(3)	Interest and dividends on investments		6.2
(4)	Sale of store fixtures		4.9
			3,072.0
	Budgeted cash payments:		
(5)	Purchases of inventory	$1,906.2	
(6)	Operating expenses	561.0	
(7)	Expansion of existing stores	106.4	
(8)	Opening of new stores	344.6	
(9)	Payment of long-term debt	148.7	
(10)	Payment of dividends	219.0	3,285.9
(11)	Cash available (needed) before new financing		(213.9)
(12)	Budgeted cash balance, January 31, 20X6		(200.0)
(13)	Cash available for additional investments, or (New financing needed)		$ (413.9)

Reporting Cash on the Balance Sheet

Most companies have numerous bank accounts, but they usually combine all cash amounts into a single total called "Cash and Cash Equivalents." Cash equivalents include liquid assets such as time deposits and certificates of deposit, which are interest-bearing accounts that can be withdrawn with no penalty. Slightly less liquid than cash, they are sufficiently similar to be reported along with cash. The balance sheet of Merrill Lynch (repeated from page 172) reported the following:

Merrill Lynch & Co.,
Balance Sheet (Excerpts, adapted)
For the Year Ended December 31, 2003

	(In millions)
Assets	
Cash and cash equivalents	$119
Cash pledged as collateral	296

Compensating Balance Agreements

The Cash account on the balance sheet reports the liquid assets available for day-to-day use. None of the cash balance is restricted in any way.

Any restricted amount of cash should *not* be reported as Cash on the balance sheet. For example, on the Merrill Lynch balance sheet, *cash pledged as collateral* is reported separately because that cash is not available for day-to-day use. Instead, Merrill Lynch has pledged the cash as security (collateral) for a loan. If Merrill Lynch fails to pay the loan, the lender can take the pledged cash. For this reason, the pledged cash is less liquid.

Also, banks often lend money under a compensating balance agreement. The borrower agrees to maintain a minimum balance in a checking account at all times. This minimum balance becomes a long-term asset and is therefore not cash in the normal sense.

Suppose **Pier 1 Imports** borrowed $5 million at 7% from First Interstate Bank and agreed to keep 10% ($500,000) on deposit at all times. The net result of the compensating balance agreement is that Pier 1 Imports actually borrowed only $4.5 million. And by paying 7% interest on the full $5 million, Pier 1's actual interest rate is higher than 7%.

Ethics and Accounting

An article in the *Wall Street Journal* quoted a Russian entrepreneur as saying that he was getting ahead in business by breaking laws. He stated, "Older people have an ethics problem. By that I mean they *have* ethics." Conversely, Roger Smith, former chairman of General Motors, said: "Ethical practice is, quite simply, good business." First and foremost, practicing good ethics is the right thing to do. Second, unethical behavior always comes back to haunt you.

Corporate and Professional Codes of Ethics

Most large companies have a code of ethics designed to encourage ethical behavior by employees. But codes of conduct are not enough: Senior management must set a high ethical tone that is steadily reinforced by management words and actions. Managers must make it clear that the Company will not tolerate unethical conduct. In the chapter-opening story, Ms. Lopez went to prison for her theft. Merrill Lynch meant it when it required "the highest standards of ethical conduct."

Check Point 4-11

As professionals, accountants are expected to maintain higher standards than society in general. Their ability to do business depends entirely on their reputations. Most independent accountants are members of the American Institute of Certified Public Accountants (AICPA) and must abide by the *AICPA Code of Professional Conduct*. Accountants who are members of the Institute of Management Accountants are bound by the *Standards of Ethical Conduct for Management Accountants*. Unacceptable actions can result in expulsion from the organization—a penalty that makes it difficult to remain in the accounting profession.

Ethical Issues in Accounting

OBJECTIVE

5 **Weigh** ethical judgments in business

In many situations, the ethical choice is clear-cut. The computer programmer (Page 178) who bought a Lexus with discarded amounts from the computer was stealing from the company and lost his job. Equity Funding (page 180) defrauded thousands of investors and went out of business. MCI (page 181) got into trouble with the Securities and Exchange Commission (SEC) by putting out inaccurate financial statements. In accounting, the fundamental ethical issue is whether the accounting data that are made available to the public are complete and accurate. The Securities Exchange Act of 1934 gives investors broad powers to obtain a legal judgment against a company whose financial statements are incomplete.

A conflict of interest creates an ethical dilemma: someone plays two roles that directly compete. For example, a judge will not decide a lawsuit when a relative is involved in the case. Judges *recuse* themselves from the case because of the natural temptation to favor a relative.

As CFO of Enron Corporation, Andrew Fastow managed Enron's finances. In this position he was honor-bound to act in the best interest of Enron stockholders. In his capacity as the principal of the outside partnerships he was also honor-bound to act in the best interest of the investors who owned those partnerships. But Fastow negotiated transactions between Enron and the partnerships. Exhibit 4-15 illustrates the conflict of interest:

■ EXHIBIT 4-15

Conflict of Interest

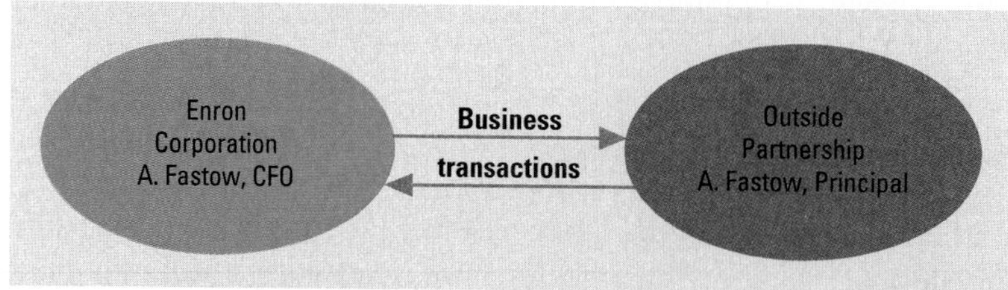

A conflict of interests arose when Enron did business with the outside partnerships. Andrew Fastow negotiated both sides of the deal, so the values of the items bought and sold may have been rigged to come out too low or too high. Investors considering buying Enron stock received financial statements based on faulty values. Flawed income amounts led investors to pay unreasonable amounts for Enron stock. Then, when the truth came out, Enron's stock tumbled and a lot of people lost money.

How could the conflict of interest have been avoided? Enron's board of directors should not have let CFO Andrew Fastow transact business with partnerships that he controlled. Then the values that came out of the transactions would have been more objective. This is only one of the problems that affected Enron, but it illustrates an important ethical issue.

Equipment purchases:

a. Bill Milburn Homes policy calls for construction supervisors to request the equipment needed for construction jobs. The home office then purchases the equipment and has it shipped to the construction site.

b. Ken Cooper Construction policy calls for project supervisors to purchase the equipment needed for jobs. The supervisors then submit the paid receipts to the home office for reimbursement. This policy enables supervisors to get the equipment quickly and keep construction jobs moving.

Correcting an internal control weakness (Obj. 1)

writing assignment ■

E4-4 Consider this story from a *Wall Street Journal* article:

> Tokyo—**Sumitomo Corp.** the giant Japanese trading company, said unauthorized trades by its former head of copper trading over the past decade caused it huge losses that may total $1.8 billion. Sumitomo said it learned of the damage after Yasuo Hamanaka confessed to making unauthorized trades over a 10-year period. Hamanaka admitted to concealing the losses by falsifying Sumitomo's books and records.

Identify two internal control weaknesses at Sumitomo. How could the company have avoided and/or limited the size of the loss?

Classifying bank reconciliation items (Obj. 2)

E4-5 The following items may appear on a bank reconciliation:

1. Book error: We debited Cash for $200. The correct debit was $2,000
2. Outstanding checks
3. Bank error: The bank charged our account for a check written by another customer.
4. Service charge.
5. Deposits in transit.
6. NSF check.
7. Bank collection of a note receivable on our behalf.

Classify each item as (a) an addition to the bank balance, (b) a subtraction from the bank balance, (c) an addition to the book balance, or (d) a subtraction from the book balance.

Preparing a bank reconciliation (Obj. 2)

E4-6 Caye Hunter's checkbook lists the following:

Date	Check No.	Item	Check	Deposit	Balance
4/1					$525
4	622	La Petite France Bakery	$19		506
9		Dividends		$116	622
13	623	General Tire Co.	43		579
14	624	Exxon Mobil Oil Co.	58		521
18	625	Cash	50		471
26	626	Antioch Bible Church	25		446
28	627	Bent Tree Apartments	275		171
30		Paycheck		1,526	1,697

The April bank statement shows

	No.	Amount		
Balance				$525
Add: Deposits				116
Deduct checks:	No.	Amount		
	622	$19		
	623	43		
	624	85*		
	625	50		(197)
Other charges:				
NSF check			$ 8	
Service charge			12	(20)
Balance				$424

*This is the correct amount for check number 624.

(*continued*)

Required

Prepare Hunter's bank reconciliation at April 30, 20X6.

Preparing a bank reconciliation (Obj. 2)

E4-7 Darren Swanner operates four Exxon convenience stores. He has just received the monthly bank statement at July 31 from City National Bank, and the statement shows an ending balance of $1,794. Listed on the statement are an EFT rent collection of $300, a service charge of $12, two NSF checks totaling $120 and a $9 charge for printed checks. In reviewing his cash records, Swanner identifies outstanding checks totaling $603 and a July 31 deposit in transit of $1,788. During July, he recorded a $290 check for the salary of a part-time employee as $29. Swanner's Cash account shows a July 31 cash balance of $3,081. How much cash does Swanner actually have at July 31?

Making journal entries from a bank reconciliation (Obj. 2)

E4-8 By using the data from Exercise 4-7, make the journal entries that Swanner should record on July 31 to update his Cash account. Include an explanation for each entry.

Applying internal controls to the bank reconciliation (Obj. 1, 2)

E4-9 A court of law convicted the manager of Broken Spoke Dance Club of stealing cash from the company. Over a 3-year period, the manager took $20,000 and attempted to cover the theft by manipulating the bank reconciliation.

What is the most likely way that a person would manipulate a bank reconciliation to cover a theft? Be specific. What internal control arrangement could prevent this theft?

Evaluating internal control over cash receipts (Obj. 3)

writing assignment ■

E4-10 **Best Buy** stores use cash registers. The register shows the amount of each sale, the cash received from the customer, and any change returned to the customer. The machine also produces a customer receipt but keeps no record of transactions. At the end of the day, the clerk counts the cash in the register and gives it to the cashier for deposit in the company bank account.

Write a memo to convince the store manager that there is an internal control weakness over cash receipts. Identify the weakness that gives an employee the best opportunity to steal cash and state how to prevent such a theft.

Accounting for petty cash (Obj. 3)

E4-11 Assume Care Net Pregnancy Center in Albany, New York, has created a $200 imprest petty cash fund. During July, the fund custodian authorized and signed petty cash tickets as follows:

Ticket No.	Item	Account Debited	Amount
1	Delivery of pledge cards to donors	Delivery Expense	$17.50
2	Ship package by UPS	Postage Expense	15.00
3	Newsletter	Supplies Expense	134.14
4	Key to closet	Miscellaneous Expense	2.85

Required

1. How much cash should the fund custodian request in order to replenish the petty cash fund?
2. Describe the items in the fund immediately before replenishment.
3. Describe the items in the fund immediately after replenishment.
4. Describe the internal control feature for this petty cash fund.

Preparing a cash budget (Obj. 4)

■ spreadsheet

E4-12 Suppose **Sprint Corporation**, the long-distance telephone company, is preparing its cash budget for 20X8. Assume Sprint ended 20X7 with $125.8 million, and managers need to keep a cash balance of at least $100 million for operations.

Collections from customers are expected to total $11,584.2 million during 20X8, and payments for the cost of services and products should reach $6,166 million. Operating expense payments are budgeted at $2,543.6 million.

During 20X8, Sprint expects to invest $1,825.7 million in new equipment and sell older assets for $115.7 million. Debt payments scheduled for 20X8 will total $597.2 million. The company forecasts net income of $890.4 million for 20X8 and plans to pay dividends of $338 million.

Prepare Sprint's cash budget for 20X8. Will the budgeted level of cash receipts leave Sprint with the desired ending cash balance of $100 million, or will the company need additional financing?

Evaluating the ethics of conduct by government legislators (Obj. 5)

writing assignment ■

E4-13 Approximately 300 current and former members of the U.S. House of Representatives—on a regular basis—wrote $250,000 of checks without having the cash in their accounts. Later investigations revealed that no public funds were involved. The House bank was a free-standing institution that recirculated House members cash. In effect, the delinquent check writers were borrowing money from each other on an interest-free, no-service-charge basis. Nevertheless, the House closed its bank after the events became public.

Suppose you are a new congressional representative from your state. Apply the decision guidelines for ethical judgments outlined on p. 195 to decide whether you would write NSF checks on a regular basis through the House bank.

Challenge Exercises

Internal control over cash payments, ethical considerations (Obj. 3, 5)

writing assignment ■

E4-14 Maxine Hart, the owner of Happy Hart Gift Ideas, has delegated management of the business to Clyde Collins, a friend. Hart drops by to meet customers and check up on cash receipts, but Collins buys the merchandise and handles cash payments. Business has been brisk lately, and cash receipts have kept pace with the apparent level of sales. However, for a year or so, the amount of cash on hand has been too low. When asked about this, Collins explains that suppliers are charging more for goods than in the past. During the past year, Collins has taken two foreign vacations, and Hart wonders how Collins can afford these trips on his $50,000 annual salary and commissions.

List at least three ways Collins could be defrauding Hart of cash. In each instance also identify how Hart can determine whether Collins' actions are ethical. Limit your answers to the store's cash payments. The business pays all suppliers by check (no EFTs).

Preparing and using a cash budget (Obj. 4)

E4-15 Among its many products, **International Paper Company** makes paper for **JCPenney** shopping bags, the labels on **Del Monte** canned foods, and **Redbook** magazine. Marianne Parrs, the chief financial officer, is responsible for International Paper's cash budget for 20X6. The budget will help Parrs determine the amount of long-term borrowing needed to end the year with a cash balance of $200 million. Parrs' assistants have assembled budget data for 20X6, which the computer printed in alphabetical order. Not all the data items, reproduced below, are used in preparing the cash budget.

(Assumed Data)	(In millions)
Acquisition of other companies	$ 1,015
Actual cash balance, December 31, 20X5	270
Borrowing	?
Budgeted total assets	22,977
Budgeted total current assets	6,073
Budgeted total current liabilities	4,863
Budgeted total liabilities	16,180
Budgeted total stockholders' equity	7,797
Collections from customers	19,467
Dividend payments	237
Issuance of stock	516
Net income	1,153
Other cash receipts	111
Payment of long-term and short-term debt	950
Payment of operating expenses	2,349
Purchases of inventory items	14,045
Purchase of property and equipment	1,518

| *Required*

1. Prepare the cash budget of International Paper for 20X6. Does it appear that International Paper will need to borrow money in 20X6?

(continued)

2. Compute International Paper's current ratio and debt ratio at December 31, 20X6. Based on these ratio values, and on the cash budget, would you lend $100 million to International Paper? Give the reason for your decision.

Compensating balance agreement (Obj. 4)

E4-16 Assume **Hewlett-Packard** borrowed $20 million from **Citibank**, agreeing to (a) pay an interest rate of 8% and (b) maintain a compensating balance amount equal to 5% of the loan. The bank will pay no interest on the compensating balance amount. Determine Hewlett-Packard's actual effective interest rate on this loan.

Practice Quiz

Test your understanding of internal control and cash by answering the following questions. Answer each question by selecting the best choice from among the answers given.

PQ4-1 All of the following are purposes of internal control except:

a. to maximize net income
b. to safeguard assets
c. to encourage adherence to company policies
d. to ensure accurate and reliable accounting records

PQ4-2 All of the following are characteristics of an effective system of internal control except:

a. separation of duties
b. proper authorization
c. e-commerce
d. internal and external audits

PQ4-3 Requiring that an employee with no access to cash prepare the bank reconciliations is an example of which characteristic of internal control:

a. competent and reliable personnel
b. separation of duties
c. assignment of responsibility
d. proper authorization

PQ4-4 All of the following are controls over cash received over the counter except:

a. the customer should be able to see the amounts entered into the register
b. a printed receipt must be given to the customer
c. the sales clerk must have access to the cash register tape
d. the cash drawer should open only when the salesclerk enters an amount on the keys

PQ4-5 In a bank reconciliation, an outstanding check is:

a. added to the bank balance
b. deducted from the bank balance
c. added to the book balance
d. deducted from the book balance

PQ4-6 In a bank reconciliation, a bank collection of a note receivable is:

a. added to the bank balance
b. deducted from the bank balance
c. added to the book balance
d. deducted from the book balance

PQ4-7 In a bank reconciliation, an EFT cash receipt is:

a. added to the bank balance
b. deducted from the bank balance
c. added to the book balance
d. deducted from the book balance

PQ4-8 If a bookkeeper mistakenly recorded an $85 deposit as $58, the error would be shown on the bank reconciliation as a:

a. $27 addition to the book balance
b. $85 deduction from the book balance
c. $27 deduction from the book balance
d. $85 addition to the book balance

PQ4-9 If a bank reconciliation included an EFT payment of $670 for insurance, the entry to record this reconciling item would include a:

a. credit to prepaid insurance for $670
b. credit to cash for $670
c. debit to cash for $670
d. no entry is required

PQ4-10 In a bank reconciliation, interest revenue is:

a. added to the bank balance
b. deducted from the bank balance
c. added to the book balance
d. deducted from the book balance

PQ4-11 Before paying an invoice for goods received on account, the controller or treasurer should ensure that

a. the company is paying for the goods it ordered.
b. the company is paying for the goods it actually received.
c. the company has not already paid this invoice.
d. All of the above.

PQ4-12 St. Louis Bread Company is budgeting cash for 20X8. The cash balance at December 31, 20X7, was $150,000. St. Louis budgets 20X8 cash receipts at $690,000. Estimated cash payments include $390,000 for inventory, $130,000 for operating expenses, and $200,000 to expand the store. St. Louis needs a minimum cash balance of $140,000 at all times. St. Louis expects to earn net income of $90,000 during 20X8. What is the final result of St. Louis Bread Company's cash budget for 20X8?

a. $20,000 available for additional investments.
b. $120,000 available at year end.
c. Pay off $20,000 of debt.
d. Must arrange new financing for $20,000.

Problems
(Group A)

PH Grade Assist

Most of these A problems can be found within Prentice Hall Grade Assist (PHGA), an online homework and practice environment. Your instructor may ask you to complete these problems using PHGA.

Identifying the characteristics of an effective internal control system (Obj. 1)

writing assignment ■

P4-1A An employee of Crisis Management, Inc. recently stole thousands of dollars of the company's cash. The company has decided to install a new system of internal controls.

Required

As a consultant for Crisis Management, write a memo to the president explaining how a separation of duties helps to safeguard company assets.

Identifying internal control weaknesses (Obj. 1, 3)

writing assignment ■

P4-2A Each of the following situations has an internal control weakness:

a. Dick Monroe, who has no known sources of outside income, has been a trusted employee of Stone Products Company for 20 years. He performs all cash-handling and accounting duties, including opening the mail, preparing the bank deposit, accounting for cash and accounts receivable, and preparing the bank reconciliation. Monroe has just purchased a new home in an expensive suburb. Lou Dobbs, owner of the company, wonders how Monroe can afford the new home on his salary.
b. Ashley Webb employs three professional interior designers in her design studio. She is located in an area with a lot of new construction, and her business is booming. Ordinarily, Webb does all the purchasing of furniture, draperies, carpets, and other materials needed to complete jobs. During the summer, she takes a long vacation, and in her absence she allows each designer to purchase materials and labor. On her return, Webb reviews operations and observes that expenses are much higher and net income much lower than in the past.
c. Discount stores such as **Wal Mart** and **Kmart** receive a large portion of their sales revenue in cash, with the remainder in credit card sales. To reduce expenses, a store manager ceases purchasing fidelity bonds on the cashiers.
d. The office supply company from which Haught Air Conditioning Service purchases cash receipt forms recently notified Haught that the last-shipped receipts were not prenumbered. Jerry Haught, the owner, replied that he did not use the receipt numbers, so the omission is not important.
e. Digital Graphics is a software company that specializes in programs with accounting applications. The company's most popular program prepares all the accounting records and financial statements. In the company's early days, the owner and eight employees wrote the computer programs, lined up production of the diskettes, sold the products to ComputerLand and

ComputerCraft, and performed the general management and accounting of the company. As Digital has grown, the number of employees has increased dramatically. Recently, the development of a new software program stopped while the programmers redesigned Digital's accounting system. Digital's own accountants could have performed this task.

Required

1. Identify the missing internal control characteristics in each situation.
2. Identify each firm's possible problem.
3. Propose a solution to the problem.
4. How will what you learned by solving this problem help you manage a business?

Using the bank reconciliation as a control device (Obj. 2)

spreadsheet

writing assignment

P4-3A The cash data of Town & Country Builders for March 20X5 follow:

Cash

Date	Item	Jrnl. Ref.	Debit	Credit	Balance
Mar. 1	Balance				10,188
31		CR 10	9,106		19,294
31		CP 16		11,353	7,941

Cash Receipts (CR)		Cash Payments (CP)	
Date	**Cash Debit**	**Check No.**	**Cash Credit**
Mar. 4	$2,716	1413	$ 1,465
9	544	1414	1,004
11	1,655	1415	450
14	896	1416	8
17	367	1417	775
25	890	1418	88
31	2,038	1419	4,126
Total	$9,106	1420	970
		1421	200
		1422	2,267
		Total	$11,353

On March 31, 20X5, Town & Country received this bank statement:

Bank Statement for March 20X5

Beginning balance		$10,188
Deposits and other Credits:		
Mar. 1	$ 625 EFT	
5	2,716	
10	544	
11	1,655	
15	896	
18	367	
25	890	
31	1,400 BC	9,093
Checks and other Debits:		
Mar. 8	$ 441 NSF	
9	1,465	
13	1,004	
14	450	
15	8	
19	340 EFT	
22	775	
29	88	
31	4,216	
31	25 SC	(8,812)
Ending balance		$10,469

Explanation: BC—bank collection, EFT—electronic funds transfer, NSF—nonsufficient funds check, SC—service charge

Additional data for the bank reconciliation:

a. The EFT deposit was for monthly rent revenue. The EFT debit was for monthly insurance expense.
b. The NSF check was received late in February from a customer.
c. The $1,400 bank collection of a note receivable on March 31 included $122 interest revenue.
d. The correct amount of check number 1419, a payment on account, is $4,216. (The Town & Country accountant mistakenly recorded the check for $4,126.)

Required

1. Prepare the bank reconciliation of Town & Country Builders at March 31, 20X5.
2. Describe how a bank account and the bank reconciliation help managers control a firm's cash.

Preparing a bank reconciliation and the related journal entries (Obj. 2)

■ spreadsheet

writing assignment ■

P4-4A The May 31 bank statement of Teletouch Answering Service has just arrived from New Orleans National Bank. To prepare the Teletouch bank reconciliation, you gather the following data:

a. The May 31 bank balance is $9,530.82.
b. Teletouch Cash account shows a balance of $8,521.55 on May 31.
c. The following Teletouch checks are outstanding at May 31:

Check No.	Amount
616	$403.00
802	74.02
806	36.60
809	161.38
810	229.05
811	48.91

d. The bank statement includes two special deposits: $899.14, which is the amount of dividend revenue the bank collected from **General Electric Company** on behalf of TeleTouch, and $16.86, the interest revenue TeleTouch earned on its bank balance during May.
e. The bank statement lists a $6.25 bank service charge.
f. On May 31 the TeleTouch treasurer deposited $381.14, which will appear on the June bank statement.
g. The bank statement includes a $410.00 deduction for a check drawn by Telemann Music Company.
h. The bank statement includes two charges for returned checks from customers. One is a nonsufficient funds check in the amount of $67.50 received from a customer. The other is a $195.03 check received from another customer. It was returned by the customer's bank with the imprint "Unauthorized Signature."
i. A few customers pay monthly bills by EFT. The May bank statement lists an EFT deposit for service revenue of $200.23.

Required

1. Prepare the bank reconciliation for TeleTouch Answering Service at May 31.
2. Journalize the transactions needed to update the Cash account. Include an explanation for each entry.
3. How will your learning from solving this problem help you manage a business?

Identifying internal control weakness (Obj. 3)

writing assignment ■

P4-5A Pacific Irrigation Co. makes all sales on credit. Cash receipts arrive by mail, usually within 30 days of the sale. Liz Galeano opens envelopes and separates the checks from the accompanying remittance advices. Galeano forwards the checks to another employee, who makes the daily bank deposit but has no access to the accounting records. Galeano sends the remittance advices, which show the amount of cash received, to the accounting department for entry in the accounts. Galeano's only other duty is to grant sales allowances to customers.

(A *sales allowance* decreases the amount that the customer must pay.) When Galeano receives a customer check for less than the full amount of the invoice, she records the sales allowance and forwards the document to the accounting department.

Required

You are a new employee of Pacific Irrigation. Write a memo to the company president identifying the internal control weakness in this situation. Explain how to correct the weakness.

Preparing a cash budget and using cash-flow information (Obj. 4)

writing assignment ■

P4-6A Robert J. Darreta is chief financial officer of **Johnson & Johnson**, the health-care products company and is responsible for the company's budgeting process. Suppose Darreta's staff is preparing the Johnson & Johnson budget for 20X6. Assume the starting point is the statement of cash flows of the current year, 20X5, reproduced in an adapted format as follows:

Johnson & Johnson, Inc.
Consolidated Statement of Cash Flows
(Adapted)

(In millions)	20X5
Cash Flows from Operating Activities	
Collections from customers	$40,687
Interest received	177
Purchases of inventory	(11,116)
Operating expenses	(16,578)
Other cash payments	(2,575)
Net cash provided by operating activities	10,595
Cash Flows from Investing Activities	
Additions to property, plant, and equipment	(5,074)
Purchases of investments	(7,590)
Sales of investments and other	8,138
Net cash used by investing activities	(4,526)
Cash Flows from Financing Activities	
Payment of dividends	(2,746)
Payment of Short-term debt, net	(1,072)
Long-term borrowings	1,023
Long-term debt repayments	(196)
Issuance of stock	311
Repurchases of common stock	(1,183)
Net cash used by financing activities	(3,863)
Effect of foreign-currency exchange rate changes on cash and cash equivalents	277
Cash and Cash Equivalents	
Increase (decrease) in Cash and Cash Equivalents	2,483
Cash and Cash Equivalents, beginning of year	2,894
Cash and Cash Equivalents, end of year	$5,377

Required

1. Prepare the Johnson & Johnson cash budget for 20X6. Date the budget simply "20X6" and denote the beginning and ending cash balances as "beginning" and "ending." Round amounts to the nearest $1 million. Assume the company expects 20X6 to be the same as 20X5, but with the following changes:
   a. In 20X6, the company expects a 10% increase in collections from customers, an 11% increase in purchases of inventory, and a doubling of additions to property, plant, and equipment.

b. All borrowings in 20X6 will be determined by the budget and thus do not appear on the cash budget (but all long-term debt and short-term debt repayments should be the same as they were in 20X5).
c. There will be no sales of investments in 20X6.
d. Daretta hopes to end the year with a cash balance of $3,000 million.
e. Ignore the "Effect of foreign-currency exchange rates on Cash and Cash Equivalents."

2. Does the company's cash budget for 20X6 suggest that Johnson & Johnson is growing, holding steady, or decreasing in size?

Making an ethical judgment (Obj. 5)

writing assignment ■

P4-7A Yuma bank in Yuma, Arizona, has a loan receivable from Wilsonart Plastics Company. Wilsonart is 6 months late in making payments to the bank, and Leon Hess, a Yuma Bank vice president, is assisting Wilsonart to restructure its debt.

Hess learns that Wilsonart is depending on landing a job with Binswanger Glass Company, another Yuma Bank client. Hess also serves as Binswanger's loan officer at the bank. In this capacity, he is aware that Binswanger is considering bankruptcy. No one else outside Binswanger Glass knows this. Hess has been a great help to Wilsonart and Wilsonart's owner is counting on Hess's expertise in loan workouts to advise the company through this difficult process. To help the bank collect on this large loan, Hess has a strong motivation to help Wilsonart to survive.

Required

Apply the ethical judgment framework outlined in the chapter to help Leon Hess plan his next action.

(Group B)

PH Grade Assist

Some of these B problems can be found within Prentice Hall Grade Assist (PHGA), an online homework and practice environment. Your instructor may ask you to complete these problems using PHGA.

Identifying the characteristics of an effective internal control system (Obj. 1)

writing assignment ■

P4-1B Chavez Real Estate Development Company prospers during an economic expansion. When business is good, the company doesn't bother with internal controls. A recent decline in the local real estate market has caused Chavez to experience a shortage of cash. Juan Felipe Chavez, the company owner, is looking for ways to save money.

Required

As a consultant for the company, write a memorandum to convince Chavez of the company's need for a system of internal control. Be specific in telling him how an internal control system could save the company money. Include the definition of internal control, and briefly discuss each characteristic of an effective internal control system, beginning with competent, reliable, and ethical personnel.

Identifying internal control weaknesses (Obj. 1, 3)

writing assignment ■

P4-2B Each of the following situations reveals an internal control weakness.

a. In evaluating the internal control over cash payments, an auditor learns that the purchasing agent is responsible for purchasing diamonds for use in the company's manufacturing process, approving the invoices for payment, and signing the checks. No supervisor reviews the purchasing agent's work.
b. Todd Wagoner owns a firm that performs engineering services. His staff consists of 12 professional engineers, and he manages the office. Often, his work requires him to travel to meet with clients. During the past 6 months, he has observed that when he returns from a business trip, the engineering jobs in the office have not progressed satisfactorily. He learns that when he is away, several of his senior employees take over office management and neglect their engineering duties. One employee could manage the office.
c. Leah Kestner has been an employee of A&S Shoe Store for many years. Because the business is relatively small, Kestner performs all accounting duties, including opening the mail, preparing the bank deposit, and preparing the bank reconciliation.

d. Most large companies have an internal audit staff that continuously evaluate the business's internal control. Part of the auditor's job is to evaluate how efficiently the company is running. For example, is the company purchasing inventory from the least expensive wholesaler? After a particularly bad year, McGregor Cellular Company eliminates its internal audit department to reduce expenses.

e. Law firms, consulting firms, and other professional organizations use paraprofessional employees to perform routine tasks. For example, a legal paraprofessional might examine documents to assist a lawyer to prepare a lawsuit. In the firm of Dunham & Lee, Cecil Dunham, the senior partner, turns over a significant portion of his high-level legal work to his paraprofessional staff.

Required

1. Identify the missing internal control characteristic in each situation.
2. Identify each firm's possible problem.
3. Propose a solution to the problem.
4. How will what you learned by solving this problem help you manage a business?

Using the bank reconciliation as a control device (Obj. 2)

writing assignment ■

■ spreadsheet

P4-3B The cash data of Investors Brokerage Co. for April 20X4 follow:

Cash					
Date	**Item**	**Jrnl. Ref.**	**Debit**	**Credit**	**Balance**
Apr. 1	Balance				1,911
30		CR6	10,578		12,489
30		CP11		10,924	1,565

Cash Receipts (CR)		Cash Payments (CP)	
Date	**Cash Debit**	**Check No.**	**Cash Credit**
Apr. 2	$ 4,174	3113	$ 891
8	407	3114	147
10	559	3115	1,930
16	2,187	3116	664
22	1,854	3117	1,472
29	1,060	3118	1,000
30	337	3119	632
Total	$10,578	3120	1,675
		3121	100
		3122	2,413
		Total	$10,924

Investors Brokerage received the following bank statement on April 30, 20X4:

Bank Statement for April 20X4

Beginning balance		$ 1,911
Deposits and other Credits:		
Apr. 1	$ 326 EFT	
4	4,174	
9	407	
12	559	
17	2,187	
22	1,701 BC	
23	1,854	11,208

(continued)

Checks and other Debits:		
Apr. 7	$ 891	
13	1,390	
14	903 US	
15	147	
18	664	
21	219 EFT	
26	1,472	
30	1,000	
30	20 SC	(6,706)
Ending Balance		$ 6,413

Explanation: EFT—electronic funds transfer, BC—bank collection, US—unauthorized signature, SC—service charge.

Additional data for the bank reconciliation include the following:

a. The EFT deposit was a receipt of monthly rent. The EFT debit was a monthly insurance payment.
b. The unauthorized signature check was received from a customer.
c. The $1,701 bank collection of a note receivable on April 22 included $185 interest revenue.
d. The correct amount of check number 3115, a payment on account, is $1,390. (Investor's accountant mistakenly recorded the check for $1,930.)

Required

1. Prepare the Investors Brokerage Company bank reconciliation at April 30, 20X4.
2. Describe how a bank account and the bank reconciliation help the Investors Brokerage Company control its cash.

Preparing a bank reconciliation and the related journal entries (Obj. 2)

spreadsheet

P4-4B The August 31 bank statement of Palm Harbor Apartments has just arrived from Florida First Bank. To prepare the Palm Harbor bank reconciliation, your gather the following data:

a. Palm Harbor's Cash account shows a balance of $3,366.14 on August 31.
b. The August 31 bank balance is $4,484.22
c. The bank statement shows that Palm Harbor earned $38.19 of interest on its bank balance during August. This amount was added to Palm Harbor's bank balance.
d. Palm Harbor pays utilities ($750) and insurance ($290) by EFT.
e. The following Palm Harbor checks did not clear the bank by August 31:

Check No.	Amount
237	$ 46.10
288	141.00
291	578.05
293	11.87
294	609.51
295	8.88
296	101.63

f. The bank statement includes a deposit of $891.17, collected by the bank on behalf of Palm Harbor Apartments. Of the total, $811.81 is collection of a note receivable, and the remainder is interest revenue.
g. The bank statement lists a $10.50 bank service charge.
h. On August 31, the Palm Harbor treasurer deposited $16.15, which will appear on the September bank statement.
i. The bank statement includes a $300.00 deposit that Palm Harbor did not make. The bank credited Palm Harbor for another company's deposit.
j. The bank statement includes two charges for returned checks from customers. One is a $395.00 check received from a customer with the imprint "Unauthorized Signature." The other is a nonsufficient funds check in the amount of $146.67 received from another customer.

Required

1. Prepare the bank reconciliation for Palm Harbor Apartments.
2. Journalize the August 31 transactions needed to update Palm Harbor's Cash account. Include an explanation for each entry.
3. How will your learning from solving this problem help you manage a business?

Identifying internal control weakness (Obj. 3)

writing assignment ■

P4-5B Altec Sound Systems makes all sales of stereo equipment on credit. Cash receipts arrive by mail, usually within 30 days of the sale. Matt Larosz opens envelopes and separates the checks from the accompanying remittance advices. Larosz forwards the checks to another employee, who makes the daily bank deposit but has no access to the accounting records. Larosz sends the remittance advices, which show the amount of cash received, to the accounting department for entry in the accounts. Larosz's only other duty is to grant sales allowances to customers. (A *sales allowance* decreases the amount that the customer must pay.) When Larosz receives a customer check for less than the full amount of the invoice, he records the sales allowance and forwards the document to the accounting department.

Required

You are a new employee of Altec Sound Systems. Write a memo to the company president identifying the internal control weakness in this situation. State how to correct the weakness.

Preparing a cash budget and using cash-flow information (Obj. 4)

writing assignment ■

P4-6B Carol B. Tomé, executive vice president and chief financial officer of **The Home Depot**, is responsible for the company's budgeting process. Suppose Tomé's staff is preparing the Home Depot cash budget for 20X7. A key input to the budgeting process is last year's statement of cash flows, reproduced in an adapted format as follows:

The Home Depot, Inc.
Consolidated Statement of Cash Flows
(Adapted)

(In millions)	20X6
Cash Flows from Operating Activities	
Collections from customers	$64,816
Interest received	59
Purchases of inventory	(44,375)
Operating expenses	(13,944)
Other operating costs	(11)
Net cash provided by operations	6,545
Cash Flows from Investing Activities	
Capital expenditures and related	(4,321)
Purchases of investments	(159)
Sales of investments and other	484
Net cash used in investing activities	(3,996)
Cash Flows from Financing Activities	
Long-term debt repayments	(9)
Issuance of stock	227
Repurchases of common stock	(1,554)
Payment of cash dividends	(595)
Net cash used in financing activities	(1,931)
Effect of foreign-currency exchange rate changes on cash and cash equivalents	20
Increase (Decrease) in Cash and Cash Equivalents	638
Cash and Cash Equivalents at Beginning of Year	2,188
Cash and Cash Equivalents at End of Year	$2,826

Required

1. Prepare the Home Depot cash budget for 20X7. Date the budget simply "20X7" and denote the beginning and ending cash balances as "beginning" and "ending." Round amounts to the nearest $1 million. Assume the company expects 20X7 to be the same as 20X6, but with the following changes:
   a. In 20X7, the company expects a 15% increase in collections from customers and a 20% increase in purchases of inventory.
   b. The company expects to incur no "Other operating" costs in 20X7. Ignore the "Effect of foreign currency exchange rates on Cash and Cash Equivalents." There should be no sales of investments in 20X7.
   c. The amount of any borrowings in 20X7 will be determined as a result of the cash budget and thus borrowings are not causal factors for the preparation of the budget (but long-term debt repayments and repurchases of common stock should be the same in 20X7 as they were in 20X6).
   d. Home Depot plans to issue no stock in 20X7.
   e. Tomé plans to end the year with a cash balance of $3,000 million.
   f. "Capital expenditures" are purchases of property and equipment.
2. Does the company's cash budget for 20X7 suggest that Home Depot is growing, holding steady, or decreasing in size?

Making an ethical judgment.
(Obj. 5)

writing assignment ■

P4-7B Max Shauk is executive vice president of Bluegrass Investments of Lexington, Kentucky. Active in community affairs, Shauk serves on the board of directors of Army–Navy Surplus stores. Army–Navy Surplus is expanding rapidly and is considering relocating its Lexington store. At a recent meeting, Army–Navy Board members decided to buy 200 acres of land on the edge of town. The owner of the property is Jerry Staas, a client of Bluegrass Investments. Staas is completing a bitter divorce, and Shauk knows that Staas is eager to sell his property. In view of Staas's difficult situation, Shauk believes Staas would accept a low offer for the land. Realtors have appraised the property at $3.6 million.

Required

Apply the ethical judgment framework outlined in the chapter Making Managerial Decisions to help Shauk decide what role he should play in Army–Navy Surplus's attempt to buy the land from Staas.

APPLY YOUR KNOWLEDGE

Decisions Cases

Correcting an internal control weakness
(Obj. 1, 3)

Case 1. This case is based on an actual situation experienced by one of the authors. Barrett Construction, headquartered in Lansing, Michigan, built a motel in Detroit. The construction foreman, Steven Wild, hired the workers needed to complete the project. Wild had the construction workers fill out the necessary tax forms and sent the employment documents to the home office.

Work on the motel began on May 1 and ended in December. Each Thursday evening, Wild filled out a time card that listed the hours worked for each employee during the 5-day work week ended at 5 P.M. on Thursday. Wild faxed the time sheets to the home office, which prepared the payroll checks on Friday morning. Wild drove to the home office after lunch on Friday, picked up the payroll checks, and returned to the construction site. At 5 P.M. on Friday, Wild distributed the payroll checks to the workers.

a. Describe in detail the internal control weakness in this situation. Specify what negative result could occur because of the internal control weakness.

b. Describe what you would do to correct the internal control weakness.

Using the bank reconciliation to detect a theft
(Obj. 2)

Case 2. McAlister's Deli has poor internal control. Recently, Randy Phipps, the manager, has suspected the bookkeeper of stealing. Details of the business's cash position at April 30 follows.

a. The Cash account shows a balance of $23,350. This amount includes an April 30 deposit of $3,794 that does not appear on the April 30 bank statement.

b. The April 30 bank statement shows a balance of $21,872. The bank statement lists a $200 bank collection, an $8 service charge, and a $36 NSF check. The accountant has not recorded any of these items.

c. At April 30, the following checks are outstanding:

Check No.	Amount
154	$116
256	150
278	853
291	990
292	206
293	145

d. The bookkeeper receives all incoming cash and makes bank deposits. He also reconciles the monthly bank statement. Here is his April 30 reconciliation:

Balance per books, April 30		$23,350
Add: Outstanding checks		2,160
Bank collection		200
Subtotal		25,710
Less: Deposits in transit	$3,794	
Service charge	8	
NSF check	36	(3,838)
Balance per bank, April 30		$21,872

Required

Phipps has requested that you determine whether the bookkeeper has stolen cash from the business and, if so, how much. He also asks you to explain how the bookkeeper attempted to conceal the theft. To make this determination, you perform your own bank reconciliation. There are no bank or book errors. Phipps also asks you to evaluate the internal controls and to recommend any changes needed to improve them.

Ethical Issue

Morton Sams owns apartment complexes in Minneapolis and St. Paul, Minnesota. Each property has a manager who collects rent, arranges for repairs, and runs advertisements in the local newspaper. The property managers transfer cash to Sams monthly and prepare their own bank reconciliations. The manager in Minneapolis has been stealing large sums of money. To cover the theft, he understates the amount of the outstanding checks on the monthly bank reconciliation. As a result, each monthly bank reconciliation appears to balance. However, the balance sheet reports more cash than Sams actually has in the bank. While negotiating the sale of the Minneapolis property, Sams shows the balance sheet to prospective investors.

Required

1. Identify two parties other than Sams who can be harmed by this theft. In what ways can they be harmed?
2. Discuss the role accounting plays in this situation.

Focus on Financials: ■ Yum! Brands

Cash and internal control (Obj. 1, 2)

Refer to the YUM! Brands financial statements in Appendix A at the end of this book. Suppose YUM's year-end bank statement, dated December 27, 2003, has just arrived at company headquarters. Further assume the bank statement shows YUM's cash balance at $197 million and that YUM's Cash and Cash Equivalents account has a balance of $194 million on the books.

1. You must determine how much to report for cash and cash equivalents on the December 27, 2003, balance sheet. Suppose you uncover these reconciling items (all amounts are assumed and in millions):
   a. Interest earned on bank balance, $1.
   b. Outstanding checks, $8.
   c. Bank collections of various items, $2.
   d. Deposits in transit, $3.
   e. Book error—YUM overstated cash by $5.

   Prepare a bank reconciliation to show how YUM arrived at the correct amount of cash and cash equivalents to report on its December 27, 2003, balance sheet. Prove that your answer is the actual amount YUM reported.
2. Study YUM Brands' Management Responsibility for Financial Statements and indicate how that report links to specific items of internal control discussed in this chapter.

Focus on Analysis: ■ Pier 1 Imports

Analyzing internal control and cash flows (Obj. 1, 5)

Refer to **Pier 1 Imports** financial statements in Appendix B at the end of this book.

1. Focus on cash, including temporary investments (this is the same as cash and cash equivalents). Why did cash change during 2004? The statement of cash flows holds the answer to this question. Analyze the seven largest individual items on the statement of cash flows (not the summary subtotals such as "net cash provided by operating activities"). For each of the seven individual items, state how Pier 1's action affected cash. Show amounts in millions and round to the nearest million.
2. Pier 1's Report of Management describes the company's internal controls. Show how the management report corresponds to three of the four elements in the definition of internal control.

Group Project

You are promoting a rock concert in your area. Assume you organize as a corporation, with each member of your group purchasing $10,000 of the corporation's stock. Therefore, each of you is risking some hard-earned money on this venture. Assume it is April 1 and that the concert will be performed on June 30. Your promotional activities begin immediately, and ticket sales start on May 1. You expect to sell all the firm's assets, pay all the liabilities, and distribute all remaining cash to the group members by July 31.

Required

Write an internal control manual that will help to safeguard the assets of the business. The manual should address the following aspects of internal control:

1. Assigning responsibilities among the group members.
2. Authorizing individuals, including group members and any outsiders that you need to hire, to perform specific jobs.
3. Separating duties among the group and any employees.
4. Describing all documents needed to account for and safeguard the business's assets.

spotlight

HOW FORD MOTOR COMPANY MAKES ITS MONEY

Ford Motor Company and Subsidiaries
Consolidated Balance Sheet (Excerpt; Adapted)
As of December 31, 2003

(In millions)	2003
Assets	
1 Cash and cash equivalents	$ 21,770
2 Marketable and loaned securities	17,539
3 Receivables, less allowance of $384	2,721
4 Finance receivables, net	110,893
5 Other receivables	44,876
6 Inventories	9,181
7 Net property	43,598
8 All other assets	54,016
9 Total assets	$304,594

Ford Motor Company and Subsidiaries
Sector Statement of Income (Excerpt; Adapted)
For the Year Ended December 31, 2003

(In millions)	2003
Sales and revenues	
1 Automotive	$138,442
2 Financial Services	25,754
≈	≈
3 Income/(loss) before income taxes—Automotive	(1,957)
4 Income/(loss) before income taxes—Financial Services	3,327
≈	≈
5 Net income	$ 495

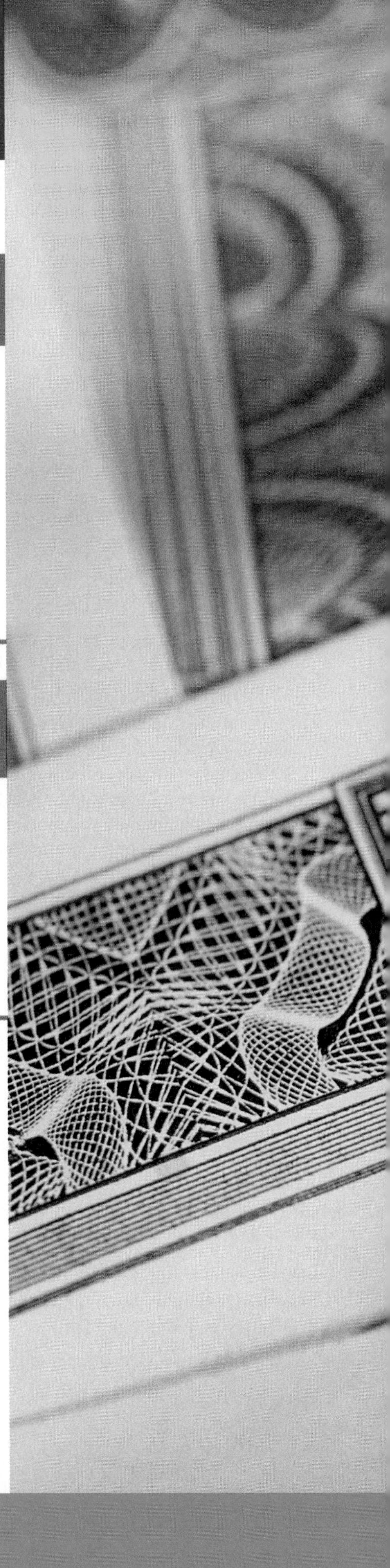

What comes to mind when you think of Ford Motor Company? Probably a Mustang convertible or an F-150 pickup truck. Did you know that Ford also owns the Volvo, Mazda, and Jaguar brands? When you think of Ford Motor Company, you probably also think it makes its money selling vehicles. You probably don't think of accounts and notes receivable.

Something startling appears on the Ford financial statements we show at the beginning of the chapter. Study Ford's balance sheet and income statement to see if you can find two surprises.

Surprise 1 **At December 31, 2003, over half of Ford's assets were receivables (Balance Sheet lines 3, 4, and 5). In fact, Ford had $158 billion of receivables and only $9 billion of inventory (line 6). Receivables are very important to Ford.**

Short-Term Investments & Receivables

LEARNING OBJECTIVES

1 **Account** for short-term investments

2 **Apply** internal controls to receivables

3 **Use** the allowance method for uncollectible receivables

4 **Account** for notes receivable

5 **Use** days' sales in receivables and the acid-test ratio to evaluate financial position

Surprise 2 **Ford's sector income statement shows that during 2003 the company lost almost $2 billion before taxes on auto sales (line 3). Ford's finance operations, based on its notes receivable, earned over $3 billion before taxes (line 4). So, Ford earns all its profits (Income Statement line 5) from lending money, not from selling cars.**

Creditor
The party to whom money is owed.

Debtor
The party who owes money.

Debt instrument
A receivable or a payable, usually some form of note.

Equity security
Stock certificate that represents the investor's ownership in a corporation.

Maturity
The date on which a debt instrument must be paid.

Term
The length of time from inception to maturity.

This chapter discusses how to account for receivables. Ford Motor Company is an interesting example because its receivables are vital to the company's financial health. Moreover, Ford has the three basic categories of receivables—accounts receivable, notes receivable, and other receivables. The chapter begins with short-term investments, another current asset of Ford Motor Company—$17 billion (Balance Sheet line 2).

We cover short-term investments along with receivables to emphasize their relative liquidity. Short-term investments are the next-most-liquid current assets after cash. We begin our discussion with short-term investments, which many companies label as Marketable Securities. But before getting into short-term investments and receivables, we need to define some key terms.

- **Creditor.** The party to whom money is owed. The creditor has a receivable.
- **Debtor.** The party who owes money. The debtor has a payable.
- **Debt instrument.** A receivable or a payable, usually some form of note.
- **Equity security.** A stock certificate that represents the investor's ownership in a corporation.
- **Maturity.** The date on which a debt instrument must be paid.
- **Term.** The length of time from inception to maturity of a debt instrument.

Short-Term Investments

OBJECTIVE

1 **Account** for short-term investments

Short-term investments
Investments that a company plans to hold for one year or less. Also called *marketable securities*

Short-term investments, also called **marketable securities**, are investments that a company plans to hold for 1 year or less. These investments allow the company to invest cash temporarily and earn a return until the cash is needed.

Short-term investments are the next-most-liquid asset after cash. This is why Ford and other companies report short-term investments immediately after cash and before receivables on the balance sheet. A short-term investment falls into one of three categories:

Three Categories of Short-Term Investments

Trading	Available-for-Sale	Held-to-Maturity
Covered in this section of the chapter	Covered in Chapter 10	Same as accounting for a note receivable, starting on page 223

The investor, such as Ford Motor Company, expects to sell a trading investment within a very short time—a few months at most. Therefore, all trading investments are current assets. The other two categories of investments can be either short term or long term, depending on how long management intends to hold them. Let's begin with trading investments.

Trading Investments

The purpose of owning a **trading investment** is to sell it for more than its cost. Trading investments can be the stock of another company. Suppose Ford Motor Company purchases **IBM** stock, intending to sell the stock within a few months. If the market value of the IBM stock increases, Ford will have a gain; if IBM's stock price drops, Ford will have a loss. Along the way, Ford will receive dividend revenue from IBM.

Trading investments
Stock investments that are to be sold in the near future with the intent of generating profits on the sale.

Suppose Ford buys the IBM stock on December 18, paying $100,000 cash. Ford records the purchase of the investment at cost:

20X5			
Dec. 18	Short-Term Investments	100,000	
	Cash		100,000
	Purchased investment.		

ASSETS	=	LIABILITIES	+	STOCKHOLDERS' EQUITY
+100,000 −100,000	=	0	+	0

Short-Term Investments	
100,000	

Assume on December 27 Ford receives a cash dividend of $4,000 from IBM. Ford records the dividend revenue as follows:

20X5			
Dec. 27	Cash	4,000	
	Dividend Revenue		4,000
	Received cash dividend.		

ASSETS	=	LIABILITIES	+	STOCKHOLDERS' EQUITY	+	REVENUES
+4,000	=				+	4,000

Ford's fiscal year ends on December 31, and Ford prepares financial statements. Assume the IBM stock has risen in value, and on December 31 Ford's investment has a current market value of $102,000. Market value is the amount the owner can receive when selling the investment. Ford has an *unrealized gain* on the investment:

- *Gain* because the market value ($102,000) is greater than Ford's cost of the investment ($100,000). A gain has the same effect as a revenue.
- *Unrealized gain* because Ford has not yet sold the investment.

Trading investments are reported on the balance sheet at their current market value, because that is the amount the investor can receive by selling the investment. Prior to financial statements on December 31, Ford adjusts the IBM investment to its current market value with this journal entry:

Check Point 5-1

20X5			
Dec. 31	Short-Term Investments	2,000	
	Unrealized Gain on Investments . . .		2,000
	Adjusted investment to market value		

ASSETS	=	LIABILITIES	+	STOCKHOLDERS' EQUITY	+	GAINS
+2,000	=	0	+	0	+	2,000

Short-Term Investments	
100,000	
2,000	

After the adjustment, Ford's investment account appears as shown above. Now the Short-Term Investments account is ready to be reported on the balance sheet—at current market value of $102,000.

If Ford's investment in IBM stock had decreased in value, say to $95,000, then Ford would have reported an unrealized loss. A *loss* has the same effect as an expense. In that case, Ford would have made a different entry at December 31. For an *unrealized loss*:

- *Debit* an Unrealized Loss account for $5,000 ($100,000 – $95,000).
- *Credit* the Short-Term Investments account for $5,000 to reduce its balance to current market value of $95,000.

Reporting on the Balance Sheet and the Income Statement

The Balance Sheet. Short-term investments are current assets. They appear on the balance sheet immediately after cash because short-term investments are almost as liquid as cash. (*Liquid* means close to cash.) Report trading investments at their current market value.

Income Statement. Investments earn interest revenue and dividend revenue. Investments also create gains and losses. For trading investments these items are reported on the income statement as Other revenue, gains, and (losses), as shown in Exhibit 5-1.

■ **EXHIBIT 5-1**

Reporting Short-Term Investments and the Related Revenues, Gains, and Losses

Balance sheet		Income statement	
Current assets:		Revenues	$ XXX
Cash	$ XXX	Expenses	XXX
Short-term investments, at market value	102,000	Other revenue, gains and (losses).	
Accounts receivable	XXX	Interest revenue	XXX
		Dividend revenue	4,000
		Unrealized gain on investment	2,000
		Net income	$ XXX

Check Point 5-2

Check Point 5-3

A *realized* gain or loss usually occurs when the investor sells an investment. The result may be a

- Realized gain = Sale price *greater than* Investment carrying amount
- Realized loss = Sale price *less than* Investment carrying amount

Suppose Ford Motor Company sells its IBM stock during 20X6. The sale price is $98,000, and Ford makes this journal entry:

20X6			
Feb. 19	Cash	98,000	
	Loss on Sale of Investments	4,000	
	Short-Term Investments		102,000
	Sold investments at a loss.		

ASSETS	=	LIABILITIES	+	STOCKHOLDERS' EQUITY	−	LOSS
+98,000 −102,000	=					−4,000

Short-Term Investments	
100,000	
2,000	102,000

Accountants rarely use the word "Realized" in the account title. A gain (or a loss) is understood to be a realized gain (or loss) arising from a sale transaction. Ford would report Gain (or Loss) on Sale of Investments among the "Other" items of the income statement, as shown in Exhibit 5-1.

ACCOUNTING ALERT

Is That Investment Really a Current Asset?

Lending agreements often require the borrower to maintain a current ratio at some specified level, say 1.50 or greater. The lender believes a current ratio of 1.50 provides enough cushion to enable the borrower to keep paying on the loan. What happens when the borrower's current ratio falls below 1.50? The consequences can be severe: (1) The lender can call the loan for immediate payment. (2) If the borrower cannot pay, then in extreme cases the lender can take over the company.

Suppose it's December 10 and it looks like the company's current ratio will end the year at a value of 1.48. That will put the company in default on the lending agreement and create a bad situation. With three weeks remaining, how can the company improve its current ratio?

If business is good, the company can launch a major effort to spur sales. The increase in Accounts Receivable will more than offset the decrease in Inventory, and the current ratio will rise. But the lower-than-expected value of the current ratio probably means that business isn't so good. How then can the company get its current ratio up to 1.50?

If the company has some long-term investments, it can reclassify them as current. Then current assets will increase. This simple maneuver may boost the current ratio above 1.50. Is the reclassification honest? Is it ethical? If the company does in fact expect to sell the investments during the coming year, yes. But if the company expects to hold the investments longer than a year, they are long term. Amazingly, what determines whether the company defaults on its loan agreement may be the classification of an investment. Is that investment really a current asset?

The take-away lesson from this accounting alert is this:

- For a company with a weak current ratio, ask lots of questions about its current assets. How current are these assets?

MID-CHAPTER Summary Problem

Humana, Inc., is one of the largest U.S. managed health-care companies. The largest current asset on Humana's balance sheet is Short-Term Investments. Their cost is $1,660 million, and their market value is $1,677 million.

Suppose Humana holds the investments in the hope of selling them at a profit within a short time. How will Humana classify the investments? What will Humana report on the balance sheet at December 31, 20X6? What will Humana report on its 20X6 income statement? Show a T-account for Short-Term Investments.

Answer

Trading investments are current assets reported on the 20X6 balance sheet as follows (amounts in millions):

Balance Sheet

	(In millions)
Current assets	
Cash	$ XX
Short-term investments, at market value	1,677

Humana's 20X6 income statement will report:

Income Statement

	(In millions)
Other revenue and expense:	
Unrealized gain on investments ($1,677 – $1,660)	$17

Short-Term Investments

Debit	Credit
1,660	
17	

Suppose Humana sells the investment for $1,650 million in 20X7. Journalize the sale and show the Short-Term Investments T-account as it appears after the sale.

Answer

	(In millions)	
Cash	1,650	
Loss on Sale of Investments	27	
Short-Term Investments		1,677
Sold investments at a loss.		

Short-Term Investments

Debit	Credit
1,660	
17	1,677

Accounts and Notes Receivable

Receivables are the third most liquid asset—after cash and short-term investments. In the remainder of the chapter, we discuss how to account for receivables.

Types of Receivables

Receivables are monetary claims against others. They are acquired mainly by selling goods and services and by lending money. The journal entries to record the receivables can be shown as follows:

Receivables
Monetary claims against a business or an individual, acquired mainly by selling goods or services and by lending money.

Performing a Service on Account			Lending Money on a Note Receivable		
Accounts Receivable	XXX		Note Receivable.......	XXX	
Service Revenue.....		XXX	Cash............		XXX
Performed a service on account.			Loaned money to another company.		

The two major types of receivables are accounts receivable and notes receivable. A business's *accounts receivable* are the amounts collectible from customers from the sale of goods and services. Accounts receivable, which are *current assets*, are sometimes called *trade receivables* or merely receivables, as Ford Motor Company calls them on its balance sheet.

The Accounts Receivable account in the general ledger serves as a *control account* that summarizes the total amount receivable from all customers. Companies also keep a *subsidiary record* of accounts receivable with a separate account for each customer, illustrated as follows:

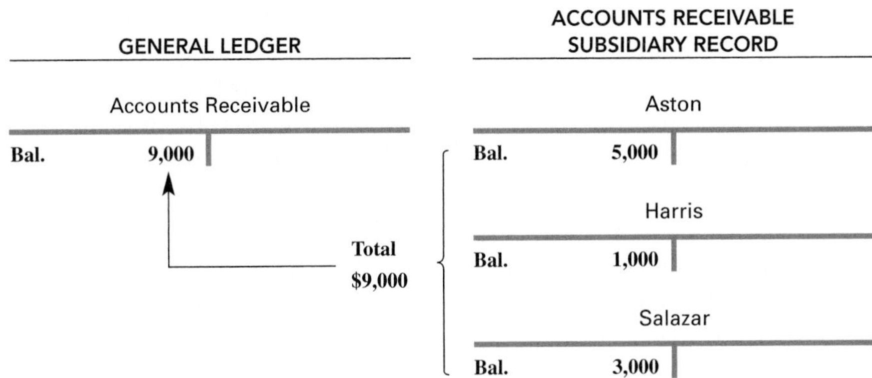

Notes receivable are more formal contracts than accounts receivable. The debtor signs a written promise to pay the creditor a definite sum at the *maturity* date. The note may require the debtor to pledge *security* for the loan. This means that the debtor gives the creditor permission to claim certain assets, called *collateral*, if the debtor fails to pay the amount due.

Notes receivable due within 1 year or less are current assets. Notes due beyond 1 year are *long-term receivables* and are reported as long-term assets. Some notes receivable are collected in installments. The portion due within 1 year is a current asset and the remainder is long term. Ford Motor Company may hold a $20,000 note receivable from you, but only the $6,000 you must pay within 1 year is a current asset.

Other receivables is a miscellaneous category that includes loans to employees and subsidiary companies. Ford reports other receivables after Finance receivables on the balance sheet. Finance receivables are Ford's notes receivable from sales of automobiles to customers.

Establishing Internal Control over Collections

OBJECTIVE

2 **Apply** internal controls to receivables

Businesses that sell on credit receive most of their cash receipts by mail. Internal control over collections is important. Chapter 4 discusses control procedures for cash receipts, but a critical element of internal control deserves emphasis here—the separation of cash-handling and cash-accounting duties. Consider the following case:

> **Butler Supply Co. is a small, family-owned business that takes pride in the loyalty of its workers. Most employees have been with the Butlers for at least 5 years. The company makes 90% of its sales on account.**
>
> **The office staff consists of a bookkeeper and a supervisor. The bookkeeper maintains the general ledger and the accounts receivable subsidiary ledger. He also makes the daily bank deposit. The supervisor prepares monthly financial statements and any special reports the Butlers require. She also takes sales orders from customers and serves as office manager.**

Can you identify the internal control weakness here? The problem is that the bookkeeper has access to both the accounts and the cash. The bookkeeper could steal an incoming customer check and write off the customer's account as uncollectible. (The bookkeeper would need to forge the endorsements of the checks and deposit them in a bank account that he controls.) The customer doesn't complain because Butler has written the account off the books and Butler therefore stops pursuing collection.

How can this weakness be corrected? The supervisor could open incoming mail and make the daily bank deposit. The bookkeeper should *not* be allowed to handle cash. Only the remittance advices would be forwarded to the bookkeeper to credit customer accounts. Removing cash handling from the bookkeeper and keeping the accounts away from the supervisor separates duties and strengthens internal control.

✔ Check Point 5-4

Using a bank lockbox achieves the same separation of duties. Customers send their payments directly to Butler Supply's bank, which records cash as it goes into Butler's account. The bank then forwards the remittance advice to Butler's bookkeeper, who credits the customer account.

■ Taking Action How Do We Manage the Risk of Not Collecting?

In Chapters 1 to 4, we use many different companies to illustrate how to account for a business. Chapter 1 began with YUM! Brands, a maker of fast foods. Chapter 2 featured Apple Computer, Inc., Chapter 3 Callaway Golf Company, and Chapter 4 Merrill Lynch, the brokerage firm. All these companies hold receivables.

By selling on account, all companies run the risk of not collecting some receivables. Unfortunately, some customers don't pay their debts. The prospect that we may fail to collect from a customer provides the biggest challenge in accounting for receivables. Making Managerial Decisions addresses this challenge.

MAKING MANAGERIAL DECISIONS

MANAGING AND ACCOUNTING FOR RECEIVABLES

Here are the management and accounting issues a business faces when it extends credit to customers. For each issue, Making Managerial Decisions proposes a plan of action. Let's look at a business situation: Suppose you and a friend open a health club near your college. Assume you will let customers use the club and charge bills to their accounts. What challenges will you encounter by extending credit to customers?

The main issues in *managing* receivables, along with a plan of action, are:

Issues	Plan of Action
1. What are the benefits and the costs of extending credit to customers?	1. Benefits—Increase in sales. Cost—Risk of not collecting.
2. Extend credit only to creditworthy customers.	2. Run a credit check on prospective customers.
3. Separate cash-handling and accounting duties to keep employees from stealing the cash collected from customers.	3. Design the internal control system to separate duties.
4. Pursue collection from customers to maximize cash flow.	4. Keep a close eye on customer pay habits. Send second, and third, statements to slow-paying customers, if necessary.

The main issues in *accounting* for receivables, and the related plans of action, are (amounts are assumed):

Issues	Plan of Action	
1. Measure and report receivables on the balance sheet at their *net realizable value*, the amount we expect to collect. This is the appropriate amount to report for receivables.	1. Report receivables at their net realizable value: **Balance sheet** Receivables . . . . Less: Allowance for uncollectibles. . . . . Receivables, net	 $1,000 (80) $ 920
2. Measure and report the expense associated with failure to collect receivables. This expense is called *uncollectible-account expense* and is reported on the income statement.	2. Measure the expense of not collecting from customers: **Income statement** Sales (or service) revenue. . . . . Expenses: Uncollectible-account expense	 $8,000 190

Accounting for Uncollectible Receivables

Selling on credit creates both a benefit and a cost:

- *Benefit:* Customers who cannot pay cash immediately can buy on credit, so sales and profits increase.
- *Cost:* The company cannot collect from some customers. Accountants label this cost **uncollectible-account expense**, **doubtful-account expense**, or **bad-debt expense**.

Uncollectible-account expense Cost to the seller of extending credit. Arises from the failure to collect from credit customers. Also called *doubtful-account expense* or *bad-debt expense*.

The extent of uncollectible-account expense varies from company to company. Ford Motor Company reports Receivables as follows on its balance sheet (in millions):

Receivables, less allowance of $384	$2,721

The allowance represents amounts that Ford does *not* expect to collect. You can see that the allowance exceeds 10% of Ford's receivables. **Wal-Mart Stores,** on the other hand, sells for cash and on credit cards and therefore has no significant amount of bad-debt expense.

Uncollectible-account expense is an operating expense along with salaries, depreciation, rent, and utilities. To measure uncollectible-account expense, accountants use the allowance method or, in certain limited cases, the direct write-off method (see page 230).

OBJECTIVE

3 Use the allowance method for uncollectible receivables

Allowance Method

Allowance method A method of recording collection losses based on estimates of how much money the business will not collect from its customers.

Allowance for Uncollectible Accounts A contra account, related to accounts receivable, that holds the estimated amount of collection losses. Another name for *Allowance for Doubtful Accounts*.

The best way to measure bad debts is by the **allowance method.** This method records collection losses based on estimates derived from the company's collection experience. The business does not wait to see which customers will not pay. Instead, the company records the estimated amount as Uncollectible-Account Expense and sets up **Allowance for Uncollectible Accounts.** Another title for this account is *Allowance for Doubtful Accounts.* This is a contra account to Accounts Receivable. The allowance shows the amount of the receivables the business expects *not* to collect.

In Chapter 3 we used the Accumulated Depreciation account to show how much of a plant asset has been expensed and is no longer a benefit to the company. Allowance for Uncollectible Receivables serves a similar purpose for Accounts Receivable. The allowance shows how much of the receivable has been expensed. You'll find this diagram helpful (amounts are assumed):

Equipment	$100,000	Accounts receivable	$10,000
Less: Accumulated		Less: Allowance for	
depreciation	(40,000)	uncollectible accounts .	(900)
Equipment, net	$ 60,000	Accounts receivable, net ...	$ 9,100

Focus on Accounts Receivable. Customers owe this company $10,000, but it expects to collect only $9,100. The net realizable value of the receivables is therefore $9,100. Another way to report these receivables is

Check Point 5-5

Accounts receivable, less allowance of $900	$9,100

You can work backward to determine the full amount of the receivable, $10,000 (net realizable value of $9,100 plus the allowance of $900).

The income statement reports Uncollectible-Account Expense among the operating expenses, as follows (using assumed figures):

Income statement (partial):

Expenses:
Uncollectible-Account Expense: $2,000

stop AND think. . .

Refer to the Ford Motor Company balance sheet on page 216. At December 31, 2003, how much did customers owe Ford? How much did Ford expect *not* to collect? How much did Ford expect to collect? What was the net realizable value of Ford's receivables?

Answer:

	Millions
Customers owed Ford	$3,105
Ford expected not to collect	384
Ford expected to collect—net realizable value	$2,721

The best way to estimate uncollectibles uses the company's history of collections from customers. There are two basic ways to estimate uncollectibles:

- Percent-of-sales-method
- Aging-of-receivables method

Percent-of-Sales. The **percent-of-sales method** computes uncollectible-account expense as a percent of revenue. This method takes an *income statement approach* because it focuses on the amount of expense to be reported on the income statement. Assume it is December 31, 2003 and Ford's accounts have these balances *before the year-end adjustments* (amounts in millions):

Percent-of-sales-method Computes uncollectible-account expense as a percentage of net sales. Also called the *income statement approach* because it focuses on the amount of expense to be reported on the income statement.

Accounts Receivable		Allowance for Uncollectible Accounts	
3,105			54

Customers owe Ford $3,105, and the Allowance amount is $54. But Ford's top managers know that the company will fail to collect more than $54. Suppose Ford's credit department estimates that uncollectible-account expense is 1% of total revenues, which were $33,000. The entry to record bad-debt expense for the year also updates the allowance as follows:

2003			
Dec. 31	Uncollectible-Account Expense ($33,000 × .01).........................	330	
	Allowance for Uncollectible Accounts.....		330
	Recorded expense for the year.		

The expense decreases assets, as shown by the accounting equation.

ASSETS	=	LIABILITIES	+	STOCKHOLDERS' EQUITY	−	EXPENSES
−330	=	0			−	330

Check Point 5-6

Now the accounts are ready for reporting in the financial statements.

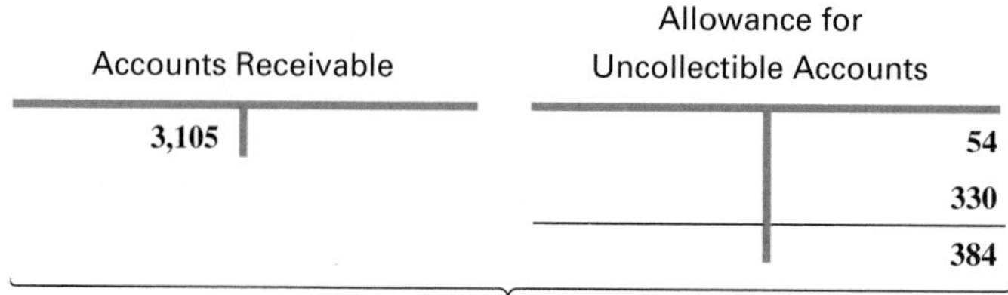

Compare these amounts to the preceding Stop and Think answer. They are the same.

Customers still owe Ford $3,105, and now the Allowance for Uncollectibles balance is realistic. Ford's balance sheet actually reported accounts receivable at their net realizable value amount of $2,721 ($3,105 – $384).

Aging-of-accounts receivable
A way to estimate bad debts by analyzing individual accounts receivable according to the length of time they have been receivable from the customer. Also called the *balance-sheet approach.*

Aging-of-Receivables. The other popular method for estimating uncollectibles is called **aging-of-receivable.** This method is a *balance-sheet approach* because it focuses on accounts receivable. In the aging method, individual receivables from specific customers are analyzed based on how long they have been outstanding.

Suppose it is December 31, 2003, and Ford Motor Company's Receivables accounts show the following before the year-end adjustment (amounts in millions):

Accounts Receivable		Allowance for Uncollectible Accounts	
3,105			170

These accounts are not yet ready for the financial statements.

Ford's computerized accounting package ages the company's accounts receivable. Exhibit 5-2 shows the aging schedule at December 31, 2003. Ford's receivables total $3,105. Of this amount, the aging schedule shows that the company will *not* collect $384 (lower right corner).

■ **EXHIBIT 5-2**

Aging the Accounts Receivable of Ford Motor Company

Age of Account (Dollar amounts in millions)

Customer	1–30 Days	31–60 Days	61–90 Days	Over 90 Days	Total Balance
Hertz Rent-A-Car					
Totals	$1,800	$ 760	$ 326	$ 219	$3,105
Estimated percent uncollectible	× 4%	× 10%	× 18.7%	× 80%	
Allowance for Uncollectible Accounts balance should be	$ 72 +	$ 76 +	$ 61 +	$ 175 =	$ 384

The aging method will bring the balance of the allowance account ($170) to the needed amount ($384) as determined by the aging schedule. The lower right corner gives the needed balance in the allowance account. To update the allowance, Ford would make this adjusting entry at year end:

2003			
Dec. 31	Uncollectible-Account Expense	214	
	Allowance for Uncollectible Accounts ($384 – $170)		214
	Recorded expense for the year.		

The expense decreases assets, as shown by the accounting equation.

ASSETS	=	LIABILITIES	+	STOCKHOLDERS' EQUITY	–	EXPENSES
–214	=	0				– 214

Now the balance sheet can report the amount that Ford actually expects to collect from customers: $2,721 ($3,105 – $384). This is the net realizable value of Ford's trade receivables.

Accounts Receivable		Allowance for Uncollectible Accounts	
3,105			170
			Adj. 214
			End. Bal. 384

Net accounts receivable, $2,721

Writing Off Uncollectible Accounts. Suppose that early in 2004, Ford's credit department determines that Ford cannot collect from customers Sarasota Pipe and Miller Auto Sales. Ford then writes off the receivables from these two delinquent customers with the following entry (using assumed data):

2004			
Mar. 31	Allowance for Uncollectible Accounts.	100	
	Accounts Receivable—Sarasota Pipe.		61
	Accounts Receivable—Miller Auto Sales . .		39
	Wrote off uncollectible receivables.		

The accounting equation shows that the write-off of uncollectibles has no effect on total assets. There is no effect on net income either.

ASSETS	=	LIABILITIES	+	STOCKHOLDERS' EQUITY
+100 –100	=	0	+	0

Check Point 5-7

Check Point 5-8

stop AND think. . .

In the preceding accounting equation (for the write-off of uncollectible receivable), why is there no effect on total assets? Why is there no effect on net income?

Answer:

There is no effect on total assets because the write-off of an uncollectible receivable decreases both Accounts Receivable and the Allowance for Uncollectibles, a contra account. Both accounts are part of net receivables, so one effect offsets the other. The result is no effect on net receivables and no effect on total assets.

There is no effect on net income because the write-off of uncollectibles affects no expense account.

Combining the Percent-of-Sales and the Aging Methods. Most companies use the percent-of-sales and aging-of-accounts methods together, as follows:

- For *interim statements* (monthly or quarterly), companies use the percent-of-sales method because it is easier to apply. The percent-of-sales method focuses on the uncollectible-account *expense*, but that is not enough.
- At the end of the year, companies use the aging method to ensure that Accounts Receivable is reported at *net realizable value*. The aging method focuses on the amount of the receivables—the *asset*—that is uncollectible.
- Using the two methods together provides good measures of both the expense and the asset. Exhibit 5-3 compares the two methods.

■ **EXHIBIT 5-3**

Comparing the Percent-of-Sales and Aging Methods for Estimating Uncollectibles

Check Point 5-9

Check Point 5-10

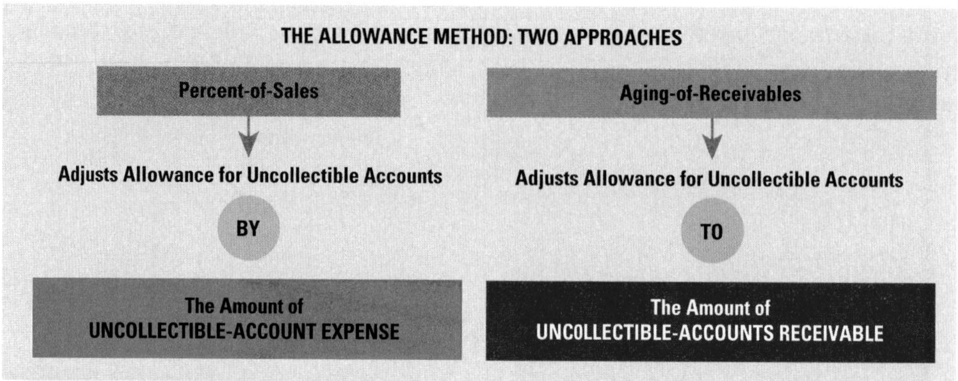

Direct Write-Off Method

Direct write-off method
A method of accounting for bad debts in which the company waits until a customer's account receivable proves uncollectible and then debits Uncollectible-Account Expense and credits the customer's Account Receivable.

There is another, less preferable, way to account for uncollectible receivables. Under the **direct write-off method**, the company waits until a specific customer's receivable proves uncollectible. Then the accountant writes off the customer's receivable account and records Uncollectible-Account Expense, as follows (using assumed data):

2004			
Jan. 2	Uncollectible-Account Expense..............	100	
	Accounts Receivable—Sarasota Pipe......		61
	Accounts Receivable—Miller Auto Sales ..		39
	Wrote off bad accounts by direct write-off method.		

The direct write-off method is defective for two reasons:

1. The direct write-off method uses no allowance for uncollectibles. As a result, receivables are always reported at their full amount, which is more than the business expects to collect. *Assets on the balance sheet are overstated.*
2. The direct write-off method causes a poor matching of uncollectible-account expense against revenue. In this example, Ford made the sales to Sarasota Pipe and Miller Auto Sales in 2003 and should have recorded the uncollectible-account expense during 2003. By recording the expense in 2004, *the company would overstate net income in 2003.* Then by recording the expense when it writes off the receivable in 2004, the company would understate net income in 2004.

Because of these deficiencies, Ford and most other companies use the allowance method. The direct write-off method is acceptable only when uncollectibles are so low that bad-debt expense is essentially the same under the allowance method and the direct write-off method.

stop AND think. . .

1. Under the allowance method, there are only two transactions to record. What are they?
2. Which transaction affects net income?
3. Which transaction affects net receivables?
4. Which transaction affects total assets?
5. Which transaction leaves net income, net receivables, and total assets unchanged?

Answers:

1. Transaction 1: Record uncollectible-account expense and set up the allowance for uncollectible accounts.
   Transaction 2: Write off uncollectible receivables.
2. Transaction 1: The expense transaction decreases net income.
3. Transaction 1: The expense transaction decreases net receivables.
4. Transaction 1: The expense transaction decreases total assets.
5. Transaction 2: The write-off transaction leaves net income, net receivables, and total assets unchanged.

Computing Cash Collections from Customers

A company earns revenue and then collects the cash from customers. There is a time lag between earning the revenue and collecting the cash. Collections from customers are the single most important source of cash for any business. You can compute a company's collections from customers by analyzing its Accounts Receivable account. Receivables typically hold only five items, as follows (amounts assumed):

Accounts Receivable

Beg. balance (left over from last period)	**200**	**Collections from customers**	**X = 1,500****
Sales (or service) revenue	**1,800***	**Write-offs of uncollectibles**	**100†**
End. balance (carries over to next period)	**400**		

*The journal entry that places revenue into the receivable account is

Accounts Receivable	1,800	
Sales (or Service) Revenue		1,800

**The journal entry that places collections into the receivable account is

Cash	1,500	
Accounts Receivable		1,500

†The journal entry for write-offs is

Allowance for Uncollectibles	100	
Accounts Receivable		100

Often write-offs are unknown and must be omitted. Then the computation of collections becomes an approximation.

ACCOUNTING ALERT

Shifting Sales into the Current Period Makes You Look Good Now, but You Pay for It Later

Suppose you are managing a company, and it's December 26. Late in the year business dried up: Your profits are running below what everyone predicted. You need a loan, and your banker requires financial statements to support your loan request. Unless you act quickly, you won't get the loan.

Fortunately, next year looks better. You have standing orders for sales of $50,000. As soon as you get the merchandise, you can ship it to customers and record the sales. An old accounting trick can solve the problem. Simply go ahead and book the $50,000 of sales in December. After all, you'll be shipping the goods on January 2 of next year. What difference does two days make?

It makes all the difference in the world. Shifting the sales into the current year will make you look better immediately. Reported profits will rise, your current ratio will improve, and you can then get the loan you need. But what are the consequences? If you are caught, you will be prosecuted for fraud and your reputation will be ruined. Remember that you shifted next year's sales into the current year. Next year's sales will be lower than the true amount, and profits will suffer. If next year turns out to be like this year, you'll be facing the same shortage again. Also, something may come up to keep you from shipping the goods on January 2.

Very few companies pull these tricks because they are dishonest, unethical, and illegal. Honesty is always the best policy.

The take-away lesson from this accounting alert is this:

- Study a company's financial-statement notes to learn when it books revenue. If too early, the company's revenues aren't there yet.

Notes Receivable

As stated earlier, notes receivable are more formal than accounts receivable. There are two parties to a note:

- The *creditor* has a note receivable.
- The *debtor* has a note payable.

Exhibit 5-4 is a typical promissory note.

OBJECTIVE

4 **Account** for notes receivable

■ **EXHIBIT 5-4** A Promissory Note

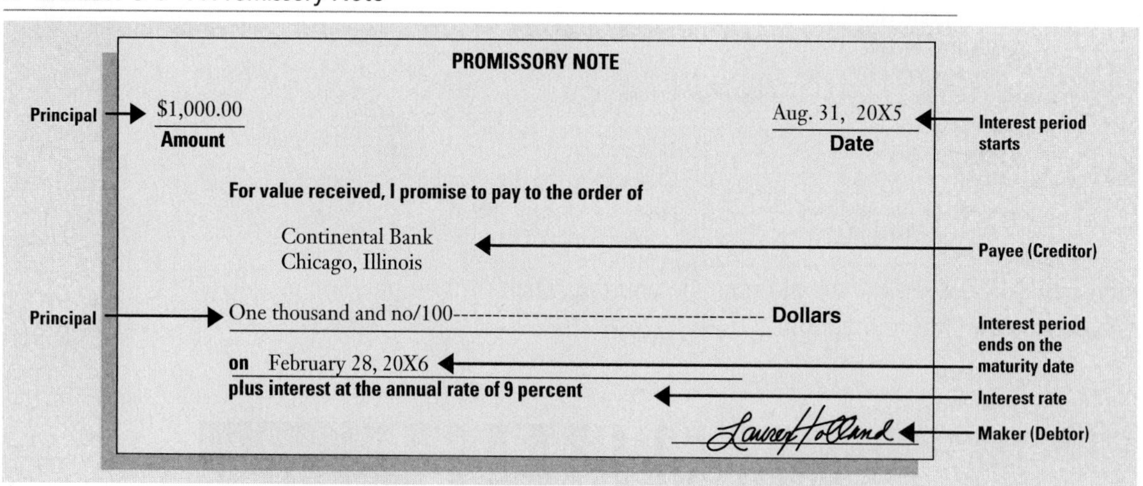

PROMISSORY NOTE

$1,000.00
Amount

Aug. 31, 20X5
Date

For value received, I promise to pay to the order of

Continental Bank
Chicago, Illinois

One thousand and no/100------------------------------------ Dollars

on February 28, 20X6

plus interest at the annual rate of 9 percent

Principal
The amount borrowed by a debtor and lent by a creditor.

The **principal** amount of the note is the amount borrowed by the debtor, lent by the creditor. Suppose the note receivable runs from August 31, 20X5, to February 28, 20X6, when Lauren Holland (the maker) promises to pay Continental Bank (the payee) the principal of $1,000 plus 9% interest. **Interest** is revenue to the lender (Continental Bank, in this case).

Accounting for Notes Receivable

Interest
The borrower's cost of renting money from a lender. Interest is revenue for the lender and expense for the borrower.

Consider the promissory note in Exhibit 5-4. After Lauren Holland signs the note, Continental Bank gives her $1,000 cash. The bank's entries follow, assuming a December 31 year end for Continental Bank:

20X5			
Aug. 31	Note Receivable—L. Holland	1,000	
	Cash		1,000
	Made a loan.		

ASSETS	=	LIABILITIES	+	STOCKHOLDERS' EQUITY
+1000 −1000	=	0	+	0

The bank gave one asset, cash, in return for another asset, a note receivable, so total assets did not change.

Continental Bank earns interest revenue during September, October, November, and December. At December 31, the bank accrues 9% interest revenue for 4 months as follows:

Dec. 31	Interest Receivable ($1,000 × .09 × 4/12)	30	
	Interest Revenue		30
	Accrued interest revenue.		

ASSETS	=	LIABILITIES	+	STOCKHOLDERS' EQUITY	+	REVENUES
+30	=	0			+	30

The bank collects the note on February 28, 20X6, and records

20X6			
Feb. 28	Cash	1,045	
	Note Receivable—L. Holland		1,000
	Interest Receivable.		30
	Interest Revenue ($1,000 × .09 × 2/12) . .		15
	Collected note at maturity.		

Check Point 5-11

ASSETS	=	LIABILITIES	+	STOCKHOLDERS' EQUITY	+	REVENUES
+1,045 −1,000 − 30	=	0			+	15

Two aspects of these entries deserve mention:

1. Interest rates are always for an annual period, unless stated otherwise. In this example, the annual interest rate is 9%. At December 31, 20X5, Continental Bank accrues interest revenue for 4 months. The interest computation is

Principal	×	Interest Rate	×	Time	=	Amount of Interest
$1,000	×	.09	×	4/12	=	$30

2. The time element is the fraction of the year that the note has been in force.

Check Point 5-12

Check Point 5-13

Check Point 5-14

Some companies sell goods and services on notes receivable (versus selling on accounts receivable). This often occurs when the payment term extends beyond the customary accounts receivable period of 30 to 60 days.

Suppose that on March 20, 20X6, Ford Motor Company sells an Explorer to Bill Dorman. Ford gets Dorman's 3-year promissory note at 10% annual interest. At the outset, Ford would debit Notes Receivable and credit Sales Revenue.

A company may also accept a note receivable from a trade customer whose account receivable is past due. The company then credits Accounts Receivable and debits Note Receivable. We would say the company "received a note receivable from a customer on account." Now let's examine some strategies to speed up cash flow.

Taking Action How to Speed Up Cash Flow

All companies want speedy cash receipts. Rapid cash flow finances new technology, research, and development. Thus, companies such as Ford Motor Company find ways to collect cash immediately. Two common strategies generate cash quickly.

Credit Card or Bankcard Sales. The merchant sells merchandise and lets the customer pay with a credit card, such as Discover or American Express, or with a bankcard, such as VISA or MasterCard. This strategy may dramatically increase sales, but the added revenue comes at a cost. Let's see how credit cards and bankcards work from the seller's perspective.

Suppose Dell, Inc., sells computers for $100,000, and the customer pays with a VISA card. Dell records the sale as follows:

Cash	97,000	
Financing Expense	3,000	
Sales Revenue		100,000
Recorded bankcard sales.		

ASSETS	=	LIABILITIES	+	STOCKHOLDERS' EQUITY	+	REVENUES	–	EXPENSES
+97,000	=	0	+		+	$100,000	–	$3,000

Dell deposits the VISA slip in its bank and immediately receives a discounted portion, say $97,000, of the $100,000 sale amount. $3,000 (3%) goes to VISA. To Dell, the financing expense is an operating expense similar to interest expense.

Selling Receivables. Ford Motor Company makes some sales—of auto parts to Pep Boys and other suppliers—on account, debiting Accounts Receivable and crediting Sales Revenue. Ford can then sell these accounts receivable to another business, called a *factor*. The factor earns revenue by paying a discounted price for the receivable and then hopefully collecting the full amount from the customer. The benefit to Ford is the immediate receipt of cash.

To illustrate selling, or factoring, accounts receivable, suppose Ford wishes to speed up cash flow and therefore sells $100,000 of trade receivables, receiving cash of $95,000. Ford would record the sale of the receivables as follows:

Cash	95,000	
Financing Expense	5,000	
Accounts Receivable		100,000
Sold accounts receivable.		

ASSETS	=	LIABILITIES	–	STOCKHOLDERS' EQUITY	–	EXPENSES
+95,000	=	0			–	5,000
–100,000						

Again, financing expense is an operating expense, with the same effect as a loss. Some companies may debit a Loss account. Discounting a note receivable is similar to selling an account receivable. However, the credit is to Notes Receivable (instead of Accounts Receivable).

Using Two Key Ratios to Make Decisions

Investors and creditors use ratios to evaluate the financial health of a company. We introduced the current ratio in Chapter 3. Other ratios, including the quick (or acid-test) ratio and the number of days' sales in receivables, help investors measure liquidity.

Days' Sales in Receivables

OBJECTIVE

5 Use days' sales in receivables and the acid-test ratio to evaluate financial position

After a business makes a credit sale, the *next* step is collecting the receivable. **Days' sales in receivables**, also called the *collection period*, tells how long it takes to collect the average level of receivables. Shorter is better because cash is coming in quickly. The longer the collection period, the less cash is available to pay bills and expand. Days' sales in receivables can be computed in two logical steps. First, compute one day's sales (or total revenues). Then divide one day's sales into average receivables for the period.

Days' sales in receivables Ratio of average net accounts receivable to one day's sales. Indicates how many days' sales remain in Accounts Receivable awaiting collection. Also called the *collection period*.

We show days' sales in receivables for Ford Motor Company and for Motorola, Inc. These companies provide an interesting contrast.

	(Dollars in millions)	
Days' Sales in Receivables	Ford Motor Company	Motorola, Inc.
1. One day's sales = $\frac{\text{Net sales}}{\text{365 days}}$	$\frac{\$138{,}442}{\text{365 days}}$ = \$379 per day	$\frac{\$27{,}058}{\text{365 days}}$ = \$74 per day
2. Days' sales in average receivables = $\frac{\text{Average receivables}^*}{\text{One day's sales}}$	$\frac{\$148{,}636}{\$379\text{ per day}}$ = 392 days	$\frac{\$4{,}437}{\$74\text{ per day}}$ = 60 days

*Average net receivables = $\frac{\text{Beginning net receivables + Ending net receivables}}{2}$

It takes Ford a whopping 392 days to collect its average level of receivables. Why so long? Because Ford finances automobiles over a several-year period. Motorola is more typical, with a days'-sales-in-receivables measure of 60 days.

Net sales come from the income statement, and the receivables amounts are taken from the balance sheet. Average receivables is the simple average of the beginning and ending balance.

The length of the collection period depends on the credit terms of the company's sales. For example, sales on net 30 terms should be collected within approximately 30 days. **Nintendo** has an average collection period of 30 days. When we offer a 2% discount for payment within 10 days, the collection period may be shorter. Terms of net 45 or net 60 result in longer collection periods.

Companies watch their collection periods closely. Whenever collections get slow, the business must find other sources of financing, such as borrowing or factoring receivables. During recessions, customers pay more slowly, and a longer collection period may be unavoidable.[1]

Acid-Test (or Quick) Ratio

The balance sheet lists assets in the order of relative liquidity:

1. Cash and cash equivalents
2. Short-term investments
3. Accounts (or trade) receivables

Ford Motor Company's balance sheet in the chapter-opening story lists these accounts in order.

Managers, stockholders, and creditors care about the liquidity of a company's assets. In Chapter 3 we saw the current ratio, which measures ability to pay current liabilities with current assets. A more stringent measure of ability to pay current liabilities is the **acid-test** (or *quick*) **ratio**:

Acid-test ratio
Ratio of the sum of cash plus short-term investments plus net current receivables to total current liabilities. Tells whether the entity can pay all its current liabilities if they come due immediately. Also called the *quick ratio*.

For Ford Motor Company 2003

(Dollars in millions)

$$\text{Acid-test ratio} = \frac{\text{Cash} + \text{Short-term investments} + \text{Net current receivables}}{\text{Total current liabilities}} = \frac{\$21{,}770 + \$17{,}539 + \$2{,}721}{\$50{,}011} = 0.84$$

The higher the acid-test ratio, the easier it is to pay current liabilities. Ford's acid-test ratio of 0.84 means that Ford has 84 cents of quick assets to pay each $1 of current liabilities. This ratio value is a little low. Traditionally, companies have wanted an acid-test ratio of 1.0 to be safe.

What is an acceptable acid-test ratio? The answer depends on the industry. Auto dealers can operate smoothly with an acid-test ratio of 0.20, roughly one-fourth of Ford's ratio value. How can auto dealers survive with so low an acid-test ratio? Ford, GM, Toyota, and the other auto manufacturers help finance their dealers' inventory. Ford can always loosen credit when a Ford dealer's cash gets tight. Most dealers, therefore, have a financial safety net. Companies without a big brother like Ford Motor Company need a higher acid-test ratio.

Check Point 5-15

[1]Another ratio, **accounts receivable turnover**, captures the same information as days' sales in receivables. Receivable turnover is computed as follows: Net sales ÷ Average net accounts receivable. During 2003, Motorola had a receivable turnover rate of 6 times ($27,058/$4,437 = 6). The authors prefer days' sales in receivables because it is easier to interpret. Days' sales in receivable can be compared directly to the company's credit sale terms.

Reporting on the Statement of Cash Flows

Receivables and short-term investments appear on the balance sheet as assets. We saw these in Ford Motor Company's balance sheet at the beginning of the chapter, and we've also seen how to report the related revenues, expenses, gains, and losses on the income statement. Because receivables and investment transactions affect cash, their effects must also be reported on the statement of cash flows.

Receivables bring in cash when the business collects from customers. These transactions are reported as *operating activities* on the statement of cash flows because they result from sales. Investments transactions show up as *investing activities* on the statement of cash flows. Chapter 12 shows how companies report their cash flows on the statement of cash flows. In that chapter we will see exactly how to report cash flows related to receivables and investment transactions.

Summary Problem

END-OF-CHAPTER

Nintendo Co. Ltd., makes popular electronic games. The company balance sheet at March 31, 20X2, reported:

	(In millions)
Notes and trade accounts receivable	$382
Allowance for doubtful accounts	(52)

Nintendo uses both the percent-of-sales and the aging approaches to account for uncollectible receivables.

Required

1. How much of the March 31, 20X2, balance of notes and accounts receivables did Nintendo expect to collect? Stated differently, what was the expected realizable value of these receivables?
2. Journalize, without explanations, 20X3 entries for Nintendo, assuming
   a. Estimated Doubtful-Account Expense of $40 million, based on the percent-of-sales method, all during the year
   b. Write-offs of uncollectible accounts receivable totaling $58 million
   c. March 31, 20X3, aging of receivables, which indicates that $46 million of the total receivables of $409 million is uncollectible at year end
3. Show how Nintendo's receivables and related allowance will appear on the March 31, 20X3, balance sheet.
4. Show what Nintendo's income statement will report for the foregoing transactions.

Answers

Requirement 1

	(In millions)
Expected realizable value of receivables ($382 – $52)	$330

Requirement 2

a. Doubtful-Account Expense	40	
Allowance for Doubtful Accounts		40
b. Allowance for Doubtful Accounts	58	
Accounts Receivable		58

Allowance for Doubtful Accounts

		Dec. 31, 20X2	52
20X3 Write-offs	58	20X3 Expense	40
		20X3 Balance prior to December 31, 20X3	34

c. Doubtful-Account Expense ($46 – $34)	12	
Allowance for Doubtful Accounts		12

Allowance for Doubtful Accounts

	34
	12
	46

Requirement 3

	(In millions)
Notes and trade accounts receivable	$409
Allowance for doubtful accounts	(46)

Requirement 4

	(In millions)
Expenses: Doubtful-account expense for 20X8 ($40 + $12)	$52

REVIEW RECEIVABLES AND INVESTMENTS

Chapter Review Quiz

1. **American Express Company** held trading investments valued at $995 million at December 31, 2003. Assume these investments cost American Express $950 million. When did American Express purchase the trading investments?
   a. Some time early in 2003
   b. Some time early in 2002
   c. Some time late in 2003
   d. Some time late in 2002

2. Return to American Express Company in question 1. How much appeared on the American Express balance sheet at December 31, 2003, for the trading investments?
   a. $995 million
   b. $45 million
   c. $950 million
   d. Cannot tell from the data given

Use the following information to answer questions 3–7.
Ray Company had the following information relating to credit sales in 20X3:

Accounts receivable 12/31/X3	$ 8,000
Allowance for uncollectible accounts 12/31/X3 (before adjustment)	750
Credit sales during 20X3	38,000
Cash sales during 20X3	12,000
Collections from customers on account during 20X3	41,000

3. Uncollectible accounts are determined by the percent-of-sales method to be 2% of credit sales. How much is uncollectible-account expense for 20X3?
   a. $1,000
   b. $760
   c. $750
   d. $10

4. Using the percent-of-sales method, what is the adjusted balance in the Allowance account at year end 20X3?
   a. $750
   b. $760
   c. $1,750
   d. $1,510

5. If uncollectible accounts are determined by the aging-of-receivables method to be $1,140, the uncollectible account expense for 20X3 would be:
   a. $1,140
   b. $750
   c. $390
   d. $760

6. Using the aging-of-receivables method, the balance of the Allowance account after the adjusting entry would be:
   a. $1,140
   b. $1,890
   c. $390
   d. $750

7. Assuming the aging-of-receivables method is used, the net realizable value of accounts receivable on the 12/31/X3 balance sheet would be:
   a. $8,000
   b. $7,250
   c. $6,110
   d. $6,860

8. Accounts Receivable has a debit balance of $2,300, and the Allowance for Uncollectible Accounts has a credit balance of $200. An $80 account receivable is written off. What is the amount of net receivables (net realizable value) after the write-off?
   a. $2,100
   b. $2,220
   c. $2,020
   d. $2,180

9. Highmark Corporation began 20X1 with Accounts Receivable of $500,000. Sales for the year totaled $2,000,000. Highmark ended the year with customers owing the company $580,000. Highmark's bad-debt losses are minimal. How much cash did Highmark collect from customers in 20X1?
   a. $2,000,000
   b. $2,080,000
   c. $1,920,000
   d. $2,580,000

10. Cosmos Company received a two-month, 8%, $1,500 note receivable on December 15. The adjusting entry on December 31 will:
    a. debit Interest Receivable $10
    b. debit Cash $10
    c. credit Interest Revenue $5
    d. credit Interest Revenue $120

11. What is the maturity value of a $30,000, 12%, 3-month note?
    a. $30,000
    b. $30,900
    c. $33,600
    d. $3,600

12. If the adjusting entry to accrue interest on a note receivable is omitted, then:
    a. assets, net income, and stockholders' equity are overstated.
    b. assets, net income, and stockholders' equity are understated.
    c. liabilities are understated, net income is overstated, and stockholders' equity is overstated.
    d. assets are overstated, net income is understated, and stockholders' equity is understated.
    e. none of the above.

13. Net sales total $600,000. Beginning and ending accounts receivable are $52,000 and $38,000, respectively. Calculate days' sales in receivables.
    a. 32 days
    b. 23 days
    c. 43 days
    d. 27 days

14. From the following list of accounts, calculate the quick ratio.

Cash	$ 3,000	Accounts Payable	$5,000
Accounts Receivable	6,000	Salary Payable	2,000
Inventory	10,000	Notes Payable (due in 2 years)	8,000
Prepaid insurance	2,000		

    a. 3.0
    b. 1.3
    c. .6
    d. 1.4

Answers:

1. c
2. a
3. b ($38,000 × .02)
4. d ($750 + $760)
5. c ($1,140 – $750)
6. a
7. d ($8,000 – $1,140)
8. a ($2,300 – $200)
9. c ($500,000 + $2,000,000 – $580,000)
10. c ($1,500 × .08 × 16/365)
11. b [$30,000 + ($30,000 × .12 × 3/12)]
12. b
13. d [($52,000 + $38,000)/2] ÷ ($600,000/365)
14. b [($3,000 + $6,000)/($5,000 + $2,000)]

Accounting Vocabulary

acid-test ratio (p. 236)
accounts receivable turnover (p. 236)
aging-of-accounts receivable (p. 228)
Allowance for Doubtful Accounts (p. 226)
Allowance for Uncollectible Accounts (p. 226)
allowance method (p. 226)
bad-debt expense (p. 226)
balance-sheet approach (p. 228)
creditor (p. 218)
days' sales in receivables (p. 235)
debt instrument (p. 218)
debtor (p. 218)
direct write-off method (p. 230)
doubtful-account expense (p. 226)
equity security (p. 218)
income-statement approach (p. 227)
interest (p. 232)
marketable securities (p. 218)
maturity (p. 218)
percent-of-sales method (p. 227)
principal (p. 232)
quick ratio (p. 236)
receivables (p. 223)
short-term investments (p. 218)
term (p. 218)
trading investments (p. 219)
uncollectible-account expense (p. 226)

ASSESS YOUR PROGRESS

Check Points

Classifying investments as current or long-term (Obj. 1)

CP5-1 (p. 219) Answer these questions about investments.

1. What is the amount to report on the balance sheet for a trading investment?
2. Why is a trading investment always a current asset? Explain.

Accounting for a trading investment (Obj. 1)

CP5-2 (p. 220) **United Health Group** (UHG) holds short-term trading investments. Suppose that on November 16, UHG paid $80,000 for a short-term trading investment in **Microsoft stock**. At December 31, the market value of Microsoft stock is $74,000. For this situation, show everything that UHG would report on its December 31 balance sheet and on its income statement for the year ended December 31.

Accounting for a trading investment (Obj. 1)

CP5-3 (p. 220) Return to page 220 and the example of **Ford Motor Company's** short-term trading investment in **IBM** stock.

1. How much did Ford pay for the short-term investment in IBM stock? Stated differently, what was Ford's cost of the IBM stock?
2. Suppose the IBM stock decreased in value to $98,000 at December 31. Make the Ford journal entry to adjust the Short-Term Investment account to market value.
3. Show how Ford would report the short-term investment on its balance sheet and the unrealized gain or loss on its income statement.

Internal control over the collection of receivables (Obj. 2)

CP5-4 (p. 224) Return to the Accounts Receivable T-accounts on page 227. Suppose Rex Jennings is the accountant responsible for these records. What duty will a good internal control system withhold from Jennings? Why?

writing assignment ■

Applying the allowance method (percent-of-sales) to account for uncollectibles (Obj. 3)

CP5-5 (p. 226) During its first year of operations, Spitzer Xcel Corporation had net sales of $900,000, all on account. Industry experience suggests that Spitzer's bad debts will amount to 1% of net credit sales. At December 31, 20X4, Spitzer's accounts receivable total $90,000. The company uses the allowance method to account for uncollectibles.

1. Make Spitzer's journal entry for uncollectible-account expense using the percent-of-sales method.
2. Show how Spitzer should report accounts receivable on its balance sheet at December 31, 20X4. Follow the reporting format illustrated in the middle of page 226.

Applying the allowance method (percent-of-sales) to account for uncollectibles (Obj. 3)

CP5-6 (p. 228) This exercise continues the situation of Check Point 5-5, in which Spitzer Xcel Corporation ended the year 20X4 with accounts receivable of $90,000 and an allowance for uncollectible accounts of $9,000.

During 20X5, Spitzer completed the following transactions:

1. Net credit sales, $800,000.
2. Collections on account, $780,000.
3. Write-offs of uncollectibles, $5,000
4. Uncollectible-account expense, 1% of net credit sales

Journalize the 20X5 transactions for Spitzer. Explanations are not required.

Applying the allowance method (percent-of-sales) to account for uncollectibles (Obj. 3)

CP5-7 (p. 229) Use the solution to Check Point 5-6 to answer these questions about Spitzer Xcel Corporation.

1. Start with Accounts Receivable's beginning balance ($90,000) and then post to the Accounts Receivable T-account. How much do Spitzer's customers owe the company at December 31, 20X5?
2. Start with the Allowance account's beginning credit balance ($9,000) and then post to the Allowance for Uncollectible Accounts T-account. How much of the receivables at December 31, 20X5, does Spitzer expect *not* to collect?
3. At December 31, 20X5, how much cash does Spitzer expect to collect on its accounts receivable?
4. Show what Spitzer should report on its 20X5 balance sheet and income statement. Do not report cash.

Applying the allowance method (aging-of-accounts-receivable) to account for uncollectibles (Obj. 3)

CP5-8 (p. 229) Davis & Baker, a law firm, started 20X6 with accounts receivable of $100,000 and an allowance for uncollectible accounts of $8,000. The 20X6 revenues on account totaled $700,000, and cash collections on account totaled $720,000. During 20X6,

Practice Quiz

Test your understanding of receivables by answering the following questions. Select the best choice from among the possible answers given.

PQ5-1 **Wells Fargo,** the nationwide banking company, owns lots of investments. Assume that Wells Fargo paid $500,000 for trading investments on December 3. Two weeks later Wells Fargo received a $15,000 cash dividend. At December 31, these trading investments were quoted at a market price of $493,000. Wells Fargo's December income statement should report

a. Dividend revenue of $15,000
b. Unrealized loss of $7,000
c. Both a and b
d. None of the above

PQ5-2 Refer to the Wells Fargo data in question 1. At December 31, Wells Fargo's balance sheet should report

a. Dividend revenue of $15,000
b. Unrealized loss of $7,000
c. Short-term investment of $500,000
d. Short-term investment of $493,000

PQ5-3 Under the allowance method for uncollectible receivables, the entry to record uncollectible-account expense has what effect on the financial statements?

a. Increases expenses and increases owners' equity.
b. Decreases assets and has no effect on net income.
c. Decreases owners' equity and decreases assets.
d. Decreases net income and increases liabilities.

PQ5-4 Mead Company uses the aging method to adjust the allowance for uncollectible accounts at the end of the period. At December 31, 20X1, the balance of accounts receivable is $220,000 and the allowance for uncollectible accounts has a credit balance of $3,200 (before adjustment). An analysis of accounts receivable produced the following age groups:

Not yet due	$150,000
60 days past due	60,000
Over 60 days past due	10,000
	$220,000

Based on past experience, Mead Company estimates that the percentage of accounts that will prove to be uncollectible within the three age groups is 2%, 8%, and 20%, respectively. Based on these facts, the adjusting entry for uncollectible accounts should be made in the amount of

a. $3,200
b. $6,600
c. $9,800
d. $13,000

PQ5-5 Refer to Question 4. The net receivables on the balance sheet is ______________.

PQ5-6 Barkus Company uses the percent-of-sales method to estimate uncollectibles. Net credit sales for the current year amount to $1,000,000 and management estimates 3% will be uncollectible. Allowance for doubtful accounts prior to adjustment has a credit balance of $2,000. The amount of expense to report on the income statement will be:

a. $30,000
b. $32,000
c. $28,000
d. $2,000

PQ5-7 Refer to Question 6. The balance of Allowance for Doubtful Accounts, after adjustment, will be:

a. $30,000
b. $32,000
c. $28,000
d. $2,000
e. Cannot be determined from the information given

PQ5-8 Draw a T-account to illustrate the information in question 6 and 7. Then early the following year, Barkus wrote off $25,000 of old receivables as uncollectible. The balance in the Allowance account is now ______________.

The next four questions use the following data:

On August 1, 20X7, Andover Company sold equipment and accepted an 8-month, 7%, $6,000 note receivable. Andover's year-end is December 31.

PQ5-9 How much interest revenue should Andover accrue on December 31, 20X7?

a. $210
b. $420
c. $175
d. some other amount

PQ5-10 If Andover Company fails to make an adjusting entry for the accrued interest,

a. net income will be overstated and liabilities will be understated.
b. net income will be overstated and assets will be overstated.
c. net income will be understated and liabilities will be overstated.
d. net income will be understated and assets will be understated.

PQ5-11 How much interest does Andover Company expect to collect on the maturity date (April 1, 20X8)?

a. $420
b. $280
c. $105
d. some other amount

PQ5-12 Which of the following accounts will Andover credit in the journal entry on April 1, 20X8, assuming collection in full?

a. Interest Receivable
b. Note Receivable
c. Interest Revenue
d. All of the above

PQ5-13 Write the journal entry for question 12.

PQ5-14 Which of the following is excluded from the calculation of the acid-test ratio?

a. inventory and accounts receivable
b. prepaid expenses and cash
c. inventory and short-term investment
d. inventory and prepaid expenses

PQ5-15 A company with net sales of $730,000, beginning net receivables of $90,000, and ending net receivables of $110,000, has a days' sales in accounts receivable of:

a. 50 days
b. 55 days
c. 100 days
d. 110 days

PQ5-16 The company in question 15 sells on credit terms of "net 30 days." Its days' sales in receivables is

a. Too high
b. Too low
c. About right
d. Cannot be evaluated from the data given.

Problems
(Group A)

PH Grade Assist

Most of these A problems can be found within Prentice Hall Grade Assist (PHGA), an online homework and practice environment. Your instructor may ask you to complete these problems using PHGA.

P5-1A During the fourth quarter of 20X4, the operations of York Air Conditioning Company generated excess cash, which the company invested in securities, as follows:

Accounting for a trading investment (Obj. 1)

Dec. 2	Purchased 2,000 shares of common stock as a trading investment, paying $12.75 per share.
21	Received semiannual cash dividend of $0.45 per share on the trading investment.
31	Adjusted the trading investment to its market value of $31,000.

Required

1. Prepare T-accounts for Cash, balance of $400,000; Short-Term Investment; Dividend Revenue; and Unrealized Gain (Loss) on Investment.
2. Journalize the foregoing transactions and post to the T-accounts.
3. Show how to report the short-term investments on York's balance sheet at December 31.
4. Show how to report whatever should appear on York's income statement.
5. On January 9, 20X5, York sold the trading investment for $29,000. Journalize the sale.

Controlling cash receipts from customers (Obj. 2)

writing assignment ■

P5-2A Ingall's Custom Lamps distributes merchandise to furniture stores. All sales are on credit, so virtually all cash receipts arrive in the mail. Akbar Kuwaja, the company president, has just returned from a trade association meeting with new ideas for the business. Among other things, Kuwaja plans to institute stronger internal controls over cash receipts from customers.

Required

Take the role of Akbar Kuwaja, the company president. Write a memo to employees outlining procedures to ensure that all cash receipts are deposited in the bank and that the total amounts of each day's cash receipts are posted to customer accounts receivable.

Accounting for revenue, collections, and uncollectibles; percent-of-sales method (Obj. 3)

P5-3A This problem takes you through the accounting for revenue, receivables, and uncollectibles for **America Online, Inc.,** the Internet service company. AOL sells for cash and on account. By selling on credit, AOL cannot expect to collect 100% of its accounts receivable. At December 31, 20X4, and 20X3, respectively, AOL reported the following on its balance sheet (all amounts adapted and in millions of dollars):

	December 31,	
	20X4	20X3
Accounts receivable	$561	$443
Less Allowance for uncollectibles	(97)	(58)
Accounts receivable, net	$464	$385

During the year ended December 31, 20X4, AOL earned service revenue and collected cash from customers. Assume uncollectible-account expense for the year was 4% of service revenue and that AOL wrote off uncollectible accounts receivable. At year end AOL ended with the foregoing December 31, 20X4, balances.

Required

1. Prepare T-accounts for Accounts Receivable and Allowance for Uncollectibles, and insert the December 31, 20X3, balances as given.
2. Journalize the following assumed transactions of AOL for the year ended December 31, 20X4 (explanations are not required):
   a. Service revenue on account, $7,703 million.
   b. Collections from customers on account, $7,316 million.
   c. Uncollectible-account expense, 4% of service revenue (rounded to the nearest $1 million).
   d. Write-offs of uncollectible accounts receivable, $? You must solve for the amount of write-offs.
3. Post to the Accounts Receivable and Allowance for Uncollectibles T-accounts.
4. Compute the ending balances for the two T-accounts and compare to the actual December 31, 20X4, amounts. They should be the same.
5. At December 31, 20X4, how much did customers owe AOL? How much did AOL expect to collect from customers?
6. Show what AOL would report on its income statement for the year ended December 31, 20X4.

P5-4A The September 30, 20X8, records of DodgeRam Auto Supply include these accounts:

Using the aging approach for uncollectibles (Obj. 3)

■ **general ledger**

Accounts Receivable	$265,000
Allowance for Doubtful Accounts	(7,100)

During the year DodgeRam estimates doubtful-account expense at 2% of credit sales. At year end, the company ages its receivables and adjusts the balance in Allowance for Doubtful Accounts to correspond to the aging schedule. During the last quarter of 20X8, DodgeRam completed the following selected transactions:

20X8	
Nov. 22	Wrote off the following accounts receivable as uncollectible: Monet Corporation $1,300; Blocker, Inc., $2,100; and M Street Plaza, $700.
Dec. 31	Adjusted the Allowance for Doubtful Accounts and recorded doubtful-account expense at year end, based on the aging of receivables:

	Age of Accounts			
Total Balance	**1–30 Days**	**31–60 Days**	**61–90 days**	**Over 90 Days**
$289,000	$160,000	$80,000	$34,000	$15,000
Estimated uncollectible	.5%	1.0%	5.0%	50.0%

Required

1. Record the transactions in the journal. Explanations are not required.
2. Prepare a T-account for Allowance for Doubtful Accounts and post to that account.
3. Show how DodgeRam Auto Supply will report its accounts receivable in a comparative balance sheet for 20X8 and 20X7. Use the reporting format on page 226. At December 31, 20X7, the company's Accounts Receivable balance was $271,000 and the Allowance for Doubtful Accounts stood at $8,700.

P5-5A Bzensky Corporation is preparing for an initial public offering of the company's stock. Top managers of Bzensky seek the counsel of **KPMG**, the accounting firm, and learn that Bzensky must make some changes to bring its financial statements into conformity with generally accepted accounting principles (GAAP). At December 31, 20X5, Bzensky's accounts include the following:

Short-term investments, uncollectibles, notes, and the ratios (Obj. 1, 3, 4, 5)

Cash	$ 18,000
Short-term trading investments, at cost	34,000
Accounts receivable	49,000
Notes receivable	42,000
Inventory	54,000
Prepaid expenses	5,000
Total current assets	$202,000
Accounts payable	$ 76,000
Other current liabilities	69,000
Total current liabilities	$145,000

Assume KPMG drew the following conclusions:

- Cash includes $8,000 that is deposited in a compensating balance account that will be tied up until 20X8.
- The market value of the short-term trading investments is $22,000. Bzensky purchased the investments in early December.

- Bzensky has been using the direct write-off method to account for uncollectibles. During 20X5, the company wrote off bad receivables of $7,000. KPMG believes uncollectible-account expense should be 3% of sales, which for 20X5 totaled $400,000. An aging of receivables at year end indicated uncollectibles of $4,000.
- The notes receivable will be collected in installments starting in 20X8.
- Bzensky reported net income of $65,000 for 20X5.

Required

1. Restate all current accounts to conform to GAAP.
2. Compute Bzensky's current ratio and acid-test ratio both before and after your corrections.
3. Determine Bzensky's correct net income for 20X5.
4. Evaluate the overall effect of KPMG's suggestions on Bzensky's financial appearance.

Notes receivable and accrued interest revenue (Obj. 4)

■ **general ledger**

P5-6A Assume that **Sherwin-Williams,** the paint company, completed the following selected transactions:

20X4	
Nov. 30	Sold goods to **Kelly Moore Paint Company,** receiving a $60,000, 3-month, 10% note.
Dec. 31	Made an adjusting entry to accrue interest on the Kelly Moore note.
20X5	
Feb. 18	Received a 90-day, 10%, $5,000 note from Altex Company on account.
Feb. 20	Sold the Altex note to First State Bank, receiving cash of $4,600.
Feb. 28	Collected the Kelly Moore note.
Nov. 11	Loaned $50,000 cash to Consolidated, Inc., receiving a 90-day, 9% note.
Dec. 31	Accrued the interest on the Consolidated, Inc. note.

Required

1. Record the transactions in Sherwin-Williams' journal. Explanations are not required.
2. Show what Sherwin-Williams will report on its comparative classified balance sheet at December 31, 20X5, and December 31, 20X4.

Using ratio data to evaluate a company's financial position (Obj. 5)

writing assignment ■

■ **spreadsheet**

P5-7A The comparative financial statements of Crain's Stationery Company for 20X6, 20X5, and 20X4 included the following selected data:

	20X6	20X5	20X4
		(In millions)	
Balance sheet:			
Current assets:			
Cash	$ 27	$ 26	$ 22
Short-term investments	93	101	69
Receivables, net of allowance for doubtful accounts of $7, $6 and $4, respectively	206	154	127
Inventories	408	383	341
Prepaid expenses	32	31	25
Total current assets	766	695	584
Total current liabilities	540	446	388
Income statement:			
Net sales	$2,671	$2,505	$1,944
Cost of sales	1,380	1,360	963

Required

1. Compute these ratios for 20X6 and 20X5:
   a. Current ratio b. Acid-test ratio c. Days' sales in receivables
2. Write a memo explaining to top management which ratio values showed improvement from 20X5 to 20X6 and which ratio values deteriorated. State whether this trend is favorable or unfavorable for the company and give the reason for your evaluation.

(Group B)

PH Grade Assist

Some of these B problems can be found within Prentice Hall Grade Assist (PHGA), an online homework and practice environment. Your instructor may ask you to complete these problems using PHGA.

Accounting for a trading investment (Obj. 1)

P5-1B During the fourth quarter of 20X8. Four Seasons, Inc., generated excess cash, which the company invested in securities, as follows:

Nov.	3	Purchased 5,000 shares of common stock as a trading investment, paying $9.25 per share.
	14	Received cash dividend of $0.32 per share on the trading investment.
Dec.	31	Adjusted the trading investment to its market value of $7.40 per share

Required

1. Prepare T-accounts for: Cash, balance of $400,000; Short-Term Investment; Dividend Revenue; Unrealized Gain (Loss) on Investment.
2. Journalize the foregoing transactions and post to the T-accounts.
3. Show how to report the short-term investment on the Four Seasons balance sheet at December 31.
4. Show how to report whatever should appear on Four Seasons' income statement.
5. Four Seasons sold the trading investment for $39,000 on January 6, 20X9. Journalize the sale.

Controlling cash receipts from customers (Obj. 2)

writing assignment ■

P5-2B Tony the Tiger, Inc., manufactures toys and sells to Levine's and other toy stores. All sales are made on account. Joy Loudermilk, accountant for the company, receives and opens the mail. Company procedure requires Loudermilk to separate customer checks from the remittance slips, which list the amounts that Loudermilk posts as credits to customer accounts receivable. Loudermilk deposits the checks in the bank. At the end of each day she computes the day's total amount posted to customer accounts and matches this total to the bank deposit slip. This procedure ensures that all receipts are deposited in the bank.

Required

As a consultant hired by Tony the Tiger, Inc., write a memo to management evaluating the company's internal controls over cash receipts from customers. If the system is effective, identify its strong features. If the system has flaws, propose a way to strengthen the controls.

Accounting for revenue, collections, and uncollectibles; percent-of-sales method (Obj. 3)

P5-3B This problem takes you through the accounting for sales, receivables, and uncollectibles for **Nike, Inc.**, the sports manufacturer. By selling on credit, Nike cannot expect to collect 100% of its accounts receivable. At May 31, 20X1, and 20X0, respectively, Nike reported the following on its balance sheet (adapted and in millions of dollars):

	May 31,	
	20X1	20X0
Accounts receivable	$1,693	$1,635
Less Allowance for uncollectibles	(72)	(65)
Accounts receivable, net	$1,621	$1,570

During the year ended May 31, 20X1, Nike earned sales revenue and collected cash from customers. Assume uncollectible-account expense for the year was 1% of sales revenue and that Nike wrote off uncollectible receivables. At year end Nike ended with the foregoing May 31, 20X1, balances.

Required

1. Prepare T-accounts for Accounts Receivable and Allowance for Uncollectibles and insert the May 31, 20X0, balances as given.
2. Journalize the following assumed transactions of Nike, Inc. for the year ended May 31, 20X1 (explanations are not required).
   a. Sales revenue on account, $9,489 million.
   b. Collections on account, $9,343 million.
   c. Uncollectible-account expense, 1% of sales revenue (round to the nearest $1 million).
   d. Write-offs of uncollectible accounts receivable, $? You must solve for the amount of write-offs.
3. Post your entries to the Accounts Receivable and the Allowance for Uncollectibles T-accounts.
4. Compute the ending balances for the two T-accounts and compare your balances to the actual May 31, 20X1 amounts. They should be the same.
5. At May 31, 20X1, how much did customers owe Nike? How much did Nike expect to collect from customers?
6. Show what Nike would report on its income statement for the year ended May 31, 20X1.

Using the aging approach for uncollectibles (Obj. 3)

general ledger

P5-4B The September 30, 20X4, records of Precision Tool Company include these accounts:

Accounts Receivable	$143,000
Allowance for Doubtful Accounts	(3,200)

During the year, Precision Tool estimates doubtful-account expense at 1 1/2% of credit sales. At year end, the company ages its receivables and adjusts the balance in Allowance for Doubtful Accounts to correspond to the aging schedule. During the last quarter of 20X4, the company completed the following selected transactions:

20X4	
Nov. 18	Wrote off as uncollectible the $700 account receivable from Bliss Company and the $400 account receivable from Micro Data.
Dec. 31	Adjusted the Allowance for Doubtful Accounts and recorded doubtful-account expense at year end, based on the aging of receivables:

	Age of Accounts			
Total Balance	**1–30 Days**	**31–60 Days**	**61–90 Days**	**Over 90 Days**
$163,000	$100,000	$40,000	$14,000	$9,000
Estimated uncollectible	.1%	.5%	5.0%	30.0%

Required

1. Record the transactions in the journal. Explanations are not required.
2. Prepare a T-account for Allowance for Doubtful Accounts and post to that account.
3. Show how Precision Tool Company will report its accounts receivable on a comparative balance sheet for 20X4 and 20X3. Use the reporting format on page 226. At December 31, 20X3, the company's Accounts Receivable balance was $112,000 and the Allowance for Doubtful Accounts stood at $2,200.

Short-term investments, uncollectibles, notes, and the ratios
(Obj. 1, 3, 4, 5)

P5-5B Ciliotta, Inc. is hoping to offer its stock to the public and seeks the advice of **Pricewaterhouse Coopers (PWC)**, the accounting firm. Assume PWC advises Ciliotta that its financial statements must be changed to conform to GAAP. At December 31, 20X7, Ciliotta's accounts include the following:

Cash	$ 21,000
Short-term trading investments, at cost	19,000
Accounts receivable	37,000
Note receivable	50,000
Inventory	61,000
Prepaid expenses	14,000
Total current assets	$202,000
Accounts payable	$ 62,000
Other current liabilities	41,000
Total current liabilities	$103,000

PWC advised Ciliotta that

- Cash includes $10,000 that is deposited in a compensating balance account that is tied up until 20X9.
- The market value of the short-term trading investments is $7,000. Ciliotta purchased the investments in November.
- Ciliotta has been using the direct write-off method to account for uncollectible receivables. During 20X7, Ciliotta wrote off bad receivables of $6,000. PWC states that uncollectible-account expense should be 2.5% of service revenue, which totaled $600,000 in 20X7. PWC's aging of Ciliotta's receivables at year end indicated uncollectibles of $9,000.
- The notes receivable are scheduled to be collected in 20X9.
- Ciliotta reported net income of $72,000 in 20X7.

Required

1. Restate Ciliotta's current accounts to conform to GAAP.
2. Compute Ciliotta's current ratio and acid-test ratio both before and after your corrections.
3. Determine Ciliotta's correct net income for 20X7.
4. Evaluate the overall effect of PWC's suggestions on Ciliotta's financial appearance.

Notes receivable and accrued interest revenue
(Obj. 4)

general ledger

P5-6B Assume that **Green Giant Foods** famous for canned and frozen fruits and vegetables, completed the following selected transactions.

20X5	
Oct. 31	Sold goods to Kroger, Inc., receiving a $30,000, 3-month, 6% note.
Dec. 31	Made an adjusting entry to accrue interest on the Kroger note.
20X6	
Jan. 31	Collected the Kroger note.
Mar. 31	Received a 90-day, 7%, $4,000 note from Bliss Company on account.
31	Sold the Bliss Company note to Lakewood Bank, receiving cash of $3,800.
Nov. 16	Loaned $45,000 cash to McNeil, Inc., receiving a 90-day, 12% note.
Dec. 31	Accrued the interest on the McNeil, Inc. note.

Required

1. Record the transactions in Green Giant's journal. Explanations are not required.
2. Show what Green Giant will report on its comparative classified balance sheet at December 31, 20X6, and December 31, 20X5.

Using ratio data to evaluate a company's financial position (Obj. 5)

writing assignment ■

■ spreadsheet

P5-7B The comparative financial statements of Braswell-Davis Organic Gardening Supply for 2006, 2005, and 2004 included the following selected data.

	2006	2005	2004
		(In millions)	
Balance sheet:			
Current assets:			
Cash	$ 36	$ 80	$ 60
Short-term investments	140	154	122
Receivables, net of allowance for doubtful accounts of $27, $21, and $15, respectively	297	285	178
Inventories	319	341	342
Prepaid expenses	21	27	46
Total current assets	813	887	748
Total current liabilities	603	528	413
Income statement:			
Net sales	$4,989	$5,295	$4,206
Cost of sales	2,734	2,636	2,418

Required

1. Compute these ratios for 2006 and 2005:
   a. Current ratio **b.** Acid-test ratio **c.** Days' sales in receivables
2. Write a memo explaining to top management which ratio values improved from 2005 to 2006 and which ratio values deteriorated. State whether this trend is favorable or unfavorable and give the reason for your evaluation.

APPLY YOUR KNOWLEDGE

Decision Cases

Estimating the collectibility of accounts receivable (Obj. 3)

Case 1. Assume that you work in the corporate loan department of Prime Meridian Bank. Martha Agee, owner of Triad Sales Company, has come to you seeking a loan for $1 million to expand operations. Agee proposes to use accounts receivable as collateral for the loan and has provided you with the following information from the company's most recent financial statements:

	20X7	20X6	20X5
		(In thousands)	
Sales	$1,475	$1,589	$1,502
Cost of goods sold	876	947	905
Gross profit	599	642	597
Other expenses	518	487	453
Net profit or (loss) before taxes	$ 81	$ 155	$ 144
Accounts receivable	$ 458	$ 387	$ 374
Allowance for doubtful accounts	23	31	29

Required

Analyze the trends of sales, days' sales in receivables, and cash collections from customers. Would you make the loan to Agee? Support you decision with facts and figures.

Revenues, collections, and bad debts on receivables (Obj. 3)

Case 2. Providence Medical Clinic serves the area around Santa Fe. The clinic extends credit to indigent patients and collects cash from individuals, Medicare, Medicaid, and various insurance companies. Rising population has caused the need for expansion, and the clinic needs a loan to finance new construction.

After opening in 20X5, Providence earned service revenue of $800,000 and collected $600,000 during the remainder of the year. The clinic's accountant estimated uncollectible receivables at 8% of revenue, and write-offs for the year totaled $30,000. There was no aging of receivables at December 31, 20X5.

At December 31, 20X6, the chief executive of Providence is astonished to learn that records of the clinic's revenues and most expenses are missing. The bank requires at least a summary income statement to support the loan. The only accounting data for 20X6 that Providence can come up with follow—all balances at December 31, 20X6:

Accounts receivable	$260,000
Less Allowance for bad debts	(52,000)*
Total expenses, excluding bad-debt expense	870,000
Collections from customers	950,000
Write-offs of bad receivables	60,000

*Determined by the aging of receivables

Prepare a summary income statement for Providence Medical Clinic for the year ended December 31, 20X6. Was the clinic profitable in 20X6?

Uncollectible accounts and evaluating a business (Obj. 3, 4)

Case 3. Nature's Best Health Foods sells to health food stores either for cash or on notes receivable. The business uses the direct write-off method to account for bad debts. Ross Earley, the owner, has prepared the company's financial statements. The most recent comparative income statements, for 20X5 and 20X4, follow:

	20X5	20X4
Total revenue	$220,000	$190,000
Total expenses	130,000	115,000
Net income	$ 90,000	$ 75,000

Due to the increase in net income, Earley seeks to expand operations. He asks you to invest $50,000 in the business. Earley states that notes receivable from customers were $200,000 at the end of 20X3 and $400,000 at the end of 20X4. Also, total revenues for 20X5 and 20X4 include interest at 10% on the year's beginning notes receivable balance. Total expenses include doubtful-account expense of $2,000 each year, based on the direct write-off method. Earley estimates that doubtful-account expense would be 5% of sales revenue if the allowance method were used.

Required

1. Prepare for Nature's Best Health Foods a comparative single-step income statement that identifies sales revenue, interest revenue, doubtful-account expense, and other expenses, all computed in accordance with GAAP.
2. Consider whether sales revenue or interest revenue caused net income to increase during 20X5. Is Nature's Best's future as promising as Earley's income statement makes it appear? Give the reason for your answer.

Ethical Issue

La Vega Credit Company is in the consumer loan business. It borrows from banks and loans out the money at higher interest rates. La Vega's bank requires La Vega to submit quarterly financial statements to keep its line of credit. La Vega's main asset is Notes Receivable. Therefore, Uncollectible-Account Expense and Allowance for Uncollectible Accounts are important accounts.

Dee Cranston, the company's owner, prefers for net income to increase in a smooth pattern, rather than increase in some periods and decrease in other periods. To report smoothly increasing net income, Cranston underestimates Uncollectible-Account Expense in some periods. In other periods, Cranston overestimates the expense. She reasons that the income overstatments roughly offset the income understatements over time.

Required

Is La Vega Credit's practice of smoothing income ethical? Why or why not?

Focus on Financials: ■ YUM! Brands

Short-term investments and accounts receivable (Obj. 1, 3, 4)

Refer to YUM! Brands financial statements in Appendix A at the end of this book.

1. Assume that YUM! Brands purchased no short-term investments and had no market-value write-downs during 2003. The statement of cash flows reports that YUM sold short-term investments during 2003. How much gain or loss did YUM have on the sale of short-term investments?
2. How much did customers owe YUM at the end of 2002 and at the end of 2003? As of these dates, how much did YUM expect to collect from customers?
3. How much cash did YUM collect from customers and franchisees during 2003? Assume that write-offs of uncollectibles totaled $14 million during 2003. Show your work.

Focus on Analysis: ■ Pier 1 Imports

Analyzing accounts receivable (Obj. 3)

This case is based on the Pier 1 Imports financial statements in Appendix B at the end of this book.

1. Consider only Pier 1's "Other accounts receivable." How much did Pier 1's customers owe the company at the end of 2004? Of this amount, how much did Pier 1 expect to collect? How much did Pier 1 expect *not* to collect?
2. Were Pier 1's "Other accounts receivable" of higher quality at the end of 2004 or at the end of 2003? How can you tell?
3. Would you predict that Pier 1's doubtful-account expense increased or decreased during 2004 as compared to 2003? Indicate how you formed your opinion.

Group Project

Jillian Michaels and Dee Childress worked for several years as sales representatives for Xerox Corporation. During this time, they became close friends as they acquired expertise with the company's full range of copier equipment. Now they see an opportunity to put their expertise to work and fulfill lifelong desires to establish their own business. Navarro Community College, located in their city, is expanding, and there is no copy center within 5 miles of the campus. Business in the area is booming, office buildings and apartments are springing up, and the population of the Navarro section of the city is growing.

Michaels and Childress want to open a copy center, similar to **Kinko's**, near the Navarro campus. A small shopping center across the street from the college has a vacancy that would fit their needs. Michaels and Childress each have $35,000 to invest in the business, but they forecast the need for $200,000 to renovate the store and purchase some of the equipment they will need. Xerox Corporation will lease two large copiers to them at a total monthly rental of $6,000. With enough cash to see them through the first 6 months of operation, they are confident they can make the business succeed. The two women work very well together, and both have excellent credit ratings. Michaels and Childress must borrow $130,000 to start the business, advertise its opening, and keep it running for its first 6 months.

Required

Assume two roles: (1) Michaels and Childress, the partners who will own Navarro Copy Center; and (2) loan officers at Synergy Bank.

1. As a group, visit a copy center to familiarize yourselves with its operations. If possible, interview the manager or another employee. Then write a loan request that Michaels and Childress will submit to Synergy Bank with the intent of borrowing $130,000 to be paid back over 3 years. The loan will be a personal loan to the partnership of Michaels and Childress, not to Navarro Copy Center. The request should specify all the details of Michaels' and Childress's plan that will motivate the bank to grant the loan. Include a budget for each of the first 6 months of operation of the proposed copy center.
2. As a group, interview a loan officer in a bank. Write Synergy Bank's reply to the loan request. Specify all the details that the bank should require as conditions for making the loan.
3. If necessary, modify the loan request or the bank's reply in order to reach agreement between the two parties.

spotlight

PIER 1 IMPORTS

Pier 1's customers thrive on creativity, and Pier 1 wants to be their resource, their outlet for expression. You may have furnished your dorm room or your apartment with items from Pier 1. The company operates 1,000 stores scattered across all 50 states. With home ownership at 68% and increasing, Pier 1 sees room for much growth.

This chapter focuses on merchandise inventory, and something Pier 1 has lots of—chairs, tables, and other home furnishings. Examine Pier 1's balance sheet. Inventory is by far the largest asset, comprising over half of Pier 1's current assets. This is in sharp contrast to Ford Motor Company, which we examined in Chapter 5. Ford manufactures automobiles—millions of automobiles—but inventories make up only a small portion of its current assets.

Different companies operate in different ways. Ford makes cars to order and therefore doesn't keep on hand any more inventory than needed. It's the Ford dealers who stockpile cars and trucks. Pier 1 Imports is more like a local Ford dealer. To show customers what's available, Pier 1 keeps lots of inventory on hand. Let's see how to manage and account for merchandise inventory. (Often this asset is referred to simply as *inventory*.)

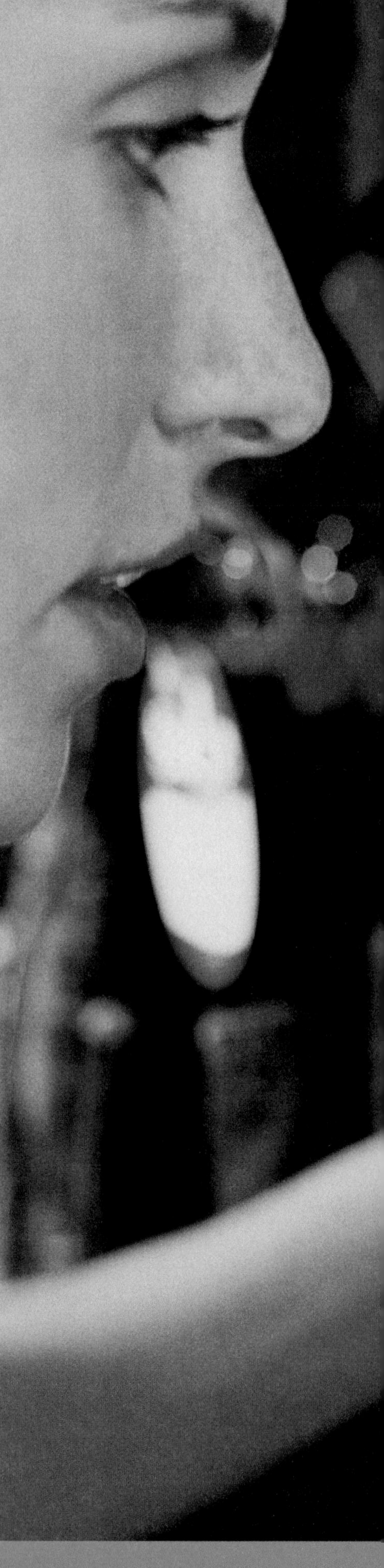

Pier 1 Imports, Inc.
Consolidated Balance Sheets (Adapted)

(In thousands)

	2003	2002
Assets		
Current assets:		
Cash	$ 16,232	$ 22,121
Short-term investments	225,882	213,488
Receivables, net of allowance for doubtful accounts of $236 and $275, respectively	51,958	50,825
Inventories	333,350	275,433
Prepaid expenses and other current assets	36,179	43,286
Total current assets	663,601	605,153
Properties, net	254,503	209,954
Other noncurrent assets	49,383	47,565
	$967,487	$862,672
Liabilities and Shareholders' Equity		
Current liabilities	$243,589	$208,396
Long-term debt	25,000	25,356
Other noncurrent liabilities	54,962	43,264
Shareholders' equity	643,936	585,656
	$967,487	$862,672

Merchandise Inventory and Cost of Goods Sold

6

LEARNING OBJECTIVES

1 **Account** for inventory transactions

2 **Analyze** the various inventory methods

3 **Identify** the income and the tax effects of the inventory methods

4 **Use** the gross profit percentage and inventory turnover to evaluate a business

5 **Estimate** inventory by the gross profit method

6 **Show** how inventory errors affect cost of goods sold and income

Pier 1 Imports, Inc.
Consolidated Statements of Operations (Adapted)

(In thousands)

	Year Ended	
	2003	2002
Net sales	$1,754,867	$1,548,556
Operating costs and expenses:		
Cost of sales	1,001,462	898,795
Operating expenses	548,751	490,948
Operating income	204,654	158,813
Nonoperating income	720	184
Income before income taxes	205,374	158,997
Income tax expense	75,988	58,788
Net income	$ 129,386	$ 100,209

Inventory
The merchandise that a company sells to customers.

Cost of goods sold
Cost of the inventory the business has sold to customers.

Merchandise inventory is the heart of a merchandising business. **Inventory** includes everything from Pier 1 furniture to Dell computers to Ford trucks. As long as Pier 1 holds a chair, the furniture is an asset. When Pier 1 sells the chair, Pier 1's $300 cost is no longer an asset. The $300 becomes an expense. We call this expense **cost of goods sold**. Cost of goods sold is the most important expense for a company that sells goods rather than services. This chapter covers the accounting for inventory and cost of goods sold. It also shows you how to analyze financial statements with respect to inventory, cost of goods sold, and profits and losses.

This chapter introduces you to a number of key concepts that help you do business in a competitive environment. We begin by showing how the financial statements of a merchandiser such as Pier 1 Imports differ from those of service entities. The financial statements in Exhibit 6-1 show how service entities differ from merchandisers (dollar amounts are assumed).

Accounting for Inventory

The basic concept of accounting for merchandise inventory can be illustrated with a simple example. Suppose Pier 1 Imports has in stock three chairs that cost $300 each. Pier 1 marks the chairs up by $200 and sells two chairs for $500 each. Pier 1's balance sheet reports the one chair that the company still holds in inventory, and the income statement reports the cost of the two chairs sold, as shown in Exhibit 6-2.

Sale Price vs. Cost of Inventory

Note the difference between the sale price of inventory and the cost of inventory. In particular:

- Sales revenue is based on the *sale price* of the inventory sold ($500 per chair in Exhibit 6-2).
- Cost of goods sold is based on the *cost* of the inventory sold ($300 per chair for Pier 1 Imports).
- Inventory on the balance sheet is based on the *cost* of the goods still on hand ($300 per chair for Pier 1 Imports).

(continued at bottom of next page)

■ **EXHIBIT 6-1** Contrasting a Service Company with a Merchandiser

Service Company
Century 21 Real Estate
Income Statement
Year Ended December 31, 20XX

Service revenue	$XXX
Expenses:	
Salary expense	X
Depreciation expense	X
Income tax expense	X
Net income	$ X

Merchandising Company
Pier 1 Imports, Inc.
Income Statement
Year Ended December 31, 20XX

Sales revenue	$1,755
Cost of goods sold	1,001
Gross profit	754
Operating *expenses:*	
Salary expense	X
Depreciation, expense	X
Income tax expense	X
Net income	$ 129

Century 21 Real Estate
Balance Sheet
December 31, 20XX

Assets	
Current assets	
Cash	$ X
Short-term investments	X
Accounts receivable, net	X
Prepaid expenses	X

Pier 1 Imports, Inc.
Balance Sheet
December 31, 20XX

Assets	
Current assets	
Cash	$ X
Short-term investments	X
Accounts receivable, net	X
Inventory	333
Prepaid expenses	X

Merchandisers have two accounts that service entities don't need
- cost of goods sold on the income statement
- inventory on the balance sheet

■ **EXHIBIT 6-2**
Inventory and Cost of Goods Sold When Inventory Cost Is Constant

Balance Sheet (partial)		Income Statement (partial)	
Current assets:		Sales revenue	
Cash	$XXX	(2 chairs @ sale price of $500)	$1,000
Short-term investments	XXX	Cost of goods sold	
Accounts receivable	XXX	(2 chairs @ cost of $300)	600
Inventory (1 chair @ cost of $300)	300	Gross profit	$ 400
Prepaid expenses	XXX		

Gross profit, also called *gross margin,* is the excess of sales revenue over cost of goods sold. It is called *gross profit* because operating expenses have not yet been subtracted. Exhibit 6-3 shows actual inventory and cost of goods sold data adapted from the financial statements of Pier 1 Imports.

Gross profit
Sales revenue minus cost of goods sold. Also called *gross margin.*

✔ Check Point 6-1

Pier 1's inventory of $333 million represents

$$\text{Inventory (balance sheet)} = \text{Number of units of inventory } \textit{on hand} \times \text{Cost per unit of inventory}$$

Pier 1's cost of goods sold ($1,001 million) represents

$$\text{Cost of goods sold (income statement)} = \text{Number of units of inventory } \textit{sold} \times \text{Cost per unit of inventory}$$

■ **EXHIBIT 6-3**

Pier 1 Imports Inventory and Cost of Goods Sold (Cost of Sales)

Pier 1 Imports, Inc.
Balance Sheets (Adapted)
February 28, 2003, and 2002

Assets (In millions)	2003	2002
Current assets		
Cash	$ 16	$ 22
Short-term investments	226	213
Receivables, net	52	51
Inventories	333	275

Pier 1 Imports, Inc.
Statements of Income (Adapted)
Years Ended February 28, 2003, and 2002

(In millions)	2003	2002
Net sales	$1,755	$1,549
Cost of sales (same as cost of goods sold)	1,001	899
Gross profit	754	650

Number of Units of Inventory. The number of inventory units on hand is determined from the accounting records, backed up by a physical count of the goods at year end. Companies do not include in their inventory any goods that they hold on *consignment* because those goods belong to another company. But they do include their own inventory that is out on consignment and held by another company.

Cost Per Unit of Inventory. The cost per unit of inventory poses a challenge because companies purchase goods at different prices throughout the year. Which unit costs go into ending inventory? Which unit costs go to cost of goods sold?

The next section shows how different accounting methods determine ending inventory on the balance sheet and cost of goods sold for the income statement. First, however, you need to understand how inventory accounting systems work.

OBJECTIVE

1 **Account** for inventory transactions

Periodic inventory system
An inventory system in which the business does not keep a continuous record of the inventory on hand. Instead, at the end of the period, the business makes a physical count of the inventory on hand and applies the appropriate unit costs to determine the cost of the ending inventory.

Perpetual inventory system
An inventory system in which the business keeps a continuous record for each inventory item to show the inventory on hand at all times.

Accounting for Inventory in the Perpetual System

There are two main types of inventory accounting systems: the periodic system and the perpetual system. The **periodic inventory system** is used by businesses that sell inexpensive goods. A fabric store or a lumber yard may not keep a running record of every bolt of fabric and every two-by-four. Instead, these stores count their inventory periodically—at least once a year—to determine the quantities on hand. Businesses such as restaurants and hometown nurseries also use the periodic system because the accounting cost is low.

A **perpetual inventory system** keeps a running record of inventory on hand with the use of computer software. This system achieves control over goods such as Pier 1 Imports furniture, Ford automobiles, jewelry, and most other types of inventory. Most businesses use the perpetual inventory system.

Even with a perpetual system, the business still counts the inventory on hand annually. The physical count establishes the correct amount of ending inventory for the financial statements and also serves as a check on the perpetual records.

Perpetual Inventory System	Periodic Inventory System
• Keeps a running record of all goods bought and sold	• Does not keep a running record of all goods bought and sold
• Inventory counted at least once a year	• Inventory counted at least once a year
• Used for all types of goods	• Used for inexpensive goods

How the Perpetual System Works. How does a perpetual inventory system work? Let's use an everyday situation. When you check out of a Foot Locker, a Best Buy, or a Pier 1 store, the clerk scans the bar codes on the product labels of the items you buy. Exhibit 6-4 illustrates a typical bar code. Suppose you are buying a desk lamp from Pier 1 Imports. The bar code on the ticket holds lots of information. The optical scanner reads the bar code, and the electronic signal activates the computer to perform the following operations:

■ **EXHIBIT 6-4**

Bar Code for Electronic Scanner

- Record the sale, debiting Cash and crediting Sales Revenue.
- Update the perpetual inventory record for the lamps, recording both Cost of Goods Sold and Inventory. This entry records cost of goods sold and keeps a running record of inventory on hand.

Recording Transactions in the Perpetual System. In the perpetual system, the business records each purchase of inventory. When Pier 1 makes a sale, two entries are needed. The company records the sale—debits Cash or Accounts Receivable and credits Sales Revenue for the sale price of the goods. Pier 1 also debits Cost of Goods Sold and credits Inventory for the cost of the inventory sold.

Exhibit 6-5, page 266, shows the accounting for inventory in a perpetual system. Panel A gives the journal entries and the T-accounts, and Panel B shows the income statement and the balance sheet. All amounts are assumed. (The chapter's Appendix 6A illustrates the accounting for these transactions in a periodic inventory system.)

In Exhibit 6-5, Panel A, the first entry to Inventory summarizes a lot of detail. The cost of the inventory, $560,000, is the *net* amount of the purchases, determined as follows (using assumed amounts):

Purchase price of the inventory	$600,000
+ **Freight-in** (the cost to transport the goods from seller to buyer)	4,000
− **Purchase returns** for unsuitable goods returned to the seller	(25,000)
− **Purchase allowances** granted by the seller	(5,000)
− **Purchase discounts** for early payment	(14,000)
= Net purchases of inventory	$560,000

Freight-in is the transportation cost, paid by the buyer, to move goods from the seller to the buyer. Freight-in is accounted for as part of the cost of inventory. A **purchase return** is a decrease in the cost of inventory because the buyer returned the goods to the seller. A **purchase allowance** also decreases the cost of inventory because the buyer got an allowance (a deduction) from the amount owed. Throughout this book, we often refer to net purchases simply as Purchases.

Purchase return
A decrease in the cost of purchases because the buyer returned the goods to the seller.

Purchase allowance
A decrease in the cost of purchases because the seller has granted the buyer a subtraction (an allowance) from the amount owed.

(continued at bottom of next page)

EXHIBIT 6-5 Recording and Reporting Inventory—Perpetual System (Amounts Assumed)

PANEL A—Recording Transactions and the T-accounts (All amounts are assumed)

1. Inventory	560,000	
Accounts Payable..........		560,000
Purchased inventory on account.		

ASSETS	=	LIABILITIES	+	STOCKHOLDERS' EQUITY
560,000	=	560,000	+	0

2. Accounts Receivable	900,000	
Sales Revenue		900,000
Sold inventory on account.		

ASSETS	=	LIABILITIES	+	STOCKHOLDERS' EQUITY	+	REVENUES
900,000	=	0			+	900,000

Cost of Goods Sold	540,000	
Inventory		540,000
Recorded cost of goods sold.		

ASSETS	=	LIABILITIES	+	STOCKHOLDERS' EQUITY	−	EXPENSES
− 540,000	=	0			−	540,000

The T-accounts show the following:

Inventory

Beginning balance	**100,000***		
Purchases	**560,000**	**Cost of goods sold**	**540,000**
Ending balance	**120,000**		

*Beginning inventory was $100,000.

Cost of Goods Sold

Cost of goods sold	**540,000**	

PANEL B—Reporting in the Financial Statements

Income Statement (Partial)

Sales revenue	$900,000
Cost of goods sold	540,000
Gross profit	$360,000

Ending Balance Sheet (Partial)

Current assets:	
Cash	$ XXX
Short-term investments	XXX
Accounts receivable	XXX
Inventory	120,000
Prepaid expenses	XXX

Check Point 6-2

Check Point 6-3

Purchase discount
A decrease in the cost of purchases earned by making an early payment to the vendor.

A **purchase discount** is a decrease in the cost of inventory that is earned by paying quickly. Many companies offer payment terms of "2/10 n/30." This means the buyer can take a 2% discount for payment within 10 days, with the final amount due within 30 days. Another common credit term is "net 30," which directs the customer to pay the full amount within 30 days. In summary,

Net purchases = Purchases
− Purchase returns and allowances
− Purchase discounts
+ Freight-in

Net sales are computed exactly the same as net purchases, but with no freight-in.

Net sales	= Sales revenue
	– Sales returns and allowances
	– Sales discounts

Freight-out paid by the seller is not part of the cost of inventory. Instead, freight-out is delivery expense, the expense of delivering merchandise to customers. (Appendix 6A shows the accounting for these same transactions in a periodic accounting system.) Now study Exhibit 6-5 (p. 266).

Inventory Costing

Inventory is the first asset for which a manager can decide which accounting methods to use. This decision has significant consequences, for the accounting method effects the profits to be reported, the amount of income tax to be paid, and the values of the ratios derived from the balance sheet.

What Goes into Inventory Cost?

The cost of inventory on Pier 1's balance sheet represents all the costs that Pier 1 incurred to bring its inventory to the point of sale. The following cost principle applies to all assets:

The cost of any asset, such as inventory, is the sum of all the costs incurred to bring the asset to its intended use, less any discounts.

After a Pier 1 chair is sitting in the showroom, other costs, such as advertising and sale commissions, are expensed. These are *not* included as the cost of inventory.

■ Taking Action Which Inventory Method Will Help Us Accomplish Our Goals?

OBJECTIVE

2 **Analyze** the various inventory methods.

Determining the cost of inventory is easy when the unit cost remains constant, as in Exhibit 6-2. But the unit cost usually changes. For example, prices often rise. The desk lamp that cost Pier 1 $10 in January may cost $14 in June and $18 in October. Suppose Pier 1 sells 1,000 lamps in November. How many of those lamps cost $10, how many cost $14, and how many cost $18?

To compute cost of goods sold and the cost of ending inventory still on hand, we must assign unit cost to the items. Accounting uses four generally accepted inventory methods:

1. **Specific unit cost**
2. **Average cost**
3. **First-in, first-out (FIFO)** cost
4. **Last-in, first-out (LIFO)** cost

A company can use any of these methods. They can have very different effects on reported profits, income taxes, and cash flow. Therefore, companies select their inventory method with great care.

FIFO (first-in, first out) method Inventory costing method by which the first costs into inventory are the first costs out to cost of goods sold. Ending inventory is based on the costs of the most recent purchases.

LIFO (last-in, first-out) method Inventory costing method by which the last costs into inventory are the first costs out to cost of goods sold. This method leaves the oldest costs—those of beginning inventory and the earliest purchases of the period—in ending inventory.

Specific Unit Cost. Some businesses deal in unique inventory items, such as antique furniture, jewels, and real estate. These businesses cost their inventories at the specific cost of the particular unit. For instance, a Ford dealer may have two vehicles in the showroom—a "stripped-down" model that costs $19,000 and a "loaded" model that costs $24,000. If the dealer sells the loaded model, the cost of goods sold is $24,000. The stripped-down auto will be the only unit left in inventory, and so ending inventory is $19,000.

Specific-unit-cost method
Inventory cost method based on the specific cost of particular units of inventory.

The **specific-unit-cost method** is also called the *specific identification* method. This method is too expensive to use for inventory items that have common characteristics, such as bushels of wheat, gallons of paint, or auto tires.

The other inventory accounting methods—average, FIFO, and LIFO—are fundamentally different. These other methods do not use the specific cost of a particular unit. Instead, they assume different flows of inventory costs. To illustrate average, FIFO, and LIFO costing, we use a common set of data, given in Exhibit 6-6.

■ EXHIBIT 6-6

Inventory Data Used to Illustrate Inventory Costing Methods

Inventory

Begin. bal.	**(10 units @ $10)**	**100**		
Purchases:			**Cost of goods sold**	
No. 1	**(25 units @ $14)**	**350**	**(40 units @ $?)**	**?**
No. 2	**(25 units @ $18)**	**450**		
Ending bal.	**(20 units @ $?)**	**?**		

In Exhibit 6-6, Pier 1 began the period with 10 lamps that cost $10 each; the beginning inventory was therefore $100. During the period Pier 1 bought 50 more lamps, sold 40 lamps, and ended the period with 20 lamps, summarized in the T-account and as follows:

GOODS AVAILABLE		NUMBER OF UNITS	TOTAL COST
Goods available	=	10 + 25 + 25 = 60 units	$100 + $350 + $450 = $900
Cost of goods sold	=	40 units	?
Ending inventory	=	20 units	?

The big accounting questions are

1. What is the cost of goods sold?
2. What is the cost of the ending inventory?

It all depends on which inventory method Pier 1 uses. Pier 1 actually uses the average-cost method, so let's look at average costing first.

Average-cost method
Inventory costing method based on the average cost of inventory during the period. Average cost is determined by dividing the cost of goods available by the number of units available. Also called the *weighted-average method.*

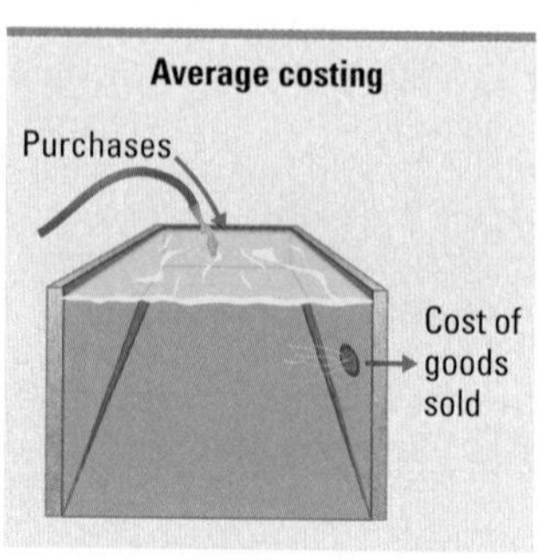

Average Cost. The **average-cost method**, sometimes called the *weighted-average method*, is based on the average cost of inventory during the period. Average cost per unit is determined as follows (data from Exhibit 6-6):

$$\text{Average cost per unit} = \frac{\text{Cost of goods available*}}{\text{Number of units available*}} = \frac{\$900}{60} = \$15$$

*Goods available = Beginning inventory + Purchases

Cost of goods sold	= Number of units sold	× Average cost per unit		
	= 40 units	×	$15	= $600
Ending inventory	= Number of units on hand	× Average cost per unit		
	= 20 units	×	$15	= $300

The following T-account shows the effects of average costing:

Inventory (at Average cost)

Begin. bal.	**(10 units @ $10)**	**100**		
Purchases:				
No. 1	**(25 units @ $14)**	**350**		
No. 2	**(25 units @ $18)**	**450**	Cost of goods sold (40 units @ average cost of $15 per unit)	600
Ending bal.	(20 units @ average cost of $15 per unit)	300		

FIFO Cost. Under the FIFO method, the first costs into inventory are the first costs assigned to cost of goods sold—hence, the name *first-in, first-out.* The diagram in the margin shows the effect of FIFO costing. The following T-account shows how to compute FIFO cost of goods sold and ending inventory for the Pier 1 lamps (data from Exhibit 6-6):

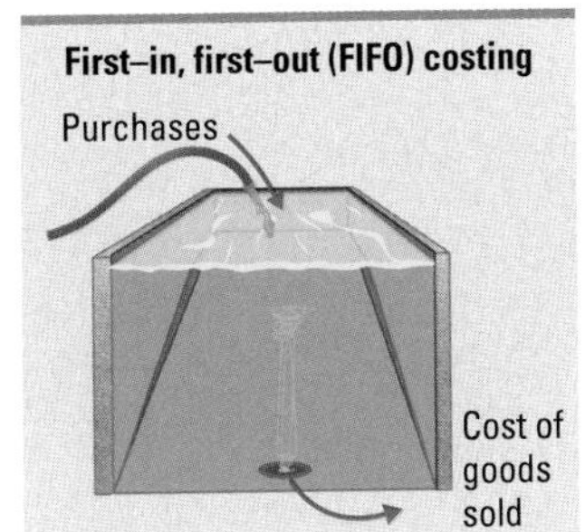

Inventory (at FIFO cost)

Begin. bal.	**(10 units @ $10)**	**100**			
Purchases:			Cost of goods sold (40 units):		
No. 1	**(25 units @ $14)**	**350**	(10 units @ $10)	100	
No. 2	**(25 units @ $18)**	**450**	(25 units @ $14)	350	540
			(5 units @ $18)	90	
Ending bal.	(20 units @ $18)	360			

Under FIFO, the cost of ending inventory is always based on the latest costs incurred—in this case $18 per unit.

LIFO Cost. LIFO costing is the opposite of FIFO. Under LIFO, the last costs into inventory go immediately to cost of goods sold, as shown in the diagram. Compare LIFO and FIFO, and you will see a vast difference.

The following T-account shows how to compute the LIFO inventory amounts for the Pier 1 lamps (data from Exhibit 6-6).

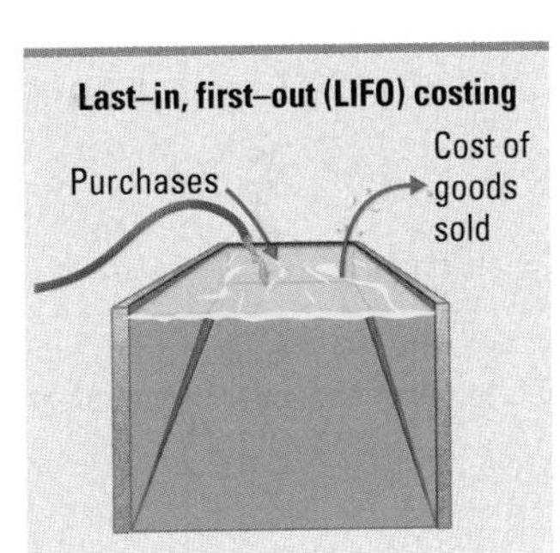

Inventory (at LIFO cost)

Begin bal.	**(10 units @ $10)**	**100**			
Purchases:			Cost of goods sold (40 units):		
No. 1	**(25 units @ $14)**	**350**	(25 units @ $18)	450	660
No. 2	**(25 units @ $18)**	**450**	(15 units @ $14)	210	
Ending bal.	(10 units @ $10) 100	240			
	(10 units @ $14) 140				

Under LIFO, the cost of ending inventory is always based on the oldest costs—from beginning inventory plus the early purchases of the period—$10 and $14 per unit.

Income Effects of FIFO, LIFO and Average Cost

Check Point 6-4
Check Point 6-5
Check Point 6-6

In our Pier 1 example, the cost of inventory rose from $10 to $14 to $18. When inventory unit costs change this way, the various inventory methods produce different cost-of-goods sold figures. Exhibit 6-7 summarizes the income effects (sales –

cost of goods sold = gross profit) of the three inventory methods, (remember that prices are rising). Study the exhibit carefully, focusing on cost of goods sold and gross profit.

■ **EXHIBIT 6-7**

Income Effects of the FIFO, LIFO, and Average Inventory Methods

	FIFO	LIFO	Average
Sales revenue (assumed)	$1,000	$1,000	$1,000
Cost of goods sold	540 (lowest)	660 (highest)	600
Gross profit	$ 460 (highest)	$ 340 (lowest)	$ 400

When inventory costs are increasing,

- LIFO cost of goods sold is *highest* because it is based on the most recent costs. Gross profit is *lowest*.
- FIFO cost of goods sold is *lowest* because it is based on the oldest costs. Gross profit is the *highest*.

When inventory costs are decreasing,

- FIFO cost of goods sold is *highest*
- LIFO cost of goods sold is *lowest*

Financial analysts search the stock markets for companies with good prospects for income growth. Analysts sometimes need to compare the net income of a company that uses LIFO with the net income of a company that uses FIFO. Appendix 6B, pages 312–313, shows how to convert a LIFO company's net income to the FIFO basis in order to make a clear-cut comparison.

Tax Advantage of LIFO

OBJECTIVE

3 **Identify** the income and the tax effects of the inventory methods

Inventory methods directly affect income taxes, to be paid in cash. When prices are rising, LIFO results in the *lowest taxable income* and thus the *lowest income taxes*. Let's use the gross profit data of Exhibit 6-7 to illustrate.

	FIFO	LIFO
Gross profit	$460	$340
Operating expenses (assumed)	260	260
Income before income tax	$200	$ 80
Income tax expense (40%)	$ 80	$ 32

Income tax expense is lowest under LIFO ($32) and highest under FIFO ($80). The most attractive feature of LIFO is low income tax payments, which is why about one-third of all companies use this method. During periods of inflation, many companies prefer LIFO for its tax and cash-flow advantage. Exhibit 6-8, based on an American Institute of Certified Public Accountants (AICPA) survey of 600 companies, indicate that FIFO remains the most popular inventory method.

stop AND think. . .

If LIFO saves on income tax, then why do more companies use the FIFO method (see Exhibit 6-8)? There are two main reasons: What are they?

Answer:

1. Some companies prefer to report higher profits, which FIFO provides when prices are rising.
2. Some companies are in declining-cost industries. These companies, therefore, use FIFO to save on income taxes.

There's also a third reason for FIFO's popularity. When prices aren't changing much, FIFO, LIFO, and average cost all produce similar results. FIFO is much less expensive to apply in actual practice.

Check Point 6-7

Comparison of the Inventory Methods

Let's compare the average, FIFO, and LIFO inventory methods.

1. How well does each method measure income by matching inventory expense—cost of goods sold—against revenue? LIFO results in the most realistic net income figure. LIFO best matches the current cost of goods sold with revenue because it assigns the most recent inventory costs to expense. In contrast, FIFO matches old inventory costs against revenue—a poor matching of expense with revenue. FIFO income is therefore less realistic than income under LIFO.
2. Which method reports the most up-to-date inventory cost on the balance sheet? FIFO. LIFO, on the other hand, can value inventory at very old costs because LIFO leaves the oldest prices in ending inventory.
3. What effects do the methods have on income taxes? LIFO results in the lowest income tax when prices are *rising*. Taxes are highest under FIFO.

   However, when inventory prices are *decreasing*, income taxes are highest under LIFO and lowest under FIFO. The average cost method produces amounts between the extremes of LIFO and FIFO.

■ **EXHIBIT 6-8**

Use of the Various Inventory Methods

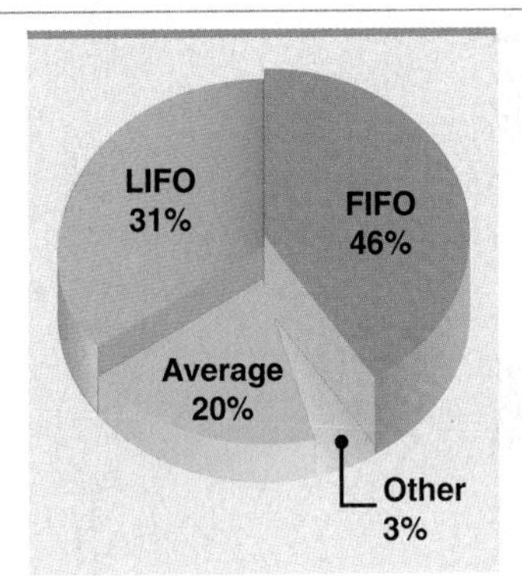

Exhibit 6-9 graphs the flow of costs under FIFO and LIFO during both increasing costs (Panel A) and decreasing costs (Panel B). Study this exhibit carefully; it will help you *really* understand FIFO and LIFO.

LIFO and Managing Reported Income. LIFO allows managers to manipulate net income by timing their purchases of inventory. When inventory prices are rising rapidly and a company wants to show less income (in order to pay less taxes), managers can buy a large amount of inventory near the end of the year. Under LIFO, these high inventory costs go to cost of goods sold immediately. As a result, net income is decreased.

If the business is having a bad year, management may need to report higher income. It can delay the purchase of high-cost inventory until next year and avoid decreasing current-year income. In the process, the company draws down inventory quantities, a practice known as *LIFO inventory liquidation*.

Check Point 6-8

■ **EXHIBIT 6-9**

Cost of Goods Sold and Ending Inventory—FIFO and LIFO Increasing Costs and Decreasing Costs

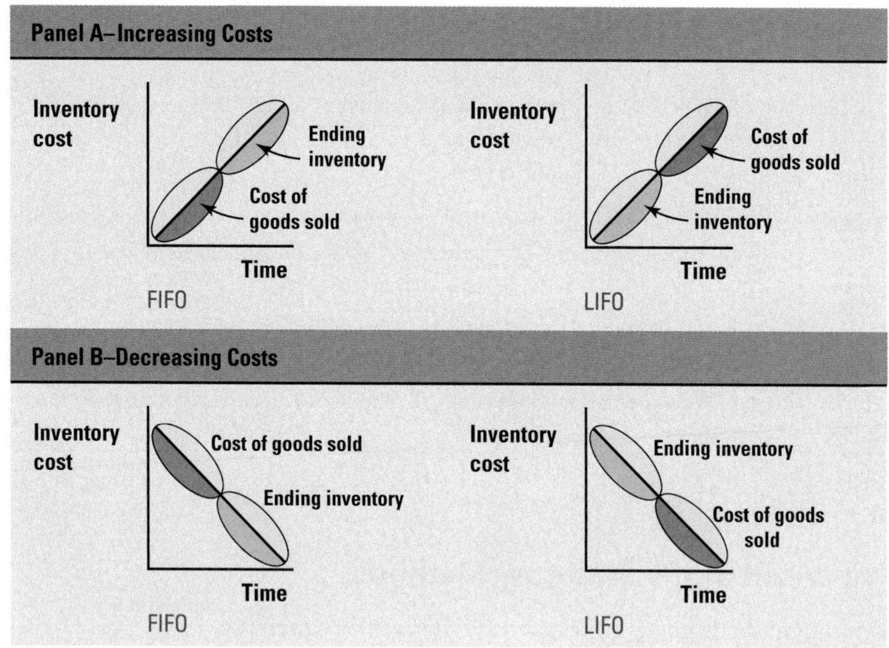

LIFO Liquidation. When LIFO is used and inventory quantities fall below the level of the previous period, the situation is called a *LIFO liquidation*. To compute cost of goods sold, the company must dip into older layers of inventory cost. Under LIFO, and when prices are rising, that action shifts older, lower costs into cost of goods sold. The result is higher net income. Managers try to avoid a LIFO liquidation because it increases income taxes. For example, **Owens-Corning**, the world's leading supplier of glass fiber materials, reported that LIFO liquidations added $2.7 million to its net income. As a result, Owens-Corning had to pay more income tax.

International Perspective. Many U.S. companies that use the LIFO method must use another inventory method in foreign countries. Why? LIFO is not allowed in some countries. Australia and the United Kingdom, for example, do not permit the use of LIFO. Virtually all countries permit FIFO and the average cost method.

MID-CHAPTER Summary Problem

Suppose a division of **IBM Corporation** that handles computer components has these inventory records for January 20X6:

Date	Item	Quantity	Unit Cost
Jan. 1	Beginning inventory	100 units	$ 8
6	Purchase	60 units	9
21	Purchase	150 units	9
27	Purchase	90 units	10

Company accounting records reveal that operating expense for January was $1,900, and sales of 310 units generated sales revenue of $6,770.

Required

1. Prepare the January income statement, showing amounts for FIFO, LIFO, and average cost. Label the bottom line "Operating income." (Round figures to whole-dollar

amounts.) Show your computations, and use T-accounts as on page 269 to compute cost of goods sold.

2. Suppose you are the financial vice president of IBM. Which inventory method will you use if your motive is to
   a. Minimize income taxes?
   b. Report the highest operating income?
   c. Report operating income between the extremes of FIFO and LIFO?
   d. Report inventory on the balance sheet at the most current cost?
   e. Attain the best measure of net income for the income statement?

   State the reason for each of your answers.

Answers

Requirement 1

IBM Corporation
Income Statement for Component
Month Ended January 31, 20X6

	FIFO		LIFO		Average	
Sales revenue		$6,770		$6,770		$6,770
Cost of goods sold:						
Beginning inventory	$ 800		$ 800		$ 800	
Purchases	2,790		2,790		2,790	
Goods available†	3,590		3,590		3,590	
Ending inventory	(900)		(720)		(808)	
Cost of goods sold		2,690		2,870		2,782
Gross profit		4,080		3,900		3,988
Operating expenses		1,900		1,900		1,900
Operating income		$2,180		$2,000		$2,088

Computations

Beginning inventory:	100 × $8	= $800
Purchases:	(60 × $9) + (150 × $9) + (90 × $10) = $2,790	
Ending inventory—FIFO:	90* × $10	= $900
LIFO:	90 × $8	= $720
Average:	90 × $8.975**	= $808 (rounded from $807.75)

†Number of units available = 100 + 60 + 150 + 90 = 400
*Number of units in ending inventory = 100 + 60 + 150 + 90 − 310 = 90
**$3,590/400 units† = $8.975 per unit

Requirement 2

a. Use LIFO to minimize income taxes. Operating income under LIFO is lowest when inventory unit costs are increasing, as they are in this case (from $8 to $10). (If inventory costs were decreasing, income under FIFO would be lowest.)

b. Use FIFO to report the highest operating income. Income under FIFO is highest when inventory unit costs are increasing, as in this situation.

c. Use the average cost method to report an operating income amount between the FIFO and LIFO extremes. This is true in this situation and in others when inventory unit costs are increasing or decreasing.

d. Use FIFO to report inventory on the balance sheet at the most current cost. The oldest inventory costs are expensed as cost of goods sold, leaving in ending inventory the most recent (most current) costs of the period.

e. Use LIFO to attain the best measure of net income. LIFO produces the best matching of current expense with current revenue. The most recent (most current) inventory costs are expensed as cost of goods sold.

Inventory turnover
Ratio of cost of goods sold to average inventory. Indicates how rapidly inventory is sold.

retailers, must keep some goods on hand. **Inventory turnover**, the ratio of cost of goods sold to average inventory, indicates how rapidly inventory is sold. The 2003 computation for Pier 1 Imports follows (data in millions from Exhibit 6-3, page 264):

$$\text{Inventory turnover} = \frac{\text{Cost of goods sold}}{\text{Average inventory}} = \frac{\text{Cost of goods sold}}{\left(\text{Beginning inventory} + \text{Ending inventory}\right) \div 2}$$

$$= \frac{\$1{,}001}{(\$333 + \$275)/2} = \begin{matrix}\text{3.3 times per year} \\ \text{(every 111 days)}\end{matrix}$$

The inventory turnover statistic shows how many times the company sold (or turned over) its average level of inventory during the year. Inventory turnover varies from industry to industry.

Pier 1 Imports and other specialty retailers turn their inventory over slowly. Retailers must keep lots of inventory on hand because visual appeal is critical in retailing. Department stores such as Lord & Taylor and discounters Wal-Mart and Target also keeps lot of inventory on hand. Exhibit 6-13 shows the inventory turnover rates for three leading retailers.

■ **EXHIBIT 6-13**
Inventory Turnover Rates of Three Leading Retailers

Check Point 6-10

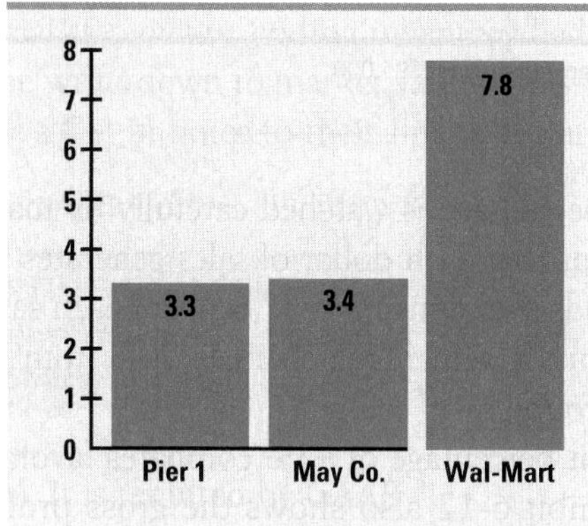

stop AND think. . .

Examine Exhibits 6-12 and 6-13. What do those ratio values say about the merchandising (pricing) strategies of Pier 1 Imports, May Department Stores, and Wal-Mart?

Answer:

It's obvious that Pier 1 and May sell high-end merchandise. Their gross profit percentages are much higher than Wal-Mart's. Wal-Mart's discounting strategy shows up in its much faster rate of inventory turnover and its lower gross profit percentage. The lower the price, the faster the turnover and vice versa.

Additional Inventory Issues

Using the Cost-of-Goods-Sold Model

Cost-of-goods-sold model
Formula that brings together all the inventory data for the entire accounting period: Beginning inventory + Purchases = Goods available. Then, Goods available – Ending inventory = Cost of goods sold.

Exhibit 6-14 presents the **cost-of-goods-sold model.** Some accountants view this model as related to the periodic inventory system. But it's used by all companies, including those with perpetual inventory systems. The model is extremely powerful because it captures all the inventory information for an entire accounting period. Study this model carefully (all amounts are assumed).

■ **EXHIBIT 6-14**

The Cost-of-Goods-Sold Model

Cost-of-goods sold:	
Beginning inventory	$1,200
+ Purchases	6,300
= Goods available	7,500
– Ending inventory	(1,500)
= Cost of goods sold	$6,000

Pier 1 Imports uses a perpetual inventory accounting system. Let's see how Pier 1 can use the cost-of-goods-sold model to manage the business effectively.

1. What's the single most important question for Pier 1 to address? What merchandise should Pier 1 offer to its customers? This is a marketing question that requires market research. If Pier 1 continually stocks up on the wrong merchandise, it will go out of business.
2. What's the second most important question for Pier 1? How much inventory should Pier 1 buy? **This is an accounting questions faced by all merchandisers.** If Pier 1 buys too much merchandise, it will have to lower prices and may lose money. If Pier 1 buys too little inventory, customers will go elsewhere. Buying the right quantity of inventory is critical for success. This question can be answered with the cost-of-goods-sold model. Let's see how it works.

We must rearrange the cost-of-goods-sold formula. Then we can help a Pier 1 manager know how much inventory to buy, as follows (using amounts from Exhibit 6-14):

1	Cost of goods sold (based on the budget for the next period)	$6,000
2	+ Ending inventory (based on the budget for the next period)	1,500
3	= Goods available as budgeted	7,500
4	– Beginning inventory (actual amount left over from the prior period)	(1,200)
5	= Purchases (how much inventory the manager needs to buy)	$6,300

In this case the manager should buy $6,300 of merchandise to reach his target cost of goods sold and ending inventory for the upcoming period.

Estimating Inventory by the Gross Profit Method

OBJECTIVE

5 **Estimate** inventory by the gross profit method

Often a business must *estimate* the value of its goods. A fire may destroy inventory, and the insurance company requires an estimate of the value of its loss. In this case, the business must estimate the cost of ending inventory because it cannot count it.

The **gross profit method**, also known as the *gross margin method*, is widely used to estimate ending inventory. This method uses the familiar cost-of-goods-sold model (amounts are assumed):

Gross profit method
A way to estimate inventory based on a rearrangement of the cost-of-goods-sold model: Beginning inventory + net purchases = Goods available – Cost of goods sold = Ending inventory. Also called the *gross margin method*.

Beginning inventory	$1,000
+ Purchases	6,000
= Goods available	7,000
– Ending inventory	(2,000)
= Cost of goods sold	$5,000

We rearrange *ending inventory* and *cost of goods sold* as follows:

Beginning inventory	$1,000
+ Purchases	6,000
= Goods available	7,000
− Cost of goods sold	(5,000)
= Ending inventory	$2,000

Suppose a fire destroys some of Pier 1's inventory. To collect insurance, Pier 1 must estimate the cost of the ending inventory. Beginning inventory, net purchases, and net sales can be taken directly from the accounting records. Using Pier 1's *actual gross profit rate* of 43% (that is, gross profit divided by net sales), you can estimate the cost of goods sold. Then subtract cost of goods sold from goods available to estimate ending inventory. Exhibit 6-15 shows the calculations for the gross profit method.

■ **EXHIBIT 6-15**

Gross Profit Method of Estimating Inventory (Amounts Assumed)

Beginning inventory		$14,000
Purchases		66,000
Goods available		80,000
Cost of goods sold:		
Net sales revenue	$100,000	
Less estimated gross profit of 43%	(43,000)	
Estimated cost of goods sold		57,000
Estimated cost of *ending inventory*		$23,000

Check Point 6-11

Accountants, managers, and auditors use the gross profit method to test the reasonableness of an ending inventory amount determined by a physical count. This method also helps to detect large errors.

stop AND think. . .

Beginning inventory is $70,000, net purchases total $365,000, and net sales are $500,000. With a normal gross profit rate of 30% of sales, how much is ending inventory?

Answer:

$85,000 = [$70,000 + $365,000 – (0.70 × $500,000)]

OBJECTIVE

6 **Show** how inventory errors affect cost of goods sold and income

Effects of Inventory Errors

Businesses count their inventories at the end of the period, and errors sometimes occur. An error in the ending inventory creates errors for cost of goods sold and gross profit for two accounting periods. In Exhibit 6-16 start with period 1, in which ending inventory is *overstated* and cost of goods sold is *understated*—each by $5,000. Then compare period 1 with period 3, which is correct. *Period 1 should look exactly like period 3.*

Recall that period 1's ending inventory becomes period 2's beginning amount. Thus, the error in period 1 carries over into period 2. Trace the ending inventory of $15,000 from period 1 to period 2. Then compare periods 2 and 3. *Period 2 should also look exactly like period 3.* All the Exhibit 6-16 amounts in color are incorrect.

■ **EXHIBIT 6-16** Inventory Errors: An Example

	Period 1		Period 2		Period 3	
	Ending Inventory Overstated by $5,000		Beginning Inventory Overstated by $5,000		Correct	
Sales revenue		$100,000		$100,000		$100,000
Cost of goods sold:						
Beginning inventory	$10,000		$15,000		$10,000	
Purchases	50,000		50,000		50,000	
Cost of goods available for sale	60,000		65,000		60,000	
Ending inventory	(15,000)		(10,000)		(10,000)	
Cost of goods sold		45,000		55,000		50,000
Gross profit		$ 55,000		$ 45,000		$ 50,000
		$100,000 (Periods 1 and 2 combined)				

Source: The authors thank Carl High for this example.

Beginning inventory and ending inventory have opposite effects on cost of goods sold (beginning is added; ending is subtracted). Therefore, after two periods, an inventory error washes out (counterbalances) as illustrated in Exhibit 6-16. Notice that total gross profit for periods 1 and 2 combined is correct ($100,000) even though each year's gross profit is wrong by $5,000. The correct gross profit is $50,000 for each period, as shown in Period 3. We must have accurate information for all periods. Exhibit 6-17 summarizes the effects of inventory accounting errors.

✓Check Point 6-12

✓Check Point 6-13

■ **EXHIBIT 6-17**
Effects of Inventory Errors

	Period 1		Period 2	
Inventory Error	**Cost of Goods Sold**	**Gross Profit and Net Income**	**Cost of Goods Sold**	**Gross Profit and Net Income**
Period 1 Ending inventory **overstated**	Understated	Overstated	Overstated	Understated
Period 1 Ending inventory **understated**	Overstated	Understated	Understated	Overstated

ACCOUNTING ALERT

Cooking the Books to Increase Reported Income

No area of accounting has a deeper ethical dimension than inventory. Managers of companies whose profits do not meet stockholder expectations are sometimes tempted to "cook the books" to increase reported income. That may trick investors into thinking the business is more successful than it really is.

What do managers hope to gain from fraudulent accounting? In some cases, their bonuses are tied to reported income: The higher the company's net income, the higher the manager's bonus. There are two main inventory schemes for cooking the books.

- The easiest is to overstate ending inventory. The upward-pointing arrows indicate an overstatement—report more assets and equity than the company actually has.

ASSETS	=	LIABILITIES	+	STOCKHOLDERS' EQUITY
↑	=	0	+	↑

- The second way to cook the books overstates sales revenue. Consider two examples of real companies. **Datapoint Corporation** and **MiniScribe**, both computer-related concerns, were charged with creating fictitious sales to boost reported profits.

  Datapoint is alleged to have hired drivers to transport its inventory around San Antonio so that the goods could not be physically counted. The scheme fell apart when the trucks returned the goods to Datapoint's warehouse, and Datapoint had unrealistic amounts of sales returns. What would you think of a company with $10 million in sales and $3 million of sales returns? No company produces that many defective computers.

  MiniScribe is alleged to have shipped boxes of bricks labeled as computers parts to customers right before year end. The bogus transactions increased the company's sales by $4 million—but only temporarily. The scheme boomeranged when MiniScribe had to record the returns. In virtually every area, accounting imposes a discipline that brings frauds to light.

Check Point 6-14

The take-away lesson from this accounting alert is this:

- Watch out for excessive sales returns. Some of the sales revenue may have been phony.

The Making Managerial Decisions feature summarizes the situations that call for a particular inventory accounting system and the motivation for using each costing method.

MAKING MANAGERIAL DECISIONS

ACCOUNTING FOR INVENTORY

Suppose a Pier 1 store stocks two basic categories of merchandise:

- Furniture pieces that are unique
- Small items of low value, near the checkout stations

Jacob Stiles, the store manager, is considering how accounting will affect the business. Let's examine several decisions Stiles must make to properly account for the store's inventory.

Decision	Guidelines	System or Method
Which inventory system to use?	• Expensive merchandise • Cannot control inventory by visual inspection	→ Perpetual system for the furniture
	• Can control inventory by visual inspection	→ Periodic system for the small, low-value items
Which costing method to use?	• Unique inventory items	→ Specific unit cost for art objects because they are unique
	• Most current cost of ending inventory • Maximizes reported income when costs are rising	→ FIFO
	• Most current measure of cost of goods sold and net income • Minimizes income tax when costs are rising	→ LIFO
	• Middle-of-the-road approach for income tax and reported income	→ Average

END-OF-CHAPTER Summary Problem

Mesa Hardware Company began 20X6 with 60,000 units of inventory that cost $36,000. During 20X6, Mesa purchased merchandise on account for $352,500 as follows:

Purchase 1	(100,000 units costing)	$ 65,000
Purchase 2	(270,000 units costing)	175,500
Purchase 3	(160,000 units costing)	112,000

Cash payments on account totaled $326,000 during the year.

Mesa's sales during 20X6 consisted of 520,000 units of inventory for $660,000, all on account. The company uses the FIFO inventory method.

Cash collections from customers were $630,000. Operating expenses totaled $240,500, of which Mesa paid $211,000 in cash. Mesa credited Accrued Liabilities for the remainder. At December 31, Mesa accrued income tax expense at the rate of 35% of income before tax.

Required

1. Make summary journal entries to record Mesa Hardware's transactions for the year, assuming the company uses a perpetual inventory system.
2. Determine the FIFO cost of Mesa's ending inventory at December 31, 20X6 two ways:
   a. Use a T-account.
   b. Multiply the number of units on hand by the unit cost.
3. Show how Mesa would compute cost of goods sold for 20X6. Follow the FIFO example on page 269.
4. Prepare Mesa Hardware's income statement for 20X6. Show totals for the gross profit and income before tax.
5. Determine Mesa's gross profit percentage, rate of inventory turnover, and net income as a percentage of sales for the year. In the hardware industry, a gross profit percentage of 40%, an inventory turnover of six times per year, and a net income percentage of 7% are considered excellent. How well does Mesa compare to these industry averages?

Answers

Requirement 1

Inventory ($65,000 + $175,500 + $112,000)	$352,500	
Accounts Payable		352,500
Accounts Payable	326,000	
Cash		326,000
Accounts Receivable	660,000	
Sales Revenue		660,000
Cost of Goods Sold	339,500	
Inventory		339,500
[$36,000 + $65,000 + $175,500 + $63,000 (90,000 units × $0.70)]		
($112,000 ÷ 160,000 units = $0.70 per unit from Purchase 3)		
Cash	630,000	
Accounts Receivable		630,000
Operating Expenses	240,500	
Cash		211,000
Accrued Liabilities		29,500
Income Tax Expense	28,000	
Income Tax Payable		28,000
($660,000 – $339,500 – $240,500) × .35 = $28,000		

Requirement 2

a.

Inventory	
36,000	
352,500	339,500
49,000	

b.

Number of units in ending inventory (60,000 + 100,000 + 270,000 + 160,000 – 520,000)	70,000
Unit cost of ending inventory at FIFO ($112,000 ÷ 160,000 from Purchase 3)	× $ 0.70
FIFO cost of ending inventory	$49,000

Requirement 3

Cost of goods sold (520,000 units):	
60,000 units costing	$ 36,000
100,000 units costing	65,000
270,000 units costing	175,500
90,000 units costing $0.70 each*	63,000
Cost of goods sold	$339,500

*From Purchase 3: $112,000/160,000 units = $0.70 per unit.

Requirement 4

Mesa Hardware Company
Income Statement
Year Ended December 31, 20X6

Sales revenue	$660,000
Cost of goods sold	339,500
Gross profit	320,500
Operating expenses	240,500
Income before tax	80,000
Income tax expense	28,000
Net income	$ 52,000

Requirement 5

Gross profit percentage: $\$320{,}500 \div \$660{,}000 = 48.6\%$

Inventory turnover: $\dfrac{\$339{,}500}{(\$36{,}000 + \$49{,}000)/2} = 8 \text{ times}$

Net income as a percent of sales: $\$52{,}000 \div \$660{,}000 = 7.9\%$

Mesa's statistics are better than the industry averages.

REVIEW MERCHANDISE INVENTORY

Chapter Review Quiz

1. All of the following statements are true except one. Which statement is false?
   a. The Sales account is used to record the sale of assets no longer needed in the business.
   b. The invoice is the seller's request for payment from the purchaser.
   c. Gross profit is the excess of the sales revenue over cost of goods sold.
   d. A merchandising firm purchases products from suppliers and then sells them.

2. Sales discounts should appear in the financial statements:
   a. As a deduction from accounts receivable
   b. As a deduction from sales
   c. As an operating expense
   d. Among the current liabilities
   e. As an addition to sales

3. How is the inventory classified in the financial statements?
   a. as an expense
   b. as a liability
   c. as an asset
   d. as a revenue
   e. as a contra account to Cost of Goods Sold

Questions 4–6 use the following data of Coastal Company.

	Units	Unit Cost	Total Cost	Units Sold
Beginning inventory	20	$6	$120	
Purchase on May 23	45	7	315	
Purchase on Nov. 5	15	8	120	
Sales	50	?	?	

4. Coastal uses a FIFO inventory system. Cost of goods sold for the period is:
   a. $330
   b. $347
   c. $355
   d. $365

5. Coastal Company's LIFO cost of ending inventory would be:
   a. $161
   b. $190
   c. $208
   d. $225

6. Assuming that Coastal uses the average method, the cost of ending inventory is:
   a. $161
   b. $190
   c. $208
   d. $225

7. When applying lower-of-cost-or-market to inventory, "market" generally means
   a. replacement cost
   b. original cost
   c. resale value
   d. original cost, less physical deterioration

8. During a period of rising prices, the inventory method that will yield the highest net income and asset value is:
   a. Specific identification
   b. Average cost
   c. FIFO
   d. LIFO

9. All of the following statements are false except one. Which statement is true?
   a. The inventory method that best matches current expense with current revenue is LIFO.
   b. Application of the lower-of-cost-or-market rule often results in higher inventory.
   c. An error overstating ending inventory in 20X1 will also understate 20X2 ending inventory.
   d. When prices are rising, the inventory method that results in the highest inventory value is LIFO.

10. The ending inventory of Bar Harbor Co. was $44,000. If beginning inventory was $50,000 and goods available totaled $104,000, the cost of goods sold would be:
    a. $112,000
    b. $198,000
    c. $50,000
    d. $60,000
    e. none of the above

11. Dell Company had cost of goods sold of $132,000. The beginning and ending inventories were $14,000 and $20,000, respectively. Purchases for the period must have been:
    a. $82,000
    b. $94,000
    c. $132,000
    d. $142,000
    e. $138,000

Use the following information for questions 12–14.

12. Lipton Company had a $24,000 beginning inventory and a $26,000 ending inventory. Net sales were $160,000; purchases, $86,000; purchase returns and allowances, $5,000 and freight-in, $6,000. Cost of goods sold for the period is
    a. $69,000
    b. $49,000
    c. $81,000
    d. $85,000
    e. none of the above

13. What is Lipton's gross profit percentage (rounded to the nearest percentage)?
    a. 53%
    b. 88%
    c. 47%
    d. none of the above

14. What is Lipton's rate of inventory turnover?
    a. 3.4 times
    b. 3.3 times
    c. 6.4 times
    d. 6.2 times

15. Beginning inventory is $60,000, purchases are $70,000 and sales total $120,000. The normal gross margin is 28%. Using the gross margin method, how much is ending inventory?
    a. $20,000
    b. $106,400
    c. $71,000
    d. $43,600
    e. None of the above; $(fill in the blank).

16. An overstatement of ending inventory in one period results in:
    a. no effect on net income of the next period
    b. an overstatement of net income of the next period
    c. an understatement of net income of the next period
    d. an understatement of the beginning inventory of the next period

Answers:

1. a
2. b
3. c
4. a [(20 × $6) + (30 × $7) = $330]
5. b [(20 × $6) + (10 × $7) = $190]
6. c [30 × ($555/80) = $208]
7. a
8. c
9. a
10. d [($104,000 – $44,000) = $60,000]
11. e ($14,000 + X – $20,000 = $132,000; X = $138,000)
12. d [($24,000 + $86,000 – $5,000 + $6,000 – $26,000) = $85,000]
13. c [($160,000 – $85,000)/$160,000 = .469]
14. a [$85,000 ÷ ($24,000 + $26,000)/2 = 3.4]
15. d {$60,000 + $70,000 – [$120,000 × (1 – .28)] = $43,600}
16. c

Accounting Vocabulary

average-cost method (p. 268)
conservatism (p. 275)
consistency principle (p. 274)
cost of goods sold (p. 262)
cost-of-goods-sold model (p. 278)
disclosure principle (p. 275)
first-in, first-out (FIFO) cost (method) (p. 267)
gross margin (p. 263)
gross margin method (p. 279)
gross margin percentage (p. 276)
gross profit (p. 263)
gross profit method (p. 279)
gross profit percentage (p. 276)
inventory (p. 262)
inventory turnover (p. 278)
last-in, first-out (LIFO) cost (method) (p. 267)
lower-of-cost-or-market (LCM) rule (p. 275)
periodic inventory system (p. 264)
perpetual inventory system (p. 264)
purchase allowance (p. 265)
purchase discount (p. 266)
purchase return (p. 265)
specific-unit-cost method (p. 268)
weighted-average method (p. 268)

Assess Your Progress

Check Points

Basic concept of accounting for inventory (Obj. 1)

CP6-1 (p. 263) Suppose **Nissan** North America purchased 1,000 door locks as units of inventory for $80 each and marked them up by $40 per unit. Nissan then sold 700 units to **Auto Zone** stores. For these transactions, show what Nissan would report on its balance sheet at December 31, 20X6, and on its income statement for the year ended December 31, 20X6, for these items. Include a complete heading for each statement.

Accounting for inventory transactions (Obj. 1)

CP6-2 (p. 266) Maxidrive Computer Peripherals purchased inventory costing $100,000 and sold 60% of the goods for $140,000. All purchases were on account. Sales were on account, with Maxidrive collecting 20% up front.

1. Journalize these two transactions for Maxidrive, which uses the perpetual inventory system.
2. For these transactions, show what Maxidrive will report for inventory, revenues, and expenses on its financial statements. Report gross profit on the appropriate statement.

Accounting for inventory transactions (Obj. 1)

CP6-3 (p. 266) Journalize the following transactions for **PepsiCo.** Show amounts in billions.

- Cash purchases of inventory, $6.4 billion
- Sales on account, $28.5 billion
- Cost of goods sold (perpetual inventory system), $6.2 billion
- Collections on account, $26.3 billion

Applying the FIFO, LIFO, and average inventory methods (Obj. 2)

CP6-4 (p. 269) Study the perpetual Inventory T-accounts on page 269, and answer these questions.

1. Are the company's inventory costs stable, increasing, or decreasing during the period? Cite specific figures to support your answer.
2. Which inventory method results in the *highest* cost of ending inventory (give this figure)? Explain when this method produces the highest cost of ending inventory. Does this method result in the highest, or the lowest, cost of goods sold? Explain why this occurs. Does this method result in the highest, or the lowest, gross profit? Explain your answer.
3. Which inventory method results in the *lowest* cost of ending inventory (give this figure)? Explain when this method produces the lowest cost of ending inventory. Does this method result in the highest or the lowest cost of goods sold? Explain why this occurs. Does this method result in the highest, or the lowest, gross profit? Explain your answer.

Applying the average, FIFO, and LIFO methods (Obj. 2)

CP6-5 (p. 269) Return to Exhibit 6-6, page 268, and assume that the business sold 50 units of inventory during the period (instead of 40 units as in the exhibit). Compute cost of goods sold and ending inventory for each of the following costing methods:

a. Average cost b. FIFO c. LIFO

Applying the average, FIFO, and LIFO methods (Obj. 2)

CP6-6 (p. 269) **Kinko's Copy Centers** use laser printers. Assume Kinko's started the year with 100 containers of ink (average cost of $9.20 each, FIFO cost of $9 each, LIFO cost of $8 each). During the year, Kinko's purchased 700 containers of ink at $10 and sold 600 units for $20 each. Kinko's paid operating expenses throughout the year, a total of $4,000. Assume Kinko's is not subject to income tax.

Prepare Kinko's income statement for the current year ended December 31 under the average, FIFO, and LIFO inventory costing methods. Include a complete statement heading.

Income tax effects of the inventory costing methods (Obj. 3)

CP6-7 (p. 271) This check point should be used in conjunction with Check Point 6-6. Kinko's in Check Point 6-6 is a corporation subject to a 40% income tax. Compute Kinko's income tax expense under the average, FIFO, and LIFO inventory costing methods. Which method would you select to (a) maximize income before tax and (b) minimize income tax expense? Format your answer as shown on page 270.

Income and tax effects of LIFO (Obj. 3)

writing assignment ■

CP6-8 (p. 271) **Lands' End, Inc.**, has used the LIFO method to account for inventory. Suppose Lands' End is having an unusually bad year, with net income below expectations.

Assume Lands' End inventory costs are rising rapidly. What can Lands' End managers do immediately before the end of the year to increase reported profits? Explain how this action increases reported income.

Applying the lower-of-cost-or-market-rule to inventory (Obj. 2)

CP6-9 (p. 276) Return to the **Pier 1 Imports** data in Exhibit 6-3, page 264. At February 28, 2003, the controller of the company applied the lower-of-cost-or-market rule to Pier 1 inventories. Suppose the controller determined that the current replacement cost (current market value) of the inventory was $330 million. Show what Pier 1 would report for inventory and cost of goods sold.

Using ratio data to evaluate operations (Obj. 4)

CP6-10 (p. 278) Use the inventory data in the FIFO and the LIFO T-accounts on page 269 to compute the company's gross profit percentage and rate of inventory turnover under

1. FIFO
2. LIFO

Sales revenue totaled $1,000. Which method makes the company look better on

3. Gross profit percentage?
4. Inventory turnover?

Estimating ending inventory by the gross profit method (Obj. 5)

CP6-11 (p. 280) Answer the following questions:

1. BXI Software began the year with inventory of $300,000. Inventory purchases for the year totaled $1,600,000. BXI managers estimate that the cost of goods sold for the year will be $1,800,000. How much is BXI's estimated cost of ending inventory? Use the gross profit method.
2. BXI Systems, a related company, began the year with inventory of $300,000 and purchased $1,600,000 of goods during the year (same as in question 1). Sales for the year are $3,000,000, and BXI's gross profit percentage is 40% of sales. Compute BXI's estimated cost of ending inventory by using the gross profit method. Compare this answer to your answer in question 1; they should be the same.

Assessing the effect of an inventory error—1 year only (Obj. 6)

CP6-12 (p. 281) Examine the Pier 1 Imports financial data in Exhibit 6-3, on page 264. Suppose Pier 1's inventory at February 28, 2003, as reported, is understated by $3 million. What are correct amounts for Pier 1 (a) inventory, (b) net sales, (c) cost of goods sold, and (d) gross profit?

Assessing the effect of an inventory error on 2 years (Obj. 6)

CP6-13 (p. 281) Maggie Lang, staff accountant of an **OfficeMax** store, learned that OfficeMax's $4 million cost of inventory at the end of last year was understated by $1.6 million. She notified the company president of the error. Michael LeVan, president of OfficeMax, explained to Lang that there is no need to report the error to lenders because the error will counterbalance this year. LeVan reasons that gross profit for both years combined will be the same whether or not OfficeMax corrects its error.

1. Was last year's reported gross product of $4 million overstated, understated, or correct? What was the correct amount of gross profit last year?
2. Is this year's gross profit of $4.8 million overstated, understated, or correct? What is the correct amount of gross profit for the current year?
3. Whose perspective is better, Lang's or LeVan's? Give your reason. Consider the trend of reported gross profit both without the correction and with the correction.

Ethical implications of inventory actions (Obj. 2, 5)

writing assignment ■

CP6-14 (p. 282) Determine whether each of the following actions in buying, selling, and accounting for inventories is ethical or unethical. Give your reason for each answer.

1. DTE Photo Film purchased lots of inventory shortly before year end to increase the LIFO cost of goods sold and decrease reported income for the year.
2. Edison Electrical Products delayed the purchase of inventory until after December 31, 20X4, to keep 20X3's cost of goods sold from growing too large. The delay in purchasing inventory helped net income of 20X4 to reach the level of profit demanded by the company's investors.
3. Dover Sales Company deliberately overstated ending inventory in order to report higher profits (net income).
4. Brazos Corporation consciously overstated purchases to produce a high figure for cost of goods sold (low amount of net income). The real reason was to decrease the company's income tax payments to the government.

(continued)

5. In applying the lower-of-cost-or-market rule to inventories, Fort Wayne Industries recorded an excessively low market value for ending inventory. This allowed the company to keep from paying income tax for the year.

Exercises

PH Grade Assist

Most of the even-numbered exercises can be found within Prentice Hall Grade Assist (PHGA), an online homework and practice environment. Your instructor may ask you to complete these exercises using PHGA.

Accounting for inventory transactions (Obj. 1, 2)

■ **general ledger**

E6-1 Accounting records for Goldwater Sales Co. yield the following data for the year ended December 31, 20X5 (amounts in thousands):

Inventory, December 31, 20X4	$ 370
Purchases of inventory (on account)	2,200
Sales of inventory—80% on account; 20% for cash (cost $2,100)	3,500
Inventory at FIFO cost, December 31, 20X5	?

Required

1. Journalize Goldwater's inventory transactions for the year under the perpetual system. Show all amounts in thousands. Use Exhibit 6-5 as a model.
2. Report ending inventory, sales, cost of goods sold, and gross profit on the appropriate financial statement (amounts in thousands).

Analyzing inventory transactions (Obj. 1, 2)

E6-2 Suppose **Microsoft Corporation's** inventory records for a particular software program show the following at October 31:

Oct. 1	Beginning inventory	5 units @ $160
8	Purchase	4 units @ 160
15	Purchase	11 units @ 170
26	Purchase	5 units @ 180

At October 31, eight of these software programs are on hand. *Journalize for Microsoft:*

1. Total October purchases in one summary entry. All purchases were on credit.
2. Total October sales and cost of goods sold in two summary entries. The selling price was $500 per unit and all sales were on credit. Assume that Microsoft uses the FIFO inventory method.
3. Under FIFO, how much gross profit would Microsoft earn on these transactions? What is the FIFO cost of Microsoft's ending inventory?

Determining ending inventory and cost of goods sold by four methods (Obj. 2)

■ **spreadsheet**

E6-3 Use the assumed data for **Microsoft Corporation** in Exercise 6-2 to answer the following questions.

Required

1. Compute cost of goods sold and ending inventory, using each of the following methods:
   a. Specific unit cost, assuming three $160 units and five $180 units are on hand
   b. Average cost
   c. First-in, first-out
   d. Last-in, first-out
2. Which method produces the highest cost of goods sold? Which method produces the lowest cost of goods sold? What causes the difference in cost of goods sold?

Computing the tax advantage of LIFO over FIFO (Obj. 3)

E6-4 Use the data in Exercise 6-2 to illustrate Microsoft's income tax advantage from using LIFO over FIFO. Assume sales revenue is $6,000, operating expenses are $1,100, and the income tax rate is 35%. How much in taxes would Microsoft save by using the LIFO method?

Determining ending inventory and cost of goods sold—FIFO vs. LIFO (Obj. 2)

E6-5 VPA, Inc. specializes in printing equipment. Because each inventory item is expensive, VPA uses a perpetual inventory system. Company records indicate the following data for a line of printers:

Date	Item	Quantity	Unit Cost	Sale Price
May 1	Balance	5	$90	
6	Purchase	12	95	
8	Sale	3		$150
17	Sale	4		155
30	Sale	3		155

Required

1. Determine the amounts that VPA should report for cost of goods sold and ending inventory two ways:
   a. FIFO
   b. LIFO
2. Assume VPA uses the FIFO method. Prepare VPA's income statement reporting gross profit for May. Operating expenses totaled $310, and the income tax rate was 40%.

Measuring gross profit—FIFO vs. LIFO (Obj. 2)

E6-6 Suppose a **Target** store in Dayton, Ohio, ended May 20X6 with 800,000 units of merchandise that cost an average of $7 each. Suppose the store then sold 600,000 units for $4.9 million during June. Further, assume the store made two large purchases during June as follows:

June	6	100,000 units @ $6 = $ 600,000
	21	400,000 units @ $5 = 2,000,000

1. At June 30, the store manager needs to know the store's gross profit under both FIFO and LIFO. Supply this information.
2. What caused the FIFO and LIFO gross profit figures to differ? Does the gross-profit difference go in the direction you would predict? Explain in detail.

Managing income taxes under the LIFO method (Obj. 3)

writing assignment ■

E6-7 Tabor Plastics Corporation is nearing the end of its best year ever. With 3 weeks until year end, it appears that net income for the year will have increased by 70% over last year. Rick Tabor, the president and principal stockholder, is pleased with the year's success but worried about the high income taxes the business will have to pay.

Tabor asks you, the financial vice president, to come up with a way to decrease the business's income tax burden. Inventory quantities are a little lower than normal because sales have been especially strong during the last few months. Tabor uses the LIFO inventory method, and inventory costs have risen dramatically during the latter part of the year.

Required

Write a memorandum to Rick Tabor to explain how the company can decrease its income taxes for the current year. Explain your reasoning in detail. Tabor is a man of integrity, so your plan must be completely honest and ethical.

Identifying income, tax, and other effects of the inventory methods (Obj. 3)

E6-8 This exercise tests your understanding of the various inventory methods. In the space provided, write the name of the inventory method that best fits the description. Assume that the cost of inventory is rising.

1. ____ Used to account for automobiles, jewelry, and art objects.
2. ____ Provides a middle-ground measure of ending inventory and cost of goods sold.
3. ____ Maximizes reported income.
4. ____ Matches the most current cost of goods sold against sales revenue.
5. ____ Results in an old measure of the cost of ending inventory.
6. ____ Generally associated with saving income taxes.
7. ____ Results in a cost of ending inventory that is close to the current cost of replacing the inventory.

8. ____ Enables a company to buy high-cost inventory at year end and thereby decrease reported income.

9. ____ Enables a company to keep reported income from dropping lower by liquidating older layers of inventory.

10. ____ Writes inventory down when replacement cost drops below historical cost.

Applying the lower-of-cost-or-market rule to inventories (Obj. 2)

E6-9 Jeffrey Corporation uses a perpetual inventory system. Jeffrey has these account balances at December 31, 20X4, prior to releasing the financial statements for the year:

Inventory

Beg. bal.	**12,400**	
End bal.	**18,000**	

Cost of Goods Sold

Bal.	**110,000**	

Sales Revenue

	Bal.	**225,000**

A year ago, when Jeffrey prepared its 20X3 financial statements, the replacement cost of ending inventory was $13,050. Jeffrey has determined that the replacement cost of the December 31, 20X4, ending inventory was $17,000.

Required

Prepare Jeffrey Corporation's 20X4 income statement through gross profit to show how the company would apply the lower-of-cost-or-market rule to its inventories.

Change from LIFO to FIFO (Obj. 2, 3)

spreadsheet

E6-10 Whitewater Canoe Sales is considering a change from LIFO to FIFO for inventory. Managers are concerned about the effect of this change on income tax expense and reported net income. If the change is made, it will become effective on January 1. Inventory on hand at January 1 is $63,000. During January, Whitewater managers expect sales of $260,000; net purchases between $159,000 and $182,000; and operating expenses, excluding income tax, of $83,000. The income tax rate is 40%. Inventories at January 31 are budgeted as follows: FIFO, $85,000; LIFO, $78,000.

	A	B	C	D	E
1	Whitewater Canoe Sales				
2	Estimated Income under FIFO and LIFO				
3	January 20XX				
4		**Purchase $159,000**		**Purchase $182,000**	
5		**FIFO**	**LIFO**	**FIFO**	**LIFO**
6					
7	Sales	$260,000	$260,000	$260,000	$260,000
8					
9	Cost of goods sold				
10	Beginning inventory	63,000	63,000	63,000	63,000
11	Purchases	159,000	159,000	182,000	182,000
12					
13	Goods available				
14	Ending inventory	(85,000)	(78,000)	(85,000)	(78,000)
15					
16	Cost of goods sold				
17					
18	Gross profit				
19	Operating expenses	83,000	83,000	83,000	83,000
20					
21	Income from operations				
22	Income tax expense				
23					
24	Net income	$	$	$	$
25					

Required

Create a spreadsheet model to compute estimated net income for January under FIFO and LIFO. Format your answer as shown here.

Determining amounts for the income statement (Obj. 2)

E6-11 Supply the missing income statement amounts for each of the following companies (amounts adapted, and in millions):

Company	Net Sales	Beginning Inventory	Purchases	Ending Inventory	Cost of Goods Sold	Gross Profit
Coca Cola	$ 19,564	$ (a)	$ 7,344	$ 1,294	$7,105	$ (b)
Wal-Mart	191,329	19,793	(c)	21,442	(d)	41,074
Intel	33,726	1,478	13,413	2,241	(e)	21,076
Estee Lauder	(f)	513	1,005	(g)	972	3,395

Prepare the income statement for The Coca-Cola Company using the cost-of-goods-sold model to compute cost of goods sold. Coca-Cola's operating and other expenses, as adapted, for the year were $7,886. Assume the income tax rate was 33.3%.

Note: Exercise 6-12 builds on Exercise 6-11 with a profitability analysis of these four actual companies.

Measuring profitability (Obj. 4)

■ **general ledger**

E6-12 Refer to the data in Exercise 6-11. Which company has the highest, and the lowest, gross profit percentage? Which company has the highest, and the lowest rate of inventory turnover? Explain how your answers to these questions describe the merchandising philosophies of these companies. Be specific. Based on your figures, which company appears to be the most profitable?

Measuring gross profit and reporting cash flows (Obj. 4)

E6-13 **The Home Depot** made sales of $45.7 billion in the year ended January 31, 20X1. Collections from customers totaled $45.5 billion. The company began the year with $5.5 billion in inventories and ended with $6.6 billion. During the year purchases of inventory added up to $33.2 billion. Of the purchases, Home Depot paid $35.2 billion to suppliers.

As an investor searching for a good investment, suppose you identify several critical pieces of information about Home Depot's operations during the year.

Compute Home Depot's gross profit, gross profit percentage, and rate of inventory turnover during 20X1. Use the cost-of-goods-sold model as needed.

Budgeting inventory purchases (Obj. 2)

E6-14 **Toys "Я" Us** is budgeting for the fiscal year ended January 31, 20X4. During the preceding year ended January 31, 20X3, sales totaled $9,400 million and cost of goods sold was $6,500 million. At January 31, 20X3, inventory stood at $1,900 million.

During the upcoming 20X4 year, suppose Toys "Я" Us expects sales and cost of goods sold to increase by 8%. The company budgets next year's inventory at $2,200 million.

Required

One of the most important decisions a manager makes is how much inventory to buy. How much inventory should Toys "Я" Us purchase during the upcoming year to reach its budgeted figures?

Estimating inventory by the gross profit method (Obj. 5)

■ **spreadsheet**

E6-15 Raleigh Technologies began January with inventory of $48,000. The business made net purchases of $136,000 and had net sales of $200,000 before a fire destroyed its merchandise inventory. For the past several years, Raleigh's gross profit percentage has been 40%. Estimate the cost of the inventory destroyed by the fire. Identify another reason managers use the gross profit method to estimate ending inventory.

Correcting an inventory error (Obj. 6)

E6-16 Allergan, maker of contact lens solutions, reported the following comparative income statement for the years ended September 30, 20X5, and 20X4:

Allergan, Inc. Income Statement Years Ended September 30, 20X5, and 20X4				
	20X5		20X4	
Sales revenue		$149,000		$122,000
Cost of goods sold				
Beginning inventory	$18,000		$12,000	
Purchases	72,000		66,000	
Goods available	90,000		78,000	
Ending inventory	(16,000)		(18,000)	
Cost of goods sold		74,000		60,000
Gross profit		75,000		62,000
Operating expenses		30,000		20,000
Net income		$ 45,000		$ 42,000

Allergan, Inc.'s, president and shareholders are thrilled by the company's boost in sales and net income during 20X5. Then they discover that ending 20X4 inventory was understated by $9,000. Prepare the corrected comparative income statement for the 2-year period. How well did Allergan really perform in 20X5, as compared with 20X4? What caused the evaluation of 20X5 to change so dramatically? Explain in detail.

Correcting an inventory error (Obj. 6)

E6-17 **Pharmacia Corporation** uses a perpetual inventory system and reports inventory at the lower of cost or market. Assume that prior to releasing its December 20X0 financial statements, the Pharmacia preliminary income statement is as follows:

Income Statement (Partial)	
	Millions
Sales revenue	$18,144
Cost of goods sold	5,456
Gross profit	$12,688

During the year, Pharmacia purchased inventory at a cost of $5,798 million. Assume that the company has learned that beginning inventory was overstated by $100 million. The ending inventory at December 31, 20X0, is $2,927 million and this amount is correct.

Show how Pharmacia should report the preceding data on its 20X0 income statement.

Challenge Exercises

Inventory policy decisions (Obj. 2)

E6-18 For each of the following situations, identify the inventory method that you would use or, given the use of a particular method, state the strategy that you would follow to accomplish your goal:

a. Company management, like that of **IBM** and **Pier 1 Imports**, prefers a middle-of-the-road inventory policy that avoids extremes.
b. Inventory costs are decreasing, and your company's board of directors wants to minimize income taxes.
c. Your inventory turns over slowly. Inventory costs are increasing, and the company prefers to report high income.
d. Inventory costs have been stable for several years, and you expect costs to remain stable for the indefinite future. (Give the reason for your choice of method.)
e. Inventory costs are increasing. Your company uses LIFO and is having an unexpectedly good year. It is near year end, and you need to keep net income from increasing too much.
f. Suppliers of your inventory are threatening a labor strike, and it may be difficult for your company to obtain inventory. This situation could increase your income taxes.

Measuring the effect of a LIFO liquidation (Obj. 2, 3)

E6-19 Suppose **Neiman Marcus**, the specialty retailer, had these records for ladies' evening gowns during 20X9.

Beginning inventory (40 @ $1,000)	$ 40,000
Purchase in February (20 @ $1,100)	22,000
Purchase in June (50 @ $1,200)	60,000
Purchase in December (30 @ $1,300)	39,000
Goods available	$161,000

Assume sales of evening gowns totaled 130 units during 20X9 and that Neiman Marcus uses the LIFO method to account for inventory. The income tax rate is 40%.

Required

1. Compute Neiman Marcus's cost of goods sold for evening gowns in 20X9.
2. Compute what cost of goods sold would have been if Neiman Marcus had purchased enough inventory in December—at $1,300 per evening gown—to keep year-end inventory at the same level it was at the beginning of the year.
3. How much did the LIFO liquidation boost Neiman Marcus's gross profit and net income? How much did the LIFO liquidation cost the company in income tax? Was the LIFO liquidation good or bad for the company? State the reason for your answer.

Evaluating a company's profitability (Obj. 4)

E6-20 Z Mart, Inc., declared bankruptcy. Let's see why. Z mart reported these figures:

Z Mart, Inc.
Statement of Income
Years Ended December 31, 20X7, 20X6, and 20X5

Millions	20X7	20X6	20X5
Sales	$37.0	$35.9	$33.7
Cost of sales	29.7	28.1	26.3
Selling, general, and administrative expenses	7.4	6.5	6.2
Other expenses	0.1	0.9	0.7
Net income (net loss)	$ (0.2)	$ 0.4	$ 0.5

Required

Evaluate the trend of Z Mart's results of operations during 20X5 through 20X7. Consider the trends of sales, gross profit, and net income. Track the gross profit percentage (to three decimal places) and the rate of inventory turnover (to one decimal place) in each year. Z Mart inventories at December 31, 20X4, 20X5, 20X6, and 20X7 were $6.4, $6.5, $7.1, and $6.4 million, respectively. Also discuss the role that selling expenses must have played in Z Mart's difficulties.

Practice Quiz

Test your understanding of accounting for inventory by answering the following questions. Select the best choice from among the possible answers given.

PQ6-1 Florence Company began January with $2,000 of merchandise inventory. During January, Florence made the following entries pertaining to its merchandise inventory:

Inventory	6,000	
Accounts Payable		6,000
Accounts Receivable	7,200	
Sales Revenue		7,200
Cost of Goods Sold	5,500	
Inventory		5,500

How much was Florence's *gross profit* for January?

a. Zero
b. $500
c. $1,200
d. $1,700

PQ6-2 Use the data in question 1. What will Florence report on its balance sheet at the end of January?

a. Inventory of $500
b. Inventory of $2,500
c. Inventory of $1,500
d. Cost of goods sold of $5,500

PQ6-3 When does the cost of inventory become an expense?

a. When inventory is sold to a customer.
b. When inventory is purchased from the supplier.
c. When payment is made to the supplier.
d. When cash is collected from the customer.

The next two questions use the following facts. Acme Paper Company wants to know the effect of different inventory costing methods on its financial statements. Inventory and purchases data for 20X5 follow.

		Units	Unit Cost	Total Cost
Jan. 1	Beginning inventory	2,000	$10.00	$20,000
April 4	Purchase	1,500	10.30	15,450
June 23	Purchase	3,400	10.75	36,550
July 9	Sale	(1,000)		
Oct. 31	Sale	(2,400)		
31	Ending inventory	3,500		

PQ6-4 If Acme uses the FIFO method, the *cost of the ending inventory* will be

a. $35,450
b. $35,000
c. $37,580
d. $37,625

PQ6-5 If Acme uses the LIFO method, *cost of goods sold* will be

a. $34,420
b. $37,580
c. $35,450
d. $36,550

PQ6-6 In a period of rising prices,

a. Gross profit under FIFO will be higher than under LIFO.
b. LIFO inventory will be greater than FIFO inventory.
c. Cost of goods sold under LIFO will be less than under FIFO.
d. Net income under LIFO will be higher than under FIFO.

PQ6-7 The income statement for Floyd Company shows gross profit of $144,000, operating expenses of $130,000, and cost of goods sold of $216,000. What is the amount of net sales revenue?

a. $274,000
b. $230,000
c. $490,000
d. $360,000

PQ6-8 The word "market" as used in "the lower of cost or market" generally means

a. Original cost
b. Retail market price
c. Replacement cost
d. Liquidation price

PQ6-9 The sum of (a) ending inventory and (b) cost of goods sold is

a. Gross margin
b. Net purchases
c. Goods available
d. Beginning inventory

PQ6-10 The following data come from the inventory records of Charger Company:

Net sales revenue	$620,000
Beginning inventory	70,000
Ending inventory	40,000
Net purchases	400,000

Based on these facts, the gross profit for Charger Company is

a. $150,000
b. $220,000
c. $190,000
d. Some other amount

PQ6-11 Eufala Company ended the month of May with inventory of $10,000. Eufala expects to end the month of June with inventory of $15,000 after cost of goods sold of $90,000. How much inventory must Eufala purchase during June in order to accomplish these results?

a. $85,000
b. $95,000
c. $105,000
d. Cannot be determined from the data given.

PQ6-12 Two financial ratios that clearly distinguish a discount retailer such as **Target** from a high-end retailer such as **Saks Fifth Avenue** are the gross profit percentage and the rate of inventory turnover. Which set of relationships is most likely for Target?

	Gross profit percentage	Inventory turnover
a.	High	High
b.	Low	Low
c.	Low	High
d.	High	Low

PQ6-13 Sales are $500,000 and the gross profit is $200,000. Beginning and ending inventories are $25,000 and $35,000, respectively. How many times did the company turn its inventory over during this period?

a. 16.7 times
b. 6.7 times
c. 8 times
d. 10 times

PQ6-14 Muskogee Corporation reported the following data:

Sales returns	$ 10,000	Freight in	$ 20,000
Purchase returns	6,000	Purchases	230,000
Sales	490,000	Beginning inventory	50,000
Ending inventory	40,000	Purchase discounts	4,000

Muskogee's gross profit percentage is

a. 47.9%
b. 52.1%
c. 53.1%
d. 54.0%

PQ6-15 Grant Company had the following for the first quarter of 20X3:

Beginning inventory, $53,500 Net purchases, $75,500
Net sales revenue, $93,000 Gross profit rate, 30%

Based on these facts, the ending inventory should be

a. $65,100
b. $63,900
c. $28,100
d. $100,800

PQ6-16 An error caused Baylor Corporation's December 31, 20X3, ending inventory to be understated by $40,000. What effect will this error have on ending total assets, cost of goods sold, and net income for 20X3?

	Assets	Cost of goods sold	Net income
a.	Understate	Understate	Understate
b.	Understate	Overstate	Understate
c.	No effect	No effect	No effect
d.	No effect	Overstate	Overstate

PQ6-17 What is the effect of Baylor Corporation's 20X3 inventory error on cost of goods sold, net income, and ending stockholders' equity for 20X4?

	Cost of goods sold	Net income	Stockholders' equity
a.	Understate	Overstate	Correct
b.	Understate	Overstate	Overstate
c.	Overstate	Understate	Correct
d.	Correct	Correct	Correct

Problems
(Group A)

PH Grade Assist

Most of these A problems can be found within Prentice Hall Grade Assist (PHGA), an online homework and practice environment. Your instructor may ask you to complete these problems using PHGA.

Accounting for inventory in a perpetual system (Obj. 1, 2)

■ **general ledger**

P6-1A The **May Department Stores Company** operates more than 300 department stores in the United States, including Lord & Taylor, Hecht's, Foley's, Robinson-May, Kaufmann's, and Filene's Basement. The company's fiscal year ends each January 31.

Assume the Lord & Taylor store in Atlanta began fiscal year 20X0 with an inventory of 50,000 units that cost $1,500,000. During the year the store purchased merchandise on account as follows:

March (60,000 units @ cost of $32)	$1,920,000
August (40,000 units @ cost of $34)	1,360,000
October (180,000 units @ cost of $35)	6,300,000
Total purchases	$9,580,000

Cash payments on account totaled $9,110,000.

During fiscal year 20X0, the store sold 290,000 units of merchandise for $13,400,000, of which $4,700,000 was for cash and the balance was on account. Lord & Taylor uses the LIFO method for inventories.

Operating expenses for the year were $2,130,000. Lord & Taylor paid two-thirds in cash and accrued the rest. The store accrued income tax at the rate of 40%.

Required

1. Make summary journal entries to record the Lord & Taylor store's transactions for the year ended January 31, 20X0. The company uses a perpetual inventory system.
2. Determine the LIFO cost of the store's ending inventory at January 31, 20X0. Use a T-account.
3. Prepare the Lord & Taylor store's income statement for the year ended January 31, 20X0. Show totals for the gross profit, income before tax, and net income.

Measuring cost of goods sold and ending inventory—perpetual system (Obj. 2, 3)

P6-2A Assume an **Eddie Bauer** store began March with 50 backpacks that cost $19 each. The sale price of each backpack was $36. During March, Eddie Bauer completed these inventory transactions:

		Units	Unit Cost	Unit Sale Price
March 2	Purchase	12	$20	$37
8	Sale	27	19	36
13	Sale	23	19	36
	Sale	1	20	37
17	Purchase	24	20	37
22	Sale	25	20	37
29	Purchase	24	21	39

Required

1. The preceding data are taken from the store's perpetual inventory records. Which cost method does Bauer use? How can you tell?
2. Determine the store's cost of goods sold for March. Also compute gross profit for March.
3. What is the cost of the store's March 31 inventory of backpacks?

Computing inventory by three methods—perpetual system (Obj. 2, 3)

P6-3A Hot Wheels Motorcycles, Inc., began December with 140 racing helmets that cost $76 each. During December, the store made the following purchases at cost:

Dec. 3	217 @ $81
12	95 @ 82
18	210 @ 84
24	248 @ 87

Hot Wheels sold 696 helmets and ended December with 214 helmets. The sale price of each helmet was $130.

Required

1. Determine the cost of goods sold and ending inventory amounts under the average, FIFO, and LIFO cost methods. Round average cost per unit to four decimal places, and round all other amounts to the nearest dollar.
2. Explain why cost of goods sold is highest under LIFO. Be specific.
3. Prepare Hot Wheels' income statement for December. Report gross profit. Operating expenses totaled $22,000. Hot Wheels uses the LIFO method for inventory. The income tax rate is 40%.

Applying the different inventory costing methods—perpetual system (Obj. 2, 3)

P6-4A The records of Blockbuster Digital Images include the following for a line of compact discs at December 31 of the current year:

Inventory

Jan. 1	**Balance**	**300 units @ $3.00**	**1,215**		
		100 units @ 3.15			
Feb. 6	**Purchase**	**800 units @ 3.15**	**2,520**		
May 19	**Purchase**	**600 units @ 3.35**	**2,010**		
Aug. 12	**Purchase**	**400 units @ 3.50**	**1,400**		
Oct. 4	**Purchase**	**700 units @ 3.70**	**2,590**		

Sales Revenue

	Dec. 31	**2,500 units**	**11,200**

Required

1. Prepare a partial income statement through gross profit under the average, FIFO, and LIFO cost methods. Round average cost per unit to four decimal places.
2. Which inventory method would you use to report the highest net income? Explain why this method produces the highest reported income.

Applying the lower-of-cost-or-market rule to inventories—perpetual system (Obj. 2)

writing assignment ■

P6-5A LM Electronics has recently been plagued with lackluster sales. The rate of inventory turnover has dropped, and some of the company's merchandise is gathering dust. At the same time, competition has forced some of LM's suppliers to lower the prices that LM will pay when it replaces its inventory. It is now December 31, 20X4. The current replacement cost of LM's ending inventory is $1,500,000 below what the company paid for the goods, which was $8,900,000. Before any adjustments at the end of the period, LM's Cost of Goods Sold account has a balance of $27,400,000.

What action should LM take in this situation? Give any journal entry required. At what amount should LM report Inventory on the balance sheet? At what amount should the company report Cost of Goods Sold on the income statement? Discuss the accounting principle or concept that is most relevant to this situation.

Using gross profit percentage and inventory turnover to evaluate two leading companies (Obj. 4)

writing assignment ■

P6-6A **Hershey Foods Corporation**, famous for chocolate, and **Target Corporation**, the discount retailer, reported these amounts:

Hershey Foods Corporation
Consolidated Statement of Income (Adapted)

	Years Ended December 31	
(Amounts in millions)	20X4	20X3
Net Sales	$4,221	$3,971
Cost of sales	2,471	2,355
Selling, marketing, and administrative expenses	1,127	1,058

Hershey Foods Corporation
Consolidated Balance Sheet (Adapted)

	December 31,	
(Amounts in millions)	20X4	20X3
Assets		
Cash and cash equivalents	$ 32	$118
Accounts receivable—trade	380	353
Inventories	605	602

Target Corporation
Consolidated Statement of Operations (Adapted)

	Year Ended	
(Amounts in millions)	20X4	20X3
Sales	$36,362	$33,212
Cost of sales	25,295	23,029
Selling, general, and administrative expenses	8,190	7,490

Target Corporation
Consolidated Financial Position (Adapted)

	Year Ended	
(Amounts in millions)	20X4	20X3
Cash and cash equivalents	$ 356	$ 220
Receivable-backed securities	1,941	1,724
Inventory	4,248	3,798

Required

1. Compute both companies' gross profit percentage and their rate of inventory turnover during 20X4.

2. Can you tell from these statistics which company should be more profitable in percentage terms? Why? What important category of expenses do the gross profit percentage and the inventory turnover ratio fail to consider?

Estimating inventory by the gross profit method; preparing the income statement (Obj. 5)

■ spreadsheet

P6-7A Assume **Kinko's,** the copy center, lost some inventory in a fire. To file an insurance claim, Kinko's must estimate its ending inventory by the gross profit method. Assume for the past 2 years, Kinko's gross profit has averaged 40% of net sales. Suppose the company's inventory records reveal the following data:

Inventory, March 1	$1,292,000
Transactions during March:	
Purchases	6,585,000
Purchase discounts	149,000
Purchase returns	8,000
Sales	8,657,000
Sales returns	17,000

Required

1. Estimate the cost of the ending inventory lost in the fire using the gross profit method.
2. Prepare Kinko's March income statement for this inventory through gross profit. Show the detailed computations of cost of goods sold in a separate schedule.

Determining the amount of inventory to purchase (Obj. 1)

P6-8A Condensed versions of a **Stop-n-Go** conveniences store's income statement and balance sheet reported the following. The business is organized as a proprietorship, so it pays no corporate income tax.

The owner is budgeting for 20X4. He expects sales and cost of goods sold to increase by 5%. To meet customer demand, ending inventory will need to be $80,000 at December 31, 20X4. The owner can lower operating expenses by doing some of the work himself. He hopes to earn a net income of $150,000 next year.

Stop-n-Go Store
Income Statement
Year Ended December 31, 20X3

Sales	$960,000
Cost of sales	720,000
Gross profit	240,000
Operating expenses	110,000
Net income	$130,000

Stop-n-Go Store
Balance Sheet
December 31, 20X3

Assets		Liabilities and Capital	
Cash	$ 40,000	Accounts payable	$ 30,000
Inventories	70,000	Note payable	190,000
Land and buildings net	270,000	Total liabilities	220,000
		Owner, capital	160,000
Total assets	$380,000	Total liabilities and capital	$380,000

Required

1. One of the most important decisions a business owner makes is the amount of inventory to purchase. Show how to determine the amount of inventory to purchase in 20X4.
2. Prepare the store's budgeted income statement for 20X4 to reach the target net income of $150,000.

Correcting inventory errors over a 3-year period (Obj. 6)

P6-9A The accounting records of Monaco Gemstones, Inc. (top of page 302) show these data (adapted, in millions):

Assume internal auditors discovered that the ending inventory for 2005 was understated by $50 million and that the ending inventory for 2006 was overstated by $20 million. The ending inventory at December 31, 2007, was correct.

Monaco Gemstones, Inc.						
(Amounts in thousands)	2007		2006		2005	
Net sales revenue		$1,412		$1,231		$1,138
Cost of goods sold:						
Beginning inventory	$ 269		$259		$234	
Purchases	859		729		663	
Goods available	1,128		988		897	
Less ending inventory	(311)		(269)		(259)	
Cost of goods sold		817		719		638
Gross profit		595		512		500
Total operating expenses		500		437		420
Net income		$ 95		$ 75		$ 80

Required

1. Show correct income statements for the 3 years.
2. State whether each year's net income as reported here is understated or overstated. For each incorrect figure, indicate the amount of the understatement or overstatement.
3. How much did these assumed corrections add to, or take away from, Monaco Gemstones' total net income over the 3-year period? How did the corrections affect the trend of net income?

(Group B)

PH Grade Assist

Some of these B problems can be found within Prentice Hall Grade Assist (PHGA), an online homework and practice environment. Your instructor may ask you to complete these problems using PHGA.

Accounting for inventory in a perpetual system (Obj. 1, 2)

■ **general ledger**

P6-1B Toys "Я" Us purchases inventory in crates of merchandise; each unit of inventory is a crate of toys. The fiscal year of Toys "Я" Us ends each January 31.

Assume you are dealing with a single Toys "Я" Us store in San Antonio, Texas, and that the store experienced the following: The San Antonio store began fiscal year 20X5 with an inventory of 20,000 units that cost a total of $1,200,000. During the year, the store purchased merchandise on account as follows:

April (30,000 units @ cost of $65)	$ 1,950,000
August (50,000 units @ cost of $65)	3,250,000
November (90,000 units @ cost of $70)	6,300,000
Total purchases	$11,500,000

Cash payments on account totaled $11,390,000.

During fiscal year 20X5, the store sold 180,000 units of merchandise for $16,400,000, of which $5,300,000 was for cash and the balance was on account. Toys "Я" Us uses the LIFO method for inventories.

Operating expenses for the year were $4,000,000. The store paid 80% in cash and accrued the rest. The store accrued income tax at the rate of 40%.

Required

1. Make summary journal entries to record the store's transactions for the year ended January 31, 20X5. Toys "Я" Us uses a perpetual inventory system.
2. Determine the LIFO cost of the store's ending inventory at January 31, 20X5. Use a T-account.
3. Prepare the store's income statement for the year ended January 31, 20X5. Show totals for the gross profit, income before tax, and net income.

Measuring cost of goods sold and ending inventory—perpetual system (Obj. 2, 3)

P6-2B Assume a **Reebok** outlet store began August 20X0 with 50 pairs of hiking boots that cost $40 each. The sale price of these boots was $70. During August, the store completed these inventory transactions:

			Units	Unit Cost	Unit Sale Price
Aug.	3	Sale	16	$40	$70
	8	Purchase	80	41	72
	11	Sale	34	40	70
	19	Sale	9	41	72
	24	Sale	32	41	72
	30	Purchase	18	42	73
	31	Sale	8	41	72

Required

1. The preceding data are taken from the store's perpetual inventory records. Which cost method does the store use? Explain how you arrived at your answer.
2. Determine the store's cost of goods sold for August. Also compute gross profit for August.
3. What is the cost of the store's August 31 inventory of hiking boots?

Computing inventory by three methods—perpetual system (Obj. 2, 3)

P6-3B Calico Corners, Inc., an upscale fabric store, began March with 73 yards of fabric that cost $23 per yard. During the month, Calico Corners made the following purchases at cost:

March 4	113 yards @ $27
12	81 yards @ 29
19	167 yards @ 32
25	44 yards @ 35

Calico Corners sold 418 yards of fabric, and at March 31 the ending inventory consists of 60 yards. The sale price of the fabric was $60 per yard.

Required

1. Determine the cost of goods sold and ending inventory amounts for March under (1) average cost, (2) FIFO cost, and (3) LIFO cost. Round average cost per unit to four decimal places, and round all other amounts to the nearest dollar.
2. Explain why cost of goods sold is highest under LIFO. Be specific.
3. Prepare Calico Corner's income statement for March. Report gross profit. Operating expenses totaled $8,000. Calico Corners uses average costing for inventory. The income tax rate is 40%.

Applying the different inventory costing methods—perpetual system (Obj. 2, 3)

P6-4B The records of Schlosstein Restaurant Supply include the following accounts for cases of coffee cups at December 31 of the current year:

Inventory

Jan. 1	Balance 700 units	@ $7.00	4,900		
Jan. 6	Purchase 300 units	@ $7.05	2,115		
Mar. 19	Purchase 1,100 units	@ 7.35	8,085		
June 22	Purchase 8,400 units	@ 7.50	63,000		
Oct. 4	Purchase 500 units	@ 8.50	4,250		

Sales Revenue

			Dec. 31	10,000 units	134,970

Required

1. Prepare a partial income statement through gross profit under the average, FIFO, and LIFO methods. Round average cost per unit to four decimal places.
2. Which inventory method would you use to minimize income tax? Explain why this method causes income tax to be the lowest.

Applying the lower-of-cost-or-market rule to inventories—perpetual system (Obj. 2)

writing assignment ■

P6-5B Rebecca Arden Cosmetics has recently been plagued with lackluster sales. The rate of inventory turnover has dropped, and some of the company's merchandise is gathering dust. At the same time, competition has forced Arden's suppliers to lower the prices that the company will pay when it replaces its inventory. It is now December 31, 20X4, and the current replacement cost of Arden's ending inventory is $600,000 below what Arden actually paid for the goods, which was $4,900,000. Before any adjustments at the end of the period, the Cost of Goods Sold account has a balance of $29,600,000.

What action should Arden take in this situation? Give any journal entry required. At what amount should Arden report Inventory on the balance sheet? At what amounts should the company report Cost of Goods Sold on the income statement? Discuss the accounting principle or concept that is most relevant to this situation.

Using gross profit percentage and inventory turnover to evaluate two retailers (Obj. 4)

writing assignment ■

P6-6B Grant Thornton, a specialty retailer, and Easy-Buy Stores, a discount merchandiser, reported these figures, which have been disguised to hide the companies identities.

Required

1. Compute the gross profit percentage and the inventory turnover ratio for Company A and for Company B during 20X1.
2. Is Company A Grant Thornton, or is it Easy-Buy? Is Company B Grant Thornton or Easy-Buy? State the reasoning for your answer, based solely on the ratios you computed.

Company A
Consolidated Statement of Income (Adapted)

(Amounts in millions)	Fiscal Years Ended January 31, 20X1	20X0
Revenues:		
Net sales	$191	$165
Other income—net	2	2
	193	167
Costs and Expenses:		
Cost of sales	150	130
Operating, selling, and general expenses	32	27

Company A
Consolidated Balance Sheet (Adapted)

(Amounts in millions)	January 31, 20X1	20X0
Assets		
Current assets:		
Cash and cash equivalents	$ 2	$ 2
Receivables	2	1
Inventories	21	20
Prepaid expenses and other	1	1
Total Current Assets	$26	$24

Company B
Consolidated Statement of Operations (Adapted)

(Amounts in millions)	Year Ended 20X1	20X0
Net sales	$1,412	$1,231
Cost of sales	817	719
Selling, general and administrative expenses	400	349

Company B Consolidated Balance Sheet (Adapted)		
	Year End	
(Amounts in millions)	20X1	20X0
Assets		
Current assets:		
Cash and temporary investments	$ 47	$ 50
Accounts receivable, net	84	59
Inventories	311	269

Estimating inventory by the gross profit method; preparing the income statement (Obj. 5)

■ **spreadsheet**

P6-7B Assume **Procter & Gamble Company** lost some Pringles potato chips inventory in a fire. To file an insurance claim, Proctor & Gamble must estimate its inventory by the gross profit method. Assume that for the past 2 years, the gross profit has averaged 40% of net sales. Suppose the company's inventory records reveal the following data:

Inventory, July 1	$ 367,000
Transactions during July:	
Purchases	5,789,000
Purchase discounts	26,000
Purchase returns	12,000
Sales	6,430,000
Sales returns	250,000

Required

1. Estimate the cost of the lost inventory, using the gross profit method.
2. Prepare the July income statement for this product through gross profit. Show the detailed computation of cost of goods sold in a separate schedule.

Determining the amount of inventory to purchase (Obj. 1)

P6-8B Assume condensed versions of **Ben's Short Stop** convenience store's most recent income statement and balance sheet reported as follows. Because the business is organized as a proprietorship, it pays no corporate income tax.

Ben's Short Stop Store Income Statement Year Ended December 31, 20X4	
Sales	$900,000
Cost of sales	690,000
Gross profit	210,000
Operating expenses	80,000
Net income	$130,000

Ben's Short Stop Store Balance Sheet December 31, 20X4			
Assets		**Liabilities and Capital**	
Cash	$ 70,000	Accounts payable	$ 35,000
Inventories	35,000	Note payable	280,000
Land and buildings, net	360,000	Total liabilities	315,000
		Owner, capital	150,000
Total assets	$465,000	Total liabilities and capital	$465,000

The owner is budgeting for 20X5. He expects sales and cost of goods sold to increase by 10%. To meet customer demand for the increase in sales, ending inventory will need to be $45,000 at December 31, 20X5. He hopes to earn a net income of $150,000 next year.

Required

1. One of the most important decisions a manager makes is the amount of inventory to purchase. Show how to determine the amount of inventory to purchase in 20X5.
2. Prepare the store's budgeted income statement for 20X5 to reach the target net income of $150,000.

Correcting inventory errors over a 3-year period (Obj. 6)

P6-9B McPhail Corporation reported these data (adapted, in billions):

	20X2		20X1		20X0	
Net sales revenue		$36		$33		$30
Cost of goods sold:						
Beginning inventory	$ 4		$ 3		$ 2	
Purchases	25		24		22	
Goods available	29		27		24	
Less ending inventory	(4)		(4)		(3)	
Cost of goods sold		25		23		21
Gross profit		11		10		9
Total operating expenses		10		9		8
Net income		$ 1		$ 1		$ 1

Assume internal auditors discovered that the ending inventory for 20X0 was overstated by $1 billion and that the ending inventory for 20X1 was understated by $1 billion. The ending inventory at year-end 20X2 was correct.

Required

1. Show corrected income statements for the 3 years.
2. State whether each year's net income as reported here is understated or overstated. For each incorrect figure, indicate the amount of the understatement or overstatement.
3. How much did these assumed corrections add to or take away from McPhail's total net income over the 3-year period? How did the corrections affect the trend of net income?

APPLY YOUR KNOWLEDGE

Decision Cases

Assessing the impact of a year-end purchase of inventory (Obj. 1, 2)

writing assignment

Case 1. Caledonia Corporation is nearing the end of its first year of operations. The company made inventory purchases of $745,000 during the year, as follows:

January	1,000 units @	$100.00 =	$100,000
July	4,000	121.25	485,000
November	1,000	160.00	160,000
Totals	6,000		$745,000

Sales for the year will be 5,000 units for $1,200,000 of revenue. Expenses other than cost of goods sold and income taxes will be $200,000. The president of the company is undecided about whether to adopt the FIFO method or the LIFO method for inventories.

The company has storage capacity for 5,000 additional units of inventory. Inventory prices are expected to stay at $160 per unit for the next few months. The president is considering purchasing 1,000 additional units of inventory at $160 each before the end of the year. He wishes to know how the purchase would affect net income under both FIFO and LIFO. The income tax rate is 40%.

Required

1. To aid company decision making, prepare income statements under FIFO and under LIFO, both *without* and *with* the year-end purchase of 1,000 units of inventory at $160 per unit.
2. Compare the net income under FIFO *without* and *with* the year-end purchase. Make the same comparison under LIFO. Under which method does the year-end purchase affect net income?
3. Under which method can a year-end purchase be made in order to manage net income?

Case 2. The inventory costing method a company chooses can affect the financial statements and thus the decisions of the people who use those statements.

Assessing the impact of the inventory costing method on the financial statements (Obj. 2, 3)

writing assignment ■

Required

1. A leading accounting researcher stated that one inventory costing method reports the most recent costs in the income statement, whereas another method reports the most recent costs in the balance sheet. In this person's opinion, the result is that one or the other of the statements is "inaccurate" when prices are rising. What did the researcher mean?
2. Conservatism is an accepted accounting concept. Would you want management to be conservative in accounting for inventory if you were (a) a shareholder or (b) a prospective shareholder? Give your reason.
3. Outback Cycle Company follows conservative accounting and writes the value of its inventory of bicycles down to market, which has declined below cost. The following year, an unexpected cycling craze results in a demand for bicycles that far exceeds supply, and the market price increases above the previous cost. What effect will conservatism have on the income of Outback over the 2 years?

Ethical Issue

During 20X5, Balmoral Corporation changed to the LIFO method of accounting for inventory. Suppose that during 20X6, Balmoral changes back to the FIFO method and the following year switches back to LIFO again.

Required

1. What would you think of a company's ethics if it changed accounting methods every year?
2. What accounting principle would changing methods every year violate?
3. Who can be harmed when a company changes its accounting methods too often? How?

Focus on Financials: ■ YUM! Brands

Analyzing inventories (Obj. 2, 4)

The notes are part of the financial statements. They give details that would clutter the statements. This case will help you learn to use a company's inventory notes. Refer to YUM! Brands' statements and related notes in Appendix A at the end of the book and answer the following questions:

1. How much was YUM's merchandise inventory at December 27, 2003? At December 28,2002?
2. How does YUM value its inventories? Which cost method does the company use?
3. How much were Yum's purchases of food and paper inventory during the year ended December 27, 2003?
4. Did YUM's gross profit percentage on company sales improve or deteriorate in 2003 compared to 2002?
5. Would you rate YUM's rate of inventory turnover as fast or slow in comparison to most other companies? Explain your answer.

Focus on Analysis: ■ Pier 1 Imports

Measuring critical inventory amounts (Obj. 1, 2, 4)

Refer to the **Pier 1 Imports** financial statements in Appendix B at the end of this book. Show amounts in millions and round to the nearest $1 million.

1. Three important pieces of inventory information are (a) the cost of inventory on hand, (b) the cost of goods sold, and (c) the cost of inventory purchases. Identify or compute each of these items for Pier 1 at the end of 2004.
2. Which item in requirement 1 is most directly related to cash flow? Why?
3. Assume that all inventory purchases were made on account, and that only inventory purchases increased Accounts Payable. Compute Pier 1's cash payments for inventory during 2004.

(continued)

4. How does Pier 1 value its inventories? Which costing method does Pier 1 use?
5. Did Pier 1's gross profit percentage and rate of inventory turnover improve or deteriorate in 2004 (versus 2003)? Consider the overall effect of these two ratios. Did Pier 1 improve during 2004? How did these factors affect net income for 2004? Pier 1's inventories totaled $275 million at the end of 2002. Round decimals to 3 places.

Group Project

Comparing companies' inventory turnover ratios
(Obj. 4)

writing assignment ■

Obtain the annual reports of 10 companies, 2 from each of five different industries. Most companies' financial statements can be downloaded from their Web sites.

1. Compute each company's gross profit percentage and rate of inventory turnover for the most recent 2 years. If annual reports are unavailable or do not provide enough data for multiple-year computations, you can gather financial statement data from *Moody's Industrial Manual*.
2. For the industries of the companies you are analyzing, obtain the industry averages for gross profit percentage and inventory turnover from Robert Morris Associates, *Annual Statement Studies*; Dun and Bradstreet, *Industry Norms and Key Business Ratios*; or Leo Troy, *Almanac of Business and Industrial Financial Ratios*.
3. How well does each of your companies compare to the other company in its industry? How well do your companies compare to the average for their industry? What insight about your companies can you glean from these ratios?
4. Write a memo to summarize your findings, stating whether your group would invest in each of the companies it has analyzed.

APPENDIX A TO CHAPTER 6

Accounting for Inventory in the Periodic System

In the periodic inventory system, the business keeps no running record of the merchandise. Instead, at the end of the period, the business counts inventory on hand and applies the unit costs to determine the cost of ending inventory. This inventory figure appears on the balance sheet and is used to compute cost of goods sold.

Recording Transactions in the Periodic System

In the periodic system, throughout the period the Inventory account carries the beginning balance left over from the preceding period. The business records purchases of inventory in the Purchases account (an expense). Then, at the end of the period, the Inventory account must be updated for the financial statements. A journal entry removes the beginning balance by crediting Inventory and debiting Cost of Goods Sold. A second journal entry sets up the ending inventory balance, based on the physical count. The final entry in this sequence transfers the amount of Purchases to Cost of Goods Sold. These end-of-period entries can be made during the closing process.

Exhibit 6A-1 illustrates the accounting in the periodic system. After the process is complete, Inventory has its correct ending balance of $120,000, and Cost of Goods Sold shows $540,000.

■ EXHIBIT 6-A1 Recording and Reporting Inventories—Periodic System (Amounts assumed)

Panel A—Recording Transactions and the T-accounts (All amounts are assumed)

1. Purchases	560,000	
Accounts Payable		560,000
Purchased inventory on account		
2. Accounts Receivable	900,000	
Sales Revenue		900,000
Sold inventory on account		

3. End-of-period entries to update Inventory and record Cost of Goods Sold:

a. Cost of Goods Sold	100,000	
Inventory (beginning balance)		100,000
Transferred beginning inventory to COGS.		
b. Inventory (ending balance)	120,000	
Cost of Goods Sold		120,000
Set up ending inventory based on physical count.		
c. Cost of Goods Sold	560,000	
Purchases		560,000
Transferred purchases to COGS.		

The T-accounts show the following:

Inventory		Cost of Goods Sold	
100,000*	100,000	100,000	120,000
120,000		560,000	
		540,000	

*Beginning Inventory was $100,000.

Types of Assets

There are two categories of long-lived assets used in a business and not held for sale, as shown in Exhibit 7-1.

■ **EXHIBIT 7-1**
Plant Asset Terminology

Asset Account (Balance Sheet)	Related Expense Account (Income Statement)
Plant Assets	
Land	None
Buildings, Machinery and Equipment	Depreciation
Furniture and Fixtures	Depreciation
Land Improvements	Depreciation
Natural Resources	Depletion
Intangibles	Amortization

Plant asset
Long-lived assets, such as land, buildings, and equipment, used in the operation of the business. Also called *fixed assets*.

Intangible asset
An asset with no physical form, a special right to current and expected future benefits.

- **Plant assets**, or *fixed assets*, are long-lived assets that are tangible—for instance, land, buildings, and equipment. The expense associated with plant assets is called *depreciation*. Of the plant assets, land is unique. Land is not expensed over time because its usefulness does not decrease. Most companies report plant assets as Property, plant, and equipment on the balance sheet. **United Parcel Service (UPS)** uses these categories (lines 6–10).
- **Intangible assets** are useful because of the special rights they carry. They have no physical form. Patents, copyrights, and trademarks are intangible assets; so is goodwill. Accounting for intangibles is similar to accounting for plant assets. UPS reports Goodwill and Intangible Assets on its balance sheet (line 14).

Accounting for plant assets and intangibles has its own terminology. Different names apply to the individual plant assets and their corresponding expenses, as shown in Exhibit 7-1.

Check Point 7-1

Unless stated otherwise, we describe accounting in accordance with generally accepted accounting principles for financial-statement reporting to outsiders, as distinguished from reporting to the IRS for income tax purposes. Later, we cover depreciation for tax purposes. Before examining the various types of plant assets, let's see how to value them.

■ Taking Action How to Value Plant Assets—At Cost or at Market Value?

The accounting profession is moving toward market value accounting, which would report assets at their current value on the date of the balance sheet. *Market value* is the price the asset could be sold for. But the business community is not yet ready to apply market value accounting to tangible plant assets. Market values are too hard to determine for most plant assets because there is no established market to determine their prices. Consider a UPS facility. How much are all the delivery trucks worth? No one but UPS or **FedEx** could use all those brown trucks, and FedEx may not want them! This is why we report plant assets at their historical cost. *Historical cost* is the price the company actually paid to acquire the asset. It is an objective but often outdated measure of a plant asset.

OBJECTIVE

1 **Determine** the cost of a plant asset

Here is a basic working rule for determining the cost of an asset:

The cost of any asset is the sum of all the costs incurred to bring the asset to its intended use. The cost of a plant asset includes purchase price, plus any taxes, commissions, and other amounts paid to make the asset ready for use. Because the specific costs differ for the various types of plant assets, we discuss the major groups individually.

Land

The cost of land includes its purchase price (cash plus any note payable given), brokerage commission, survey fees, legal fees, and any back property taxes that the purchaser pays. Land cost also includes expenditures for grading and clearing the land and for demolishing or removing unwanted buildings.

The cost of land does *not* include the cost of fencing, paving, security systems, and lighting. These are separate plant assets—called *land improvements*—and they are subject to depreciation.

Suppose UPS signs a $300,000 note payable to purchase 20 acres of land for a new shipping site. UPS also pays $10,000 for real estate commission, $8,000 of back property tax, $5,000 for removal of an old building, a $1,000 survey fee, and $260,000 to pave the parking lot—all in cash. What is UPS's cost of this land?

Purchase price of land		$300,000
Add related costs:		
Real estate commission	$10,000	
Back property tax	8,000	
Removal of building	5,000	
Survey fee	1,000	
Total related		24,000
Total cost of land		$324,000

Check Point 7-2

Note that the cost to pave the parking lot, $260,000, is *not* included in the land's cost, because the pavement is a land improvement. UPS would record the purchase of this land as follows:

Land	324,000	
Note Payable		300,000
Cash		24,000

ASSETS	=	LIABILITIES	+	STOCKHOLDERS' EQUITY
+324,000 −24,000	=	+300,000	+	0

The purchase increases both assets and liabilities. There is no effect on equity.

Buildings, Machinery, and Equipment

The cost of constructing a building includes architectural fees, building permits, contractors' charges, and payments for material, labor, and overhead. If the company constructs its own building, the cost will also include the cost of interest on money borrowed to finance the construction.

When an existing building (new or old) is purchased, its cost includes the purchase price, brokerage commission, sales and other taxes paid, and all expenditures to repair and renovate the building for its intended purpose.

The cost of UPS's machinery and equipment includes its purchase price (less any discounts), plus transportation, insurance while in transit, sales and other taxes, purchase commission, installation costs, and any expenditures to test the asset before it is placed in service. The equipment cost will also include the cost of any special platforms. Then after the asset is up and running, insurance, taxes, and maintenance costs are recorded as expenses, not as part of the asset's cost.

Land Improvements and Leasehold Improvements

For a UPS shipping terminal, the cost to pave a parking lot ($260,000) would be recorded in a separate account entitled Land Improvements. This account includes costs for such other items as driveways, signs, fences, and sprinkler systems. Although these assets are located on the land, they are subject to decay, and their cost should therefore be depreciated.

UPS leases some of its airplanes and other assets. The company customizes these assets for its special needs. For example, UPS paints its logo on airplanes and delivery trucks. These improvements are assets of UPS even though the company may not own the airplane or truck. The cost of improvements to leased assets appears on the company's balance sheet under other property and equipment. The cost of leasehold improvements should be depreciated over the term of the lease. Most companies call the depreciation on leasehold improvements *amortization*, which is the same concept as *depreciation*.

Lump-Sum (or Basket) Purchases of Assets

Businesses often purchase several assets as a group, or a "basket," for a single lump-sum amount. For example, UPS may pay one price for land and a building. The company must identify the cost of each asset. The total cost is divided among the assets according to their relative sales (or market) values. This technique is called the *relative-sales-value method.*

Suppose UPS purchases land and a building in Kansas City. The building sits on two acres of land, and the combined purchase price of land and building is $2,800,000. An appraisal indicates that the land's market value is $300,000 and that the building's market value is $2,700,000.

UPS first figures the ratio of each asset's market value to the total market value. Total appraised value is $2,700,000 + $300,000 = $3,000,000. Thus, the land, valued at $300,000, is 10% of the total market value. The building's appraised value is 90% of the total. These percentages are then used to determine the cost of each asset, as follows:

Asset	Market (Sales) Value		Total Market Value		Percentage of Total Market Value		Total Cost		Cost of Each Asset
Land	$ 300,000	÷	$3,000,000	=	10%	×	$2,800,000	=	$ 280,000
Building	2,700,000	÷	3,000,000	=	90%	×	$2,800,000	=	2,520,000
Total	$3,000,000				100%				$2,800,000

If UPS pays cash, the entry to record the purchase of the land and building is

Land	280,000	
Building	2,520,000	
Cash		2,800,000

Check Point 7-3

ASSETS	=	LIABILITIES	+	STOCKHOLDERS' EQUITY
+280,000	=			
+2,520,000	=	0	+	0
−2,800,000	=			

stop AND think. . .

How would UPS divide a $120,000 lump-sum purchase price for land, building, and equipment with estimated market values of $40,000, $95,000, and $15,000, respectively?

Answer:

	Estimated Market Value	Percentage of Total Market Value	×	Total Cost	=	Cost of Each Asset
Land	$ 40,000	26.7%*	×	$120,000	=	$ 32,040
Building	95,000	63.3%	×	120,000	=	75,960
Equipment ..	15,000	10.0%	×	120,000	=	12,000
....	$150,000	100.0%				$120,000

*$40,000/$150,000 = 0.267, and so on

■ Taking Action Capital Expenditure vs. Immediate Expense

When a company spends money on a plant asset, it must decide whether to record an asset or an expense. Examples of these expenditures range from UPS's purchase of package-handling equipment to replacing the windshield wipers on a UPS delivery truck.

Expenditures that increase the asset's capacity or extend its useful life are called **capital expenditures**. For example, the cost of a major overhaul that extends the useful life of a UPS delivery truck is a capital expenditure. Capital expenditures are said to be *capitalized*, which means the cost is added to an asset account and not expensed immediately.

Capital expenditure Expenditure that increases an asset's capacity or efficiency or extends its useful life. Capital expenditures are debited to an asset account.

Costs that do not extend the asset's capacity or its useful life, but merely maintain the asset or restore it to working order, are recorded as expenses. For example, Repair Expense is reported on the income statement and matched against revenue. The costs of repainting a UPS delivery truck, repairing a dented fender, and replacing tires are also expensed immediately. Exhibit 7-2 illustrates the distinction between capital expenditures and immediate expenses for delivery truck expenditures.

■ **EXHIBIT 7-2**

Capital Expenditure or Immediate Expense for Costs Associated with a Delivery Truck

Record an Asset for Capital Expenditures	Record Repair and Maintenance Expense, and Not an Asset, for an Expense
Extraordinary repairs:	**Ordinary repairs:**
Major engine overhaul	Repair of transmission or other mechanism
Modification of body for new use of truck	Oil change, lubrication, and so on
Addition to storage capacity of truck	Replacement of tires and windshield, or a paint job

A major decision in accounting for plant assets is whether to capitalize or to expense a certain cost. The distinction between a capital expenditure and an expense requires judgment: Does the cost extend the asset's usefulness or its useful life? If so, record an asset. If the cost merely repairs or maintains the asset or returns it to its prior condition, then record an expense.

Most companies expense all small costs, say, below $1,000. For higher costs, they follow the rule we gave above: they capitalize costs that extend the asset's usefulness or its useful life, and they expense all other costs. A conservative policy is one that avoids overstating assets and profits. Companies that overstate their assets may get into trouble and have to defend themselves in court. Whenever investors lose money because a company overstated its profits or its assets, the investors file a lawsuit. The courts tend to be sympathetic to investor losses caused by shoddy accounting. The Accounting Alert provides an example.

Check Point 7-4

ACCOUNTING ALERT

Is *That* Cost Really an Asset?

There is a world of difference between a capital expenditure and an expense. Just ask **MCI**. MCI WorldCom (now just MCI) got in hot water by missing the mark in its accounting for capital expenditures.

A few years ago—before cellular phones became so popular—long-distance (LD) phone service was extremely profitable for **Sprint** and MCI. These companies invested huge amounts on LD phone networks. MCI was one of the hottest stocks on Wall Street.

Almost overnight cellular companies **Cingular** and **Verizon** began to siphon profits away from MCI. Profits grew thin and then turned to losses. MCI needed to protect its pacesetter image. But how?

MCI's CFO, Scott Sullivan, made some highly unusual journal entries, as follows:

Line-Cost Assets	$Billions	
Line-Cost Expenses		$Billions
To reclassify expenses as assets.		

These *line costs* were payments MCI made to other companies (such as **AT&T** and Sprint) to transmit LD calls for MCI customers. It's a common practice for these companies to rent competitors' phone lines. But it's most unusual to record an expense and then later reclassify the expense as an asset.

The fundamental question is this: Is MCI's rental payment to transmit customer calls an expense or an asset?

Scott Sullivan rationalized that the rental payments were assets because they provided future business for MCI. Independent CPAs from **KPMG** disagreed. KPMG stated flat out that the rental payments were expenses because the LD calls lasted only minutes and provided no future benefit for MCI. KPMG was right. MCI was wrong. MCI's improper accounting created a scandal.

The take-away lesson from this accounting alert:

- Label expenses as expenses and assets as assets!

Measuring Plant Asset Depreciation

Plant assets wear out, grow obsolete, and lose value over time. To account for this process we allocate a plant asset's cost to expense over its life—a process called *depreciation*. The depreciation process matches the asset's expense against revenue to measure income, as the matching principle directs. Exhibit 7-3 illustrates the depreciation process for the purchase of a Boeing 737 jet by UPS.

■ **EXHIBIT 7-3**

Depreciation and the Matching of Expense with Revenue

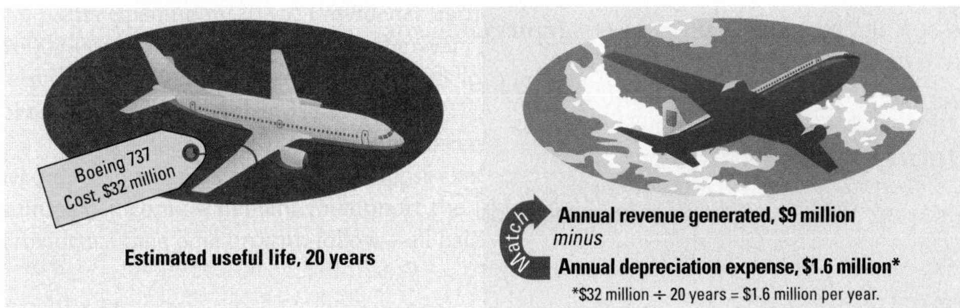

Only land has an unlimited life and is not depreciated for accounting purposes. For most plant assets, depreciation is caused by:

- ***Physical wear and tear.*** For example, physical deterioration takes its toll on the usefulness of UPS airplanes, delivery trucks, and buildings.
- ***Obsolescence.*** Computers and other electronic equipment may become *obsolete* before they deteriorate. An asset is obsolete when another asset can do the job more efficiently. An asset's useful life may be shorter than its physical life. UPS and other companies depreciate their computers over a short period of time—perhaps 4 years—even though the computers will remain in working condition much longer.

Suppose UPS buys a computer for use in tracking packages. UPS believes it will get 4 years of service from the computer, which will then be worthless. Under straight-line depreciation, UPS expenses one-quarter of the asset's cost in each of its 4 years of use.

Let's contrast what depreciation accounting is with what it is *not*

1. ***Depreciation is not a process of valuation.*** Businesses do *not* record depreciation based on changes in the market value of their plant assets. Instead, businesses allocate the asset's cost to the period of its useful life based on a specific depreciation method.
2. ***Depreciation does not mean setting aside cash to replace assets as they wear out.*** Any cash fund is entirely separate from depreciation.

How to Measure Depreciation

To measure depreciation for a plant asset, we must know its

1. Cost 2. Estimated useful life 3. Estimated residual value

We have already discussed cost, which is a known amount. The other two factors must be estimated.

Estimated useful life is the length of service expected from using the asset. Useful life may be expressed in years, units of output, miles, or some other measure. For example, the useful life of a building is stated in years. The useful life of a UPS airplane or delivery truck may be expressed as the number of miles the vehicle is expected to travel. Companies base such estimates on past experience and industry and government publications.

Estimated useful life
Length of a service that a business expects to get from an asset. May be expressed in years, units of output, miles, or other measures.

Estimated residual value—also called *scrap value* or *salvage value*—is the expected cash value of an asset at the end of its useful life. For example, UPS may believe that a package-handling machine will be useful for 7 years. After that time,

Estimated residual value
Expected cash value of an asset at the end of its useful life. Also called *residual value, scrap value*, or *salvage value*.

UPS may expect to sell the machine as scrap metal. The amount UPS believes it can get for the machine is the estimated residual value. In computing depreciation, the asset's estimated residual value is *not* depreciated because UPS expects to receive this amount from selling the asset. If there's no expected residual value, the full cost of the asset is depreciated. A plant asset's **depreciable cost** is measured as follows:

Depreciable cost
The cost of a plant asset minus its estimated residual value.

Depreciable cost = Asset's cost – Estimated residual value

Depreciation Methods

OBJECTIVE

2 **Account** for depreciation

There are three main depreciation methods:

- Straight-line
- Units-of-production
- Double-declining-balance—an accelerated depreciation method

These methods allocate different amounts of depreciation to each period. However, they all result in the same total amount of depreciation, which is the asset's depreciable cost. Exhibit 7-4 presents the data we use to illustrate depreciation computations for a UPS truck.

■ **EXHIBIT 7-4**
Data for Depreciation Computations—A UPS Truck

Data Item	Amount
Cost of truck	$41,000
Less Estimated residual value	(1,000)
Depreciable cost	$40,000
Estimated useful life:	
Years	5 years
Units of production	100,000 units [miles]

Straight-line (SL) method
Depreciation method in which an equal amount of depreciation expense is assigned to each year of asset use.

Straight-Line Method. In the **straight-line (SL) method**, an equal amount of depreciation is assigned to each year (or period) of asset use. Depreciable cost is divided by useful life in years to determine the annual depreciation expense. Applied to the UPS truck data from Exhibit 7-4, SL depreciation is

$$\text{Straight-line depreciation per year} = \frac{\text{Cost} - \text{Residual value}}{\text{Useful life, in years}}$$

$$= \frac{\$41{,}000 - \$1{,}000}{5}$$

$$= \$8{,}000$$

The entry to record depreciation is

Depreciation Expense.................	8,000	
Accumulated Depreciation.........		8,000

ASSETS	=	LIABILITIES	+	STOCKHOLDERS' EQUITY	–	EXPENSES
–8,000	=	0			–	8,000

Observe that depreciation decreases the asset (through Accumulated Depreciation) and also decreases equity (through Depreciation Expense). Let's assume that UPS purchased this truck on January 1, 20X3. UPS's accounting year ends on December 31. Exhibit 7-5 gives a *straight-line depreciation schedule* for the truck. The final column of the exhibit shows the *asset's book value*, which is cost less accumulated depreciation.

■ **EXHIBIT 7-5** Straight-Line Depreciation for a UPS Truck

		Depreciation for the Year						
Date	Asset Cost	Depreciation Rate		Depreciable Cost		Depreciation Expense	Accumulated Depreciation	Asset Book Value
1- 1-20X3	$41,000							$41,000
12-31-20X3		0.20*	×	$40,000	=	$8,000	$ 8,000	33,000
12-31-20X4		0.20	×	40,000	=	8,000	16,000	25,000
12-31-20X5		0.20	×	40,000	=	8,000	24,000	17,000
12-31-20X6		0.20	×	40,000	=	8,000	32,000	9,000
12-31-20X7		0.20	×	40,000	=	8,000	40,000	1,000

* $\frac{1}{5}$ year = .20 per year

As an asset is used in operations, accumulated depreciation increases, and the book value of the asset decreases. An asset's final book value is its *residual value* ($1,000 in Exhibit 7-5). At the end of its useful life, the asset is said to be *fully depreciated.*

stop AND think. . .

A UPS sorting machine that cost $10,000, has a useful life of 5 years, and residual value of $2,000, was purchased on January 1. What is SL depreciation for each year?

Answer:
$1,600 = ($10,000 – $2,000)/5

Units-of-Production Method. In the **units-of-production (UOP) method**, a fixed amount of depreciation is assigned to each *unit of output*, or service, produced by the asset. Depreciable cost is divided by useful life, in units of production, to determine this amount. This per-unit depreciation expense is then multiplied by the number of units produced each period to compute depreciation. The UOP depreciation for the UPS truck data in Exhibit 7-4 (page 322) is

Units-of-production (UOP) method
Depreciation method by which a fixed amount of depreciation is assigned to each unit of output produced by the plant asset.

$$\text{Units-of-production depreciation per unit of output} = \frac{\text{Cost} - \text{Residual value}}{\text{Useful life, in units of production}}$$

$$= \frac{\$41,000 - \$1,000}{100,000 \text{ miles}} = \$0.40 \text{ per mile}$$

Assume that UPS expects to drive the truck 20,000 miles during the first year, 30,000 during the second, 25,000 during the third, 15,000 during the fourth, and 10,000 during the fifth. Exhibit 7-6 shows the UOP depreciation schedule.

■ **EXHIBIT 7-6** Units-of-Production Depreciation for a UPS Truck

		Depreciation for the Year						
Date	Asset Cost	Depreciation Per Unit		Number of Units		Depreciation Expense	Accumulated Depreciation	Asset Book Value
1- 1-20X3	$41,000							$41,000
12-31-20X3		$0.40*	×	20,000	=	$ 8,000	$ 8,000	33,000
12-31-20X4		0.40	×	30,000	=	12,000	20,000	21,000
12-31-20X5		0.40	×	25,000	=	10,000	30,000	11,000
12-31-20X6		0.40	×	15,000	=	6,000	36,000	5,000
12-31-20X7		0.40	×	10,000	=	4,000	40,000	1,000

*($41,000 – $1,000)/100,000 miles = $0.40 per mile.

The amount of UOP depreciation varies with the number of units the asset produces. In our example, the total number of units produced is 100,000. UOP depreciation does not depend directly on time, as do the other methods.

Accelerated depreciation method
A depreciation method that writes off a relatively larger amount of the asset's cost nearer the start of its useful life than the straight-line method does.

Double-declining-balance (DDB) method
An accelerated depreciation method that computes annual depreciation by multiplying the asset's decreasing book value by a constant percentage, which is 2 times the straight-line rate.

Double-Declining-Balance Method. An **accelerated depreciation method** writes off a larger amount of the asset's cost near the start of its useful life than the straight-line method does. Double-declining-balance is the main accelerated depreciation method. **Double-declining-balance (DDB) depreciation** computes annual depreciation by multiplying the asset's declining book value by a constant percentage, which is 2 times the straight-line depreciation rate. DDB amounts are computed as follows:

- *First*, compute the straight-line depreciation rate per year. A 5-year truck has a straight-line depreciation rate of 1/5, or 20% each year. A 10-year asset has a straight-line rate of 1/10, or 10%, and so on.
- *Second*, multiply the straight-line rate by 2 to compute the DDB rate. For a 5-year asset, the DDB rate is 40% (20% × 2). A 10-year asset has a DDB rate of 20% (10% × 2).
- *Third*, multiply the DDB rate by the period's beginning asset book value (cost less accumulated depreciation). Under the DDB method, ignore the residual value of the asset in computing depreciation, except during the last year. The DDB rate for the UPS truck in Exhibit 7-4 (page 322) is

$$\text{DDB depreciation rate per year} = \frac{1}{\text{Useful life, in years}} \times 2$$
$$= \frac{1}{5\text{ years}} \times 2$$
$$= 20\% \times 2 = 40\%$$

Check Point 7-5

- *Fourth*, determine the final year's depreciation amount—that is, the amount needed to reduce asset book value to its residual value. In Exhibit 7-7, the fifth and final year's DDB depreciation is $4,314—book value of $5,314 less the $1,000 residual value. *The residual value should not be depreciated* but should remain on the books until the asset is disposed of.

EXHIBIT 7-7 Double-Declining-Balance Depreciation for a UPS Truck

		Depreciation for the Year						
Date	Asset Cost	DDB Rate		Asset Book Value		Depreciation Expense	Accumulated Depreciation	Asset Book Value
1- 1-20X3	$41,000							$41,000
12-31-20X3		0.40	×	$41,000	=	$16,400	$16,400	24,600
12-31-20X4		0.40	×	24,600	=	9,840	26,240	14,760
12-31-20X5		0.40	×	14,760	=	5,904	32,144	8,856
12-31-20X6		0.40	×	8,856	=	3,542	35,686	5,314
12-31-20X7						4,314*	40,000	1,000

*Last-year depreciation is the "plug" amount needed to reduce asset book value to the residual amount ($5,314 – $1,000 = $4,314).

The DDB method differs from the other methods in two ways:

1. Residual value is ignored initially; first-year depreciation is computed on the asset's full cost.
2. Depreciation expense in the final year is the "plug" amount needed to reduce the asset's book value to the residual amount.

stop AND think. . .

What is the DDB depreciation of the asset in the Stop and Think on page 323 for each year?

Answers:
Yr. 1: $4,000 ($10,000 × 40%)
Yr. 2: $2,400 ($6,000 × 40%)
Yr. 3: $1,440 ($3,600 × 40%)
Yr. 4: $160 ($10,000 – $4,000 – $2,400 – $1,440 – $2,000)*
Yr. 5: $0

*The asset is not depreciated below residual value of $2,000.

Comparing Depreciation Methods

Let's compare the three methods in terms of the yearly amount of depreciation. The yearly amount varies by method, but the total $40,000 depreciable cost is the same under all methods.

	Amount of Depreciation Per Year		
Year	Straight-Line	Units-of-Production	Accelerated Method Double-Declining Balance
1	$ 8,000	$ 8,000	$16,400
2	8,000	12,000	9,840
3	8,000	10,000	5,904
4	8,000	6,000	3,542
5	8,000	4,000	4,314
Total	$40,000	$40,000	$40,000

Generally accepted accounting principles (GAAP) say to match an asset's depreciation against the revenue the asset produces. For a plant asset that generates revenue evenly over time, the straight-line method best meets the matching principle. The units-of-production method best fits those assets that wear out because of physical use rather than obsolescence. The accelerated method (DDB) applies best to assets that generate more revenue earlier in their useful lives and less in later years.

Exhibit 7-8 graphs annual depreciation amounts for the straight-line, units-of-production, and accelerated depreciation (DDB) methods. The graph of straight-line depreciation is flat through time because annual depreciation is the same in all periods. Units-of-production depreciation follows no particular pattern because annual depreciation depends on the use of the asset. Accelerated depreciation is greatest in the first year and less in the later years.

Exhibit 7-9 shows the percentage of companies that use each depreciation method from a survey of 600 companies by the American Institute of CPAs.

■ **EXHIBIT 7-8**

Depreciation Patterns Through Time

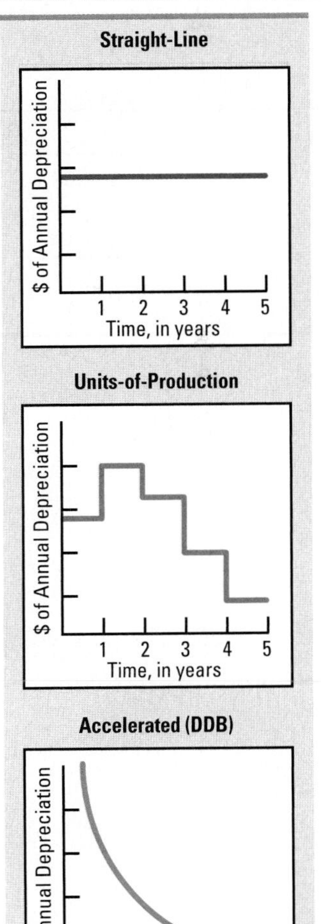

■ **EXHIBIT 7-9**

Depreciation Methods Used by 600 Companies

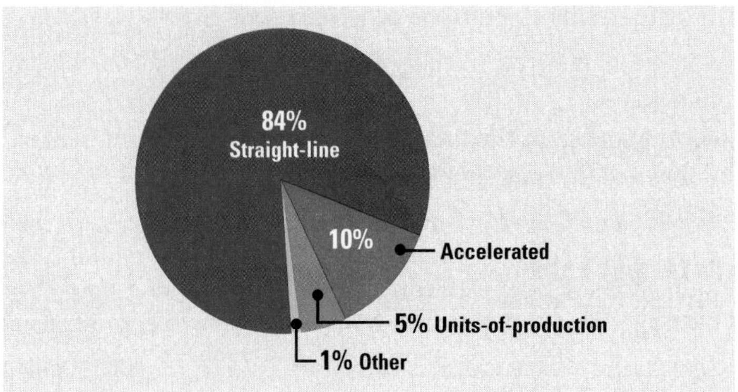

Check Point 7-6

For reporting in the financial statements, straight-line depreciation is most popular. As we shall see, however, accelerated depreciation is most popular for income-tax purposes.

MID-CHAPTER Summary Problem

Suppose UPS purchased equipment on January 1, 20X7, for $44,000. The expected useful life of the equipment is 10 years or 100,000 units of production, and its residual value is $4,000. Under three depreciation methods, the annual depreciation expense and the balance of accumulated depreciation at the end of 20X7 and 20X8 are as follows:

	Method A		*Method B*		*Method C*	
Year	Annual Depreciation Expense	Accumulated Depreciation	Annual Depreciation Expense	Accumulated Depreciation	Annual Depreciation Expense	Accumulated Depreciation
20X7	$4,000	$4,000	$8,800	$ 8,800	$1,200	$1,200
20X8	4,000	8,000	7,040	15,840	5,600	6,800

Required

1. Identify the depreciation method used in each instance, and show the equation and computation for each. (Round to the nearest dollar.)
2. Assume continued use of the same method through year 20X9. Determine the annual depreciation expense, accumulated depreciation, and book value of the equipment for 20X7 through 20X9 under each method, assuming 12,000 units of production in 20X9.

Answers

Requirement 1

Method A: Straight-Line

Depreciable cost = $40,000 ($44,000 – $4,000)

Each year: $40,000/10 years = $4,000

Method B: Double-Declining-Balance

$$\text{Rate} = \frac{1}{10 \text{ years}} \times 2 = 10\% \times 2 = 20\%$$

20X7: 0.20 × $44,000 = $8,800

20X8: 0.20 × ($44,000 – $8,800) = $7,040

Method C: Units-of-Production

$$\text{Depreciation per unit} = \frac{\$44{,}000 - \$4{,}000}{100{,}000 \text{ units}} = \$0.40$$

20X7: $0.40 × 3,000 units = $1,200

20X8: $0.40 × 14,000 units = $5,600

Requirement 2

Method A: Straight-Line

Year	Annual Depreciation Expense	Accumulated Depreciation	Book Value
Start			$44,000
20X7	$4,000	$ 4,000	40,000
20X8	4,000	8,000	36,000
20X9	4,000	12,000	32,000

Method B: Double-Declining-Balance

Year	Annual Depreciation Expense	Accumulated Depreciation	Book Value
Start			$44,000
20X7	$8,800	$ 8,800	35,200
20X8	7,040	15,840	28,160
20X9	5,632	21,472	22,528

Method C: Units-of-Production

Year	Annual Depreciation Expense	Accumulated Depreciation	Book Value
Start			$44,000
20X7	$1,200	$ 1,200	42,800
20X8	5,600	6,800	37,200
20X9	4,800	11,600	32,400

Computations for 20X9

Straight-line	$40,000/10 years = $4,000
Double-declining-balance	$28,160 × 0.20 = $5,632
Units-of-production	12,000 units × $0.40 = $4,800

Other Issues in Accounting for Plant Assets

Plant assets are complex because of their long lives. Depreciation affects income taxes, and companies may have gains or losses when they sell plant assets.

Depreciation for Tax Purposes

OBJECTIVE

3 **Select** the best depreciation method

UPS and most other companies use straight-line depreciation for reporting to stockholders and creditors on their financial statements. They also keep a separate set of depreciation records for computing income taxes. For tax purposes, most companies use an accelerated depreciation method.

Suppose you are a business manager. The IRS allows an accelerated depreciation method, which most managers prefer to straight-line depreciation. Why? Because accelerated depreciation provides the fastest deductions, thus decreasing immediate tax payments. You can then reinvest the cash back into your business.

To understand the relationships between cash flow, depreciation, and income tax, recall our earlier depreciation example for a UPS truck:

- First-year depreciation is $8,000 under straight-line and $16,400 under double-declining-balance (DDB).
- DDB is permitted for income tax reporting.

Assume that this UPS office has $400,000 in revenue and $300,000 in cash operating expenses during the truck's first year and an income tax rate of 30%. The cash-flow analysis appears in Exhibit 7-10.

■ EXHIBIT 7-10

The Cash-Flow Advantage of Accelerated Depreciation over Straight-Line Depreciation for Income Tax Purposes

		SL	Accelerated
1	Cash revenues	$400,000	$400,000
2	Cash operating expenses	300,000	300,000
3	Cash provided by operations before income tax	100,000	100,000
4	Depreciation expense (a noncash expense)	8,000	16,400
5	Income before income tax	$ 92,000	$ 83,600
6	Income tax expense (30%)	$ 27,600	$ 25,080
	Cash-flow analysis:		
7	Cash provided by operations before tax	$100,000	$100,000
8	Income tax expense	27,600	25,080
9	Cash provided by operations	$ 72,400	$ 74,920
10	Extra cash available for investment if DDB is used ($74,920 – $72,400)		$ 2,520

Check Point 7-7

Exhibit 7-10 highlights an important fact: The higher the depreciation expense, the lower the income before tax and thus the lower the tax payment. Therefore, accelerated depreciation helps conserve cash for the business. Exhibit 7-10 shows that UPS will have $2,520 (line 10) more cash at the end of the first year if it uses accelerated depreciation instead of SL.

stop AND think. . .

Which depreciation method makes UPS look better to its stockholders? How much better? Show how you arrive at your answer.

Answer:

Straight-line depreciation makes UPS look better. Net income under

- Straight-line depreciation is $64,400 ($92,000 – $27,600).
- Accelerated depreciation is $58,520 ($83,600 – $25,080).

Under straight-line depreciation, UPS reports $5,880 ($64,400 – $58,520) more net income. Therefore, most managers prefer to use straight-line depreciation for their financial statements.

There is a special depreciation method—used only for income tax purposes—called the **Modified Accelerated Cost Recovery System (MACRS)**. Under this method assets are grouped into one of eight classes identified by asset life (Exhibit 7-11). Depreciation for the first four classes is computed by the double-declining-balance method. Depreciation for 15-year assets and 20-year assets is computed by the 150%-declining-balance method. Under this method, the annual depreciation rate is computed by multiplying the straight-line rate by 1.50 (instead of 2.00, as for DDB). For a 20-year asset, the straight-line rate is 0.05 per year (1/20 = 0.05), so the annual MACRS depreciation rate is 0.075 (0.05 × 1.50 = 0.075). The taxpayer computes annual depreciation by multiplying asset book value by 0.075, in a manner similar to the way the DDB method works. Most real estate is depreciated by the straight-line method (see the last two categories in Exhibit 7-11).

Modified Accelerated Cost Recovery System (MACRS)
A special depreciation method used only for income tax purposes. Assets are grouped into classes, and for a given class depreciation is computed by the double-declining-balance method, the 150%-declining balance method, or, for most real estate, the straight-line method.

■ **EXHIBIT 7-11**

Details of the Modified Accelerated Cost Recovery System (MACRS) Depreciation Method

Class Identified by Asset Life (years)	Representative Assets	Depreciation Method
3	Race horses	DDB
5	Automobiles, light trucks	DDB
7	Equipment	DDB
10	Equipment	DDB
15	Sewage-treatment plants	150% DB
20	Certain real estate	150% DB
27½	Residential rental property	SL
39	Nonresidential rental property	SL

Depreciation for Partial Years

Companies purchase plant assets whenever they need them. They do not wait until the beginning of a year or a month. Therefore, companies must compute *depreciation for partial years*. Suppose UPS purchases a warehouse building on April 1 for $500,000. The building's estimated life is 20 years, and its estimated residual value is $80,000. UPS's accounting year ends on December 31. Let's consider how the company computes depreciation for April through December:

- First, compute depreciation for a full year.
- Second, multiply the full year's depreciation by the fraction of the year that you held the asset. Assuming the straight-line method, the year's depreciation for UPS's building is $15,750, as follows:

$$\text{Full-year depreciation } \frac{\$500{,}000 - \$80{,}000}{20} = \$21{,}000$$

$$\text{Partial year depreciation } \$21{,}000 \times 9/12 = \$15{,}750$$

What if UPS bought the asset on April 18? Many businesses record no monthly depreciation on assets purchased after the 15th of the month, and they record a full month's depreciation on an asset bought on or before the 15th.

Most companies use computerized systems to account for fixed assets. Each asset has a unique identification number that links to the asset's cost, estimated life, residual value, and depreciation method. The system will automatically calculate the depreciation expense for each period. Both Accumulated Depreciation and book value are automatically updated.

Check Point 7-8

Changing the Useful Life of a Depreciable Asset

After an asset is in use, managers may refine their estimate of its useful life on the basis of experience and new information. **The Walt Disney Company** made such a change, called a *change in accounting estimate*. Disney recalculated depreciation on the basis of revised useful lives of several of its theme park assets. The following note in Walt Disney's financial statements reports this change in accounting estimate:

> **Note 5**
> **. . . [T]he Company extended the estimated useful lives of certain theme park ride and attraction assets based upon historical data and engineering studies. The effect of this change was to decrease depreciation by approximately $8 million (an increase in net income of approximately $4.2 million . . .).**

Assume that a Disney hot dog stand cost $50,000 and that the company originally believed the asset had a 10-year useful life with no residual value. Using the straight-line method, the company would record $5,000 depreciation each year ($50,000/10 years = $5,000). Suppose Disney used the asset for 4 years. Accumulated depreciation reached $20,000, leaving a remaining depreciable book value (cost *less* accumulated depreciation *less* residual value) of $30,000 ($50,000 – $20,000). From its experience, management believes the asset will remain useful for an additional 10 years. The company would spread the remaining depreciable book value over the asset's remaining life as follows:

Asset's remaining depreciable book value	÷	(New) Estimated useful life remaining	=	(New) Annual depreciation
$30,000	÷	10 years	=	$3,000

The yearly depreciation entry based on the new estimated useful life is

Check Point 7-9

Depreciation Expense—Hot Dog Stand	3,000	
Accumulated Depreciation—Hot Dog Stand . . .		3,000

ASSETS	=	LIABILITIES	+	STOCKHOLDERS' EQUITY	–	EXPENSES
–3,000	=	0			–	3,000

■ Taking Action Is It Ethical to Keep Two Sets of Depreciation Records?

Is it ethical for UPS, **Home Depot**, and **GM** to keep two sets of depreciation records—one for its financial statements and the other for reporting to the IRS? Yes, that's perfectly okay because the two sets of depreciation records serve two very different purposes.

The depreciation records illustrated in this chapter are designed for the income statement and the balance sheet. The purpose here is to measure accounting income and asset values for reporting to stockholders and creditors. The driving force behind these depreciation amounts is to provide relevant information for investment and credit decisions.

Depreciation amounts for income tax purposes march to the beat of a different drummer. Congress designs tax depreciation to raise tax revenue for the government. Political considerations enter the world of taxes, so tax depreciation may differ from basic accounting depreciation.

Fully Depreciated Assets

A *fully depreciated asset* is an asset that has reached the end of its estimated useful life. Suppose UPS has fully depreciated equipment with zero residual value (cost was $60,000). UPS accounts will appear as follows:

Equipment		Accumulated Depreciation	
60,000			60,000

The equipment's book value is zero, but that doesn't mean the equipment is worthless. UPS may continue using the equipment for a few more years, but UPS will not record any more depreciation on a fully depreciated asset.

When UPS disposes of the equipment, UPS will remove both the asset's cost ($60,000) and its accumulated depreciation ($60,000) from the books. The next section shows how to account for plant asset disposals.

Accounting for Disposal of Plant Assets

OBJECTIVE

4 **Analyze** the effect of a plant asset disposal

Eventually, a plant asset ceases to serve a company's needs. The asset may wear out, become obsolete, or for some other reason cease to be useful. Before accounting for the disposal of the asset, the business should bring depreciation up to date to measure the asset's final book value and also record the expense up to the date of sale.

To account for disposal, remove the asset and its related accumulated depreciation from the books. Suppose the final year's depreciation expense has just been recorded for a machine that cost $60,000 and is estimated to have zero residual value. The machine's accumulated depreciation thus totals $60,000. Assuming that this asset is junked, the entry to record its disposal is:

Accumulated Depreciation—Machinery	60,000	
Machinery		60,000
To dispose of fully depreciated machine.		

ASSETS	=	LIABILITIES	+	STOCKHOLDERS' EQUITY
+60,000 −60,000	=	0	+	0

There is no gain or loss on this disposal, so there is no effect on equity.

If assets are junked before being fully depreciated, the company incurs a loss on the disposal. Suppose UPS disposes of equipment that cost $60,000 in this manner. Accumulated depreciation is $50,000, and book value is, therefore, $10,000. Junking this equipment results in a loss equal to the asset's book value, as follows:

Accumulated Depreciation—Equipment	50,000	
Loss on Disposal of Equipment	10,000	
Equipment		60,000
To dispose of equipment.		

ASSETS	=	LIABILITIES	+	STOCKHOLDERS' EQUITY	−	LOSSES
+50,000 −60,000	=	0			−	10,000

UPS got rid of an asset with $10,000 book value and received nothing. The result is a $10,000 loss, which decreases equity.

The Loss on Disposal of Equipment is reported as Other income (expense) on the income statement. Losses decrease net income exactly as expenses do. Gains increase net income in the same manner as revenues.

Selling a Plant Asset. Suppose UPS sells equipment on September 30, 20X4, for $5,000 cash. The equipment cost $10,000 when purchased on January 1, 20X1, and has been depreciated on a straight-line basis. UPS originally estimated a 10-year useful life and no residual value. Prior to recording the sale, the UPS accountants must update the asset's depreciation. UPS uses the calendar year as its accounting period. Partial-year depreciation must be recorded for the asset's expense from January 1, 20X4, to the sale date. The straight-line depreciation entry at September 30, 20X4, is

Sept. 30	Depreciation Expense ($10,000/10 years × 9/12) . . .	750	
	Accumulated Depreciation—Equipment		750
	To update depreciation.		

ASSETS	=	LIABILITIES	+	STOCKHOLDERS' EQUITY	−	EXPENSES
−750	=	0			−	750

The Equipment account and the Accumulated Depreciation account appear as follows. Observe that the equipment's book value is $6,250 ($10,000 − $3,750).

Equipment			−	Accumulated Depreciation		
Jan. 1, 20X1	10,000				Dec. 31, 20X1	1,000
					Dec. 31, 20X2	1,000
					Dec. 31, 20X3	1,000
					Sep. 30, 20X4	750
					Balance	3,750

= Book value $6,250

Suppose UPS sells the equipment for $7,000 cash. The gain on the sale is $750, determined as follows:

Cash received from sale of the asset		$7,000
Book value of asset sold:		
Cost	$10,000	
Less accumulated depreciation	(3,750)	6,250
Gain (loss) on sale of the asset		$ 750

The entry to record sale of the equipment for $7,000 cash is

Sept. 30	Cash	7,000	
	Accumulated Depreciation—Equipment	3,750	
	Equipment.		10,000
	Gain on Sale of Equipment.		750
	To sell equipment.		

Check Point 7-10

ASSETS	=	LIABILITIES	−	STOCKHOLDERS' EQUITY	+	GAINS
+ 7,000						
+ 3,750	=	0			+	750
−10,000						

Gains are recorded as credits, in the same manner as revenues. Gains and losses on asset disposals appear on the income statement as Other Income (Expense).

stop AND think. . .

Suppose UPS's comparative income statement for 2 years included these items:

	(In billions) 20X2	20X1
Net revenues	$30.2	$28.0
Income from operations	2.7	3.2
Other income (expense):		
Gain on sale of equipment	0.8	
Income before income taxes	$ 3.5	$ 3.2

Which was a better year for UPS—20X2 or 20X1?

Answer:

From a revenue standpoint, 20X2 was better because revenues were higher. But from an *income* standpoint, 20X1 was better.

In 20X1, shipping operations—the company's core business—generated $3.2 billion of income from operations. In 20X2, operations produced only $2.7 billion of operating income. Almost $1 billion of the company's income in 20X2 came from selling equipment (gain of $0.8 billion). A business cannot hope to continue on this path very long. This example shows why investors and creditors care about the sources of a company's profits.

Accounting Alert: Avoid companies that generate most of their income from nonoperating sources such as Gains on Sale of Equipment.

Exchanging Plant Assets. Managers often trade in old plant assets for new ones. For example, a pizzeria may trade in a 5-year-old delivery car for a newer model. In many cases, the business simply transfers the book value of the old asset plus any cash payment into the new asset account. For example, assume Mazzio Pizzeria's old delivery car cost $9,000 and has accumulated depreciation of $8,000. The old car's book value is $1,000. If Mazzio trades in the old automobile and pays cash of $10,000, the cost of the new delivery car is $11,000 (book value of the old asset, $1,000, plus cash given, $10,000). The pizzeria records the exchange transaction as follows:

Delivery Auto (new)	11,000	
Accumulated Depreciation (old)	8,000	
Delivery Auto (old)		9,000
Cash		10,000
Traded in old delivery car for new auto.		

ASSETS	=	LIABILITIES	+	STOCKHOLDERS' EQUITY
+11,000				
+ 8,000	=	0	+	0
− 9,000				
−10,000				

There was no gain or loss on this exchange, so there was no effect on equity.

Accounting for Natural Resources

OBJECTIVE

5 **Account** for natural resources and depletion

Depletion expense
That portion of a natural resource's cost that is used up in a particular period. Depletion expense is computed in the same way as units-of-production depreciation.

Natural resources are plant assets of a special type, such as iron ore, petroleum (oil), and timber. As plant assets are expensed through depreciation, so natural resource assets are expensed through *depletion*. **Depletion expense** is that portion of the cost of a natural resource that is used up in a particular period. Depletion expense is computed in the same way as units-of-production depreciation.

An oil lease may cost **ExxonMobil** $100,000 and contain an estimated 10,000 barrels of oil. The depletion rate would be $10 per barrel ($100,000/10,000 barrels). If 3,000 barrels are extracted, depletion expense is $30,000 (3,000 barrels × $10 per barrel). The depletion entry is

Depletion Expense (3,000 barrels × $10)	30,000	
Accumulated Depletion—Oil		30,000

ASSETS	=	LIABILITIES	+	STOCKHOLDERS' EQUITY	−	EXPENSES
−30,000	=	0			−	30,000

Both assets and equity decrease. Why equity? Because the depletion expense decreases net income and then also decreases retained earnings.

If 4,500 barrels are removed the next year, that period's depletion is $45,000 (4,500 barrels × $10 per barrel). Accumulated Depletion is a contra account similar to Accumulated Depreciation.

Natural resource assets can be reported on ExxonMobil's balance sheet as follows (amounts assumed):

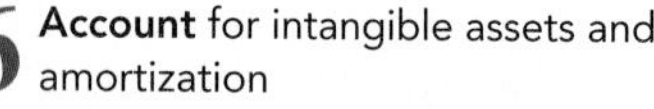

Property, Plant, and Equipment:		
Equipment	$960,000	
Less: Accumulated depreciation	(410,000)	$550,000
Oil	$340,000	
Less: Accumulated depletion	(70,000)	270,000
Total property, plant, and equipment		$820,000

Accounting for Intangible Assets

OBJECTIVE

6 **Account** for intangible assets and amortization

Amortization
The systematic reduction of a lump-sum amount. Expense that applies to intangible assets in the same way depreciation applies to plant assets and depletion applies to natural resources.

As we saw earlier, *intangible assets* are long-lived assets with no physical form. Intangibles are valuable because they carry special rights from patents, copyrights, trademarks, franchises, leaseholds, and goodwill. Like buildings and equipment, an intangible asset is recorded at its acquisition cost. Cost is then systematically expensed through **amortization** over the intangible's estimated useful life unless the asset is determined to have an indefinite life.

Amortization is the same concept as depreciation, but applied to intangibles it is called amortization. Amortization is often computed on a straight-line basis. Amortization expense for an intangible asset can be written off directly against the asset account rather than held in an accumulated amortization account. The residual value of most intangibles is zero.

Assume that **Sony** purchases a patent on a new DVD process. Legally, the patent may run for 20 years. But Sony realizes that new technologies will limit the process's life to 4 years. If the patent cost $80,000, each year's amortization expense is $20,000 ($80,000/4). The balance sheet reports the patent at its acquisition cost less amortization expense to date. After 1 year, the patent has a $60,000 balance ($80,000 – $20,000), after 2 years a $40,000 balance, and so on.

Types of Intangible Assets

Each type of intangible asset is unique, and the accounting can vary from one intangible to another.

Patents. **Patents** are federal government grants that give the holder the exclusive right for 20 years to produce and sell an invention. The invention may be a product or a process—for example, Sony compact disc players and the Dolby noise-reduction process. Like any other asset, a patent may be purchased. Suppose a company pays $170,000 to acquire a patent on January 1, and the business believes the expected useful life of the patent is 5 years. Amortization expense is $34,000 per year ($170,000/5 years). Sony records the acquisition and amortization for this patent as follows:

Patent
A federal government grant giving the holder the exclusive right for 20 years to produce and sell an invention.

Jan. 1	Patents	170,000	
	Cash		170,000
	To acquire a patent.		

ASSETS	=	LIABILITIES	+	STOCKHOLDERS' EQUITY
+170,000 –170,000	=	0	+	0

Dec. 31	Amortization Expense—Patents ($170,000/5)	34,000	
	Patents		34,000
	To amortize the cost of a patent.		

ASSETS	=	LIABILITIES	+	STOCKHOLDERS' EQUITY	–	EXPENSES
–34,000	=	0			–	34,000

Both assets and equity decrease because of the amortization expense.

Copyrights. **Copyrights** are exclusive rights to reproduce and sell a book, musical composition, film, or other work of art. Copyrights also protect computer software programs, such as **Microsoft's** Windows® and **Excel**. Issued by the federal government, copyrights extend 70 years beyond the author's (composer's, artist's, or programmer's) life. The cost of obtaining a copyright from the government is low, but a company may pay a large sum to purchase an existing copyright from the owner. For example, a publisher may pay the author of a popular novel $1 million or more for the book copyright. Because the useful life of a copyright is usually no longer than 2 or 3 years, each period's amortization amount is a high proportion of the copyright cost.

Copyright
Exclusive right to reproduce and sell a book, musical composition, film, other work of art, or computer program. Issued by the federal government, copyrights extend 70 years beyond the author's life.

Trademarks and Trade Names. **Trademarks** and **trade names** (or *brand names*) are distinctive identification of a product or service. The "eye" symbol that flashes across our television screens is the trademark that identifies the **CBS** television network. You are probably also familiar with **NBC's** peacock. Advertising slogans that are legally protected include **United Airlines**' "Fly the friendly skies®" and **Avis Rental Car's** "We try harder®." These are distinctive identifications of products or services, marked with the symbol ™ or ®.

Trademark, trade name
A distinctive identification of a product or service. Also called a *brand name*.

The cost of a trademark or trade name may be amortized over its useful life. But if the trademark is expected to generate cash flow for the indefinite future, the business should not amortize the trademark's cost.

Franchises and licenses
Privileges granted by a private business or a government to sell a product or service in accordance with specified conditions.

Franchises and Licenses. **Franchises** and **licenses** are privileges granted by a private business or a government to sell a product or service in accordance with specified conditions. The Chicago Cubs baseball organization is a franchise granted to its owner by the National League. **McDonald's** restaurants and **Holiday Inns** are popular franchises. The useful lives of many franchises and licenses are indefinite and, therefore, are not amortized.

Goodwill
Excess of the cost of an acquired company over the sum of the market values of its net assets (assets minus liabilities).

Goodwill. In accounting, **goodwill** has a very specific meaning. It is defined as the excess of the cost of purchasing another company over the sum of the market values of its net assets (assets minus liabilities). A purchaser is willing to pay for goodwill when it buys another company with abnormal earning power.

UPS has expanded into Mexico, Canada, Europe, and other countries. Suppose UPS acquires Europa Company at a cost of $10 million. The sum of the market values of Europa's assets is $9 million, and its liabilities total $1 million so Europa's *net* assets total $8 million at current market value. In this case, UPS paid $2 million for goodwill, computed as follows:

Purchase price paid for Europa Company		$10 million
Sum of the market values of Europa Company's assets	$9 million	
Less: Europa Company's liabilities	(1 million)	
Market value of Europa Company's net assets		8 million
Excess is called *goodwill*		$ 2 million

UPS's entry to record the acquisition of Europa Company, including its goodwill, would be

Assets (Cash, Receivables, Inventories, Plant Assets, all at market value)	9,000,000	
Goodwill	2,000,000	
Liabilities		1,000,000
Cash		10,000,000

Check Point 7-12

ASSETS	=	LIABILITIES	+	STOCKHOLDERS' EQUITY
+ 9,000,000				
+ 2,000,000	=	+1,000,000	+	0
−10,000,000				

Note that UPS has acquired both Europa's assets *and* its liabilities.

Goodwill in accounting has special features, as follows:

1. Goodwill is recorded *only* when it is purchased in the acquisition of another company. A purchase transaction provides objective evidence of the value of goodwill. Companies never record goodwill that they create for their own business.
2. According to generally accepted accounting principles (GAAP), goodwill is not amortized because the goodwill of many entities increases in value.

Accounting for the Impairment of an Intangible Asset

Some intangibles—such as goodwill, licenses, and some trademarks—have indefinite lives and therefore are not subject to amortization. But all intangibles are subject to a write-down when their value decreases. **PepsiCo** is a major company with vast amounts of purchased goodwill due to its acquisition of other companies.

Each year, PepsiCo determines whether the goodwill it has purchased has increased or decreased in value. If PepsiCo's goodwill is worth more at the end of the year than at the beginning, no increase in the asset is permitted. But if PepsiCo's goodwill has decreased in value, say from $500 million to $470 million, then PepsiCo will record a $30 million loss as follows (in millions):

20X6			
Dec. 31	Loss on Goodwill ($500 – $470)	30	
	Goodwill		30

ASSETS	=	LIABILITIES	+	STOCKHOLDERS' EQUITY	–	EXPENSES
–30	=	0			–	30

PepsiCo's financial statements will report the following (in millions):

	20X6	20X5
Balance sheet		
Intangible assets:		
Goodwill	$470	$500
Income statement		
(Loss) on goodwill	(30)	—

Accounting for Research and Development Costs

Accounting for research and development (R&D) costs is one of the most difficult issues in accounting. R&D is the lifeblood of companies such as **Procter & Gamble**, **General Electric**, **Intel**, and **Boeing**. It can be argued that R&D is one of these companies' most valuable (intangible) assets. But, in general, companies do not report R&D assets on their balance sheets.

GAAP requires companies to expense R&D costs as they incur them. Only in limited circumstances may the company capitalize R&D cost as an asset. For example, a company may incur R&D cost under a contract guaranteeing that the company will recover R&D costs from a customer. This R&D cost is an asset, and the company records an intangible R&D asset when it incurs the cost. But this is the exception to the general rule.

✔ Check Point 7-13

Reporting Plant Asset Transactions on the Statement of Cash Flows

OBJECTIVE

7 **Report** plant asset transactions on the statement of cash flows

Three main types of plant asset transactions appear on the statement of cash flows: acquisitions, sales, and depreciation (including amortization and depletion).

Acquisitions and sales are *investing* activities. A company invests in plant assets by paying cash or by incurring a liability. The cash payments for plant and equipment are investing activities that appear on the statement of cash flows. The sale of plant assets results in a cash receipt, as illustrated in Exhibit 7-12, which excerpts data from the cash-flow statement of United Parcel Service (UPS). The acquisitions, sales, and depreciation of plant assets are denoted in color (lines 5, 6, and 2).

■ EXHIBIT 7-12

Reporting Plant Asset Transactions on UPS's Statement of Cash Flows

United Parcel Service, Inc.
Statement of Cash Flows (partial, adapted)
Year Ended December 31, 2003

Cash Flows from Operating Activities:		
1	Net income	$2,898
	Adjustments to reconcile net income to net cash provided by operating activities:	
2	Depreciation and amortization	1,549
3	Other items (summarized)	199
4	Net cash from operating activities	4,646
Cash Flows from Investing Activities:		
5	Capital expenditures	(1,947)
6	Disposals of property, plant, and equipment	118
7	Other items (summarized)	(113)
8	Net cash (used in) investing activities	(1,942)
Cash Flows from Financing Activities		
9	Net cash (used in) financing activities	(2,180)
10	Other items	216
11	Net increase in cash and cash equivalents	740
12	Cash and cash equivalents, beginning of period	2,211
13	Cash and cash equivalents, end of period	$2,951

Check Point 7-14

Let's examine the investing activities first. During 2003, UPS paid $1,947 million for plant assets (line 5). UPS also sold property and equipment, receiving cash of $118 million (line 6). UPS labels the cash received as Disposals of property, plant, and equipment. The $118 million is the amount of cash received from the sale of plant assets.

UPS's statement of cash flows reports Depreciation and amortization (line 2). Observe that "Depreciation and amortization" is listed as a positive item under Adjustments to reconcile net income to Cash provided by operating activities. You may be wondering why depreciation appears on the cash-flow statement. After all, depreciation does not affect cash.

In this format, the operating activities section of the cash-flow statement starts with net income (line 1) and reconciles to net cash from operating activities (line 4). Depreciation decreases net income but does not affect cash. Depreciation is therefore added back to net income to measure cash flow from operations. The add-back of depreciation to net income offsets the earlier subtraction of the expense. The sum of net income plus depreciation, therefore, helps to reconcile net income (on the accrual basis) to cash flow from operations (a cash-basis amount). We revisit this topic in the full context of the statement of cash flows in Chapter 12.

Incidentally, UPS's cash flows are exceptionally strong. Operations generated $4,646 million of cash, and UPS spent $1,947 million on new property and equipment. The company is not standing still.

stop AND think. . .

Test your ability to use the cash-flow statement.

1. Make the journal entry to record UPS's purchases of property and equipment during the year.
2. Suppose the book value of the property and equipment that UPS sold was $51 million (cost of $72 million minus accumulated depreciation of $21 million). Record the company's transaction to sell the property and equipment. Also write a sentence to explain why the sale transaction results in a gain for UPS.
3. Where would UPS report any gain or loss on the sale of the property and equipment—on which financial statement, under what heading?

Answers:

	(In millions)	
1. Property and Equipment	1,947	
Cash		1,947
Made capital expenditures.		
2. Cash	118	
Accumulated Depreciation	21	
Property and Equipment		72
Gain on Sale of Property and Equipment		67
Sold property and equipment.		

The company sold for $118 million assets that had book value of $51 million. The result of the sale was a gain of $67 million ($118 million received – $51 million of asset book value given up).

3. Report the gain on the *income statement* under the heading *Other income (expense)*.

MAKING MANAGERIAL DECISIONS

PLANT ASSETS AND RELATED EXPENSES

United Parcel Service, like all other companies, must make some decisions about how to account for its plant assets and intangibles. Let's review some of these decisions.

Decision	Guidelines
Capitalize or expense a cost?	General rule: Capitalize all costs that provide *future* benefit for the business such as a new package-handling system. Expense all costs that provide no *future* benefit, such as a repair to an airplane.
Capitalize or expense: • Cost associated with a new asset?	Capitalize all costs that bring the asset to its intended use, including asset purchase price, transportation charges, and taxes paid to acquire the asset.
• Cost associated with an existing asset?	Capitalize only those costs that add to the asset's usefulness or to its useful life. Expense all other costs as maintenance or repairs.
Which depreciation method to use • For financial reporting?	Use the method that best matches depreciation expense against the revenues produced by the asset. Most companies use the straight-line method.
• For income tax?	Use the method that produces the fastest tax deductions (MACRS). A company can use different depreciation methods for financial reporting and for income tax purposes. In the United States, this practice is considered both legal and ethical.
• How to account for natural resources?	Capitalize the asset's acquisition cost and all later costs that add to the natural resource's future benefit. Then record depletion expense, as computed by the units-of-production method.
• How to account for intangibles?	Capitalize acquisition cost and all later costs that add to the asset's future benefit. For intangibles with finite lives, record amortization expense. For intangibles with indefinite lives, do not record amortization. But if an intangible asset loses value, then record a loss in the amount of the decrease in asset value.

END-OF-CHAPTER Summary Problem

1. The figures that follow appear in the *Answers to the Mid-Chapter Summary Problem*, Requirement 2, on page 327.

	Method A: Straight-Line			*Method B: Double-Declining-Balance*		
Year	Annual Depreciation Expense	Accumulated Depreciation	Book Value	Annual Depreciation Expense	Accumulated Depreciation	Book Value
Start			$44,000			$44,000
20X7	$4,000	$ 4,000	40,000	$8,800	$ 8,800	35,200
20X8	4,000	8,000	36,000	7,040	15,840	28,160
20X9	4,000	12,000	32,000	5,632	21,472	22,528

Required

Suppose the income tax authorities permitted a choice between these two depreciation methods. Which method would UPS select for income tax purposes? Why?

2. Suppose UPS purchased the equipment described in the table on January 1, 20X7. Management has depreciated the equipment by using the double-declining-balance method. On July 1, 20X9, UPS sold the equipment for $27,000 cash.

Required

Record depreciation for 20X9 and the sale of the equipment on July 1, 20X9.

Answers

1. For tax purposes, most companies select the accelerated method because it results in the most depreciation in the earliest years of the asset's life. Accelerated depreciation minimizes taxable income and income tax payments in the early years of the asset's life, thereby maximizing the business's cash at the earliest possible time.

2. To record depreciation to date of sale, and then the sale of the equipment:

20X9			
July 1	Depreciation Expense—Equipment ($5,632 × 1/2 year) . . .	2,816	
	Accumulated Depreciation—Equipment		2,816
	To update depreciation.		
July 1	Cash	27,000	
	Accumulated Depreciation—Equipment ($15,840 + $2,816).	18,656	
	Equipment		44,000
	Gain on Sale of Equipment		1,656
	To record sale of equipment.		

REVIEW PLANT ASSETS, NATURAL RESOURCES, AND INTANGIBLES

Chapter Review Quiz

1. Harrington Corp. purchased a tract of land, a small office building, and some equipment for $1,500,000. The appraised value of the land was $850,000, the building $675,000, and the equipment $475,000. What is the cost of the land?
   a. $481,667
   b. $637,500
   c. $850,000
   d. None of the above.

2. One of the following statements about depreciation is false. Which statement is false?
   a. Depreciation is a process of allocating the cost of a plant asset over its useful life.
   b. The cost of a plant asset minus accumulated depreciation equals the asset's book value.
   c. Recording depreciation creates a fund to replace the asset at the end of its useful life.
   d. Depreciation is based on the matching principle because it matches the cost of the asset with the revenue generated over the asset's useful life.

Use the following data for questions 3–6.

On 8/1/X3, Conlee Grain Co. purchased a new piece of equipment that cost $25,000. The estimated useful life is 5 years and estimated residual value is $2,500.

3. What is depreciation expense for 20X3 if Conlee uses the straight-line method of depreciation:
   a. $1,875
   b. $1,500
   c. $2,083
   d. $4,500

4. Assume Conlee purchased the equipment on 1/1/X3. If Conlee uses the straight-line method for depreciation, what is the asset's book value at 12/31/X4:
   a. $13,500
   b. $16,000
   c. $18,625
   d. $15,000

5. Assume Conlee purchased the equipment on 1/1/X3. If Conlee uses the double-declining-balance method of depreciation, what is depreciation for the year ended 12/31/X4:
   a. $5,400
   b. $7,500
   c. $6,000
   d. $8,333

6. Return to Conlee's original purchase date of 8/1/X3. Assume that Conlee uses the straight-line method of depreciation and sells the equipment for $11,500 on 8/1/X6. The result of the sale of the equipment is a gain (loss) of
   a. $11,500
   b. $13,500
   c. $(9,000)
   d. $0

7. A company bought a new machine for $17,000 on January 1. The machine is expected to last 4 years and have a residual value of $2,000. If the company uses the double-declining-balance method, accumulated depreciation at the end of year 2 will be:
   a. $10,880
   b. $11,250
   c. $12,750
   d. $15,000

8. Which of the following is *not* a capital expenditure:
   a. The addition of a building wing.
   b. A complete overhaul of an air-conditioning system.
   c. The cost of installing a piece of equipment.
   d. Replacement of an old motor with a new one in a piece of equipment.
   e. A tune-up of a company vehicle.

9. Which of the following assets is *not* subject to a decreasing book value through depreciation, depletion, or amortization:
   a. Natural resources
   b. Intangibles
   c. Land improvements
   d. Land

10. Why would a business select an accelerated method of depreciation for tax purposes?
    a. Accelerated depreciation generates higher depreciation expense immediately, and therefore lower tax payments in the early years of the asset's life.
    b. Accelerated depreciation generates a greater amount of depreciation over the life of the asset than does straight-line depreciation.
    c. Accelerated depreciation is easier to calculate because salvage value is ignored.
    d. All of the above are valid reasons.

11. A company purchases an oil well for $200,000. It estimates that the well contains 50,000 barrels, has a 10-year life, and has no salvage value. If the company extracts and sells 4,000 barrels during the first year, how much depletion expense should be recorded:
    a. $16,000
    b. $40,000
    c. $20,000
    d. $100,000
    e. $24,000

12. Which item among the following is *not* an intangible asset:
    a. A trademark
    b. An account receivable
    c. A patent
    d. Goodwill
    e. All of the above are intagible assets

Answers:

1. b {[$850,000/($850,000 + $675,000 + $475,000)] × $1,500,000 = $637,500}
2. c
3. a ($25,000 – $2,500)/5 × 5/12 = $1,875)
4. b [($25,000 – $2,500)/5 × 2 = $9,000; $25,000 – $9,000 = $16,000]
5. c [$25,000 × 2/5 = $10,000; ($25,000 – $10,000) × 2/5 = $6,000]
6. d [($25,000 – $2,500)/5 × 3 = $13,500; $25,000 – $13,500 = $11,500; $11,500 – $11,500 = 0]
7. c [$17,000 × 2/4 = $8,500; ($17,000 – $8,500) × 2/4 = $4,250; $8,500 + $4,250 = $12,750]
8. e
9. d
10. a
11. a [$200,000 × (4,000/50,000) = $16,000]
12. b

Accounting Vocabulary

accelerated depreciation method (p. 324)
amortization (p. 334)
brand name (p. 335)
capital expenditure (p. 319)
copyright (p. 335)
depletion expense (p. 334)
depreciable cost (p. 322)
double-declining-balance (DDB) method (p. 324)
estimated residual value (p. 321)
estimated useful life (p. 321)
franchises and licenses (p. 336)
goodwill (p. 336)
intangible assets (p. 316)
Modified Accelerated Cost Recovery System (MACRS) (p. 329)
patent (p. 335)
plant assets (p. 316)
straight-line (SL) method (p. 322)
trademark, trade name (p. 335)
units-of-production (UOP) method (p. 323)

Assess Your Progress

Check Points

Cost and book value of a company's plant assets (Obj. 1)

CP7-1 (p. 316) Examine the balance sheet of **UPS** at the beginning of this chapter. Answer these questions about the company:

1. What is UPS's largest category of assets?
2. What was UPS's cost of property and equipment at December 31, 2003? What was the book value of property and equipment on this date? Why is book value less than cost?

Measuring the cost of a plant asset (Obj. 1)

writing assignment ■

CP7-2 (p. 317) Page 317 of this chapter lists the costs included for the acquisition of land. First is the purchase price of the land, which is obviously included in the cost of the land. The reasons for including the other costs are not so obvious. For example, property tax is ordinarily an expense, not part of the cost of an asset. State why the other costs listed on page 317 are included as part of the cost of the land. After the land is ready for use, will these other costs be capitalized or expensed?

Lump-sum purchase of assets (Obj. 1)

CP7-3 (p. 318) Return to the UPS Stop and Think feature on page 319. Suppose at the time of your acquisition, the land has a current market value of $80,000, the building's market value is $60,000, and the equipment's market value is $20,000. Journalize UPS's lump-sum purchase of the three assets for a total cost of $150,000. You sign a note payable for this amount.

Capitalizing versus expensing plant asset costs (Obj. 1)

CP7-4 (p. 320) Assume **American Airlines** repaired a Boeing 777 aircraft at a cost of $1.6 million, which American paid in cash. Further, assume the American accountant erroneously capitalized this cost as part of the cost of the plane.

Show the effects of the accounting error on American Airlines' income statement and balance sheet. To answer this question, determine whether plant assets, total expenses, net income, total assets, and owners' equity would be overstated or understated by the accounting error.

Computing depreciation by three methods—first year only (Obj. 2)

CP7-5 (p. 324) Assume that at the beginning of 20X0, **FedEx**, a UPS competitor, purchased a used Boeing 737 aircraft at a cost of $20,000,000. FedEx expects the plane to remain useful for 5 years (5 million miles) and to have a residual value of $6,000,000. UPS expects to fly the plane 750,000 miles the first year, 1,250,000 miles each year 2 through 4, and 500,000 miles the last year.

1. Compute FedEx's first-year depreciation on the plane using the following methods:
   a. Straight-line b. Units-of-production c. Double-declining-balance
2. Show the airplane's book value at the end of the first year under each depreciation method.

Computing depreciation by three methods—third year only (Obj. 2)

CP7-6 (p. 326) Use the assumed FedEx data in Check Point 7-5 to compute FedEx's third-year depreciation on the plane using the following methods:
   a. Straight-line b. Units-of-production c. Double-declining balance

Selecting the best depreciation method for income tax purposes (Obj. 3)

CP7-7 (p. 328) This exercise uses the assumed FedEx data from Check Point 7-6. Assume FedEx is trying to decide which depreciation method to use for income tax purposes.

1. Which depreciation method offers the tax advantage for the first year? Describe the nature of the tax advantage.
2. How much income tax will FedEx save for the first year of the airplane's use as compared with using the straight-line depreciation method? The combined federal and state income tax rate is 40%. Ignore any earnings from investing the extra cash.

Partial-year depreciation (Obj. 2)

CP7-8 (p. 329) Assume that on March 31, 20X4, **Lufthansa**, the German airline, purchased a used Airbus aircraft at a cost of €40,000,000 (€ is the symbol for the euro). Lufthansa expects the plane to remain useful for 5 years (5,000,000 miles) and to have a residual value of €5,000,000. Lufthansa will fly the plane 500,000 miles during the remainder of 20X4. Compute Lufthansa's depreciation on the plane for the year ended December 31, 20X4, using the following methods:
   a. Straight-line b. Units-of-production c. Double-declining-balance

Which method would produce the highest net income for 20X4? Which method produces the lowest net income?

Computing and recording depreciation after a change in useful life of the asset (Obj. 2)

CP7-9 (p. 330) Return to the example of the Disney World hot dog stand on page 000. Suppose that after using the hot dog stand for 4 years, **The Walt Disney Company** determines that the asset will remain useful for only 2 more years. Record Disney's depreciation on the hot dog stand for year 5 by the straight-line method.

Recording a gain or loss on disposal under two depreciation methods (Obj. 4)

CP7-10 (p. 332) Return to the UPS delivery-truck depreciation example in Exhibits 7-5 (page 323) and 7-7 (page 324). Suppose UPS sold the truck on January 1, 20X5, for $10,000 cash, after using the truck for two full years.

1. Record the sale of the truck under
   a. Straight-line depreciation (Exhibit 7-5, page 323)
   b. Double-declining-balance depreciation (Exhibit 7-7, page 324).
2. Why is there such a big difference between the gain or loss on disposal under the two depreciation methods?

Accounting for the depletion of a company's natural resources (Obj. 5)

CP7-11 (p. 334) **ExxonMobil**, the giant oil company, holds reserves of oil and gas assets. At the end of 20X4, assume the cost of ExxonMobil's mineral assets totaled approximately $120 billion, representing 12 billion barrels of oil in the ground.

1. Which depreciation method do ExxonMobil and other oil companies use to compute their annual depletion expense for the minerals removed from the ground?
2. Suppose ExxonMobil removed 0.6 billion barrels of oil during 20X5. Record ExxonMobil's depletion expense for the year.
3. At December 31, 20X4, ExxonMobil's Accumulated Depletion account stood at $85.0 billion. If ExxonMobil did not add any new oil and gas reserves during 20X5, what

would be the book value of the company's oil and gas reserves at December 31, 20X5? Cite a specific figure from your answer to illustrate why exploration activities are so important for companies such as ExxonMobil.

Measuring and recording goodwill (Obj. 6)

CP7-12 (p. 336) **PepsiCo, Inc.** dominates the snack-food industry with its Frito-Lay brand. Assume that PepsiCo, Inc. purchased Hot Chips, Inc., for $8.5 million cash. The market value of Hot Chips' assets is $14 million, and Hot Chips has liabilities of $11 million.

Required

1. Compute the cost of the goodwill purchased by PepsiCo.
2. Explain how PepsiCo will account in future years for any goodwill that PepsiCo purchased.

Accounting for patents and research and development cost (Obj. 6)

CP7-13 (p. 337) This exercise summarizes the accounting for patents, which like copyrights, trademarks, and franchises, provide the owner with a special right or privilege. It also covers research and development costs.

Suppose Ling Software paid $500,000 to research and develop a new software program. Ling also paid $300,000 to acquire a patent on the new software. After readying the software for production, Ling's sales revenue for the first year totaled $1,500,000. Cost of goods sold was $200,000, and selling expenses were $400,000. All these transactions occurred during 20X4. Ling expects the patent to have a useful life of 3 years.

1. Prepare Ling Software's income statement for the year ended December 31, 20X4, complete with a heading.
2. What should Ling's outlook for future profits be on the new software program?

Reporting investing activities on the statement of cash flows (Obj. 7)

CP7-14 (p. 338) During 20X5, Troy Satellite Systems purchased two other companies for $180 million. Assume Troy financed this purchase by paying cash of $160 million and borrowing the remainder. Also during fiscal 20X5, Troy made capital expenditures of $45 million to expand its transmission capabilities. During the year, Troy sold its cable operations, receiving cash of $123 million. Overall, Troy reported a net loss of $1.4 million during 20X5.

Show what Troy Satellite Systems would report for cash flows from investing activities on its statement of cash flows for 20X5. Report a total amount for net cash provided by (used for) investing activities.

Exercises

Most of the even-numbered exercises can be found within Prentice Hall Grade Assist (PHGA), an online homework and practice environment. Your instructor may ask you to complete these exercises using PHGA.

Determining the cost of plant assets (Obj. 1)

E7-1 Mae Davis Enterprises purchased land, paying $200,000 cash as a down payment and signing a $150,000 note payable for the balance. Davis also had to pay delinquent property tax of $2,000, title insurance costing $2,500, and $5,500 to level the land and to remove an unwanted building. The company paid $80,000 to remove earth for the foundation and then constructed an office building at a cost of $1,200,000. It also paid $93,000 for a fence around the property, $10,400 for the company sign near the property entrances, and $6,000 for lighting of the grounds. Determine the cost of the company's land, land improvements, and building.

Allocating costs to assets acquired in a lump-sum purchase; disposing of a plant asset (Obj. 1, 4)

E7-2 Four-D Products bought three used machines in a $90,000 lump-sum purchase. An independent appraiser valued the machines as follows:

Machine No.	Appraised Value
1	$27,000
2	45,000
3	36,000

Four-D paid one-fourth in cash and signed a note payable for the remainder. What is each machine's individual cost? Immediately after making this purchase Four-D sold machine 2 for its appraised value. What is the result of the sale? Round decimals to three places.

Distinguishing capital expenditures from expenses (Obj. 1)

E7-3 Assume **UPS** purchased a piece of conveyor-belt machinery. Classify each of the following expenditures as a capital expenditure or an immediate expense related to machinery: (a) purchase price, (b) sales tax paid on the purchase price, (c) transportation and insurance while machinery is in transit from seller to buyer, (d) installation, (e) training of personnel for initial operation of the machinery, (f) special reinforcement to the machinery platform, (g) income tax paid on income earned from the sale of products manufactured by the machinery, (h) major overhaul to extend useful life by 3 years, (i) ordinary repairs to keep the machinery in good working order, (j) lubrication of the machinery before it is placed in service and (k) periodic lubrication after the machinery is placed in service.

Measuring, depreciating, and reporting plant assets (Obj. 1, 2)

■ **general ledger**

E7-4 During 20X4, **Saab Auto Sales** paid $500,000 for land and built a store in Madison, Wisconsin. Prior to construction, the city of Madison charged Saab $1,000 for a building permit, which Saab paid. Saab also paid $20,000 for architect's fees. The construction cost of $830,000 was financed by a long-term note payable, with interest cost of $39,000 paid at December 31, 20X4. The building was completed September 30, 20X4. Saab depreciates the building by the straight-line method over 35 years, with estimated residual value of $190,000.

1. Journalize transactions for
   a. Purchase of the land
   b. All the costs chargeable to the building in a single entry
   c. Depreciation on the building

   Explanations are not required.
2. Report Saab's plant assets on the company's balance sheet at December 31, 20X4.
3. What will Saab's income statement for the year ended December 31, 20X4, report for this situation?

Explaining the concept of depreciation (Obj. 2)

writing assignment ■

E7-5 Nicole Smeenk has just slept through the class in which Professor Cassell explained the concept of depreciation. Because the next test is scheduled for Wednesday, Smeenk telephones Mark McCreary to get the lecture notes. McCreary's notes are concise: "Depreciation—Sounds like Greek to me." Smeenk next tries Akbar Khuwaja who says depreciation is what happens when an asset wears out. Kelly Kasiak is confident that depreciation is the process of building up a cash fund to replace an asset at the end of its useful life. Explain the concept of depreciation for Smeenk. Evaluate the statements of Khuwaja and Kasiak. Be specific.

Determining depreciation amounts by three methods (Obj. 2, 3)

writing assignment ■

■ **spreadsheet**

E7-6 **Domino's Pizza** bought a used Chevy Luv delivery van on January 2, 20X4, for $15,000. The van was expected to remain in service 4 years (100,000 miles). At the end of its useful life, Domino's officials estimated that the van's residual value would be $3,000. The van traveled 34,000 miles the first year, 28,000 the second year, 18,000 the third year, and 20,000 in the fourth year. Prepare a schedule of *depreciation expense* per year for the van under the three depreciation methods. Show your computations.

Which method best tracks the wear and tear on the van? Which method would Domino's prefer to use for income tax purposes? Explain in detail why Domino's prefers this method.

Reporting plant assets, depreciation, and cash flow (Obj. 1, 2, 7)

E7-7 In January 20X6, Rudy's Restaurant purchased a building, paying $70,000 cash and signing a $130,000 note payable. The restaurant paid another $60,000 to remodel the building. Furniture and fixtures cost $40,000, and dishes and supplies—a current asset—were obtained for $9,000.

Rudy's Restaurant is depreciating the building over 20 years by the straight-line method, with estimated residual value of $50,000. The furniture and fixtures will be replaced at the end of 5 years and are being depreciated by the double-declining-balance method, with zero residual value. At the end of the first year, the restaurant still has dishes and supplies worth $2,000.

Show what the restaurant will report for supplies, plant assets, and cash flows at the end of the first year on its

- Income statement
- Balance sheet
- Statement of cash flows (investing only)

Show all computations.

Note: The purchase of dishes and supplies is an operating cash flow because supplies are a current asset.

Units-of-production depreciation (Obj. 2)

E7-8 Laser Gym purchased Cybex exercise equipment at a cost of $100,000. In addition, Laser paid $2,000 for a special platform on which to stabilize the equipment for use. Freight costs of $1,200 to ship the equipment were borne by Cybex. Laser will depreciate the equipment by the units-of-production method, based on an expected useful life of 50,000 hours of exercise. The estimated residual value of the equipment is $10,000. How many hours of usage can Laser Gym expect from the machine if depreciation expense is $3,680 for the year 20X5?

Selecting the best depreciation method for income tax purposes (Obj. 3)

E7-9 On June 30, 20X6, Bongo Board Corp. paid $210,000 for equipment that is expected to have a 7-year life. In this industry, the residual value of equipment is approximately 10% of the asset's cost. Bongo Board cash revenues for the year are $100,000 and cash expenses total $60,000.

Select the appropriate MACRS depreciation method for income tax purposes. Then determine the extra amount of cash that Bongo Board Corp. can invest by using MACRS depreciation, versus straight-line for the year ended December 31, 20X6. The income tax rate is 40%.

Changing a plant asset's useful life (Obj. 2)

E7-10 Assume the **Salvation Army** purchased a building for $900,000 and depreciated it on a straight-line basis over 40 years. The estimated residual value was $100,000. After using the building for 20 years, the Salvation Army realized that the building will remain useful only 10 more years. Starting with the 21st year, the Salvation Army began depreciating the building over the newly revised total life of 30 years and decreased the estimated residual value to $50,000. Record depreciation expense on the building for years 20 and 21.

Analyzing the effect of a sale of a plant asset; DDB depreciation (Obj. 4)

E7-11 Assume that on January 2, 20X4, a **McDonald's** restaurant purchased fixtures for $8,700 cash, expecting the fixtures to remain in service 5 years. McDonald's has depreciated the fixtures on a double-declining-balance basis, with $1,000 estimated residual value. On September 30, 20X5, McDonald's sold the fixtures for $800 cash. Record both the depreciation expense on the fixtures for 20X5 and then the sale of the fixtures. Apart from your journal entry, also show how to compute the gain or loss on McDonald's disposal of these fixtures.

Measuring a plant asset's cost, using UOP depreciation, and trading in a used asset (Obj. 1, 2, 4)

E7-12 MoPac Express is a large trucking company that operates throughout the midwestern United States. MoPac uses the units-of-production (UOP) method to depreciate its trucks.

MoPac Express trades in its trucks often to keep driver morale high and to maximize fuel efficiency. Consider these facts about one **Volvo** truck in the company's fleet: When acquired in 20X2, the tractor-trailer rig cost $285,000 and was expected to remain in service for 5 years or 1,000,000 miles. Estimated residual value was $35,000. During 20X2, the truck was driven 75,000 miles; during 20X3, 120,000 miles; and during 20X4, 210,000 miles. After 35,000 miles in 20X5, the company traded in the Volvo truck for a **Mack** rig. MoPac Express paid cash of $120,000. Determine MoPac Express's cost of the new truck. Journal entries are not required.

Recording natural resource assets and depletion (Obj. 5)

E7-13 Cheyenne Ore Deposits paid $398,500 for the right to extract ore from a 200,000-ton mineral deposit. In addition to the purchase price, Cheyenne also paid a $500 filing fee, a $1,000 license fee to the state of Utah, and $60,000 for a geologic survey of the property. Because the company purchased the rights to the minerals only, it expected the asset to have zero residual value when fully depleted. During the first year of production, Cheyenne removed 50,000 tons of ore. Make journal entries to record (a) purchase of the mineral rights, (b) payment of fees and other costs, and (c) depletion for first-year production. What is the mineral asset's book value at the end of the year?

Recording intangibles, amortization, and a change in the asset's useful life (Obj. 6)

E7-14 Magnetic Imaging, Inc. (MII) has recently purchased for $400,000 a patent for the design of a new resonance imaging machine. Although it gives legal protection for 20 years, the patent is expected to provide MII with a competitive advantage for only 5 years. Assuming the straight-line method of amortization, make journal entries to record (a) the purchase of the patent and (b) amortization for year 1.

After using the patent for 2 years, Magnetic Imaging's research director learns at a professional meeting that **Ingersoll-Rand** is designing a more efficient machine. On the basis of this new information, MII determines that the patent's total useful life is only 4 years. Record amortization for year 3.

Computing and accounting for goodwill (Obj. 6)

E7-15 **Safeway Inc.** operates over 1,800 grocery stores in all sections of the United States but the Northeast. The company has grown in part by purchasing other grocery chains. One such acquisition was the **Randalls** food stores in Texas. Assume Safeway paid $25 million to purchase Randalls. Assume further that Randalls had the following summarized data at the time of the Safeway acquisition (amounts in millions):

Randalls Food Stores			
Assets		**Liabilities and Equity**	
Current assets	$ 10	Total Liabilities	$ 60
Long-term assets	90	Stockholders' equity	40
	$100		$100

Randalls' long-term assets had a current market value of only $70 million.

Required

1. Compute the cost of goodwill purchased by Safeway.
2. Journalize Safeway's purchase of Randalls food stores.
3. Explain how Safeway will account for goodwill in the future.

Business acquisitions and cash flows (Obj. 6, 7)

E7-16 Assume **Campbell Soup Company's** 20X3 statement of cash flows reported:

	20X3
Cash Flows from Investing Activities	Millions
Businesses acquired	$(1,255)

Assume Campbell Soup's balance sheet reported:

	20X3	20X2
Intangible assets:	Millions	
Goodwill	$1,583	$452

Required

Answer these questions:

1. Explain the meaning of the (a) $1,255 million that Campbell Soup reported on the statement of cash flows and (b) $1,583 million on the balance sheet.
2. Assume $1,200 million of the $1,255 purchase price for businesses acquired was for goodwill. What must have happened in 20X3 to cause $452 million + $1,200 million to not equal $1,583 million? Describe the transaction and give its dollar amount.

Interpreting a cash-flow statement (Obj. 7)

E7-17 The following items are excerpted from an annual report of **Pier 1 Imports, Inc.**:

Pier 1 Imports, Inc. Consolidated Statement of Cash Flows (Partial, adapted)	
(Millions of dollars)	**20X3**
Cash flow from operating activities:	
Net income	$129
Adjustments to reconcile to net cash provided by operating activities:	
Depreciation and amortization	46
Cash flow from investing activities:	
Capital expenditures	$(99)
Disposals of properties	6

Required

Answer these questions:

1. Why are depreciation and amortization listed on the statement of cash flows?
2. Explain in detail each investing activity.

Reporting cash flows for property and equipment (Obj. 7)

E7-18 Assume **Pier 1 Imports, Inc.**, completed the following transactions. For each transaction, show what Pier 1 would report for investing activities on its statement of cash flows. Show negative amounts in parentheses.

a. Sold a building for $650,000. The building had cost Pier 1 $2,000,000, and at the time of the sale its accumulated depreciation totaled $1,500,000.
b. Lost a store building in a fire. The warehouse cost $5,000,000 and had accumulated depreciation of $2,800,000. The insurance proceeds received by Pier 1 were $2,500,000.
c. Renovated a store at a cost of $300,000, paying half in cash and borrowing the remainder on a 3-year note payable.
d. Purchased store fixtures for $100,000. The fixtures are expected to remain in service for 10 years and then be sold for $15,000. Pier 1 uses the straight-line depreciation method.

Challenge Exercises

Determining the sale price of property and equipment (Obj. 4)

E7-19 **Target Corporation**, the discount chain, reported the following for property and equipment (in millions):

	Year End	
	20X1	20X0
Property and equipment	$15,759	$13,824
Accumulated depreciation	(4,341)	(3,925)

During 20X1, Target paid $2,528 million for new property and equipment. Depreciation for the year totaled $940 million. Assume that during 20X1, Target sold property and equipment at a loss of $31 million. For how much did Target sell the property and equipment?

Determining net income after a change in depreciation method (Obj. 2)

E7-20 **Fossil, Inc.**, the company known for its popular lines of wristwatches and sunglasses, reported net income of $68.30 million for 20X3. Depreciation expense for the year totaled $18.90 million. Assume Fossil depreciates plant assets over approximately 8 years using the straight-line method and no residual value. The company's income tax rate is 40%.

Assume that Fossil's plant assets are 3 years old and that Fossil switches over to double-declining-balance (DDB) depreciation at the start of 20X4. Further, assume that 20X4 is expected to be the same as 20X3 except for the change in depreciation method. How much net income can Fossil, Inc., expect to earn during 20X4? Round to two decimal places.

Capitalizing versus expensing; measuring the effect of an error (Obj. 1)

E7-21 **Agence France Press (AFP)** is a major French telecommunication conglomerate. Assume that early in year 1, AFP purchased equipment at a cost of 4 million euros (€4 million). Management expects the equipment to remain in service 4 years and estimated residual value to be negligible. AFP uses the straight-line depreciation method. *Through an accounting error, AFP expenses the entire cost of the equipment at the time of purchase.* Because the company is operated as a partnership, it pays no income tax.

Required

Prepare a schedule to show the overstatement or understatement in the following items at the end of each year over the 4-year life of the equipment:

1. Total current assets 2. Equipment, net 3. Net income

2. Ahmadi reports to stockholders and creditors in the financial statements using the depreciation method that maximizes reported income in the early years of asset use. For income tax purposes, however, the company uses the depreciation method that minimizes income tax payments in those early years. Consider the first year Ahmadi uses the computer. Identify the depreciation methods that meet Ahmadi's objectives, assuming the income tax authorities would permit the use of any of the methods.
3. Assume that cash provided by operations before income tax is $200,000 for the computer's first year. The income tax rate is 35%. For the two depreciation methods identified in Requirement 2, compare the net income and cash provided by operations (cash flow). Show which method gives the net-income advantage and which method gives the cash-flow advantage.

Analyzing plant asset transactions from a company's financial statements (Obj. 2, 4, 7)

P7-6B **Fossil, Inc.** features high-fashion wristwatches and sunglasses. The company's motto is "Never a dull moment." The excerpts that follow are adapted from Fossil's financial statements for 2003.

Balance Sheet (dollars in millions)	December 31, 2003	2002
Assets		
Total current assets	$439	$356
Property, plant, and equipment	173	144
Less Accumulated depreciation	(57)	(41)
Intangibles	28	22

Statement of Cash Flows (dollars in millions)	Year Ended December 31, 2003	2002
Operating activities:		
Net income	$68	$59
Noncash items affecting net income:		
Depreciation	16	14
Investing activities:		
Additions to property, plant, and equipment	(29)	(27)
Business acquisitions	(104)	(4,373)

Required

Answer these questions about Fossil's plant assets:

1. How much was Fossil's cost of plant assets at December 31, 2003? How much was the book value of plant assets? Show computations.
2. The financial statements give four evidences that Fossil purchased plant assets and intangible assets during 2003. What are they?
3. Prepare T-accounts for Property, Plant, and Equipment; Accumulated Depreciation, and Intangibles. Then show all the activity in these accounts during 2003. Label each increase or decrease and give its dollar amount. Assume there was no amortization of intangibles and no loss on intangibles during 2003.
4. Why is depreciation added to net income on the statement of cash flows?

Accounting for intangibles, natural resources, and the related expenses (Obj. 5, 6)

P7-7B *Part 1.* **Collins Food Group, Inc.**, is the majority owner of Sizzler Restaurants in Australia. The company's balance sheet reports the asset Cost in Excess of Net Assets of Purchased Businesses. Assume that Collins purchased this asset as part of the acquisition of another company, which carried these figures:

Book value of assets	$2.4 million
Market value of assets	5.1 million
Liabilities	2.2 million

Required

1. What is another title for the asset Cost in Excess of Net Assets of Purchased Businesses?
2. Record a journal entry for Collins' purchase of the other company for $6.1 million cash.
3. Assume that Collins Foods determined that Cost in Excess of Net Assets of Purchased Businesses increased in value by $800,000. Make whatever journal entry is needed to record this transaction. Then, suppose Cost in Excess of Net Assets of Purchased Businesses decreased in value by $800,000. Make the needed journal entry for this transaction.

Part 2. **Georgia-Pacific Corporation** is one of the world's largest forest products companies. The company's balance sheet includes the assets Natural Gas, Oil, and Coal.

Suppose Georgia-Pacific paid $3.8 million cash for a lease giving the firm the right to work a mine that contained an estimated 100,000 tons of coal. Assume that the company paid $60,000 to remove unwanted buildings from the land and $45,000 to prepare the surface for mining. Further assume that Georgia-Pacific signed a $30,000 note payable to a landscaping company to return the land surface to its original condition after the lease ends. During the first year, Georgia-Pacific removed 35,000 tons of coal, which it sold on account for $67 per ton. Operating expenses for the first year totaled $240,000, all paid in cash. In addition, the company accrued income tax at the tax rate of 30%.

Required

1. Record all of Georgia-Pacific's transactions for the year.
2. Prepare the company's income statement for its coal operations for the first year. Evaluate the profitability of the coal operations.

Reporting plant asset transactions on the statement of cash flows (Obj. 7)

writing assignment ■

P7-8B At the end of 20X0, **The Coca-Cola Company** had total assets of $20.8 billion and total liabilities of $11.5 billion. Included among the assets were property, plant, and equipment with a cost of $6.6 billion and accumulated depreciation of $2.4 billion.

Assume that Coca-Cola completed the following selected transactions during 20X1: The company earned total revenues of $20.5 billion and incurred total expenses of $18.3 billion, which included depreciation of $0.7 billion. During the year, Coca-Cola paid $0.7 billion for new property, plant, and equipment and sold old plant assets for $0.5 billion. The cost of the assets sold was $0.8 billion, and their accumulated depreciation was $0.4 billion.

Required

1. Explain how to determine whether Coca-Cola had a gain or loss on the sale of old plant assets during the year. What was the amount of the gain or loss, if any?
2. Show how Coca-Cola would report property, plant, and equipment on the balance sheet at December 31, 20X1. What was the book value of property, plant and equipment?
3. Show how Coca-Cola would report operating activities and investing activities on its statement of cash flows for 20X1. Ignore gains and losses.

APPLY YOUR KNOWLEDGE

Decision Cases

Measuring profitability based on different inventory and depreciation methods (Obj. 2, 3)

writing assignment ■

Case 1. Suppose you are considering investing in two businesses. **360 Communications** and **Beeper Unlimited**. The two companies are virtually identical, and both began operations at the beginning of the current year. Assume that during the year, each company purchased inventory as follows:

Jan. 4	10,000 units at $4 =	$ 40,000
Apr. 6	5,000 units at 5 =	25,000
Aug. 9	7,000 units at 6 =	42,000
Nov. 27	10,000 units at 7 =	70,000
Totals	32,000	$177,000

During the first year, both companies sold 25,000 units of inventory.

In early January, both companies purchased equipment costing $150,000 that had a 10-year estimated useful life and a $20,000 residual value. 360 uses the inventory and depreciation methods that maximize reported income. By contrast, Beepers uses the inventory and depreciation methods that minimize income tax payments. Assume that both companies' trial balances at December 31 included the following:

Sales revenue	$370,000
Operating expenses	50,000

The income tax rate is 35%.

Required

1. Prepare both companies' income statements.
2. Write an investment newsletter to address the following questions for your clients: Which company appears to be more profitable? Which company has more cash to invest in promising projects? If prices continue rising over the long term, which company would you prefer to invest in? Why?

Plant assets and intangible assets (Obj. 1, 6)

writing assignment ■

Case 2. The following questions are unrelated except that they all apply to fixed assets and intangible assets:

1. It has been suggested that because many intangible assets have no value except to the company that owns them, they should be valued at $1.00 or zero on the balance sheet. Many accountants disagree with this view. Which view do you support? Why?
2. The manager of Horizon Software regularly buys plant assets and debits the cost to Repairs and Maintenance Expense. Why would he do that, since he knows this action violates GAAP?
3. The manager of Central Transportation Systems regularly debits the cost of repairs and maintenance of plant assets to Plant and Equipment. Why would she do that, since she knows she is violating GAAP?

Ethical Issue

writing assignment ■

United Kansas Bank of Topeka purchased land and a building for the lump sum of $4.3 million. To get the maximum tax deduction, the bank's managers allocated 80% of the purchase price to the building and only 20% to the land. A more realistic allocation would have been 60% to the building and 40% to the land.

Required

1. Explain the tax advantage of allocating too much to the building and too little to the land.
2. Was United Kansas Bank's allocation ethical? If so, state why. If not, why not? Identify who was harmed.

Focus on Financials: ■ YUM! Brands

Analyzing plant assets (Obj. 2, 3, 6)

Refer to **YUM! Brands'** financial statements in Appendix A at the end of the book, and answer the following questions:

1. Which depreciation method does YUM use for reporting to stockholders and creditors in the financial statements? What type of depreciation method does the company probably use for income tax purposes? Why is this method preferable for tax purposes?
2. Depreciation expense is embedded in the expense amounts listed on the income statement. It is reported elsewhere in the financial statements. How much was YUM's depreciation and amortization expense during fiscal year 2003? How much was YUM's accumulated depreciation and amortization at the end of 2003? Explain why accumulated depreciation and amortization exceeds depreciation and amortization expense for the current year.

3. Explain why YUM adds depreciation and amortization expense back to net income in the computation of net cash from operating activities on the statement of cash flows.
4. How much did YUM spend on property, plant, and equipment during 2003? Evaluate the trend in these capital expenditures as to whether it conveys good news or bad news for YUM. Explain.
5. YUM reports two separate intangible assets. What are they? How does YUM account for each of these intangibles over its lifetime?

Focus on Analysis: ■ Pier 1 Imports

Explaining plant asset activity (Obj. 2, 4, 7)

Refer to the **Pier 1 Imports** financial statements in Appendix B at the end of this book. This case leads you through a comprehensive analysis of Pier 1's long-term assets. Its purpose is to show you how to account for plant asset (properties) transactions in summary form. Show amounts in millions, and round to the nearest $1 million.

1. On the statement of cash flows, how much did Pier 1 pay for capital expenditures during 2004? How much cash did Pier 1 receive from the disposition of properties (fixed assets) during 2004? Consider the loss on disposal of fixed assets reported under Cash Flow from Operating Activities, and determine the book value of plant assets sold during 2004.
2. Use the answer to requirement 1, plus the amount of depreciation and amortization reported on the statement of cash flows, to explain all the activity in the Properties, Net account during 2004. Of the total depreciation and amortization for 2004, assume that $13 million related to Other Noncurrent Assets and not to Properties. Use either a T-account or an equation for your analysis.
3. Which depreciation method does Pier 1 use? Over what useful life does Pier 1 depreciate buildings, equipment, furniture, and fixtures?
4. During 2004, Pier 1 added $121 million of new plant assets. Therefore, it is possible that the company's plant assets at the end of 2004 were proportionately newer than the assets the company held at the end of 2003. Were plant assets proportionately newer or older at the end of 2004 (versus 2003)? Explain your answer.

Group Project

Visit a local business.

Required

1. List all its plant assets.
2. If possible, interview the manager. Gain as much information as you can about the business's plant assets. For example, try to determine the assets' costs, the depreciation method the company is using, and the estimated useful life of each asset category. If an interview is impossible, then develop your own estimates of the assets' costs, useful lives, and book values, assuming an appropriate depreciation method.
3. Determine whether the business has any intangible assets. If so, list them and gain as much information as possible about their nature, cost, and estimated useful lives.
4. Write a detailed report of your findings and be prepared to present your results to the class.

spotlight

TOUGH TIMES FOR THE AIRLINES

The airlines are some of the most volatile companies around. During good times, people travel a lot, and the airlines earn lots of money. But when times get tough, people drive instead of fly, and the airlines suffer. Air travel isn't a basic commodity such as milk and toothpaste; it's mostly discretionary. So analysts label the airlines as cyclicals—meaning they ride the economic cycles up and down.

Recent years have been tough for the airlines: 9/11, a weak economy, and high fuel prices have driven AMR Corporation (American Airlines) to the brink. UAL Corporation (United Airlines) is working its way out of bankruptcy. What makes these companies so vulnerable? Their balance sheets tell the story. Look at AMR's and UAL's liabilities and stockholders' equity. AMR's equity is only $46 *million* dollars, compared to total liabilities of over $29 *billion*. UAL's equity is almost $6 billion negative, which means that UAL has $6 billion more liabilities than assets. That's what bankruptcy means: Your liabilities exceed your assets.

AMR Corporation (American Airlines)
Balance Sheet (Adapted)
December 31, 2003

(In millions)

Assets		Liabilities and Stockholders' Equity	
Current Assets		Current Liabilities	
Cash	$ 120	Accounts payable	$ 967
Other current assets	4,562	Salaries and wages payable	528
Total current assets	4,682	Current maturities of long-term debt	603
Equipment and property, net	19,460	Other current liabilities	4,461
Other assets	5,188	Total current liabilities	6,559
		Long-term debt	11,901
		Other long-term liabilities	10,824
		Stockholders' Equity	46
Total assets	$29,330	Total liabilities and equity	$29,330

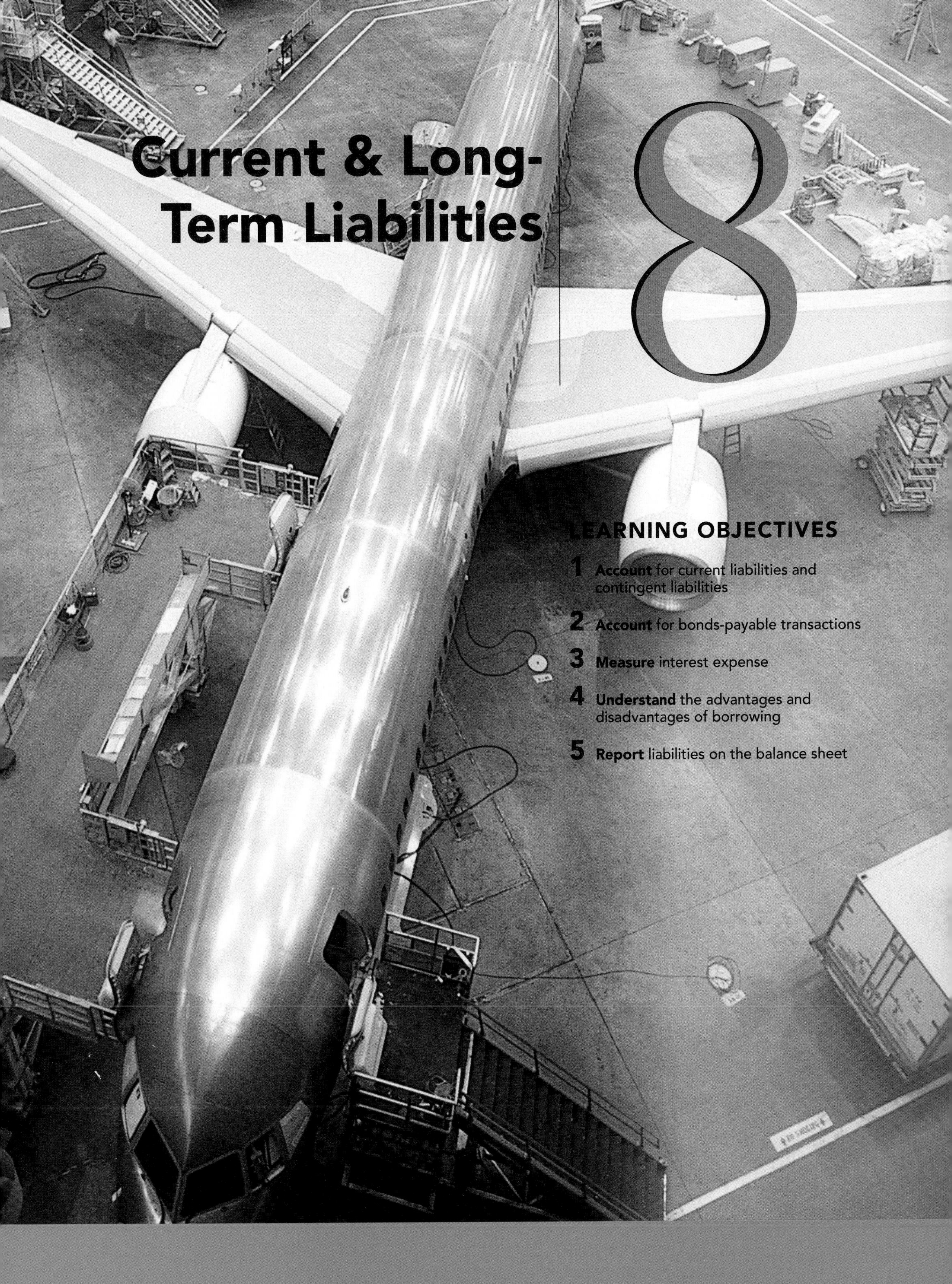

Current & Long-Term Liabilities

8

LEARNING OBJECTIVES

1 **Account** for current liabilities and contingent liabilities

2 **Account** for bonds-payable transactions

3 **Measure** interest expense

4 **Understand** the advantages and disadvantages of borrowing

5 **Report** liabilities on the balance sheet

UAL Corporation (United Airlines)
Debtor and Debtor-in-Possession
Balance Sheet (Adapted)
December 31, 2003

(In millions)

Assets		Liabilities and Stockholders' Equity	
Current Assets		Current Liabilities	
Cash	$ 1,640	Accounts payable	$ 501
Other current assets	2,384	Unearned ticket revenue	1,330
Total current assets	4,024	Current maturities of	
Operating property		long-term obligations	689
and equipment, net	15,038	Other current liabilities	3,592
Other assets	2,917	Total current liabilities	6,112
		Long-term liabilities	21,783
		Stockholders' Equity	(5,916)
Total assets	$21,979	Total liabilities and equity	$21,979

Why are airlines so volatile? Because airplanes are so expensive, their liabilities are high, and their debt ratios are high. Any company that finances with a lot of debt will be risky. In good times, profits soar. But bad times can be really bad.

This chapter shows how to account for liabilities—both current and long-term. We begin with current liabilities.

Current Liabilities

OBJECTIVE

1 **Account** for current liabilities and contingent liabilities

Current liabilities are obligations due within 1 year or within the company's normal operating cycle if longer than a year. Obligations due beyond that period of time are classified as *long-term liabilities*.

Current liabilities are of two kinds: known amounts and estimated amounts. We look first at current liabilities of a known amount.

Current Liabilities of Known Amount

Current liabilities of known amount include accounts payable, short-term notes payable, sales tax payable, current portion of long-term debt, accrued expenses payable, payroll liabilities, and unearned revenues.

Accounts Payable. Amounts owed for products or services purchased on account are *accounts payable*. For example, AMR and UAL purchase snack meals on accounts payable. We have seen many other accounts payable examples in preceding chapters. One of a merchandiser's most common transactions is the credit purchase of inventory. **Home Depot** and **Saks Fifth Avenue** buy their inventory on account. A computer integrates the accounts payable and inventory systems. When merchandise dips below a certain level, the computer prints a purchase order. The goods are received, and the computer increases Inventory and Accounts Payable.

Short-term note payable
Note payable due within one-year.

Short-Term Notes Payable. **Short-term notes payable**, a common form of financing, are notes payable due within 1 year. **H.J. Heinz Company**, famous for ketchup, lists its short-term notes payable as *short-term debt*. Heinz may issue short-term notes payable to borrow cash or to purchase assets. On its notes payable, Heinz must accrue interest expense and interest payable at the end of the period. The following sequence of entries covers the purchase of inventory, accrual of interest expense, and payment of a short-term note payable.

20X5			
Jan. 30	Inventory	8,000	
	Note Payable, Short-Term		8,000
	Purchase of inventory by issuing a 1-year 10% note payable.		

This transaction increases both an asset and a liability.

ASSETS	=	LIABILITIES	+	STOCKHOLDERS' EQUITY
+8,000	=	+8,000	+	0

The H.J. Heinz fiscal year ends each April 30. At year end, Heinz must accrue interest expense for February, March, and April:

Apr. 30	Interest Expense ($8,000 × .10 × 3/12)	200	
	Interest Payable		200
	Adjusting entry to accrue interest expense at year end.		

ASSETS	=	LIABILITIES	+	STOCKHOLDERS' EQUITY	–	EXPENSES
0	=	+200			–	200

The balance sheet at year end will report the Note Payable of $8,000 and the related Interest Payable of $200 as current liabilities. The income statement will report interest expense of $200.

The following entry records the note's payment at maturity.

20X6			
Jan. 30	Note Payable, Short-Term	8,000	
	Interest Payable	200	
	Interest Expense ($8,000 × 0.10 × 9/12)	600	
	Cash [8,000 + ($8,000 × .10)]		8,800
	Payment of a note payable and interest at maturity		

Check Point 8-1

Check Point 8-2

ASSETS	=	LIABILITIES	+	STOCKHOLDERS' EQUITY	–	EXPENSES
–8,800	=	–8,000			–	600
		– 200				

The debits zero out the payables and also record the interest expense of year 20X6.

Sales Tax Payable. Most states levy a sales tax on retail sales. Retailers collect the tax from customers and thus have a liability to the state for the sales tax collected. Suppose one Saturday's sales at a Home Depot store totaled $200,000. Home Depot collected an additional 5% ($10,000) of sales tax. The store would record that day's sales as follows:

Cash ($200,000 × 1.05)	210,000	
Sales Revenue		200,000
Sales Tax Payable ($200,000 × .05) ..		10,000
To record cash sales and the related sales tax.		

ASSETS	=	LIABILITIES	+	STOCKHOLDERS' EQUITY	+	REVENUES
+210,000	=	+10,000			+	200,000

Current installment of long-term debt
The amount of the principal that is payable within one year.

Current Portion of Long-Term Debt. Some long-term debt must be paid in installments. The **current installment of long-term debt** (also called *current portion*) is the amount of the principal that is payable within 1 year. At the end of each year, a company reclassifies (from long-term debt to a current liability) the amount of its long-term debt that must be paid during the upcoming year.

Both AMR Corporation and UAL Corporation (pages 362 and 364) report Current Maturities of Long-Term Obligations as a current liability. They also report Long-Term Debt, which excludes the current maturities. *Long-term debt* refers to the notes payable and bonds payable, which we cover in the second half of this chapter.

stop AND think. . .

Study AMR Corporation's balance sheet and answer these questions about the company's current and long-term debt:

1. At December 31, 2003, how much in total did AMR owe on current and long-term debt?
2. How much of the long-term debt did AMR have to pay during the year ended December 31, 2004? How much was the company scheduled to pay during later years?

Answers:

1. $12,504 million ($603 + $11,901)
2. Pay next year—$603 million. Pay later—$11,901 million

Accrued expense
An expense incurred but not yet paid in cash. Also called *accrued liability*.

Accrued Expenses (Accrued Liabilities). An **accrued expense** is an expense the business has incurred but not yet paid. Therefore, an accrued expense is also a liability, which explains why it is also called an *accrued liability*. AMR's salaries and wages payable occur as employees work for the company. There are several categories of accrued expenses:

- Salaries and Wages Payable
- Interest Payable
- Income Taxes Payable

Salaries and Wages Payable (also called Accrued Salaries and Wages Payable) is the company's liabilities for salaries, wages, and related payroll expenses not yet paid at the end of the period. This category includes payroll taxes withheld from employee paychecks. Interest Payable is the company's interest payable on long-term debt. Income Taxes Payable is the amount of income tax the company still owes at year end.

Payroll
Employee compensation, a major expense of many businesses.

Payroll Liabilities. **Payroll**, also called *employee compensation*, is a major expense. For service organizations—such as law firms, real estate brokerage, and travel agencies—compensation is *the* major expense, just as cost of goods sold is the largest expense for a merchandising company.

Employee compensation takes different forms. A *salary* is employee pay stated at a yearly or monthly rate. A *wage* is employee pay stated at an hourly rate. Sales employees earn a *commission*, which is a percentage of the sales the employee has made. A *bonus* is an amount over and above regular compensation. Accounting for all forms of compensation follows the pattern illustrated in Exhibit 8-1 (using assumed figures).

EXHIBIT 8-1

Accounting for Payroll Expenses and Liabilities

Salary Expense	10,000	
Employee Income Tax Payable		1,200
FICA Tax Payable		800
Salary Payable to Employees [take-home pay]		8,000
To record salary expense.		

ASSETS	=	LIABILITIES	+	STOCKHOLDERS' EQUITY	−	EXPENSES
		+1,200			−	10,000
0	=	+800				
		+8,000				

Salary expense represents *gross pay* (that is, employee pay before subtractions for taxes and other deductions). Salary expense creates several payroll liabilities:

- *Salary Payable* to employees is their net (take-home) pay.
- *Employee Income Tax Payable* is the employees' income tax that has been withheld from paychecks.
- *FICA Tax Payable* includes the employees' Social Security tax and Medicare tax, which also are withheld from paychecks. (FICA stands for the Federal Insurance Contributions Act, which created the Social Security tax.)

Companies must also pay some *employer* payroll taxes and expenses for employee benefits. Accounting for these expenses is similar to the illustration in Exhibit 8-1.

Unearned Revenues. *Unearned revenues* are also called *deferred revenues* and *revenues collected in advance*. All these account titles indicate that the business has received cash from customers before earning the revenue. The company has an obligation to provide goods or services to the customer. Let's consider an example.

United Airlines sells tickets and collects cash in advance. UAL Corporation therefore reports Unearned Ticket Revenue for airline tickets sold in advance. At December 31, 2003, UAL owed customers $1,330 million of air travel (see page 364). Let's see how UAL accounts for unearned revenue.

Assume that UAL collects $1,200 for a round-trip ticket from Chicago to London and back. UAL records the cash collection and related liability as follows:

20X6			
Dec. 15	Cash	1,200	
	Unearned Ticket Revenue		1,200
	Received cash in advance for ticket sales.		

ASSETS	=	LIABILITIES	+	STOCKHOLDERS' EQUITY
+1,200	=	+1,200		

Unearned Ticket Revenue

	1,200

Suppose the customer flies to London late in December. UAL records the revenue earned as follows:

20X6			
Dec. 28	Unearned Ticket Revenue	600	
	Ticket Revenue (1,200 × 1/2)		600
	Earned revenue that was collected in advance.		

ASSETS	=	LIABILITIES	+	STOCKHOLDERS' EQUITY	+	REVENUES
0	=	−600			+	600

Unearned Ticket Revenue	
600	1,200

Ticket Revenue	
	600

At year end, UAL reports

- $600 of unearned ticket revenue (a liability) on the balance sheet
- $600 of ticket revenue on the income statement

The customer returns to Chicago in January 20X7, and UAL makes this journal entry:

20X7			
Jan.4	Unearned Ticket Revenue	600	
	Ticket Revenue ($1,200 × 1/2)		600
	Earned revenue that was collected in advance.		

ASSETS	=	LIABILITIES	+	STOCKHOLDERS' EQUITY	+	REVENUES
0	=	−600			+	600

Unearned Ticket Revenue	
600	1,200
600	

Now UAL has no liability for unearned ticket revenue.

Current Liabilities That Must Be Estimated

A business may know that a liability exists and not know the exact amount. But the business must report the liability on the balance sheet. Estimated liabilities vary among companies. Let's look first at Estimated Warranty Payable, a liability account most merchandisers have.

Estimated Warranty Payable. Many companies guarantee their products under *warranty* agreements. The warranty period may extend for 90 days to a year for consumer products. Automobile companies—BMW, General Motors, and Toyota—accrue liabilities for vehicle warranties.

Whatever the warranty's life, the matching principle demands that the company record the *warranty expense* in the same period that the business records sales revenue. After all, the warranty motivates customers to buy products, so the company must record warranty expense. At the time of the sale, however, the company does not know which products are defective. The exact amount of warranty expense cannot be known with certainty, so the business must estimate warranty expense and the related warranty liability.

Assume that **Black & Decker**, which manufactures products sold in Home Depot stores, made sales of $200,000,000 subject to product warranties. Assume that in past years between 2% and 4% of products proved defective. Black & Decker could estimate that 3% of sales will require repair or replacement. Black & Decker would estimate warranty expense of $6,000,000 ($200,000,000 × 0.03) for the year and make the following entry:

Warranty Expense	6,000,000	
Estimated Warranty Payable		6,000,000
To accrue warranty expense.		

ASSETS	=	LIABILITIES	+	STOCKHOLDERS' EQUITY	–	EXPENSES
0	=	+6,000,000			–	6,000,000

Assume that defects add up to $5,800,000, and Black & Decker will replace the defective products. Black & Decker then records the following:

Estimated Warranty Payable	5,800,000	
Inventory		5,800,000
To replace defective products sold under warranty.		

If Black & Decker paid cash to satisfy the warranty, then the credit would be to Cash rather than to Inventory.

ASSETS	=	LIABILITIES	+	STOCKHOLDERS' EQUITY
–5,800,000	=	–5,800,000	+	0

Check Point 8-3

Check Point 8-4

stop AND think. . .

In the preceding sequence, what would Black & Decker report on its income statement and balance sheet?

Answer:

Income statement:	Warranty expense	$6,000,000
Balance sheet:	Estimated warranty payable ($6,000,000 – $5,800,000)	$ 200,000

Contingent Liabilities. A *contingent liability* is not an actual liability. Instead, it is a potential liability that depends on a *future* event arising out of past events. The Financial Accounting Standards Board (FASB) provides these guidelines to account for contingent losses (or expenses) and their related liabilities:

1. Record an actual liability if it is *probable* that the loss (or expense) will occur and the *amount can be reasonably estimated*. Warranty expense is an example.
2. Report the contingency in a financial statement note if it is *reasonably possible* that a loss (or expense) will occur. Lawsuits in progress are a prime example. AMR Corporation includes a lengthy note on its financial statements to report contingent liabilities.

3. There is no need to report a contingent loss that is unlikely to occur. Instead, wait until an actual transaction clears up the situation. For example, suppose **Del Monte Foods** grows vegetables in Nicaragua, and the Nicaraguan government issues a mild threat to confiscate the assets of all foreign companies. Del Monte will report nothing about the contingency if the probability of a loss is considered remote.

AMR Corporation reported its contingencies (type 2 above) in the following note:

> **Note 4, Commitments, Contingencies, and Guarantees (excerpt)**
> **The company is involved in certain claims and litigation related to its operations. In the opinion of management, liabilities, if any, arising from these claims and litigation would not have a material adverse effect on the Company's consolidated financial position, results of operations, or cash flows.**

Check Point 8-5

The contingent liability may arise from lawsuits that claim wrongdoing by AMR and seek damages through the courts. If the court rules in favor of AMR, there is no liability. But if the ruling favors the plaintiff, then AMR will have an actual liability. It would be unethical to omit these disclosures from the financial statements. Investors need this information to properly evaluate AMR's stock.

ACCOUNTING ALERT

Are All Your Liabilities Reported on the Balance Sheet?

The big danger with liabilities is that you may fail to report a significant debt on your balance sheet. What is the consequence of missing a liability or two? You will definitely overstate your current ratio and your acid-test ratio, and you may also overstate your net income. In short, your financial statements will make you look better than you really are. Any such error, if significant, hurts a company's credibility.

The unrecorded-liability problem is so well understood that auditors run a standard *test for unrecorded liabilities*. Which type of liability is easiest to overlook? It's not notes payable, because they are written promises signed by the debtor. Most other types of long-term liabilities also have documentary evidence that is hard to overlook.

The easiest liabilities to miss are accounts payable and accrued expenses payable. Most companies such as AMR Corporation, UAL Corporation, and Home Depot owe thousands of creditors on account. It is easy to miss a few accounts payable. Accrued expenses payable are the easiest to overlook because accrued expenses are not always supported by specific documents. Take, for example, interest payable. Unless the interest payment date falls on December 31, you must accrue the interest expense you still owe at year end. At December 31, you don't get a bill for interest payable due next April; you just have to know to accrue the interest expense at year end. Likewise for estimated warranty payable, employee vacation pay, and payroll taxes. You don't get a bill for these liabilities, so you must take special care to accrue them.

Contingent liabilities are very easy to overlook because they aren't actual debts. How would you feel if you owned stock in a company that failed to report a large contingency? Suppose the contingency materialized and put the company out of business. If you had known of the contingency, you might have sold the stock and avoided the loss. In this case, you would hire a lawyer to file suit against the company for negligent financial reporting.

To sniff out any unrecorded liabilities, auditors examine all the client's cash payments immediately after year end. Most payments during January will be for liabilities that you owed at December 31. Auditors trace all January payments back to the December 31 list of liabilities. Any payments that don't match up with December 31 liabilities may signal an unrecorded liability. The auditor then forces the client to add all unrecorded liabilities to the list and report them on the December 31 balance sheet.

The take-away lesson from this accounting alert is this:

- Examine contingent liabilities carefully. They aren't real liabilities yet, but if they go the wrong way, they may kill the company.

MID-CHAPTER Summary Problem

Assume that the **Estée Lauder Companies, Inc.** faced the following liability situations at June 30, 20X4, the end of the company's fiscal year:

a. Long-term debt totals $100 million and is payable in annual installments of $10 million each. The interest rate on the debt is 7%, and the interest is paid each December 31.

b. The company pays royalties on its purchased trademarks. Royalties for the trademarks are equal to a percentage of Estée Lauder's sales. Assume that sales in 20X4 were $400 million and were subject to a royalty rate of 3%. At June 30, 20X4, Estée Lauder owes two-thirds of the year's royalty, to be paid in July.

c. Salary expense for the last payroll period of the year was $900,000. Of this amount, employees' withheld income tax totaled $88,000 and FICA taxes were $61,000. These payroll amounts will be paid in early July.

d. On fiscal year 20X4 sales of $400 million, management estimates warranty expense of 2%. One year ago, at June 30, 20X3, Estimated Warranty Liability stood at $3 million. Warranty payments were $9 million during the year ended June 30, 20X4.

Show how Estée Lauder would report these liabilities on its balance sheet at June 30, 20X4.

Answer

a. Current liabilities:	
Current installment of long-term debt	$10,000,000
Interest payable ($100,000,000 × 0.07 × 6/12)	3,500,000
Long-term debt ($100,000,000 − $10,000,000)	90,000,000
b. Current liabilities:	
Royalties payable ($400,000,000 × 0.03 × 2/3)	8,000,000
c. Current liabilities:	
Salary payable ($900,000 − $88,000 − $61,000)	751,000
Employee income tax payable	88,000
FICA tax payable	61,000
d. Current liabilities:	
Estimated warranty payable	2,000,000
[$3,000,000 + ($400,000,000 × 0.02) − $9,000,000]	

Long-Term Liabilities: Bonds

Bonds payable
Groups of notes payable (bonds) issued to multiple lenders called *bondholders*.

Large companies such as AMR Corporation, Home Depot, and **DaimlerChrysler Corporation** cannot borrow billions from a single lender. So how do large corporations borrow huge amounts? They issue (sell) bonds to the public. **Bonds payable** are groups of notes payable issued to multiple lenders, called *bondholders*. AMR needs airplanes and can borrow large amounts by issuing bonds to thousands of individual investors, who each lend it a modest amount. AMR receives the cash it needs, and each investor limits risk by diversifying investments—not putting all the "eggs in one basket." Here we treat bonds payable and notes payable together because their accounting is the same.

Bonds: An Introduction

Each bond payable is, in effect, a note payable. Bonds payable are debts of the issuing company.

Purchasers of bonds receive a bond certificate, which carries the issuing company's name. The certificate also states the *principal*, which is typically stated in units of $1,000;

■ **EXHIBIT 8-2** Bond (Note) Certificate

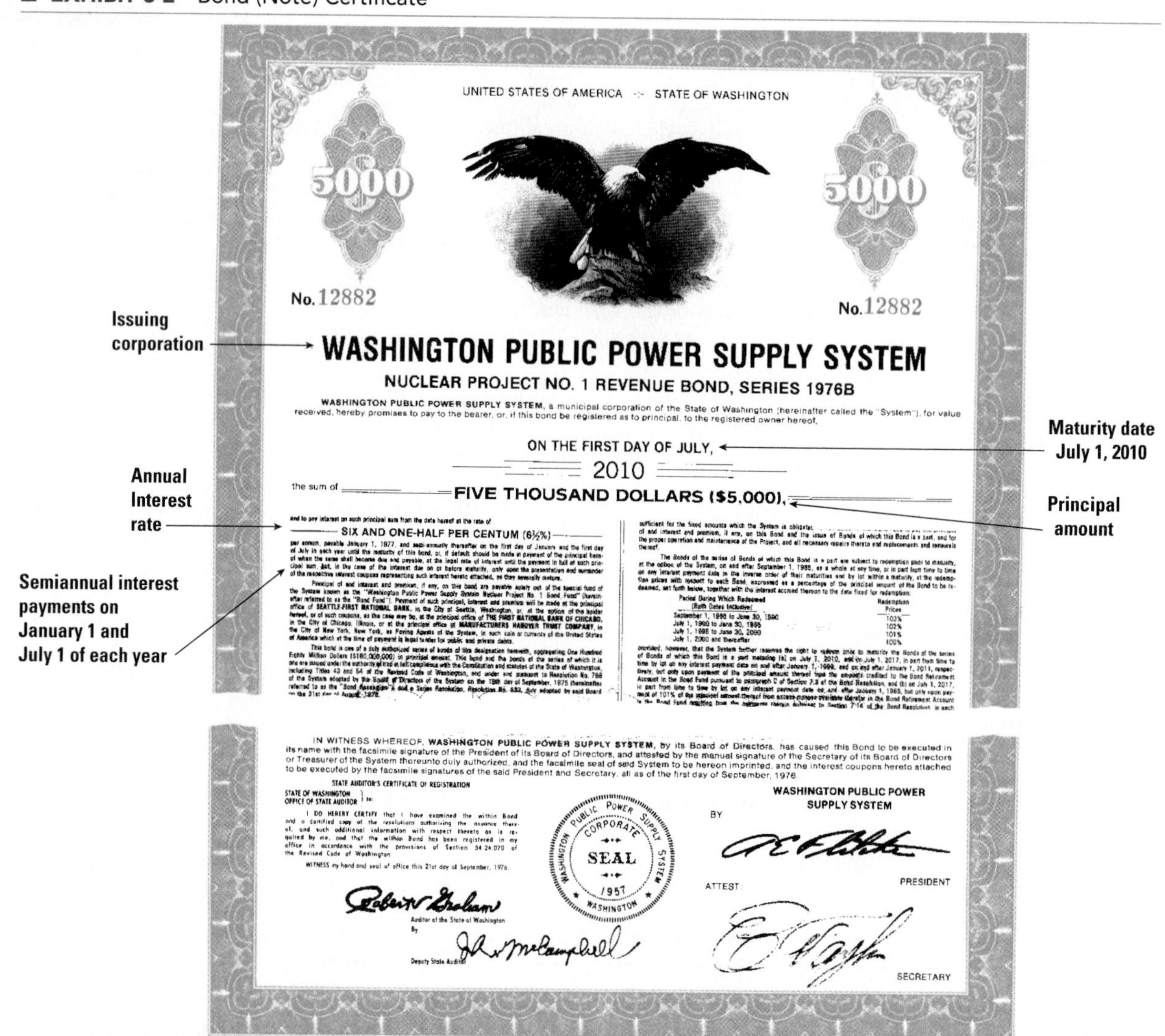

principal is also called the bond *face value*, *maturity value*, or *par value*. The bond obligates the issuing company to pay the debt at a specific future time called the *maturity date*.

Bondholders loan their money to companies for a price: *interest*. Interest is the rental fee on money borrowed. The bond certificate states the interest rate that the issuer will pay the holder and the dates that the interest payments are due (generally twice a year). Exhibit 8-2, on the previous page, shows an actual bond certificate.

Issuing bonds usually requires the services of a securities firm, such as Merrill Lynch, to act as the underwriter of the bond issue. The **underwriter** purchases the bonds from the issuing company and resells them to its clients, or it may sell the bonds to its clients and earn a commission on the sale.

Underwriter
Organization that purchases the bonds from an issuing company and resells them to its clients or sells the bonds for a commission, agreeing to buy all unsold bonds.

Types of Bonds. All the bonds in a particular issue may mature at a specified time (**term bonds**) or in installments over a period of time (**serial bonds**). Serial bonds are like installment notes payable. AMR Corporation's long-term debts are serial in nature because they are payable in installments.

Secured, or *mortgage*, *bonds* give the bondholder the right to take specified assets of the issuer if the company *defaults*—that is, fails to pay interest or principal. *Unsecured bonds*, called **debentures**, are backed only by the good faith of the borrower. Debentures carry a higher rate of interest than secured bonds because debentures are riskier investments.

Term bonds
Bonds that all mature at the same time for a particular issue.

Serial bonds
Bonds that mature in installments over a period of time.

Debentures
Unsecured bonds—bonds backed only by the good faith of the borrower.

Bond Prices and the Time Value of Money. Investors may buy and sell bonds through bond markets. The most famous bond market is the *New York Exchange*, which lists several thousand bonds. Bond prices are quoted at a percentage of their maturity value. For example, a $1,000 bond quoted at 100 is bought or sold for $1,000, which is 100% of its face value. The same bond quoted at 101.5 has a market price of $1,015 (101.5% of face value = $1,000 × 1.015). Prices are quoted as percentages. A $1,000 bond quoted at 88.375 is priced at $883.75 ($1,000 × 0.88375).

Exhibit 8-3 contains actual price information for the bonds of **Ohio Edison Company**, taken from *The Wall Street Journal*. On this particular day, 12 of Ohio Edison's 9½%, $1,000 face-value bonds maturing in the year 2006 (indicated by 06) were traded. The bonds' highest price on this day was $795 ($1,000 × 0.795). The lowest price of the day was $785 ($1,000 × 0.785). The closing price (last sale price of the day) was $795. This price was 2 points higher than the closing price of the preceding day. What was the bonds' closing price the preceding day? It was 77.5 (79.5 − 2).

Check Point 8-6

■ **EXHIBIT 8-3**
Bond Price Information for Ohio Edison Company (OhEd)

Bonds	Volume	High	Low	Close	Net Change
OhEd 9½ 06	12	79.5	78.5	79.5	+2

A bond issued at a price above its face (par) value is said to be issued at a **premium**, and a bond issued at a price below face (par) value has a **discount**. As a bond nears maturity, its market price moves toward par value. On the maturity date, a bond's market value exactly equals its par value because the company that issued the bond pays that amount to retire the bond.

Premium (on a bond)
Excess of a bond's issue price over its face (par) value.

Discount (on a bond)
Excess of a bond's face (par value) over its issue price.

A dollar received today is worth more than a dollar to be received in the future. You may invest today's dollar immediately and earn income from it. But if you must wait to receive the dollar, you forgo the interest revenue. Money earns income over time, a fact called the *time value of money*. Let's examine how the time value of money affects the pricing of bonds.

Assume that a bond with a face value of $1,000 reaches maturity 3 years from today and carries no interest. Would you pay $1,000 to purchase the bond? No, because the payment of $1,000 today to receive the same amount in the future provides you with no income on the investment. You would not be taking advantage of the time value of money. Just how much would you pay today to receive $1,000 at the end of 3 years? The answer is some amount *less* than $1,000. Let's suppose that you feel $750 is a good price. By investing $750 now to receive $1,000 later, you earn $250 interest revenue over the 3 years. The issuing company sees the transaction this way: It pays you $250 interest for the use of your $750 for 3 years.

Present value
Amount a person would invest now to receive a greater amount at a future date.

The amount that a person would invest *at the present time* to receive a greater amount at a future date is called the **present value** of a future amount. In our example, $750 is the present value of the $1,000 to be received 3 years later.

Our $750 bond price is a reasonable estimate. The exact present value of any future amount depends on

1. The amount of the future payment
2. The length of time from the investment date to the date when the future amount is to be paid
3. The interest rate during the period

Present value is always less than the future amount. We discuss how present value is computed in Appendix C at the end of the book (pages 679–688).

How Bond Interest Rates Determine Bond Prices. Bonds are always sold at their *market price*, which is the amount investors are willing to pay. Market price is the bond's present value, which equals the present value of the principal payment plus the present value of the cash interest payments (which are made semiannually [twice a year], annually, or quarterly over the term of the bond).

Two interest rates work to set the price of a bond.

Stated interest rate
Interest rate that determines the amount of cash interest the borrower pays and the investor receives each year.

Market interest rate
Interest rate that investors demand for loaning their money. Also called *effective interest rate*.

- The **stated interest rate** is the interest rate that determines the amount of cash interest the borrower pays—and the investor receives—each year. For example, AMR Corporation's 9% bonds have a stated interest rate of 9%. Thus, AMR pays $9,000 of interest annually on each $100,000 bond. Each semiannual payment is $4,500 ($100,000 × 0.09 × $\frac{6}{12}$).
- The **market interest rate**, or *effective interest rate*, is the rate that investors demand for loaning their money. The market rate varies by the minute.

  A company may issue bonds with a stated interest rate that differs from the prevailing market interest rate.

Exhibit 8-4 shows how the stated interest rate and the market interest rate interact to determine the issuance price of a bond payable for three separate cases. AMR, for example, may issue its 9% bonds when the market rate has risen to 10%. Will the AMR bonds attract investors in this market? No, because investors can earn 10% on other bonds of similar risk. Therefore, investors will purchase AMR bonds only at a price less than their par value. The difference between the lower price and face value is a *discount* (Exhibit 8-4). Conversely, if the market interest rate is 8%, AMR's 9% bonds will be so attractive that investors will pay more than face value for them. The difference between the higher price and face value is a *premium*.

■ **EXHIBIT 8-4**

How the Stated Interest Rate and the Market Interest Rate Interact to Determine the Price of a Bond

Issuance Price of Bonds Payable				
Case A:				
Stated interest rate on a bond payable	equals	Market interest rate	Therefore,	Price of par (face, or maturity) value
Example: 9%	=	9%	→	*Par: $1,000 bond issued for $1,000*
Case B:				
Stated interest rate on a bond payable	less than	Market interest rate	Therefore,	Discount price (price *below* par)
Example: 9%	<	10%	→	*Discount: $1,000 bond issued for a price* below *$1,000*
Case C:				
Stated interest rate on a bond payable	greater than	Market interest rate	Therefore,	Premium price (price *above* par)
Example: 9%	>	8%	→	*Premium: $1,000 bond issued for a price* above *$1,000*

Check Point 8-7

Issuing Bonds Payable at Par Value

OBJECTIVE

2 **Account** for bonds payable transactions

Suppose AMR Corporation has $50 million in 9% bonds that mature in 5 years. Assume that AMR issues these bonds at par on January 1, 2006. The issuance entry is

2006			
Jan. 1	Cash	50,000,000	
	Bonds Payable		50,000,000
	To issue bonds at par.		

ASSETS	=	LIABILITIES	+	STOCKHOLDERS' EQUITY
+50,000,000	=	+50,000,000	+	0

AMR, the borrower, makes a one-time entry to record the receipt of cash and the issuance of bonds. Afterward, investors buy and sell the bonds through the bond markets. These later buy-and-sell transactions between outside investors do *not* involve AMR at all.

Interest payments occur each January 1 and July 1. AMR's entry to record the first semiannual interest payment is:

2006			
July 1	Interest Expense ($50,000,000 × 0.09 × 6/12)	2,250,000	
	Cash		2,250,000
	To pay semiannual interest.		

ASSETS	=	LIABILITIES	+	STOCKHOLDERS' EQUITY	−	EXPENSES
−2,250,000	=	0	+		−	2,250,000

At year end, AMR accrues interest expense and interest payable for 6 months (July through December), as follows:

2006			
Dec. 31	Interest Expense ($50,000,000 × 0.09 × 6/12)	2,250,000	
	Interest Payable		2,250,000
	To accrue interest.		

ASSETS	=	LIABILITIES	+	STOCKHOLDERS' EQUITY	–	EXPENSES
0	=	+2,250,000	+		–	2,250,000

At maturity, AMR pays off the bonds as follows:

Check Point 8-8

2011			
Jan. 1	Bonds Payable	50,000,000	
	Cash		50,000,000
	To pay bonds payable at maturity.		

ASSETS	=	LIABILITIES	+	STOCKHOLDERS' EQUITY
–50,000,000	=	–50,000,000		

Issuing Bonds Payable at a Discount

Market conditions may force a company to issue bonds at a discount. Suppose AMR Corporation issues $100,000 of its 9%, 5-year bonds when the market interest rate is 10%. The market price of the bonds drops, and AMR receives $96,149[1] at issuance. The transaction is recorded as follows:

2006			
Jan. 1	Cash	96,149	
	Discount on Bonds Payable	3,851	
	Bonds Payable		100,000
	To issue bonds at a discount.		

ASSETS	=	LIABILITIES	+	STOCKHOLDERS' EQUITY
+96,149	=	–3,851	+	0
		+100,000		

Now the bonds payable accounts have a net balance of $96,149 as follows:

Bonds Payable		Discount on Bonds Payable		Net carrying amount of bonds payable
100,000	–	3,851	=	$96,149

AMR's balance sheet immediately after issuance of the bonds would report the following:

Total current liabilities		$ XXX
Long-term liabilities:		
Bonds payable, 9%, due 2011	$100,000	
Less: Discount on bonds payable	(3,851)	96,149

[1]Appendix C at the end of this book shows how to determine the price of this bond.

Discount on Bonds Payable is a contra account to Bonds Payable, a decrease in the company's liabilities. Subtracting the discount from Bonds Payable yields the *carrying amount* of the bonds. Thus, AMR's liability is $96,149, which is the amount the company borrowed.

■ Taking Action What Is AMR Corporation's Interest Expense on These Bonds Payable?

OBJECTIVE

3 **Measure** interest expense

AMR pays interest on its bonds semiannually, which is common practice. Each semiannual interest *payment* remains the same over the life of the bonds:

$$\text{Semiannual interest payment} = \$100{,}000 \times 0.09 \times 6/12 = \$4{,}500$$

This payment amount is fixed by the bond contract. But AMR's interest *expense* increases from period to period as the bonds march toward maturity because these bonds were issued at a discount.

Panel A of Exhibit 8-5 repeats the AMR Corporation bond data we've been using so far. Panel B provides an amortization table that does two things:

- Determines the periodic interest expense
- Shows the bond carrying amount

■ EXHIBIT 8-5 Debt Amortization for a Bond Discount

Panel A—Bond Data

Issue date—January 1, 2006
Maturity (face, or par) value—$100,000
Stated interest rate—9%
Interest paid—4 ½% semiannually, $4,500 = $100,000 × 0.09 × 6/12
Maturity date—January 1, 2011
Market interest rate at time of issue—10% annually, 5% semiannually
Issue price—$96,149

Panel B—Amortization Table

	A	B	C	D	E
Semiannual Interest Date	Interest Payment (4 ½% of Maturity Value)	Interest Expense (5% of Preceding Bond Carrying Amount)	Discount Amortization (B – A)	Discount Account Balance (Preceding D – C)	Bond Carrying Amount ($100,000 – D)
Jan. 1, 2006				$3,851	$ 96,149
July 1	$4,500	$4,807	$307	3,544	96,456
Jan. 1, 2007	4,500	4,823	323	3,221	96,779
July 1	4,500	4,839	339	2,882	97,118
Jan. 1, 2008	4,500	4,856	356	2,526	97,474
July 1	4,500	4,874	374	2,152	97,848
Jan. 1, 2009	4,500	4,892	392	1,760	98,240
July 1	4,500	4,912	412	1,348	98,652
Jan. 1, 2010	4,500	4,933	433	915	99,085
July 1	4,500	4,954	454	461	99,539
Jan. 1, 2011	4,500	4,961*	461	-0-	100,000

*Adjusted for effect of rounding

Notes
- Column A The semiannual interest payments are constant—fixed by the bond contract.
- Column B The interest expense each period = the preceding bond carrying amount × the market interest rate. Interest expense increases as the bond carrying amount (E) increases.
- Column C The discount amortization (C) is the excess of interest expense (B) over interest payment (A).
- Column D The discount balance (D) decreases when amortized.
- Column E The bond carrying amount (E) increases from $96,149 at issuance to $100,000 at maturity.

Study the exhibit carefully because the amounts we will be using come directly from the amortization table. This exhibit is an example of the *effective-interest method of amortization*, which is the correct way to measure interest expense.

Interest Expense on Bonds Issued at a Discount

In Exhibit 8-5, AMR Corporation borrowed $96,149 cash but must pay $100,000 when the bonds mature. What happens to the $3,851 balance of the discount account over the life of the bond issue?

The $3,851 is additional interest expense to AMR over and above the stated interest that AMR pays each 6 months. Exhibit 8-6 graphs the interest expense and the interest payment on the AMR bonds over their lifetime. Observe that the semiannual interest payment is fixed—by contract—at $4,500 (column A). But the amount of interest expense (column B) increases as the bond marches toward maturity.

■ **EXHIBIT 8-6**

Interest Expense on Bonds Payable Issued at a Discount

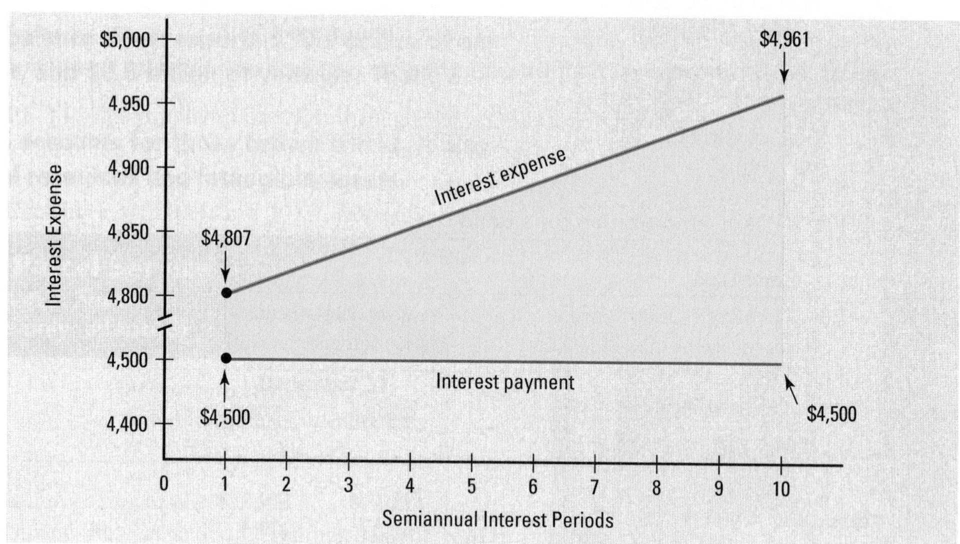

The discount is allocated to interest expense through amortization over the term of the bonds. Exhibit 8-7 illustrates the amortization of the bonds from $96,149 at issuance to $100,000 at maturity. These amounts come from Exhibit 8-5, column E.

■ **EXHIBIT 8-7**

Amortizing Bonds Payable Issued at a Discount

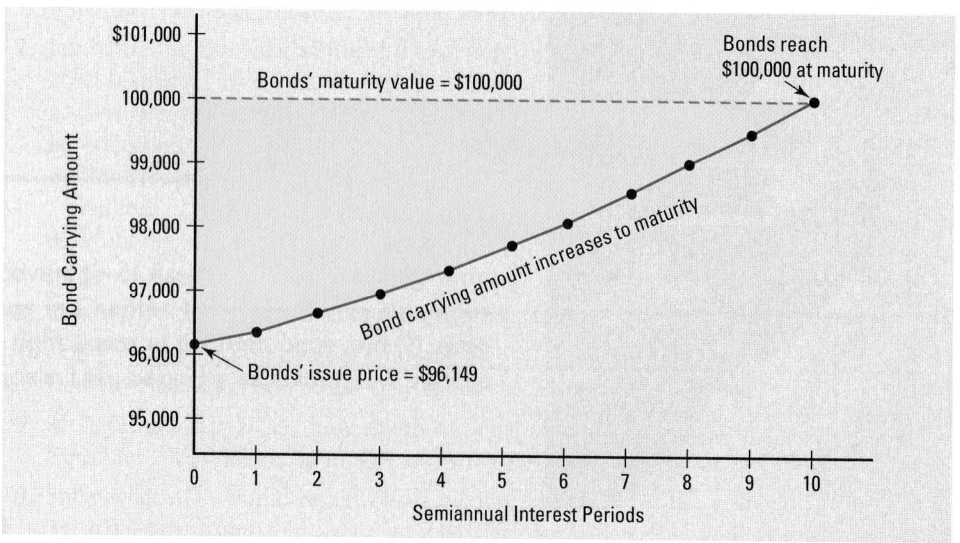

stop AND think. . .

What explains the difference between interest expense and the cash payment of interest for bonds issued at a discount? Why is interest expense always greater than the cash payment?

Answer:
Amortization of the bond discount is the difference between interest expense and the cash payment of interest. Interest expense exceeds the interest payment because AMR borrowed $96,149 but must pay $100,000 at maturity.

Now let's see how AMR accounts for these bonds issued at a discount. AMR issued its bonds on January 1, 2006. On July 1, AMR made the first semiannual interest payment. But AMR's interest expense is greater than its payment of $4,500. AMR's journal entry to record interest expense and the interest payment for the first 6 months follows (with all amounts taken from Exhibit 8-5):

2006			
July 1	Interest Expense	4,807	
	Discount on Bonds Payable		307
	Cash		4,500
	To pay semiannual interest and amortize bond discount.		

ASSETS	=	LIABILITIES	+	STOCKHOLDERS' EQUITY	−	EXPENSES
−4,500	=	+ 307			−	4,807

The credit to Discount on Bonds Payable accomplishes two purposes:

- It amortizes the bonds as they march toward maturity value.
- It amortizes the discount to interest expense.

At December 31, 2006, AMR accrues interest and amortizes the bonds for July through December with this entry (amounts from Exhibit 8-5):

2006			
Dec. 31	Interest Expense	4,823	
	Discount on Bonds Payable		323
	Interest Payable		4,500
	To accrue semiannual interest and amortize bond discount.		

ASSETS	=	LIABILITIES	+	STOCKHOLDERS' EQUITY	−	EXPENSES
0	=	+ 323			−	4,823
		+4,500				

At December 31, 2006, AMR's bond accounts appear as follows:

Bonds Payable		Discount on Bonds Payable	
	100,000	**3,851**	**307**
			323
		Bal. 3,221	

Bond carrying amount, $96,779 = ($100,000 − $3,221) from Exhibit 8-5

stop AND think. . .

What would AMR Corporation's 2006 income statement and year-end balance sheet report for these bonds?

Answer:

Income Statement for 2006		
Interest expense ($4,807 + $4,823)		$ 9,630
Balance Sheet at December 31, 2006		
Current liabilities:		
Interest payable		$ 4,500
Long-term liabilities:		
Bonds payable	$100,000	
Less: Discount on bonds payable	(3,221)	96,779

Check Point 8-9

Check Point 8-10

At maturity on January 1, 2011, the discount will have been amortized to zero, and the bonds' carrying amount will be $100,000. AMR will retire the bonds by paying $100,000 to the bondholders.

Issuing Bonds Payable at a Premium

Let's modify the AMR Corporation bond example to illustrate issuance of the bonds at a premium. Assume that AMR issues $100,000 of 5-year, 9% bonds that pay interest semiannually. If the 9% bonds are issued when the market interest rate is 8%, their issue price is $104,100.[2] The premium on these bonds is $4,100, and Exhibit 8-8 shows how to amortize the bonds by the effective-interest method. In practice, bond premiums are rare because few companies issue their bonds to pay cash interest above the market interest rate. We cover bond premiums for completeness.

AMR's entries to record issuance of the bonds on January 1, 2006, and to make the first interest payment and amortize the bonds on July 1, are as follows:

2006			
Jan. 1	Cash	104,100	
	Bonds Payable		100,000
	Premium on Bonds Payable		4,100
	To issue bonds at a premium.		

ASSETS	=	LIABILITIES	+	STOCKHOLDERS' EQUITY
+104,100	=	+100,000	+	0
		+4,100		

2006			
July 1	Interest Expense	4,164	
	Premium on Bonds Payable	336	
	Cash		4,500
	To pay semiannual interest and amortize bond premium.		

ASSETS	=	LIABILITIES	+	STOCKHOLDERS' EQUITY	–	EXPENSES
–4,500	=	–336			–	4,164

[2]Again, Appendix C at the end of the book shows how to determine the price of this bond.

■ **EXHIBIT 8-8** Debt Amortization for a Bond Premium

Panel A—Bond Data

Issue date—January 1, 2006	Maturity date—January 1, 2011
Maturity (face, or par) value—$100,000	Market interest rate at time of issue—8% annually, 4% semiannually
Stated interest rate—9%	Issue price—$104,100

Interest paid—4 ½% semiannually, $4,500 = $100,000 × 0.09 × 6/12

Panel B—Amortization Table

	A	B	C	D	E
Semiannual Interest Date	**Interest Payment (4 ½% of Maturity Value)**	**Interest Expense (4% of Preceding Bond Carrying Amount)**	**Premium Amortization (A – B)**	**Premium Account Balance (Preceding D – C)**	**Bond Carrying Amount ($100,000 + D)**
Jan. 1, 2006				$4,100	$104,100
July 1	$4,500	$4,164	$336	3,764	103,764
Jan. 1, 2007	4,500	4,151	349	3,415	103,415
July 1	4,500	4,137	363	3,052	103,052
Jan. 1, 2008	4,500	4,122	378	2,674	102,674
July 1	4,500	4,107	393	2,281	102,281
Jan. 1, 2009	4,500	4,091	409	1,872	101,872
July 1	4,500	4,075	425	1,447	101,447
Jan. 1, 2010	4,500	4,058	442	1,005	101,005
July 1	4,500	4,040	460	545	100,545
Jan. 1, 2011	4,500	3,955*	545	-0-	100,000

*Adjusted for effect of rounding

Notes

- Column A — The semiannual interest payments are constant—fixed by the bond contract.
- Column B — The interest expense each period = the preceding bond carrying amount × the market interest rate. Interest expense decreases as the bond carrying amount (E) decreases.
- Column C — The premium amortization (C) is the excess of interest payment (A) over interest expense (B).
- Column D — The premium balance (D) decreases when amortized.
- Column E — The bond carrying amount (E) decreases from $104,100 at issuance to $100,000 at maturity.

Immediately after issuing the bonds at a premium on January 1, 2006, AMR Corporation would report the bonds payable on the balance sheet as follows:

Total current liabilities		$ XXX
Long-term liabilities:		
Bonds payable	$100,000	
Premium on bonds payable	4,100	104,100

A premium is *added* to the balance of bonds payable to determine the carrying amount.

In Exhibit 8-8 AMR Corporation borrowed $104,100 cash but must pay only $100,000 at maturity. The $4,100 premium is a reduction in AMR's interest expense over the term of the bonds. Exhibit 8-9 graphs AMR's interest payments (column A from Exhibit 8-8) and interest expense (column B).

The premium decreases interest expense through amortization each period over the term of the bonds. Exhibit 8-10 diagrams the amortization of the bonds from the issue price of $104,100 to maturity value of $100,000. All amounts are taken from Exhibit 8-8.

■ **EXHIBIT 8-9**

Interest Expense on Bonds Payable Issued at a Premium

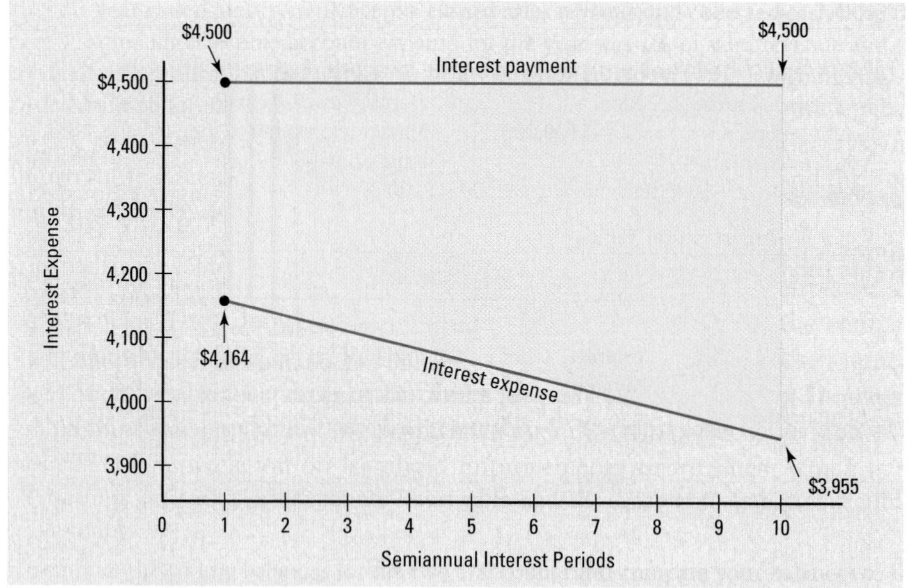

■ **EXHIBIT 8-10**

Amortizing Bonds Payable Issued at a Premium

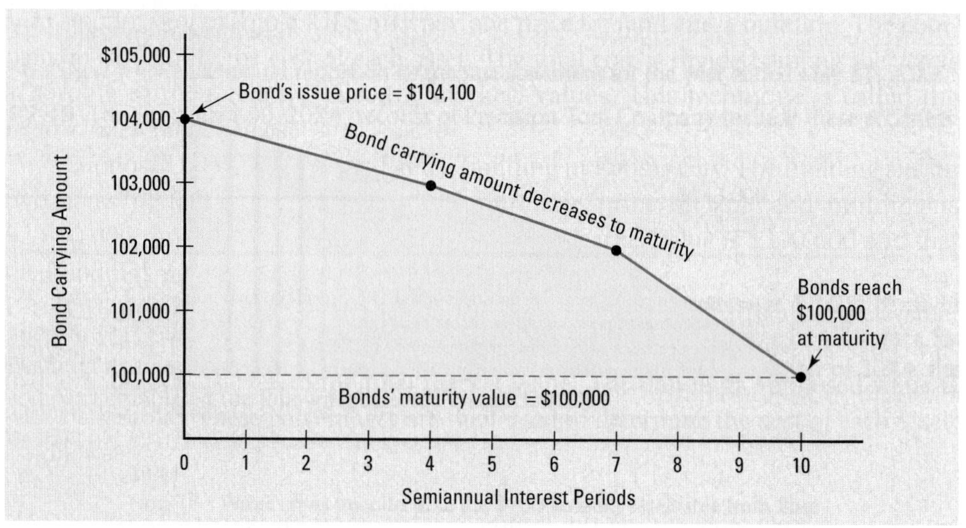

The Straight-Line Amortization Method: A Quick and Dirty Way to Measure Interest Expense

There is a less precise way to amortize bond discount or premium. Called the *straight-line amortization method*, it divides a bond discount (or premium) into equal periodic amounts over the bond's term. The amount of interest expense is thus the same for each interest period.

Let's apply the straight-line method to the AMR bonds issued at a discount and illustrated in Exhibit 8-5 (p. 377). Suppose AMR's financial vice president is considering issuing the 9% bonds at $96,149. To estimate semiannual interest expense on the bonds, the executive can use the straight-line amortization method for the bond discount.

	Semiannual cash interest payment ($100,000 × 0.09 × 6/12)	$4,500
+	Semiannual amortization of discount ($3,851 ÷ 10)	385
=	Estimated semiannual interest expense	$4,885

AMR's entry to record interest and amortization of the bond discount under the straight-line amortization method would be

2006			
July 1	Interest Expense	4,885	
	Discount on Bonds Payable		385
	Cash		4,500
	To pay semiannual interest and amortize bond discount.		

Check Point 8-11

Check Point 8-12

ASSETS	=	LIABILITIES	+	STOCKHOLDERS' EQUITY	–	EXPENSES
–4,500	=	+ 385			–	4,885

Generally accepted accounting principles (GAAP) permit the straight-line amortization method only when its amounts differ insignificantly from the amounts determined by the effective-interest method.

Taking Action Should We Retire Bonds Payable Before Maturity?

Normally, companies wait until maturity to pay off, or *retire*, their bonds payable. But companies sometimes retire bonds early. The main reason for doing so is to relieve the pressure of making interest payments. Also, the company may be able to borrow at a lower interest rate.

Some bonds are **callable**, which means that the issuer may *call*, or pay off, those bonds at a specified price whenever the issuer so chooses. The call price is often a percentage point or two above the par value, perhaps 101 or 102. Callable bonds give the issuer the benefit of being able to pay off the bonds whenever it is most favorable to do so. The alternative to calling the bonds is to purchase them in the open market at their current market price.

Callable bonds
Bonds that the issuer may call (pay off) at a specified price whenever the issuer wants.

AMR Corporation has $300 million of debenture bonds outstanding. Assume the unamortized discount is $30 million. Lower interest rates may convince management to pay off these bonds now. Assume that the bonds are callable at 102. If the market price of the bonds is 99, will AMR call the bonds or purchase them in the open market? Market price is the better choice because the market price is lower than the call price. Retiring the bonds at 99 results in a loss of $27 million, computed as follows:

	Millions
Par value of bonds being retired	$300
Less: Unamortized discount	(30)
Carrying amount of the bonds	270
Market price ($300 × .99)	297
Loss on retirement of bonds payable	$ 27

Gains and losses on early retirement of debt are reported as Other income (loss) on the income statement.

stop AND think. . .

Several years ago Quill Corporation issued $300,000 of 10-year bonds at a discount. The carrying value of the bonds is $299,000. Quill retires half the bonds by paying the market price of 96. What is the amount of Quill's gain or loss on retirement of the bonds payable?

Answer:

Carrying amount of Quill Corp.'s bonds payable	$299,000
Portion being retired	× .50
Carrying amount of bonds being retired	$149,500
Call price of the bonds ($150,000 × .96)	144,000
Gain on retirement of bonds payable	$ 5,500

Convertible Bonds and Notes

Convertible bonds (or notes) Bonds (or notes) that may be converted into the issuing company's common stock at the investor's option.

Some corporate bonds may be converted into the issuing company's common stock. These bonds are called **convertible bonds** (or **notes**). For investors they combine the safety of assured receipt of interest and principal on the bonds with the opportunity for gains on the stock. The conversion feature is so attractive that investors usually accept a lower interest rate than they would on nonconvertible bonds. The lower cash interest payments benefit the issuer. If the market price of the issuing company's stock gets high enough, the bondholders will convert the bonds into stock.

AMR Corporation has convertible notes payable of $300 million. If AMR stock price rises significantly, the noteholders will convert the notes into the company's common stock. Conversion of the notes payable into stock will decrease AMR's debt and increase its equity.

Assume the noteholders convert half the notes into 4 million shares of AMR Corporation common stock ($1 par) on May 14. AMR makes the following entry in its accounting records:

May 14	Notes Payable ($300,000,000 × ½)	$150,000,000	
	Common Stock (4,000,000 × $1 par) . .		4,000,000
	Paid-in Capital in Excess of Par-Common		146,000,000
	To record conversion of notes payable.		

ASSETS	=	LIABILITIES	+	STOCKHOLDERS' EQUITY
0	=	−150,000,000		+4,000,000 + 146,000,000

The carrying amount of the notes ($150 million) becomes stockholders' equity. Common Stock is recorded at its *par value*, which is a dollar amount assigned to each share of stock. In this case, the credit to Common Stock is $4,000,000 (4,000,000 shares × $1 par value per share). The extra carrying amount of the notes payable ($146,000,000) is credited to another stockholders' equity account, Paid in Capital in Excess of Par—Common. We'll be using this account in various ways in the next chapter.

■ Taking Action Financing Operations with Bonds or Stock?

OBJECTIVE

4 **Understand** the advantages and disadvantages of borrowing

Managers must decide how to pay for assets. The money to purchase an asset may be financed by retained earnings, by issuing stock, or by borrowing on bonds payable. Each strategy has its advantages:

1. ***Issuing stock*** creates no liabilities or interest expense and is less risky to the issuing corporation.
2. ***Issuing notes or bonds payable*** does not dilute stock ownership or control of the corporation. It results in higher earnings per share because the earnings on borrowed money usually exceed interest expense.

Earnings per share (EPS) is the amount of a company's net income for each share of its stock. EPS is perhaps the single most important statistic used to evaluate companies because it is a standard measure of operating performance for comparing companies of different sizes and from different industries.

Earnings per share (EPS) Amount of a company's net income per share of its outstanding common stock.

Suppose AMR Corporation needs $50,000 for expansion. AMR has net income of $300,000 and 100,000 shares of commons stock outstanding. Management is considering two financing plans. Plan 1 is to issue $500,000 of 10% bonds payable, and plan 2 is to issue 50,000 shares of common stock for $500,000. Management believes the new cash can be invested in operations to earn income of $200,000 before interest and taxes.

Exhibit 8-11 shows the earnings-per-share advantage of borrowing. As you can see, AMR Corporation's EPS amount is higher if the company borrows by issuing bonds (compare lines 9 and 10). AMR earns more on the investment ($90,000) than the interest it pays on the bonds ($50,000). This is called **trading on the equity**, or using *leverage*. It is widely used to increase earnings per share of common stock.

Trading on the equity Earning more income on borrowed money than the related interest expense, thereby increasing the earnings for the owners of the business. Also called *leverage*.

■ **EXHIBIT 8-11** Earnings-Per-Share Advantage of Borrrowing

	Plan 1 Borrow $500,000 at 10%		Plan 2 Issue 50,000 Shares of Common Stock for $500,000	
1 Net income before expansion		$300,000		$300,000
2 Expected project income before interest and income tax	$200,000		$200,000	
3 Less interest expense ($500,000 × .10)	(50,000)		0	
4 Expected project income before income tax	150,000		200,000	
5 Less income tax expense (40%)	(60,000)		(80,000)	
6 Expected project net income		90,000		120,000
7 Total company net income		$390,000		$420,000
8 Earnings per share after expansion:				
9 Plan 1 ($390,000/100,000 shares)		$3.90		
10 Plan 2 ($420,000/150,000 shares)				$2.80

In this case borrowing results in higher earnings per share than issuing stock. Borrowing has its disadvantages, however. Interest expense may be high enough to eliminate net income and lead to a cash crisis or even bankruptcy. Also, borrowing creates liabilities that accrue during bad years as well as good years. In contrast, a company that issues stock can omit its dividends during a bad year. The Making Managerial Decisions feature provides some guidance to help decide how to finance operations.

Check Point 8-13

MAKING MANAGERIAL DECISIONS

FINANCING WITH DEBT OR WITH STOCK

El Chico is the leading chain of Tex-Mex restaurants in the United States, begun by the Cuellar family in the Dallas area. Suppose El Chico is expanding into neighboring states. Take the role of Miguel Cuellar and assume you must make some key decisions about how to finance the expansion.

Decision	Guidelines
How will you finance El Chico's expansion?	Your financing plan depends on El Chico's ability to generate cash flow, your willingness to give up some control of the business, the amount of financing risk you are willing to take, and El Chico's credit rating.
Do El Chico's operations generate enough cash to meet all its financing needs?	If yes, the business needs little outside financing. There is no need to borrow. If no, the business will need to issue additional stock or borrow the money.
Are you willing to give up some of your control of the business?	If yes, then issue stock to other stockholders, who can vote their shares to elect the company's directors. If no, then borrow from bondholders, who have no vote in the management of the company.
How much financing risk are you willing to take?	If much, then borrow as much as you can, and you may increase El Chico's earnings per share. But this will increase the business's debt ratio and the risk of being unable to pay its debts. If little, then borrow sparingly. This will hold the debt ratio down and reduce the risk of default on borrowing agreements. But El Chico's earnings per share may be lower than if you were to borrow.
How good is the business's credit rating?	The better the credit rating, the easier it is to borrow on favorable terms. A good credit rating also makes it easier to issue stock. Neither stockholders nor creditors will entrust their money to a company with a bad credit rating.

■ Taking Action How Much Debt Can We Manage—The Times-Interest-Earned Ratio

We have just seen how the wise use of borrowing can increase EPS. But too much debt can lead to bankruptcy if the business cannot pay liabilities as they come due. UAL Inc. fell into this trap. Managers and lenders use ratios to determine how much credit risk they are taking.

Times-interest-earned ratio Ratio of income from operations to interest expense. Measures the number of times that operating income can cover interest expense. Also called the *interest-coverage ratio*.

The debt ratio measures the effect of debt on the company's *financial position* but says nothing about the ability to pay interest expense. Analysts use a second ratio—the **times-interest-earned ratio**—to relate income to interest expense. To compute this ratio, we divide *income from operations* (also called *operating income*) by interest expense. This ratio measures the number of times that operating income can *cover* interest expense. The ratio is also called the *interest-coverage ratio*. A high times-interest-earned ratio indicates ease in paying interest expense; a low value suggests difficulty. Let's see how two well-known companies, Home Depot and H.J. Heinz, compare on the times-interest-earned ratio (dollar amounts in millions).

				Home Depot	H.J. Heinz Company
Times-interest earned ratio	=	Operating income / Interest expense	=	$6,846 / $62	$1,174 / $224
				= 110 times	= 5 times

Home Depot's income from operations covers its interest expense 110 times. Heinz's interest-coverage ratio is 5 times. H.J. Heinz is much more risky on this ratio than Home Depot.

Check Point 8-14

stop AND think. . .

Which company, Home Depot or Heinz, would you expect to have the higher debt ratio? Compute the two companies' debt ratios to confirm your opinion. Summarized balance sheets follow.

	Millions	
	Home Depot	**Heinz**
Total assets	$34,437	$9,225
Total liabilities	$12,030	$8,026
Stockholders' equity	22,407	1,199
Total liabilities and equity	$34,437	$9,225

Answer:

As expected, Heinz has a much higher debt ratio than Home Depot, as follows (dollar amounts in millions):

				Home Depot	H.J. Heinz
Debt ratio	=	Total liabilities / Total assets	=	$12,030 / $34,437	$8,026 / $9,225
				= 0.35	= 0.87

Long-Term Liabilities: Leases and Pensions

A **lease** is a rental agreement in which the tenant (**lessee**) agrees to make rent payments to the property owner (**lessor**) in exchange for the use of the asset. Leasing allows the lessee to acquire the use of a needed asset without having to make the large up-front payment that purchase agreements require. Accountants distinguish between two types of leases: operating and capital.

Lease
Rental agreement in which the tenant (lessee) agrees to make rent payments to the property owner (lessor) in exchange for the use of the asset.

Lessee
Tenant in a lease agreement.

Lessor
Property owner in a lease agreement.

Types of Leases

Operating leases are often short-term or cancelable. They give the lessee the right to use the asset but provide no continuing rights to the asset. The lessor retains the usual risks and rewards of owning the leased asset. To account for an operating lease,

Operating lease
Usually a short-term or cancelable rental agreement.

the lessee debits Rent Expense (or Lease Expense) and credits Cash for the amount of the lease payment. The lessee's books do not report the leased asset or any lease liability. Nevertheless, operating leases require the lessee to make rent payments. Therefore, an operating lease creates a liability even though the liability does not appear on the balance sheet.

Capital lease
Lease agreement that meets any one of four criteria: (1) The lease transfers title of the leased asset to the lessee. (2) The lease contains a bargain purchase option. (3) The lease term is 75% or more of the estimated useful life of the leased asset. (4) The present value of the lease payments is 90% or more of the market value of the leased asset.

Most businesses use capital leasing to finance the acquisition of some assets. A **capital lease** is a long-term and noncancelable financing obligation that is a form of debt. How do you distinguish a capital lease from an operating lease? *FASB Statement No. 13* provides the guidelines. To be classified as a capital lease, a particular lease agreement must meet any *one* of the following criteria:

1. The lease transfers title of the leased asset to the lessee at the end of the lease term. Thus, the lessee becomes the legal owner of the leased asset.
2. The lease contains a *bargain purchase option*. The lessee can be expected to purchase the leased asset and become its legal owner.
3. The lease term is 75% or more of the estimated useful life of the leased asset. The lessee uses up most of the leased asset's service potential.
4. The present value of the lease payments is 90% or more of the market value of the leased asset. In effect, the lease payments are the same as installment payments for the leased asset.

Accounting for a capital lease is much like accounting for the purchase of an asset by the lessee. The lessee enters the asset into its own accounts and records a lease liability at the beginning of the lease term. Thus, the lessee capitalizes the asset in its own financial statements even though it may never take legal title to the property.

Most companies lease some of their plant assets. AMR Corporation leases airplanes under capital leases. At December 31, 2003, AMR reported its capital leases in Note 5 of its financial statements, excerpted as follows:

Note 5 Leases (partial)
The future minimum lease payments required under capital leases [. . .] at December 31, 2003 were (in millions):

Year Ending December 31	Capital Lease Payments	
2004	$ 325	
2005	256	
2006	256	
2007	187	
2008	224	
2009 and subsequent	1,111	*This is AMR*
	2,359	*Corporation's*
Less amount representing interest	(933)	*liability under its*
Present value of . . . lease payments	$1,426 ←	*capital leases.*

The note reveals that AMR Corporation must pay a total of $2,359 million on its capital leases. The present value of this liability is $1,426 million. The present value is included in the liability figures reported on AMR's balance sheet.

■ Taking Action Do Lessees Prefer Operating Leases or Capital Leases?

Suppose you were the chief financial officer (CFO) of AMR Corporation. AMR leases assets valued at over $2 billion. AMR is the lessee (the renter) in the transaction. The lease can be structured either as an operating lease or as a capital lease. Which type of lease would you prefer for AMR? Why? Computing AMR's debt ratio two ways (new lease as an operating lease; new lease as a capital lease) will make your decision clear (using assumed figures in billions):

(dollar amounts in billions)	Operating Lease	Capital Lease
Debt ratio = $\frac{\text{Total liabilities}}{\text{Total assets}}$ =	$\frac{\$15}{\$29}$ = 0.52	$\frac{\$15 + \$2}{\$29 + \$2} = \frac{\$17}{\$31}$ = 0.55

AMR may prefer an operating lease because an operating lease adds no assets and no liabilities to the balance sheet. By contrast, a capital lease forces AMR to capitalize the leased asset and record a lease liability as though it had purchased the asset with long-term debt. As a result, a capital lease would increase AMR's debt ratio. For this reason, lessees generally prefer operating leases.

Pensions and Postretirement Liabilities

Most companies have pension plans for their employees. A **pension** is employee compensation that will be received during retirement. Companies also provide postretirement benefits, such as medical insurance for retired former employees. Because employees earn these benefits by their service, the company records pension and retirement-benefit expense while employees work for the company.

Pension
Employee compensation that will be received during retirement.

Pensions are one of the most complex areas of accounting. As employees earn their pensions and the company pays into the pension plan, the plan's assets grow. The obligation for future pension payments to employees also accumulates. At the end of each period, the company compares

- The fair market value of the assets in the pension plan—cash and investments—with
- The plan's *accumulated benefit obligation*, which is the present value of promised future pension payments to retirees.

If the plan assets exceed the accumulated benefit obligation, the plan is said to be *overfunded*. In this case, the asset and obligation amounts are to be reported only in the notes to the financial statements. However, if the accumulated benefit obligation (the pension liability) exceeds plan assets, the plan is *underfunded*, and the company must report the excess liability amount as a long-term pension liability on the balance sheet.

At December 31, 2003, the pension plan of AMR Corporation was underfunded. It had

- Assets with a fair market value of $6,230 million
- Accumulated pension benefit obligations totaling $8,894 million

AMR's balance sheet, therefore, included a Long-Term Pension Liability of $2,664 million ($8,894 – $6,230). This amount is included among Other Long-Term Liabilities.

Reporting Liabilities

Reporting on the Balance Sheet

OBJECTIVE

5 **Report** liabilities on the balance sheet

This chapter began with the liabilities reported on the balance sheets of AMR Corporation and UAL Corporation. Exhibit 8-12 repeats the liabilities section of AMR's balance sheet.

■ **EXHIBIT 8-12** Reporting Liabilities of AMR Corporation

AMR Corporation
Balance Sheet
(Partial, adapted)

Liabilities (in millions)	
Current Liabilities:	
Accounts payable	$ 967
Salaries and wages payable	528
Current maturities of long-term debt	603
Other current liabilities	4,461
Total current liabilities	6,559
Long-term debt	11,901
Other long-term liabilities	10,824

Note 6, Indebtedness (adapted)
Long-term debt consists of (in millions);

Secured indebtedness due through 2021, 1.61%–9.16%	$ 6,041
Equipment trust certificates payable through 2011, 1.8%–9.1%	3,747
Debentures payable through 2021, 9–10.2%	330
Senior convertible notes payable due 2023, 4.25%	300
Other long-term debt	2,086
Total long-term indebtedness	12,504
Less current maturities	(603)
Long-term debt	$11,901

Exhibit 8-12 includes Note 6 from AMR's financial statements, which gives additional details about the company's liabilities. Note 6 shows the interest rates and the maturity dates of AMR's long-term debt. Investors need these data to evaluate the company. The note also reports

- Current installments of long-term debt ($603 million) as a current liability
- Long-term debt, excluding current installments, of $11,901 million

Trace these amounts from Note 6 to the company's balance sheet. Working back and forth between the financial statements and the related notes is an important part of financial analysis. You now have the tools to understand the liabilities reported on an actual balance sheet.

Check Point 8-15

Reporting the Fair Market Value of Long-Term Debt

FASB Statement No. 107 requires companies to report the fair market value of their long-term debt. At December 31, 2003, AMR Corporation's Note 7 included this excerpt:

> **The . . . estimated fair values of the Company's long-term debt . . . were . . . $11,227 [million].**

Overall, the fair market value of AMR's long-term debt is about $1.3 billion less than its carrying amount on AMR's books.

Reporting Financing Activities on the Statement of Cash Flows

The AMR balance sheet (page 362) shows that the company finances most of its operations with debt. In fact, AMR's debt ratio is 99.8%. Let's examine AMR's financing activities as reported on its statement of cash flows. Exhibit 8-13 is an excerpt from the company's cash-flow statement.

■ **EXHIBIT 8-13**

Statement of Cash Flows (partial; adapted) for AMR Corporation

AMR Corporation
Statement of Cash Flows

(In millions)	Year Ended December 31, 2003
Cash Flow from Operating Activities:	
Net cash provided by operating activities	$ 601
Cash Flow from Investing Activities:	
Net cash used for investing activities	$(645)
Cash Flow from Financing Activities:	
Issuance of long-term debt	$ 945
Payments on long-term debt	(886)

During the year ended December 31, 2003, AMR borrowed $945 million by issuing long-term debt. The company paid $886 million on its long-term debt. These were the only financing transactions that affected the company's liabilities during the year. AMR had to finance most of its asset purchases with borrowing, which is troubling.

Summary Problem

END-OF-CHAPTER

The **Cessna Aircraft Company** has outstanding an issue of 8% convertible bonds that mature in 2018. Suppose the bonds are dated October 1, 2008, and pay interest each April 1 and October 1.

Required

1. Complete the following effective-interest amortization table through October 1, 2010.

   Bond Data
   Maturity value—$100,000
   Stated interest rate—8%
   Interest paid—4% semiannually, $4,000 ($100,000 × 0.08 × 6/12)
   Market interest rate at the time of issue—9% annually, $4\frac{1}{2}$% semiannually
   Issue price—93.5

Amortization Table

	A	B	C	D	E
Semiannual Interest Date	Interest Payment (4% of Maturity Amount)	Interest Expense (4 ½% of Preceding Bond Carrying Amount)	Discount Amortization (B – A)	Discount Account Balance (Preceding D – C)	Bond Carrying Amount ($100,000 – D)
10-1-08					
4-1-09					
10-1-09					
4-1-10					
10-1-10					

2. Using the amortization table, record the following transactions:
   a. Issuance of the bonds on October 1, 2008.
   b. Accrual of interest and amortization of the bonds on December 31, 2008.
   c. Payment of interest and amortization of the bonds on April 1, 2009.
   d. Conversion of one-third of the bonds payable into no-par stock on October 2, 2010. For no-par stock, transfer the bond carrying amount into the Common Stock account. There is no Additional Paid-in Capital.
   e. Retirement of two-thirds of the bonds payable on October 2, 2010. Purchase price of the bonds was based on their call price of 102.

Answers

Requirement 1

	A	B	C	D	E
Semiannual Interest Date	Interest Payment (4% of Maturity Amount)	Interest Expense (4 ½% of Preceding Bond Carrying Amount)	Discount Amortization (B – A)	Discount Account Balance (Preceding D – C)	Bond Carrying Amount ($100,000 – D)
10-1-08				$6,500	$93,500
4-1-09	$4,000	$4,208	$208	6,292	93,708
10-1-09	4,000	4,217	217	6,075	93,925
4-1-10	4,000	4,227	227	5,848	94,152
10-1-10	4,000	4,237	237	5,611	94,389

Requirement 2

a. 2008			
Oct. 1	Cash ($100,000 × 0.935)	93,500	
	Discount on Bonds Payable	6,500	
	Bonds Payable		100,000
	To issue bonds at a discount.		
b. Dec. 31	Interest Expense ($4,208 × 3/6)	2,104	
	Discount on Bonds Payable ($208 × 3/6)		104
	Interest Payable ($4,000 × 3/6)		2,000
	To accrue interest and amortize the bonds.		
c. 2009			
Apr. 1	Interest Expense	2,104	
	Interest Payable	2,000	
	Discount on Bonds Payable ($208 × 3/6)		104
	Cash		4,000
	To pay semiannual interest, part of which was accrued, and amortize the bonds.		

d. 2010			
Oct. 2	Bonds Payable ($100,000 × 1/3)	33,333	
	Discount on Bonds Payable (5,611 × 1/3)		1,870
	Common Stock ($94,389 × 1/3)		31,463
	To record conversion of bonds payable		

e. Oct. 2	Bonds Payable ($100,000 × 2/3)	66,667	
	Loss on Retirement of Bonds	5,074	
	Discount on Bonds Payable ($5,611 × 2/3)		3,741
	Cash ($100,000 × 2/3 × 1.02)		68,000
	To retire bonds payable before maturity.		

REVIEW CURRENT & LONG-TERM LIABILITIES

Chapter Review Quiz

1. Which of the following is *not* an estimated liability?
   a. Property taxes
   b. Product warranties
   c. Income taxes
   d. Sales taxes

2. Recording estimated income tax expense in the current year *best* follows which accounting principle?
   a. Consistency
   b. Matching
   c. Full disclosure
   d. Historical cost
   e. Materiality

3. Sound Advice grants a 90-day warranty on all stereos. Historically, approximately 2 1/2% of all sales prove to be defective. Sales in July are $194,600. In August, $2,900 of defective units are returned for replacement. What entry must Sound Advice make at the end of July to record the warranty expense?
   a. Debt Warranty Expense and credit Estimated Warranty Payable, $2,900.
   b. Debit Warranty Expense and credit Cash, $4,865.
   c. Debit Warranty Expense and credit Estimated Warranty Payable, $4,865.
   d. No entry is needed at July 31.

4. Neff, Inc. was organized to sell a single product for $400 per unit, including a 60-day warranty against defects. Engineering estimates indicate that 5% of the units sold will prove defective and require an average repair cost of $45 per unit. During Neff's first month of operations, total sales were $144,000; by the end of the month, 6 units had been reported defective and repaired. The liability for product warranties at month-end should be:
   a. $270
   b. $540
   c. $18,000
   d. $810
   e. None of these

5. A contingent liability is an obligation that depends on the occurrence of a future event and that should be recorded in the accounts:
   a. if the related future event will probably occur.
   b. if the amount is due in cash within one year.
   c. if the amount can be reasonably estimated.
   d. Both a and c.
   e. None of these.

6. An unsecured bond is a
   a. registered bond.
   b. bond indenture.
   c. term bond.
   d. debenture bond.
   e. serial bond.

7. The Discount on Bonds Payable account
   a. has a normal credit balance.
   b. is a miscellaneous revenue account.
   c. is an expense account.
   d. is expensed at the bond's maturity.
   e. is a contra account to Bonds Payable.

8. The discount on a bond payable becomes
   a. a reduction in interest expense the year the bonds mature.
   b. a reduction in interest expense over the life of the bonds.
   c. a liability in the year the bonds are sold.
   d. additional interest expense the year the bonds are sold.
   e. additional interest expense over the life of the bonds.

9. A bond that matures in installments is called a
   a. serial bond.
   b. zero coupon
   c. secured bond.
   d. term bond.
   e. callable bond.

10. The carrying value of Bonds Payable equals
   a. Bonds Payable – Premium on bonds Payable.
   b. Bonds Payable + Accrued Interest.
   c. Bonds Payable + Discount on Bonds Payable.
   d. Bonds Payable – Discount on Bonds Payable.

11. A corporation issues bonds that pay interest each March 1 and September 1. The corporation's December 31 adjusting entry may include a
   a. debit to Cash.
   b. credit to Discount on Bonds Payable.
   c. credit to Bond Interest Revenue.
   d. debit to Interest Payable.
   e. credit to Cash.

Use this information to answer questions 12–16.
Waco Publishing Company issued $225,000 of 9 1/2% 5-year bonds. The bonds are dated and sold on 1/1/X2. Interest payment dates are 1/1 and 7/1. The bonds are issued for $220,657 to yield the market interest rate of 10%.

12. What is the amount of interest expense that Waco Publishing Company will record on 7/1/X2, the first semiannual interest payment date?
   a. $11,108
   b. $11,670
   c. $11,033
   d. $10,688

13. What is the amount of discount amortization that Waco Publishing Company will record on 7/1/X2, the first semiannual interest payment date?
   a. $210
   b. $840
   c. $420
   d. None of the above; the answer is ____.

14. What is the total cash payment for interest during 20X2?
   a. $11,108
   b. $10,688
   c. $21,375
   d. $11,250

15. What is the carrying amount of the bonds on the 12/31/X2 balance sheet?
   a. $221,365
   b. $221,640
   c. $221,080
   d. $221,500

16. Using straight-line amortization, the carrying amount of Waco Publishing's bonds at 12/31/X2 is
   a. $221,526
   b. $225,869
   c. $219,788
   d. $220,657

Answers

1. d
2. b
3. c ($194,600 × 0.025 = $4,865)
4. b [$144,000 ÷ $400 = 360 units sold
   360 × 0.05 × $45 = warranty expense of $810;
   repaired $45 × 6 = $270;
   year-end liability = $540 ($810 − $270)]
5. d
6. d
7. e
8. e
9. a
10. d
11. b
12. c ($220,657 × .10 × 6/12 = $11,033)
13. d [Int. exp. = $11,032.85 ($220,657 × .10 × 6/12)
    Int. payment = $10,687.50 ($225,000 × .095 × 6/12)
    $11,032.85 − $10,687.50 = $345.35]
14. c ($225,000 × .095 = $21,375)
15. a (See Amortization Schedule)

Date	Interest Payment	Interest Expense	Discount Amortiz.	Bond Carry Amt.
1/1/X2				$220,657
7/1/X2	$10,687.50	$11,032.85	$345	221,002
1/1/X3	10,687.50	11,050.10	363	221,365

16. a {$220,657 + [($225,000 − $220,657) × 1/5] = $221,526}

Accounting Vocabulary

accrued expense (p. 366)
accrued liability (p. 366)
bonds payable (p. 372)
callable bonds (p. 383)
capital lease (p. 388)
convertible bonds (or notes) (p. 384)
current installment of long-term debt (p. 366)
debentures (p. 373)
discount (on a bond) (p. 373)
earnings per share (EPS) (p. 385)
interest-coverage ratio (p. 386)
lease (p. 387)
lessee (p. 387)
lessor (p. 387)
leverage (p. 385)
market interest rate (p. 374)
operating lease (p. 387)
payroll (p. 366)
pension (p. 389)
premium (on a bond) (p. 373)
present value (p. 374)
serial bonds (p. 373)
short-term notes payable (p. 364)
stated interest rate (p. 374)
term bonds (p. 373)
times-interest-earned ratio (p. 386)
trading on the equity (p. 385)
underwriter (p. 373)

Assess Your Progress

Check Points

Accounting for a note payable (Obj. 1)

CP8-1 (p. 365) Return to the $8,000 purchase of inventory on a short-term note payable that begins on page 365. Assume that the purchase of inventory occurred on March 31, 20X5, instead of January 30, 20X5. Journalize the company's (a) purchase of inventory, (b) accrual of interest expense on December 31, 20X5, and (c) payment of the note plus interest on March 31, 20X6.

Reporting a short-term note payable and the related interest in the financial statements (Obj. 1)

CP8-2 (p. 365) This check point works with Check Point 8-1.

1. Refer to the data in Check Point 8-1. Show what the company would report on its balance sheet at December 31, 20X5, and on its income statement for the year ended on that date.
2. What one item will the financial statements for the year ended December 31, 20X6 report? Identify the financial statement, the item, and its amount.

Accounting for warranty expense and estimated warranty payable (Obj. 1)

CP8-3 (p. 369) **DaimlerChrysler Corporation** guarantees some automobiles against defects for 4 years or 50,000 miles, whichever comes first. Suppose Chrysler can expect warranty costs during the 4-year period to add up to 5% of sales.

Assume that Four Corners Dodge in Durango, Colorado, made sales of $500,000 during 20X0. Four Corners Dodge received cash for 20% of the sales and took notes receivable for the remainder. Payments to satisfy customer warranty claims totaled $22,000 during 20X0.

1. Record the sales, warranty expense, and warranty payments for Four Corners Dodge. Ignore any reimbursement Four Corners Dodge may receive from Daimler-Chrysler Corporation.
2. Post to the Estimated Warranty Payable T-account. The beginning balance was $7,000. At the end of 20X0, how much in estimated warranty payable does Four Corners Dodge owe its customers? Why must the warranty payable amount be estimated?

Applying GAAP; reporting warranties in the financial statements (Obj. 1)

CP8-4 (p. 369) Refer to the data given in Check Point 8-3. What amount of warranty expense will Four Corners Dodge report during 20X0? Which accounting principle addresses this situation? Does the warranty expense for the year equal the year's cash payments for warranties? Explain how the accounting principle works for measuring warranty expense.

writing assignment ■

Interpreting a company's contingent liabilities (Obj. 1)

writing assignment ■

CP8-5 (p. 370) **Harley-Davidson, Inc.**, the motorcycle manufacturer, included the following note in its annual report:

NOTES TO CONSOLIDATED FINANCIAL STATEMENTS
7 (In Part): Commitments and Contingencies

The Company self-insures its product liability losses in the United States up to $3 million (catastrophic coverage is maintained for individual claims in excess of $3 million up to $25 million). Outside the United States, the Company is insured for product liability up to $25 million per individual claim and in the aggregate.

1. Why are these *contingent* (versus *real*) liabilities?
2. In the United States, how can the contingent liability become a real liability for Harley-Davidson? What are the limits to the company's product liabilities in the United States? Explain how these limits work.
3. How can a contingency outside the United States become a real liability for the company? How does Harley-Davidson's potential liability differ for claims outside the United States?

Pricing bonds (Obj. 2)

CP8-6 (p. 373) Compute the price of the following bonds:

a.	$100,000 quoted at 97.50	c.	$2,000,000 quoted at 89.75
b.	$400,000 quoted at 102.625	d.	$500,000 quoted at 110.375

Determining bond prices at par, discount, or premium (Obj. 2)

CP8-7 (p. 375) Determine whether the following bonds payable will be issued at par value, at a premium, or at a discount:

a. Ephesus Corporation issued 8% bonds when the market interest rate was $6\frac{7}{8}$%.
b. Antioch Company issued bonds payable that pay cash interest at the stated interest rate of 7%. At the date of issuance, the market interest rate was $8\frac{1}{4}$%.
c. The market interest rate is 9%. Corinth, Inc., issues bonds payable with a stated rate of $8\frac{1}{2}$%.
d. Macedonia Corporation issued $7\frac{1}{2}$% bonds payable when the market rate was $7\frac{1}{2}$%.

Journalizing basic bond payable transactions; bonds issued at par (Obj. 2)

CP8-8 (p. 376) Suppose **Washington Public Power Supply System (WPPSS)** issued the 10-year bond in Exhibit 8-2, page 372, when the market interest rate was $6\frac{1}{2}$%. Assume that the accounting year of WPPSS ends on December 31. Journalize the following transactions for WPPSS, including an explanation for each entry:

a. Issuance of the bond payable on July 1, 2000.
b. Accrual of interest expense on December 31, 2000 (rounded to the nearest dollar).
c. Payment of cash interest on January 1, 2001.
d. Payment of the bonds payable at maturity. (Give the date.)

Issuing bonds payable and amortizing bonds by the effective-interest method (Obj. 3)

CP8-9 (p. 380) **Borden Food Products** issued $500,000 of 7%, 10-year bonds payable at a price of 87 on January 31, 20X8. The market interest rate at the date of issuance was 9%, and the Borden bonds pay interest semiannually.

1. Prepare an effective interest amortization table for the bonds through the first three interest payments. Use Exhibit 8-5, page 377, as a guide and round amounts to the nearest dollar.
2. Record Borden's issuance of the bonds on January 31, 20X8, and, on July 31, 20X8, payment of the first semiannual interest amount and amortization of the bonds. Explanations are not required.

Analyzing data on long-term debt (Obj. 3)

CP8-10 (p. 380) Use the amortization table that you prepared for Borden Food Products in Check Point 8-9 to answer these questions about the company's long-term debt:

1. How much cash did Borden borrow on January 31, 20X8? How much cash will Borden pay back at maturity on January 31, 20X18?
2. How much cash interest will Borden pay each 6 months?
3. How much interest expense will Borden report on July 31, 20X8, and on January 31, 20X9? Why does the amount of interest expense increase each period? Explain in detail.

Determining bonds payable amounts; amortizing bonds by the straight-line method (Obj. 3)

CP8-11 (p. 383) WPPSS borrowed money by issuing the bond payable in Exhibit 8-2, page 372. Assume the issue price was 98 on July 1, 2000.

1. How much cash did WPPSS receive when it issued the bond payable?
2. How much must WPPSS pay back at maturity? When is the maturity date?
3. How much cash interest will WPPSS pay each 6 months? Carry the interest amount to the nearest cent.
4. How much interest expense will WPPSS report each 6 months? Assume the straight-line amortization method and carry the interest amount to the nearest cent.

Issuing bonds payable, accruing interest, and amortizing bonds by the straight-line method (Obj. 3)

CP8-12 (p. 383) Return to the WPPSS bond in Exhibit 8-2, page 372. Assume that WPPSS issued the bond payable on July 1, 2000, at a price of 96. Also assume that WPPSS's accounting year ends on December 31. Journalize the following transactions for WPPSS, including an explanation for each entry:

a. Issuance of the bonds on July 1, 2000.
b. Accrual of interest expense and amortization of bonds on December 31, 2000. (Use the straight-line amortization method, and round amounts to the nearest dollar.)
c. Payment of the first semiannual interest amount on January 1, 2001.

Earnings-per-share effects of financing with bonds versus stock (Obj. 4)

CP8-13 (p. 385) **Motel 6** needs $1 million to expand the company. Motel 6 is considering the issuance of either

- $1,000,000 of 7% bonds payable to borrow the money
- 100,000 shares of common stock at $10 per share

Before any new financing, Motel 6 expects to earn net income of $400,000, and the company already has 200,000 shares of common stock outstanding. Motel 6 believes the expansion will increase income before interest and income tax by $200,000. Motel 6's income tax rate is 40%.

Prepare an analysis similar to Exhibit 8-11, page 385, to determine which plan is likely to result in the higher earnings per share. Based solely on the earnings-per-share comparison, which financing plan would you recommend for Motel 6? Why does the plan with the lower net income result in higher earnings per share?

Computing the times-interest-earned ratio (Obj. 4)

CP8-14 (p. 387) **Sprint Corporation** reported the following data in 20X3 (adapted, in billions):

Net operating revenues	$26.2
Operating expenses	25.3
Operating income	0.9
Nonoperating items:	
Interest expense	(1.4)
Other	(0.2)
Net income (net loss)	$(0.7)

Compute Sprint's times-interest-earned ratio, and write a sentence to explain what the ratio value means. Would you be willing to lend Sprint $1 billion? State your reason.

Reporting liabilities, including capital lease obligations (Obj. 5)

CP8-15 (p. 390) Mayflower Energy Company has the following selected accounts at December 31, 20X7:

Interest payable (due March 1, 20X8)	$ 7,000	Bonds payable	$350,000
Accounts payable	27,000	Equipment	114,000
Discount on bonds payable (all long-term)	6,000	Current portion of bonds payable	50,000
Accounts receivable	31,000	Notes payable, long-term	60,000

Prepare the liabilities section of Mayflower's balance sheet at December 31, 20X7, to show how Mayflower would report these items. Report total current liabilities.

Exercises

PH Grade Assist

Most of the even-numbered exercises can be found within Prentice Hall Grade Assist (PHGA), an online homework and practice environment. Your instructor may ask you to complete these exercises using PHGA.

Accounting for warranty expense and the related liability (Obj. 1)

■ **general ledger**

E8-1 Assume the accounting records of Centex Dodge-Hyundai included the following balances at the end of the period:

Estimated Warranty Payable		Sales Revenue		Warranty Expense	
	Beg. bal 8,000		**150,000**		

In the past, Centex's warranty expense has been 8% of sales. During the current period, the business paid $9,000 to satisfy the warranty claims of customers.

Required

1. Record Centex's warranty expense for the period and the company's cash payments to satisfy warranty claims. Explanations are not required.
2. Show what Centex will report on its income statement and balance sheet for this situation.
3. Which data item from requirement 2 will affect Centex's current ratio? Will Centex's current ratio increase or decrease as a result of this item?

Recording and reporting current liabilities (Obj. 1)

■ **general ledger**

E8-2 Assume **The Denver Post** publishing company completed the following transactions during 20X6:

Sept. 30	Sold a 1-year subscription, collecting cash of $300, plus sales tax of 4%.
Dec. 15	Remitted (paid) the sales tax to the state of Colorado.
31	Made the necessary adjustment at year end.

Journalize these transactions (explanations not required). Then report any liability on the company's balance sheet.

Reporting payroll expense and liabilities (Obj. 1)

E8-3 Friends for Life, Inc., has an annual payroll of $300,000. In addition, the company incurs payroll tax expense of 9%. At December 31, Friends for Life owes salaries of $4,000 and FICA and other payroll tax of $400. The company will pay these amounts early next year.

Show what the Friends for Life will report for the foregoing on its income statement and year-end balance sheet.

E8-4 Assume that Sewell Lexus completed the following note-payable transactions.

Recording note payable transactions (Obj. 1)

20X6	
July 1	Purchased wheel-balancing equipment costing $100,000 by issuing a 1-year, 8% note payable.
Dec. 31	Accrued interest on the note payable.
20X7	
July 1	Paid the note payable at maturity.

Answer these questions for Sewell Lexus:

1. How much interest expense must be accrued at December 31, 20X6?
2. Determine the amount of Sewell's final payment on July 1, 20X7.
3. How much interest expense will Sewell report for 20X6 and for 20X7?

E8-5 Assume the following for **Campbell Soup Company**. At December 31, 20X4, Campbell Soup Company reported a current liability for income tax payable of $217 million. During 20X5, Campbell Soup earned income of $924 million before income tax. The company's income tax rate during 20X5 was 32%. Also during 20X5, Campbell Soup paid income taxes of $225 million.

Accounting for income tax (Obj. 1)

How much income tax payable did Campbell Soup Company report on its balance sheet at December 31, 20X5? How much income tax expense did Campbell Soup report on its 20X5 income statement? Round amounts to the nearest $1 million.

E8-6 Geodesic Domes, Inc., builds environmentally sensitive structures. The company's 20X4 revenues totaled $2,790 million, and at December 31, 20X4, the company had $653 million in current assets. The December 31, 20X4, balance sheet reported the liabilities and stockholders' equity as follows.

Analyzing liabilities (Obj. 1, 5)

At year end (In millions)	20X4	20X3
Liabilities and Shareholders' Equity		
Current Liabilities		
Accounts payable	$ 138	$ 176
Accrued expenses	157	178
Employee compensation and benefits	37	25
Current portion of long-term debt	5	14
Total Current Liabilities	337	393
Long-Term Debt	1,489	1,316
Postretirement Benefits Payable	132	126
Other Liabilities	21	17
Shareholders' Equity	2,021	1,783
Total Liabilities and Shareholders' Equity	$4,000	$3,635

Required

1. Describe each of Geodesic Domes, Inc.'s liabilities and state how the liability arose.
2. What were the company's total assets at December 31, 20X4? Was the company's debt ratio high, low, or in a middle range?

E8-7 **Wyeth Pharmaceuticals** is a global leader in pharmaceuticals and consumer health-care products such as Advil and Chapstick. Revenues for 20X3 totaled $15.9 billion. As with most pharmaceutical companies, Wyeth is a defendant in lawsuits related to its products. Note 11 of Wyeth's Annual Report for 20X3 reported:

Reporting a contingent liability (Obj. 1)

writing assignment ■

11. Contingencies

The company is involved in various legal proceedings. . . . It is the Company's policy to accrue for amounts related to these legal matters if it is probable that a liability has been incurred and an amount is reasonably estimable.

Required

1. Suppose Wyeth's lawyers believe that a significant legal judgment against the company is reasonably possible. Should Wyeth disclose this situation in its financial statements? If so, how?
2. Suppose Wyeth's lawyers believe it is probable that a $100 million judgment will be rendered against the company. Report this situation in Wyeth's financial statements. Journalize any entry required by GAAP. Explanations are not required.

Reporting current liabilities (Obj. 1, 5)

E8-8 Assume the top management of **The Home Depot, Inc.**, examines company accounting records at January 24, one week before the end of the fiscal year (amounts in billions):

Total current assets	$13.3
Noncurrent assets	21.1
	$34.4
Total current liabilities	$ 9.6
Noncurrent liabilities	12.8
Owners' equity	12.0
	$34.4

Suppose Home Depot's top management wants to achieve a current ratio of 1.5. How much in current liabilities should Home Depot pay off within the next week to achieve its goal?

Reporting current and long-term liabilities (Obj. 1, 5)

E8-9 Assume that **Titleist Golf Corporation** completed these selected transactions during December 20X4.

a. **Sport Spectrum**, a chain of sporting goods stores, ordered $100,000 of golf equipment. With its order, Sport Spectrum sent a check for $100,000, and Titleist shipped $55,000 of the goods. Titleist will ship the remainder of the goods on January 3, 20X5.
b. The December payroll of $120,000 is subject to employee withheld income tax of 9% and FICA tax of 8%. On December 31, Titleist pays employees their take-home pay and accrues all tax amounts.
c. Sales of $2,000,000 are subject to estimated warranty cost of 3%. The estimated warranty payable at the beginning of the year was $18,000, and warranty payments for the year totaled $55,000.
d. On December 1, Titleist signed a $100,000 note payable that requires annual payments of $10,000 plus 9% interest on the unpaid balance each December 1.

Required

Classify each liability as current or long-term and report the amount that would appear for these items on the Titleist Golf Corporation balance sheet at December 31, 20X4. Show a total for current liabilities.

Issuing bonds payable, paying and accruing interest, and amortizing the bonds by the straight-line method (Obj. 2)

E8-10 On January 31, Dover China Company issues 10-year, 7% bonds payable with a face value of $1,000,000. The bonds were issued at 98 and pay interest on January 31 and July 31. Dover amortizes bonds by the straight-line method. Record (a) issuance of the bonds on January 31, (b) the semiannual interest payment on July 31, and (c) the interest accrual on December 31.

Measuring cash amounts for a bond; amortizing the bonds by the straight-line method (Obj. 2, 3)

E8-11 Solitaire Factory Outlets has $200 million of 8.88% debenture bonds outstanding. The bonds mature in 2024. The bonds were issued at 101 in 2004.

Required

1. How much cash did Solitaire receive when it issued these bonds?
2. How much cash in *total* will Solitaire pay the bondholders through the maturity date of the bonds?

(continued)

3. Take the difference between your answers to Requirements 1 and 2. This difference represents Solitaire's total interest expense over the life of the bonds.
4. Compute Solitaire's annual interest expense by the straight-line amortization method. Multiply this amount by 20. Your 20-year total should be the same as your answer to Requirement 3.

Issuing bonds payable; recording interest payments and the related bond amortization (Obj. 2, 3)

■ **spreadsheet**

E8-12 Assume Dollar General Stores, Inc., is authorized to issue $500,000 of 7%, 10-year bonds payable. On December 31, 20X6, when the market interest rate is 8%, the company issues $400,000 of the bonds and receives cash of $372,660. Dollar General amortizes bonds by the effective-interest method. The semiannual interest dates are June 30 and December 31.

Required

1. Prepare a bond amortization table for the first four semiannual interest periods.
2. Record issuance of the bonds payable on December 31, 20X6, the semiannual interest payment on June 30, 20X7, and the payment on December 31, 20X7.

Issuing bonds payable; recording interest accrual and payment and the related bond amortization (Obj. 2, 3)

■ **spreadsheet**

E8-13 On July 1, 2008, the market interest rate is 7%. Electronic Financial Group, Inc. (EFG) issues $300,000 of 8%, 20-year bonds payable at 110.625. The bonds pay interest on January 1 and July 1. EFG amortizes bonds by the effective-interest method.

Required

1. Prepare a bond amortization table for the first four semiannual interest periods.
2. Record issuance of the bonds on July 1, 2008, the accrual of interest at December 31, 2008, and the semiannual interest payment on January 1, 2009.

Debt payment and bond amortization schedule (Obj. 3)

E8-14 Highland Park Realty issued $600,000 of 8 3/8 % (0.8375), 5-year bonds payable on January 1, 20X5, when the market interest rate was 9 1/2 % (.095). The company pays interest annually at year end. The issue price of the bonds was $574,082.

Required

Create a spreadsheet model to prepare a schedule to amortize the bonds. Use the effective-interest method of amortization. Round to the nearest dollar and format your answer as shown here.

	A	B	C	D	E	F
2						Bond
3		Interest	Interest	Discount	Discount	Carrying
4	Date	Payment	Expense	Amortization	Balance	Amount
5	1-1-X5				$☐	$574,082
6	12-31-X5	$☐	$☐	$☐		☐
7	12-31-X6					
8	12-31-X7					
9	12-31-X8					
10	12-31-X9					
		600,000*.08375	+F5*.095	+C6–B6	600,000–F5	+F5+D6

Recording conversion of notes payable (Obj. 2)

E8-15 Beverly Hills Security Corporation issued $400,000 of 8 1/2 % notes payable on December 31, 20X5, at a price of 98.5. The notes' term to maturity is 10 years. After 3 years, the notes may be converted into Beverly Hills Security common stock. Each $1,000 face amount of notes is convertible into 40 shares of $1 par stock. On December 31, 20X9, noteholders exercised their right to convert the notes into common stock.

Required

1. Without making journal entries, compute the carrying amount of the notes payable at December 31, 20X9, immediately before the conversion. Beverly Hills Security uses the straight-line method to amortize bonds.
2. All amortization has been recorded properly. Journalize the conversion transaction at December 31, 20X9.

(continued)

3. Identify the two ratios affected most directly in the future by the conversion transaction. Will the conversion increase or decrease each ratio? After the conversion, will Beverly Hills Security look more or less risky?

Measuring the times-interest-earned ratio (Obj. 4)

E8-16 Companies that operate in different industries may look very different on their financial ratios. These differences may grow even wider when we compare companies located in different countries.

Let's compare three leading companies on their current ratio, debt ratio, and times-interest-earned ratio. Compute these three ratios for **Safeway** (the U.S. grocery chain), **Sony** (the Japanese electronics manufacturer), and **DaimlerChrysler** (the German auto company).

Income data (Amounts in millions or billions)	Safeway	Sony	DaimlerChrysler
Total revenues	$34,301	¥7,315	€136,437
Total operating expenses	31,712	7,090	130,751
Interest expense	447	43	911
Net income	1,254	17	448

Asset and liability data (Amounts in millions or billions)	Safeway	Sony	DaimlerChrysler
Total current assets	$ 3,312	¥3,477	€ 65,051
Long-term assets	14,151	4,351	159,513
Total current liabilities	3,883	2,647	70,542
Long-term liabilities	7,690	2,866	110,586
Stockholders' equity	5,890	2,315	43,436

Note: ¥ is the symbol for a Japanese yen; € for a euro. In May 2003, ¥1 = $0.009, €1 = $1.20.

Based on your computed ratio values, which company looks the most risky?

Analyzing alternative plans for raising money (Obj. 4)

writing assignment ■

E8-17 Sunamerica Securities is considering two plans for raising $500,000 to expand operations. Plan A is to borrow at 8%, and plan B is to issue 100,000 shares of common stock. Before any new financing, Sunamerica has net income of $600,000 and 100,000 shares of common stock outstanding. Assume you own most of Sunamerica's existing stock. Management believes the company can use the new funds to earn additional income of $420,000 before interest and taxes. The income tax rate is 40%.

Required

1. Analyze Sunamerica's situation to determine which plan will result in higher earnings per share. Use Exhibit 8-11 (page 385) as a model.
2. Which plan results in the higher earnings per share? Which plan allows you to retain control of the company? Which plan creates more financial risk for the company? Which plan do you prefer? Why? Present your conclusion in a memo to Sunamerica's board of directions.

Challenge Exercises

Refinancing old bonds payable with new bonds (Obj. 2, 3, 5)

E8-18 **United Brands**, famous for Chiquita bananas, completed one of the most famous debt refinancings in history. A debt refinancing occurs when a company issues new bonds payable to retire old bonds.

United had $125 million of 5 3/8% bonds payable outstanding, with 21 years to maturity. United retired these old bonds by issuing $75 million of new 9% bonds payable to the holders of the old bonds and paying the bondholders $13 million in cash. United issued both groups of bonds at par. At the time of the debt refinancing, United Brands had total assets of $500 million and total liabilities of $360 million. Net income for the most recent year was $6.5 million on sales of $1 billion.

P8-3A Assume the board of directors of **Rose Bowl Pasadena, Inc.**, authorizes the issue of $2 million of 8%, 20-year bonds payable. The semiannual interest dates are March 31 and September 30. The bonds are issued on March 31, 20X8, at par.

Recording bond transactions (at par) and reporting bonds payable on the balance sheet (Obj. 2)

■ **general ledger**

Required

1. Journalize the following transactions:
   a. Issuance of the bonds on March 31, 20X8.
   b. Payment of interest on September 30, 20X8.
   c. Accrual of interest on December 31, 20X8.
   d. Payment of interest on March 31, 20X9.
2. Report interest payable and bonds payable as they would appear on the Rose Bowl Pasadena, Inc., balance sheet at December 31, 20X8.

P8-4A On February 28, 20X8, Malibu Amusement Park, Inc. issues 7 3/4%, 10-year notes payable with a face value of $300,000. The notes pay interest on February 28 and August 31, and Malibu amortizes bonds by the straight-line method.

Issuing notes, amortizing by the straight-line method, and reporting notes payable on the balance sheet (Obj. 2, 5)

Required

1. If the market interest rate is 8 1/2% when Malibu issues its notes, will the notes be priced at par, at a premium, or at a discount? Explain.
2. If the market interest rate is 7% when Malibu issues its notes, will the notes be priced at par, at a premium, or at a discount? Explain.
3. Assume that the issue price of the notes is 102. Journalize the following note payable transactions:
   a. Issuance of the notes on February 28, 20X8.
   b. Payment of interest and amortization of the bonds on August 31, 20X8.
   c. Accrual of interest and amortization of the bonds on December 31, 20X8.
   d. Payment of interest and amortization of the bonds on February 28, 20X9.
4. Report interest payable and notes payable as they would appear on the Malibu balance sheet at December 31, 20X8.

P8-5A

Accounting for bonds payable at a discount and amortizing by the straight-line method. (Obj. 2)

■ **general ledger**

1. Journalize the following transactions of Stoneleigh Hotels, Inc.:

20X4	
Jan. 1	Issued $500,000 of 8%, 5-year bonds payable at 94.
July 1	Paid semiannual interest and amortized the bonds by the straight-line method on our 8% bonds payable.
Dec. 31	Accrued semiannual interest expense and amortized the bonds by the straight-line method on our 8% bonds payable.
20X9	
Jan. 1	Paid the 8% bonds at maturity.

2. At December 31, 20X4, after all year-end adjustments, determine the carrying amount of Stoneleigh Hotels' bonds payable, net.
3. For the 6 months ended July 1, 20X4, determine the following for Stoneleigh Hotels, Inc.:
   a. Interest expense   b. Cash interest paid
   What causes interest expense on the bonds to exceed cash interest paid?

Analyzing a company's long-term debt and reporting the long-term debt on the balance sheet (effective-interest method) (Obj. 2, 3, 5)

■ **spreadsheet**

P8-6A The notes to the Bells.com financial statements reported the following data on September 30, year 1 (the end of the fiscal year):

Note E—Long-Term Debt	
5% bonds payable, due year 14, net of discount of $31,645,000 (market interest rate of 7.50%)	$119,855,000
Notes payable, interest rate of 8.67%, principal due in annual amounts of $26,000,000 in years 5 through 10	156,000,000

Bells.com amortizes bonds by the effective-interest method.

Required

1. Answer the following questions about Bells' long-term liabilities:
   a. What is the maturity value of the 5% bonds?
   b. What is Bells' annual cash interest payment on the 5% bonds?
   c. What is the carrying amount of the 5% bonds at September 30, year 1?
2. Prepare an amortization table through September 30, year 4, for the 5% bonds. Round all amounts to the nearest thousand dollars. Bells pays interest annually on September 30. How much is Bells' interest expense on the 5% bonds for the year ended September 30, year 4?
3. Show how Bells would report the 5% bonds payable and notes payable at September 30, year 4.

Issuing convertible bonds at a premium, by the effective-interest method, retiring bonds early, converting bonds, and reporting the bonds payable on the balance sheet (Obj. 2, 3, 5)

■ **general ledger**

P8-7A On December 31, 20X1, Dunlap Plastics issues 9%, 10-year convertible bonds with a maturity value of $300,000. The semiannual interest dates are June 30 and December 31. The market interest rate is 8%, and the issue price of the bonds is 106. Dunlap amortizes bonds by the effective-interest method.

Required

1. Prepare an effective-interest-method amortization table for the first four semiannual interest periods.
2. Journalize the following transactions:
   a. Issuance of the bonds on December 31, 20X1. Credit Convertible Bonds Payable.
   b. Payment of interest and amortization of the bonds on June 30, 20X2.
   c. Payment of interest and amortization of the bonds on December 31, 20X2.
   d. Retirement of bonds with face value of $100,000 on July 1, 20X3. Dunlap pays the market price of 104.
   e. Conversion by the bondholders on July 1, 20X3, of bonds with face value of $100,000 into 10,000 shares of Dunlap's $1-par common stock.
3. Show how Dunlap would report the remaining bonds payable on its balance sheet at December 31, 20X3.

Financing operations with debt or with stock (Obj. 4)

writing assignment ■

P8-8A Two businesses in very different circumstances are pondering how to raise $10 million.

Callnotes Voice Message Service is in the midst of its most successful period since it began operations in 2002. For each of the past several years, net income and earnings per share have increased by 25%. The outlook for the future is equally bright with new markets opening up and competitors unable to compete with Callnotes. As a result Callnotes is planning a large-scale expansion.

Lincoln Property Management Company has fallen on hard times. Net income has remained flat for 5 of the last 6 years, even falling by 10% from last year's level of profits, and cash flow also took a nosedive. Top management has experienced some turnover and has stabilized only recently. To become competitive again, Lincoln needs $10 million to invest in new real estate.

Required

1. Propose a plan for each company to raise the needed cash. Which company should borrow? Which company should issue stock? Consider the advantages and the disadvantages of raising money by borrowing and by issuing stock and discuss them in your answer.
2. How will what you learned in this problem help you manage a business?

Reporting liabilities on the balance sheet, times-interest-earned ratio (Obj. 5)

writing assignment ■

P8-9A The accounting records of Brazos Fitness Centers, Inc. include the following items at December 31, 20X6:

Interest expense	$47,000	Premium on bonds payable (all long-term)	$ 13,000
Bonds payable, current portion	60,000	Interest payable	6,200
Accumulated depreciation, building	88,000	Pension plan assets (market value)	402,000
Mortgage note payable, long term	467,000	Operating income	71,000
Bonds payable, long term	180,000	Accumulated pension benefit obligation	436,000
Building	190,000		

Required

1. Show how these items would be reported on Brazos Fitness Centers' classified balance sheet, including headings and totals for current liabilities, long-term liabilities, and so on.
2. Answer the following questions about the financial position of Brazos Fitness Centers at December 31, 20X6:
   a. What is the carrying amount of the bonds payable?
   b. Why is the interest payable amount so much less than the amount of interest expense?
3. How many times did Brazos cover its interest expense during 20X6? Do you consider this ratio value safe or risky? Why?

(Group B)

PH Grade Assist

Some of these B problems can be found within Prentice Hall Grade Assist (PHGA), an online homework and practice environment. Your instructor may ask you to complete these exercises using PHGA.

Measuring current liabilities (Obj. 1)

P8-1B Following are five pertinent facts about events during the current year at Mathers & Mathers Air Conditioning:

a. On August 31, Mathers & Mathers signed a 6-month, 7% note payable to purchase a graphics computer costing $80,000. The note requires payment of principal and interest at maturity.
b. On October 31, Mathers & Mathers received cash of $2,400 in advance for service revenue. This revenue will be earned evenly over 6 months.
c. December revenue totaled $104,000, and in addition, Mathers & Mathers collected sales tax of 6%. This amount will be sent to the state of Illinois early in January.
d. Mathers & Mathers owes $100,000 on a long-term note payable. At December 31, 6% interest for the year plus $20,000 of this principal are payable within 1 year.
e. Revenues of $909,000 were covered by Mathers & Mathers' service warranty. At January 1, estimated warranty payable was $11,300. During the year, Mathers & Mathers recorded warranty expense of $31,100 and paid warranty claims of $28,100.

Required

For each item, indicate the account and the related amount to be reported as a current liability on the Mathers & Mathers December 31 balance sheet.

Recording liability-related transactions (Obj. 1)

general ledger

P8-2B Assume the following transactions of Suzuki Piano Company occurred during 20X5 and 20X6:

20X5	
Feb. 3	Purchased a machine for $47,000, signing a 6-month, 8% note payable.
Apr. 30	Borrowed $100,000 on a 9% note payable that calls for annual installment payments of $25,000 principal plus interest. Record the short-term note payable in a separate account from the long-term note payable.
Aug. 3	Paid the 6-month, 8% note at maturity.
Dec. 31	Accrued warranty expense, which is estimated at 2% of sales of $145,000.
31	Accrued interest on the outstanding note payable.
20X6	
Apr. 30	Paid the first installment and interest for 1 year on the outstanding note payable.

Required

Record the transactions in Suzuki's journal. Explanations are not required.

Recording bond transactions (at par) and reporting bonds payable on the balance sheet (Obj. 2)

general ledger

P8-3B The board of directors of Synex Communications authorizes the issue of $3 million of 7%, 10-year bonds payable. The semiannual interest dates are May 31 and November 30. The bonds are issued on May 31, 20X5, at par.

Required

1. Journalize the following transactions:
   a. Issuance of the bonds on May 31, 20X5.
   b. Payment of interest on November 30, 20X5.
   c. Accrual of interest on December 31, 20X5.
   d. Payment of interest on May 31, 20X6.
2. Report interest payable and bonds payable as they would appear on the Synex balance sheet at December 31, 20X5.

Issuing bonds at a discount, amortizing by the straight-line method, and reporting bonds payable on the balance sheet (Obj. 2, 5)

P8-4B On February 28, 20X4, Village Green Apartments issues 8 1/2%, 20-year bonds payable with a face value of $500,000. The bonds pay interest on February 28 and August 31. Village Green amortizes bonds by the straight-line method.

Required

1. If the market interest rate is 8 7/8% when Village Green issues its bonds, will the bonds be priced at par, at a premium, or at a discount? Explain.
2. If the market interest rate is 7 3/8% when Village Green issues its bonds, will the bonds be priced at par, at a premium, or at a discount? Explain.
3. Assume that the issue price of the bonds is 97. Journalize the following bond transactions:
   a. Issuance of the bonds on February 28, 20X4.
   b. Payment of interest and amortization of the bonds on August 31, 20X4.
   c. Accrual of interest and amortization of the bonds on December 31, 20X4.
   d. Payment of interest and amortization of the bonds on February 28, 20X5.
4. Report interest payable and bonds payable as they would appear on the Village Green balance sheet at December 31, 20X4.

P8-5B

Accounting for bonds payable at a discount and amortizing by the straight-line method (Obj. 2)

■ general ledger

1. Journalize the following transactions of Oak Cliff Country Club:

2007	
Jan. 1	Issued $1,000,000 of 8%, 10-year bonds payable at 97.
July 1	Paid semiannual interest and amortized bonds by the straight-line method on the 8% bonds payable.
Dec. 31	Accrued semiannual interest expense and amortized bonds by the straight-line method on the 8% bonds payable.
2017	
Jan. 1	Paid the 8% bonds at maturity.

2. At December 31, 2007, after all year-end adjustments, determine the carrying amount of Oak Cliff Country Club bonds payable, net.
3. For the 6 months ended July 1, 2007, determine for Oak Cliff Country Club:
   a. Interest expense b. Cash interest paid
   What causes interest expense on the bonds to exceed cash interest paid?

P8-6B The notes to Oasis Landscaping financial statements reported the following data on September 30, year 1 (the end of the fiscal year):

Analyzing a company's long-term debt and reporting long-term debt on the balance sheet (effective-interest method) (Obj. 2, 3, 5)

■ spreadsheet

Note 4. Indebtedness	
Long-term debt at September 30, year 1, included the following:	
5.00% bonds payable due year 21 with a market interest rate of 9.66%, net of discount of $81,223,000	$118,777,000
Other indebtedness with an interest rate of 8.30%, due $9,300,000 in year 5 and $19,257,000 in year 6	28,557,000

Oasis amortizes bonds by the effective-interest method.

Required

1. Answer the following questions about Oasis's long-term liabilities:
   a. What is the maturity value of the 5.00% bonds?
   b. What are Oasis's annual cash interest payments on the 5.00% bonds?
   c. What is the carrying amount of the 5.00% bonds at September 30, year 1?
2. Prepare an amortization table through September 30, year 4, for the 5.00% bonds. Round all amounts to the nearest thousand dollars and assume that Oasis pays interest annually on September 30. How much is Oasis's interest expense on the 5.00% bonds for the year ended September 30, year 4? Round interest to the nearest thousand dollars.
3. Show how Oasis Landscaping would report the bonds payable and other indebtedness at September 30, year 4.

P8-7B On December 31, 20X7, Mobil Technology issues 8%, 10-year convertible bonds with a maturity value of $500,000. The semiannual interest dates are June 30 and December 31. The market interest rate is 9%, and the issue price of the bonds is 94. Mobil Technology amortizes bonds by the effective-interest method.

Issuing convertible bonds at a discount, amortizing by the effective-interest method, retiring bonds early, converting bonds, and reporting the bonds payable on the balance sheet (Obj. 2, 3, 5)

■ general ledger

Required

1. Prepare an effective-interest-method amortization table for the first four semiannual interest periods.
2. Journalize the following transactions:
   a. Issuance of the bonds on December 31, 20X7. Credit Convertible Bonds Payable.
   b. Payment of interest and amortization of the bonds on June 30, 20X8.
   c. Payment of interest and amortization of the bonds on December 31, 20X8.

(continued)

d. Retirement of bonds with face value of $200,000 July 1, 20X9. Mobil pays off the bonds at 102 in the open market.
e. Conversion by the bondholders on July 1, 20X9, of bonds with face value of $200,000 into 50,000 shares of Mobil's $1-par common stock.

3. Show how Mobil Technology would report the remaining bonds payable on its balance sheet at December 31, 20X9.

Financing operations with debt or with stock (Obj. 4)

writing assignment ■

P8-8B Marketing studies have shown that consumers prefer upscale restaurants, and recent trends in industry sales have supported the research. To capitalize on this trend, assume that **Pappadeaux's Restaurant, Inc.** is embarking on a massive expansion. Assume plans call for opening 20 new restaurants during the next 2 years. Each restaurant is scheduled to be 50% larger than the company's existing locations, furnished more elaborately, and with upgraded menus. Management estimates that company operations will provide $3 million of the cash needed for expansion. Pappadeaux's must raise the remaining $9.5 million from outsiders. The board of directors is considering obtaining the $9.5 million either through borrowing or by issuing common stock.

Required

1. Write a memo to Pappadeaux's management discussing the advantages and disadvantages of borrowing and of issuing common stock to raise the needed cash. Which method of raising the funds would you recommend?
2. How will what you learned in this problem help you manage a business?

Reporting liabilities on the balance sheet; times-interest-earned ratio (Obj. 5)

writing assignment ■

P8-9B The accounting records of Mirage Casino Corp. include the following items at December 31, 20X8:

Accumulated depreciation, equipment	$ 46,000	Mortgage note payable, current	$ 39,000
Discount on bonds payable (all long-term)	7,000	Accumulated pension benefit obligation	419,000
Operating income	315,000	Bonds payable, long-term	675,000
Equipment	137,000	Mortgage note payable, long-term	82,000
Pension plan assets (market value)	382,000	Bonds payable, current portion	75,000
Interest payable	9,000	Interest expense	57,000

Required

1. Show how how these items would be reported on the Mirage Casino Corp. classified balance sheet, including headings and totals for current liabilities, long-term liabilities, and so on.
2. Answer the following questions about Mirage's financial position at December 31, 20X8:
   a. What is the carrying amount of the bonds payable?
   b. Why is the interest-payable amount so much less than the amount of interest expense?
3. How many times did Mirage cover its interest expense during 20X8? Do you consider this ratio value safe or risky. Why?

APPLY YOUR KNOWLEDGE

Decision Cases

Analyzing alternative ways of raising $5 million (Obj. 4)

Case 1. Business is going well for **Park 'N Fly**, the company that operates remote parking lots near major airports. The board of directors of this family-owned company believes that Park 'N Fly could earn an additional $1.5 million income before interest and taxes by expanding into new markets. However, the $5 million that the business needs for growth cannot be raised within the family. The directors, who strongly wish to retain family control of the company, must consider issuing securities to outsiders. They are considering three financing plans.

Plan A is to borrow at 6%. Plan B is to issue 100,000 shares of common stock. Plan C is to issue 100,000 share of nonvoting, $3.75 preferred stock ($3.75 is the annual dividend paid on each share of preferred stock).* Park 'N Fly presently has net income of $2.5 million and 1 million shares of common stock outstanding. The company's income tax rate is 40%.

Required

1. Prepare an analysis to determine which plan will result in the highest earnings per share of common stock.
2. Recommend one plan to the board of directors. Give your reasons.

Exploring an actual bankruptcy (Obj. 2)

Case 2. In 20X2, **Enron Corporation** filed for Chapter 11 bankruptcy protection, shocking the business community: How could a company this large and this successful go bankrupt? This case explores the causes and the effects of Enron's bankruptcy.

At December 31, 20X0, and for the 4 years ended on that date, Enron reported the following (amounts in millions):

Balance Sheet (summarized)

Total assets	$65,503
Total liabilities	54,033
Total stockholders' equity	11,470

Income Statements (excerpts)

	20X0	19X9	19X8	19X7
Net income	$979*	$893	$703	$105

*Operating income = $1,953
Interest expense = $838

Unknown to investors and lenders, Enron also controlled hundreds of partnerships that owed vast amounts of money. These special-purpose entities (SPEs) did not appear on the Enron financial statements. Assume that the SPEs' assets totaled $7,000 million and their liabilities stood at $6,900 million; assume a 10% interest rate on the debt.

During the 4-year period up to 20X0, Enron's stock price shot up from $17.50 to $90.56. Enron used its escalating stock price to finance the SPEs by guaranteeing lenders that Enron would give them Enron stock if the SPEs could not pay their loans.

In 20X1, the SEC launched an investigation into Enron's accounting practices. It was alleged that Enron should have been including the SPEs in its financial statements all along. Enron then restated net income for years up to 20X0, wiping out nearly $600 million of total net income (and total assets) for this 4-year period. Enron's stock price tumbled, and the guarantees to the SPEs' lenders added millions to Enron's liabilities (assume the full amount of the SPEs' debt). To make matters worse, the assets of the SPEs lost much of their value; assume that their market value is only $500 million.

Required

1. Compute the debt ratio that Enron reported at the end of 20X0. Recompute this ratio after including the SPEs in Enron's financial statements. Also compute Enron's times-interest-earned ratio both ways for 20X0. Assume that the changes to Enron's financial position occurred during 20X0.
2. Why does it appear that Enron failed to include the SPEs in its financial statements? How do you view Enron after including the SPEs in the financial statements?

*For a discussion of preferred stock, see Chapter 9.

Ethical Issues

writing assignment ■

Issue 1. The Boeing Company, manufacturer of jet aircraft, was the defendant in numerous lawsuits claiming unfair trade practices. Boeing has strong incentives not to disclose these contingent liabilities. However, GAAP requires that companies report their contingent liabilities.

Required

1. Why would a company prefer not to disclose its contingent liabilities?
2. Describe how a bank could be harmed if a company seeking a loan did not disclose its contingent liabilities.
3. What is the ethical tightrope that companies must walk when they report their contingent liabilities?

writing assignment ■

Issue 2. SolarTech, manufacturer of solar energy panels, borrowed heavily to exploit the advantage of financing operations with debt. At first, SolarTech was able to earn operating income much higher than its interest expense and was therefore quite profitable. However, cheaper energy sources emerged, and SolarTech's debt burden pushed the company to the brink of bankruptcy. Operating income was less than interest expense.

Required

Is it unethical for managers to saddle a company with a high level of debt? Or is it just risky? Who could be hurt by a company's taking on too much debt? Discuss.

Focus on Financials: ■ YUM! Brands

Analyzing current and contingent liabilities (Obj. 1, 2, 5)

Refer to **YUM! Brands**, financial statements in Appendix A at the end of this book.

1. YUM's balance sheet reports a combined total for Accounts payable and other current liabilities. Give the breakdown of the reported total.
2. Income tax provision is another title for income tax expense. Why is YUM's income tax provision larger than income taxes payable at the end of each year?
3. Did YUM borrow more or pay off more short-term and long-term debt during 2003? How can you tell?
4. How would experienced analysts rate YUM's overall debt position—risky, safe, or average? Compute the ratio at December 27, 2003, that answers this question.

Focus on Analysis: ■ Pier 1 Imports

Analyzing current liabilities and long-term debt (Obj. 1, 2, 3, 5)

Pier 1 Imports' financial statements in Appendix B at the end of this book report a number of liabilities. Show amounts in thousands.

1. How would experienced analysts rate Pier 1's overall debt position—risky, safe, or average? Compute the ratio that enables you to answer this question.
2. Assume that Pier 1 completed two notes payable and long-term debt transactions during 2004. Journalize those transactions.
3. Use the data on the faces of Pier 1's 2004 income statement and balance sheet to estimate Pier 1's average interest rate during 2004 on all company borrowings. For this calculation, combine notes payable and long-term debt into a single amount, and use the beginning balance for 2004.

Group Projects

Project 1. Consider three different businesses:

1. A bank
2. A magazine publisher
3. A department store

For each business, list all of its liabilities—both current and long-term. Then compare the three lists to identify the liabilities that the three businesses have in common. Also identify the liabilities that are unique to each type of business.

Project 2. Alcenon Corporation leases the majority of the assets that it uses in operations. Alcenon prefers operating leases (versus capital leases) in order to keep the lease liability off its balance sheet and maintain a low debt ratio.

Alcenon is negotiating a 10-year lease on an asset with an expected useful life of 15 years. The lease requires Alcenon to make 10 annual lease payments of $20,000 each, with the first payment due at the beginning of the lease term. The leased asset has a market value of $135,180. The lease agreement specifies no transfer of title to the lessee and includes no bargain purchase option.

Write a report for Alcenon's management to explain what conditions must be present for Alcenon to be able to account for this lease as an operating lease.

spotlight

IHOP GOES PUBLIC

IHOP Corp.
Consolidated Balance Sheet (Adapted)
December 31, 2003

(In thousands, except share amounts)

Assets	
Current assets	
Total current assets	$127,081
Long-term receivables	354,036
Property and equipment, net	314,221
Other assets	47,666
Total assets	$843,004
Liabilities and Stockholders' Equity	
Current liabilities	
Total current liabilities	$ 45,373
Long-term debt	139,615
Other long-term liabilities	275,656
1 Stockholders' equity	
2 Preferred stock, $1 par value, 10,000,000 shares authorized; shares issued and outstanding: none	—
3 Common stock, $.01 par value, 40,000,000 shares authorized: 21,994,068 shares issued and 21,389,939 shares outstanding	220
4 Additional paid-in capital	104,661
5 Retained earnings	295,448
6 Treasury stock, at cost (604,129 shares)	(19,443)
7 Other	1,474
8 Total stockholders' equity	382,360
Total liabilities and stockholders' equity	$843,004

If you're like most college students, you've eaten at an IHOP restaurant. In this chapter you'll see a side of IHOP that you probably never considered before—the company's capital structure.

IHOP started in California and expanded across the country. To grow the company, IHOP management needed more capital and faced a decision: Do we keep control, or do we go outside and raise the money to expand? For the people who start up a company, this can be a tough decision. IHOP managers took the plunge and went public.

In its initial public offering of stock, IHOP issued common stock at $10 per share. The shares got off to a good start, and the stock has traded at $35.70 lately.

Stockholders' Equity

9

LEARNING OBJECTIVES

1. **Explain** the advantages and disadvantages of a corporation
2. **Measure** the effect of issuing stock on a company's financial position
3. **Describe** how treasury stock transactions affect a company
4. **Account** for dividends and measure their impact on a company
5. **Use** different stock values in decision making
6. **Evaluate** a company's return on assets and return on common equity
7. **Report** stockholders' equity transactions on the statement of cash flows

What does it mean to "go public," as **IHOP** did? A corporation *goes public* when it sells its stock to the general public. A common reason for going public is to raise money for expansion. By offering its stock to the public, a company can raise more money than if the stockholders remain private. The IHOP Corporation balance sheet (lines 3 and 4) indicates that through the end of 2003, the company had received almost $105 million from its stockholders.

Chapters 4 to 8 discussed accounting for the assets and the liabilities of a company. By this time, you should be familiar with all the assets and liabilities listed on IHOP's balance sheet. Let's focus now on the last part of the balance sheet—IHOP's stockholders' equity. In this chapter we discuss some of the decisions a company faces when issuing stock and buying back its stock and when paying dividends. Let's begin by reviewing how a corporation is organized.

Taking Action What Is the Best Way to Organize a Business?

OBJECTIVE

1 **Explain** the advantages and disadvantages of a corporation

Anyone starting a business must decide whether to organize the entity as a proprietorship, a partnership, or a corporation. Many businesses choose the corporation form. Why is the corporate form of business so attractive? The ways in which corporations differ from proprietorships and partnerships provide some reasons.

Stockholder
A person who owns stock in a corporation. Also called a *shareholder*.

Separate Legal Entity. A corporation is a business entity formed under state law. It is a distinct entity, an artificial person that exists apart from its owners, who are called **stockholders** or *shareholders*. The corporation has many of the rights that a person has. For example, a corporation may buy, own, and sell property. Assets and liabilities in the business belong to the corporation rather than to its owners. The corporation may enter into contracts, sue, and be sued.

Nearly all well-known companies, such as **IHOP**, **Motorola**, and **Pier 1 Imports**, are corporations. Their full names may include *Corporation* or Incorporated (abbreviated *Corp.* and *Inc.*) to indicate that they are corporations, for example, IHOP Corp. and Pier 1 Imports, Inc.

Continuous Life and Transferability of Ownership. Corporations have *continuous lives* regardless of changes in the ownership of their stock. The stockholders of IHOP or any corporation may transfer stock as they wish. They may sell or trade the stock to another person, give it away, bequeath it in a will, or dispose of it in any other way. The transfer of the stock does not affect the continuity of the corporation. In contrast, proprietorships and partnerships terminate when ownership changes.

Limited liability
No personal obligation of a stockholder for corporation debts. A stockholder can lose no more on an investment in a corporation's stock than the cost of the investment.

Limited Liability. Stockholders have **limited liability** for the corporation's debts. They have no personal obligation for corporate liabilities. The most that a stockholder can lose on an investment in a corporation's stock is the cost of the investment. In contrast, proprietors and partners are personally liable for all the debts of their businesses. Limited liability is one of the most attractive features of the corporate form of organization. It enables corporations to raise more capital from a wider group of investors than proprietorships and partnerships can.

Separation of Ownership and Management. Stockholders own the corporation, but the *board of directors*—elected by the stockholders—appoints officers to manage the business. Thus, stockholders may invest $1,000 or $1 million in the corporation without having to manage the business or disrupt their personal affairs.

Management's goal is to maximize the firm's value for the stockholders. But the separation between owners and managers may create problems. Corporate officers may run the business for their own benefit and not for the stockholders. For example, the chairman and CEO of **Tyco Corporation** was accused of looting Tyco of $600 million. The CFO of **Enron Corporation** set up outside partnerships and paid himself millions to manage the partnerships—unknown to Enron stockholders.

Corporate Taxation. Corporations are separate taxable entities. They pay several taxes not borne by proprietorships or partnerships, including an annual franchise tax levied by the state. The franchise tax is paid to keep the corporate charter in force. Corporations also pay federal and state income taxes.

Corporate earnings are subject to **double taxation** on their income. First, corporations pay income taxes on their corporate income. Then stockholders pay personal income tax on the cash dividends that they receive from corporations. Proprietorships and partnerships pay no business income tax. Instead, the tax falls solely on the owners.

Double taxation
Corporations pay income taxes on corporate income. Then, the stockholders pay personal income tax on the cash dividends that they receive from corporations.

Government Regulation. Because stockholders have only limited liability for corporation debts, outsiders doing business with the corporation can look no further than the corporation if it fails to pay. To protect the creditors and the stockholders of a corporation, both federal and state governments monitor corporations. The regulations mainly ensure that corporations disclose the information that investors and creditors need to make informed decisions. Accounting provides much of this information.

Exhibit 9-1 summarizes the advantages and disadvantages of the corporate form of business organization.

■ **EXHIBIT 9-1**

Advantages and Disadvantages of a Corporation

Advantages	Disadvantages
1. Can raise more capital than a proprietorship or partnership can	1. Separation of ownership and management
2. Continuous life	2. Corporate taxation
3. Ease of transferring ownership	3. Government regulation
4. Limited liability of stockholders	

Organizing a Corporation

The process of creating a corporation begins when its organizers, called the *incorporators*, obtain a charter from the state. The charter includes the authorization for the corporation to issue a certain number of shares of stock. A share of stock is the basic unit of ownership for a corporation. The incorporators pay fees, sign the charter, and file documents with the state. They agree to a set of **bylaws**, which act as the constitution for governing the corporation. The corporation then comes into existence.

Ultimate control of the corporation rests with the stockholders. The stockholders elect a **board of directors**, which sets policy and appoints officers. The board elects a **chairperson**, who usually is the most powerful person in the organization. The board also designates the **president**, who is the chief operating officer in charge of day-to-day operations. Most corporations also have vice presidents in charge of sales, manufacturing, accounting and finance (the chief financial officer, or CFO), and other key areas. Exhibit 9-2 shows the authority structure in a corporation.

Bylaws
Constitution for governing a corporation.

Board of directors
Group elected by the stockholders to set policy for a corporation and to appoint its officers.

Chairperson
Elected by a corporation's board of directors, usually the most powerful person in the corporation.

President
Chief operating officer in charge of managing the day-to-day operations of a corporation.

■ **EXHIBIT 9-2**
Authority Structure in a Corporation

Check Point 9-1

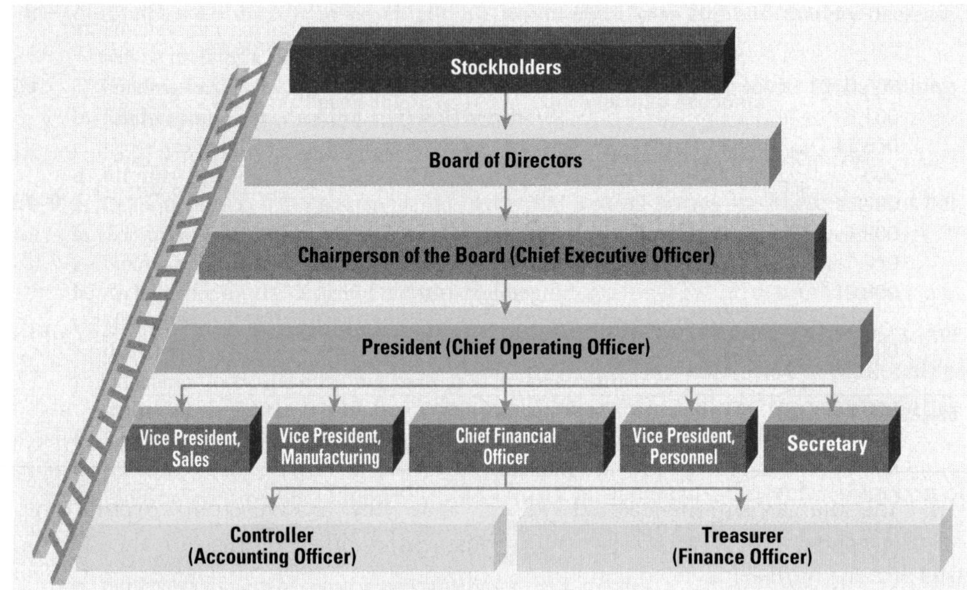

Stockholders' Rights

Ownership of stock entitles stockholders to four basic rights, unless specific rights are withheld by agreement with the stockholders:

1. *Vote.* The right to participate in management by voting on matters that come before the stockholders. This is the stockholder's sole voice in the management of the corporation. A stockholder is entitled to one vote for each share of stock owned.
2. *Dividends.* The right to receive a proportionate part of any distributed payment, or dividend. Each share of stock in a particular class receives an equal dividend.
3. *Liquidation.* The right to receive a proportionate share (based on number of shares held) of any assets remaining after the corporation pays its liabilities in liquidation. Liquidation means to go out of business, sell the entity's assets, pay its liabilities, and distribute any remaining cash to the owners.
4. *Preemption.* The right to maintain one's proportionate ownership in the corporation. Suppose you own 5% of a corporation's stock. If the corporation issues 100,000 new shares, it must offer you the opportunity to buy 5% (5,000) of the new shares. This right, called the *preemptive right*, is usually withheld from the stockholders.

Stockholders' Equity

Stockholders' equity
The stockholders' ownership interest in the assets of a corporation.

Paid-in capital
The amount of stockholders' equity that stockholders have contributed to the corporation. Also called *contributed capital*.

Retained earnings
The amount of stockholders' equity that the corporation has earned through profitable operation of the business and has not given back to stockholders.

As we saw in Chapter 1, **stockholders' equity** represents the stockholders' ownership interest in the assets of a corporation. Stockholders' equity is divided into two main parts:

1. **Paid-in capital**, also called *contributed capital*. This is the amount of stockholders' equity the stockholders have contributed to the corporation. Paid-in capital includes the stock accounts and any additional paid-in capital.
2. **Retained earnings.** This is the amount of stockholders' equity the corporation has earned through profitable operations and has not used for dividends.

Companies report stockholders' equity by source. They report paid-in capital separately from retained earnings because most states prohibit the declaration of cash dividends from paid-in capital. Thus, cash dividends are declared from retained earnings.

The owners' equity of a corporation is divided into shares of **stock**. A corporation issues *stock certificates* to its owners in exchange for their investment in the business. Because stock represents the corporation's capital, it is often called *capital stock*. The basic unit of capital stock is called a *share*. A corporation may issue a stock certificate for any number of shares it wishes—one share, 100 shares, or any other number—but the total number of *authorized* shares is limited by charter. Exhibit 9-3 shows an actual stock certificate for 288 shares of Central Jersey Bancorp common stock.

Stock
Shares into which the owners' equity of a corporation is divided.

■ **EXHIBIT 9-3** Stock Certificate

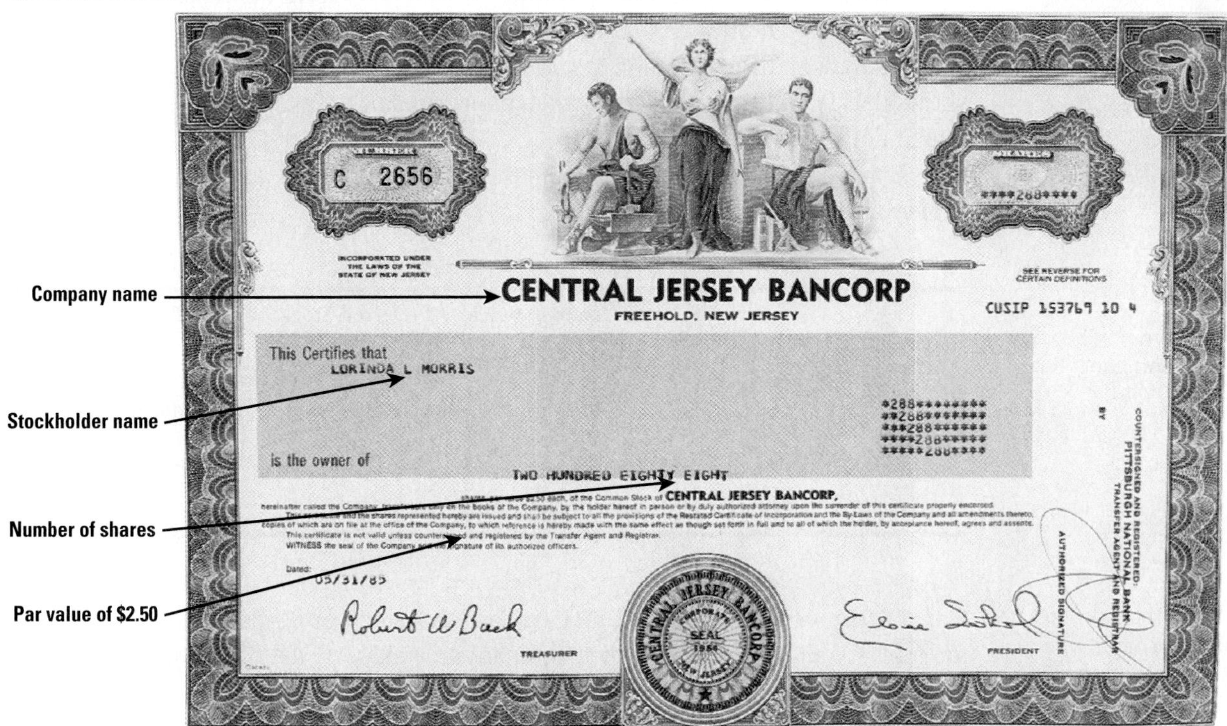

Stock in the hands of a stockholder is said to be **outstanding**. The total number of shares of stock outstanding at any time represents 100% ownership of the corporation.

Outstanding stock
Stock in the hands of stockholders.

Classes of Stock

Corporations issue different types of stock to appeal to a variety of investors. The stock of a corporation may be either

- Common or preferred
- Par or no-par

Common and Preferred. Every corporation issues **common stock**, the basic form of capital stock. Unless designated otherwise, the word *stock* is understood to mean "common stock." Common stockholders have the four basic rights of stock ownership, unless a right is specifically withheld. For example, some companies issue Class A common stock, which usually carries the right to vote, and Class B common stock, which may be nonvoting. In describing a corporation, we would say the common stockholders are the owners of the business.

Common stock
The most basic form of capital stock. The common stockholders own a corporation.

Preferred stock gives its owners certain advantages over common stockholders. Preferred stockholders receive dividends before the common stockholders and receive assets before the common stockholders if the corporation liquidates. Owners of

Preferred stock
Stock that gives its owners certain advantages, such as the priority to receive dividends before the common stockholders and the priority to receive assets before the common stockholders if the corporation liquidates.

preferred stock also have the four basic stockholder rights, unless a right is specifically denied. Companies may issue different classes of preferred stock (Class A and Class B or Series A and Series B, for example). Each class is recorded in a separate account.

Check Point 9-2

■ **EXHIBIT 9-4**

Preferred Stock

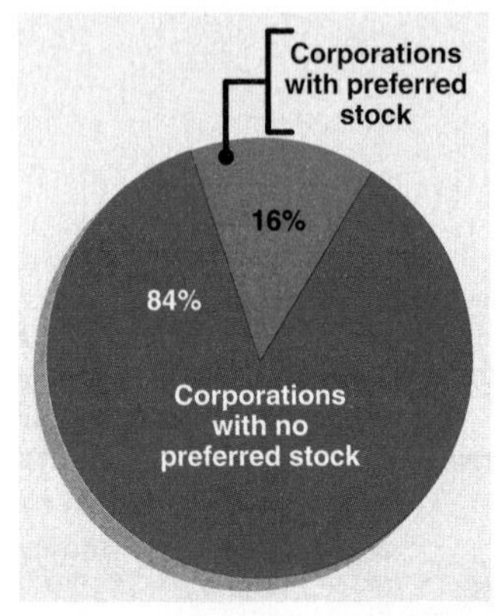

Preferred stock is a hybrid between common stock and long-term debt. Like debt, preferred stock pays a fixed dividend amount to the investor. But like stock, the dividend is not required to be paid unless the board of directors has declared the dividend. Also, companies have no obligation to pay back true preferred stock. Preferred stock that must be redeemed (paid back) by the corporation is a liability masquerading as a stock.

Preferred stock is rarer than you might think. A recent survey of 600 corporations revealed that only 16% of them had preferred stock outstanding (Exhibit 9-4). All corporations have common stock. The balance sheet of IHOP Corp. (page 416) shows that IHOP is authorized to issue preferred stock. To date, however, IHOP has issued none of the preferred stock.

Exhibit 9-5 summarizes the similarities and differences among common stock, preferred stock, and long-term debt.

■ **EXHIBIT 9-5**

Comparison of Common Stock, Preferred Stock, and Long-Term Debt

	Common Stock	Preferred Stock	Long-Term Debt
1. Corporate obligation to repay principal	No	No	Yes
2. Dividends/interest	Dividends not tax-deductible	Dividends not tax-deductible	Tax-deductible interest expense
3. Corporate obligation to pay dividends/interest	Only after declaration	Only after declaration	At fixed dates

Par value
Arbitrary amount assigned by a company to a share of its stock.

Legal capital
Minimum amount of stockholders' equity that a corporation must maintain for the protection of creditors. For corporations with par-value stock, legal capital is the par value of the stock issued.

Stated value
An arbitrary amount assigned to no-par stock; similar to par value.

Par Value and No-Par. Stock may be par-value stock or no-par stock. **Par value** is an arbitrary amount assigned by a company to a share of its stock. Most companies set the par value of their common stock low to avoid legal difficulties from issuing their stock below par. Most states require companies to maintain a minimum amount of stockholders' equity for the protection of creditors, and this minimum is often called the corporation's legal capital. For corporations with par-value stock, **legal capital** is the par value of the shares issued.

The par value of **PepsiCo** common stock is 1 $\frac{2}{3}$ cents per share. **Amazon.com** common stock carries a par value of $0.01 per share, and **Pier 1 Imports** common stock par value is $1 per share. Per value of preferred stock is sometimes higher.

No-par stock does not have par value. But some no-par stock has a **stated value**, which makes it similar to par-value stock. The stated value is an arbitrary amount similar to par value. In a recent survey, only 9% of the companies had no-par stock outstanding.

Issuing Stock

OBJECTIVE

2 **Measure** the effect of issuing stock on a company's financial position

Large corporations such as IHOP, PepsiCo, and **Microsoft** need huge quantities of money to operate. Corporations may sell stock directly to the stockholders or use the service of an *underwriter*, such as the brokerage firms **Merrill Lynch** and **Salomon Smith Barney**. Companies often advertise the issuance of their stock to attract investors. The *Wall Street Journal* is the most popular medium for such advertisements, which are also called *tombstones*. Exhibit 9-6 is a reproduction of IHOP's tombstone, which appeared in the *Wall Street Journal*.

■ **EXHIBIT 9-6** Announcement of Public Offering of IHOP Stock (Adapted)

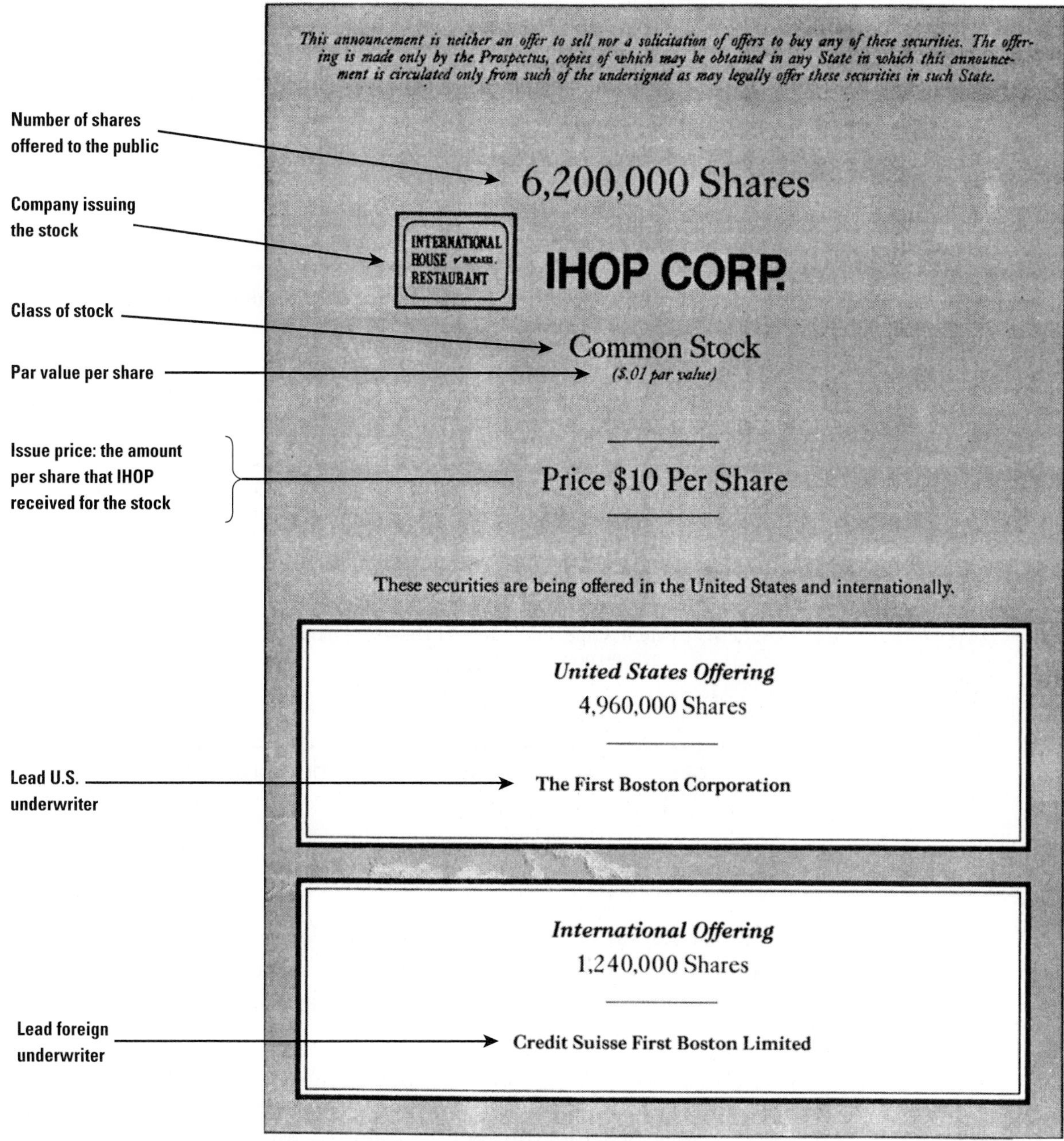

The lead underwriter of IHOP's public offering was the First Boston Group of Credit Suisse First Boston. Several other domestic brokerage firms and investment bankers sold IHOP stock to their clients. In its initial public offering (illustrated in Exhibit 9-6), IHOP sought to raise $62 million of capital.

Common Stock

Common Stock at Par. Suppose IHOP's common stock carried a par value of $10 per share. The entry for issuance of 6.2 million shares of stock at par would be

Jan. 8	Cash (6,200,000 × $10)........	62,000,000	
	Common Stock..........		62,000,000
	To issue common stock.		

IHOP's assets and stockholders' equity increase by the same amount.

ASSETS	=	LIABILITIES	+	STOCKHOLDERS' EQUITY
+62,000,000	=	0		+62,000,000

Common Stock Above Par. Most corporations set par value at a low amount, then issue common stock for a price above par. IHOP's common stock has a par value of \$0.01 (1 cent) per share. The \$9.99 difference between issue price (\$10) and par value (\$0.01) is additional paid-in capital. Both the par value of the stock and the additional amount are part of paid-in capital.

Check Point 9-3

Because the entity is dealing with its own stockholders, a sale of stock is not gain, income, or profit to the corporation. This situation illustrates one of the fundamentals of accounting: *A company neither earns a profit nor incurs a loss when it sells its stock to, or buys its stock from, its own stockholders.*

With a par value of \$0.01, IHOP's entry to record the issuance of the stock is

July 23	Cash (6,200,000 × \$10)	62,000,000	
	Common Stock (6,200,000 × \$0.01). . . .		62,000
	Paid-in Capital in Excess of Par—Common (6,200,000 × \$9.99).		61,938,000
	To issue common stock.		

ASSETS	=	LIABILITIES	+	STOCKHOLDERS' EQUITY
+62,000,000	=	0		+62,000
				+61,938,000

Another title for Paid-in Capital in Excess of Par—Common is Additional Paid-in Capital—Common, as used by IHOP Corporation. At the end of the year, IHOP could report stockholders' equity on its balance sheet as follows:

Stockholders' Equity	
Common stock, \$0.01 par, 40 million shares authorized, 6.2 million shares issued	\$ 62,000
Paid-in capital in excess of par	61,938,000
Total paid-in capital	62,000,000
Retained earnings	194,000,000
Total stockholders' equity	\$256,000,000

Check Point 9-4

All the transactions recorded in this section include a receipt of cash by the corporation as it issues *new* stock. These transactions are different from those reported in the financial press. In those transactions, one stockholder sells stock to another investor, and the corporation makes no journal entry.

stop AND think. . .

Examine IHOP's balance sheet at December 31, 2003, given at the beginning of the chapter (page 416). Answer these questions about IHOP's actual stock transactions (amounts in thousands, except per share):

1. What was IHOP's total paid-in capital at December 31, 2003?
2. How many shares of common stock had IHOP issued through the end of 2003?
3. What was the average issue price of the IHOP stock that the company issued through the end of 2003?

Answers:

	December 31, 2003
1. Total paid-in capital	$220 + $104,661 = $104,881
2. Number of shares issued	21,994

$$3.\ \text{Average issue price of stock through the end of 2003} = \frac{\text{Total received from issuance of stock}}{\text{New shares issued}} = \frac{\$104{,}881}{21{,}994}$$

$$= \$4.77 \text{ per share}$$

Apparently IHOP has issued a lot of its stock at a price below its initial price of $10 per share.

No-Par Common Stock. To record the issuance of no-par stock, the company debits the asset received and credits the stock account for the cash value of the asset received. Glenwood Corporation, which manufactures skateboards, issues 3,000 shares of no-par common stock for $20 per share. The stock issuance entry is

Aug. 14	Cash (3,000 × $20)	60,000	
	Common Stock		60,000
	To issue no-par common stock.		

ASSETS	=	LIABILITIES	+	STOCKHOLDERS' EQUITY
+60,000	=	0		+60,000

Glenwood Corporation's charter authorizes Glenwood to issue 100,000 shares of no-par stock, and the company has $46,000 in retained earnings. The corporation reports stockholders' equity on the balance sheet as follows

Stockholders' Equity	
Common stock, no par, 100,000 shares authorized, 3,000 shares issued	$ 60,000
Retained earnings	46,000
Total stockholders' equity	$106,000

No-Par Common Stock with a Stated Value. Accounting for no-par stock with a stated value is identical to accounting for par-value stock. The excess over stated value is credited to Additional Paid-in Capital.

Common Stock Issued for Assets Other Than Cash. When a corporation issues stock in exchange for assets other than cash, it records the assets received at their current market value and credits the capital accounts accordingly. The assets' prior book value does not matter because the stockholder will demand stock equal to the market value of the asset given. Kahn Corporation issued 15,000 shares of its $1 par common stock for equipment worth $4,000 and a building worth $120,000. Kahn's entry is

Check Point 9-5

Nov. 12	Equipment........................	4,000	
	Building	120,000	
	Common Stock (15,000 × $1)		15,000
	Paid-in Capital in Excess of Par—Common ($124,000 – $15,000)..........		109,000
	To issue common stock in exchange for equipment and a building.		

ASSETS	=	LIABILITIES	+	STOCKHOLDERS' EQUITY
+4,000				+15,000
	=	0		
+120,000				+109,000

ACCOUNTING ALERT

A Stock Issuance for Other Than Cash Can Pose an Accounting Problem

Generally accepted accounting principles say to record stock at the fair market value of whatever the corporation receives in exchange for the stock. When the corporation receives cash, the cash received provides clear evidence of the value of the stock because cash is worth its face amount.

Many entrepreneurs start up companies with an asset other than cash. They invest the asset and receive the new corporation's stock. A computer whiz may contribute some computer hardware and software. The software may be market-tested or it may be new. It may be worth millions or it may be worthless. An artist may contribute paintings or sculpture to start an art gallery. A real-estate agent may invest in a building to start a realty company.

The corporation must record the asset received and the stock given with a journal entry such as the following:

Software............................	XXX	
Common Stock		XXX
Issued stock in exchange for software.		

In effect, the new corporation is buying the software and paying for it by issuing common stock. Therefore, the business must assign a value to the software and to the common stock. The market value of the software determines the value assigned to the common stock. What is the software really worth? Let's consider two possibilities:

Situation 1. The software has been on the market for several months and is selling well. The creator of the software has standing orders for 2,000 copies, and an industry expert values the software at $500,000. To start up the new corporation, the company makes this entry:

Software............................	500,000	
Common Stock		500,000
Issued stock in exchange for software.		

Situation 2. The software is new and untested. The entrepreneur believes it is worth millions but decides to be conservative and values it at $500,000. For its first transaction, the company makes this entry:

Software	500,000	
Common Stock		500,000
Issued stock in exchange for software.		

Suppose both entrepreneurs need $200,000 to market the software. They invite you to invest in their new business. Both balance sheets look identical:

Gee-Whiz Computer Solutions
Balance Sheet
December 31, 20X8

ASSETS		LIABILITIES	
Compute software . . .	$500,000		$ -0-
		STOCKHOLDER EQUITY	
		Common stock	500,000
Total assets	$500,000	Total liabilities and equity . .	$500,000

Both companies are debt-free and both appear to have a valuable asset. Which company will you invest in? Here are three takeaway lessons:

- Be careful when you invest your money.
- Some accounting values are more solid than others.
- Not all financial statements mean exactly what they say—unless they are audited by independent CPAs.

Preferred Stock

Accounting for preferred stock follows the pattern we illustrated for common stock. The company records a Preferred Stock account at its par value, with any excess credited to Paid-in Capital in Excess of Par—Preferred. This is an entirely separate account from Paid-in-Capital in Excess of Par—Common. Accounting for no-par preferred stock follows the pattern for no-par common stock. When reporting stockholders' equity on the balance sheet, a corporation lists preferred stock, common stock, and retained earnings—in that order, as illustrated for IHOP on page 416.

Ethical Considerations

Issuance of stock for *cash* poses no serious ethical challenge. The company simply receives cash and records the stock at the amount received, as illustrated in the preceding sections of this chapter. There is no difficulty in valuing stock issued for cash because the values of the cash—and the stock—are obvious.

Issuing stock for assets other than cash can pose an ethical challenge. The company issuing the stock often wishes to record a large amount for the noncash asset received (such as land or a building) and for the stock it is issuing. Large asset and stockholders' equity amounts on the balance sheet make the business look more prosperous and more creditworthy.

A company is supposed to record an asset received at its current market value. But one person's perception of a particular asset's market value can differ from another person's opinion. The ethical course of action is to record the asset at its current fair market value, as determined by a good-faith estimate of market value from independent appraisers. It is rare for a public corporation to be found guilty of *understating* the asset values on its balance sheet, but companies have been embarrassed by *overstating* these values. Investors who rely on the financial statements may be able to prove in a court of law that an overstatement of asset values caused them to pay too much for the company's stock.

Interestingly, the stockholder doesn't have to prove that he/she relied on the false financial statements. Under the Securities Acts of 1933/1934, the stockholders must only prove that (a) he/she lost money on the investment and (b) the company's financial statements were flawed. The court will then decide in favor of the stockholder and assess damages against the company.

MID-CHAPTER Summary Problems

1. Test your understanding of the first half of this chapter by deciding whether each of the following statements is true or false.
   a. The policy-making body in a corporation is called the board of directors.
   b. The owner of 100 shares of preferred stock has greater voting rights than the owner of 100 shares of common stock.
   c. Par-value stock is worth more than no-par stock.
   d. Issuance of 1,000 shares of $5 par-value stock at $12 increases contributed capital by $12,000.
   e. The issuance of no-par stock with a stated value is fundamentally different from issuing par-value stock.
   f. A corporation issues its preferred stock in exchange for land and a building with a combined market value of $200,000. This transaction increases the corporation's owners' equity by $200,000 regardless of the assets' prior book values.
   g. Preferred stock is a riskier investment than common stock.
2. The brewery **Adolph Coors Company** has two classes of common stock. Only the Class A common stockholders are entitled to vote. The company's balance sheet included the following presentation:

Stockholders' Equity	
Capital stock	
Class A common stock, voting, $1 par value, authorized and issued 1,260,000 shares	$ 1,260,000
Class B common stock, nonvoting, no par value, authorized and issued 46,200,000 shares	11,000,000
	12,260,000
Additional paid-in capital	2,011,000
Retained earnings	872,403,000
	$886,674,000

Required

a. Record the issuance of the Class A common stock. Use the Coors account titles.
b. Record the issuance of the Class B common stock. Use the Coors account titles.
c. How much of Coors' stockholders' equity was contributed by the stockholders? How much was provided by profitable operations? Does this division of equity suggest that the company has been successful? Why or why not?
d. Write a sentence to describe what Coors' stockholders' equity means.

Answers

1. a. True b. False c. False d. True e. False f. True g. False

2. a.

Cash	3,271,000	
Class A Common Stock		1,260,000
Additional Paid-in Capital		2,011,000
To record issuance of Class A common stock.		

b.

Cash	11,000,000	
Class B Common Stock		11,000,000
To record issuance of Class B common stock		

c. Contributed by the stockholders: $14,271,000 ($12,260,000 + $2,011,000). Provided by profitable operations: $872,403,000.
This division suggests that the company has been successful because most of its stockholders' equity has come from profitable operations.

Check Point 9-6

d. A Coors stockholders' equity of $886,674,000 means that the company's stockholders own $886,674,000 of the business's assets.

Check Point 9-7

Treasury Stock Transactions

OBJECTIVE

3 **Describe** how treasury stock transactions affect a company

A company's own stock that it has issued and later reacquired is called **treasury stock**.[1] In effect, the corporation holds the stock in its treasury. Corporations may purchase their own stock for several reasons:

Treasury stock
A corporation's own stock that it has issued and later reacquired.

1. The company has issued all its authorized stock and needs the stock for distributions to employees under stock purchase plans.
2. The business is trying to increase net assets by buying its shares low and hoping to resell them for a higher price.
3. Management wants to avoid a takeover by an outside party.

■ Taking Action Should a Company Buy Back Its Own Stock?

Let's illustrate the accounting for treasury stock by IHOP Corp. We use rounded amounts, as adapted, and stated in thousands. If IHOP had not purchased any treasury stock, the company could have reported the following stockholders' equity at December 31, 2003 (all amounts in thousands):

(Before Purchase of Treasury Stock)	
Common Stock	$ 220
Paid-in capital in excess of par—common	105,000
Retained earnings	295,000
Total equity	$400,220

[1]In this text, we illustrate the *cost* method of accounting for treasury stock because it is used most widely. Other methods are presented in intermediate accounting courses.

Assume that during 2004, IHOP paid $19,000 to purchase some of its common stock as treasury stock. IHOP would record the purchase of treasury stock as follows (in thousands):

2004			
Nov. 12	Treasury Stock	19,000	
	Cash		19,000
	Purchased treasury stock.		

Treasury stock is recorded at cost—without regard to par value. The Treasury Stock account has a debit balance, the opposite of the other equity accounts. Therefore, *Treasury Stock is contra stockholders' equity*, reported beneath Retained Earnings on the balance sheet. Treasury Stock's balance is subtracted from equity as follows (amounts in thousands):

(After Purchase of Treasury Stock)	
Common stock	$ 220
Paid-in capital in excess of par—common	105,000
Retained earnings	295,000
Less Treasury stock (300 shares at cost)	(19,000)
Total equity	$381,220

Compare IHOP's total equity before the purchase of treasury stock ($400,220) and after ($381,220). IHOP's total equity decreased by $19,000, the cost of the treasury stock. The purchase of treasury stock has the opposite effect of issuing stock:

- Issuing stock *grows* a company's assets and equity.
- Purchasing treasury stock *shrinks* assets and equity.

Treasury stock is so named because it is held in the company treasury awaiting resale. Now let's see how to account for the sale of treasury stock.

Sale of Treasury Stock

Selling treasury stock grows assets and equity exactly as issuing new stock does. Suppose IHOP resells its treasury stock in 2005 for $25,000. The sale increases assets and equity by the full amount of cash received. IHOP would record this sale of treasury stock as follows (in thousands):

2005			
July 22	Cash	25,000	
	Treasury Stock		19,000
	Paid-in Capital from Treasury Stock Transactions (or Additional Paid-in Capital—Common)		6,000
	Sold treasury stock.		

If IHOP had sold the treasury stock for a price below cost then IHOP could have debited Retained Earnings for the difference.

stop AND think. . .

All amounts are in thousands.

Report IHOP's stockholders' equity after selling the treasury stock for $25,000.

Answer:

	Thousands
Common stock	$ 220
Paid-in capital in excess of par—common ($105,000 + $6,000)	111,000
Retained earnings	295,000
Total equity	$406,220

Now compare total equity before and after selling the treasury stock. What was the net effect of selling the treasury stock?

Answer:

Stockholders' equity increased by the full sale price received for the treasury stock, as follows:

	Thousands
Total equity after sale of treasury stock	$406,220
Total equity before selling the treasury stock	381,220
Increase in stockholders' equity	$ 25,000

Check Point 9-8

Check Point 9-9

Retirement of Stock

A corporation may purchase its own stock and *retire* it by canceling the stock certificates. Retirements of preferred stock occur more often than retirements of common stock, to avoid paying dividends on the preferred stock. The retired stock cannot be reissued. When a company retires its stock, the journal entry debits the stock account and any additional paid-in capital on the stock and credits Cash.

Retained Earnings, Dividends, and Splits

We have seen that the equity section of the balance sheet is called *stockholders' equity* or *shareholders' equity*. The paid-in capital accounts and retained earnings make up the stockholders' equity section.

The Retained Earnings account carries the balance of the business's net income less its net losses and less any declared dividends accumulated over the corporation's lifetime. *Retained* means "held onto." Successful companies grow by reinvesting back into the business the assets they generate through profitable operations. IHOP Corp. is an example; the majority of its equity comes from retained earnings.

The Retained Earnings account is not a reservoir of cash waiting for the board of directors to pay dividends to the stockholders. In fact, the corporation may have a large balance in Retained Earnings but not have the cash to pay a dividend. Cash and Retained Earnings are two separate accounts with no particular relationship. A $500,000 balance in Retained Earnings simply means that $500,000 of owners' equity has been created by profits reinvested in the business. It says nothing about the company's Cash balance.

A *credit* balance in Retained Earnings is normal, indicating that the corporation's lifetime earnings exceed its lifetime losses and dividends. A *debit* balance in Retained Earnings arises when a corporation's lifetime losses and dividends exceed its lifetime earnings. Called a **deficit**, this amount is subtracted from the sum of the other equity

■ **EXHIBIT 9-7**

Retained Earnings of the *Accounting Trends & Techniques 600* Companies

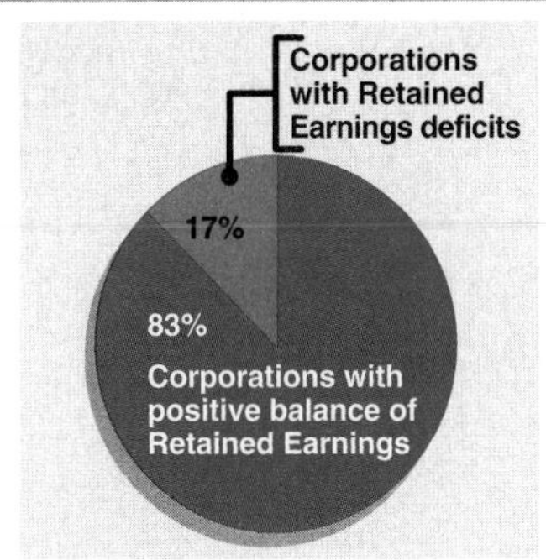

Deficit
Debit balance in the Retained Earnings account.

accounts to determine total stockholders' equity. In a recent survey, 17% had a retained earnings deficit (Exhibit 9-7).

■ Taking Action Should the Company Declare and Pay Cash Dividends?

Dividend
Distribution (usually cash) by a corporation to its stockholders.

A **dividend** is a corporation's return to its stockholders of the benefits of earnings. Most dividends are cash dividends. Corporate finance courses address the question of how a company decides on its dividend policy. Accounting tells a company if it can pay a dividend. To do so, a company must have both

- Enough retained earnings to *declare* the dividend
- Enough cash to *pay* the dividend

A corporation declares a dividend before paying it. Only the board of directors has the authority to declare a dividend. The corporation has no obligation to pay a dividend until the board declares one, but once declared, the dividend becomes a legal liability of the corporation. Three relevant dates for dividends are as follows:

1. ***Declaration date, June 19.*** On the declaration date, the board of directors announces the dividend, and that creates a liability for the corporation. Declaration is recorded by debiting Retained Earnings and crediting Dividends Payable. Assume a $50,000 dividend.

June 19	Retained Earnings[2]	50,000	
	Dividends Payable		50,000
	Declared a cash dividend.		

2. ***Date of record, July 1.*** As part of the declaration, the corporation announces the record date, which follows the declaration date by a few weeks. The stockholders on the record date will receive the dividend. There is no journal entry for the date of record.
3. ***Payment date, July 10.*** Payment of the dividend usually follows the record date by a week or two. Payment is recorded by debiting Dividends Payable and crediting Cash.

July 10	Dividends Payable	50,000	
	Cash		50,000
	Paid cash dividend.		

Dividends on Preferred Stock

OBJECTIVE

4 **Account** for dividends and measure their impact on a company

When a company has issued both preferred and common stock, the preferred stockholders receive their dividends first. The common stockholders receive dividends only if the total dividend is large enough to pay the preferred stockholders first.

Pinecraft Industries, Inc., a furniture manufacturer, has 100,000 shares of $1.50 preferred stock outstanding in addition to its common stock. The $1.50 designation means that the preferred stockholders receive an annual dividend of $1.50 per share.

[2]In the early part of this book, we debited a Dividends account to clearly identify the purpose of the payment. From here on, we follow the more common practice of debiting the Retained Earnings account for dividend declarations.

In 20X6, Pinecraft declares an annual dividend of $1,000,000. The allocation to preferred and common stockholders is:

Preferred dividend (100,000 shares × $1.50 per share)	$ 150,000
Common dividend (remainder: $1,000,000 – $150,000)	850,000
Total dividend	$1,000,000

If Pinecraft declares only a $200,000 dividend, preferred stockholders receive $150,000, and the common stockholders receive the remainder, $50,000 ($200,000 – $150,000).

Two Ways to Express the Dividend Rate on Preferred Stock. Dividends on preferred stock are stated either as a

- Percentage rate or
- Dollar amount

For example, preferred stock may be "6% preferred," which means that owners of the preferred stock receive an annual dividend of 6% of the stock's par value. If par value is $100 per share, preferred stockholders receive an annual cash dividend of $6 per share (6% of $100). Alternatively, the preferred stock may be "$3 preferred," which means that the preferred stockholders receive an annual dividend of $3 per share regardless of the stock's par value. The dividend rate on no-par preferred stock is stated in a dollar amount per share.

Dividends on Cumulative and Noncumulative Preferred Stock. The allocation of dividends may be complex if the preferred stock is *cumulative*. Corporations sometimes fail to pay a dividend to preferred stockholders. This is called *passing the dividend*, and the passed dividends are said to be *in arrears*. The owners of **cumulative preferred stock** must receive all dividends in arrears plus the current year's dividend before the corporation can pay dividends to the common stockholders. *The law considers preferred stock cumulative unless it is specifically labeled as noncumulative.* Therefore, most preferred stock is cumulative.

Cumulative preferred stock
Preferred stock whose owners must receive all dividends in arrears before the corporation can pay dividends to the common stockholders.

The preferred stock of Pinecraft Industries is cumulative. Suppose the company passed the 20X6 preferred dividend of $150,000. Before paying dividends to its common stockholders in 20X7, the company must first pay preferred dividends of $150,000 for both 20X6 and 20X7, a total of $300,000.

Assume that Pinecraft Industries passes its 20X6 preferred dividend. In 20X7, the company declares a $500,000 dividend. The entry to record the declaration is

Sept. 6	Retained Earnings	500,000	
	Dividends Payable, Preferred ($150,000 × 2)		300,000
	Dividends Payable, Common ($500,000 – $300,000)		200,000
	To declare a cash dividend.		

Check Point 9-10

Check Point 9-11

If the preferred stock is *noncumulative*, the corporation is not obligated to pay dividends in arrears. A liability for either preferred or common dividends arises only when the board of directors declares the dividend.

■ Taking Action Why Issue a Stock Dividend?

A **stock dividend** is a proportional distribution by a corporation of its own stock to its stockholders. Stock dividends increase the stock account and decrease Retained Earnings. Total equity is unchanged, and no asset or liability is affected.

Stock dividend
A proportional distribution by a corporation of its own stock to its stockholders.

The corporation distributes stock dividends to stockholders in proportion to the number of shares they already own. If you own 300 shares of IHOP common stock and IHOP distributes a 10% common stock dividend, you will receive 30 (300 × .10) additional shares. You would then own 330 shares of the stock. All other IHOP stockholders would also receive additional shares equal to 10% of their prior holdings.

In distributing a stock dividend, the corporation gives up no assets. Why, then, do companies issue stock dividends? A corporation may choose to distribute stock dividends for the following reasons:

1. ***To continue dividends but conserve cash.*** A company may want to keep cash for operations and yet wish to continue dividends in some form. So the corporation may distribute a stock dividend. Stockholders pay no income tax on stock dividends.
2. ***To reduce the per-share market price of its stock.*** Distribution of a stock dividend may cause the market price of a share of the company's stock to fall because of the increased supply of the stock. The objective is to make the stock less expensive and thus most attractive to a wider range of investors.

Suppose IHOP declared a 10% stock dividend in 2006. At the time, assume IHOP had 20,000,000 shares of common stock outstanding. Generally accepted accounting principles (GAAP) label a stock dividend of 25% or less as *small* and suggest that the dividend be recorded at the market value of the shares distributed. At the time of the stock dividend, assume IHOP's stock is trading for $15 per share. IHOP would record this stock dividend as follows:

2006			
May 19	Retained Earnings (20,000,000 shares of common outstanding × 0.10 stock dividend × $15 market value per share of common)	30,000,000	
	Common Stock (20,000,000 × 0.10 × $0.01 par value per share)		20,000
	Paid-in Capital in Excess of Par—Common. . .		29,980,000
	Distributed a 10% stock dividend.		

GAAP identifies stock dividends above 25% as *large* and permits large stock dividends to be recorded at par value. For a large stock dividend, therefore, IHOP would debit Retained Earnings and credit Common Stock for the par value of the shares distributed in the dividend. Large stock dividends are rare.

Check Point 9-12

stop AND think. . .

A corporation issued 1,000 shares of its $10-par common as a stock dividend when the stock's market price was $25 per share. Assume that the 1,000 dividend shares are equal to (1) 10% of the outstanding shares and (2) 100% of the outstanding shares. How much is the debit to Retained Earnings for each dividend?

Answer:

1. 10% = Small stock dividend. Debit Retained Earnings for market value of $25,000 (1,000 shares × $25 market value per share).
2. 100% = Large stock dividend. Debit Retained Earnings for par value of $10,000 (1,000 shares × $10 per value per share).

Stock Splits

A **stock split** is an increase in the number of authorized, issued, and outstanding shares of stock, coupled with a proportionate reduction in the stock's par value. For example, if the company splits its stock 2 for 1, the number of outstanding shares is doubled and each share's par value is halved. A stock split, like a large stock dividend, decreases the market price of the stock—with the intention of making the stock more attractive in the market. Most leading companies in the United States—**IBM, Ford Motor Company, Giant Food, Inc.**—have split their stock.

Stock split
An increase in the number of authorized, issued, and outstanding shares of stock coupled with a proportionate reduction in the stock's par value.

The market price of a share of **Quaker Oats** common stock has been approximately \$25. Assume that Quaker Oats wishes to decrease the market price to approximately \$12.50. Quaker may decide to split its common stock 2 for 1. A 2-for-1 stock split means that the company would have twice as many shares of stock outstanding after the split as it had before and that each share's par value would be cut in half. Before the split, Quaker had approximately 170 million shares of \$5 par common stock issued and outstanding. Compare Quaker Oats stockholders' equity before and after a 2-for-1 stock split:

Quaker Oats Stockholders' Equity (Adapted)

Before 2-for-1 Stock Split:	(In millions)	After 2-for-1 Stock Split	(In millions)
Common stock, \$5 par, 400 million shares authorized, 170 million shares issued	\$ 850	Common stock, \$2.50 par, 800 million shares authorized, 340 million shares issued	\$ 850
Additional paid-in capital	136	Additional paid-in capital	136
Retained earnings	1,062	Retained earnings	1,062
Other	(1,683)	Other	(1,683)
Total stockholders' equity	\$ 365	Total stockholders' equity	\$ 365

All account balances are the same after the stock split, as before. Only the par value per share of common, the number of shares authorized, and the number of shares issued are affected. Total equity does not change.

Measuring the Value of Stock

The business community measures *stock values* in various ways, depending on the purpose of the measurement. These values include market value, redemption value, liquidation value, and book value.

Market, Redemption, Liquidation, and Book Value

OBJECTIVE

5 Use different stock values in decision making

A stock's **market value**, or *market price*, is the price a person can buy or sell a share of the stock for. The issuing corporation's net income, financial position, and future prospects and the general economic conditions determine market value. *In almost all cases, stockholders are more concerned about the market value of a stock than about any of the other values discussed next.* In the chapter opening story, IHOP's most recent stock price was quoted at \$35.70. Therefore, if IHOP were issuing 1,000 shares of its common stock, IHOP would receive \$35,700 (1,000 shares × \$35.70 per share).

Market value (of a stock)
Price for which a person could buy or sell a share of stock.

Preferred stock that requires the company to redeem (pay to retire) the stock at a set price is called *redeemable preferred stock*. The company is *obligated* to redeem the preferred stock, so redeemable preferred stock is really not stockholders' equity but instead is a liability. The price the corporation agrees to pay for the stock, which is set when the stock is issued, is called the *redemption value*. *Liquidation value* is the amount that a company must pay a preferred stockholder in the event the company liquidates (sells out) and closes its doors.

Book value (of a stock)
Amount of owners' equity on the company's books for each share of its stock.

The **book value** per share of common stock is the amount of owners' equity on the company's books for each share of its stock. If the company has only common stock outstanding, its book value is computed by dividing total equity by the number of shares of common *outstanding*. *Outstanding* stock is *issued* stock minus *treasury* stock. For example, a company with stockholders' equity of $180,000 and 5,000 shares of common stock outstanding has a book value of $36 per share ($180,000 ÷ 5,000 shares).

If the company has both preferred stock and common stock outstanding, the preferred stockholders have the first claim to owners' equity. Preferred stock often has a specified liquidation or redemption value. The preferred equity is its redemption value plus any cumulative preferred dividends in arrears. Book value per share of common is then computed as follows:

$$\text{Book value per share of common stock} = \frac{\text{Total stockholders' equity} - \text{Preferred equity}}{\text{Number of shares of common stock outstanding}}$$

Assume that the company balance sheet reports the following amounts:

Stockholders' Equity	
Preferred stock, 6%, $100 par, 400 shares issued, redemption value $130 per share	$ 40,000
Additional paid-in capital—preferred	4,000
Common stock, $10 par, 5,500 shares issued	55,000
Additional paid-in capital—common	72,000
Retained earnings	85,000
Treasury stock—common, 500 shares at cost	(15,000)
Total stockholders' equity	$241,000

Suppose that 4 years (including the current year) of cumulative preferred dividends are in arrears and observe that preferred stock has a redemption value of $130 per share. The book-value-per-share computations for this corporation are as follows:

Preferred Equity	
Redemption value (400 shares × $130)	$ 52,000
Cumulative dividends ($40,000 × 0.06 × 4 years)	9,600
Preferred equity	$ 61,600*
Common Equity	
Total stockholders' equity	$241,000
Less preferred equity	(61,600)
Common equity	$179,400
Book value per share [$179,400 ÷ 5,000 shares outstanding (5,500 shares issued minus 500 treasury shares)]	$ 35.88

*If the preferred stock had no redemption value, then preferred equity would be $40,000 + $4,000 + preferred dividends in arrears.

■ Taking Action Using Book Value Per Share

Companies negotiating the purchase of a corporation may wish to know the book value of its stock, which may figure into the negotiated purchase price. Corporations—especially those whose stock is not publicly traded—may buy out a retiring executive, agreeing to pay the book value of the person's stock in the company.

Some investors compare the book value of a company's stock with the stock's market value. Some believe that a share selling below its book value is underpriced and thus a good buy. Let's compare two companies, IHOP and **Intel**:

Book Value Per Share

Amounts in thousands

Company	Recent Stock Price	(Common stock-holders' equity)	/	(Number of shares of common stock outstanding)	Book Value
IHOP	$35.70	$382,360	÷	21,390	= $17.88
Intel	$28.37	$37,846,000	÷	6,487,000	= $ 5.83

Check Point 9-13

Neither company's stock is selling below its book value. But IHOP's book value per share is closer to its market value than Intel's. Does this mean IHOP's stock is the better investment? Not necessarily. Investment decisions should be based on more than one ratio.

Relating Profitability to a Company's Stock

OBJECTIVE

6 **Evaluate** a company's return on assets and return on common equity

Investors and creditors are constantly evaluating managers' ability to earn profits. Investors search for companies whose stocks are likely to increase in value. Investment decisions often include a comparison of companies. But a comparison of IHOP Corp.'s net income with the net income of a new restaurant chain is not meaningful. IHOP's profits run into the millions of dollars, which far exceed a new company's net income. Does this automatically make IHOP a better investment? Not necessarily. To compare companies of different size, investors use some standard measures. Two widely used measures of operating performance are return on assets and return on equity.

Rate of return on total assets
Net income plus interest expense divided by average total assets. This ratio measures a company's success in using its assets to earn income for the persons who finance the business. Also called *return on assets.*

Return on Assets. The **rate of return on total assets**, or simply *return on assets (ROA)*, measures a company's use of its assets to earn income for the two groups who finance the business:

- Creditors to whom the corporation owes money and who, therefore, earn interest
- Stockholders who own the corporation's stock and expect it to earn net income

The sum of interest expense and net income is the return to the two groups who finance a corporation, and this is the numerator of the return-on-assets ratio. The denominator is average total assets. ROA is computed as follows, using actual data from the 2003 annual report of IHOP Corp. (dollars in thousands):

$$\text{Rate of return on total assets} = \frac{\text{Net income} + \text{Interest expense}}{\text{Average total assets}}$$

$$= \frac{\$36,782 + \$27,283}{(\$819,800 + \$843,004)/2} = \frac{\$64,065}{\$831,402} = 0.077$$

Net income and interest expense are taken from the income statement. Average total assets is computed from the beginning and ending balance sheets.

What is a good rate of return on total assets? 10% is considered strong for most companies. However, rates of return vary by industry. For example, successful high-technology companies earn much higher returns than do utility companies, groceries, and manufacturers of consumer goods such as toothpaste and paper towels. IHOP's return on assets (7.7%) is low.

Rate of return on common stockholders' equity
Net income minus preferred dividends, divided by average common stockholders' equity. A measure of profitability. Also called *return on equity*.

Return on Equity. **Rate of return on common stockholders' equity**, often called *return on equity (ROE)*, shows the relationship between net income and average common stockholders' equity. Return on equity is computed only on common stock because the return to preferred stockholders is the specified dividend (for example, 5%).

The numerator of return on equity is net income minus preferred dividends. The denominator is *average common stockholders' equity*—total stockholders' equity minus preferred equity. IHOP Corp.'s ROE for 2003 is computed as follows (dollars in thousands):*

$$\text{Rate of return on common stockholders' equity} = \frac{\text{Net income} - \text{Preferred dividends}}{\text{Average common stockholders' equity}}$$

$$= \frac{\$36{,}782 - \$0}{(\$364{,}389* + \$382{,}360*)/2} = \frac{\$36{,}782}{\$373{,}375} = 0.099$$

Check Point 9-14

Check Point 9-15

Because IHOP Corp. has no preferred stock, preferred dividends are zero. With no preferred stock outstanding, average *common* stockholders' equity is the same as average *total* equity—the average of the beginning and ending amounts.

IHOP's return on equity (9.9%) is higher than its return on assets (7.7%), as it should be for a successful company. Investors and creditors use ROE in much the same way they use ROA—to compare companies. The higher the rate of return, the more successful the company. In most industries, 15% is considered a good ROE. Therefore, the IHOP's 9.9% return on common stockholders' equity is on the low side.

The Making Managerial Decisions feature (page 440) offers suggestions for what to consider when investing in stock.

Reporting Stockholders' Equity Transactions

Statement of Cash Flows

OBJECTIVE

7 **Report** stockholders' equity transactions on the statement of cash flows

Many of the transactions discussed in this chapter are reported on the statement of cash flows. Equity transactions are *financing activities* because the company is dealing with its owners, the stockholders who finance the company. Financing transactions that affect equity and cash fall into three main categories: issuance of stock, treasury stock, and dividends.

Issuances of Stock. *Issuances of stock* include those transactions in which a company issues its stock for cash. During 2003, IHOP Corp. issued stock. IHOP's statement of cash flows (Exhibit 9-8) reports the cash received from issuing stock as a financing activity.

*Beginning stockholders' equity comes from the 2002 balance sheet; ending equity comes from page 416.

Cash Flows from Financing Activities	(In thousands)
Issuance of common stock	$10,262
Purchase of treasury stock	(18,634)
Payment of dividends	(16,102)

■ **EXHIBIT 9-8**
IHOP Corp's Financing Activities (Adapted)

Treasury Stock. As we discussed earlier, a company can repurchase its stock as treasury stock. During 2003, IHOP purchased treasury stock and reported the payment as a financing activity.

Dividends. Most companies, including IHOP, pay cash dividends to their stockholders. Dividend payments are a type of financing transaction because the company is paying its stockholders for the use of their money. Stock dividends are not reported on the statement of cash flows because the company pays no cash.

In Exhibit 9-8, cash receipts appear as positive amounts and cash payments as negative amounts, denoted by parentheses.

Check Point 9-16

Variations in Reporting Stockholders' Equity

Businesses often use terms and formats for stockholders' equity that differ from our examples. We use a detailed format in this book to help you learn all the components of stockholders' equity. Companies assume that readers of their statements already understand the details.

One of the most important skills you will learn in this course is the ability to understand the financial statements of real companies. Exhibit 9-9 presents a side-by-side comparison of our general teaching format and the format you are more likely to encounter in real-world balance sheets.

■ **EXHIBIT 9-9** Formats for Reporting Stockholders' Equity

General Teaching Format

Stockholders' Equity

Paid-in capital:	
Preferred stock, 8%, $10 par, 30,000 shares authorized and issued	$ 300,000
Paid-in capital in excess of par—preferred	10,000
Common stock, $1 par, 100,000 shares authorized, 60,000 shares issued	60,000
Paid-in capital in excess of par—common	2,140,000
Paid-in capital from treasury stock transactions, common	9,000
Paid-in capital from retirement of preferred stock	11,000
Total paid-in capital	2,530,000
Retained earnings	1,565,000
Subtotal	4,095,000
Less treasury stock, common (1,400 shares at cost)	(42,000)
Total stockholders' equity	$4,053,000

Real-World Format

Stockholders' Equity

Preferred stock, 8%, $10 par, 30,000 shares authorized and issued	$ 310,000
Common stock, $1 par, 100,000 shares authorized, 60,000 shares issued	60,000
Additional paid-in capital	2,160,000
Retained earnings	1,565,000
Less treasury stock, common (1,400 shares at cost)	(42,000)
	$4,053,000

In general:

- Preferred Stock comes first and is usually reported as a single amount
- Common Stock lists par value per share, the number of shares authorized and the number of shares issued. The balance of the Common Stock account is determined as follows:

$$\text{Common stock} = \text{Number of shares issued} \times \text{Par value per share}$$

- Additional paid-in capital combines Paid-in Capital in Excess of Par plus Paid-in Capital from Treasury Stock Transactions plus Paid-in Capital from Retirement of Preferred Stock. Additional paid-in capital belongs to the common stockholders.
- Retained Earnings comes after the paid-in capital accounts.
- Treasury Stock can come last, as a subtraction in arriving at total stockholders' equity.
- Outstanding stock equals issued stock minus treasury stock.

MAKING MANAGERIAL DECISIONS

INVESTING IN STOCK

Suppose you've saved $5,000 to invest. You visit a nearby **Edward Jones** office, where the broker probes for your risk tolerance. Are you investing mainly for dividends or for growth in the stock price? You must make some key decisions.

Investor Decision	Guidelines
Which category of stock to buy for:	
• A safe investment?	Preferred stock is safer than common, but for even more safety, invest in high-grade corporate bonds or government securities.
• Steady dividends?	Cumulative preferred stock. However, the company is not obligated to declare preferred dividends, and the dividends are unlikely to increase.
• Increasing dividends?	Common stock, as long as the company's net income is increasing and the company has adequate cash flow to pay a dividend after meeting all obligations and other cash demands.
• Increasing stock price?	Common stock, but again only if the company's net income and cash flow are increasing.
How to identify a good stock to buy?	There are many ways to pick stock investments. One strategy that works reasonably well is to invest in companies that consistently earn higher rates of return on assets and on equity than competing firms in the same industry. Also, select industries that are expected to grow.

Summary Problems

END-OF-CHAPTER

1. The balance sheet of Trendline Corp. reported the following at December 31, 20X6.

Stockholders' Equity	
Preferred stock, 4%, $10 par, 10,000 shares authorized and issued (redemption value, $110,000)	$100,000
Common stock, no-par, $5 stated value, 100,000 shares authorized, 50,000 shares issued	250,000
Paid-in capital in excess of par or stated value:	
Common stock	239,500
Retained earnings	395,000
Less: Treasury stock, common (1,000 shares)	(8,000)
Total stockholders' equity	$976,500

Required

a. Is the preferred stock cumulative or noncumulative? How can you tell?
b. What is the total amount of the annual preferred dividend?
c. How many shares of common stock are outstanding?
d. Compute the book value per share of the common stock. No preferred dividends are in arrears, and Trendline has not yet declared the 20X6 dividend.

2. Use the following accounts and related balances to prepare the classified balance sheet of Whitehall, Inc., at September 30, 20X7. Use the account format of the balance sheet.

Common stock, $1 par, 50,000 shares authorized, 20,000 shares issued	$ 20,000	Long-term note payable	$ 80,000
Dividends payable	4,000	Inventory	85,000
Cash	9,000	Property, plant, and equipment, net	226,000
Accounts payable	28,000	Accounts receivable, net	23,000
Paid-in capital in excess of par—common	115,000	Preferred stock, $3.75, no-par, 10,000 shares authorized, 2,000 shares issued	24,000
Treasury stock, common, 1,000 shares at cost	6,000	Accrued liabilities	3,000
		Retained earnings	75,000

Answers

1. a. The preferred stock is cumulative because it is not specifically labeled otherwise.
   b. Total annual preferred dividend: $4,000 ($100,000 × 0.04).
   c. Common shares outstanding: 49,000 (50,000 issued – 1,000 treasury).
   d. Book value per share of common stock:

Common:	
Total stockholders' equity	$976,500
Less stockholders' equity allocated to preferred	(114,000)*
Stockholders' equity allocated to common	$862,500
Book value per share ($862,500 ÷ 49,000 shares)	$17.60

*Redemption value	$110,000
Cumulative dividend ($100,000 × 0.04)	4,000
Stockholders' equity allocated to preferred	$114,000

2.

Whitehall, Inc.
Balance Sheet
September 30, 20X7

Assets		Liabilities		
Current		Current		
Cash	$ 9,000	Accounts payable		$ 28,000
Accounts receivable, net	23,000	Dividends payable		4,000
Inventory	85,000	Accrued liabilities		3,000
Total current assets	117,000	Total current liabilities		35,000
Property, plant, and equipment, net	226,000	Long-term note payable		80,000
		Total liabilities		115,000
		Stockholders' Equity		
		Preferred stock, $3.75, no par, 10,000 shares authorized, 2,000 shares issued	$ 24,000	
		Common stock, $1 par, 50,000 shares authorized, 20,000 shares issued	20,000	
		Paid-in capital in excess of par—common	115,000	
		Retained earnings	75,000	
		Treasury stock, common, 1,000 shares at cost	(6,000)	
		Total stockholders' equity		228,000
Total assets	$343,000	Total liabilities and stockholders' equity		$343,000

REVIEW STOCKHOLDERS' EQUITY

Chapter Review Quiz

1. Lauren Company is authorized to issue 40,000 shares of $10 par common stock. On January 15, 20X8, it issued 10,000 shares at $15 per share. Lauren's journal entry to record these facts should include a
   a. credit to Common Stock for $400,000.
   b. credit to Paid-in Capital in Excess of Par for $50,000.
   c. debit to Cash for $100,000.
   d. all of the above.

Questions 2–5 use some of the following account balances of ABC Co. at March 31, 20X7:

Cash	$ 74,000	Dividends Payable	22,000
Common Stock, $1 par	180,000	Preferred Stock, $100 par	500,000
Retained Earnings	231,000	Paid-in Capital in Excess of Par—Common	450,000
Paid-in Capital in Excess of Par—Preferred	45,000		

2. The average issue price of a share of ABC's common stock was
   a. $1.00
   b. $1.25
   c. $3.50
   d. Some other amount

3. ABC's total paid-in capital at March 31, 20X7, is
   a. $495,000
   b. $680,000
   c. $1,175,000
   d. Some other amount

4. ABC's total stockholders' equity as of March 31, 20X7, is
   a. $1,406,000
   b. $1,249,000
   c. $1,175,000
   d. $1,480,000

5. What would ABC's total stockholders' equity be if there was $5,000 of Treasury Stock?
   $__________

6. Charlie Company purchased treasury stock in 20X2 at a price of $30 per share and resold it in 20X3 at a price of $40 per share. What amount should Charlie Company report on its income statement for 20X3?
   a. $0
   b. $10
   c. $30
   d. $40

7. The stockholders' equity section of a corporation's balance sheet reports

	Treasury Stock	*Discount on Bonds Payable*
a.	Yes	Yes
b.	No	Yes
c.	Yes	No
d.	No	No

8. The purchase of treasury stock
   a. increases one asset and decreases another asset.
   b. decreases total assets and decreases total liabilities.
   c. has no effect on total assets, total liabilities, or total stockholders' equity.
   d. decreases total assets and decreases total stockholders' equity.

9. When does a cash dividend become a legal liability?
   a. On the date of declaration.
   b. On the date of record.
   c. On the date of payment.
   d. It never becomes a liability because it is paid.

10. When do dividends decrease stockholders' equity? On the date of __________.

11. Wallace Corporation has 15,000 shares of 5%, $20 par cumulative preferred stock and 100,000 shares of $1 par common stock outstanding. At the beginning of the current year preferred dividends were three years in arrears. Wallace's board of directors wants to pay a $1.25 cash dividend on each share of outstanding common stock. To accomplish this, what total amount of dividends must Wallace declare?

    First, determine the annual preferred dividend amount: $__________
    a. $170,000
    b. $185,000
    c. $125,000
    d. Some other amount $__________

12. Stock dividends
    a. are distributions of cash to stockholders.
    b. have no effect on total stockholders' equity.
    c. reduce the total assets of the company.
    d. All of the above.

13. What is the effect of a stock dividend and a stock split on total assets?

	Stock dividend	*Stock split*
a.	Decrease	No effect
b.	Decrease	Decrease
c.	No effect	Decrease
d.	No effect	No effect

14. A 2-for-1 stock split has the same effect on the number of shares being issued as a
    a. 100% stock dividend.
    b. 20% stock dividend.
    c. 200% stock dividend.
    d. 50% stock dividend.

15. The numerator for computing the rate of return on total assets is
    a. net income.
    b. net income plus interest expense.
    c. net income minus interest expense.
    d. net income minus preferred dividends.

16. The numerator for computing the rate of return on common equity is
    a. net income plus preferred dividends.
    b. net income minus interest expense.
    c. net income minus preferred dividends.
    d. net income.

Answers

1. b [10,000 shares × ($15 – $10) = $50,000]
2. c [($180,000 + $450,000)/($180,000 ÷ $1 par) = $3.50 per share]
3. c ($180,000 + $45,000 + $500,000 + $450,000 = $1,175,000)
4. a ($1,175,000 + $231,000 = $1,406,000)
5. $1,401,000 = $1,406,000 – $5,000
6. a [No gain or loss (for the income statement) on treasury stock]
7. c
8. d
9. a
10. Declaration, because of the debit to Retained Earnings
11. b [First, annual preferred dividend = $15,000 (15,000 × $20 × .05)]
    [($15,000 × 4) + (100,000 × $1.25) = $185,000]
12. b
13. d
14. a
15. b
16. c

Accounting Vocabulary

board of directors (p. 419)
book value (of a stock) (p. 436)
bylaws (p. 419)
chairperson (p. 419)
common stock (p. 421)
contributed capital (p. 420)
cumulative preferred stock (p. 433)
deficit (p. 431)
dividends (p. 432)
double taxation (p. 419)
legal capital (p. 422)
limited liability (p. 418)
market value (of a stock) (p. 435)
outstanding stock (p. 421)
paid-in capital (p. 420)
par value (p. 422)
preferred stock (p. 421)
president (p. 419)
rate of return on common stockholders' equity (p. 438)
rate of return on total assets (p. 437)
retained earnings (p. 420)
return on assets (p. 437)
return on equity (p. 438)
shareholders (p. 418)
stated value (p. 422)
stock (p. 421)
stock dividend (p. 433)
stockholders (p. 418)
stockholders' equity (p. 420)
stock split (p. 435)
treasury stock (p. 429)

Assess Your Progress

Check Points

Authority structure in a corporation (Obj. 1)

CP9-1 (p. 420) Consider the authority structure in a corporation, as diagrammed in Exhibit 9-2, page 420.

1. What group holds the ultimate power in a corporation?
2. Who is the most powerful person in the corporation?
3. Who is in charge of day-to-day operations?
4. Who has primary responsibility for the corporation's cash?
5. Who manages the accounting?

Characteristics of preferred and common stock (Obj. 1)

CP9-2 (p. 422) Answer the following questions about the characteristics of a corporation's stock:

1. Which right clearly distinguishes a stockholder from a creditor (who has lent money to the corporation)?
2. Which stockholders are the real owners of a corporation?
3. What privileges do preferred stockholders have over common stockholders?
4. Which class of stockholders reap greater benefits from a highly profitable corporation? Why?

Effect of a stock issuance on net income (Obj. 2)

CP9-3 (p. 424) Study **IHOP's** July 23 stock issuance entry given on page 423 and answer these questions about the nature of the IHOP transaction.

1. IHOP received $62,000,000 for the issuance of its stock. The par value of the IHOP stock was only $62,000. Was the excess amount of $61,938,000 a profit to IHOP? If not, what was it?
2. Suppose the par value of the IHOP stock had been $1 per share, $5 per share, or $10 per share. Would a change in the par value of the company's stock affect IHOP's total paid-in capital? Give the reason for your answer.

Issuing stock and analyzing retained earnings (Obj. 2)

CP9-4 (p. 424) At December 31, 2003, **eBay Inc.** reported the following on its comparative balance sheet, which included 2002 amounts for comparison (adapted, with all amounts except par value in thousands):

	December 31, 2003	December 31, 2002
Common stock $0.001 par value		
Authorized: 900,000 shares		
Issued: 649,000 shares in 2003	$ 649	
623,000 shares in 2002		$ 623
Additional paid-in capital	3,937,160	3,108,131
Retained earnings	856,245	414,474

1. How much did eBay's total paid-in capital increase during 2003? What caused total paid-in capital to increase? How can you tell?
2. Journalize eBay's issuance of stock for cash during 2003.
3. Did eBay have a profit or a loss for 2003? How can you tell?

Issuing stock to finance the purchase of assets (Obj. 2)

CP9-5 (p. 426) This Check Point shows the similarity and the difference between two ways to acquire plant assets.

Case A—Issue stock and buy the assets in separate transactions:	*Case B—Issue stock to acquire the assets in a single transaction:*
Stagecoach Corporation issued 10,000 shares of its $5 par common stock for cash of $500,000. In a separate transaction, Stagecoach used the cash to purchase a warehouse building for $400,000 and equipment for $100,000. Journalize the two transactions.	Stagecoach Corporation issued 10,000 shares of its $5 par common stock to acquire a warehouse building valued at $400,000 and equipment worth $100,000. Journalize this transaction.

Compare the balances in all accounts after making both sets of entries. Are the account balances similar or different?

Preparing the stockholders' equity section of a balance sheet (Obj. 2)

CP9-6 (p. 428) **Paychex, Inc.** provides employer services for other companies. The financial statements of Paychex, Inc. reported the following accounts (adapted, dollar amounts in millions except for par value):

Total revenues	$1,099	Paid-in capital in excess of par	$198
Accounts payable	22	Other stockholders' equity	29
Retained earnings	846	Common stock $0.01 par;	
Other current liabilities	2,566	376 million shares issued	4
Total expenses	805	Long-term liabilities	25

Prepare the stockholders' equity section of the Paychex, Inc. balance sheet. Net income has already been closed to Retained Earnings.

Using stockholders' equity data (Obj. 2)

CP9-7 (p. 428) Use the **Paychex, Inc.**, data in Check Point 9-6 to compute Paychex's

a. Net income
b. Total liabilities
c. Total assets (use the accounting equation)

Accounting for the purchase and sale of treasury stock (Obj. 3)

CP9-8 (p. 431) **General Dynamics Corporation**, manufacturer of fighter aircraft, Army tanks, and Navy ships, reported the following stockholders' equity (adapted in millions):

Common stock	$ 243
Additional paid-in capital	297
Retained earnings	2,159
Treasury stock	(691)
Total stockholders' equity	$2,008

During the next year, General Dynamics purchased treasury stock at a cost of $28 million and resold treasury stock for $7 million (this treasury stock had cost General Dynamics $3 million).

Record the purchase and resale of General Dynamics treasury stock. Overall, how much did stockholders' equity increase or decrease as a result of the two treasury stock transactions?

Explaining treasury stock transactions (Obj. 3)

CP9-9 (p. 431) Return to the **General Dynamics** data of Check Point 9-8. Explain how General Dynamics can have a larger balance of Treasury Stock than the sum of Common Stock and Additional Paid-In Capital. Does it mean that General Dynamics has more shares of treasury stock than the number of shares of stock the company has issued?

Accounting for cash dividends (Obj. 4)

writing assignment ■

CP9-10 (p. 433) Turnberry Company earned net income of $60,750 during the year ended December 31, 20X6. On December 15, Turnberry declared the annual cash dividend on its $4\frac{1}{2}$% preferred stock (10,000 shares with total par value of $50,000) and a $0.50 per share cash dividend on its common stock (25,000 shares with total par value of $250,000). Turnberry then paid the dividends on January 4, 20X7.

Journalize for Turnberry Company:

a. Declaring the cash dividends on December 15, 20X6.
b. Paying the cash dividends on January 4, 20X7.

Did Retained Earnings increase or decrease during 20X6? By how much?

Dividing cash dividends between preferred and common stock (Obj. 4)

CP9-11 (p. 433) Refer to the allocation of dividends for Pinecraft Industries on page 433. Answer these questions about Pinecraft's cash dividends.

1. How much in dividends must Pinecraft declare each year before the common stockholders receive cash dividends for the year?
2. Suppose Pinecraft declares cash dividends of $300,000 for 20X6. How much of the dividends go to preferred? How much goes to common?
3. Is Pinecraft's preferred stock cumulative or noncumulative? How can you tell?
4. Pinecraft passed the preferred dividend in 20X5 and 20X6. Then in 20X7, Pinecraft declares cash dividends of $650,000. How much of the dividends go to preferred? How much goes to common?

Recording a small stock dividend (Obj. 4)

CP9-12 (p. 434) Highland Corporation has 60,000 shares of $1 par common stock outstanding. Suppose Highland distributes a 5% stock dividend when the market value of its stock is $11.50 per share.

1. Journalize Highland's distribution of the stock dividend on August 12. An explanation is not required.
2. What was the overall effect of the stock dividend on Highland's total assets? On total liabilities? On total stockholders' equity?

Computing book value per share (Obj. 5)

CP9-13 (p. 437) Refer to the Real-World Format of Stockholders' Equity in Exhibit 9-9, page 439. That company has passed its preferred dividends for the current year. Compute the book value of a share of the company's common stock.

Computing and explaining return on assets and return on equity (Obj. 6)

writing assignment ■

CP9-14 (p. 438) Give the formula for computing (a) rate of return on common stockholders' equity (ROE) and (b) rate of return on total assets (ROA). Then answer these questions about the rate-of-return computations.

1. Why are preferred dividends subtracted from net income to compute ROE? Why are preferred dividends *not* subtracted from net income to compute ROA?
2. Why is interest expense added to net income in the computation of ROA?

Computing return on assets and return on equity for a leading company (Obj. 6)

CP9-15 (p. 438) **Sara Lee's** 2003 financial statements reported the following items, with 2002 figures given for comparison (adapted, in millions). Compute Sara Lee's return on assets and return on common equity for 2003. Evaluate the rates of return as strong or weak.

	2003	2002
Balance sheet		
Total assets	$15,084	$13,753
Total liabilities	$13,032	$12,011
Total stockholders' equity (substantially all common)	2,052	1,742
Total liabilities and equity	$15,084	$13,753
Income statement		
Net sales	$18,291	
Operating expense	16,620	
Interest expense	276	
Other expense	174	
Net income	$ 1,221	

Measuring cash flows from financing activities (Obj. 7)

CP9-16 (p. 439) During fiscal year 20X1 **Kmart Corporation** incurred a net loss of $244 million. The company borrowed $397 million and paid off $151 million of debt. Kmart raised $53 million by issuing common stock and paid $139 million to purchase treasury stock. Determine the amount of Kmart's *net cash flow from financing activities* during 20X1.

Exercises

 PH Grade Assist	Most of the even-numbered exercises can be found within Prentice Hall Grade Assist (PHGA), an online homework and practice environment. Your instructor may ask you to complete these exercises using PHGA.

Organizing a corporation (Obj. 1)

writing assignment ■

E9-1 Katy Jax and Marta Fraser are opening a deli to be named **Schmaltz's**. They need outside capital, so they plan to organize the business as a corporation. Because your office is in the same building, they come to you for advice. Write a memorandum informing them of the steps in forming a corporation. Identify specific documents used in this process, and name the different parties involved in the ownership and management of a corporation.

Issuing stock and reporting stockholders' equity (Obj. 2)

■ general ledger

E9-2 Steakley Mazda, Inc., obtained a corporate charter that authorized the issuance of 100,000 shares of common stock and 5,000 shares of preferred stock. During its first year, the business completed the following stock issuance transactions:

Feb. 19	Issued 1,000 shares of \$2.50 par common stock for cash of \$6.50 per share.
Mar. 3	Sold 500 shares of \$1.50 no-par preferred stock for \$50,000 cash.
11	Received inventory valued at \$11,000 and equipment with market value of \$8,500 for 3,300 shares of the \$2.50 par common stock.

▌Required

1. Journalize the transactions. Explanations are not required.
2. Prepare the stockholders' equity section of Steakley's balance sheet. The ending balance of retained earnings is a deficit of \$42,000.

Stockholders' equity section of a balance sheet (Obj. 2)

E9-3 The charter of **Austin-Healey Corporation** authorizes the issuance of 5,000 shares of preferred stock and 10,000 shares of common stock. During a 2-month period, Austin-Healey completed these stock-issuance transactions:

June 23	Issued 1,000 shares of \$1 par common stock for cash of \$22 per share.
July 2	Sold 300 shares of \$4.50, no-par preferred stock for \$20,000 cash.
12	Received inventory valued at \$25,000 and equipment with market value of \$43,000 for 3,000 shares of the \$1 par common stock.

▌Required

Prepare the stockholders' equity section of the Austin-Healey balance sheet for the transactions given in this exercise. Retained earnings has a balance of \$88,000. Journal entries are not required.

Measuring the paid-in capital of a corporation (Obj. 2)

E9-4 Laser Medical Corporation was recently organized. The company issued common stock to an attorney who provided legal services of \$20,000 to help organize the corporation. Laser Medical issued common stock to an inventor in exchange for his patent with a market value of \$150,000. In addition, Laser Medical received cash both for the issuance of 5,000 shares of its preferred stock at \$110 per share and for the issuance of 50,000 shares of its common stock at \$15 per share. During the first year of operations, Laser Medical earned net income of \$85,000 and declared a cash dividend of \$26,000. Without making journal entries, determine the total paid-in capital created by these transactions.

Stockholders' equity section of a balance sheet (Obj. 2, 3)

■ spreadsheet

E9-5 Avon Products, Inc., the cosmetics company, had the following selected account balances at December 31, 20X3 (adapted, in millions, except par value per share). Prepare the stockholders' equity section of Avon's balance sheet (in millions).

Common stock, $0.25 par per share, 800 shares authorized, 361 shares issued	$ 90	Inventory	$ 653
Retained earnings	2,202	Property, plant, and equipment, net	857
Accounts receivable, net	600	Paid-in capital in excess of par	1,188
Notes payable	1,122	Treasury stock, 126 shares at cost	2,380
		Other stockholders' equity	(729)*

*Debit balance

How can Avon have a larger balance of treasury stock than the sum of Common Stock and Paid-in Capital in Excess of Par?

Recording treasury stock transactions and measuring their effects on stockholders' equity (Obj. 2, 3)

■ **general ledger**

E9-6 Journalize the following assumed transactions of **Johnson & Johnson**:

Jan. 19	Issued 10,000 shares of $1 par common stock at $5 per share.
Oct. 22	Purchased 900 shares of treasury stock at $7 per share.
Dec. 11	Sold 800 shares of treasury stock at $12 per share.

What was the overall effect of these transactions on Johnson & Johnson's stockholders' equity?

Recording stock issuance, treasury stock, and dividend transactions (Obj. 2, 3, 4)

E9-7 At December 31, 20X3, **Spandex Corporation** reported the stockholders' equity accounts shown here (as adapted, with dollar amounts in millions, except par value per share).

Common stock $1.50 par value per share, 1,829 million shares issued	$ 2,744
Capital in excess of par value	10,076
Retained earnings	261
Treasury stock, at cost	-0-
Total stockholders' equity	$13,081

Spandex's 20X4 transactions included the following:

a. Net income, $440 million.
b. Issuance of 6 million shares of common stock for $15.50 per share.
c. Purchase of 1 million shares of treasury stock for $14 million.
d. Declaration and payment of cash dividends of $30 million.

Journalize Spandex's transactions in b, c, and d. Explanations are not required.

Reporting stockholders' equity after a sequence of transactions (Obj. 2, 3, 4)

E9-8 Use the **Spandex Corporation** data in Exercise 9-7 to prepare the stockholders' equity section of the company's balance sheet at December 31, 20X4.

Inferring transactions from a company's stockholders' equity (Obj. 2, 3, 4, 5)

E9-9 Delta Corporation reported the following shareholders' equity on its balance sheet:

Shareholders' Equity (Dollars and shares in millions)	December 31, 20X4	20X3
Preferred stock—$1 per share par value; authorized 20 shares; Convertible Preferred Stock; issued and outstanding: 20X4 and 20X3—0 and 2 shares, respectively	$ -0-	$ 2
Common stock—$1 per share par value; authorized 1,000.0 shares; issued: 20X4 and 20X3—408 and 364 shares, respectively	408	364
Additional paid-in capital	7,706	5,536
Retained earnings	6,280	5,006
Treasury stock, common—at cost 20X4—29 shares; 20X3—9 shares	(1,235)	(215)
Total Shareholders' Equity	13,159	10,693
Total Liabilities and Shareholders' Equity	$53,756	$49,539

Required

1. What caused Delta's preferred stock to decrease during 20X4? Cite all the causes.
2. What caused Delta's common stock to increase during 20X4? Identify all the causes.
3. How many shares of Delta common stock were outstanding at December 31, 20X4?
4. Assume that during 20X4, Delta sold no treasury stock. What average price per share did Delta pay for the treasury stock the company purchased during the year? During 20X4, the market price of Delta's common stock ranged from a low of $38.25 to a high of $53.13. Compare the average price Delta paid for its treasury stock during 20X4 to the range of market prices during the year.
5. Delta's net income during 20X4 was $1,680 million. How much were Delta's dividends during the year?

Computing dividends on preferred and common stock (Obj. 4)

E9-10 Gulf States Financial Corporation reported the following:

Gulf States Financial Corporation Stockholders' Equity	
Preferred stock, cumulative, $1 par, 6%, 60,000 shares issued ...	$ 60,000
Common stock, $0.10 par, 9,130,000 shares issued	913,000

Gulf States Financial has paid all preferred dividends through 20X1.

Required

Compute the total amounts of dividends to both preferred and common for 20X4 and 20X5 if total dividends are $100,000 in 20X4 and $100,000 in 20X5.

Recording a stock dividend and reporting stockholders' equity (Obj. 4)

E9-11 The stockholders' equity for Electronic Motor Systems, Inc. (EMS) on December 31, 2004, follows (adapted in millions, except for par value per share):

Stockholders' Equity	
Common stock, $0.10 par, 2,000 shares authorized, 500 shares issued	$ 50
Paid-in capital in excess of par—common	962
Retained earnings	7,122
Other	(1,643)
Total stockholders' equity	$6,491

On April 15, 2005, the market price of EMS common stock was $51.50 per share. Assume EMS distributed a 10% stock dividend on this date.

Required

1. Journalize the distribution of the stock dividend.
2. Prepare the stockholders' equity section of the balance sheet after the stock dividend.
3. Why is total stockholders' equity unchanged by the stock dividend?
4. Suppose EMS had a cash balance of $3,000 million on April 16, 2005. What is the maximum amount of cash dividends EMS can declare?

Measuring the effects of stock issuance, dividends, and treasury stock transactions (Obj. 2, 3, 4)

E9-12 Identify the effects—both the direction and the dollar amount—of these assumed transactions on the total stockholders' equity of **Best Buy, Inc.** Each transaction is independent.

a. 10% stock dividend. Before the dividend, 69 million shares of $1 par common stock were outstanding; the market value was $7.625 at the time of the dividend.
b. A 50% stock dividend. Before the dividend, 69 million shares of $1 par common stock were outstanding; the market value was $13.75 at the time of the dividend.

c. Purchase of 2,000 shares of treasury stock (par value $1) at $4.25 per share.
d. Sale of 600 shares of $1 par treasury stock for $5.00 per share. Cost of the treasury stock was $4.25 per share.
e. A 3-for-1 stock split. Prior to the split, 69 million shares of $1 par common were outstanding.

Reporting stockholders' equity after a stock split (Obj. 4)

E9-13 Zap Corp. had the following stockholders' equity (adapted) at January 31 (dollars in millions):

Common stock, $0.05 par, 500 million shares authorized, 440 million shares issued	$ 22
Additional paid-in capital	318
Retained earnings	2,393
Other	(1,149)
Total stockholders' equity	$1,584

Assume that on March 7, Zap split its $0.05 par common stock 2 for 1. Prepare the stockholders' equity section of the balance sheet immediately after the split.

Measuring the book value per share of common stock (Obj. 5)

E9-14 The balance sheet of Frost Bank Corporation reported the following, with all amounts, including shares, in thousands:

Redeemable preferred stock, 6%, redemption value $5,900; outstanding 100 shares	$ 4,800
Common stockholders' equity 10,500 shares issued and outstanding	87,200
Total stockholders' equity	$92,000

Required

1. Compute the book value per share for the common stock, assuming all preferred dividends are fully paid up (none in arrears).
2. Compute the book value per share of the common stock, assuming that 3 years' preferred dividends including the current year, are in arrears.
3. Frost's common stock recently traded at market value of $7.75. Does this mean that Frost's stock is a good buy at $7.75?

Evaluating profitability (Obj. 6)

writing assignment ■

E9-15 Elsimate, Inc., reported these figures for 20X4 and 20X3 (adapted, in millions):

	20X4	20X3
Balance sheet:		
Total assets	$21,695	$20,757
Common stock and additional paid-in capital	43	388
Retained earnings	11,519	16,510
Other equity	(2,914)	(9,294)
Income statement:		
Operating income	$ 4,021	$ 3,818
Interest expense	219	272
Net income	2,662	2,543

Compute Elsimate's return on assets and return on common stockholders' equity for 20X4. Do these rates of return suggest strength or weakness? Give your reason.

Evaluating profitability (Obj. 6)

writing assignment ■

E9-16 **Kraft Foods, Inc.**, included the following items in its financial statements for 20X4, the current year (amounts in millions):

Dividends paid	$ 225	Payment of long-term debt	$17,055
Interest expense:		Proceeds from issuance	
Current year	1,437	of common stock	8,425
Preceding year	597	Total liabilities:	
Net income:		Current year end	32,320
Current year	1,882	Preceding year end	38,023
Preceding year	2,001	Total stockholders' equity:	
Operating income:		Current year end	23,478
Current year	4,884	Preceding year end	14,048
Preceding year	4,012	Borrowings	6,582

Compute Kraft's return on assets and return on common equity during 20X4 (the current year). Kraft has no preferred stock outstanding. Do Kraft's rates of return look strong or weak? Give your reason.

Challenge Exercises

Reporting cash flows from financing activities (Obj. 7)

E9-17 Use the Kraft Foods data in Exercise 9-16 to show how Kraft reported cash flows from financing activities during 20X4 (the current year). List items in descending order from largest to smallest dollar amount.

Reconstructing transactions from the financial statements (Obj. 2, 3, 4)

E9-18 Golinda Corporation began operations on January 1, 20X7, and immediately issued its stock, receiving cash. Golinda's balance sheet at December 31, 20X7, reported the following stockholders' equity:

Common stock, $1 par	$ 50,000
Additional paid-in capital	200,600
Retained earnings	38,000
Treasury stock, 500 shares	(2,000)
Total stockholders' equity	$286,600

During 20X7, Golinda

a. Issued stock for $5 per share.
b. Reacquired 800 shares of its own stock for the corporate treasury, paying $4 per share.
c. Resold some of the treasury shares.
d. Earned net income of $56,000 and declared and paid cash dividends.

Required

Journalize all of Golinda's stockholders' equity transactions during the year. Golinda's entry to close net income to Retained Earnings was:

Revenues	171,000	
Expenses		115,000
Retained Earnings		56,000

Explaining the changes in stockholders' equity (Obj. 2, 3, 4)

writing assignment ■

E9-19 Gemini Corporation reported the following stockholders' equity data (all dollars in millions except par value per share):

	December 31,	
	20X5	20X4
Preferred stock	$ 604	$ 686
Common stock, $1 par value	894	891
Additional paid-in capital	1,572	1,468
Retained earnings	20,661	19,108
Treasury stock, common	(2,843)	(2,643)

Gemini earned net income of $3,604 during 20X5. For each account except Retained Earnings, one transaction explains the change from the December 31, 20X4, balance to the December 21, 20X5, balance. Two transactions affected Retained Earnings. Give a full explanation, including the dollar amount, for the change in each account.

Accounting for changes in stockholders' equity (Obj. 2, 3, 4)

■ **spreadsheet**

E9-20 Northeast Powersports, Inc., began 20X6 with 8 million shares of $1 par common stock issued and outstanding. Beginning additional paid-in capital was $13 million, and retained earnings totaled $40 million. In March 20X6, Northeast issued 2 million shares of common stock at a price of $2 per share. In May, the company distributed a 10% stock dividend at a time when Northeast's common stock had a market value of $3 per share. Then in October, Northeast's stock price dropped to $1 per share and the company purchased 2 million shares of treasury stock. For the year, Northeast earned net income of $26 million and declared cash dividends of $17 million.

Complete the following tabulation to show what Northeast should report for stockholders' equity at December 31, 20X6. Journal entries are not required.

(Amounts in millions)	Common Stock	Additional Paid-In Capital	Retained Earnings	Treasury Stock	Total
Balance, Dec. 31, 20X5	$8	$13	$40		$61
Issuance of stock					
Stock dividend					
Purchase of treasury stock				$	
Net income					
Cash dividends					
Balance, Dec. 31, 20X6	$	$	$	$	$

Practice Quiz

Test your understanding of stockholders' equity by answering the following questions. Select the best choice from among the possible answers given.

PQ9-1 Which of the following would be considered a characteristic of the corporation?

a. unlimited liability of stockholders
b. separate legal entity
c. mutual agency
d. both a and b

PQ9-2 Custard Corporation has outstanding 500 shares of 7% cumulative preferred stock, $100 par value, and 1,200 shares of common stock, $20 par value. In 20X8, the corporation declares dividends of $14,300. The correct entry is:

a. Retained Earnings	14,300	
Dividends Payable, Preferred		3,500
Dividends Payable, Common		10,800
b. Dividends Expense	4,300	
Cash		14,300
c. Retained Earnings	14,300	
Dividends Payable, Preferred		7,150
Dividends Payable, Common		7,150
d. Dividends Payable, Preferred	3,500	
Dividends Payable, Common	10,800	
Cash		14,300

PQ9-3 National Corporation issues 240,000 shares of no-par stock, stated value $2 per share, for $5 per share. The journal entry is:

a. Cash	480,000	
Common Stock		480,000
b. Cash	1,200,000	
Common Stock		480,000
Gain on the Sale of Stock		720,000

c. Cash	1,200,000	
Common Stock		1,200,000
d. Cash	1,200,000	
Common Stock		480,000
Paid-in Capital in Excess of Stated Value—Common		720,000

Use the following information for questions 4–6:

These selected account balances at December 31 relate to Centura Corporation:

Accounts Payable	$ 51,700	Paid-in Capital in Excess of Par—Common	$280,285
Accounts Receivable	81,350	Paid-in Capital in Excess of Par—Preferred	12,160
Common Stock	313,000	Preferred Stock, 10%, $100 Par	89,000
Treasury Stock	5,000	Retained Earnings	71,890
Bonds Payable	3,400	Notes Receivable	12,500

PQ9-4 What is total paid-in capital for Centura Corporation at December 31?

a. $699,445
b. $701,345
c. $694,445
d. $292,445
e. None of the above.

PQ9-5 What is total stockholders' equity for Centura Corporation at December 31?

a. $761,335
b. $771,335
c. $766,335
d. $764,735
e. None of the above.

PQ9-6 Ignore Treasury Stock. If Centura's net income for the period is $119,600 and beginning common stockholders' equity is $681,425, calculate Centura's return on common stockholders' equity.

a. 17.7%
b. 15.3%
c. 16.5%
d. 15.6%

PQ9-7 Which of the following is *not* true about a 10% stock dividend?

a. Par value decreases.
b. Paid-in Capital increases.
c. Retained Earnings decreases.
d. The market value of the stock is needed to record the stock dividend.
e. Total stockholders' equity remains the same.

PQ9-8 A corporation has 40,000 shares of 8% cumulative preferred stock authorized and 20,000 shares issued. Also, there are 20,000 shares of common stock outstanding. Par value for each is $100. If a $350,000 dividend is paid, how much goes to preferred stockholders?

a. None
b. $350,000
c. $160,000
d. $120,000
e. $320,000

PQ9-9 Assume the same facts as in question 8. What is the amount of dividends per share on common stock?

a. $8.00
b. $9.50
c. $17.50
d. $1.50
e. None of these.

PQ9-10 The contributed capital portion of stockholders' equity does not include

a. Retained Earnings
b. Paid-in Capital in Excess of Stated Value
c. Preferred Stock
d. Paid-in Capital in Excess of Par Value
e. Common Stock

PQ9-11 Dividends in arrears

a. should be shown on the balance sheet as a current liability.
b. should be disclosed as a footnote.
c. should be shown on the income statement as an expense.
d. should be disclosed as a contra account in the stockholders' equity section of the balance sheet.
e. should not be disclosed in the financial statements or as a footnote.

PQ9-12 Par value

a. represents what a share of stock is worth.
b. represents the original selling price for a share of stock.
c. is established for a share of stock after it is issued.
d. is an arbitrary amount that establishes the legal capital for each share.
e. may exist for common stock but not for preferred stock.

PQ9-13 Which of the following classifications represents the *most* shares of common stock?

a. Issued shares
b. Outstanding shares
c. Treasury shares
d. Unissued shares
e. Authorized shares

PQ9-14 Preferred stock is *least* likely to have which of the following characteristics?

a. Preference as to assets on liquidation of the corporation
b. Represent the basic ownership of the corporation
c. The right of the holder to convert to common stock
d. Preference as to dividends

PQ9-15 Which of the following statements about stock dividends and stock splits is false?

a. A stock split has no effect on paid-in capital; a stock dividend increases paid-in capital.
b. A stock split increases the shares authorized, whereas a small stock dividend does not.
c. Neither a stock split nor a small stock dividend has an effect on total stockholder's equity.
d. A stock split increases the shares outstanding, whereas a stock dividend does not.

PQ9-16 Stockholders are eligible for a dividend if they own the stock on the date of:

a. declaration
b. record
c. payment
d. issuance

PQ9-17 Saxton Company has return on assets of 12.5% for 20X0. If Saxton's 20X0 net income and interest expense, respectively, are $44,000 and $4,000, how much are Saxton's average total assets?

a. $192,000
b. $6,000
c. $320,000
d. $384,000

PQ9-18 A company declares a 5% stock dividend. The debit to Retained Earnings is an amount equal to:

a. the par value of the shares to be issued.
b. the market value of the shares to be issued.
c. the book value of the shares to be issued.
d. the excess of the market price over the original issue price of the shares to be issued.

PQ9-19 A company paid $20 per share to purchase 500 shares of its common stock ($10 par) as treasury stock. The stock was originally issued at $15 per share. The journal entry to record the purchase of the treasury stock is:

a. Treasury Stock	10,000	
Cash		10,000
b. Treasury Stock	7,500	
Retained Earnings	2,500	
Cash		10,000

c. Treasury Stock	5,000	
Paid-in Capital in Excess of Par	5,000	
Cash		10,000
d. Common Stock	10,000	
Cash		10,000

PQ9-20 When treasury stock is sold for less than its cost, the entry should include a debit to:

a. Gain on Sale of Treasury Stock.
b. Loss on Sale of Treasury Stock.
c. Paid-in Capital in Excess of Par
d. Retained Earnings

PQ9-21 Which of the following statements is *not* true about a 3-for-1 stock split?

a. Par value is reduced to one-third of what it was before the split.
b. Total contributed capital increases.
c. The market price of each share of stock will decrease.
d. A stockholder with 10 shares before the split owns 30 shares after the split.
e. Retained Earnings remains the same.

PQ9-22 A company purchases 200 shares of its $50 par value stock at $55 per share. It then reissues 30 shares at $58 per share. The entry to reissue the stock would include a

a. credit to Cash for $1,740.
b. credit to Treasury Stock for $1,740.
c. credit to Retained Earnings for $240.
d. credit to Paid-in Capital, Treasury Stock for $90.
e. debit to Retained Earnings for $90.

Problems
(Group A)

PH Grade Assist

Most of these A problems can be found within Prentice Hall Grade Assist (PHGA), an online homework and practice environment. Your instructor may ask you to complete these problems using PHGA.

Explaining the features of a corporation's stock (Obj. 1, 3, 4)

writing assignment ■

P9-1A The board of directors of Akin & Gump, Inc., investment bankers, is meeting to address the concerns of stockholders. Stockholders have submitted the following questions for discussion at the board meeting. Answer each question.

1. Why did Akin & Gump organize as a corporation if a corporation must pay an additional layer of income tax?
2. How is preferred stock similar to common stock? How is preferred stock similar to debt?
3. Akin & Gump purchased treasury stock for $50,000 and a year later sold it for $65,000. Explain to the stockholders whether the $15,000 excess is profit to be reported on the company's income statement. Explain your answer.
4. Would Akin & Gump investors prefer to receive cash dividends or stock dividends? Explain your reasoning.

Recording corporate transactions and preparing the stockholders' equity section of the balance sheet (Obj. 2)

■ general ledger

P9-2A The partnership of Grant and Hoffman needed additional capital to expand into new markets, so the business incorporated as GH, Inc. The charter from the state of Illinois authorizes GH, Inc. to issue 10,000 shares of 6%, $100 par preferred stock and 100,000 shares of no-par common stock with a stated value of $5 per share. In its first month, GH, Inc. completed the following transactions:

Feb. 2	Issued 300 shares of common stock to the promoter for assistance with issuance of the common stock. The promotional fee was $1,800. Debit the asset account Organization Cost.
2	Issued 9,000 shares of common stock to Grant and 12,000 shares to Hoffman in return for cash equal to the stock's market value of $6 per share.
10	Issued 400 shares of preferred stock to acquire a patent with a market value of $40,000.
16	Issued 2,000 shares of common stock for cash of $12,000.

Required

1. Record the transactions in the journal.
2. Prepare the stockholders' equity section of the GH, Inc. balance sheet at February 28. The ending balance of Retained Earnings is $119,000.

Preparing the stockholders' equity section of the balance sheet (Obj. 2, 4)

P9-3A The following summary provides the information needed to prepare the stockholders' equity section of the Eli Jackson Company balance sheet:

Jackson's charter authorizes the company to issue 5,000 shares of 5%, $100 par preferred stock and 500,000 shares of no-par common stock. Jackson issued 1,000 shares of the preferred stock at $105 per share. It issued 100,000 shares of the common stock for $519,000. The company's retained earnings balance at the beginning of 20X4 was $61,000. Net income for 20X4 was $80,000, and the company declared a 5% cash dividend on preferred stock for 20X4. Preferred dividends for 20X3 were in arrears.

Required

Prepare the stockholders' equity section of Eli Jackson Company's balance sheet at December 31, 20X4. Show the computation of all amounts. Journal entries are not required.

Fighting off a takeover of the corporation (Obj. 3)

writing assignment ■

P9-4A Guilford Distributing Company is positioned ideally in the clothing business. Located in Concord, New Hampshire, Guilford is the only company with a distribution network for its imported goods. The company does a brisk business with specialty stores such as **Bloomingdale's, I. Magnin**, and **Bonwit Teller**. Guilford's recent success has made the company a prime target for a takeover. Against the wishes of Guilford's board of directors, an investment group from Cincinnati is attempting to buy 51% of Guilford's outstanding stock. Board members are convinced that the Cincinnati investors would sell off the most desirable pieces of the business and leave little of value. At the most recent board meeting, several suggestions were advanced to fight off the hostile takeover bid.

Required

Suppose you are a significant stockholder of Guilford Distributing Company. Write a short memo to the board to propose an action that would make it difficult for the investor group to take over Guilford. Include in your memo a discussion of the effect your proposed action would have on the company's assets, liabilities, and total stockholders' equity.

Measuring the effects of stock issuance, treasury stock, and dividend transactions on stockholders' equity (Obj. 2, 3, 4)

P9-5A The corporate charter of House of Carpets, granted by the state of Georgia, authorizes the company to issue 5,000,000 shares of $1 par common stock and 50,000 shares of $50 par preferred stock.

In its initial public offering during 20X4, House of Carpets issued 500,000 shares of its $1 par common stock for $5.00 per share. Over the next 5 years, House of Carpets' stock price increased in value and the company issued 400,000 more shares at prices ranging from $6 to $10.75. The average issue price of these shares was $8.50.

During 20X6, the price of House of Carpets' common stock dropped to $7, and the company purchased 60,000 shares of its common stock for the treasury. After the market price of the common stock rose in 20X7, House of Carpets sold 40,000 shares of the treasury stock for $8 per share.

During the 5 years 20X4 through 20X8, House of Carpets earned net income of $1,020,000 and declared and paid cash dividends of $640,000. Stock dividends of $220,000 were distributed to the stockholders in 20X7, with $35,000 transferred to common stock and $185,000 transferred to additional paid-in capital. At December 31, 20X8, the company has total assets of $13,100,000 and total liabilities of $6,920,000.

Required

Show the computation of House of Carpets' total stockholders' equity at December 31, 20X8. Present a detailed computation of each element of stockholders' equity.

Analyzing the stockholders' equity and dividends of a corporation (Obj. 2, 4)

P9-6A **Bethlehem Steel Corporation** is the nation's largest steel company. Bethlehem included the following stockholders' equity on its balance sheet:

Stockholders' Equity	($ Millions)
Preferred stock—	
Authorized 20,000,000 shares in each class; issued:	
$5.00 Cumulative Convertible Preferred Stock,	
at $50.00 stated value, 2,500,000 shares	$ 125
$2.50 Cumulative Convertible Preferred Stock,	
at $25.00 stated value, 4,000,000 shares	100
Common stock—$8 par value—	
Authorized 80,000,000 shares, issued 48,308,516 shares	621
Retained earnings	529
	$1,375

Observe that Bethlehem reports no Paid-in Capital in Excess of Par or Stated Value. Instead, the company combines those items in the stock accounts.

Required

1. Identify the different issues of stock Bethlehem has outstanding.
2. Which class of stock did Bethlehem issue at par or stated value, and which class did it issue above par or stated value?
3. Suppose Bethlehem passed its preferred dividends for 1 year. Would the company have to pay these dividends in arrears before paying dividends to the common stockholders? Why?
4. What amount of preferred dividends must Bethlehem declare and pay each year to avoid having preferred dividends in arrears?
5. Assume preferred dividends are in arrears for 20X7. Journalize the declaration of a $61 million dividend for 20X8. No explanation is needed.

Accounting for stock issuance, dividends, and treasury stock (Obj. 2, 3, 4)

general ledger

P9-7A Safety Network Corporation reported the following summarized balance sheet at December 31, 20X8:

Assets	
Current assets	$33,400
Property and equipment, net	51,800
Total assets	$85,200
Liabilities and Equity	
Liabilities	$37,800
Stockholders' equity	
$0.50 cumulative preferred stock, $5 par	2,000
Common stock, $1 par	6,000
Paid-in capital in excess of par, common	17,400
Retained earnings	22,000
Total liabilities and equity	$85,200

During 20X9, Safety Network Corporation completed these transactions that affected stockholders' equity:

Mar. 13	Issued 2,000 shares of common stock for $4 per share.
July 7	Declared the regular cash dividend on the preferred stock.
24	Paid the cash dividend.
Sept. 9	Distributed a 10% stock dividend on the common stock. Market price of the common stock was $5 per share.
Oct. 26	Reacquired 500 shares of common stock as treasury stock, paying $7 per share.
Nov. 20	Sold 200 shares of the treasury stock for $8 per share.

Required

1. Journalize Safety Network's transactions. Explanations are not required.
2. Report Safety Network's stockholders' equity at December 31, 20X9. Net income for 20X9 was $27,000.

Measuring the effects of dividend and treasury stock transactions on a company (Obj. 3, 4)

P9-8A Assume that **IHOP Corporation** completed the following selected transactions during the current year:

April 18	Distributed a 10% stock dividend on the 9.7 million shares of common stock outstanding. The market value of the common stock was $25 per share.
May 23	Declared a cash dividend on the 5%, $100 par preferred stock (1,000 shares outstanding).
July 30	Paid the cash dividends.
Oct. 26	Purchased 2,500 shares of the company's own common stock at $24 per share.
Nov. 8	Sold 1,000 shares of treasury common stock for $27 per share.

Required

Analyze each transaction in terms of its effect on the accounting equation of IHOP.

Preparing a corporation's balance sheet; measuring profitability (Obj. 3, 6)

■ **general ledger**

P9-9A The following accounts and related balances of InterMax Graphics, Inc., are arranged in no particular order.

Accounts payable	$ 31,000	Dividends payable	$ 3,000
Retained earnings	?	Total assets, November 30, 20X6	481,000
Common stock, $5 par; 100,000 shares authorized, 42,000 shares issued	210,000	Net income	36,200
Inventory	170,000	Common stockholders' equity, November 30, 20X6	383,000
Property, plant, and equipment, net	181,000	Interest expense	12,800
Goodwill, net	6,000	Treasury stock, common, 1,600 shares at cost	11,000
Preferred stock, 4%, $10 par, 25,000 shares authorized, 3,700 shares issued	37,000	Prepaid expenses	13,000
Cash	32,000	Patent, net	31,000
Additional paid-in capital—common	140,000	Accrued liabilities	17,000
		Long-term note payable	7,000
		Accounts receivable, net	102,000

Required

1. Prepare InterMax's classified balance sheet in the account format at November 30, 20X7.
2. Compute rate of return on total assets and rate of return on common stockholders' equity for the year ended November 30, 20X7.
3. Do these rates of return suggest strength or weakness? Give your reason.

Analyzing the statement of cash flows
(Obj. 7)

writing assignment ■

P9-10A Assume the statement of cash flows of Mayfair International, Inc. reported the following for the year ended December 31, 20X6.

Cash flows from financing activities—*amounts in millions*	
Dividends [declared and] paid	$ (28.3)
Proceeds from issuance of common stock	14.1
Payments of short-term notes payable	(36.9)
Repayments of long-term debt	(1.3)
Proceeds from long-term debt	632.1
Repurchases of common stock	(686.3)

Required

1. Make the journal entry that Mayfair used to record each of these transactions.
2. From these transactions, would you expect Mayfair's total liabilities, total stockholders' equity, and total assets to have grown or shrunk during 20X6? Mayfair's net income for 20X6 was $135 million. Show your work.

(Group B)

PH Grade Assist

Some of these B problems can be found within Prentice Hall Grade Assist (PHGA), an online homework and practice environment. Your instructor may ask you to complete these problems using PHGA.

Explaining the features of a corporation's stock
(Obj. 1, 2, 5)

writing assignment ■

P9-1B Grabow & Eisenbarth, an engineering firm, is conducting a special meeting of its board of directors to address some concerns raised by its stockholders. Stockholders have submitted the following questions. Answer each question.

1. Why are capital stock and retained earnings shown separately in the shareholders' equity section of the balance sheet?
2. Ann Martinelli, a shareholder of Grabow & Eisenbarth, proposes to give some land she owns to the company in exchange for shares of the company stock. How should Grabow & Eisenbarth determine the number of shares of our stock to issue for the land?
3. Preferred shares generally are preferred with respect to dividends and in the event of our liquidation. Why would investors buy our common stock when preferred stock is available?
4. What does the redemption value of our preferred stock require us to do?
5. One of our stockholders owns 100 shares of Grabow & Eisenbarth stock and someone has offered to buy his shares for their book value. Our stockholder asks us the formula for computing the book value of *his* stock.

Recording corporate transactions and preparing the stockholders' equity section of the balance sheet
(Obj. 2)

■ general ledger

P9-2B The partners who own Bhanapol & Cink (B&C) wished to avoid the unlimited personal liability of the partnership form of business, so they incorporated as B&C Exploration, Inc. The charter from the state of Wyoming authorizes the corporation to issue 10,000 shares of 6%, $100 par preferred stock and 250,000 shares of no-par common stock with a stated value of $5 per share. In its first month, B&C Exploration completed the following transactions:

Dec. 3	Issued 500 shares of common stock to the promoter for assistance with issuance of the common stock. The promotional fee was $5,000. Debit the asset account Organization Cost.
3	Issued 5,100 shares of common stock to Bhanapol and 3,800 shares to Cink in return for cash equal to the stock's market value of $10 per share;.
12	Issued 1,000 shares of preferred stock to acquire a patent with a market value of $110,000.
22	Issued 1,500 shares of common stock for $10 cash per share.

Required

1. Record the transactions in the journal.
2. Prepare the stockholders' equity section of the B&C Exploration, Inc., balance sheet at December 31. The ending balance of Retained Earnings is $89,000.

Preparing the stockholders' equity section of the balance sheet (Obj. 2, 4)

P9-3B Srixon Inc. has the following stockholders' equity information:

Srixon's charter authorizes the company to issue 10,000 shares of $2.50 preferred stock with par value of $100 and 120,000 shares of no-par common stock. The company issued 1,000 shares of the preferred stock at $104 per share. It issued 40,000 shares of the common stock for a total of $220,000. The company's retained earnings balance at the beginning of 20X3 was $40,000, and net income for the year was $90,000. During 20X3, Srixon declared the specified dividend on preferred and a $0.50 per-share dividend on common. Preferred dividends for 20X2 were in arrears.

Required

Prepare the stockholders' equity section of Srixon Inc.'s balance sheet at December 31, 20X3. Show the computation of all amounts. Journal entries are not required.

Purchasing treasury stock to fight off a takeover of the corporation (Obj. 3)

writing assignment ■

P9-4B Yuma Corporation is positioned ideally in its line of business. Located in Nogales, Arizona, Yuma is the only company between Texas and California with reliable sources for its imported gifts. The company does a brisk business with specialty stores such as **Pier 1 Imports**. Yuma's recent success has made the company a prime target for a takeover. An investment group from Mexico City is attempting to buy 51% of Yuma's outstanding stock against the wishes of Yuma's board of directors. Board members are convinced that the Mexico City investors would sell the most desirable pieces of the business and leave little of value.

At the most recent board meeting, several suggestions were advanced to fight off the hostile takeover bid. The suggestion with the most promise is to purchase a huge quantity of treasury stock. Yuma has the cash to carry out this plan.

Required

1. Suppose you are a significant stockholder of Yuma Corporation. Write a memorandum to explain to the board how the purchase of treasury stock would make it more difficult for the Mexico City group to take over Yuma. Include in your memo a discussion of the effect that purchasing treasury stock would have on stock outstanding and on the size of the corporation.
2. Suppose Yuma management is successful in fighting off the takeover bid and later sells the treasury stock at prices greater than the purchase price. Explain what effect these sales will have on assets, stockholders' equity, and net income.

Measuring the effects of stock issuance, treasury stock, and dividend transactions on stockholders' equity (Obj. 2, 3, 4)

P9-5B The corporate charter of Hebrides Woolens, Inc., granted by the state of Delaware, authorizes the company to issue 1,000,000 shares of $1 par common stock and 100,000 shares of $50 par preferred stock.

In its initial public offering during 20X2, Hebrides issued 200,000 shares of its $1 par common stock for $6.50 per share. Over the next 5 years, Hebrides' common stock price increased in value, and the company issued 100,000 more shares at prices ranging from $7 to $11. The average issue price of these shares was $9.25.

During 20X4, the price of Hebrides' common stock dropped to $8, and Hebrides purchased 30,000 shares of its common stock for the treasury. After the market price of the common stock increased in 20X5, Hebrides sold 20,000 shares of the treasury stock for $9 per share.

During the 5 years 20X2 to 20X6, Hebrides' earned net income of $295,000 and declared and paid cash dividends of $119,000. Stock dividends of $110,000 were distributed to the stockholders in 20X3, with $14,000 transferred to common stock and $96,000 transferred to additional paid-in capital. At December 31, 20X6, total assets of the company are $5,365,000, and liabilities add up to $3,024,000.

Required

Show the computation of Hebrides Woolens' total stockholders' equity at December 31, 20X6. Present a detailed computation of each element of stockholders' equity.

Analyzing the stockholders' equity and dividends of a corporation (Obj. 2, 4)

P9-6B U and I Group, which makes food products and livestock feeds, included the following stockholders' equity on its year-end balance sheet at February 28:

Stockholders' Equity	(In Thousands)
Voting Preferred stock, 5.5% cumulative—par value $23 per share; authorized 100,000 shares in each class;	
Class A—issued 75,473 shares	$ 1,736
Class B—issued 92,172 shares	2,120
Common stock—par value $5 per share; authorized 5,000,000 shares; issued 2,870,950 shares	14,355
[Additional] Paid-in capital	5,548
Retained earnings	8,336
	$32,095

Required

1. Identify the different issues of stock U and I has outstanding.
2. Give the summary entries to record issuance of all the U and I stock. Assume that all the stock was issued for cash and that the additional paid-in capital applies to the common stock. Explanations are not required.
3. Suppose U and I passed its preferred dividends for 3 years. Would the company have to pay those dividends in arrears before paying dividends to the common stockholders? Give your reason.
4. What amount of preferred dividends must U and I declare and pay each year to avoid having preferred dividends in arrears?
5. Assume that preferred dividends are in arrears for 20X4. Record the declaration of an $800,000 dividend in the year ended February 28, 20X5. An explanation is not required.

Accounting for stock issuance, dividends, and treasury stock (Obj. 2, 3, 4)

general ledger

P9-7B Yankee Internet Corporation reported the following summarized balance sheet at December 31, 20X2:

Assets	
Current assets	$18,200
Property and equipment, net	34,700
Total assets	$52,900
Liabilities and Equity	
Liabilities	$ 6,200
Stockholders' equity:	
$5 cumulative preferred stock, $100 par	1,800
Common stock, $1 par	2,400
Paid-in capital in excess of par, common	23,500
Retained earnings	19,000
Total liabilities and equity	$52,900

During 20X3, Yankee completed these transactions that affected stockholders' equity:

Jan. 22	Issued 1,000 shares of common stock for $14 per share.
Aug. 4	Declared the regular cash dividend on the preferred stock.
24	Paid the cash dividend.
Oct. 9	Distributed a 10% stock dividend on the common stock. Market price of the common stock was $15 per share.
Nov. 19	Reacquired 800 shares of common stock as treasury stock, paying $12 per share.
Dec. 8	Sold 600 shares of the treasury stock for $15 per share.

Required

1. Journalize Yankee's transactions. Explanations are not required.
2. Report Yankee's stockholders' equity at December 31, 20X3. Net income for 20X3 was $39,000.

P9-8B Assume **Steak & Shake, Inc.** completed the following transactions during 20X6:

Measuring the effects of dividend and treasury stock transactions on a company (Obj. 3, 4)

Jan. 18	Purchased 2,000 shares of the company's own common stock at $12 per share.
Mar. 22	Sold 700 shares of treasury common stock for $16 per share.
July 6	Declared a cash dividend on the 10,000 shares of $1.70 no-par preferred stock.
Aug. 1	Paid the cash dividends.
Nov. 18	Distributed a 10% stock dividend on the 30,000 shares of $1 par common stock outstanding. The market value of the common stock was $15 per share.

Required

Analyze each transaction in terms of its effect on the accounting equation of Steak & Shake, Inc.

P9-9B The following accounts and related balances of Air Control Specialists, Inc., as of September 30, 20X5, are arranged in no particular order.

Preparing a corporation's balance sheet; measuring profitability (Obj. 3, 6)

■ **spreadsheet**

Interest expense	$ 6,100	Cash	$13,000
Property, plant, and equipment, net	357,000	Accounts receivable, net	24,000
Common stock, $1 par, 500,000 shares authorized, 115,000 shares issued	115,000	Paid-in capital in excess of par—common	19,000
Prepaid expenses	10,000	Accrued liabilities	26,000
Common stockholders' equity, September 30, 20X4	192,000	Long-term note payable	72,000
Net income	31,000	Inventory	59,000
Total assets, September 30, 20X4	404,000	Dividends payable	9,000
Treasury stock, common, 18,000 shares at cost	22,000	Retained earnings	?
Goodwill, net	14,000	Accounts payable	31,000
		Trademark, net	9,000
		Preferred stock, $0.20, no-par, 10,000 shares authorized and issued	27,000

Required

1. Prepare the company's classified balance sheet in the account format at September 30, 20X5.
2. Compute rate of return on total assets and rate of return on common stockholders' equity for the year ended September 30, 20X5.
3. Do these rates of return suggest strength or weakness? Give your reason.

P9-10B The statement of cash flows of **PepsiCo, Inc.** reported the following (adapted) for the year ended December 31, 20X1:

Analyzing the statement of cash flows (Obj. 7)

writing assignment ■

Cash flows from financing activities—*amounts in millions*	
Cash dividends paid	$ (994)
Issuance of common stock	623
Proceeds from issuance of long-term debt	324
Purchases of treasury stock	(1,731)
Payments of long-term debt	(573)
Reissuance of treasury stock (cost, $374)	524

Required

1. Make the journal entry that PepsiCo would use to record each of these transactions.
2. From these transactions, would you expect PepsiCo's total liabilities, total stockholders' equity, and total assets to have grown or shrunk during 20X1? PepsiCo's net income for 20X1 was $2,662 million. Show your work.

Apply Your Knowledge

Decision Cases

Evaluating the financial position and profitability of a real company (Obj. 2, 3, 4, 5)

Case 1. At December 31, 20X4, **Enron Corporation** reported the following data (condensed in millions):

Stockholders' equity	$11,470	Total current liabilities	$28,406
Long-term liabilities	25,627	Investments and other assets	23,379
Property, plant, equipment, net	11,743	Total current assets	30,381
Total expenses for 20X4	99,810	Total revenues for 20X4	100,789

During 20X5, Enron restated company financial statements for 20X1 to 20X4, after reporting that some data had been omitted from those prior-year statements. Assume that the startling events of 20X5 included the following:

- Several related companies should have been, but were not, included in the Enron statements for 20X4. These companies had revenues of $90 million, total assets of $5,700 million, expenses of $220 million, and liabilities totaling $5,600 million.
- In January 20X5, Enron's stockholders got the company to exchange $2,000 million of 12% long-term notes payable for their common stock. Interest is accrued at year end.

Take the role of an analyst with **Moody's Investors Service**. It is your job to analyze Enron Corporation and rate the company's long-term debt.

Required

1. Measure Enron's expected net income for 20X5 two ways:
   a. Assume 20X5's net income should be approximately the same as the amount of net income that Enron actually reported for 20X4.
   b. Recompute expected net income for 20X5 taking into account all the new developments of 20X5.
   c. Evaluate Enron's likely trend of net income for the future. Discuss *why* this trend is developing. Ignore income tax.
2. Write Enron's accounting equation two ways:
   a. As actually reported at December 31, 20X4.
   b. As adjusted for the events of 20X5.
3. Measure Enron's debt ratio as reported at December 31, 20X4, and after again making the adjustments for the events of 20X5.
4. Based on your analysis, make a recommendation to the Debt-Rating Committee of Moody's Investor Services. Would you recommend upgrading, downgrading, or leaving Enron's debt rating undisturbed (currently, it is "high-grade").

Evaluating alternative ways of raising capital (Obj. 2)

Case 2. John Vines and Larry Price have written a computer program for a video game that they believe will rival Playstation and Xbox. They need additional capital to market the product, and they plan to incorporate their partnership. They are considering alternative capital structures for the corporation. Their primary goal is to raise as much capital as possible without giving up control of the business. The partners plan to receive 110,000 shares of the corporation's common stock in return for the net assets of the partnership. After the partnership books are closed and the assets adjusted to current market value, Vines' capital balance will be $60,000, and Price's balance will be $50,000.

The corporation's plans for a charter include an authorization to issue 5,000 shares of preferred stock and 500,000 shares of $1 par common stock. Vines and Price are uncertain about the most desirable features for the preferred stock. Prior to incorporating, the partners are discussing their plans with two investment groups. The corporation can obtain capital from outside investors under either of the following plans:

- Plan 1. Group 1 will invest $160,000 to acquire 1,400 shares of 6%, $100 par nonvoting, noncumulative preferred stock.
- Plan 2. Group 2 will invest $105,000 to acquire 1,000 shares of $5, no-par preferred stock and $70,000 to acquire 70,000 shares of common stock. Each preferred share receives 50 votes on matters that come before the stockholders.

Required

Assume that the corporation is chartered.

1. Journalize the issuance of common stocks to Vines and Price. Debit each partner's capital account for its balance.
2. Journalize the issuance of stock to the outsiders under both plans.
3. Assume that net income for the first year is $120,000 and total dividends are $19,000. Prepare the stockholders' equity section of the corporation's balance sheet under both plans.
4. Recommend one of the plans to Vines and Price. Give your reasons.

Analyzing cash dividends and stock dividends (Obj. 4)

Case 3. United Parcel Service (UPS), Inc. had the following stockholders' equity amounts on December 31, 20X5 (adapted, in millions):

Common stock and additional paid-in capital; 1,135 shares issued	$ 278
Retained earnings	9,457
Total stockholders' equity	$9,735

During 20X5, UPS paid a cash dividend of $0.715 per share. Assume that, after paying the cash dividends, UPS distributed a 10% stock dividend. Assume further that the following year UPS declared and paid a cash dividend of $0.65 per share.

Suppose you own 10,000 shares of UPS common stock, acquired 3 years ago, prior to the 10% stock dividend. The market price of UPS stock was $61.02 per share before the stock dividend.

Required

1. How does the stock dividend affect your proportionate ownership in UPS? Explain.
2. What amount of cash dividends did you receive last year? What amount of cash dividends will you receive after the above dividend action?
3. Assume that immediately after the stock dividend was distributed, the market value of UPS' stock decreased from $61.02 per share to $55.47 per share. Does this decrease represent a loss to you? Explain.
4. Suppose UPS announces at the time of the stock dividend that the company will continue to pay the annual $0.715 *cash* dividend per share, even after distributing the *stock* dividend. Would you expect the market price of the stock to decrease to $55.47 per share as in Requirement 3? Explain.

Ethical Issues

writing assignment ■

Ethical Issue 1. *Note: This case is based on a real situation*

George Campbell paid $50,000 for a franchise that entitled him to market Success Associates software programs in the countries of the European Union. Campbell intended to sell individual franchises for the major language groups of western Europe—German, French,

English, Spanish, and Italian. Naturally, investors considering buying a franchise from Campbell asked to see the financial statements of his business.

Believing the value of the franchise to be greater than $50,000, Campbell sought to capitalize his own franchise at $500,000. The law firm of McDonald & LaDue helped Campbell form a corporation chartered to issue 500,000 shares of common stock with par value of $1 per share. Attorneys suggested the following chain of transactions:

a. A third party borrows $500,000 and purchases the franchise from Campbell.
b. Campbell pays the corporation $500,000 to acquire all its stock.
c. The corporation buys the franchise from the third party, who repays the loan.

In the final analysis, the third party is debt-free and out of the picture. Campbell owns all the corporation's stock, and the corporation owns the franchise. The corporation balance sheet lists a franchise acquired at a cost of $500,000. This balance sheet is Campbell's most valuable marketing tool.

Required

1. What is unethical about this situation?
2. Who can be harmed in this situation? How can they be harmed? What role does accounting play here?

writing assignment ■

Ethical Issue 2. St. Genevieve Petroleum Company is an independent oil producer in Baton Parish, Louisiana. In February, company geologists discovered a pool of oil that tripled the company's proven reserves. Prior to disclosing the new oil to the public, St. Genevieve quietly bought most of its stock as treasury stock. After the discovery was announced, the company's stock price increased from $6 to $27.

Required

1. Did St. Genevieve managers behave ethically? Explain your answer.
2. Identify the accounting principle relevant to this situation.
3. Who was helped and who was harmed by management's action?

Focus on Financials: ■ YUM! Brands

Analyzing common stock, retained earnings, return on equity, and return on assets (Obj. 2, 3, 6)

YUM! Brands' financial statements appear in Appendix A at the end of this book.

1. YUM reports common stock in a single total. Why is there no paid-in capital in excess of par?
2. YUM's common stock balance decreased during 2003. What caused the decrease? The statement of stockholders' equity reveals the reason for the decrease.
3. Prove that only one item affected YUM's retained earnings during 2003. Identify the item and its amount.
4. How much had YUM's stockholders paid into the company through December 27, 2003, net of amounts paid back to retire company stock?
5. Compute YUM's return on equity and return on assets for 2003. Which is larger? Is this a sign of financial strength or weakness? Explain.

Focus on Analysis: ■ Pier 1 Imports

Analyzing treasury stock and retained earnings (Obj. 2, 3, 4)

This case is based on the financial statements of **Pier 1 Imports**, given in Appendix B at the end of this book. In particular, this case uses Pier 1's statement of shareholders' equity for the year 2004.

1. During 2004, Pier 1 purchased treasury stock and also sold treasury stock under the company's stock option plan and stock purchase plan. Was Pier 1's average price per share higher for the treasury stock the company purchased or for the treasury stock sold? What was the difference in price per share between the two transactions?
2. Journalize the purchase of treasury stock and the sale of treasury stock during the year ended February 28, 2004. Also journalize the exercise-of-stock option transaction (Pier 1 issued stock to its executives).

■ **EXHIBIT 10-2**

Reporting Investments on the Balance Sheet

Current Assets:		
Cash	$X	
Short-term investments	X	
Accounts receivable	X	
Inventories	X	
Prepaid expenses	X	
Total current assets		$X
Long-term investments [or simply Investments]		X
Property, plant, and equipment		X
Intangible assets		X
Other assets		X

Assets are listed in order of liquidity. Long-Term Investments are less liquid than Current Assets but more liquid than Property, Plant, and Equipment. GE reports investment securities immediately after cash.

The accounting rules for investments in stock depend on the percentage of ownership by the investor. The closer the relationship, the tighter the accounting bond, as shown in Exhibit 10-3.[1]

■ **EXHIBIT 10-3**

Accounting Methods for Long-Term Investments Based on Level of Ownership

Percentage Ownership by the Investor	Similar to a Man/Woman Relationship	GAAP Accounting Method
Up to 20%	Dating Relationship	Available-for-Sale
20–50%	Girlfriend/Boyfriend	Equity
Greater than 50%	Married	Consolidation

An investment up to 20% is casual because the investor usually has almost no influence on the investee company. This is like a dating relationship. Ownership between 20% and 50% provides the investor with the opportunity to significantly influence the investee, similar to a girlfriend/boyfriend arrangement. An investment above 50% of the investee's stock is like a marriage. The investor should be able to have lots of influence—perhaps control—over the investee company. Let's examine the related accounting methods for long-term investments in stock.

Available-for-Sale Investments

OBJECTIVE

1 **Account** for available-for-sale investments

Available-for-sale investments are stock investments other than trading securities. They are classified as current assets if the business expects to sell them within the next year. All other available-for-sale investments are classified as long term (Exhibit 10-2).

Available-for-sale investments All investments not classified as held-to-maturity or trading securities.

Accounting for Available-for-Sale Investments

Available-for-sale investments are accounted for at market value because the company expects to sell the stock at its market price. *Cost* is used only as the initial amount for recording the investments. These investments are reported on the balance sheet as *current market value*.

[1]Professor Mark Miller suggested this characterization of investments.

Suppose GE purchases 1,000 shares of **Hewlett-Packard** common stock at the market price of $35.75. GE intends to hold this investment for longer than a year and therefore treats it as an available-for-sale investment. GE's entry to record the investment is:

20X7			
Oct. 23	Long-term Investment (1,000 × $35.75)....	35,750	
	Cash		35,750
	Purchased investment.		

ASSETS	=	LIABILITIES	+	STOCKHOLDERS' EQUITY
+35,750 −35,750	=	0	+	0

Assume that GE receives a $0.20 quarterly cash dividend on the Hewlett-Packard stock. GE's entry to record receipt of the dividend is

20X7			
Nov. 14	Cash (1,000 × $0.20)......................	200	
	Dividend Revenue		200
	Received cash dividend.		

ASSETS	=	LIABILITIES	+	STOCKHOLDERS' EQUITY	+	REVENUES
+200	=	0	+			+200

Receipt of a *stock* dividend is different from receipt of a cash dividend. For a stock dividend, the investor records no dividend revenue. Instead, the investor makes a memorandum entry in the accounting records to denote the new number of shares of stock held as an investment. Because the number of shares of stock held has increased, the investor's cost per share of the stock decreases. To illustrate, suppose GE receives a 5% stock dividend from Hewlett-Packard Company. GE would receive 50 shares (5% of 1,000 shares previously held) and make this memorandum entry in its accounting methods:

MEMORANDUM—Receipt of stock dividend: Received 50 shares of Hewlett-Packard common stock in 5% stock dividend. New cost per share is $34.05 (cost of $35,750 ÷ 1,050 shares).

In all future transactions affecting this investment, GE's cost per share is now $34.05.

■ Taking Action What Value of an Investment Is Most Relevant?

Market value is the amount that you can buy or sell an investment for. Because of the relevance of market values for decision making, available-for-sale investments in stock are reported on the balance sheet at their market value. On the balance-sheet date we therefore adjust available-for-sale investments from their last carrying amount to current market value. Assume that the market value of the Hewlett-Packard common stock is $36,400 on December 31, 20X7. In this case, GE makes the following entry to bring the investment to market value.

20X7			
Dec. 31	Allowance to Adjust Investment to Market ($36,400 – $35,750)	650	
	Unrealized Gain on Investment		650
	Adjusted investment to market value.		

The increase in the investment's market value creates new equity for the investor.

ASSETS	=	LIABILITIES	+	STOCKHOLDERS' EQUITY
+650	=	0		+650

Allowance to Adjust Investment to Market is a companion account to Long-Term Investment. In this case, the investment's cost ($35,750) plus the Allowance ($650) equals the investment carrying amount ($36,400), as follows:

Long-Term Investment	Allowance to Adjust Investment to Market
35,750	650

Investment carrying amount = Market value of $36,400

Here the Allowance has a debit balance because the market value of the investment increased. If the investment's market value declines, the Allowance is credited. In that case the carrying amount is its cost minus the Allowance.

The other side of the adjustment entry (top of this page) is a credit to Unrealized Gain on Investment. If the market value of the investment declines, the company debits Unrealized Loss on Investment. *Unrealized* gains and losses result from changes in market value, not from sales of investments. For available-for-sale investments, the Unrealized Gain account or the Unrealized Loss account is reported in two places in the financial statements:

- *Other comprehensive income*, which can be reported on the *income statement* in a separate section below net income
- *Accumulated other comprehensive income*, which is a separate section of stockholders' equity, below retained earnings, on the *balance sheet*

The following display shows how GE could report its investment and the related unrealized gain in its financial statements at the end of 20X7 (all other figures are assumed for illustration in context):

Balance sheet

Assets:	
Total current assets	$ XXX
Long-term investments—at market value ($35,750 + $650)	$36,400
Property, plant, and equipment, net	XXX
Stockholders' equity:	
Common stock	$ 1,000
Retained earnings	2,000
Accumulated other comprehensive income:	
Unrealized gain on investments	390
Total stockholders' equity	$ 3,390

Income statement

Revenues		$10,000
Expenses, including income tax		6,000
Net income		$ 4,000
Other comprehensive income:		
Unrealized gain on investments	$650	
Less Income tax 40%	(260)	390
Comprehensive income		$ 4,390

Check Point 10-1

The unrealized gain appears on the balance sheet; it is not part of net income. The unrealized gain is reported at its net-of-tax amount ($390) because it comes after net income, which also is an after-tax figure. The investments appear on the balance sheet at current market value. The balance sheet also reports the unrealized gain in a separate section of stockholders' equity, Accumulated other comprehensive income, which comes after Retained Earnings.

Selling an Available-for-Sale Investment

The sale of an available-for-sale investment usually results in a *realized* gain or loss. Realized gains and losses measure the difference between the amount received from the sale and the cost of the investment.

Suppose GE sells its investment in Hewlett-Packard stock for $34,000 during 20X9. GE would record the sale as follows:

20X9			
May 19	Cash.	$34,000	
	Loss on Sale of Investment	1,750	
	Long-Term Investment (cost)		35,750
	Sold investment.		

ASSETS	=	LIABILITIES	+	STOCKHOLDERS' EQUITY	−	LOSSES
+34,000 −35,750	=	0	+		−	1,750

GE would report Loss on Sale of Investments as an "Other" item on the income statement. Then at December 31, 20X9, GE must update the Allowance to Adjust Investment to Market and the Unrealized Gain on Investment accounts to their current balances. These adjustments are covered in intermediate accounting courses.

✓Check Point 10-2

stop AND think. . .

Suppose **Intel Corporation** holds the following available-for-sale securities as long-term investments at December 31, 20X9:

Stock	Cost	Current Market Value
The Coca-Cola Company	$ 85,000	$71,000
Eastman Kodak Company	16,000	12,000
	$101,000	$83,000

Show how Intel will report long-term investments on its December 31, 20X9, balance sheet.

Answer:

Assets

Long-term investments, at market value $83,000

ACCOUNTING ALERT

When Should We Sell That Investment in Hewlett-Packard Stock?

In January we announced that earnings per share (EPS) should hit $2.40 for the year. That would give us a nice increase over last year. The stock market likes steady increases in EPS, and we've been delivering for the past 5 years. If we reach our EPS goal, our stock price should stay up. But if we fail to meet our EPS target, . . .

Its December 15, and net income for the year is disappointing. The accounting department has run our numbers, and it appears that EPS will come in at $2.38. Everyone knows that investors will punish us for missing our forecast. Top managers of the company may lose their jobs.

Wait a minute! We own some Hewlett-Packard stock that we bought for $35,750. The investment is now worth $86,000, and we can sell it for a $50,250 gain. The gain will increase our net income, and EPS should rise by two cents. We can meet our earnings target, and investors should be happy. Let's go ahead and unload the stock.

This scenario is played out across the country. It reveals an interesting fact about gains and losses on the sale of investments. Companies control when they sell investments, and that helps them control when they book gains and losses. Suppose a bad year hits and we hold an investment that has appreciated in value. We can sell the investment, record the gain, and boost our reported income.

The cost principle of accounting provides this opportunity to "manage" earnings. If companies had to account for all investments at pure market value, there would be no gains or losses on the sale. Instead, all gains and losses would be recorded when the market value of the asset changes. That would eliminate part of management's ability to "manage" earnings. But the business community isn't ready to fully embrace market-value accounting.

The takeaway lessons from this accounting alert are

- Ask questions when a company barely meets its EPS target.
- Did the company "manage" to meet its goal by selling an investment?
- If so, that's not as good as if the income had come from operations.

Equity-Method Investments

We use the **equity method** to account for investments in which the investor owns 20% to 50% of the investee's stock.

Equity method
The method used to account for investments in which the investor has 20–50% of the investee's voting stock and can significantly influence the decisions of the investee.

Buying a Large Stake in Another Company

An investor with a stock holding between 20% and 50% of the investee's voting stock may significantly influence the investee (as in a girlfriend/boyfriend relationship). Such an investor can probably affect dividend policy, product lines, and other important matters.

General Motors (GM), for example, owns nearly 40% of **Isuzu Motors Overseas Distribution Corporation**. These investee companies are often referred to as *affiliates*; thus Isuzu is an affiliate of GM. And because GM has a voice in shaping the policy and operations of Isuzu, some measure of Isuzu's success or failure should be included in GM's accounting for the investment.

Accounting for Equity-Method Investments

OBJECTIVE

2 **Use** the equity method for investments

Investments accounted for by the equity method are recorded initially at cost. Suppose Phillips Petroleum Company pays $400 million for 30% of the common stock of White Rock Natural Gas Corporation. Phillips' entry to record the purchase of this investment follows (in millions):

Jan. 6	Long-Term Investment	400	
	Cash		400
	To purchase equity-method investment.		

ASSETS	=	LIABILITIES	+	STOCKHOLDERS' EQUITY
+400 −400	=	0	+	0

The Investor's Percentage of Investee Income. Under the equity method, Phillips, as the investor, applies its percentage of ownership—30%, in our example—in recording its share of the investee's net income and dividends. If White Rock reports net income of $250 million for the year, Phillips records 30% of this amount as follows (in millions):

Dec. 31	Long-Term Investment ($250 × 0.30)...........	75	
	Equity-Method Investment Revenue........		75
	To record investment revenue.		

ASSETS	=	LIABILITIES	+	STOCKHOLDERS' EQUITY	+	REVENUES
+75	=	0	+		+	75

Because of the close relationship between the two companies, the investor increases the Investment account and records Investment Revenue when the investee reports income. As the investee's owners' equity increases, so does the Investment account on the investor's books.

Receiving Dividends under the Equity Method. Phillips records its proportionate part of cash dividends received from White Rock. When White Rock declares and pays a cash dividend of $100 million, Phillips receives 30% of this dividend and records this entry (in millions):

Dec. 31	Cash ($100 × 0.30)	30	
	Long-Term Investment		30
	To receive cash dividend on equity-method investment.		

ASSETS	=	LIABILITIES	+	STOCKHOLDERS' EQUITY
+30 −30	=	0	+	0

The Investment account is *decreased* for the receipt of a dividend on an equity-method investment. Why? Because the dividend decreases the investee's owners' equity and thus the investor's investment.

After the preceding entries are posted, Phillips' Investment account reflects its equity in the net assets of White Rock (in millions):

Long-Term Investment

Jan. 6	**Purchase**	**400**	**Dec. 31**	**Dividends**	**30**
Dec. 31	**Net income**	**75**			
Dec. 31	**Balance**	**445**			

✔Check Point 10-3

Phillips would report the long-term investment on the balance sheet and the equity-method investment revenue on the income statement as follows:

	Millions
Balance sheet (partial):	
Assets	
Total current assets	$XXX
Long-term investments, at equity	445
Property, plant, and equipment, net	XXX
Income statement (partial):	
Income from operations	$XXX
Other revenue:	
Equity-method investment revenue	75
Net income	$XXX

Gain or loss on the sale of an equity-method investment is measured as the difference between the sale proceeds and the carrying amount of the investment. For example, sale of 20% of the White Rock common stock for $81 million would be recorded as follows:

Feb. 13	Cash	81	
	Loss on Sale of Investment	8	
	Long-Term Investment ($445,000 × 0.20)		89
	Sold 20% of investment.		

✔Check Point 10-4

ASSETS	=	LIABILITIES	+	STOCKHOLDERS' EQUITY	–	LOSSES
+81 –89	=	0	+		–	8

Summary of the Equity Method. The following T-account illustrates the accounting for equity-method investments:

Equity-Method Investment

Original cost	**Share of losses**
Share of income	**Share of dividends**
Balance	

Consolidated Subsidiaries

OBJECTIVE

3 **Understand** consolidated financial statements

Companies buy a significant stake in another company in order to *influence* the other company's operations. In this section we cover the situation in which a corporation buys enough of another company to actually *control* that company. GE's ownership of GE Capital Services is an example.

Controlling (majority) interest
Ownership of more than 50% of an investee company's voting stock.

Parent company
An investor company that owns more than 50% of the voting stock of a subsidiary company.

Subsidiary company
An investee company in which a parent company owns more than 50% of the voting stock.

■ Taking Action Why Buy Another Company?

Most large corporations own controlling interests in other companies. A **controlling** (or **majority**) **interest** is the ownership of more than 50% of the investee's voting stock. Such an investment enables the investor to elect a majority of the members of the investee's board of directors and thus control the investee. The investor is called the **parent company**, and the investee company is called the **subsidiary**. For example, **NBC** is a subsidiary of GE, the parent. Therefore, the stockholders of GE control NBC, as diagrammed in Exhibit 10-4.

■ **EXHIBIT 10-4**
Ownership Structure of General Electric and NBC

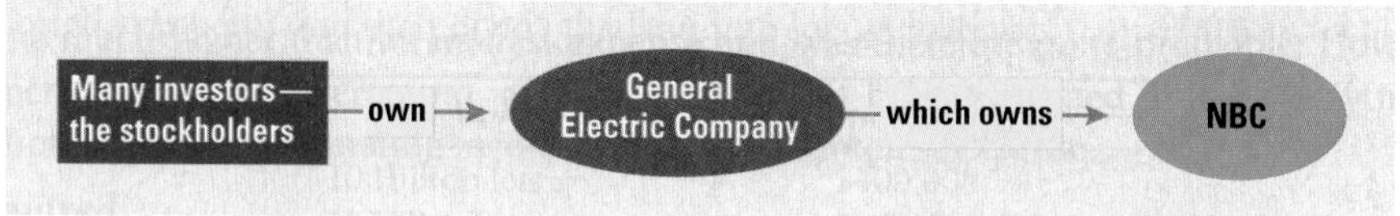

Exhibit 10-5 shows some of the more interesting subsidiaries of GE Company.

■ **EXHIBIT 10-5** Selected Subsidiaries of General Electric Company

GE Aircraft Engines	GE Appliances
GE Capital Services	GE Lighting
NBC	GE Transportation Services

■ **EXHIBIT 10-6**
Accounting Methods for Stock Investment by Percentage of Ownership

Consolidation Accounting

Consolidation accounting is a method of combining the financial statements of all the companies that are controlled by the same stockholders. Consolidation can be likened to marriage. This method reports a single set of financial statements for the consolidated entity, which carries the name of the parent company. Exhibit 10-6 summarizes the accounting methods used for stock investments.

Consolidated statements combine the balance sheets, income statements, and cash-flow statements of the parent company with those of majority-owned subsidiaries. The result is an overall set of statements as if the parent and its subsidiaries were a single entity. Investors can gain a better perspective on total operations than they could by examining the reports of each individual subsidiary.

In consolidated statements the assets, liabilities, revenues, and expenses of each subsidiary are added to the parent's accounts. For example, the balance in NBC's Cash account is added to the balance in the GE Cash account. The sum of the two amounts is presented as a single amount in the GE consolidated balance sheet. Each account balance of a subsidiary, such as NBC or GE Capital Services, loses its identity in the consolidated statements, which bear the name of the parent, General Electric Company.

Consolidated statements
Financial statements of the parent company plus those of majority-owned subsidiaries as if the combination were a single legal entity.

Exhibit 10-7 diagrams a corporate structure whose parent corporation owns controlling interests in five subsidiaries and an equity-method investment in another investee company.

■ **EXHIBIT 10-7**

Parent Company with Consolidated Subsidiaries and an Equity-Method Investment

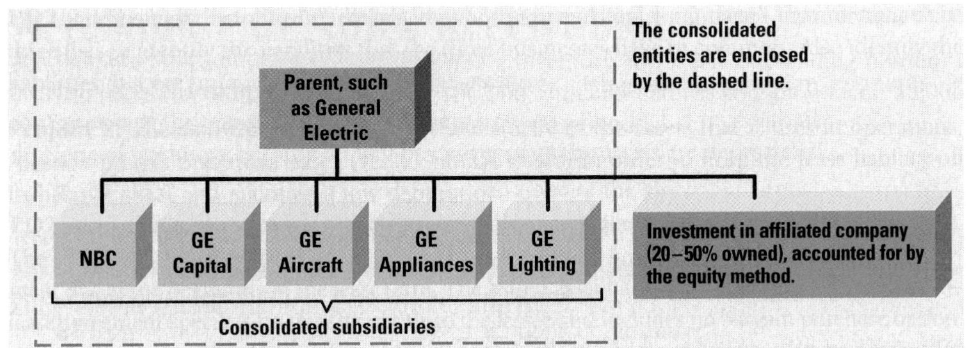

The Consolidated Balance Sheet and the Related Work Sheet

GE has purchased all (100%) the outstanding common stock of NBC. Both GE and NBC keep separate sets of books. GE, the parent company, uses a work sheet to prepare the consolidated statements of GE and its consolidated subsidiaries. Then GE's consolidated balance sheet shows the combined assets and liabilities of both GE and all its subsidiaries.

Exhibit 10-8 shows the work sheet for consolidating the balance sheets of Parent Corporation and Subsidiary Corporation. We use these hypothetical entities to illustrate the consolidation process. Consider elimination entry (a) for the parent-subsidiary ownership accounts. Entry (a) credits the parent's Investment account to eliminate its debit balance. Entry (a) also eliminates the subsidiary's stockholders' equity accounts by debiting the subsidiary's Common Stock and Retained Earnings for their full balances. Without this elimination, the consolidated financial statements would include both the parent company's investment in the subsidiary and the subsidiary company's equity. But these accounts represent the same thing—Subsidiary's equity—and so they must be eliminated from the consolidated totals. If they weren't, the same resources would be counted twice.

■ **EXHIBIT 10-8** Work Sheet for a Consolidated Balance Sheet

	Parent Corporation	Subsidiary Corporation	Eliminations Debit	Eliminations Credit	Parent and Subsidiary Consolidated Amounts
Assets					
Cash	12,000	18,000			30,000
Note receivable from Subsidiary	80,000	—		(b) 80,000	—
Inventory	104,000	91,000			195,000
Investment in Subsidiary	150,000	—		(a) 150,000	—
Other assets	218,000	138,000			356,000
Total	564,000	247,000			581,000
Liabilities and Stockholders' Equity					
Accounts payable	43,000	17,000			60,000
Notes payable	190,000	80,000	(b) 80,000		190,000
Common stock	176,000	100,000	(a) 100,000		176,000
Retained earnings	155,000	50,000	(a) 50,000		155,000
Total	564,000	247,000	230,000	230,000	581,000

The resulting Parent and Subsidiary consolidated balance sheet (far-right column) reports no Investment in Subsidiary account. Moreover, the consolidated totals for Common Stock and Retained Earnings are those of Parent Corporation only. Study the final column of the consolidation work sheet.

In this example, Parent Corporation has an $80,000 note receivable from Subsidiary, and Subsidiary has a note payable to Parent. The parent's receivable and the subsidiary's payable represent the same resources—all entirely within the consolidated entity. Both, therefore, must be eliminated. Entry (b) accomplishes this. The $80,000 credit in the elimination column of the work sheet zeros out Parent's Note Receivable from Subsidiary. The $80,000 debit in the elimination column zeros out the Subsidiary's Note Payable to Parent. The resulting consolidated amount for notes payable is the amount owed to creditors outside the consolidated entity, which is appropriate. After the work sheet is complete, the consolidated amount for each account represents the total asset, liability, and equity amounts controlled by Parent Corporation.

Check Point 10-5

stop AND think. . .

Examine Exhibit 10-8. Why does the consolidated stockholders' equity ($176,000 + $155,000) *exclude* the equity of Subsidiary Corporation?

Answer:
The stockholders' equity of the consolidated entity is that of the parent only. Also, the subsidiary's equity and the parent company's investment balance represent the same resources. Including both would amount to double counting.

Goodwill and Minority Interest

Goodwill and Minority Interest are two accounts that only a consolidated entity can have. *Goodwill*, which we studied in Chapter 7, arises when a parent company pays more to acquire a subsidiary company than the market value of the subsidiary's net assets. As we saw in Chapter 7, goodwill is the intangible asset that represents the parent company's excess payment to acquire the subsidiary. GE reports goodwill on its balance sheet.

Minority interest
A subsidiary company's equity that is held by stockholders other than the parent company.

Minority interest arises when a parent company purchases less than 100% of the stock of a subsidiary company. For example, GE owns less than 100% of some of the companies it controls. The remainder of the subsidiaries' stock is minority interest to GE. Minority Interest is included along with the liabilities on the balance sheet of the parent company. GE reports minority interest on its balance sheet.

Check Point 10-6

Income of a Consolidated Entity

The income of a consolidated entity is the net income of the parent plus the parent's proportion of the subsidiaries' net income. Suppose Parent Company owns all the stock of Subsidiary S-1 and 60% of the stock of Subsidiary S-2. During the year just ended, Parent earned net income of $330,000, S-1 earned $150,000, and S-2 had a net loss of $100,000. Parent Company would report net income of $420,000, computed as follows:

	Net Income (Net Loss) of Each Company		Parent's Ownership of Each Company		Parent's Consolidated Net Income (Net Loss)
Parent Company	$330,000	×	100%	=	$330,000
Subsidiary S-1	150,000	×	100%	=	150,000
Subsidiary S-2	(100,000)	×	60%	=	(60,000)
Consolidated net income . .					$420,000

Long-Term Investments in Bonds and Notes

OBJECTIVE 4 **Account** for long-term investments in bonds

The major investors in bonds are financial institutions—pension plans, mutual funds, and insurance companies such as GE Capital Services. The relationship between the issuing corporation and the investor (bondholder) may be diagrammed as follows:

Investor (Bondholder)		Issuing Corporation
Investment in bonds	←——→	Bonds payable
Interest revenue	←——→	Interest expense

An investment in bonds is classified either as short-term (a current asset) or as long-term. Short-term investments in bonds are rare. Here, we focus on long-term investments called **held-to-maturity investments**.

Held-to-maturity investments Bonds and notes that an investor intends to hold until maturity.

Bond investments are recorded at cost. Years later, at maturity, the investor will receive the bonds' face value. Often bond investments are purchased at a premium or a discount. When there is a premium or discount, held-to-maturity investments are amortized to account for interest revenue and the bonds' carrying amount. Held-to-maturity investments are reported at their *amortized cost*, which determines the carrying amount.

Suppose an investor purchases $10,000 of 6% CBS bonds at a price of 95.2 on April 1, 20X5. The investor intends to hold the bonds as a long-term investment until their maturity. Interest dates are April 1 and October 1. Because these bonds mature on April 1, 20X9, they will be outstanding for 4 years (48 months). In this case the investor paid a discount price for the bonds (95.2% of face value). The investor must amortize the bonds' carrying amount from cost of $9,520 up to $10,000 over their term to maturity. Assume amortization of the bonds by the straight-line method. The following are the entries for this long-term investment:

20X5			
Apr. 1	Long-Term Investment in Bonds		
	($10,000 × 0.952)	9,520	
	Cash		9,520
	To purchase bond investment.		
Oct. 1	Cash ($10,000 × 0.06 × 6/12)	300	
	Interest Revenue		300
	To receive semiannual interest.		
Oct. 1	Long-Term Investment in Bonds		
	[($10,000 – $9,520)/48] × 6	60	
	Interest Revenue		60
	To amortize bond investment.		

At December 31, the year-end adjustments are

20X5			
Dec. 31	Interest Receivable ($10,000 × 0.06 × 3/12) . . .	150	
	Interest Revenue		150
	To accrue interest revenue.		
Dec. 31	Long-Term Investment in Bonds		
	[($10,000 – $9,520)/48] × 3	30	
	Interest Revenue		30
	To amortize bond investment.		

This amortization entry has two effects:

Check Point 10-7

- It increases the Long-Term Investment account on its march toward maturity value.
- It records the interest revenue earned from the increase in the carrying amount of the investment.

Check Point 10-8

The financial statements at December 31, 20X5 report the following for this investment in bonds:

Balance sheet at December 31, 20X5:	
Current assets:	
Interest receivable	$ 150
Long-term investments in bonds ($9,520 + $60 + $30)	9,610
Property, plant, and equipment	X,XXX
Income statement for the year ended December 31, 20X5:	
Other revenues:	
Interest revenue ($300 + $60 + $150 + $30)	$540

MAKING MANAGERIAL DECISIONS

ACCOUNTING METHODS FOR LONG-TERM INVESTMENTS

These guidelines show which accounting method to use for each type of long-term investment.

General Electric Company has all types of investments—stocks, bonds, 25% interests, and controlling interests. How should GE account for its various investments?

Type of Long-Term Investment	Accounting Method
GE owns less than 20% of investee stock	Available-for-sale
GE owns between 20% and 50% of investee/affiliate stock	Equity
GE owns more than 50% of investee stock	Consolidation
GE owns long-term investment in bonds (held-to-maturity investment)	Amortized cost

Summary Problems

MID-CHAPTER

1. Identify the appropriate accounting method for each of the following situations:
   a. Investment in 25% of investee's stock
   b. 10% investment in stock
   c. Investment in more than 50% of investee's stock
2. At what amount should the following available-for-sale investment portfolio be reported on the December 31 balance sheet? All the investments are less than 5% of the investee's stock.

Stock	Investment Cost	Current Market Value
DuPont	$ 5,000	$ 5,500
ExxonMobil	61,200	53,000
Procter & Gamble	3,680	6,230

   Journalize any adjusting entry required by these data.
3. Investor paid $67,900 to acquire a 40% equity-method investment in the common stock of Investee. At the end of the first year, Investee's net income was $80,000, and Investee declared and paid cash dividends of $55,000. What is Investor's ending balance in its Equity-Method Investment account?
4. Parent company paid $85,000 for all the common stock of Subsidiary Company, and Parent owes Subsidiary $20,000 on a note payable. Complete the consolidation work sheet below.

	Parent Company	Subsidiary Company	Eliminations Debit	Eliminations Credit	Consolidated Amounts
Assets					
Cash	7,000	4,000			
Note receivable from Parent	—	20,000			
Investment in Subsidiary	85,000	—			
Other assets	108,000	99,000			
Total	200,000	123,000			
Liabilities and Stockholders' Equity					
Accounts payable	15,000	8,000			
Notes payable	20,000	30,000			
Common stock	120,000	60,000			
Retained earnings	45,000	25,000			
Total	200,000	123,000			

Answers

1. a. Equity b. Available-for-sale c. Consolidation
2. Report the investments at market value: $64,730.

Stock	Investment Cost	Current Market Value
DuPont	$ 5,000	$ 5,500
ExxonMobil	61,200	53,000
Procter & Gamble	3,680	6,230
Totals	$69,880	$64,730

Adjusting entry:

	Debit	Credit
Unrealized Loss on Investments ($69,880 – $64,730)	5,150	
Allowance to Adjust Investment to Market		5,150
To adjust investments to current market value.		

3. Equity-Method Investment

Cost	67,900	Dividends	22,000**
Income	32,000*		
Balance	77,900		

*$80,000 × .40 = $32,000
**$55,000 × .40 = $22,000

4. Consolidation work sheet:

	Parent Company	Subsidiary Company	Eliminations Debit	Eliminations Credit	Consolidated Amounts
Assets					
Cash	7,000	4,000			11,000
Note receivable from Parent	—	20,000		(a) 20,000	—
Investment in Subsidiary	85,000	—		(b) 85,000	—
Other assets	108,000	99,000			207,000
Total	200,000	123,000			218,000
Liabilities and Stockholders' Equity					
Accounts payable	15,000	8,000			23,000
Notes payable	20,000	30,000	(a) 20,000		30,000
Common stock	120,000	60,000	(b) 60,000		120,000
Retained earnings	45,000	25,000	(b) 25,000		45,000
Total	200,000	123,000	105,000	105,000	218,000

Accounting for International Operations

It is common for U.S. companies to do a large part of their business abroad. **Coca-Cola**, **Intel**, and **General Electric**, among many others, are very active in other countries. In fact, Coca-Cola earns 70% of its revenue outside the United States. Exhibit 10-9 shows the percentages of international sales for these companies.

■ **EXHIBIT 10-9**
Extent of International Business

Company	Percentage of International Sales
Coca-Cola	70%
Intel	75
General Electric	45

Accounting for business activities across national boundaries is called *international accounting*. Electronic communication makes international accounting more important because as the world grows smaller, investors around the world need the same data to make decisions. Therefore, the accounting in Australia needs to be the same as in Brazil and the United States. The International Accounting Standards Board (IASB) is working on a uniform set of accounting standards for the whole world.

Foreign Currencies and Exchange Rates

Most countries use their own national currency. An exception is a group of European nations (the European Union)—France, Germany, Italy, Belgium, and so on—most of which use a common currency, the *euro*, whose symbol is €. If GE, a U.S. company, sells jet engines to Air France, will GE receive U.S. dollars or euros? If the transaction is in dollars, Air France must buy dollars to pay GE in U.S. currency. If the transaction is in euros, GE must sell euros for dollars.

The price of one nation's currency may be stated in terms of another's monetary unit. This measure of one currency against another is called the **foreign-currency exchange rate**. In Exhibit 10-10, the dollar value of a euro is $1.20. This means that one euro can be bought for $1.20. Other currencies are also listed in Exhibit 10-10.

Foreign-currency exchange rate The measure of one country's currency against another country's currency.

■ **EXHIBIT 10-10**

Foreign-Currency Exchange Rates

Country	Monetary Unit	U.S. Dollar Value	Country	Monetary Unit	U.S. Dollar Value
Brazil	Real (R)	$0.31	United Kingdom	Pound (£)	$1.79
Canada	Dollar ($)	0.73	Italy	Euro (€)	1.20
France	Euro (€)	1.20	Japan	Yen (¥)	0.0089
Germany	Euro (€)	1.20	Mexico	Peso (P)	0.086

Source: *The Wall Street Journal* (May 24, 2004), p. C11.

We can convert the cost of an item given in one currency to its cost in a second currency. We call this conversion a *translation*. Suppose an item costs 200 euros. To compute its cost in dollars, we multiply the euro amount by the conversion rate: 200 euros × $1.20 = $240.

Two main factors affect supply and demand for a particular currency:

1. The ratio of a country's imports to its exports.
2. The rate of return available in the country's capital markets.

The Import/Export Ratio. Japanese exports often surpass Japan's imports. Customers of Japanese companies must buy yen (the Japanese unit of currency) to pay for their purchases. This strong demand drives up the price—the foreign exchange rate—of the yen. In contrast, the United States imports more goods than it exports. American businesses must sell dollars to buy the foreign currencies needed to acquire the foreign goods. As the supply of the dollar increases, its price decreases.

The Rate of Return. The rate of return available in a country's capital markets affects the amount of investment funds flowing into the country. When rates of return are high in a politically stable country such as the United States, international investors buy stocks, bonds, and real estate in that country. This activity increases the demand for the nation's currency and drives up its exchange rate.

Currencies are often described as "strong" or "weak." The exchange rate of a **strong currency** is rising relative to other nations' currencies. The exchange rate of a **weak currency** is falling relative to other currencies.

Strong currency A currency whose exchange rate is rising relative to other nations' currencies.

Suppose *The Wall Street Journal* listed the exchange rate for the British pound as $1.78 on May 24. On May 25, that rate may change to $1.80. We would say that the dollar has weakened against the pound. Because the pound has become more expensive, the dollar now buys fewer pounds. That makes travel in England more expensive for Americans.

Weak currency A currency whose exchange rate is falling relative to that of other nations.

OBJECTIVE

5 **Account** for international operations

Managing Cash in International Transactions. International transactions are common. **D.E. Shipp Belting**, a small family-owned company in Waco, Texas, provides an example. Shipp Belting makes conveyor belts used in a variety of industries. Farmers along the Texas–Mexico border use Shipp conveyor belts to process vegetables. Some of these customers are in Mexico, so Shipp makes sales in pesos, the Mexican monetary unit. Shipp Belting purchases inventory from Swiss companies, and some of these transactions are in Swiss francs.

■ Taking Action Do We Collect Cash in Dollars or in Foreign Currency? Do We Pay in Dollars or in Foreign Currency?

Consider Shipp Belting's sale of conveyor belts to Artes de Mexico, a vegetable grower in Matamoros, Mexico. The sale can be conducted in dollars or in pesos. If Artes de Mexico agrees to pay in dollars, Shipp avoids the complication of dealing in a foreign currency, and the transaction is the same as selling to M&M Mars across town. But suppose Artes de Mexico orders 1 million pesos (approximately $130,000) worth of conveyor belts from Shipp. Further suppose that Artes demands to pay in pesos and that Shipp agrees to receive pesos instead of dollars.

Shipp will need to convert the pesos to dollars, so the transaction poses a challenge. What if the peso weakens before Shipp collects from Artes? In that case, Shipp will collect as many dollars as expected. The following example shows how to account for international sales stated in a foreign currency.

Shipp Belting sells goods to Artes de Mexico for a price of 1 million pesos on July 28. On that date, a peso is worth $0.086. One month later, on August 28, the peso has weakened against the dollar so that a peso is worth only $0.083. Shipp receives 1 million pesos from Artes on August 28, but the dollar value of Shipp's cash receipt is $3,000 less than expected. Shipp ends up earning less than hoped for on the transaction. The following journal entries show how Shipp would account for these transactions:

July 28	Accounts Receivable—Artes		
	(1,000,000 pesos × $0.086)	86,000	
	Sales Revenue.		86,000
	Sale on account.		

ASSETS	=	LIABILITIES	+	STOCKHOLDERS' EQUITY	+	REVENUES
+86,000	=	0	+		+	86,000

Aug. 28	Cash (1,000,000 pesos × $0.083).	83,000	
	Foreign-Currency Transaction Loss	3,000	
	Accounts Receivable—Artes		86,000
	Collection on account.		

ASSETS	=	LIABILITIES	+	STOCKHOLDERS' EQUITY	−	LOSSES
+83,000 −86,000	=	0	+		−	3,000

Check Point 10-9

If Shipp had required Artes to pay at the time of the sale, Shipp would have received pesos worth $86,000. But by selling on account, Shipp exposed itself to *foreign-currency exchange risk*. Shipp therefore had a $3,000 foreign-currency transaction loss when it received $3,000 less cash than expected. If the peso had increased in value, Shipp would have had a foreign-currency transaction gain.

When a company holds a receivable denominated in a foreign currency, it wants the foreign currency to strengthen so that it can be converted into more dollars. Unfortunately, that did not occur for Shipp Belting.

Purchasing in a foreign currency also exposes a company to foreign-currency exchange risk. To illustrate, assume Shipp Belting buys inventory from Gesellschaft Ltd., a Swiss company. The price is 20,000 Swiss francs. On September 15 Shipp receives the goods, and the Swiss franc is quoted at $0.80. When Shipp pays 2 weeks later, the Swiss franc has weakened against the dollar—to $0.78. Shipp would record the purchase and payment as follows:

Sept. 15	Inventory (20,000 Swiss francs × $0.80).....	16,000	
	Accounts Payable—Gesellschaft Ltd....		16,000
	Purchase on account.		

ASSETS	=	LIABILITIES	+	STOCKHOLDERS' EQUITY
+16,000	=	16,000	+	0

Sept. 29	Accounts Payable—Gesellschaft Ltd	16,000	
	Cash (20,000 Swiss francs × $0.78)		15,600
	Foreign-Currency Transaction Gain		400
	Payment on account.		

ASSETS	=	LIABILITIES	+	STOCKHOLDERS' EQUITY	+	GAINS
−15,600	=	−16,000	+		+	400

Check Point 10-10

The Swiss franc could have strengthened against the dollar, and Shipp would have had a foreign-currency transaction loss. A company with a payable denominated in a foreign currency wants the dollar to get stronger: The payment then costs fewer dollars.

Reporting Gains and Losses on the Income Statement

The Foreign-Currency Transaction Gain account holds gains on transactions settled in a foreign currency. Likewise, the Foreign-Currency Transaction loss account holds losses on transactions conducted in foreign currencies. Report the *net amount* of these two accounts on the income statement as Other Revenues and Gains, or Other Expenses and Losses, as the case may be. For example, Shipp Belting would combine the $3,000 foreign-currency loss and the $400 gain and report the net loss of $2,600 on the income statement as follows:

Other Expenses and Losses:	
Foreign-currency transaction loss, net	$2,600

These gains and losses fall into the "Other" category because they arise from buying and selling foreign currencies, not from the company's main business (in the case of D.E. Shipp Belting, selling conveyor belts).

■ Taking Action Should We Hedge Our Foreign-Currency-Transaction Risk?

One way for U.S. companies to avoid foreign-currency transaction losses is to insist that international transactions be settled in dollars. This requirement puts the burden of currency translation on the foreign party. But this approach may alienate

Hedging
To protect oneself from losing money in one transaction by engaging in a counterbalancing transaction.

customers and decrease sales. Another way for a company to protect itself is by hedging. **Hedging** means to protect oneself from losing money in one transaction by engaging in a counterbalancing transaction.

A U.S. company selling goods to be collected in Mexican pesos expects to receive a fixed number of pesos in the future. If the peso is losing value, the U.S. company would expect the pesos to be worth fewer dollars than the amount of the receivable—an expected loss situation, as we saw for Shipp Belting.

The U.S. company may have accumulated payables in a foreign currency, such as Shipp's payable to the Swiss company. Losses on pesos may be offset by gains on Swiss francs. Most companies do not have equal amounts of receivables and payables in foreign currency. To obtain a more precise hedge, companies can buy *futures contracts*. There are contracts for foreign currencies to be received in the future. Futures contracts can create a payable to exactly offset a receivable, and vice versa. Many companies that do business internationally use hedging techniques.

Consolidation of Foreign Subsidiaries

A U.S. company with a foreign subsidiary must consolidate the subsidiary's financial statements into its own statements for reporting to the public. The consolidation of a foreign subsidiary poses two special challenges:

1. Many foreign countries require accounting treatments that differ from American accounting principles. For reporting to the American public, the subsidiary's statements must conform to American generally accepted accounting principles (GAAP).
2. The subsidiary's statements may be expressed in a foreign currency. First, we must translate the subsidiary's statements into dollars. Then the two companies' financial statements can be consolidated as illustrated in Exhibit 10-8.

The process of translating a foreign subsidiary's financial statements into dollars usually creates a *foreign-currency translation adjustment*. This item appears in the financial statements of most multinational companies and is reported as part of other comprehensive income on the income statement and as part of stockholders' equity on the consolidated balance sheet.

A translation adjustment arises due to changes in the foreign exchange rate over time. In general, *assets* and *liabilities* are translated into dollars at the current exchange rate on the date of the statements. *Stockholders' equity* is translated into dollars at older, historical exchange rates. This difference in exchange rates creates an out-of-balance condition on the balance sheet. The translation adjustment brings the balance sheet back into balance. Let's use an example to see how the translation adjustment works.

U.S. Express Corporation owns Italian Imports, Inc., whose financial statements are expressed in euros (the European currency). U.S. Express must consolidate the Italian subsidiary's financials into its own statements. When U.S. Express acquired Italian Imports in 20X2, a euro was worth $1.30. When Italian Imports earned its retained income during 20X2–20X6, the average exchange rate was $1.26. On the balance sheet date in 20X6, a euro is worth $1.20. Exhibit 10-11 shows how to translate Italian Imports' balance sheet into dollars.

Foreign-currency translation adjustment
The balancing figure that brings the dollar amount of the total liabilities and stockholders' equity of the foreign subsidiary into agreement with the dollar amount of its total assets.

The **foreign-currency translation adjustment** is the balancing amount that brings the dollar amount of liabilities and equity of a foreign subsidiary into agreement with the dollar amount of total assets (in Exhibit 10-11, total assets equal $960,000). Only after the translation adjustment of $22,000 do total liabilities and equity equal total assets stated in dollars.

■ **EXHIBIT 10-11**

Translation of a Foreign-Currency Balance Sheet into Dollars

Italian Imports, Inc., Amounts	Euros	Exchange Rate	Dollars
Assets	800,000	$1.20	$960,000
Liabilities	500,000	1.20	$600,000
Stockholders' equity			
Common stock	100,000	1.30	130,000
Retained earnings	200,000	1.26	252,000
Accumulated other comprehensive income:			
Foreign-currency translation adjustment			(22,000)
	800,000		$960,000

What caused the negative translation adjustment? The euro weakened after the acquisition of Italian Imports. When U.S. Express acquired the foreign subsidiary in 20X2, a euro was worth $1.30. When Italian Imports earned its retained income during 20X2 through 20X6, the average exchange rate was $1.26. On the balance sheet date in 20X6, a euro is worth only $1.20. Thus, Italian Imports' equity (assets minus liabilities) are translated into only $360,000 ($960,000 – $600,000).

To bring stockholders' equity to $360,000 requires a $22,000 negative amount. In a sense, a negative translation adjustment is like a loss, reported as a contra item in the stockholders' equity section of the balance sheet, as in Exhibit 10-11. Italian Imports' dollar figures in Exhibit 10-11 are what U.S. Express would include in its consolidated balance sheet. The consolidation procedures would follow those illustrated beginning on page 478.

International Accounting Standards

In this text, we focus on the accounting principles that are generally accepted in the United States. Most accounting methods are consistent throughout the world. Double-entry accounting, the accrual system, and the basic financial statements are used worldwide. Differences, however, do exist among countries, as shown in Exhibit 10-12.

■ **EXHIBIT 10-12** Some International Accounting Differences

Country	Inventories	Goodwill	Research and Development Costs
United States	Specific unit cost, FIFO, LIFO, and average cost	Record any loss in value of goodwill	Expensed as incurred
Germany	Similar to U.S.	Amortized over 5 years	Expensed as incurred
Japan	Similar to U.S.	Amortized over 5 years	May be capitalized and amortized over 5 years
United Kingdom	LIFO is unacceptable for tax purposes and is not widely used	Amortized over useful life or not amortized if life indefinite	Expense research costs. Some development costs may be capitalized

In discussing depreciation (Chapter 7), we emphasized that in the United States, the methods used for reporting to tax authorities differ from the methods used for reporting to shareholders. However, tax reporting and shareholder reporting are identical in many countries.

✔ Check Point 10-11

Several organizations are working to achieve worldwide harmony of accounting standards. Chief among these is the *IASB*, which operates much as the Financial

Accounting Standards Board (FASB) in the United States. It has the support of the accounting professions in the United States, most of the British Commonwealth countries, Japan, France, Germany, the Netherlands, and Mexico. However, the IASB has no authority to require compliance. It must rely on cooperation by the various national accounting professions.

Investing Activities on the Statement of Cash Flows

OBJECTIVE

6 **Report** investing transactions on the statement of cash flows

The statement of cash flows reports operating activities, investing activities, and financing activities. Investing activities include many types of transactions. In Chapter 7, we covered the purchase and sale of long-term assets such as plant and equipment. In this chapter, we examine investments in stocks and bonds.

Exhibit 10-13 provides excerpts from General Electric's statement of cash flows. During 2003, GE spent $10 billion on plant assets and $14 billion to acquire other companies. The company loaned $14 billion of cash. Overall, GE invested $23 billion more than it received from selling assets. This is one reason GE stays ahead of competitors: It invests in the future.

✔Check Point 10-12

■ **EXHIBIT 10-13**

General Electric Company Consolidated Statement of Cash Flows (Partial, Adapted)

General Electric Company
Statement of Cash Flows

(In billions)	2003
Cash flows—investing activities	
Additions to property, plant, and equipment	$(10)
Dispositions of property, plant, and equipment	5
Loans to others	(14)
Payments for other companies	(14)
All other investing activities	11
Cash used for investing activities	(22)

END-OF-CHAPTER Summary Problem

Translate the balance sheet of the Brazilian subsidiary of **Wrangler Corporation**, a U.S. company, into dollars. When Wrangler acquired this subsidiary, the exchange rate of the Brazilian currency, the real, was $0.40. The average exchange rate applicable to retained earnings is $0.41. The real's current exchange rate is $0.43.

Before performing the translation, predict whether the translation adjustment will be positive or negative. Does this situation generate a foreign-currency translation gain or loss? Give your reasons.

	Reals
Assets	900,000
Liabilities	600,000
Stockholders' equity:	
Common stock	30,000
Retained earnings	270,000
	900,000

Answer

Translation of foreign-currency balance sheet:

This situation will generate a *positive* translation adjustment, which is like a gain. The gain occurs because the real's current exchange rate, which is used to translate net assets (assets minus liabilities), exceeds the historical exchange rates used for stockholders' equity.

The calculation follows.

	Reals	Exchange Rate	Dollars
Assets	900,000	0.43	$387,000
Liabilities	600,000	0.43	$258,000
Stockholders' equity:			
Common stock	30,000	0.40	12,000
Retained earnings	270,000	0.41	110,700
Accumulated other comprehensive income:			
Foreign-currency translation adjustment	—		6,300
	900,000		$387,000

Review Long-Term Investments and International Operations

Chapter Review Quiz

1. An investment in less than 1% of GE's stock, which you expect to hold for 2 years and then sell, is which type of investment?
   a. Trading
   b. Available-for-sale
   c. Equity
   d. Consolidation

2. Meadows Corporation purchased an available-for-sale investment in 1,000 shares of GE stock for $35.70 per share. On the next balance-sheet date, GE stock is trading for $31.70 per share. Meadows' balance sheet should report
   a. unrealized gain of $4,000.
   b. unrealized gain of $31,700.
   c. investments of $31,700.
   d. investments of $35,700.

3. Use the Meadows Corporation data in question 2. Meadows' income statement should report
   a. unrealized gain of $4,000.
   b. unrealized loss of $4,000.
   c. investments of $31,700.
   d. nothing.

4. Use the Meadows Corporation data in question 2. Meadows sold the GE stock for $40,000 two years later. Meadows' income statement should report
   a. unrealized gain of $4,000.
   b. gain on sale of $4,300.
   c. unrealized gain of $4,300.
   d. nothing.

5. Bazinski Corporation paid $100,000 for 20% of the common stock of Sellers Co. Sellers earned net income of $50,000 and paid dividends of $25,000. The carrying value of Bazinski's investment is
   a. $105,000
   b. $125,000
   c. $150,000
   d. $100,000

6. Ellis, Inc., owns 90% of Navarro Corporation, and Navarro owns 90% of Henderson Company. During 20X6, these companies' net incomes are as follows before any consolidations:
   - Ellis $100,000
   - Navarro $64,000
   - Henderson $40,000

   How much net income should Ellis report for 20X6?
   a. $100,000
   b. $164,000
   c. $190,000
   d. $204,000

7. **iPod, Inc.**, holds an investment in GE bonds that pay interest each June 30. iPod's financial statements at December 31 should report

	Balance Sheet	*Income Statement*
a. Interest receivable	Yes	No
b. Interest payable	Yes	No
c. Interest revenue	Yes	No
d. Interest expense	Yes	No

8. You are taking a vacation to France, and you buy euros for $1.22. On your return you cash in your unused euros for $1.19. During your vacation
   a. the euro rose against the dollar.
   b. the dollar lost value.
   c. the dollar rose against the euro.
   d. the euro gained value.

9. McLennan County, Texas, purchased earth-moving equipment from a Canadian company. The cost was $1,000,000 Canadian, and the Canadian dollar was quoted at $0.73. A month later, McLennan County paid its debt, and the Canadian dollar was quoted at $0.75. What was McLennan County's cost of the equipment?
   a. $1,000,000
   b. $750,000
   c. $730,000
   d. $20,000

10. GE owns numerous foreign subsidiary companies. When GE consolidates its British subsidiary, GE should translate the subsidiary's assets into dollars at the
    a. historical exchange rate when GE purchased the British company.
    b. current exchange rate.
    c. average exchange rate during the period GE owned the British subsidiary.
    d. none of the above. There's no need to translate the subsidiary's assets into dollars.

Answers

1. b
2. c (1,000 shares × $31.70 = $31,700)
3. d
4. b [$40,000 – (1,000 shares × $35.70)]
5. a [$100,000 + 0.20($50,000) – .20($25,000) = $105,000]
6. c {$100,000 + 0.90[$64,000 + .90($40,000)] = $190,000}
7. a
8. c
9. c ($1,000,000 Canadian × $0.73 = $730,000)
10. b

Accounting Vocabulary

available-for-sale investments (p. 471)
consolidated statements (p. 478)
controlling interest (p. 478)
equity method (p. 475)
foreign-currency exchange rate (p. 485)
foreign-currency translation adjustment (p. 488)
hedging (p. 488)
held-to-maturity investments (p. 481)
long-term investments (p. 470)
majority interest (p. 478)
marketable securities (p. 470)

minority interest (p. 480)
parent company (p. 478)
short-term investments (p. 470)
strong currency (p. 485)
subsidiary company (p. 478)
weak currency (p. 485)

Assess Your Progress

Check Points

Accounting for an available-for-sale investment; unrealized gain or loss (Obj. 1)

CP10-1 (p. 473) Assume **DuPont Corporation** completed these long-term available-for-sale investment transactions during 20X8:

20X8	
Jan. 14	Purchased 300 shares of Sysco stock, paying $19 per share. DuPont intends to hold the investment for the indefinite future.
Aug. 22	Received a cash dividend of $1.25 per share on the Sysco stock.
Dec. 31	Adjusted the Sysco investment to its current market value of $5,170.

1. Journalize DuPont's investment transactions. Explanations are not required.
2. Show how to report the investment and any unrealized gain or loss on DuPont's balance sheet at December 31, 20X8. Ignore income tax.

Accounting for the sale of an available-for-sale investment (Obj. 1)

CP10-2 (p. 474) Use the data given in Check Point 10-1. On August 4, 20X9, DuPont sold its investment in Sysco stock for $20.75 per share.

1. Journalize the sale. No explanation is required.
2. How does the gain or loss that you recorded differ from the gain or loss that was recorded at December 31, 20X8?

Accounting for a 40% investment in another company (Obj. 2)

CP10-3 (p. 477) Suppose on January 6, 20X8, **General Motors** paid $220 million for its 40% investment in **Isuzu Motors**. Assume Isuzu earned net income of $45 million and paid cash dividends of $20 million during 20X8.

1. What method should General Motors use to account for the investment in Isuzu? Give your reason?
2. Journalize these three transactions on the books of General Motors. Show all amounts in millions of dollars and include an explanation for each entry.
3. Post to the Long-Term Investment T-account. What is its balance after all the transactions are posted?

Accounting for the sale of an equity-method investment (Obj. 3)

CP10-4 (p. 477) Use the data given in Check Point 10-3. Assume that in January 20X9, General Motors sold half its investment in Isuzu to Toyota. The sale price was $140 million. Compute General Motors' gain or loss on the sale.

Understanding consolidated financial statements (Obj. 3)

writing assignment ■

CP10-5 (p. 480) Answer these questions about consolidation accounting:

1. Define *parent company*. Define *subsidiary company*.
2. How do consolidated financial statements differ from the financial statements of a single company?
3. Which company's name appears on the consolidated financial statements? How much of the subsidiary's stock must the parent own before reporting consolidated statements?

Understanding goodwill and minority interest (Obj. 3)

writing assignment ■

CP10-6 (p. 480) Two accounts that arise from consolidation accounting are goodwill and minority interest.

1. What is goodwill, and how does it arise? Which company reports goodwill, the parent or the subsidiary? Where is goodwill reported?
2. What is minority interest, and which company reports it, the parent or the subsidiary? Where is minority interest reported?

Working with a bond investment (Obj. 4)

CP10-7 (p. 482) **GMAC**, the financing subsidiary of General Motors Corporation, owns vast amounts of corporate bonds. Suppose GMAC buys $5,000,000 of **CitiCorp** bonds at a price of 101. The CitiCorp bonds pay cash interest at the annual rate of 7% and mature at the end of 5 years.

1. How much did GMAC pay to purchase the bond investment? How much will GMAC collect when the bond investment matures?
2. How much cash interest will GMAC receive each year from CitiCorp?
3. Will GMAC's annual interest revenue on the bond investment be more or less than the amount of cash interest received each year? Give your reason.
4. Compute GMAC's annual interest revenue on this bond investment. Use the straight-line method to amortize the investment.

Recording bond investment transactions (Obj. 4)

CP10-8 (p. 482) Return to Check Point 10-7, the **GMAC** investment in **CitiCorp** bonds. Journalize on GMAC's books:

a. Purchase of the bond investment on January 2, 2007. GMAC expects to hold the investment to maturity.
b. Receipt of annual cash interest on December 31, 2007.
c. Amortization of the bonds on December 31, 2007.
d. Collection of the investment's face value at the maturity date on January 2, 2012. (Assume the receipt of 2011 interest and the amortization of bonds for 2011 have already been recorded, so ignore these entries.)

Accounting for transactions stated in a foreign currency (Obj. 5)

CP10-9 (p. 486) Suppose **Seven-Up** sells soft drink syrup to a Russian company on March 14. Seven-Up agrees to accept 200,000 Russian rubles. On the date of sale, the ruble is quoted at $0.32. Seven-Up collects half the receivable on April 19, when the ruble is worth $0.30. Then on May 10, when the foreign-exchange rate of the ruble is $0.35, Seven-Up collects the final amount.

Journalize these three transactions for Seven-Up.

Accounting for transactions stated in a foreign currency (Obj. 5)

CP10-10 (p. 487) Page 486 includes a sequence of **Shipp Belting** journal entries for transactions denominated in Mexican pesos. Suppose the foreign-exchange rate for a peso is $0.090 on August 28. Record Shipp Belting's collection of cash on August 28.

On page 487, Shipp Belting buys inventory for which it must pay Swiss francs. Suppose a Swiss franc costs $0.81 on September 29. Record Shipp Belting's payment of cash on September 29.

In these two scenarios, which currencies strengthened? Which currencies weakened?

International accounting differences (Obj. 5)

writing assignment ■

CP10-11 (p. 489) Exhibit 10-11, page 489, outlines some differences between accounting in the United States and accounting in other countries. American companies transact a lot of business with British companies. But there are important differences between American and British accounting. In your own words, describe these differences for inventories, goodwill, and research and development.

Reporting cash flows (Obj. 6)

CP10-12 (p. 490) Companies divide their cash flows into three categories for reporting on the statement of cash flows.

1. List the three categories of cash flows in the order they appear on the statement of cash flows. Which category of cash flows is most closely related to this chapter?
2. Identify two types of transactions that companies report as cash flows from investing activities.

Exercises

PH Grade Assist

Most of the even-numbered exercises can be found within Prentice Hall Grade Assist (PHGA), an online homework and practice environment. Your instructor may ask you to complete these exercises using PHGA.

Journalizing transactions for an available-for-sale investment (Obj. 1)

■ **general ledger**

E10-1 Journalize the following long-term available-for-sale investment transactions of Rivera Securities:

a. Purchased 400 shares of **AOL Time Warner** common stock at $22 per share, with the intent of holding the stock for the indefinite future.
b. Received cash dividend of $1 per share on the AOL investment.
c. At year end, adjusted the investment account to current market value of $25 per share.
d. Sold the AOL stock for the market price of $23 per share.

Accounting for long-term investments (Obj. 1)

E10-2 Manatee Corporation bought 3,000 shares of ProStar common stock at $37.375; 600 shares of **Coca-Cola** stock at $46.75; and 1,400 shares of **Panasonic** stock at $79—all as available-for-sale investments. At December 31, **The Wall Street Journal** reports ProStar stock at $29.125, Coca-Cola at $48.50, and Panasonic at $68.25.

Required

1. Determine the cost and the market value of the long-term investment portfolio at December 31.
2. Record Manatee's adjusting entry at December 31.
3. What would Manatee report on its income statement and balance sheet for the information given? Make the necessary disclosures. Ignore income tax.

Accounting for transactions under the equity method (Obj. 2)

E10-3 **JCPenney Company** owns equity-method investments in several companies. Suppose Penney paid $2,400,000 to acquire a 25% investment in Thai Imports Company. Assume that Thai Imports reported net income of $640,000 for the first year and declared and paid cash dividends of $420,000. Record the following in JCPenney's journal: (a) purchase of the investment, (b) JCPenney's proportion of Thai Imports' net income, and (c) receipt of the cash dividends. What is the ending balance in JCPenney's investment account?

Measuring gain or loss on the sale of an equity-method investment (Obj. 2)

E10-4 Without making journal entries, record the transactions of Exercise 10-3 directly in the **JCPenney** account, Long-Term Investment in Thai Imports. Assume that after all the noted transactions took place, JCPenney sold its entire investment in Thai Imports for cash of $2,700,000. How much is JCPenney's gain or loss on the sale of the investment?

Applying the appropriate accounting method for a 30% investment (Obj. 2)

E10-5 MidContinent Investors paid $400,000 for a 30% investment in the common stock of eTrav, Inc. For the first year, eTrav reported net income of $210,000 and at year end declared and paid cash dividends of $90,000. On the balance-sheet date, the market value of MidContinent's investment in eTrav stock was $384,000.

Required

1. Which method is appropriate for MidContinent Investors to use in accounting for its investment in eTrav? Why?
2. Show everything that MidContinent would report for the investment and any investment revenue in its year-end financial statements.

Preparing a consolidated balance sheet (Obj. 3)

■ spreadsheet

E10-6 **Mercedes, Inc.** owns **Benz Corp.** The two companies' individual balance sheets follow:

	Mercedes	Benz
Assets		
Cash	$ 49,000	$ 14,000
Accounts receivable, net	82,000	53,000
Note receivable from Mercedes	—	12,000
Inventory	55,000	77,000
Investment in Benz	100,000	—
Plant assets, net	186,000	129,000
Other assets	22,000	8,000
Total	$494,000	$293,000
Liabilities and Stockholders' Equity		
Accounts payable	$ 44,000	$ 26,000
Notes payable	47,000	36,000
Other liabilities	82,000	131,000
Common stock	210,000	80,000
Retained earnings	111,000	20,000
Total	$494,000	$293,000

Required

1. Prepare the consolidated balance sheet of Mercedes, Inc. It is sufficient to complete the consolidation work sheet.
2. What is the amount of stockholders' equity for the consolidated entity?

Recording bond investment transactions (Obj. 4)

E10-7 Assume that on March 31, 20X3, **Hyundai, Inc.** paid 97 for 5 1/2% bonds of **Daewoo Corporation** as a long-term held-to-maturity investment. The maturity value of the bonds will be $20,000 on March 31, 20X8. The bonds pay interest on March 31 and September 30.

Required

1. What method should Hyundai use to account for its investment in the Daewoo bonds?
2. Using the straight-line method of amortizing the bonds, journalize all of Hyundai's transactions on the bonds for 20X3.
3. Show how Hyundai would report everything related to the bond investment on its balance sheet at December 31, 20X3.

Managing and accounting for foreign-currency transactions (Obj. 5)

writing assignment ■

E10-8 Assume that **Best Buy, Inc.** completed the following foreign-currency transactions:

Nov. 17	Purchased DVD players as inventory on account from **Sony**. The price was 200,000 yen, and the exchange rate of the yen was $0.0086.
Dec. 16	Paid Sony when the exchange rate was $0.0082.
19	Sold merchandise on account to BonTemps, a French company, at a price of 60,000 euros. The exchange rate was $1.20
30	Collected from BonTemps when the exchange rate was $1.17.

1. Journalize these transactions for Best Buy. Focus on the gains and losses caused by changes in foreign-currency rates.
2. On November 18, immediately after the purchase, and on December 20, immediately after the sale, which currencies did Best Buy want to strengthen? Which currencies did in fact strengthen? Explain your reasoning in detail.

Translating a foreign-currency balance sheet into dollars (Obj. 5)

■ spreadsheet

E10-9 Translate into dollars the balance sheet of Lenox Crystal's Italian subsidiary. When Lenox acquired the foreign subsidiary, a euro was worth $1.01. The current exchange rate is

$1.22. During the period when retained earnings were earned, the average exchange rate was $1.15 per euro.

	Euros
Assets	500,000
Liabilities	300,000
Stockholders' equity:	
Common stock	50,000
Retained earnings	150,000
	500,000

During the period covered by this situation, which currency was stronger, the dollar or the euro?

Preparing and using the statement of cash flows (Obj. 6)

E10-10 During fiscal year 20X4, **The Home Depot, Inc.**, reported net income of $4,304 million and paid $215 million to acquire other businesses. Home Depot made capital expenditures, as adapted, of $4,106 million and sold property, plant, and equipment for $265 million. The company purchased long-term investments at a cost of $159 million and sold other long-term investments for $219 million.

Required

Prepare the investing activities section of The Home Depot's statement of cash flows. Based solely on Home Depot's investing activities, does it appear that the company is growing or shrinking? How can you tell?

Using the statement of cash flows (Obj. 6)

E10-11 Moonbeam Corporation earns one-fourth of its net income from financial services through its wholly-owned subsidiary, Moonbeam Financial Corporation. As a result, Finance Receivables is the largest single long-term asset on Moonbeam's balance sheet. At the end of the year, Moonbeam's statement of cash flows reported the following for investment activities:

Moonbeam Corporation
Consolidated Statement of Cash Flows (Partial)

	(In millions)
Cash Flows from Investing Activities	
Finance receivables collected	$ 3,110
Purchases of short-term investments	(3,457)
Proceeds from sales of equipment	1,409
Proceeds from sales of investments	461
Expenditures for property and equipment	(1,761)
Net cash used by investing activities	$ (238)

Required

For each item listed, make the journal entry that placed the item on Moonbeam's statement of cash flows. The equipment that Moonbeam sold had a book value equal to its sale price. The cost of the investments that Moonbeam sold was $419 million.

Challenge Exercises

Accounting for various types of investments (Obj. 1, 2, 3, 5)

E10-12 This exercise summarizes the accounting for investments. Suppose **Motorola, Inc.** owns the following investments at December 31, 20X1:

a. Investments that Motorola is holding to sell cost $900 million. These investments declined in value by $400 million during 20X1, but they paid cash dividends of $16 million to Motorola. At December 31, 20X0, the market value of these investments was $1,100 million.
b. 25% of the common stock of Motorola Financing Associates. During 20X1, Motorola Financing earned net income of $300 million and declared and paid cash dividends of $80 million. The carrying amount of this investment was $700 million at December 31, 20X0.

c. 100% of the common stock of Motorola United Kingdom, which holds assets of £800 million and owes a total of £600 million. At December 31, 20X1, the current exchange rate of the pound (£) is £1 = \$1.80. The translation rate of the pound applicable to stockholders' equity is £1 = \$1.60. During 20X1, Motorola United Kingdom earned net income of £100 million, and the average exchange rate for the year was £1 = \$1.75. Motorola United Kingdom paid cash dividends of £40 million during 20X1.

Required

1. Which method is used to account for each investment?
2. By how much did these investments increase or decrease Motorola's net income during 20X1?
3. For investments a and b, show how Motorola would report these investments on its balance sheet at December 31, 20X1.

Explaining and analyzing accumulated other comprehensive income (Obj. 1, 6)

E10-13 Interfax Corporation reported stockholders' equity on its balance sheet at December 31, as follows:

Interfax Corporation
Balance Sheet (Partial)

	(In millions) December 31, 20X3
Shareholders' Equity	
Common stock, \$0.10 par value—800 million shares authorized, 299 million shares issued	\$ 30
Additional paid-in capital	1,088
Retained earnings	6,250
Accumulated other comprehensive (loss)	(?)
Less Treasury stock, at cost	(50)

Required

1. Identify the two components that make up Accumulated other comprehensive income.
2. For each component of Accumulated other comprehensive income, describe the event that can cause a *positive* balance. Also describe the events that can cause a *negative* balance for each component.
3. At December 31, 20X2, Interfax's Accumulated other comprehensive (loss) was \$53 million. Then during 20X3, Interfax had a positive foreign-currency translation adjustment of \$29 million and an unrealized loss of \$16 million on available-for-sale investments. What was Interfax's balance of Accumulated other comprehensive income (loss) at December 31, 20X3?
4. How does Interfax's Accumulated other comprehensive income affect net income? How does it affect total stockholders' equity?

Practice Quiz

Test your understanding of long-term investments and international operations by answering the following questions. Select the best choice from among the possible answers given.

Questions 1–3 use the following data:

Mondavi Motorcycles owns the following long-term available-for-sale investments:

Company	Number of Shares	Cost Per Share	Current Market Value Per Share	Dividend Per Share
Northwestern Life	1,000	\$60	\$71	\$2
Jim Stewart Realty	200	9	11	—
Mini-Cooper Express	500	20	16	1

PQ10-1 Mondavi's balance sheet should report

a. investments of $71,800.
b. investments of $81,200.
c. dividend revenue $2,500.
d. unrealized loss of $13,400.

PQ10-2 Mondavi's income statement should report

a. investments of $71,800.
b. gain on sale of investment of $13,400.
c. dividend revenue of $2,500.
d. unrealized gain of $13,400.

PQ10-3 Suppose Mondavi sells the Northwestern Life stock for $71 per share. Journalize the sale.

PQ10-4 Dividends received on an equity-method investment.

a. decrease the investment account.
b. increase the investment account.
c. increase dividend revenue.
d. Increase owners' equity.

PQ10-5 The starting point in accounting for all investments is

a. market value on the balance-sheet date.
b. equity value.
c. cost minus dividends.
d. cost.

PQ10-6 Consolidation accounting

a. combines the accounts of the parent company and those of the subsidiary companies.
b. eliminates all intercompany receivables and payables.
c. Reports the stockholders' equity of the parent company only.
d. All of the above.

PQ10-7 On January 1, 20X1, IKON Systems purchased $100,000 face value of the 6% bonds of Mail Frontier, Inc. at 105. The bonds mature on January 1, 20X6. For the year ended December 31, 20X1, IKON Systems received cash interest of

a. $5,000
b. $6,000
c. $6,400
d. $7,000

PQ10-8 Return to IKON Systems' bond investment in the preceding question. For the year ended December 31, 20X1, IKON earned interest revenue of

a. $5,000
b. $6,000
c. $6,400
d. $7,000

PQ10-9 IKON Systems purchased inventory on account from **SONY**. The price was ¥100,000, and a yen was quoted at $0.0090. IKON paid the debt in yen a month later, when the price of a yen was $0.0082. IKON

a. paid $880.
b. debited Inventory for $820.
c. debited Inventory for $900.
d. recorded a Foreign-Currency Transaction Loss of $80.
e. None of the above.

PQ10-10 One way to hedge a foreign-currency transaction loss is to

a. pay in the foreign currency
b. collect in the foreign currency.
c. offset foreign-currency receivables and payables.
d. pay debts as late as possible.

PQ10-11 Foreign-currency transaction gains and losses are reported on the

a. balance sheet.
b. income statement.
c. statement of cash flows.
d. consolidation work sheet.

PQ10-12 Consolidation of a foreign subsidiary usually results in a

a. gain or loss on consolidation.
b. LIFO/FIFO difference.
c. foreign-currency transaction gain or loss.
d. foreign-currency translation adjustment.

Problems
(Group A)

 PH Grade Assist	Most of these A problems can be found within Prentice Hall Grade Assist (PHGA), an online homework and practice environment. Your instructor may ask you to complete these exercises using PHGA.

Reporting investments on the balance sheet and the related revenue on the income statement (Obj. 1, 2)

P10-1A Jefferson-Pilot Corporation, a financial service concern headquartered in Greensboro, North Carolina, owns numerous investments in the stock of other companies. Assume that Jefferson-Pilot completed the following long-term investment transactions:

20X4	
May 1	Purchased 8,000 shares, which make up 25% of the common stock of Venus Company at total cost of $640,000.
Sep. 15	Received semiannual cash dividend of $1.40 per share on the Venus investment.
Oct. 12	Purchased 1,000 shares of Mercury Corporation common stock as an available-for-sale investment paying $22.50 per share.
Dec. 14	Received semiannual cash dividend of $0.75 per share on the Mercury investment.
Dec. 31	Received annual report from Venus Company. Net income for the year was $350,000.

At year end the current market value of the Mercury stock is $20,700. The market value of the Venus stock is $740,000.

Required

1. For which investment is current market value used in the accounting? Why is market value used for one investment and not the other?
2. Show what Jefferson-Pilot would report on its year-end balance sheet and income statement for these investment transactions. (It is helpful to use a T-account for the investment in Venus stock.) Ignore income tax.

Accounting for available-for-sale and equity-method investments (Obj. 1, 2)

general ledger

P10-2A The beginning balance sheet of Charter Investment Bankers, Ltd. included the following:

Long-Term Investments in Affiliates (equity-method investments) . .	$657,000

Charter completed the following investment transactions during the year:

Feb. 16	Purchased 5,000 shares of BCM Software common stock as a long-term available-for-sale investment, paying $9.25 per share.
May 14	Received cash dividend of $0.82 per share on the BCM investment.
Oct. 15	Received cash dividend of $29,000 from an affiliated company.
Dec. 31	Received annual reports from affiliated companies. Their total net income for the year was $620,000. Of this amount, Charter's proportion is 25%.

The market values of Charter's investments are BCM, $45,100; affiliated companies, $947,000.

Required

1. Record the transactions in the journal of Charter Investment Bankers.
2. Post entries to the Long-Term Investments in Affiliates T-account and determine its balance at December 31.
3. Show how to report Long-Term Available-for-Sale Investments and Long-Term Investments in Affiliates on Charter's balance sheet at December 31.

Analyzing consolidated financial statements (Obj. 3)

P10-3A This problem demonstrates the dramatic effect that consolidation accounting can have on a company's ratios. **General Motors Corporation (GM)** owns 100% of **General Motors Acceptance Corporation (GMAC)**, its financing subsidiary. GM's main operations consist of manufacturing automotive products. GMAC mainly helps people finance the purchase of automobiles from GM and its dealers. The two companies' individual balance sheets are summarized as follows (amounts in billions):

	General Motors (Parent)	GMAC (Subsidiary)
Total assets	$132.6	$94.6
Total liabilities	$109.3	$86.3
Total stockholders' equity	23.3	8.3
Total liabilities and equity	$132.6	$94.6

Assume that GMAC's liabilities include $5.1 billion owed to General Motors, the parent company.

Required

1. Compute the debt ratio of GM Corporation considered alone.
2. Determine the consolidated total assets, total liabilities, and stockholders' equity of GM after consolidating the financial statements of GMAC into the totals of GM, the parent company.
3. Recompute the debt ratio of the consolidated entity. Why do companies prefer not to consolidate their financing subsidiaries into their own financial statements?

Consolidating a wholly owned subsidiary (Obj. 3)

■ **spreadsheet**

P10-4A Water Resources Corporation paid $179,000 to acquire all the common stock of Hydra Park, Inc., and Hydra Park owes Water Resources $55,000 on a note payable. Immediately after the purchase on June 30, 20X6, the two companies' balance sheets were as follows:

	Water Resources	Hydra Park
Assets		
Cash	$ 18,000	$ 32,000
Accounts receivable, net	264,000	43,000
Note receivable from Hydra Park	55,000	—
Inventory	193,000	153,000
Investment in Hydra Park	179,000	—
Plant assets, net	305,000	138,000
Total	$1,014,000	$366,000
Liabilities and Stockholders' Equity		
Accounts payable	$ 76,000	$ 37,000
Notes payable	118,000	123,000
Other liabilities	144,000	27,000
Common stock	282,000	90,000
Retained earnings	394,000	89,000
Total	$1,014,000	$366,000

Required

1. Prepare Water Resources' consolidated balance sheet. (It is sufficient to complete a consolidation work sheet.)
2. Why aren't total assets of the consolidated entity equal to the sum of total assets for both companies combined? Why isn't consolidated equity equal to the sum of the two companies' stockholders' equity combined?

Accounting for a bond investment purchased at a discount
(Obj. 4)

P10-5A Financial institutions such as investment companies and pension plans hold large quantities of bond investments. Suppose **Paine Webber** purchases $500,000 of 6% bonds of **General Motors Corporation** for 92 on January 31, 20X0. These bonds pay interest on January 31 and July 31 each year. They mature on July 31, 20X8. At December 31, 20X0, the market price of the bonds is 93.

Required

1. Journalize Paine Webber's purchase of the bonds as a long-term investment on January 31, 20X0 (to be held to maturity), receipt of cash interest and amortization of the bond investment on July 31, 20X0, and accrual of interest revenue and amortization at December 31, 20X0. The straight-line method is appropriate for amortizing the bond investment.
2. Show all financial statement effects of this long-term bond investment on Paine Webber's balance sheet and income statement at December 31, 20X0.

Recording foreign-currency transactions and reporting the transaction gain or loss
(Obj. 5)

general ledger

P10-6A Suppose **Big Red Company**, which features a strawberry soda, completed the following international transactions:

June 4	Sold soft-drink syrup on account to a Mexican company for $43,000. The exchange rate of the Mexican peso is $0.101, and the customer agrees to pay in dollars.
13	Purchased inventory on account from a Canadian company at a price of Canadian $100,000. The exchange rate of the Canadian dollar is $0.65, and payment will be in Canadian dollars.
20	Sold goods on account to an English firm for 70,000 British pounds. Payment will be in pounds, and exchange rate of the pound is $1.80.
27	Collected from the Mexican company.
July 21	Paid the Canadian company. The exchange rate of the Canadian dollar is $0.62.
Aug. 17	Collected from the English firm. The exchange rate of the British pound is $1.70.

Required

1. Record these transactions in Big Red's journal and show how to report the transaction gain or loss on the income statement.
2. How will what you learned in this problem help you structure international transactions.

Measuring and explaining the foreign-currency translation adjustment
(Obj. 5)

P10-7A International Pastries, Inc. owns a subsidiary based in Denmark.

Required

1. Translate the foreign-currency balance sheet of the Danish subsidiary of International Pastries, Inc., into dollars. When International Pastries acquired this subsidiary, the Danish krone was worth $0.17. The current exchange rate is $0.12. During the period when the subsidiary earned its income, the average exchange rate was $0.16 per krone.

	Kroner
Assets	3,000,000
Liabilities	1,000,000
Stockholders' equity:	
Common stock	300,000
Retained earnings	1,700,000
	3,000,000

Before you perform the foreign-currency translation calculation, indicate whether International Pastries, Inc. has experienced a positive or a negative foreign-currency translation adjustment. State whether the adjustment is a gain or loss, and show where it is reported in the financial statements.

2. To which company does the translation adjustment "belong"? In which company's financial statements will the translation adjustment be reported?
3. How will what you learned in this problem help you understand published financial statements?

Using a cash-flow statement (Obj. 6)

writing assignment ■

P10-8A Excerpts from **The Coca-Cola Company** statement of cash flows, as adapted, appear as follows:

The Coca-Cola Company and Subsidiaries
Consolidated Statements of Cash Flows
(Adapted)

(In millions)	Years Ended December 31, 20X4	20X3
Operating Activities		
Net cash provided by operating activities	$ 4,110	$ 1,165
Investing Activities		
Purchases of property, plant, and equipment	(769)	(733)
Acquisitions and investments, principally trademarks and bottling companies	(651)	(397)
Purchases of investments	(456)	(508)
Proceeds from disposals of investments	455	290
Proceeds from disposals of property, plant, and equipment	91	45
Other investing activities	142	138
Net cash used in investing activities	(1,188)	(1,165)
Financing activities		
Issuances of debt (borrowing)	3,011	3,671
Payments of debt	(3,937)	(4,256)
Issuances of stock	164	331
Purchases of stock for treasury	(277)	(133)
Dividends	(1,791)	(1,685)
Net cash used in financing activities	(2,830)	(2,072)

Required

As the chief executive officer of The Coca-Cola Company, your duty is to write the management letter to your stockholders explaining Coca-Cola's major investing activities during 20X4. Compare the company's level of investment with previous years and indicate how the company financed its investments during 20X4. Net income for 20X4 was $3,969 million.

(Group B)

PH Grade Assist

Some of these B problems can be found within Prentice Hall Grade Assist (PHGA), an online homework and practice environment. Your instructor may ask you to complete these exercises using PHGA.

Reporting investments on the balance sheet and the related revenue on the income statement (Obj. 1, 2)

P10-1B **Wells Fargo & Company**, headquartered in San Francisco, owns banks in most states west of the Mississippi River. Wells Fargo owns numerous investments in the stock of other companies. Assume that Wells Fargo completed the following long-term investment transactions during 20X6:

20X6	
Feb. 12	Purchased 20,000 shares, which make up 35% of the common stock of Demski Corporation at total cost of $490,000.
Aug. 9	Received annual cash dividend of $1.26 per share on the Demski investment.
Oct. 16	Purchased 800 shares of Busy Beaver, Inc., common stock as an available-for-sale investment, paying $41.50 per share.
Nov. 30	Received semiannual cash dividend of $0.60 per share on the Busy Beaver investment.
Dec. 31	Received annual report from Demski Corporation. Net income for the year was $510,000.

At year end the current market value of the Busy Beaver stock is $29,800. The market value of the Demski stock is $652,000.

Required

1. For which investment is current market value used in the accounting? Why is market value used for one investment and not the other?
2. Show what Wells Fargo & Company would report on its year-end balance sheet and income statement for these investment transactions. It is helpful to use a T-account for the investment in Demski stock. Ignore income tax.

Accounting for available-for-sale and equity-method investments (Obj. 1, 2)

■ general ledger

P10-2B The beginning balance sheet of Montgomery Investment Corporation included the following:

Long-Term Investments in **UPS, Inc.** (equity-method investment)	$344,000

Montgomery completed the following investment transactions during the year:

Apr. 2	Purchased 2,000 shares of ATI, Inc. common stock as a long-term available-for-sale investment, paying $12.25 per share.
June 21	Received cash dividend of $0.75 per share on the ATI investment.
Nov. 17	Received cash dividend of $81,000 from UPS, Inc.
Dec. 31	Received annual report from UPS, Inc.; total net income for the year was $550,000. Of this amount, Montgomery's proportion is 22%.

At year end, the market values of Montgomery's investments are ATI, $26,800; UPS, Inc., $500,000.

Required

1. Record the transactions in the journal of Montgomery Investment Corporation.
2. Post entries to the Long-Term Investments in UPS, Inc., T-account and determine its balance at December 31.
3. Show how to report the Long-Term Available-for-Sale Investments and the Long-Term Investments in UPS accounts on Montgomery's balance sheet at December 31.

Analyzing consolidated financial statements (Obj. 3)

P10-3B This problem demonstrates the dramatic effect that consolidation accounting can have on a company's ratios. **Ford Motor Company (Ford)** owns 100% of **Ford Motor Credit Corporation (FMCC)**, its financing subsidiary. Ford's main operations consist of manufacturing automotive products. FMCC mainly helps people finance the purchase of automobiles from Ford and its dealers. The two companies' individual balance sheets are adapted and summarized as follows (amounts in billions):

	Ford (Parent)	FMCC (Subsidiary)
Total assets	$89.6	$170.5
Total liabilities	$65.1	$156.9
Total stockholders' equity	24.5	13.6
Total liabilities and equity	$89.6	$170.5

Assume that FMCC's liabilities include $1.6 billion owed to Ford, the parent company.

Required

1. Compute the debt ratio of Ford Motor Company considered alone.
2. Determine the consolidated total assets, total liabilities, and stockholders' equity of Ford Motor Company after consolidating the financial statements of FMCC into the totals of Ford, the parent company.
3. Recompute the debt ratio of the consolidated entity. Why do companies prefer not to consolidate their financing subsidiaries into their own financial statements?

Consolidating a wholly owned subsidiary (Obj. 3)

spreadsheet

P10-4B Assume **Tejas Logistics, Inc.**, paid $266,000 to acquire all the common stock of Volunteer Corporation, and Volunteer owes Tejas $81,000 on a note payable. Immediately after the purchase on September 30, 20X8, the two companies' balance sheets follow.

	Tejas	Volunteer
Assets		
Cash	$ 24,000	$ 20,000
Accounts receivable, net	91,000	42,000
Note receivable from Volunteer	81,000	—
Inventory	145,000	214,000
Investment in Volunteer	266,000	—
Plant assets, net	278,000	219,000
Total	$885,000	$495,000
Liabilities and Stockholders' Equity		
Accounts payable	$ 57,000	$ 49,000
Notes payable	177,000	149,000
Other liabilities	129,000	31,000
Common stock	274,000	118,000
Retained earnings	248,000	148,000
Total	$885,000	$495,000

Required

1. Prepare the consolidated balance sheet for Tejas Logistics, Inc. (It is sufficient to complete a consolidation work sheet.)
2. Why aren't total assets of the consolidated entity equal to the sum of total assets for both companies combined? Why isn't consolidated equity equal to the sum of the two companies' stockholders' equity amounts?

Accounting for a bond investment purchased at a premium (Obj. 4)

P10-5B Financial institutions such as insurance companies and pension plans hold large quantities of bond investments. Suppose **Farm Bureau Insurance and Financial Services** purchases $600,000 of 6% bonds of Eaton, Inc., for 103 on March 1, 20X4. These bonds pay interest on March 1 and September 1 each year. They mature on March 1, 20X8. At December 31, 20X4, the market price of the bonds is 103.5

Required

1. Journalize Farm Bureau's purchase of the bonds as a long-term investment on March 1, 20X4 (to be held to maturity), receipt of cash interest, and amortization of the bond investment at December 31, 20X4. The straight-line method is appropriate for amortizing the bond investment.
2. Show all financial statement effects of this long-term bond investment on Farm Bureau Insurance and Financial Services' balance sheet and income statement at December 31, 20X4.

Recording foreign-currency transactions and reporting the transaction gain or loss (Obj. 5)

■ **general ledger**

P10-6B Suppose **Goodyear Tire & Rubber Company** completed the following international transactions:

Feb. 1	Sold inventory on account to **Fiat**, the Italian automaker, for €82,000. The exchange rate of the euro is \$1.10, and Fiat demands to pay in euros.
10	Purchased supplies on account from a Canadian company at a price of Canadian \$50,000. The exchange rate of the Canadian dollar is \$0.70, and payment will be in Canadian dollars.
17	Sold inventory on account to an English firm for 100,000 British pounds. Payment will be in pounds, and the exchange rate of the pound is \$1.80.
22	Collected from Fiat. The exchange rate is €1 = \$1.13.
Mar. 18	Paid the Canadian company. The exchange rate of the Canadian dollar is \$0.67.
24	Collected from the English firm. The exchange rate of the British pound is \$1.77.

Required

1. Record these transactions in Goodyear's journal and show how to report the transaction gain or loss on the income statement.
2. How will what you learned in this problem help you structure international transactions?

Measuring and explaining the foreign-currency translation adjustment (Obj. 5)

P10-7B Assume **Texas Instruments (TI)** has a semiconductor subsidiary company based in Japan.

Required

1. Translate into dollars the foreign-currency balance sheet of the Japanese subsidiary of TI. When TI acquired this subsidiary, the Japanese yen was worth \$0.0064. The current exchange rate is \$0.0086. During the period when the subsidiary earned its income, the average exchange rate was \$0.0070 per yen.

	Yen
Assets	300,000,000
Liabilities	80,000,000
Stockholders' equity:	
Common stock	20,000,000
Retained earnings	200,000,000
	300,000,000

Before you perform the foreign-currency translation calculations, indicate whether TI has experienced a positive or a negative translation adjustment. State whether the adjustment is a gain or a loss, and show where it is reported in the financial statements.

2. To which company does the foreign-currency translation adjustment "belong"? In which company's financial statements will the translation adjustment be reported?
3. How will what you learned in this problem help you understand published financial statements?

P10-8B Excerpts from **Intel Corporation's** statement of cash flows, as adapted, appear as follows:

Using a cash-flow statement (Obj. 6)

writing assignment ■

Intel Corporation
Consolidated Statement of Cash Flows (Adapted partial)
Years Ended December 31

(In millions)	20X4	20X3
Cash and cash equivalents, beginning of year	$ 2,976	$ 3,695
Net cash provided by operating activities	8,654	12,827
Cash flows provided by (used for) investing activities:		
Additions to property, plant, and equipment	(7,309)	(6,674)
Acquisitions of other companies	(883)	(2,317)
Purchases of available-for-sale investments	(7,141)	(17,188)
Sales of available-for-sale investments	15,138	16,144
Net cash (used for) investing activities	(195)	(10,035)
Cash flows provided by (used for) financing activities:		
Borrowing	329	215
Retirement of long-term debt	(10)	(46)
Proceeds from issuance of stock	762	797
Repurchase and retirement of common stock	(4,008)	(4,007)
Payment of dividends to stockholders	(538)	(470)
Net cash (used for) financing activities	(3,465)	(3,511)
Net increase (decrease) in cash and cash equivalents	4,994	(719)
Cash and cash equivalents, end of year	$ 7,970	$ 2,976

Required

As the chief executive officer of Intel Corporation, your duty is to write the management letter to your stockholders to explain Intel's investing activities during 20X4. Compare the company's level of investment with preceding years and indicate the major way the company financed its investment during 20X4. Net income for 20X4 was $1,291 million.

Apply Your Knowledge

Decision Cases

Case 1. United Technologies (UT) may not be an everyday name in American households, but millions of people ride on **Otis Elevators**, keep cool with **Carrier** air conditioners, and travel on airplanes powered by **Pratt & Whitney** engines. All these companies are subsidiaries of United Technologies. UT's consolidated sales for 20X6 were $26.6 billion, and expenses totaled $24.8 billion. UT operates worldwide and conducts 37% of its business outside the United States. During 20X6, UT reported the following items in its financial statements:

Making an investment decision (Obj. 1, 5)

Foreign-currency translation adjustments	$(202)
Unrealized holding ____ on available-for-sale investments	(328)

As you consider an investment in UT stock, some concerns arise. Answer each of the following questions:

1. What do the parentheses around these items signify?
2. Are these items reported as assets, liabilities, stockholders' equity, revenues, or expenses? Are they normal-balance accounts, or are they contra accounts?
3. Are these items reason for rejoicing or sorrow at UT? Are UT's emotions about these items deep or only moderate? Why?

(continued)

4. Did UT include these items in net income? in retained earnings? In the final analysis, how much net income did UT report for 20X6?
5. Should these items scare you away from investing in UT stock? Why or why not?

Making an investment sale decision (Obj. 1, 2, 4)

Case 2. Shelly Herzog is the general manager of McNamara Service Company, which provides data-management services for physicians in the Orlando, Florida, area. McNamara Service Company is having a rough year. Net income trails projections for the year by almost $75,000. This shortfall is especially important. McNamara plans to issue stock early next year and needs to show investors that the company can meet its earnings targets.

McNamara holds several investments purchased a few years ago. Even though investing in stocks is outside McNamara's core business of data-management services, Herzog thinks these investments may hold the key to helping the company meet its net income goal for the year. She is considering what to do with the following investments:

1. McNamara owns 50% of the common stock of Mid-Florida Office Systems, which provides the company's business forms that McNamara uses. Mid-Florida has lost money for the past 2 years but still has a retained earnings balance of $550,000. Herzog thinks she can get Mid-Florida's treasurer to declare a $160,000 cash dividend, half of which would go to McNamara.
2. McNamara owns a bond investment purchased 8 years ago for $250,000. The purchase price represents a discount from the bonds' maturity value of $400,000. These bonds mature 2 years from now, and their current market value is $380,000. Herzog has checked with an **Edward Jones** investment representative, and Ms. Herzog is considering selling the bonds. Edward Jones would charge a 1% commission on the sale transaction.
3. McNamara owns 5,000 shares of **Microsoft** stock valued at $53 per share. One year ago, Microsoft stock was worth only $28 per share because the company was involved in a major antitrust lawsuit. McNamara purchased the Microsoft stock for $37 per share. Herzog wonders whether McNamara should sell the Microsoft stock.

Required

Evaluate all three actions as a way for McNamara Service Company to generate the needed amount of income. Recommend the best way for McNamara to achieve its net income goal.

Ethical Issue

writing assignment ■

Media One owns 18% of the voting stock of Web Talk, Inc. The remainder of the Web Talk stock is held by numerous investors with small holdings. Austin Cohen, president of Media One and a member of Web Talk's board of directors, heavily influences Web Talk's policies.

Under the market value method of accounting for investments, Media One's net income increases as it receives dividend revenue from Web Talk. Media One pays President Cohen a bonus computed as a percentage of Media One's net income. Therefore, Cohen can control his personal bonus to a certain extent by influencing Web Talk's dividends.

A recession occurs in 20X4, and Media One's income is low. Cohen uses his power to have Web Talk pay a large cash dividend. The action requires Web Talk to borrow in order to pay the dividend.

Required

1. In getting Web Talk to pay the large cash dividend, is Cohen acting within his authority as a member of the Web Talk board of directors? Are Cohen's actions ethical? Whom can his actions harm?
2. Discuss how using the equity method of accounting for investment would decrease Cohen's potential for manipulating his bonus.

Focus on Financials: ■ YUM! Brands

Analyzing investments, consolidated subsidiaries, and international operations (Obj. 2, 3, 5)

The financial statements of **YUM! Brands, Inc.** are given in Appendix A at the end of this book.

1. YUM accounts for its investments in unconsolidated affiliates by the equity method. During 2003, YUM made no such investments. Assume YUM received no dividends from unconsolidated affiliates. What was the overall result of operations for YUM's unconsolidated affiliates during 2003?

2. What is YUM's percentage ownership of its consolidated subsidiaries? How can you tell? Which financial statement provides the evidence?
3. Does YUM have any foreign subsidiaries? What evidence answers this question? Which financial statement provides the evidence?
4. Which monetary currency was stronger, the U.S. dollar or YUM's foreign currencies, during 2001, 2002, and 2003? Give the basis for your answers.

Focus on Analysis: ■ Pier 1 Imports

Analyzing consolidated statements and international operations (Obj. 3, 5)

This case is based on the financial statements of **Pier 1 Imports, Inc.** given in Appendix B at the end of this book.

1. What indicates that Pier 1 Imports owns foreign subsidiaries? Identify the item that proves your point and the financial statement on which it appears.
2. Which currency, the U.S. dollar, or Pier 1's foreign currencies, was stronger in the year ended March 2, 2002? Which currency was stronger during 2004? Give the evidence to support each answer. Ignore the minimum pension liability adjustment.
3. At February 28, 2004, did Pier 1 Imports have a net gain or a net loss from translating its foreign subsidiaries' financial statements into dollars? How can you tell? Ignore the minimum pension liability adjustment.

Group Project

Pick a stock from *The Wall Street Journal* or other database or publication. Assume that your group purchases 1,000 shares of the stock as a long-term investment and that your 1,000 shares are less than 20% of the company's outstanding stock. Research the stock in *Value Line*, *Moody's Investor Record*, or other source to determine whether the company pays cash dividends and, if so, how much and at what intervals.

Required

1. Track the stock for a period assigned by your professor. Over the specified period, keep a daily record of the price of the stock to see how well your investment has performed. Each day, search the Corporate Dividend News in *The Wall Street Journal* to keep a record of any dividends you've received. End the period of your analysis with a month end, such as September 30 or December 31.
2. Journalize all transactions that you have experienced, including the stock purchase, dividends received (both cash dividends and stock dividends), and any year-end adjustment required by the accounting method that is appropriate for your situation. Assume you will prepare financial statements on the ending date of your study.
3. Show what you will report on your company's balance sheet, income statement, and statement of cash flows as a result of your investment transactions.

spotlight

IS SOMETHING HAPPENING TO BEST BUY?

Best Buy Co, Inc.
Consolidated Statements of Earnings (Excerpt)
For the Fiscal Years Ended
March 1, 2003, March 2, 2002, March 3, 2001

($ in millions)	2003	2002	2001
1 Revenue	$ 20,946	$17,711	$15,189
2 Cost of goods sold	15,710	13,941	12,177
3 Gross profit	5,236	3,770	3,012
4 Selling, general, and administrative expenses	4,226	2,862	2,401
5 Operating income	1,010	908	611
6 Net interest income	4	18	38
7 Earnings from continuing operations before income tax expense	1,014	926	649
8 Income tax expense	392	356	248
9 Earnings from continuing operations	622	570	401
10 Loss from discontinued operations, net of tax	(441)	—	(5)
11 Cumulative effect of change in accounting principle for goodwill, net of $24 tax	(40)	—	—
12 Cumulative effect of change in accounting principle for vendor allowances, net of $26 tax	(42)	—	—
13 Net earnings	$ 99	$ 570	$ 396
14 Basic earnings (loss) per share:			
Continuing operations	$1.93	$1.80	$1.29
Discontinued operations	(1.37)	—	(0.02)
Cumulative effect of accounting changes	(0.25)	—	—
Basic earnings per share	$ 0.31	$ 1.80	$ 1.28

Where do you buy CDs, printer ink, and electronics? It may be Best Buy, North America's number one specialty retailer of consumer electronics. The company carries good merchandise, the salespeople know their products, and the prices are competitive. Best Buy's sales and profits grew handsomely through 2002, so the company must have been doing something right. However, in 2003 net income hiccupped. The bottom line of Best Buy's income statement (line 13) shows that net income dropped to $99 million in 2003. Is Best Buy in a downward spiral?

A closer look at the income statement reveals *why* net income dipped in 2003. Best Buy took a $441 million loss on discontinued operations (line 10). Two accounting changes siphoned off $82 million (lines 11 and 12). Without these hits to income, Best Buy's net income would have been $622 million (line 9). That was Best Buy's *income from continuing operations* for 2003, up 9% over the previous year. Most companies would be delighted to increase net income by 9% year after year.

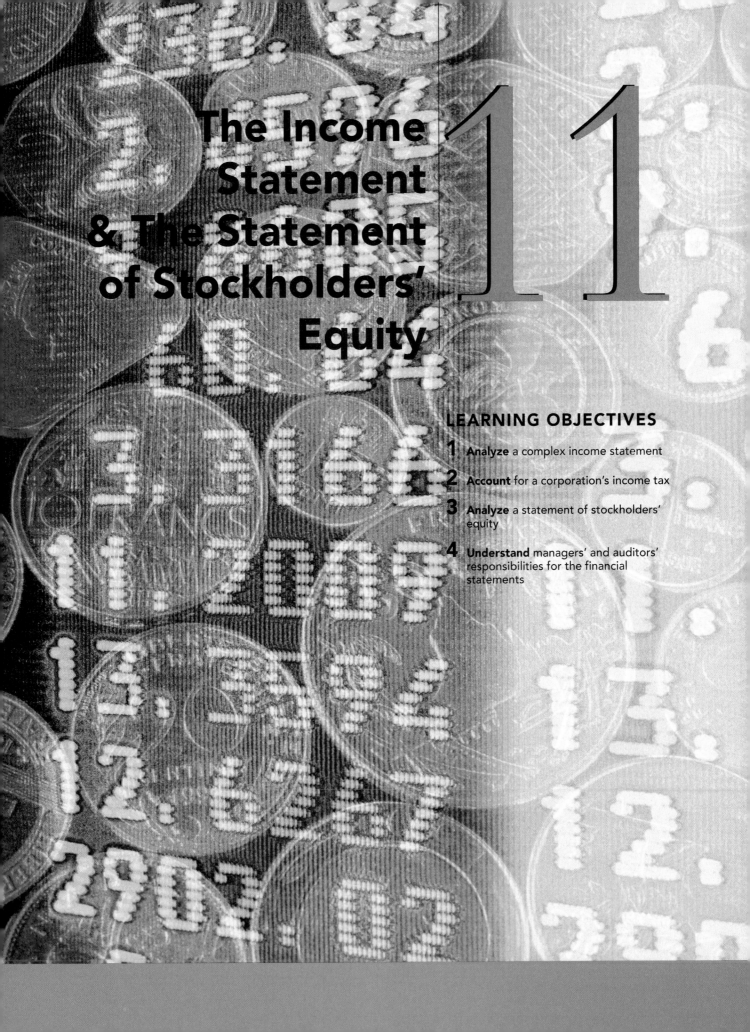

11 The Income Statement & The Statement of Stockholders' Equity

LEARNING OBJECTIVES

1. **Analyze** a complex income statement
2. **Account** for a corporation's income tax
3. **Analyze** a statement of stockholders' equity
4. **Understand** managers' and auditors' responsibilities for the financial statements

Net income. Income from continuing operations. Cumulative effect of accounting changes. Which number measures a company's progress? This chapter will help you make that decision. It covers the full-blown income statement that corporations use to report their operations to the public.

We begin with a basic question: how to evaluate the quality of earnings.

Evaluating the Quality of Earnings

OBJECTIVE

1 **Analyze** a complex income statement

A corporation's net income (net earnings) receives more attention that any other item in the financial statements. To stockholders, the larger the net income, the greater the likelihood of dividends. To creditors, the better the ability to pay debts.

Suppose you are considering investing in the stock of **Best Buy** and Brand X Superstore. Both companies earned the same net income last year, and each company has increased profits by 9% annually over the last 5 years.

The two companies, however, generate profits in different ways:

- Best Buy's income has resulted from continuing operations.
- Brand X's sales have struggled. Its growth in net income resulted from selling off land acquired years earlier.

In which company would you invest?

Best Buy holds the promise of better earnings in the future because its profits come from *continuing operations*. We may expect Best Buy to match its past earnings in the future. Brand X shows no growth from operations. Its net income results from *one-time transactions*—the selling off of assets. Sooner or later, Brand X will run out of assets to sell. Investors would say that Best Buy's earnings are of *higher quality* because they are likely to repeat in the future.

To explore the makeup of net income, let's examine its various sources. Exhibit 11-1 provides a comprehensive example that we will use throughout the chapter. It is the income statement of **Allied Electronics Corporation**, which produces electronic-control instruments.

Continuing Operations

In Exhibit 11-1, the topmost section of the income statement reports the results of continuing operations (lines 1 to 10). This part of the business is expected to continue from period to period. We use this information to predict that Allied Electronics will earn income of approximately $54,000 next year.

The continuing operations of Allied Electronics include three new items:

- During 20X5, the company *restructured* operations at a loss of $8,000 (line 6). Restructuring costs include severance pay to laid-off workers and moving expenses for employees transferred to other locations. The restructuring loss is part of continuing operations because Allied Electronics is remaining in the electronics business. But the restructuring loss is an "Other" item because restructuring falls outside Allied's core activity.
- Allied had a *gain on the sale of machinery* (line 7), also outside the company's core business. This explains why the gain isn't part of operating income (lines 1 to 5).
- *Income tax expense* (line 9) is subtracted in arriving at income from continuing operations. Corporate income tax is a significant expense. The current maximum federal income tax rate for corporations is 35%. State income taxes run about 5% in many states. Thus, we use an income tax rate of 40% in our illustrations. The $36,000 income tax expense in Exhibit 11-1 equals the pretax income from continuing operations multiplied by the tax rate ($90,000 × 0.40 = $36,000).

■ **EXHIBIT 11-1**
Allied Electronics Corporation Income Statement

Allied Electronics Corporation
Income Statement
Year Ended December 31, 20X5

Continuing Operations	1	Sales revenue	$500,000
	2	Cost of goods sold	240,000
	3	Gross margin	260,000
	4	Operating expenses (detailed)	181,000
	5	Operating income	79,000
		Other gains (losses):	
	6	Loss on restructuring operations	(8,000)
	7	Gain on sale of machinery	19,000
	8	Income from continuing operations before income tax	90,000
	9	Income tax expense	36,000
	10	Income from continuing operations	54,000
Special Items	11	Discontinued operations, $35,000, less income tax of $14,000	21,000
	12	Income before extraordinary item and cumulative effect of change in depreciation method	75,000
	13	Extraordinary flood loss, $20,000, less income tax saving of $8,000	(12,000)
	14	Cumulative effect of change in depreciation method, $10,000, less income tax of $4,000	6,000
	15	Net income	$ 69,000
Earning per Share		Earnings per share of common stock (20,000 shares outstanding):	
	16	Income from continuing operations	$2.70
	17	Income from discontinued operations	1.05
	18	Income before extraordinary item and cumulative effect of change in depreciation method	3.75
	19	Extraordinary loss	(0.60)
	20	Cumulative effect of change in depreciation method	0.30
	21	Net income	$3.45

Check Point 11-1

Check Point 11-2

Check Point 11-3

stop AND think. . .

How much was Allied Electronics' total income tax expense during 20X5? Consider lines, 9, 11, 13, and 14 of the income statement in Exhibit 11-1.

Answer:
Total income tax expense was

$46,000 = ($36,000 + $14,000 – $8,000 + $4,000)

■ Taking Action Which Income Number Predicts Future Profits?

How is income from continuing operations used in investment analysis? Suppose Paul Malone, an analyst with Prudential Securities in Detroit, is estimating the value of Allied Electronics' common stock. Malone believes that Allied Electronics can earn annual income of $54,000 each year for the indefinite future.

To estimate the value of Allied's common stock, financial analysts determine the present value (present value means the value *today*) of Allied's stream of future income. Malone must use some interest rate to compute the present value. Assume that an

Investment capitalization rate An earnings rate used to estimate the value of an investment in stock.

appropriate interest rate (i) for the valuation of Allied Electronics is 12%. This rate is based on the risk that Allied might not be able to earn annual income of $54,000 for the indefinite future. The rate is also called the **investment capitalization rate** because it is used to estimate the value of an investment. The higher the risk, the higher the rate, and vice versa. The computation of the estimated value of a stock is

$$\text{Estimated value of Allied Electronics common stock} = \frac{\text{Estimated annual income in the future}}{\text{Investment capitalization rate}} = \frac{\$54{,}000}{0.12} = \$450{,}000^{*}$$

Malone thus estimates that Allied Electronics Corporation is worth $450,000. He would then compare this estimate to the current market value of Allied Electronics' stock, which is $513,000. Allied Electronics' balance sheet reports that Allied has 108,000 shares of common stock outstanding, and *The Wall Street Journal* reports that Allied common stock is selling for $4.75 per share. The current value of Allied Stock is thus

$$\text{Current market value of the company} = \text{Number of shares of common stock outstanding} \times \text{Current market price per share}$$

$$\$513{,}000 = 108{,}000 \times \$4.75$$

The investment decision rule may be:

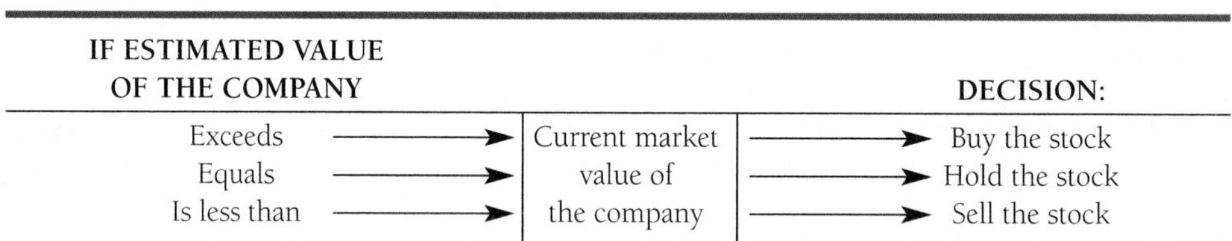

IF ESTIMATED VALUE OF THE COMPANY
DECISION:
Exceeds
Equals
Is less than
Current market value of the company
Buy the stock
Hold the stock
Sell the stock

In this case,

			DECISION:
Estimated Value of Allied $450,000	Is less than	Current market value of Allied $513,000 →	Sell the stock

Malone believes Allied's stock price should fall below its current market value of $513,000 to somewhere in a range near $450,000. Based on this analysis, Prudential would recommend that investors holding Allied stock should sell it.

Investors often value a single share of stock. They can estimate the value of one share of stock by using earnings per share (EPS) of common stock, as follows:

Check Point 11-4

$$\text{Estimated value of one share of common stock} = \frac{\text{Estimated annual earnings per share}}{\text{Investment capitalization rate}}$$

The analysis based on one share of stock follows the pattern illustrated for the company as a whole.

*This valuation model has many forms, which are covered in finance classes. Here we introduce the basic form.

Discontinued Operations

Most large corporations engage in several lines of business. For example, Best Buy has its basic Best Buy Stores in addition to Magnolia Hi-Fi stores. **Sears, Roebuck & Company** has a real estate development company (**Homart**) and an insurance company (**Allstate**) in addition to its retail stores. We call each identifiable part of a company a **segment of the business**.

Segment of the business
An identifiable part of a company.

A company may sell a segment of its business. Best Buy sold its **Musicland** subsidiary. The sale of a business segment is viewed as a one-time transaction. Best Buy's income statement reports on the Musicland segment that has been disposed of under the heading Discontinued Operations (line 10 on page 510).

Let's return to the Allied Electronics example in Exhibit 11-1 (page 513). The discontinued operations are taxed at the 40% rate. Therefore, discontinued operations are reported along with their income tax by Allied Electronics Corporation as follows (line 11, page 513).

Discontinued operations, $35,000, less income tax of $14,000	$21,000

Financial analysts typically do *not* include discontinued operations in predictions of future corporate income because the discontinued segments will not continue to generate income for the company.

Gains and losses on the sales of plant assets are *not* reported as discontinued operations. They appear in the "Other" section of the income statement (Exhibit 11-1, lines 6 and 7).

Extraordinary Gains and Losses (Extraordinary Items)

Extraordinary gains and losses, also called *extraordinary items*, are both *unusual* for the company and *infrequent*. Losses from natural disasters (such as earthquakes, floods, and tornadoes) and the expropriation of company assets by a foreign government (expropriation) are extraordinary. Best Buy had no extraordinary items during 2001–2003.

Extraordinary gains and losses
Also called *extraordinary items*, these gains and losses are both unusual for the company and infrequent.

Extraordinary items are reported along with their income tax effects. During 20X5, Allied Electronics Corporation suffered a $20,000 flood loss (Exhibit 11-1, line 13). This flood loss reduced income and therefore reduced Allied's income tax. Taxes decrease the net amount of a loss the same way they reduce net income. Another way to report an extraordinary loss along with its tax effect is as follows:

Extraordinary flood loss	$(20,000)
Less income tax saving	8,000
Extraordinary flood loss, net of tax	(12,000)

Trace this item to the income statement in Exhibit 11-1 (line 13). An extraordinary gain is reported in the same way, net of its income tax.

Gains and losses due to lawsuits, restructuring, and the sale of plant assets are *not* extraordinary items. They are considered normal business occurrences and are reported as Other gains and losses. Exhibit 11-1 (page 513, lines 6 and 7) provides an example.

Cumulative Effect of a Change in Accounting Method

Companies sometimes change from one accounting method to another, such as from double-declining-balance (DDB) to straight-line depreciation, or from first-in, first-out (FIFO) to average cost for inventory. An accounting change makes it difficult to compare one period with preceding periods. Without detailed information, investors can be misled into thinking that the current year is better or worse than the preceding year, when in fact the only difference is a change in accounting method.

To help investors separate continuing operations from changes in accounting methods, companies report accounting changes in a special section of the income statement. This section usually appears after extraordinary items. Exhibit 11-1, line 14 gives an example for Allied Electronics.

Allied Electronics Corporation changed from DDB to straight-line depreciation at the beginning of 20X5. How did this accounting change affect 20X5? First, it decreased depreciation expense for 20X5 and thereby increased 20X5 income from continuing operations. Second, the change affected previous years. If Allied had been using straight-line depreciation in previous years, depreciation expense would have been less, and net income would have been $6,000 higher ($10,000 minus the additional income tax of $4,000). Exhibit 11-1 reports the cumulative effect of this accounting change on line 14.

ACCOUNTING ALERT

Watch Out for Voluntary Accounting Changes That Increase Reported Income

Investment analysts follow companies to see if they meet their forecasted earnings targets. And managers sometimes take drastic action to increase reported earnings. Assume it's late in November and it appears that earnings will fall *below* the target for the year. A reasonable thing to do is step up sales efforts to increase sales and net income. Managers can also cut expenses. These actions are ethical and honest. Profits earned by these actions are real. Managers can take another action that is honest and legal, but its ethics are questionable. Suppose the company has been using the LIFO inventory method. Changing to FIFO can increase reported income.

Accounting changes are a quick-and-dirty way to create reported profits when the company can't earn enough from continuing operations. This is why GAAP requires companies to report changes in accounting methods, along with the effects on earnings, to let investors know where the income came from. Without these disclosures, investors would believe the income came from continuing operations when in fact it resulted solely from accounting. The stock market punishes companies—through lower stock prices—when they switch accounting methods to increase reported income. These accounting changes are *voluntary* because the company made the decision to change accounting methods.

Other accounting changes are required by new accounting rules; these are not voluntary. When the FASB issues a new standard, companies that have been using a different method must make an accounting change to comply with the new rules. The change may increase the company's reported income. How does the stock market react? Because the company was forced to make this accounting change, the stock market may view this income as real. The company's stock price may actually increase.

The take-away lesson from the accounting alert is this:

- Watch out for voluntary accounting changes that increase reported income. The company may have switched accounting methods because it couldn't earn enough income from its basic operations.

Earnings per Share of Common Stock

The final segment of the income statement reports earnings per share. **Earnings per share (EPS)** is the amount of a company's net income per share of its *outstanding common stock*. EPS is a key measure of a business's success, computed as follows:

Earnings per share (EPS) Amount of a company's net income per share of its outstanding common stock.

$$\text{Earnings per share} = \frac{\text{Net income} - \text{Preferred dividends}}{\text{Average number of shares of common stock outstanding}}$$

The corporation lists its various sources of income separately: continuing operations, discontinued operations, and so on. It also lists the EPS figure for each element of net income. Consider the EPS of Allied Electronics Corporation. The final section of Exhibit 11-1 (lines 16 to 21) shows how companies report EPS.

	Earnings per share of common stock (20,000 shares outstanding):	
16	Income from continuing operations ($54,000/20,000)	$2.70
17	Income from discontinued operations ($21,000/20,000)	1.05
18	Income before extraordinary item and cumulative effect of change in depreciation method ($75,000/20,000)	3.75
19	Extraordinary loss ($12,000/20,000)	(0.60)
20	Cumulative effect of change in depreciation method ($6,000/20,000)	0.30
21	Net income ($69,000/20,000)	$3.45

Effect of Preferred Dividends on Earnings Per Share. Recall that EPS is earnings per share of *common* stock. But the holders of preferred stock have first claim on dividends. Therefore, preferred dividends must be subtracted to compute EPS. Preferred dividends are not subtracted from discontinued operations, extraordinary items, or the cumulative effect of accounting changes.

Allied Electronics Corporation has 10,000 shares of preferred stock outstanding, each with a $1.00 dividend. Allied's annual preferred dividends are $10,000 (10,000 × $1.00). The $10,000 is subtracted from each income subtotal, resulting in the following EPS amounts (recall that Allied has 20,000 shares of common stock outstanding):

Earnings per share of common stock (20,000 shares outstanding):	
Income from continuing operations ($54,000 – $10,000)/20,000	$2.20
Income from discontinued operations ($21,000/20,000)	1.05
Income before extraordinary item and cumulative effect of change in depreciation method ($75,000 – $10,000)/20,000	3.25
Extraordinary loss ($12,000/20,000)	(0.60)
Cumulative effect of change in depreciation method ($6,000/20,000)	0.30
Net income ($69,000 – $10,000)/20,000	$2.95

Check Point 11-5

Check Point 11-6

Earnings Per Share Dilution. Some corporations have convertible preferred stock, which may be exchanged for common stock. When preferred is converted to common, the EPS is *diluted*—reduced—because more common shares are divided into net income. Corporations with complex capital structures present two sets of EPS figures:

- EPS based on actual outstanding common shares (*basic* EPS)
- EPS based on outstanding common shares plus the additional common shares that would arise from conversion of the preferred stock into common (*diluted* EPS)

Reporting Comprehensive Income

All companies report net income or net loss on their income statements. As we saw in Chapter 10, companies with unrealized gains and losses on certain investments and foreign-currency translation adjustments also report another income figure. **Comprehensive income** is the company's change in total stockholders' equity from all sources other than from the owners of the business. Comprehensive income includes net income plus:

Comprehensive income
A company's change in total stockholder's equity from all sources other than from the owners of the business.

- Unrealized gains (losses) on available-for-sale investments
- Foreign-currency translation adjustments

These items do not enter into the determination of net income or of earnings per share. They can be reported as Other comprehensive income, as shown in Exhibit 11-2. All amounts are assumed for this illustration.

■ **EXHIBIT 11-2**
Reporting Comprehensive Income

Allied Electronics Corporation
Statement of Comprehensive Income (Partial)
Year Ended December 31, 20X5

Net income			$69,000
Other comprehensive income:			
Unrealized gain on investment	$ 6,500		
Less income tax (40%)	2,600	$3,900	
Foreign-currency translation adjustment (loss)	$(9,000)		
Less income tax saving (40%)	3,600	(5,400)	
Other comprehensive income			(1,500)
Comprehensive income			$67,500

Check Point 11-7

■ Taking Action What Should You Analyze to Gain an Overall Picture of a Company?

Two key figures used in financial analysis are

- Net income
- Cash flow from operations

For any one period, Allied Electronics' net income and net cash flow from operating activities may chart different paths. Accounting income arises from the accrual process as follows:

$$\text{Total revenues and gains} - \text{Total expenses and losses} = \text{Net income (or Net loss)}$$

As we have seen, revenues and gains are recorded when they occur, regardless of when the company receives or pays cash.

Net cash flow, on the other hand, is based solely on cash receipts and cash payments. During 2006, a company may have lots of revenues and expenses and a hefty net income. But the company may have weak cash flow because it has not yet collected from customers. The reverse may also be true: The company may have abundant cash but little income.

The income statement and the cash-flow statement often paint different pictures of the company. Which statement provides better information? Neither: Both statements are needed, along with the balance sheet and statement of stockholders' equity, for an overall view of the business.

ACCOUNTING ALERT

Beware of *Pro Forma* Earnings

Investors do not wait until December 31 to learn a company's earnings. They make investment decisions throughout the year. To provide timely data, companies report forecasted (or *pro forma*) earnings. This often comes in a press release, such as the following from eBay:

> Based on eBay's current outlook . . . , 2002 pro forma earnings per share could range between $0.70 and $0.73 per [. . .] share.

Investors could compare the pro forma earnings for 2002 to the comparable EPS figure for 2001, which was $0.32. The higher expected earnings for 2002 made eBay stock look attractive.

Astute investors take pro forma earnings with a grain of salt because pro forma means "as if." In short, reader beware! As 2002 unfolded, eBay may or may not have been able to earn net income of $0.73 per share. As it turned out, eBay's EPS for 2003 was $0.87, a successful year for the company. Nevertheless, beware of pro forma earnings.

Another feature of pro forma earnings: they are not audited by independent accountants. There is no GAAP definition of pro forma earnings, so managers can report whatever figures they wish. By contrast, GAAP provides an objective way to measure net income and its components. GAAP is designed to provide reliable information.

Accounting for Corporate Income Taxes

OBJECTIVE

2 **Account** for a corporation's income tax

Corporations pay income tax as individuals do, but corporate and personal tax rates differ. The current federal tax rate on most corporate income is 35%. Most states also levy income taxes on corporations, so most corporations have a combined federal and state income tax rate of approximately 40%.

To account for income tax, the corporation measures

- *Income tax expense*, an expense on the income statement. Income tax expense helps measure net income.
- *Income tax payable*, a liability on the balance sheet. Income tax payable is the amount of tax to pay the government.

Pretax accounting income
Income before tax on the income statement.

Accounting for income tax follows the principles of accrual accounting. Suppose in 20X4 Best Buy reported income before tax (also called **pretax accounting income**) of $900 million. Best Buy's combined income tax rate is close to 40%. To start this discussion, assume income tax expense and income tax payable are the same. Then Best Buy records income tax for the year as follows (amounts in millions):

20X4			
Dec. 31	Income Tax Expense ($900 × 0.40)	360	
	Income tax Payable		360
	Recorded income tax for the year.		

ASSETS	=	LIABILITIES	+	STOCKHOLDERS' EQUITY	–	EXPENSES
0	=	+360			–	360

Best Buy's 20X4 financial statements would report these figures (partial, in millions):

Income statement		Balance sheet	
Income before income tax	$900	Current liabilities:	
Income tax expense	(360)	Income tax payable	$360
Net income	$540		

In general, income tax expense and income tax payable can be computed as follows:*

Income tax *expense*	=	Income before income tax (from the *income statement*)	×	Income tax rate

Income tax *payable*	=	Taxable income (from the *income tax return* filed with the IRS)	×	Income tax rate

*The authors thank Jean Marie Hudson for suggesting this presentation.

The income statement and the income tax return are entirely separate documents:

- The *income statement* reports the results of operations.
- The *income tax return* is filed with the Internal Revenue Service (IRS) to measure how much tax to pay the government.

Taxable income
The basis for computing the amount of tax to pay the government.

For most companies, tax expense and tax payable differ. Some revenues and expenses affect income differently for accounting and for tax purposes. The most common difference between accounting income and **taxable income** occurs when a corporation uses straight-line depreciation in its financial statements and accelerated depreciation for the tax return.

Continuing with the Best Buy illustration, suppose for 20X5 that Best Buy, has:

- Pretax accounting income of $900 million on its income statement
- Taxable income of $800 million on its income tax return

Taxable income is less than accounting income because Best Buy uses straight-line depreciation for accounting purposes and accelerated depreciation for tax purposes. Best Buy will record income tax for 20X5 as follows (dollar amounts in millions and an income tax rate of 40%):

20X5			
Dec. 31	Income Tax Expense ($900 × 0.40)	360	
	Income Tax Payable ($800 × 0.40)		320
	Deferred Tax Liability		40
	Recorded income tax for the year.		

Deferred Tax Liability is usually long-term.

ASSETS	=	LIABILITIES	+	STOCKHOLDERS' EQUITY	–	EXPENSES
0	=	+320 + 40			–	$360

Best Buy's financial statements for 20X5 will report the following:

Income statement		**Balance sheet**	
Income before income tax	$900	Current liabilities:	
Income tax expense	(360)	Income tax payable	$320
Net income	$540	Long-term liabilities:	
		Deferred tax liability	40*

Check Point 11-8

*The beginning balance of Deferred tax liability was zero.

Early in 20X6, Best Buy would pay income tax payable of $320 million because this is a current liability. The deferred tax liability can be paid later.

For a given year, Income Tax Payable can exceed Income Tax Expense. When that occurs, the company debits a Deferred Tax Asset.

Analyzing Retained Earnings

Occasionally a company records a revenue or an expense incorrectly. If the error is corrected in a later period, the balance of Retained Earnings is wrong until corrected. Corrections to Retained Earnings for errors of an earlier period are called **prior-period adjustments**. The prior-period adjustment appears on the statement of retained earnings.

Prior-period adjustment
A correction to beginning balance of retained earnings for an error of an earlier period.

Assume that **NPR Corporation** recorded 20X6 income tax expense as $30,000, but the correct amount was $40,000. This error understated expenses by $10,000 and overstated net income by $10,000. The government sent a bill in 20X7 for the additional $10,000, and this alerted NPR to the mistake.

Prior-period adjustments are not reported on the income statement because they relate to an earlier accounting period. This prior-period adjustment would appear on the statement of retained earnings, as shown in Exhibit 11-3, with all amounts assumed:

■ **EXHIBIT 11-3**
Reporting a Prior-Period Adjustment

NPR Corporation
Statement of Retained Earnings
Year Ended December 31, 20X7

Retained earnings balance, December 31, 20X6, as originally reported	$390,000
Prior-period adjustment—debit to correct error in recording income tax expense of 20X6	(10,000)
Retained earnings balance, December 31, 20X6, as adjusted	380,000
Net income for 20X7	110,000
	490,000
Dividends for 20X7	(40,000)
Retained earnings balance, December 31, 20X7	$450,000

Check Point 11-9

Analyzing the Statement of Stockholders' Equity

OBJECTIVE

3 **Analyze** a statement of stockholder's equity

Statement of stockholders' equity
Reports the changes in all categories of stockholders' equity during the period.

Companies report a statement of stockholders' equity, which includes retained earnings. The statement of stockholders' equity is formatted like a statement of retained earnings but with a column for each element of stockholders' equity. The **statement of stockholders' equity** thus reports reasons for all changes in equity during the period.

Exhibit 11-4 is the 20X5 statement of stockholders' equity for Allied Electronics Corporation. Study its format. There is a column for each element of equity, with the far-right column reporting the total. The top row (line 1) reports beginning balances, taken from last period's balance sheet. The rows report the various transactions, starting with Issuance of stock (line 2). The statement ends with the December 31, 20X5, balances (line 10). All these amounts appear on the ending balance sheet, given in Exhibit 11-5.

■ **EXHIBIT 11-4** Statement of Stockholders' Equity

Allied Electronics Corporation
Statement of Stockholders' Equity
Year Ended December 31, 20X5

	Common Stock, $1 Par	Additional Paid-in Capital	Retained Earnings	Treasury Stock	Accumulated Other Comprehensive Income: Unrealized Gain (Loss) on Investments	Accumulated Other Comprehensive Income: Foreign-Currency Translation Adjustment	Total Stockholders' Equity
1 Balance, December 31, 20X4	$80,000	$160,000	$130,000	$(25,000)	$6,000	$(10,000)	$341,000
2 Issuance of stock	20,000	65,000					85,000
3 Net income			69,000				69,000
4 Cash dividends			(21,000)				(21,000)
5 Stock dividends—8%	8,000	26,000	(34,000)				0
6 Purchase of treasury stock				(9,000)			(9,000)
7 Sale of treasury stock		7,000		4,000			11,000
8 Unrealized gain on investments					1,000		1,000
9 Foreign-currency translation adjustment						3,000	3,000
10 Balance, December 31, 20X5	$108,000	$258,000	$144,000	$(30,000)	$7,000	$ (7,000)	$480,000

Let's examine Allied Electronics' stockholders' equity during 20X5.

Issuance of Stock (Line 2). During 20X5, Allied issued common stock for $85,000. Of this total, $20,000 (par value) went into the Common Stock account, and $65,000 increased Additional Paid-in Capital. Total equity increased by $85,000.

Net Income (Line 3). During 20X5, Allied Electronics earned net income of $69,000, which increased Retained Earnings. Trace net income from the income statement (Exhibit 11-1 page 513) to the statement of stockholders' equity (Exhibit 11-4).

■ **EXHIBIT 11-5**

Stockholders' Equity Section of the Balance Sheet

Allied Electronics Corporation
Balance Sheet (Partial)
December 31, 20X5

	20X5
Total assets	$940,000
Total liabilities	$460,000
Stockholders' Equity	
Common stock, $1 par, shares issued—108,000	$108,000
Additional paid-in capital	258,000
Retained earnings	144,000
Treasury stock	(30,000)
Accumulated other comprehensive income:	
Unrealized gain on investments	7,000
Foreign-currency translation adjustment	(7,000)
Total stockholders' equity	480,000
Total liabilities and stockholders' equity	$940,000

Declaration of Cash Dividends (Line 4). Allied Electronics declared cash dividends of $21,000. Exhibit 11-4 reports the decrease in retained earnings from the declaration of the cash dividends.

Distribution of Stock Dividends (Line 5). During 20X5, Allied Electronics distributed a stock dividend to its stockholders. Prior to the stock dividend, Allied's Common Stock account had a balance of $100,000 (beginning balance of $80,000 + new issue of $20,000). The 8% stock dividend then added 8,000 shares of $1-par common stock, or $8,000, to the Common Stock account.

Allied decreased (debited) Retained Earnings for the market value of this "small" stock dividend. The difference between the market value of the dividend ($34,000) and its par value ($8,000) was credited to Additional Paid-in Capital ($26,000).

Purchase and Sale of Treasury Stock (Lines 6 and 7). Recall from Chapter 9 that treasury stock is recorded at cost. During 20X5, Allied Electronics paid $9,000 to buy treasury stock (line 6). This transaction decreased stockholders' equity. Allied later sold some treasury stock (line 7). The sale of treasury stock brought in $11,000 cash and increased total stockholders' equity by $11,000. The treasury stock that Allied sold had cost the company $4,000, and the extra $7,000 was added to Additional Paid-in Capital. At year end (line 10), Allied still owned treasury stock that cost the company $30,000. The parentheses around the treasury stock figures in Exhibit 11-4 mean that treasury stock is a negative element of stockholders' equity. Trace treasury stock's ending balance to the balance sheet in Exhibit 11-5.

Accumulated Other Comprehensive Income (Lines 8 and 9). Two categories of other comprehensive income are unrealized gains and losses on available-for-sale investments and the foreign-currency translation adjustment.

At December 31, 20X4, Allied Electronics held available-for-sale investments with an unrealized gain of $6,000. This explains the beginning balance. Then, during 20X5, the market value of the investments increased by another $1,000 (line 8). At December 31, 20X5, Allied's portfolio of investments had an unrealized gain of $7,000 (line 10). An unrealized loss on investments would appear as a negative amount.

At December 31, 20X4, Allied had a negative foreign-currency translation adjustment of $10,000 (line 1). During 20X5, the foreign-currency translation adjustment was $3,000 (line 9), and at December 31, 20X5, Allied's cumulative foreign-currency translation adjustment stood at $8,000—a negative amount that resembles an unrealized loss (line 10).

Check Point 11-10

Responsibility for the Financial Statements

Management's Responsibility

OBJECTIVE

4 **Understand** managers' and auditors' responsibilities for the financial statements

Management issues a *statement of responsibility* along with the company's financial statements. Exhibit 11-6 is an excerpt from the statement of management's responsibility for Best Buy, Inc.

Management declares its responsibility for the financial statements and states that they conform to GAAP. As we've seen throughout this book, GAAP is the standard for preparing the financial statements. GAAP is designed to produce relevant, reliable, and useful information for making investment and credit decisions.

■ **EXHIBIT 11-6**

Excerpt from Management's Responsibility for Financial Reporting—Best Buy Co., Inc.

Report of Best Buy Management (Excerpt)

To Our Shareholders:

Our management is responsible for the preparation, integrity and objectivity of the accompanying consolidated financial statements and the related financial information. The financial statements have been prepared in conformity with accounting principles generally accepted in the United States.

Auditor Report

The Securities Exchange Act of 1934 requires companies that issue their stock publicly to file audited financial statements with the Securities and Exchange Commission (SEC), a governmental agency. Companies engage outside auditors who are certified public accountants to examine their statements. The independent auditors decide whether the company's financial statements comply with GAAP and then issue an audit report. Exhibit 11-7 is the audit report on the financial statements of Best Buy Co., Inc.

The audit report is addressed to the stockholders and board of directors of the company. The auditing firm signs its name, in this case the Minneapolis office of **Ernst & Young LLP** (LLP is the abbreviation for limited liability partnership).

The audit report typically contains three paragraphs:

- The first paragraph identifies the audited statements.
- The second paragraph describes how the audit was performed, mentioning that generally accepted auditing standards are the benchmark for evaluating audit quality.
- The third paragraph states Ernst & Young's opinion that Best Buy's financial statements conform to GAAP and that people can rely on them for decision making. Best Buy's audit report contains a **clean opinion**, more properly called an *unqualified* opinion. Audit reports usually fall into one of four categories:

1. **Unqualified (clean)**. The statements are reliable.
2. **Qualified**. The statements are reliable, except for one or more items for which the opinion is said to be qualified.

Unqualified (clean) opinion
An audit opinion stating that the financial statements are reliable.

Qualified opinion
An audit opinion stating that the financial statements are reliable, except for one or more items for which the opinion is said to be qualified.

3. **Adverse**. The statements are unreliable.
4. **Disclaimer**. The auditor was unable to reach a professional opinion.

The independent audit adds credibility to the financial statements. It is no accident that financial reporting and auditing are more advanced in the United States than anywhere else in the world and that U.S. capital markets are the envy of the world.

Adverse opinion
An audit opinion stating that the financial statements are unreliable.

Disclaimer
An audit opinion stating that the auditor was unable to reach a professional opinion regarding the quality of the financial statements.

■ **EXHIBIT 11-7**

Excerpts from the Audit Report on the Financial Statements of Best Buy Co., Inc.

Auditor's Report
Independent Auditor's Report (Excerpts)

Shareholders and Board of Directors
Best Buy Co., Inc.

We have audited the accompanying consolidated balance sheets of Best Buy Co., and subsidiaries as of March 1, 2003, and March 2, 2002, and the related consolidated statements of earnings, changes in shareholders' equity, and cash flows for each of the three years in the period ended March 1, 2003. . . .

We conducted our audits in accordance with auditing standards generally accepted in the United States. . . . We believe that our audits provide a reasonable basis for our opinion.

In our opinion, the financial statements referred to above present fairly, in all material respects, the consolidated financial position of Best Buy Co., Inc. and subsidiaries at March 1, 2003, and March 2, 2002, and the consolidated results of their operations and their cash flows for each of the three years in the period ended March 1, 2003, in conformity with accounting principles generally accepted in the United States. . . .

Ernst & Young LLP

Minneapolis, Minnesota
April 1, 2003

MAKING MANAGERIAL DECISIONS

USING THE INCOME STATEMENT AND RELATED NOTES IN INVESTMENT ANALYSIS

Suppose you've completed your studies, taken a job, and been fortunate to save $10,000. Now you are ready to start investing. These guidelines provide a framework for using accounting information for investment analysis.

Decision	Factors to Consider		Decision Variable or Model
Which measure of profitability should be used for investment analysis?	Are you interested in accounting income? →	Income, including all revenues, expenses, gains, and losses? →	Net income (bottom line)
		Income that can be expected to repeat from year to year? →	Income from continuing operations
	Are you interested in cash flows? →		Cash flows from operating activities (Chapter 12)

Note: A conservative strategy may use both income and cash flows and compare the two sets of results.

Decision	Factors to Consider	Decision Variable or Model
What is the estimated value of the stock?	If you believe the company can earn the income (or cash flow) indefinitely →	$\text{Estimated value} = \frac{\text{Annual income}}{\text{Investment capitalization rate}}$
	If you believe the company can earn the income (or cash flow) for a finite number of years →	$\text{Estimated value} = \text{Annual income} \times \text{Present value of annuity (See Appendix C)}$
How does risk affect the value of the stock?	If the investment is high risk →	Increase the investment capitalization rate
	If the investment is low risk →	Decrease the investment capitalization rate

END-OF-CHAPTER Summary Problem

The following information was taken from the ledger of Kraftway Corporation:

Prior-period adjustment—credit to Retained Earnings	$ 5,000	Treasury stock, common (5,000 shares at cost)	$25,000
Gain on sale of plant assets	21,000	Selling expenses	78,000
Cost of goods sold	380,000	Common stock, no par, 45,000 shares issued	180,000
Income tax expense (saving):		Sales revenue	620,000
Continuing operations	32,000	Interest expense	30,000
Discontinued operations	8,000	Extraordinary gain	26,000
Extraordinary gain	10,000	Income from discontinued operations	20,000
Cumulative effect of change in inventory method	(4,000)	Loss due to lawsuit	11,000
Preferred stock, 8%, $100 par, 500 shares issued	50,000	General expenses	62,000
Dividends	16,000	Retained earnings, beginning, as originally reported	103,000
		Cumulative effect of change in inventory method (debit)	(10,000)

Required

Prepare a single-step income statement (with all revenues grouped together) and a statement of retained earnings for Kraftway Corporation for the current year ended December 31, 20XX. Include the earnings-per-share presentation and show computations. Assume no changes in the stock accounts during the year.

Answers

Kraftway Corporation
Income Statement
Year Ended December 31, 20XX

Revenue and gains:		
Sales revenue		$620,000
Gain on sale of plant assets		21,000
Total revenues and gains		641,000
Expenses and losses:		
Cost of goods sold	$380,000	
Selling expenses	78,000	
General expenses	62,000	
Interest expense	30,000	
Loss due to lawsuit	11,000	
Income tax expense	32,000	
Total expenses and losses		593,000
Income from continuing operatons		48,000
Discontinued operations, $20,000, less income tax, $8,000		12,000
Income before extraordinary item and cumulative effect of change in inventory method		60,000
Extraordinary gain; $26,000, less income tax, $10,000		16,000
Cumulative effect of change in inventory method, $10,000, less income tax saving, $4,000		(6,000)
Net Income		$ 70,000
Earnings per share:*		
Income from continuing operations [($48,000 – $4,000)/40,000 shares]		$1.10
Income from discontinued operations ($12,000/40,000 shares)		0.30
Income before extraordinary item and cumulative effect of change in inventory method [($60,000 – $4,000)/40,000 shares]		1.40
Extraordinary gain ($16,000/40,000 shares)		0.40
Cumulative effect of change in inventory method ($6,000/40,000 shares)		(0.15)
Net income [($70,000 – $4,000)/40,000 shares]		$1.65

*Computations:

$$\text{EPS} = \frac{\text{Income} - \text{Preferred dividends}}{\text{Common shares outstanding}}$$

Preferred dividends: $50,000 × 0.08 = $4.000

Common shares outstanding:

45,000 shares issued – 5,000 treasury shares = 40,000 shares outstanding

Kraftway Corporation
Statement of Retained Earnings
Year Ended December 31, 20XX

Retained earnings balance, beginning, as originally reported	$103,000
Prior-period adjustment—credit	5,000
Retained earnings balance, beginning, as adjusted	108,000
Net income for current year	70,000
	178,000
Dividends for current year	(16,000)
Retained earnings balance, ending	$162,000

Review The Income Statement

Chapter Review Quiz

1. The quality of earnings means:
   a. Net income is the best measure of the results of operations.
   b. Continuing operations and one-time transactions are of equal importance.
   c. Income from continuing operations is better than income from one-time transactions.
   d. Stockholders want the corporation to earn enough income to be able to pay its debts.

2. Which statement is true?
   a. Discontinued operations are a separate category on the income statement.
   b. Extraordinary items are a separate category on the income statement.
   c. Cumulative effect of accounting changes is a separate category on the income statement.
   d. All of the above are true.

3. Examine **Best Buy's** income statement on page 510. Suppose you capitalize Best Buy's income at 6%. How much are you willing to pay for a share of Best Buy stock?
   a. $32.17
   b. $5.17
   c. $165.00
   d. Some other amount

4. Return to Best Buy's income statement on page 510. Best Buy has no preferred stock outstanding. How many shares of common stock did Best Buy have outstanding during fiscal year 2003?
   a. 99 million
   b. 320 million
   c. 193 million
   d. 31 million

5. Why is it important for companies to report their accounting changes to the public?
   a. Without the reporting of accounting changes, investors could believe all the company's income came from continuing operations.
   b. Some accounting changes are more extraordinary than others.
   c. Most accounting changes increase net income, and investors need to know why the increase in net income occurred.
   d. Accounting changes affect dividends, and investors want dividends.

6. Other comprehensive income
   a. affects earnings per share.
   b. includes extraordinary gains and losses.
   c. has no effect on income tax.
   d. includes unrealized gains and losses on investments.

7. Ajax Party Rentals earned income before tax of $50,000, Taxable income was $40,000, and the income tax rate was 40%. Ajax recorded income tax with this journal entry:

a. Income Tax Payable	16,000	
Income Tax Expense		16,000
b. Income Tax Expense	20,000	
Income Tax Payable		20,000
c. Income Tax Expense	20,000	
Income Tax Payable		16,000
Deferred Tax Liability		4,000
d. Income Tax Payable	20,000	
Income Tax Expense		16,000
Deferred Tax Liability		4,000

8. Deferred Tax Liability is usually a

	Type of Account	*Reported on the*
a.	Long-term	Income statement
b.	Long-term	Balance statement
c.	Short-term	Income statement
d.	Short-term	Statement of stockholders' equity

9. The main purpose of the statement of stockholders' equity is to report
   a. financial position.
   b. results of operations.
   c. reasons for changes in the equity accounts.
   d. comprehensive income.

10. An audit report by independent accountants
    a. ensures that the financial statements are error-free.
    b. gives investors assurance that the company's stock is a safe investment.
    c. gives investors assurance that the company can pay its debts when they come due.
    d. None of the above. An audit report (fill in this blank).

Answers:

1. c
2. d
3. a ($1.93/0.06 = $32.17)
4. b ($622/$1.93 = 322; $99/$0.31 = 319)
5. a
6. d
7. c
8. b
9. c
10. d (. . . states whether the financial statements comply with GAAP)

Accounting Vocabulary

adverse opinion (p. 525)
clean opinion (p. 524)
comprehensive income (p. 518)
disclaimer (p. 525)
earnings per share (EPS) (p. 517)
extraordinary gains and losses (p. 515)
extraordinary items (p. 515)
investment capitalization rate (p. 514)
pretax accounting income (p. 520)
prior-period adjustment (p. 521)
qualified opinion (p. 524)
segment of the business (p. 515)
statement of stockholders' equity (p. 522)
taxable income (p. 520)
unqualified (clean) opinion (p. 524)

ASSESS YOUR PROGRESS

Check Points

Preparing a complex income statement (Obj. 1)

CP11-1 (p. 513) List the major parts of a complex corporate income statement for Goldberg Corporation for the year ended December 31, 20X8. Include all the major parts of the income statement, starting with net sales revenue and ending with net income (net loss). You may ignore dollar amounts and earnings per share.

Explaining the items on a complex income statement (Obj. 1)

writing assignment ■

CP11-2 (p. 513) Study the income statement of **Best Buy Co., Inc.** (page 510) and answer these questions about the company:

1. How much gross profit did Best Buy earn on the sale of its products—before deducting any operating expenses? How much was income from continuing operations? Net income?
2. What dollar amount of net income would most sophisticated investors use to predict Best Buy's net income during 20X4 and beyond? Name this item, give its amount, and state your reason.

Preparing a complex income statement (Obj. 1)

CP11-3 (p. 513) BA II Plus, Inc. reported the following items, listed in no particular order at December 31, 20X8 (in thousands):

Extraordinary gain	$ 5,000	Other gains (losses)	$ (2,000)
Cost of goods sold	71,000	Net sales revenue	182,000
Operating expenses	64,000	Gain on discontinued operations	15,000
Accounts receivable	19,000		

Income tax of 40% applies to all items.

Prepare BA II Plus's income statement for the year ended December 31, 20X8. Omit earnings per share.

Valuing a company's stock (Obj. 1)

CP11-4 (p. 514) For fiscal year 20X3, **Target Corporation** reported net sales of $46,781 million, net income of $1,841 million, and no significant discontinued operations, extraordinary items, or accounting changes.

Earnings per share was $2.02. At a capitalization rate of 6%, how much should one share of Target stock be worth? Compare your estimated stock price to Target's actual stock price as quoted in *The Wall Street Journal*, in your newspaper, or on the Internet. Based on your estimated market value, should you buy, hold, or sell Target stock?

Reporting earnings per share (Obj. 1)

CP11-5 (p. 517) Return to the BA II Plus data in CP11-3. BA II Plus had 10,000 shares of common stock outstanding during 20X8. BA II Plus declared and paid preferred dividends of $5,000 during 20X8.

Report BA II Plus's earnings per share on the income statement.

Interpreting earnings-per-share data (Obj. 1)

writing assignment ■

CP11-6 (p. 517) Raintree Corporation has preferred stock outstanding and issued additional common stock during the year.

1. Give the basic equation to compute earnings per share of common stock for net income.
2. List the income items for which Raintree must report earnings-per-share data.
3. What makes earnings per share so useful as a business statistic?

Reporting comprehensive income (Obj. 1)

CP11-7 (p. 518) Use the BA II Plus data in Check Point 11-3. In addition, BA II Plus had unrealized losses of $1,000 on investments and a $2,000 foreign-currency translation adjustment (a gain) during 20X8. Both amounts are net of tax. Start with BA II Plus's net income from CP11-3 and show how the company could report other comprehensive income on its 20X8 income statement.

Should BA II Plus report earnings per share for other comprehensive income? State why or why not.

Accounting for a corporation's income tax (Obj. 2)

CP11-8 (p. 521) Logic Growth, Inc. had income before income tax of $120,000 and taxable income of $90,000 for 20X5, the company's first year of operations. The income tax rate is 40%.

1. Make the entry to record Logic Growth's income taxes for 20X5.
2. Show what Logic Growth will report on its 20X5 income statement starting with income before income tax. Also show what Logic Growth will report for current and long-term liabilities on its December 31, 20X5, balance sheet.

Reporting a prior-period adjustment (Obj. 3)

CP11-9 (p. 521) Examine **NPR Corporation's** statement of retained earnings on page 521. Suppose instead that NPR had overstated 20X6 income tax expense by $15,000. Show how NPR would report this prior-period adjustment on the statement of retained earnings for 20X7.

Using the statement of stockholders' equity (Obj. 4)

CP11-10 (p. 524) Use the statement of stockholders' equity in Exhibit 11-4 (page 522) to answer the following questions about **Allied Electronics Corporation**:

1. How much cash did the issuance of common stock bring in during 20X5?
2. What was the effect of the stock dividends on Allied's retained earnings? on total paid-in capital? on total stockholders' equity? on total assets?
3. What was the cost of the treasury stock that Allied purchased during 20X5? What was Allied's cost of the treasury stock that Allied sold during the year? For how much did Allied sell the treasury stock during 20X5?

Exercises

PH Grade Assist

Most of the even-numbered exercises can be found within Prentice Hall Grade Assist (PHGA), an online homework and practice environment. Your instructor may ask you to complete these exercises using PHGA.

Preparing and using a complex income statement (Obj. 1)

E11-1 Quest Communications, Inc., reported a number of special items on its income statement. The following data, listed in no particular order, came from Quest's financial statements (amounts in millions):

Net sales	$13,800	Income tax expense (saving):	
Foreign-currency translation adjustment	360	Continuing operations	$290
Extraordinary loss	13	Discontinued operations	50
Income from discontinued operations	270	Extraordinary loss	(3)
Dividends declared and paid	680	Unrealized gain on available-for-sale investments	40
Total operating expenses	12,250	Short-term investments	35

Required

Show how the Quest Communications income statement for 20X6 should appear. Omit earnings per share.

Preparing and using a complex income statement (Obj. 1)

■ **spreadsheet**

E11-2 The Culinary Institute, Inc., accounting records include the following for 20X8 (in thousands):

Extraordinary loss	$ 1,300
Sales revenue	104,000
Total operating expenses	97,900
Other revenues	1,800
Income tax saving—extraordinary loss	500
Income tax expense—income from operations	3,100

Required

1. Prepare The Culinary Institute's single-step income statement for the year ended December 31, 20X8, including EPS. The Institute had 1,600 thousand shares of common stock and no preferred stock outstanding during the year.
2. Assume investors capitalize The Institute's earnings at 8%. Estimate the price of one share of the company's stock.

Using an actual income statement (Obj. 1)

writing assignment ■

E11-3 **Verizon Communication's Inc.**, the telecommunication company, reported the following income statement (adapted) for the year ended December 31, 2003.

	Millions
Operating revenues	$67,752
Operating expenses	60,258
Operating income	7,494
Other revenue (expense), net	(3,985)
Income before discontinued operations and cumulative effect of accounting change	3,509
Discontinued operations, net of tax	(935)
Cumulative effect of accounting change, net of tax	503
Net income	$ 3,077

Required

1. Were Verizon's discontinued operations and cumulative effect of the accounting change more like an expense or a revenue? How can you tell?
2. Should the discontinued operations and the cumulative effect of Verizon's accounting change be included in or excluded from net income? State your reason.
3. Suppose your are working as a financial analyst and your job is to predict Verizon's net income for 2004 and beyond. Which item from the income statement will you use for your prediction? Identify its amount. Why will you use this item?

Using income data for investment analysis (Obj. 1)

E11-4 During 20X3, **PepsiCo, Inc.** had sales of $27.0 billion, operating profit of $4.8 billion, and net income of $3.6 billion. Earnings per share (EPS) were $2.07. On June 1, 20X4, the market price of a share of PepsiCo's common stock closed at $54.36 on the New York Stock Exchange.

What investment capitalization rate did investors appear to be using to determine the value of one share of PepsiCo stock? The formula for the value of one share of stock uses EPS in the calculation. Does this capitalization rate suggest high risk or low risk? What about PepsiCo's line of business is consistent with your evaluation of the company's risk?

Computing earnings per share (Obj. 1)

E11-5 First Savings Bank provides low-cost mortgages. During 20X4, the bank earned net income of $5,800 million. First Savings Bank's balance sheet reports the following:

	Millions
Preferred stock, $50 stated value, 6%, 40 million shares issued	$2,000
Common stock, $0.50 par, 1,200 million shares issued	600
Treasury stock, common, 130 million shares at cost	5,500

Required

Compute First Savings Bank's EPS for 20X4.

Computing and using earnings per share (Obj. 1)

E11-6 Topmark Corporation operates numerous businesses, including motel, auto rental, and real estate companies. Year 20X6 was interesting for Topmark, which reported the following on its income statement (in millions):

Net revenues	$3,930
Total expenses and other	3,354
Income from continuing operations	576
Discontinued operations, net of tax	(84)
Income before extraordinary item and cumulative effect of accounting change, net of tax	492
Extraordinary gain, net of tax	8
Net income	$ 500

During 20X6, Topmark had the following (in millions, except for par value per share):

Common stock, $0.01 par value, 917 shares issued	$ 9
Treasury stock, 197 shares at cost	(3,568)

Required

Show how Topmark should report earnings per share for 20X6.

Accounting for income tax by a corporation (Obj. 2)

E11-7 For 20X6, its first year of operations, Financial Services Corporation (FSC) earned pretax accounting income (on the income statement) of $400,000. Taxable income (on the tax return filed with the Internal Revenue Service) is $350,000. The income tax rate is 40%. Record FSC's income tax for the year. Show what FSC will report on its 20X6 income statement and balance sheet for this situation. Start the income statement with income before tax.

Accounting for income tax by a corporation (Obj. 2)

E11-8 During 20X5, Ditto Inc.'s income statement reported income of $850,000 before tax. The company's income tax return filed with the IRS reported taxable income of only $810,000. During 20X5, Ditto was subject to an income tax rate of 40%.

Required

1. Journalize Ditto's income taxes for 20X5.
2. How much income tax did Ditto have to pay currently for the year 20X5?
3. At the beginning of 20X5, Ditto's balance of Deferred Tax Liability was $40,000. How much Deferred Tax Liability did Ditto report on its balance sheet at December 31, 20X5?

Reporting a prior-period adjustment on the statement of retained earnings (Obj. 3)

E11-9 Linen Depot, Inc., a household products chain, reported a prior-period adjustment in 20X5. An accounting error caused net income of prior years to be overstated by $13 million. Retained earnings at December 31, 20X4, as previously reported, stood at $344 million. Net income for 20X5 was $92 million, and dividends were $61 million.

■ **spreadsheet**

Required

Prepare the company's statement of retained earnings for the year ended December 31, 20X5. How does the prior-period adjustment affect Linen Depot's net income for 20X5?

Preparing a statement of stockholders' equity (Obj. 3)

E11-10 At December 31, 20X4, Infinity Corporation reported stockholders' equity as follows:

Common stock, $1 par, 500,000 shares authorized, 320,000 shares issued	$ 320,000
Additional paid-in capital	600,000
Retained earnings	680,000
Treasury stock, 20,000 shares at cost	(80,000)
	$1,520,000

During 20X5, Infinity completed these transactions (listed in chronological order):

a. Declared and issued a 1% stock dividend on the outstanding stock. At the time, Infinity's stock was quoted at a market price of $40 per share.
b. Sold 1,000 shares of treasury stock for $40 per share (cost was $40).
c. Issued 20,000 shares of common stock at the price of $40 per share.
d. Net income for the year, $340,000.
e. Declared cash dividends of $180,000.

Required

Prepare Infinity Corporation's statement of stockholders' equity for 20X5, using the format of Exhibit 11-4 (page 522) as a model. Then use the statement to answer the following questions:

1. Did Infinity's retained earnings increase or decrease during 20X5? What caused retained earnings to change during the year?
2. How did the stock dividend affect total stockholders' equity? How did it affect total assets? Total liabilities?
3. How would creditors feel about Infinity's sale of treasury stock? About Infinity's issuance of common stock? Why?

Using a company's statement of stockholders' equity (Obj. 3)

E11-11 Advantage Travel Associates reported the following items on its statement of shareholders' equity for the year ended December 31, 20X7 (in thousands):

	$1 Par Common Stock	Capital in Excess of Par Value	Retained Earnings	Accumulated Other Comprehensive Income	Total Shareholders' Equity
Balance, Dec. 31, 20X6 ...	$380	$1,590	$3,500	$9	$5,479
Net earnings			1,020		
Unrealized gain on investments				1	
Issuance of stock	5	215			
Cash dividends			(60)		
Balance, Dec. 31, 20X7 ...					

Required

1. Determine the December 31, 20X7, balances in Advantage's shareholders' equity accounts and total shareholders' equity on this date.
2. Advantage's total liabilities on December 31, 20X7 are $7,000 thousand. What is Advantage's debt ratio on this date?
3. Was there a profit or a loss for the year ended December 31, 20X7? How can you tell?
4. At what price per share did Advantage issue common stock during 20X7?
5. What suggests that all Advantage Travel's operations are located in the United States?

Identifying responsibility and standards for the financial statements (Obj. 4)

writing assignment ■

E11-12 The annual report of **The Gap, Inc.**, included the following reports:

The Gap, Inc.
Management's Report on Financial Information (Excerpts)

Management is responsible for the . . . financial information presented in the Annual Report. The financial statements have been prepared in accordance with accounting principles generally accepted in the United States of America. . . .

In fulfilling its responsibility for the reliability of financial information, Management has established and maintains accounting systems . . . supported by internal accounting controls. . . . The Financial Statements of the Company . . . have been audited by Deloitte & Touche LLP, independent auditors, whose report appears below.

Independent Auditors' Report (Excerpts)
To the Board of Directors and Shareholders of The Gap, Inc.:

We have audited the accompanying consolidated balance sheets of The Gap, Inc. and subsidiaries as of January 31, 2004, and February 1, 2003, and the related consolidated statements of operations, shareholders' equity and cash flows for each of the three fiscal years in the period ended January 31, 2004.

We conducted our audits in accordance with auditing standards generally accepted in the United States of America.

In our opinion, such consolidated financial statements present fairly, in all material respects, the financial position of The Gap, Inc. and subsidiaries as of January 31, 2004, and February 1, 2003, and the results of their operations and their cash flows for each of the three fiscal years in the period ended January 31, 2004, in conformity with accounting principles generally accepted in the United States of America.

Deloitte & Touche LLP
San Francisco, California
March 30, 2004

1. Who is responsible for Gap's financial statements? Is it Gap's management, or is it the auditor?
2. By what accounting standard are the financial statements prepared? Give the abbreviation of this standard.
3. Identify one concrete action that Gap management takes to fulfill its responsibility for the reliability of the company's financial information.
4. Which entity gave an outside, independent opinion on the Gap financial statement? Where was this entity located, and when did it release its opinion to the public?
5. Exactly what did the audit cover? Give names and dates.
6. By what standard did the auditor conduct the audit?
7. By what standard did the auditor evaluate Gap's financial statements?
8. What was the auditor's opinion of Gap's financial statements?

Practice Quiz

Test your understanding of the corporate income statement and the statement of stockholders equity by answering the following questions. Select the best choice from among the possible answers given.

PQ11-1 What is the best source of income for a corporation?

a. Prior-period adjustments
b. Discontinued operation
c. Extraordinary items
d. None of the above (fill in this blank).

PQ11-2 Use **Allied Electronics** income statement in Exhibit 11-1, page 513. How much net income would most investment analysts predict for Allied to earn in 20X6?

a. $90,000
b. $54,000
c. $75,000
d. $69,000

PQ11-3 Suppose you are evaluating Allied Electronics stock (page 513) as an investment. You require a 10% rate of return on investments, so you capitalize Allied's earnings at 10%. How much are you willing to pay for 1 share of Allied stock?

a. $27.00
b. $37.50
c. $34.50
d. Some other amount ____

PQ11-4 General Dollar Corporation had the following extraordinary items:

Flood loss	$ 90,000
Gain on lawsuit	110,000

Net income before extraordinary items totals $400,000, and the income tax rate is 40%. General Dollar's net income is

a. $168,00
b. $252,000
c. $380,000
d. $420,000

PQ11-5 General Dollar Corporation in question 5 has 10,000 shares of 5%, $100 par preferred stock and 100,000 shares of common stock outstanding. Earnings per share for net income is

a. $2.02
b. $2.52
c. $3.70
d. $4.20

PQ11-6 Earnings per share is *not* reported for

a. comprehensive income.
b. continuing operations.
c. discontinued operations.
d. extraordinary items.

PQ11-7 Why are pro forma earnings so risky? They are

a. backed up by GAAP.
b. usually incorrect.
c. not audited.
d. irrelevant to investment decisions.

PQ11-8 Examine **Best Buy's** income statement on page 510. Best Buy's income tax rate is closest to

a. 37%
b. 38%
c. 39%
d. 40%

PQ11-9 BILO Corporation has income before income tax of $100,000 and taxable income of $80,000. The income tax rate is 40%. BILO's income statement will report net income of

a. $32,000
b. $40,000
c. $48,000
d. $60,000

PQ11-10 BILO Corporation in the preceding question must immediately pay income tax of

a. $0
b. $8,000
c. $32,000
d. $40,000

PQ11-11 Use the BILO Corporation data in question 9. At the end of its first year of operations, BILO's deferred tax liability is

a. $0
b. $8,000
c. $32,000
d. $40,000

PQ11-12 Which of the following items is most closely related to prior-period adjustments?

a. Retained earnings
b. Earnings per share
c. Accounting changes
d. Preferred stock dividends

PQ11-13 Examine the statement of stockholders' equity of Allied Electronics Corporation in Exhibit 11-4, page 522. What was the market value of the stock that Allied gave its stockholders in the stock dividend?

a. $0
b. $8,000
c. $26,000
d. $34,000

PQ11-14 Which statement is false?

a. Management prepares the financial statements.
b. Independent auditors certify the financial statements.
c. GAAP governs the form and content of the financial statements.
d. None of the above. All the statements are true.

Problems
(Group A)

Most of these A problems can be found within Prentice Hall Grade Assist (PHGA), an online homework and practice environment. Your instructor may ask you to complete these problems using PHGA.

Preparing a complex income statement (Obj. 1)

P11-1A The following information was taken from the records of Otis Systems, Inc., at September 30, 20X3. Otis manufactures electronic control devices for elevators.

Treasury stock, common (1,000 shares at cost)	$ 11,000	Dividends	$ 15,000
Prior-period adjustment—debit to Retained Earnings	6,000	Interest revenue	4,000
Paid-in capital from treasury stock transactions	7,000	Extraordinary loss	30,000
Interest expense	11,000	Income from discontinued operations	5,000
Cost of goods sold	424,000	Loss on insurance settlement	12,000
Cumulative effect of change in depreciation method (debit)	(18,000)	General expenses	113,000
Loss on sale of plant assets	8,000	Preferred stock—5%, $40 par, 10,000 shares authorized, 5,000 shares issued	200,000
Income tax expense (saving):		Paid-in capital in excess of par—common	20,000
Continuing operations	72,000	Retained earnings, beginning, as originally reported	88,000
Discontinued operations	2,000	Selling expenses	136,000
Extraordinary loss	(12,000)	Common stock, $10 par, 25,000 shares authorized and issued	250,000
Cumulative effect of change in depreciation method	(7,000)		
Sales revenue	833,000		

Required

1. Prepare Otis Systems' single-step income statement, which lists all revenues together and all expenses together, for the fiscal year ended September 30, 20X3. Include earnings-per-share data.
2. Evaluate income for the year ended September 30, 20X3, in terms of the outlook for 20X4; 20X3 was a typical year, and Otis's top managers hoped to earn income from continuing operations equal to 10% of sales.

Preparing a statement of retained earnings (Obj. 3)

P11-2A Use the data in Problem 11-1A to prepare Otis Systems, Inc.'s statement of retained earnings for the year ended September 30, 20X3.

Using income data to make an investment decision (Obj. 1)

P11-3A Otis systems in Problem 11-1A holds significant promise for carving a niche in the electronic control device industry, and a group of Swiss investors is considering purchasing the company. Otis's common stock is currently selling for $33.75 per share.

A *Business Today* magazine story predicts that Otis's income is bound to grow. It appears that the company can earn at least its current level of income for the indefinite future. Based on this information, the investors think an appropriate investment capitalization rate for estimating the value of Otis common stock is 8%. Any capitalization rate below 8% would overvalue the stock. How much will this belief lead the investors to offer for Otis Systems? Will the existing stockholders of Otis be likely to accept this offer? Explain your answers.

Computing earnings per share and estimating the price of a stock (Obj. 1)

P11-4A The capital structure of Wells Cargo Trailer Corporation, at December 31, 20X5, included 20,000 shares of $1.25 preferred stock and 44,000 shares of common stock. During 20X6, Wells Cargo issued stock and ended the year with 58,000 shares. The average number of common shares outstanding for the year was 51,000. Income from continuing operations during 20X6 was $81,100. The company discontinued a segment of the business at a gain of $6,630, and an extraordinary item generated a gain of $16,000.

Required

1. Compute Wells Cargo's earnings per share. Start with income from continuing operations. Income and loss amounts are net of income tax.
2. Analysts believe Wells Cargo can earn its current level of income for the indefinite future. Estimate the market price of a share of Wells Cargo common stock at investment capitalization rates of 8%, 10%, and 12%. The formula for estimating the value of one share of stock uses earnings per share. Which estimate presumes an investment in Wells Cargo stock is the most risky? How can you tell?

Preparing a corrected income statement, including comprehensive income (Obj. 1)

P11-5A Colin Thatcher, accountant for British Telecom. Inc., was injured in a motorcycle accident. Another employee prepared the accompanying income statement for the year ended December 31, 20X8.

The individual *amounts* listed on the income statement are correct. However, some *accounts* are reported incorrectly, and one does not belong on the income statement at all. Also, income tax (40%) has not been applied to all appropriate figures. British Telecom issued 52,000 shares of common stock in 20X1 and held 2,000 shares as treasury stock during 20X8.

British Telecom, Inc. Income Statement 20X8		
Revenue and gains:		
Sales		£362,000
Unrealized gain on available-for-sale investments		10,000
Paid-in capital in excess of par—common		80,000
Total revenues and gains		452,000
Expenses and losses:		
Cost of goods sold	£103,000	
Selling expenses	56,000	
General expenses	61,000	
Sales returns	11,000	
Dividends paid	7,000	
Sales discounts	6,000	
Income tax expense	50,000	
Total expenses and losses		294,000
Income from operations		158,000
Other gains and losses:		
Extraordinary gain	£ 20,000	
Loss on discontinued operations	(3,000)	
Total other gains, net		17,000
Net income		£175,000
Earnings per share		£3.50

Required

Prepare a corrected statement of income (single-step, which lists all revenues together and all expenses together), including comprehensive income, for 20X8. Include earnings per share.

Accounting for a corporation's income tax (Obj. 2)

P11-6A The accounting (not the income tax) records of Yoeman Corporation provide the following comparative income statement for 20X4 and 20X5, respectively.

	20X4	20X5
Total revenue	$900,000	$990,000
Expenses:		
Cost of goods sold	$430,000	$460,000
Operating expenses	270,000	280,000
Total expenses before tax	700,000	740,000
Pretax accounting income	$200,000	$250,000

Total revenue of 20X5 includes $15,000 for cash that was received late in 20X4. This revenue is included in 20X5 total revenue because it was earned in 20X5. However, revenue collected in advance is included in the taxable income of the year when the cash is received. In calculating taxable income on the tax return, this revenue belongs in 20X4. Also, the operating expenses of each year include depreciation of $50,000 computed under the straight-line method. In calculating taxable income on the tax return, Yoeman uses the Modified Accelerated Cost Recovery System (MACRS). MACRS depreciation was $80,000 for 20X4 and $20,000 for 20X5. The income tax rate is 35%.

Required

1. Compute Yoeman Corporation's taxable income for 20X4.
2. Journalize the corporation's income taxes for 20X4.
3. Prepare the corporation's income statement for 20X4.

Using a statement of stockholders' equity (Obj. 3)

P11-7A Transpacific Communication, Inc., reported the following statement of stockholders' equity for the year ended October 31, 20X7.

Transpacific Communication, Inc.
Statement of Stockholders' Equity
Year Ended October 31, 20X7

(In millions)	Common Stock	Additional Paid-in Capital	Retained Earnings	Treasury Stock	Total
Balance, Oct. 31, 20X6 . . .	$427	$1,622	$904	$(117)	$2,836
Net income			336		336
Cash dividends			(194)		(194)
Issuance of stock (10,000,000 shares)	13	36			49
Stock dividend	22	61	(83)		—
Sale of treasury stock		9		19	28
Balance, Oct. 31, 20X7 . . .	$462	$1,728	$963	$ (98)	$3,055

Required

Answer these questions about Transpacific's stockholders' equity transactions:

1. The income tax rate is 40%. How much income before income tax did Transpacific report on the income statement?
2. What is the par value of the company's common stock?
3. At what price per share did Transpacific issue its common stock during the year?
4. What was the cost of treasury stock sold during the year? What was the selling price of the treasury stock sold? What was the increase in total stockholders' equity?
5. Transpacific's statement lists the stock transactions in the order they occurred. What was the percentage of the stock dividend? Round to the nearest percentage.

(Group B)

PH Grade Assist

Some of these B problems can be found within Prentice Hall Grade Assist (PHGA), an online homework and practice environment. Your instructor may ask you to complete these problems using PHGA.

Preparing a complex income statement (Obj. 1)

P11-1B The following information was taken from the records of Motors Unlimited, which specializes in engines for antique sports cars, at December 31, 20X3.

Dividends on common stock . . .	$31,000	Prior-period adjustment— debit to Retained Earnings . . .	$ 4,000
Interest expense	23,000	Income tax expense (saving):	
Gain on settlement of lawsuit . . .	8,000	Continuing operations	28,000
Paid-in capital from retirement of preferred stock	16,000	Income from discontinued operations	2,000
Dividend revenue	11,000	Extraordinary gain	10,800
Treasury stock, common (2,000 shares at cost)	28,000	Cumulative effect of change in depreciation method	3,000
General expenses	71,000		

(continued)

Sales revenue	$567,000	Loss on sale of plant assets	$ 10,000
Retained earnings, beginning, as originally reported	63,000	Income from discontinued operations	7,000
Selling expenses	87,000	Dividends on preferred stock	?
Common stock, no par, 22,000 shares authorized and issued	350,000	Preferred stock, 6%, $25 par, 20,000 shares authorized, 4,000 shares issued	100,000
Extraordinary gain	27,000	Cumulative effect of change in depreciation method (credit)	7,600
		Cost of goods sold	319,000

Required

1. Prepare Motors Unlimited's single-step income statement, which lists all revenues together and all expenses together, for the fiscal year ended December 31, 20X3. Include earnings-per-share data.
2. Evaluate income for the year ended December 31, 20X3, in terms of the outlook for 20X4. 20X3 was a typical year, and Motors Unlimited top managers hoped to earn income from continuing operations equal to 10% of sales.

Preparing a statement of retained earnings (Obj. 3)

P11-2B Use the data in Problem 11-1B to prepare the Motors Unlimited statement of retained earnings for the year ended December 31, 20X3.

Using income data to make an investment decision (Obj. 1)

P11-3B Motors Unlimited in Problem 11-1B holds significant promise for carving a niche in the antique auto parts industry and a group of Canadian investors is considering purchasing the company. Motors Unlimited's stock is currently selling for $42 per share.

A *Business Today* magazine story predicted the company's income is bound to grow. It appears that the company can earn at least its current level of income for the indefinite future. Based on this information, the investors think that an appropriate investment capitalization rate for estimating the value of Motors Unlimited's common stock is 6%. Any capitalization rate below 6% would overvalue the stock. How much will this belief lead the investors to offer for Motors Unlimited? Will the existing stockholders of Motors Unlimited be likely to accept this offer? Explain your answers.

Computing earnings per share and estimating the price of a stock (Obj. 1)

P11-4B Wall Street Workout, Inc. (WSWO) specializes in turning around underperforming companies. WSWO's capital structure at December 31, 20X5 included 5,000 shares of $2.50 preferred stock and 120,000 shares of common stock. During 20X6, WSWO issued stock and ended the year with 127,000 shares of common stock outstanding. Average common shares outstanding during 20X6 were 123,500. Income from continuing operations during 20X6 was $371,885. The company discontinued a segment of the business at a gain of $69,160, and an extraordinary item generated a loss of $49,510.

Required

1. Compute WSWO's earnings per share. Start with income from continuing operations. Income and loss amounts are net of income tax.
2. Analysts believe WSWO can earn its current level of income for the indefinite future. Estimate the market price of a share of WSWO common stock at investment capitalization rates of 5%, 7%, and 9%. The formula for estimating the value of one share of stock uses earnings per share. Which estimate presumes an investment in WSWO is the most risky? How can you tell?

Preparing a corrected income statement, including comprehensive income (Obj. 1)

P11-5B Blake Willis, accountant for Willis Jeep Sales, Inc. was injured in a skiing accident. Another employee prepared the following income statement for the fiscal year ended June 30, 20X4:

Willis Jeep Sales, Inc. Income Statement June 30, 20X4		
Revenue and gains:		
Sales		$733,000
Paid-in capital in excess of par—common		100,000
Total revenues and gains		833,000
Expenses and losses:		
Cost of goods sold	$383,000	
Selling expenses	103,000	
General expenses	74,000	
Sales returns	22,000	
Unrealized loss on available-for-sale investments	4,000	
Dividends paid	15,000	
Sales discounts	10,000	
Income tax expense	56,400	
Total expenses and losses		667,400
Income from operations		165,600
Other gains and losses:		
Extraordinary loss	$(30,000)	
Loss on discontinued operations	(15,000)	
Total other gains (losses)		(45,000)
Net income		$120,600
Earnings per share		$6.03

The individual *amounts* listed on the income statement are correct. However, some *accounts* are reported incorrectly, and some do not belong on the income statement at all. Also, income tax (40%) has not been applied to all appropriate figures. Willis issued 24,000 shares of common stock in 20X1 and held 4,000 shares as treasury stock during the fiscal year 20X4.

Required

Prepare a corrected statement of income (single-step, which lists all revenues together and all expenses together), including comprehensive income, for fiscal year 20X4; include earnings per share.

Accounting for a corporation's income tax (Obj. 2)

P11-6B The accounting (not the income tax) records of British Wire Wheels, Inc. provide the comparative income statement for 20X5 and 20X6, respectively:

	20X5	20X6
Total revenue	$600,000	$720,000
Expenses:		
Cost of goods sold	$290,000	$310,000
Operating expenses	180,000	190,000
Total expenses before tax	470,000	500,000
Pretax accounting income	$130,000	$220,000

Total revenue in 20X6 includes rent of $10,000 for cash that was received late in 20X5. This rent is included in 20X6 total revenue because the rent was earned in 20X6. However, rent revenue that is collected in advance is included in taxable income when the cash is received. In calculating taxable income on the tax return, this rent revenue belongs in 20X5.

In addition, operating expenses for each year include depreciation of $40,000 computed under the straight-line method. In calculating taxable income on the tax return, British Wire Wheels uses the Modified Accelerated Cost Recovery System (MACRS). MACRS depreciation was $60,000 for 20X5 and $20,000 for 20X6. The income tax rate is 35%.

Required

1. Compute British Wire Wheels taxable income for 20X5.
2. Journalize the corporation's income taxes for 20X5.
3. Prepare the corporation's income statement for 20X5.

Using a statement of stockholders' equity (Obj. 3)

P11-7B Coopers, Inc., an English company, reported the following statement of stockholders' equity for the year ended June 30, 20X4:

Coopers, Inc.
Statement of Stockholders' Equity
Year Ended June 30, 20X4

(In millions)	Common Stock	Additional Paid-in Capital	Retained Earnings	Treasury Stock	Total
Balance, June 30, 20X3	£173	£2,118	£1,702	£(18)	£3,975
Net income			520		520
Cash dividends			(117)		(117)
Issuance of stock (5,000,000 shares)	7	46			53
Stock dividend	18	272	(290)		—
Sale of treasury stock		22		11	33
Balance, June 30, 20X4	£198	£2,458	£1,815	£ (7)	£4,464

Required

Answer these questions about Coopers' stockholders' equity transactions.

1. The income tax rate is 35%. How much income before income tax did Coopers report on the income statement?
2. What is the par value of the company's common stock?
3. At what price per share did Coopers issue its common stock during the year?
4. What was the cost of treasury stock sold during the year? What was the selling price of the treasury stock sold? What was the increase in total stockholders' equity?
5. Coopers' statement of stockholders' equity lists the stock transactions in the order in which they occurred. What was the percentage of the stock dividend? Round to the nearest percentage.

Apply Your Knowledge

Decision Cases

Evaluating the components of income (Obj. 1)

Case 1. Magnetic Imaging, Inc., is having its initial public offering (IPO) of company stock. To create public interest in its stock, Magnetic's chief financial officer has blitzed the media with press releases. One, in particular, caught your eye. On November 19, Magnetic announced pro forma earnings per share (EPS) of $3.15, up 20% from last year's EPS of $2.63. A 20% increase in EPS is very good.

Before deciding to buy Magnetic Imaging stock, you investigated further and found that the company omitted several items from the determination of pro forma EPS, as follows:

- Unrealized loss on available-for-sale investments, $0.05 per share
- Gain on sale of building, $0.05 per share

- Cumulative effect of change in method of recognizing service revenue, increase in retained earnings $1.10 per share
- Restructuring expenses, $0.19 per share
- Loss on settlement of lawsuit begun 5 years ago, $0.12 per share
- Lost income due to employee labor strike, $0.14 per share
- Income from discontinued operations, $0.07 per share

Wondering how to treat these "special items," you called your stockbroker at **Merrill Lynch**. She thinks that these items are nonrecurring and outside Magnetic's core operations. Furthermore, she suggests that you ignore the items and consider Magnetic's earnings of $3.15 per share to be a good estimate of long-term profitability.

Required

What EPS number will you use to predict Magnetic Imaging's future profits? Show your work, and explain your reasoning for each item.

Using the financial statement in investment analysis (Obj. 1)

writing assignment ■

Case 2. Clayton Homes, Inc. manufactures and sells houses across the southern part of the United States. Clayton's annual report includes Note 1—Summary of Significant Accounting Policies as follows:

> **Income Recognition**
>
> [S]ales are recognized when cash payment is received or, in the case of credit sales, which represent the majority of . . . sales, when a down payment is received and the customer enters into an installment sales contract. Most of these installment sales contracts . . . are normally [collectible] over 36 to 180 months. . . .
>
> [Revenue] from . . . insurance policies [sold to customers] are recognized as income over the terms of the contracts. [E]xpenses are matched to recognize profits over the life of the contracts.

Magnuson Home Builders, Inc., a competitor of Clayton, includes the following note in its Summary of Significant Accounting Policies:

> **Accounting Policies for Revenues**
>
> Sales are recognized when cash payment is received or, in the case of credit sales, which represent the majority of . . . sales, when the customer enters into an installment sales contract. Customer down payments on credit sales are rare. Most of these installment sales contracts are normally [collectible] over 36 to 180 months. . . . Revenue from insurance policies sold to customers are recognized when the customer signs an insurance contract. Expenses are recognized over the life of the insurance contracts.

Suppose you have decided to invest in the stock of a home builder and you've narrowed your choices to Clayton and Magnuson. Which company's earnings are of higher quality? Why? Will their accounting policies affect your investment decision? If so, how? Mention specific accounts in the financial statements that will differ between the two companies.

Ethical Issue

writing assignment ■

The income statement of **General Cinema Corporation** reported the following results of operations:

Earnings before income taxes, extraordinary gain, and cumulative effect of accounting change	$187,046
Income tax expense	72,947
Earnings before extraordinary gain and cumulative effect of accounting change	114,099
Extraordinary gain, net of income tax	419,557
Cumulative effect of change in accounting, net of income tax	(39,196)
Net earnings	$494,460

Suppose General Cinema's management had reported the company's results of operations in this manner:

Earnings before income taxes	$847,111
Income tax expense	352,651
Net earnings	$494,460

Required

1. Does it really matter how a company reports its operating results? Why? Who could be helped by management's action? Who could be hurt?
2. Suppose General Cinema's management decides to report its operating results in the second manner. Evaluate the ethics of this decision.

Focus on Financials: ■ YUM! Brands

Analyzing income and investments (Obj. 1)

Refer to the **YUM! Brands, Inc.** financial statements in Appendix A at the end of this book.

1. YUM's net income includes only one "special" item. Identify the special item and its amount.
2. How much income from continuing operations did YUM earn in 2003? How can you be certain of your answer?
3. Take the role of an investor, and suppose you are determining the price to pay for a share of YUM stock. Assume you are considering three investment capitalization rates that depend on the risk of an investment in YUM: 6%, 9%, and 12%. Compute your estimated value of a share of YUM stock using each of the three capitalization rates. Which estimated value would you base your investment strategy on if you rate YUM risky? Which estimated value would you use if you consider YUM a safe investment? Use basic earnings per share for 2003.
4. Go to YUM! Brands Web site and compare your computed estimates to YUM's actual stock price. Which of your prices is most realistic?

Focus on Analysis: ■ Pier 1 Imports

Evaluating the quality of earnings, valuing investments, and analyzing stock outstanding (Obj. 1, 3)

This case is based on the **Pier 1 Imports** financial statements in Appendix B at the end of this book.

1. What is your evaluation of the quality of Pier 1's earnings? State how you formed your opinion.
2. At the end of 2004, how much would you be willing to pay for one share of Pier 1 stock if you rate the investment as high risk? as low risk? Use even-numbered investment capitalization rates in the range of 6%–12% for your analysis, and use basic earnings per share.
3. During 2004, Pier 1's average number of shares of common stock outstanding changed from the preceding year. But the balance sheet and the statement of shareholders' equity report the same amount for common stock at the end of each year. What event during 2004 altered the number of Pier 1 shares outstanding? Did this event increase or decrease the number of shares outstanding? Why didn't this event affect the Common Stock account as reported on the balance sheet?

Group Project

Select a company and research its business. Search the business press for articles about this company. Obtain its annual report by requesting it directly from the company or from the company's Web site or from *Moody's Industrial Manual* (the exercise will be most meaningful if you obtain an actual copy and do not have to use *Moody's*).

Required

1. Based on your group's analysis, come to class prepared to instruct the class on six interesting facts about the company that can be found in its financial statements and the related notes. Your group can mention only the obvious, such as net sales or total revenue, net income, total assets, total liabilities, total stockholders' equity, and dividends, in conjunction with other terms. Once you use an obvious item, you may not use that item again.
2. The group should write a paper discussing the facts that it has uncovered. Limit the paper to two double-spaced word-processed pages.

spotlight

EBAY OUTLINES GLOBAL BUSINESS STRATEGY

eBay Inc.
Consolidated Statement of Cash Flows (Adapted; in millions)
Year Ended December 31, 2003

Cash Flows from Operating Activities	
Net income	$ 442
Adjustments to reconcile net income to net cash provided by operating activities:	
Depreciation and amortization	159
Changes in assets and liabilities, net of acquired businesses	
Accounts receivable	(153)
Other current assets	(4)
Accounts payable	17
Accrued expenses and other liabilities	86
Unearned revenue	9
Income taxes payable	12
Other	306
Net cash provided by operating activities	874
Cash Flows from Investing Activities	
Purchases of property and equipment	(365)
Purchases of investments	(2,035)
Sales of investments	1,297
Purchases of other assets	(217)
Net cash used in investing activities	(1,320)
Cash Flows from Financing Activities	
Proceeds from issuance of common stock, net	701
Payments on long-term debt	(12)
Net cash provided by financing activities	689
Effect of exchange rate changes on cash and cash equivalents	29
Net increase in cash and cash equivalents	272
Cash and cash equivalents at beginning of year	1,110
Cash and cash equivalents at end of year	$1,382

San Jose, Calif.—eBay Inc. (www.ebay.com), the world's online marketplace, . . . outlined its strategy for growth through 2005. eBay executives highlighted key areas of growth, both domestically and abroad. "The depth, breadth and potential of our business gives us great confidence in the future," said Meg Whitman, president and CEO of eBay. "The eBay marketplace is thriving across . . . the services we offer our community."

The Statement of Cash Flows

12

LEARNING OBJECTIVES

1 **Identify** the purposes of the statement of cash flows

2 **Distinguish** among operating, investing, and financing cash flows

3 **Prepare** a statement of cash flows by the indirect method

4 **Prepare** a statement of cash flows by the direct method

STEP 1 Lay out the template as shown in Part 1 of Exhibit 12-3. The exhibit is comprehensive. The diagram in Part 2 gives a visual picture of the statement.

STEP 2 Use the balance sheet to determine the increase or decrease in cash during the period. The change in cash is the "check figure" for the statement of cash flows. Exhibit 12-4 gives Anchor Corporation's comparative balance sheet, with cash highlighted. Anchor's cash decreased by $20,000 during 20X2. *Why* did cash fall during the year? The statement of cash flows explains.

STEP 3 From the income statement, take net income, depreciation, depletion, and amortization expense, and any gains or losses on the sale of long-term assets. Print these items on the statement of cash flows. Exhibit 12-5 gives Anchor's income statement, with relevant items highlighted.

STEP 4 Use the income statement and balance sheet data to prepare the statement of cash flows. The statement is complete only after you have explained the year-to-year changes in all the balance sheet accounts.

■ **EXHIBIT 12-3**

Part 1: Template of the Statement of Cash Flows: Indirect Method

Anchor Corporation
Statement of Cash Flows
Year Ended December 31, 20X2

Cash flows from operating activities:
Net income
Adjustments to reconcile net income to net cash provided by operating activities:
+ Depreciation/amortization expense
+ Loss on sale of long-term assets
– Gain on sale of long-term assets
– Increases in current assets other than cash
+ Decreases in current assets other than cash
+ Increases in current liabilities
– Decreases in current liabilities
Net cash provided by operating activities

Cash flows from investing activities:
Sales of long-term assets (investments, land, building, equipment, and so on)
– Purchases of long-term assets
+ Collections of notes receivable
– Loans to others
Net cash provided by (used for) investing activities

Cash flows from financing activities
Issuance of stock
+ Sale of treasury stock
– Purchase of treasury stock
+ Borrowing (issuance of notes or bonds payable)
– Payment of notes or bonds payable
– Payment of dividends
Net cash provided by (used for) financing activities

Net increase (decrease) in cash during the year
+ Cash at December 31, 20X1
= Cash at December 31, 20X2

■ **EXHIBIT 12-3** Part 2: Positive and Negative Items on the Statement of Cash Flows: Indirect Method

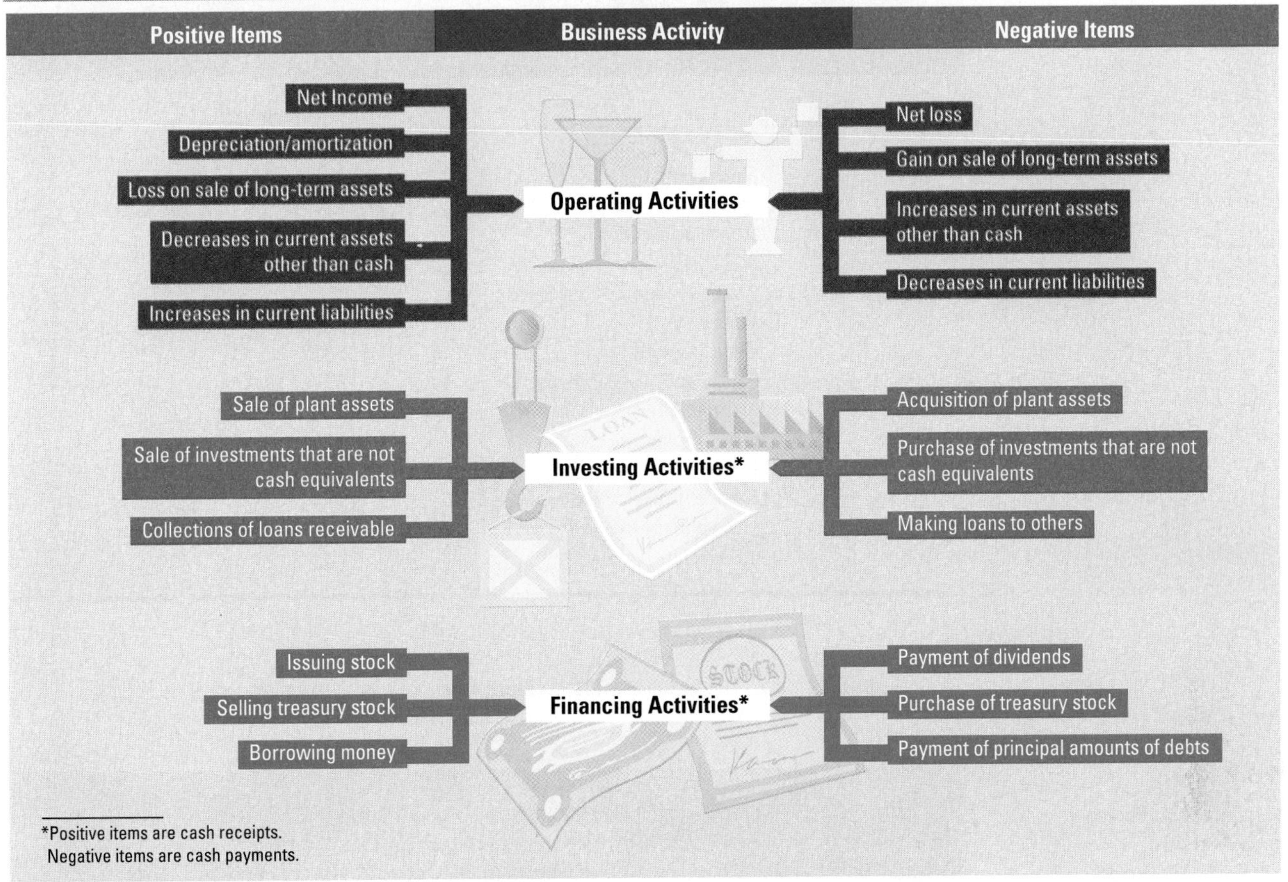

■ **EXHIBIT 12-4**
Comparative Balance Sheet

Anchor Corporation
Comparative Balance Sheet
December 31, 20X2 and 20X1

(In thousands)	20X2	20X1	Increase (Decrease)	
Assets				
Current:				
Cash	$ 22	$ 42	$(20)	*Changes in current assets—Operating*
Accounts receivable	93	80	13	
Interest receivable	3	1	2	
Inventory	135	138	(3)	
Prepaid expenses	8	7	1	
Notes receivable	11	—	11	*Changes in noncurrent assets—Investing*
Plant assets, net of depreciation	453	219	234	
Total	$725	$487	$238	
Liabilities				
Current:				
Accounts payable	$ 91	$ 57	$ 34	*Changes in current liabilities—Operating*
Salary and wage payable	4	6	(2)	
Accrued liabilities	1	3	(2)	
Long-term debt	160	77	83	*Changes in long-term liabilities and paid-in capital accounts—Financing*
Stockholders' Equity				
Common stock	359	258	101	
Retained earnings	110	86	24	*Changes due to net income—Operating* *Change due to dividends—Financing*
Total	$725	$487	$238	

■ **EXHIBIT 12-5**
Income Statement

Anchor Corporation
Income Statement
Year Ended December 31, 20X2

	(In thousands)	
Revenues and gains:		
Sales revenue	$284	
Interest revenue	12	
Dividend revenue	9	
Gain on sale of plant assets	8	
Total revenues and gains		$313
Expenses:		
Cost of goods sold	$150	
Salary and wage expense	56	
Depreciation expense	18	
Other operating expense	17	
Interest expense	16	
Income tax expense	15	
Total expenses		272
Net income		$ 41

The operating section of Anchor's statement of cash flows appears in Exhibit 12-6.

■ **EXHIBIT 12-6**
Statement of Cash Flows—Operating Activities by the Indirect Method

Anchor Corporation
Statement of Cash Flows
For the Year Ended December 31, 20X2

		(In thousands)	
	Cash flows from operating activities:		
	Net income		$41
	Adjustments to reconcile net income to net cash provided by operating activities:		
Ⓐ	Depreciation	$ 18	
Ⓑ	Gain on sale of plant assets	(8)	
Ⓒ	Increase in accounts receivable	(13)	
	Increase in interest receivable	(2)	
	Decrease in inventory	3	
	Increase in prepaid expenses	(1)	
	Increase in accounts payable	34	
	Decrease in salary and wage payable	(2)	
	Decrease in accrued liabilities	(2)	27
	Net cash provided by operating activities		$ 68

Cash Flows from Operating Activities

Operating activities are related to the transactions that make up net income.[1]

The operating section begins with the net income, taken from the income statement, and is followed by "Adjustments to reconcile net income to net cash provided by operating activities." Let's discuss these adjustments.

[1]The authors thank Alfonso Oddo for suggesting this summary.

Ⓐ **Depreciation, Depletion, and Amortization Expenses.** These expenses are added back to net income to convert net income to cash flow. Let's see why. Depreciation is recorded as follows:

Depreciation Expense	18,000	
Accumulated Depreciation		18,000

Depreciation has no effect on cash. However, depreciation, like all other expenses, decreases net income. Therefore, to convert net income to cash flows, we add depreciation back to net income. The add-back cancels the earlier deduction.

Example: Suppose you had only two transactions, a $1,000 cash sale and depreciation expense of $300. Cash flow from operations is $1,000, and net income is $700 ($1,000 – $300). To go from net income ($700) to cash flow ($1,000), we add back the depreciation ($300). Depletion and amortization are treated like depreciation.

Ⓑ **Gains and Losses on the Sale of Assets.** Sales of long-term assets are *investing* activities and there's often a gain or loss on the sale. On the statement of cash flows, the gain or loss is an adjustment to net income. Exhibit 12-6 includes an adjustment for a gain. During 20X2, Anchor sold equipment for $62,000. The book value was $54,000, so there was a gain of $8,000.

The $62,000 cash received from the sale is an investing activity, and the $62,000 includes the $8,000 gain. Net income also includes the gain, so we must remove the gain from net cash provided by operations, as shown in the statement of cash flows (Exhibit 12-7). (We explain investing activities in the next section.)

A loss on the sale of plant assets also creates an adjustment in the operating section. Losses are *added back* to net income to compute cash flow from operations.

Ⓒ **Changes in the Current Asset and Current Liability Accounts.** Most current assets and current liabilities result from operating activities. For example, accounts receivable result from sales, inventory relates to cost of goods sold, and so on. Changes in the current accounts are adjustments to net income on the cash-flow statement. The reasoning follows:

1. ***An increase in another current asset decreases cash.*** It takes cash to acquire assets. Suppose you make a sale on account. Accounts receivable are increased, but cash isn't affected yet. Exhibit 12-4 (page 553) reports that during 20X2 Anchor Corporation's Accounts Receivable increased by $13,000. To compute cash flow from operations, we must subtract the $13,000 increase in Accounts Receivable, as shown in Exhibit 12-6. The reason is this: We have *not* collected this $13,000 in cash. The same logic applies to all the other current assets. If they increase, cash decreases.
2. ***A decrease in another current asset increases cash.*** Suppose Anchor's Accounts Receivable balance decreased by $4,000. Cash receipts caused Accounts Receivable to decrease, so we add decreases in Accounts Receivable and the other current assets to net income.
3. ***A decrease in a current liability decreases cash.*** Payment of a current liability decreases both cash and the liability, so we subtract decreases in current liabilities from net income. In Exhibit 12-6, the $2,000 decrease in Accrued Liabilities is *subtracted* to compute net cash provided by operations.

Check Point 12-2

4. ***An increase in a current liability increases cash.*** Anchor's Accounts Payable increased. That can occur only if cash was not spent to pay this debt. Cash payments are therefore less than expenses and Anchor has more cash on hand. Thus, increases in current liabilities increase cash.

Check Point 12-3

■ **EXHIBIT 12-7**

Statement of Cash Flows—Indirect Method

Anchor Corporation
Statement of Cash Flows
For the Year Ended December 31, 20X2

			(In thousands)
	Cash flows from operating activities:		
	Net income		$ 41
	Adjustments to reconcile net income to net cash provided by operating activities:		
Ⓐ	Depreciation	$ 18	
Ⓑ	Gain on sale of plant assets	(8)	
Ⓒ	Increase in accounts receivable	(13)	
Ⓒ	Increase in interest receivable	(2)	
Ⓒ	Decrease in inventory	3	
Ⓒ	Increase in prepaid expenses	(1)	
Ⓒ	Increase in accounts payable	34	
Ⓒ	Decrease in salary and wage payable	(2)	
Ⓒ	Decrease in accrued liabilities	(2)	27
	Net cash provided by operating activities		68
	Cash flows from investing activities:		
	Acquisition of plant assets	$(306)	
	Loan to another company	(11)	
	Proceeds from sale of plant assets	62	
	Net cash used for investing activities		(255)
	Cash flows from financing activities:		
	Proceeds from issuance of common stock	$ 101	
	Proceeds from issuance of long-term debt	94	
	Payment of long-term debt	(11)	
	Payment of dividends	(17)	
	Net cash provided by financing avctivities		167
	Net decrease in cash		**$ (20)**
	Cash balance, December 31, 20X1		42
	Cash balance, December 31, 20X2		$ 22

Check Point 12-4

Check Point 12-5

Check Point 12-6

Evaluating Cash Flows from Operating Activities. Let's step back and evaluate Anchor's operating cash flows during 20X2. Anchor's operations provided net cash flow of $68,000. This amount exceeds net income, and it should because of the add-back of depreciation. Now let's examine Anchor's investing and financing activities, as reported in Exhibit 12-7.

Cash Flows from Investing Activities

Investing activities affect long-term assets, such as Plant Assets, Investments, and Notes Receivable.

Most of the data came from the balance sheet.

Computing Purchases and Sales of Plant Assets. Companies keep a separate account for each plant asset. But for computing cash flows, it is helpful to combine all the plant assets into a single summary account. Also, we subtract accumulated depreciation and use the net figure. It's easier to work with a single plant asset account.

To illustrate, observe that Anchor Corporation's

- Balance sheet reports beginning plant assets, net of accumulated depreciation, of $219,000. The ending balance is $453,000 (Exhibit 12-4).
- Income statement shows depreciation expense of $18,000 and an $8,000 gain on sale of plant assets (Exhibit 12-5).

Anchor's purchases of plant assets total $306,000 (see Exhibit 12-7). How much, then, are the proceeds from the sale of plant assets? First, we must determine the book value of the plant assets sold, as follows:

Plant Assets (net)

Beginning balance	+	Acquisitions	−	Depreciation	−	Book value of assets sold	=	Ending balance
$219,000	+	$306,000	−	$18,000		−X	=	$453,000
						−X	=	$453,000 − $219,000 − $306,000 + $18,000
						X	=	$54,000

The sale proceeds are $62,000, determined as follows:

Sale proceeds	=	Book value of assets sold	+	Gain	−	Loss
	=	$54,000	+	$8,000	−	$0
	=	$62,000				

Trace the sale proceeds of $62,000 to the statement of cash flows in Exhibit 12-7. The Plant Assets T-account provides another look at the computation of the book value of the asset sold.

Plant Assets (Net)

Beginning balance	**219,000**	**Depreciation**	**18,000**
Acquisitions	**306,000**	Book value of assets sold	54,000
Ending balance	**453,000**		

If the sale resulted in a loss of $3,000, the sale proceeds would be $51,000 ($54,000 – $3,000), and the statement of cash flows would report $51,000 as a cash receipt from this investing activity.

Computing Purchases and Sales of Investments, and Loans and Collections. The cash amounts of investment transactions can be computed in the manner illustrated for plant assets. Investments are easier because there is no depreciation, as shown in the following equation:

Investments (amounts assumed for illustration only)

Beginning balance	+	Purchases	−	Book value of investments sold	=	Ending balance
$100,000	+	$50,000		−X	=	$140,000
				−X	=	$140,000 − $100,000 − $50,000
				X	=	$10,000

The investments T-account provides another look.

Investments

Beginning balance	**100**		
Purchases	**50**	Book value of investments sold	10
Ending balance	**140**		

Check Point 12-7

Anchor Corporation has a long-term receivable, and the cash flows from loan transactions on notes receivable can be determined as follows (data from Exhibit 12-4):

Notes Receivable								
	Beginning balance	+	New loans made	−	Collections	=	Ending balance
	$0	+	X		−0	=	$11,000
			X			=	$11,000

Notes Receivable

Beginning balance	**0**		
New loans made	**11**	Collections	0
Ending balance	**11**		

Exhibit 12-8 summarizes the cash flows from investing activities, highlighted in color.

■ EXHIBIT 12-8 Computing Cash Flows from Investing Activities

Receipts									
From sale of plant assets	Beginning plant assets (net)	+	Acquisition cost	−	Depreciation	−	Book value of assets sold	=	Ending plant assets (net)
	Cash received	=	Book value of assets sold	+ or −	Gain on sale Loss on sale				
From sale of investments	Beginning investments	+	Purchase cost of investments	−	Cost of investments sold	=	Ending investments		
	Cash received	=	Cost of investments sold	+ or −	Gain on sale Loss on sale				
From collection of notes receivable	Beginning notes receivable	+	New loans made	−	Collections	=	Ending notes receivable		
Payments									
For acquisition of plant assets	Beginning plant assets (net)	+	Acquisition cost	−	Depreciation	−	Book value of assets sold	=	Ending plant assets (net)
For purchase of investments	Beginning investments	+	Purchase cost of investments	−	Cost of investments sold	=	Ending investments		
For new loans made	Beginning notes receivable	+	New loans made	−	Collections	=	Ending notes receivable		

Cash Flows from Financing Activities

Financing activities affect liabilities and stockholders' equity, such as Notes Payable, Bonds Payable, Long-Term Debt, Common Stock, Paid-in Capital in Excess of Par, and Retained Earnings.

Computing Issuances and Payments of Long-Term Debt. The beginning and ending balances of Long-Term Debt, Notes Payable, or Bonds Payable come from the balance sheet. If either new issuances or payments are known, the other amount can be computed. Anchor Corporation's new debt issuances total $94,000 (Exhibit 12-7). Debt payments are computed from the Long-Term Debt account (see Exhibit 12-4).

Long-Term Debt (Notes Payable, Bonds Payable)

Beginning balance	+	Issuance of new debt	−	Payments of debt	=	Ending balance
$77,000	+	$94,000		−X	=	$160,000
				−X	=	$160,000 – $77,000 – $94,000
				X	=	$11,000

Long-Term Debt

		Beginning balance	**77,000**
Payments	11,000	**Issuance of new debt**	**94,000**
		Ending balance	**160,000**

Computing Issuances of Stock and Purchases of Treasury Stock. These cash flows can be determined from the stock accounts. For example, cash received from issuing common stock is computed from Common Stock and Capital in Excess of Par. We use a single summary Common Stock account for stock as we do for plant assets. The Anchor Corporation data are

Common Stock

Beginning balance	+	Issuance of new stock	=	Ending balance
$258,000	+	$101,000	=	$359,000

Common Stock

		Beginning balance	**258,000**
		Issuance of new stock	101,000
		Ending balance	**359,000**

Anchor Corporation has no treasury stock, but cash flows from purchasing treasury stock can be computed as follows (using assumed amounts):

Treasury Stock (amounts assumed for illustration only)

Beginning balance	+	Purchase of treasury stock	=	Ending balance
$16,000	+	$3,000	=	$19,000

Treasury Stock

Beginning balance	**16,000**		
Purchase of treasury stock	3,000		
Ending balance	**19,000**		

Computing Dividend Payments. If dividend payments are not given elsewhere, they can be computed. Anchor Corporation's dividend payments are

Retained Earnings							
Beginning balance	+	Net income	−	Dividend declarations and payments	=	Ending balance
$86,000	+	$41,000		−X	=	$110,000
				−X	=	$110,000 − $86,000 − $41,000
				X	=	$17,000

The T-accounts also show the dividend computation.

Retained Earnings

Dividend declarations and payments	17,000	Beg. bal.	86,000
		Net income	41,000
		End. bal.	110,000

Check Point 12-8

Exhibit 12-9 summarizes the cash flows from financing activities, highlighted in color.

■ **EXHIBIT 12-9**

Computing Cash Flows from Financing Activities

Receipts								
From issuance of long-term debt (notes payable)	Beginning long-term debt (notes payable)	+	Cash received from issuance of long-term debt	−	Payment of debt	=	Ending long-term debt (notes payable)
From issuance of stock	Beginning stock	+	Cash received from issuance of new stock	=	Ending stock		
Payments							
Of long-term debt	Beginning long-term debt (notes payable)	+	Cash received from issuance of long-term debt	−	Payment of debt	=	Ending long-term debt (notes payable)
To purchase treasury stock	Beginning treasury stock + Purchase cost of treasury stock = Ending treasury stock						
Of dividends	Beginning retained earnings + Net income − Dividend declarations and payments = Ending retained earnings						

stop AND think. . .

Classify each of the following as an operating activity, an investing activity, or a financing activity:

a. Issuance of stock
b. Borrowing
c. Sales revenue
d. Payment of dividends
e. Purchase of land
f. Purchase of treasury stock
g. Paying bonds payable
h. Interest expense
i. Sale of equipment
j. Cost of goods sold
k. Purchase of another company
l. Making a loan

Answer:

a. Financing
b. Financing
c. Operating
d. Financing
e. Investing
f. Financing
g. Financing
h. Operating
i. Investing
j. Operating
k. Investing
l. Investing

Noncash Investing and Financing Activities

Companies make investments that do not require cash. They also obtain financing other than cash. Our examples have included none of these transactions. Now suppose Anchor Corporation issued common stock valued at $300,000 to acquire a warehouse. Anchor would journalize this transaction as follows:

Warehouse Building	300,000	
Common Stock		300,000

This transaction would not be reported as a cash payment because Anchor paid no cash. But the investment in the warehouse and the issuance of stock are important. These noncash investing and financing activities can be reported in a separate schedule under the statement of cash flows. Exhibit 12-10 illustrates noncash investing and financing activities (all amounts are assumed).

■ **EXHIBIT 12-10**

Noncash investing and Financing Activities (All Amounts Assumed)

	Thousands
Noncash Investing and Financing Activities:	
Acquisition of building by issuing common stock	$300
Acquisition of land by issuing note payable	70
Payment of long-term debt by issuing common stock	100
Total noncash investing and financing activities	$470

Now let's apply what you've learned about the statement of cash flows prepared by the indirect method.

MID-CHAPTER Summary Problem

Robins Corporation reported the following income statement and comparative balance sheet, along with transaction data for 20X5:

Robins Corporation
Income Statement
Year Ended December 31, 20X5

Sales revenue		$662,000
Cost of goods sold		560,000
Gross profit		102,000
Operating expenses		
Salary expenses	$46,000	
Depreciation expense equipment	7,000	
Amortization expense patent	3,000	
Rent expense	2,000	
Total operating expenses		58,000
Income from operations		44,000
Other items:		
Loss on sale of equipment		(2,000)
Income before income tax		42,000
Income tax expense		16,000
Net income		$ 26,000

Robins Corporation
Balance Sheet
December 31, 20X5 and 20X4

Assets	20X5	20X4	Liabilities	20X5	20X4
Current:			Current:		
Cash and equivalents	$ 19,000	$ 3,000	Accounts payable	$ 35,000	$ 26,000
Accounts receivable	22,000	23,000	Accrued liabilities	7,000	9,000
Inventories	34,000	31,000	Income tax payable	10,000	10,000
Prepaid expenses	1,000	3,000	Total current liabilities	52,000	45,000
Total current assets	76,000	60,000	Long-term note payable	44,000	—
Long-term investments	18,000	10,000	Bonds payable	40,000	53,000
Equipment, net	67,000	52,000	**Owners' Equity**		
Patent, net	44,000	10,000	Common stock	52,000	20,000
			Retained earnings	27,000	19,000
			Less: Treasury stock	(10,000)	(5,000)
Total assets	$205,000	$132,000	Total liabilities and equity	$205,000	$132,000

Transaction Data for 20X5:

Purchase of equipment	$98,000	Issuance of long-term note payable to purchase patent	$37,000
Payment of cash dividends	18,000	Issuance of long-term note payable to borrow cash	7,000
Issuance of common stock to retire bonds payable	13,000	Issuance of common stock for cash	19,000
Purchase of long-term investment	8,000	Sale of equipment (book value, 76,000)	74,000
Purchase of treasury stock	5,000		

Required

Prepare Robins Corporation's statement of cash flows (indirect method) for the year ended December 31, 20X5. Follow the four steps outlined below. For Step 4, prepare a T-account to show the transaction activity in each long-term balance sheet account. For each plant asset, use a single account, net of accumulated depreciation (for example: Equipment, Net).

Requirement 1

STEP 1 Lay out the template of the statement of cash flows.

STEP 2 From the comparative balance sheet, determine the increase in cash during the year, $16,000.

STEP 3 From the income statement, take net income, depreciation, amortization, and the loss on sale of equipment, to the statement of cash flows.

STEP 4 Complete the statement of cash flows. Account for the year-to-year change in each balance sheet account.

Answer

Robins Corporation
Statement of Cash Flows
Year Ended December 31, 20X5

Cash flows from operating activities:		
Net income		$26,000
Adjustments to reconcile net income to net cash provided by operating activities:		
Depreciation	$ 7,000	
Amortization	3,000	
Loss on sale of equipment	2,000	
Decrease in accounts receivable	1,000	
Increase in inventories	(3,000)	
Decrease in prepaid expenses	2,000	
Increase in accounts payable	9,000	
Decrease in accrued liabilities	(2,000)	19,000
Net cash provided by operating activities		45,000
Cash flows from investing activities:		
Purchase of equipment	$(98,000)	
Sale of equipment	74,000	
Purchase of long-term investment	(8,000)	
Net cash used for investing activities		(32,000)
Cash flows from financing activities:		
Issuance of common stock	$ 19,000	
Payment of cash dividends	(18,000)	
Issuance of long-term note payable	7,000	
Purchase of treasury stock	(5,000)	
Net cash provided by financing activities		3,000
Net increase in cash		**$16,000**
Cash balance, December 31, 20X4		3,000
Cash balance, December 31, 20X5		$19,000
Noncash investing and financing activities:		
Issuance of long-term note payable to purchase patent		$37,000
Issuance of common stock to retire bonds payable		13,000
Total noncash investing and financing activities		$50,000

Long-Term Investments

Debit		Credit
Bal.	**10,000**	
	8,000	
Bal.	**18,000**	

Equipment, Net

Debit		Credit
Bal.	**52,000**	
	98,000	76,000
		7,000
Bal.	**67,000**	

Patent, Net

Debit		Credit
Bal.	**10,000**	
	37,000	3,000
Bal.	**44,000**	

Long-term Note Payable

Debit	Credit	
	Bal.	**0**
		37,000
		7,000
	Bal.	**44,000**

Bond Payable

Debit	Credit	
	Bal.	**53,000**
13,000		
	Bal.	**40,000**

Common Stock

Debit	Credit	
	Bal.	**20,000**
		13,000
		19,000
	Bal.	**52,000**

Retained Earnings

Debit	Credit	
	Bal.	**19,000**
18,000		26,000
	Bal.	**27,000**

Treasury Stock

Debit		Credit
Bal.	**5,000**	
	5,000	
Bal.	**10,000**	

Preparing the Statement of Cash Flows: Direct Method

OBJECTIVE

4 Prepare a statement of cash flows by the direct method

The Financial Accounting Standards Board (FASB) prefers the direct method of reporting operating cash flows because it provides clearer information about the sources and uses of cash. But very few companies use this method because it takes more computations than the indirect method. Investing and financing cash flows are unaffected by the operating cash flows.

To illustrate the statement of cash flows, we use Anchor Corporation, a dealer in auto parts for vintage British sports cars **Austin-Healey**, **Triumph**, and **MG**. To prepare the statement of cash flows by the direct method, proceed as follows:

STEP 1 Lay out the template of the statement of cash flows by the direct method, as shown in Part 1 of Exhibit 12-11. Part 2 gives a visual picture of the statement.

STEP 2 Use the balance sheet to determine the increase or decrease in cash during the period. The change in cash is the "check figure" for the statement of cash flows. Anchor's comparative balance sheet shows that cash decreased by $20,000 during 20X2 (Exhibit 12-4, page 553). *Why* did cash fall during 20X2? The statement of cash flows explains.

(continued on next page)

■ **EXHIBIT 12-11**

Part 1: Template of the Statement of Cash Flows—Direct Method

Anchor Corporation
Statement of Cash Flows
For the Year Ended December 31, 20X2

Cash flows from operating activities:
Receipts:
Collections from customers
Interest received on notes receivable
Dividends received on investments in stock
Total cash receipts
Payments:
To suppliers
To employees
For interest
For income tax
Total cash payments
Net cash provided by operating activities
Cash flows from investing activities:
Sales of long-term assets (investments, land, building, equipment, and so on)
− Purchases of long-term assets
+ Collections of notes receivable
− Loans to others
Net cash provided by (used for) investing activities
Cash flows from financing activities:
Issuance of stock
+ Sale of treasury stock
− Purchases of treasury stock
+ Borrowing (issuance of notes or bonds payable)
− Payment of notes or bonds payable
− Payment of dividends
Net cash provided by (used for) financing activities
Net increase (decrease) in cash during the year
+ Cash at December 31, 20X1
= Cash at December 31, 20X2

■ **EXHIBIT 12-11** Part 2: Cash Receipts and Cash Payments on the Statement of Cash Flows—Direct Method

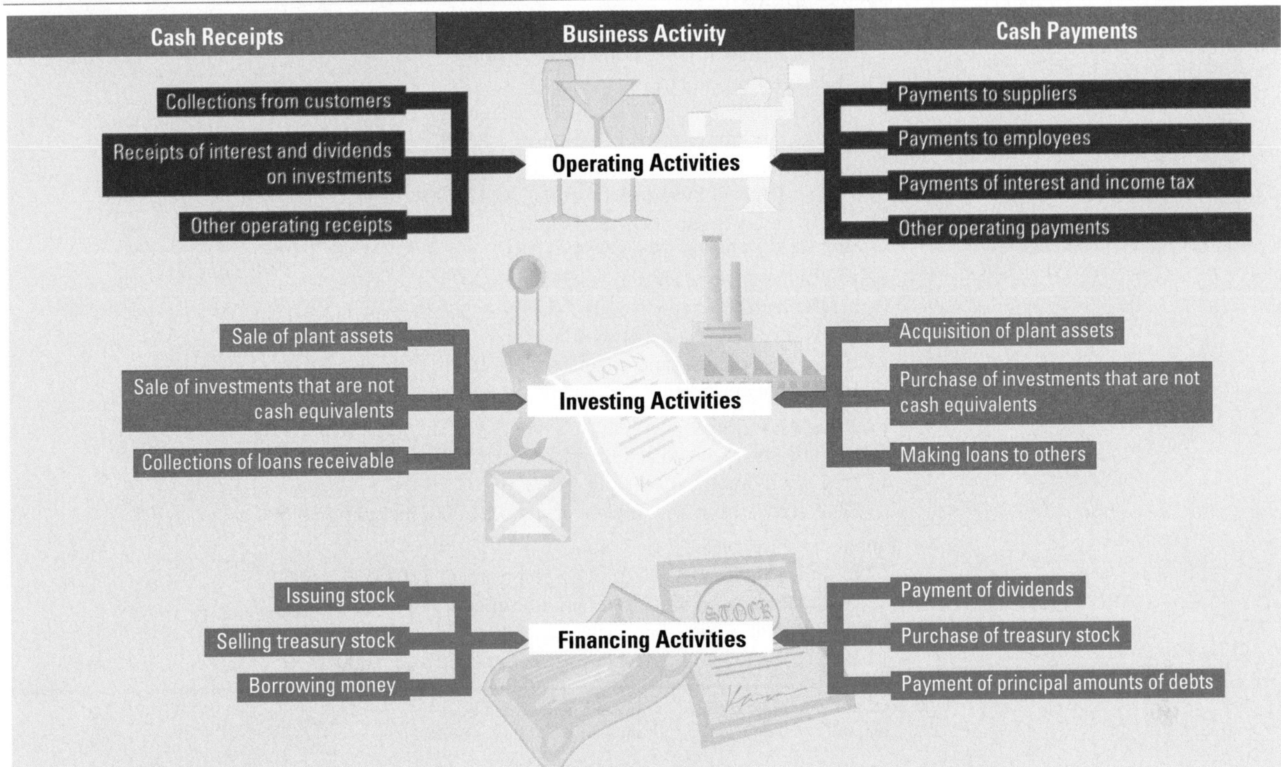

STEP 3 Use the available data to prepare the statement of cash flows. Anchor's transaction data appear in Exhibit 12-12. These transactions affected both the income statement (Exhibit 12-5, page 554) and the statement of cash flows. Some transactions affect one statement and some affect the other. For example, sales (item 1) are reported on the income statement. Cash collections (item 2) go on the statement of cash flows. Other transactions, such as the cash receipt of dividend revenue (item 5) affect both statements. *The statement of cash flows reports only those transactions with cash effects* (those with an asterisk in Exhibit 12-12). Exhibit 12-13 gives Anchor Corporation's statement of cash flows for 20X2.

Cash Flows from Operating Activities. Operating cash flows are listed first because they are most important. Exhibit 12-13 shows that Anchor Corporation is sound; operating activities were the largest source of cash.

Cash Collections from Customers. Both cash sales and collections of accounts receivable are reported on the statement of cash flows as "Collections from customers . . . $271,000" in Exhibit 12-13.

Cash Receipts of Interest. The income statement reports interest revenue. Only the cash receipts of interest appear on the statement of cash flows—$10,000 in Exhibit 12-13.

Cash Receipts of Dividends. Dividend revenue goes on the income statement, and only cash receipts are reported on the statement of cash flows—$9,000 in Exhibit 12-13. (Dividends *received* are operating activities, but dividends *paid* are financing.)

■ **EXHIBIT 12-12**

Summary of Anchor Corporation's 20X2 Transactions

Operating Activities

1. Sales on credit, $284,000
*2. Collections from customers, $271,000
3. Interest revenue, $12,000
*4. Collection of interest receivable, $10,000
*5. Cash receipt of dividend revenue, $9,000
6. Cost of goods sold, $150,000
7. Purchases of inventory on credit, $147,000
*8. Payments to suppliers, $133,000
9. Salary and wage expense, $56,000
*10. Payments of salary and wages, $58,000
11. Depreciation expense, $18,000
12. Other operating expense, $17,000
*13. Interest expense and payments, $16,000
*14. Income tax expense and payments, $15,000

Investing Activities

*15. Cash payments to acquire plant assets, $306,000
*16. Loan to another company, $11,000
*17. Proceeds from sale of plant assets, $62,000, including $8,000 gain

Financing Activities

*18. Proceeds from issuance of common stock, $101,000
*19. Proceeds from issuance of long-term debt, $94,000
*20. Payment of long-term debt, $11,000
*21. Declaration and payment of cash dividends, $17,000

*Indicates a cash flow to be reported on the statement of cash flows.
Note: Income statement data are taken from Exhibit 12-16, page 570.

■ **EXHIBIT 12-13**

Statement of Cash Flows—Direct Method

Anchor Corporation
Statement of Cash Flows
For Year Ended December 31, 20X2

	(In thousands)	
Cash flows from operating activities:		
Receipts:		
Collections from customers	$ 271	
Interest received on notes receivable	10	
Dividends received on investments in stock	9	
Total cash receipts		$290
Payments:		
To suppliers	$(133)	
To employees	(58)	
For interest	(16)	
For income tax	(15)	
Total cash payments		(222)
Net cash provided by operating activities		68
Cash flows from investing activities:		
Acquisition of plant assets	$(306)	
Loan to another company	(11)	
Proceeds from sale of plant assets	62	
Net cash used for investing activities		(255)
Cash flows from financing activities:		
Proceeds from issuance of common stock	$ 101	
Proceeds from issuance of long-term debt	94	
Payment of long-term debt	(11)	
Payment of dividends	(17)	
Net cash provided by financing activities		167
Net decrease in cash		**$(20)**
Cash balance, December 31, 20X1		42
Cash balance, December 31, 20X2		$ 22

Payments to Suppliers. Payments to suppliers include all expenditures for inventory and operating expenses except employee pay, interest, and income taxes. *Suppliers* are those entities that provide inventory and essential services. For example, a clothing store's suppliers may include **Liz Claiborne, Nike,** and **Ralph Lauren**. Other suppliers provide advertising, utilities, and office supplies. Exhibit 12-13 shows that Anchor Corporation paid suppliers $133,000.

Payments to Employees. This category includes salaries, wages, and other forms of employee pay. Accrued amounts are excluded because they have not yet been paid. The statement of cash flows reports only the cash payments ($58,000).

Payments for Interest Expense and Income Tax Expense. Interest and income tax payments are reported separately. Anchor Corporation paid all its interest and income taxes in cash. Therefore, the same amount goes on the income statement and the statement of cash flows. Interest payments are operating cash flows because the interest is an expense.

Depreciation, Depletion, and Amortization Expense. These expenses are *not* listed on the direct-method statement of cash flows because they do not affect cash.

Cash Flows from Investing Activities

Investing is critical because a company's investments affect the future. Large purchases of plant assets signal expansion. Meager investing activity means the business is not growing.

Purchases of Plant Assets; Purchasing Investments and Making Loans to Other Companies. These cash payments acquire long-term assets. Anchor Corporation's first investing activity in Exhibit 12-13 is the purchase of plant assets ($306,000). Anchor also made an $11,000 loan and got a note receivable.

Proceeds from Selling Plant Assets and Investments and from Collecting Notes Receivable. These cash receipts are also investing activities. The sale of the plant assets needs explanation. Anchor Corporation received $62,000 cash from the sale of plant assets, and there was an $8,000 gain on this transaction. What is the appropriate amount to show on the cash-flow statement? It is $62,000, the cash received from the sale, not the $8,000 gain.

Investors are often critical of a company that sells large amounts of its plant assets. That may signal an emergency. For example, problems in the airline industry have caused some companies to sell airplanes to generate cash.

Cash Flows from Financing Activities

Cash flows from financing activities include the following:

Proceeds from Issuance of Stock and Debt (Notes Payable). Issuing stock and borrowing money are two ways to finance a company. In Exhibit 12-13, Anchor Corporation received $101,000 when it issued common stock. Anchor also issued long-term debt (notes payable) to borrow $94,000.

Payment of Debt and Purchasing the Company's Own Stock. Paying debt (notes payable) is the opposite of borrowing. Anchor Corporation reports long-term debt payments of $11,000. The purchase of treasury stock is another example.

Check Point 12-9

Check Point 12-10

Check Point 12-11

Payment of Cash Dividends. Paying cash dividends is a financing activity, as shown by Anchor's $17,000 payment in Exhibit 12-13. A *stock* dividend has no effect on Cash and is *not* reported on the cash-flow statement.

Noncash Investing and Financing Activities

Companies make investments that do not require cash. They also obtain financing other than cash. Our examples thus far have included none of these transactions. Now suppose that Anchor Corporation issued common stock valued at $300,000 to acquire a warehouse. Anchor would journalize this transaction as follows:

Warehouse Building	300,000	
Common Stock		300,000

This transaction would not be reported as a cash payment because Anchor paid no cash. But the investment in the warehouse and the issuance of stock are important. These noncash investing and financing activities can be reported in a separate schedule under the statement of cash flows. Exhibit 12-14 illustrates noncash investing and financing activities (all amounts are assumed).

EXHIBIT 12-14

Noncash Investing and Financing Activities (All Amounts Assumed)

	Thousands
Noncash Investing and Financing Activities:	
Acquisition of building by issuing common stock	$300
Acquisition of land by issuing note payable	70
Payment of long-term debt by issuing common stock	100
Total noncash investing and financing activities	$470

stop AND think. . .

Classify each of the following as an operating activity, an investing activity, or a financing activity. Also identify those items that are not reported on the statement of cash flows prepared by the direct method.

a. Net income
b. Payment of dividends
c. Borrowing
d. Payment of cash to suppliers
e. Making a loan
f. Sale of treasury stock
g. Depreciation expense
h. Purchase of equipment
i. Issuance of stock
j. Purchase of another company
k. Payment of a note payable
l. Payment of income taxes
m. Collections from customers
n. Accrual of interest revenue
o. Expiration of prepaid expense
p. Receipt of cash dividends

Answer:

a. Not reported
b. Financing
c. Financing
d. Operating
e. Investing
f. Financing
g. Not reported
h. Investing
i. Financing
j. Investing
k. Financing
l. Operating
m. Operating
n. Not reported
o. Not reported
p. Operating

Now let's see how to compute the operating cash flows by the direct method.

Computing Operating Cash Flows by the Direct Method

To compute operating cash flows by the direct method, we use the income statement and the *changes* in the balance sheet accounts. Exhibit 12-15 diagrams the process. Exhibit 12-16 is Anchor Corporation's income statement, and Exhibit 12-17 is the comparative balance sheet.

■ **EXHIBIT 12-15**

Direct Method of Computing Cash Flows from Operating Activities

RECEIPTS / PAYMENTS	Income Statement Account	Change in Related Balance Sheet Account	
RECEIPTS:			
From customers	Sales Revenue	+ Decrease in Accounts Receivable − Increase in Accounts Receivable	
Of interest	Interest Revenue	+ Decrease in Interest Receivable − Increase in Interest Receivable	
PAYMENTS:			
To suppliers	Cost of Goods Sold	+ Increase in Inventory − Decrease in Inventory	+ Decrease in Accounts Payable − Increase in Accounts Payable
	Operating Expense	+ Increase in Prepaids − Decrease in Prepaids	+ Decrease in Accrued Liabilities − Increase in Accrued Liabilities
To employees	Salary (Wage) Expense	+ Decrease in Salary (Wage) Payable − Increase in Salary (Wage) Payable	
For interest	Interest Expense	+ Decrease in Interest Payable − Increase in Interest Payable	
For income tax	Income Tax Expense	+ Decrease in Income Tax Payable − Increase in Income Tax Payable	

We thank Barbara Gerrity for suggesting this exhibit.

Computing Cash Collections from Customers. Collections start with sales revenue (an accrual-basis amount). Anchor Corporation's income statement (Exhibit 12-16) reports sales of $284,000. Accounts receivable increased from $80,000 at the beginning of the year to $93,000 at year end, a $13,000 increase (Exhibit 12-17). Based on those amounts, Cash Collections equal $271,000, as follows. We must solve for cash collections (X):

Accounts Receivable

Beginning balance	+	Sales	−	Collections	=	Ending balance
$80,000	+	$284,000		−X	=	$93,000
				−X	=	$93,000 − $80,000 − $284,000
				Collections	=	$271,000

The T-account for Accounts Receivable provides another view of the same computation.

Accounts Receivable

Beginning balance	**80,000**		
Sales	**284,000**	Collections	271,000
Ending balance	**93,000**		

Accounts Receivable increased, so collections must be less than sales.

All collections of receivables are computed this way. Let's turn now to cash receipts of interest revenue. In our example, Anchor Corporation earned interest revenue. Cash receipts of interest were $10,000 (Interest revenue of $12,000 minus the $2,000 increase in Interest Receivable). Exhibit 12-15 shows how to make this computation.

Computing Payments to Suppliers. This computation includes two parts:

- Payments for inventory
- Payments for operating expenses (other than interest and income tax)

(continued at bottom of next page)

The T-accounts give another picture of the same data.

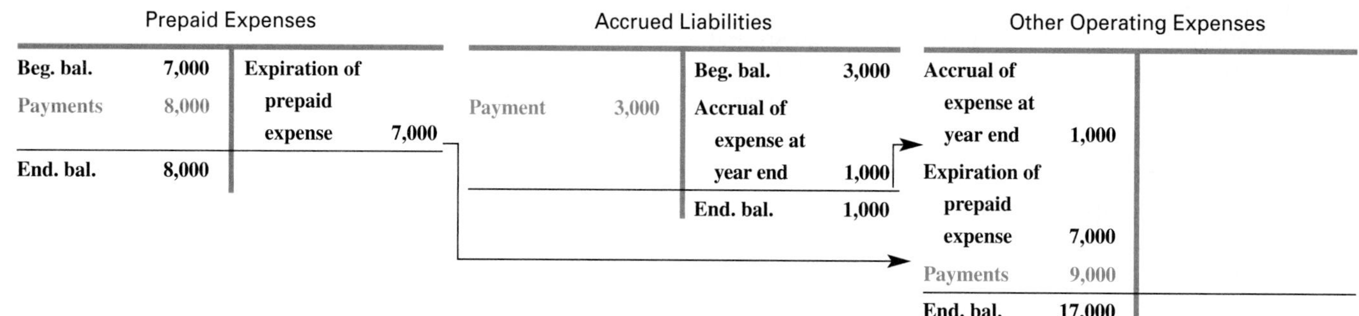

Computing Payments to Employees. It is convenient to combine all payments to employees into one account, Salary and Wage Expense. We then adjust the expense for the change in Salary and Wage Payable, as shown here:

Salary and Wage Payable							
Beginning balance	+	Salary and wage expense	−	Payments	=	Ending balance
$6,000	+	$56,000		−X	=	$4,000
				−X	=	$4,000 − $6,000 − $56,000
				Payments	=	$58,000

Salary and Wage Payable

		Beginning balance	**6,000**
Payments to employees	58,000	**Salary and wage expense**	**56,000**
		Ending balance	**4,000**

Check Point 12-13

Computing Payments of Interest and Income Taxes. Anchor Corporation's expense and payment amounts are the same for interest and income tax, so no analysis is required. If the expense and the payment differ, the payment can be computed as illustrated for payments to employees; Exhibit 12-15 summarizes the procedure.

Computing Investing and Financing Cash Flows

Investing and financing activities are explained on pages 556–560. These computations are the same for both the direct and the indirect methods.

stop AND think. . .

Vanex Company reported the following for 2006 and 2005 (in millions):

At December 31,	2006	2005
Receivables, net	$ 3,582	$ 3,964
Inventory	5,224	5,035
Accounts payable	945	1,261
Income taxes payable	865	901

Year Ended December 31,	2006	2005
Revenues	$23,223	$20,044
Cost of goods sold	14,137	11,707
Income tax expense	923	730

Based on these figures, how much cash did
- Vanex collect from customers during 2006?
- Vanex pay for inventory during 2006?
- Vanex pay for income taxes during 2006?

Answers (in millions):

Collections from customers	=	$23,605	Beginning Receivables	+	Revenues	−	Collections	=	Ending Receivables	
			$3,964	+	$23,223	−	$23,605	=	$3,582	
Payments for inventory	=	$14,642	Cost of Goods Sold	+	Increase in Inventory	+	Decrease in Accounts Payable	=	Payments	
			$14,137	+	($5,224 − $5,035)	+	($1,261 − $945)	=	$14,642	
Payment of income taxes	=	$959	Beginning Income Taxes Payable	+	Income Tax Expense	−	Payment	=	Ending Income Taxes Payable	
			$901	+	$923	−	$959	=	$865	

Measuring Cash Adequacy: Free Cash Flow

Throughout this chapter, we have focused on cash flows from operating, investing, and financing activities. Some investors want to know how much cash a company can "free up" for new opportunities. **Free cash flow** is the amount of cash available from operations after paying for planned investments in plant assets. Free cash flow can be computed as follows:

Free cash flow
The amount of cash available from operations after paying for planned investments in plant, equipment, and other long-term assets.

Free cash flow = Net cash provided by operating activities − Cash payments earmarked for investments in plant assets

PepsiCo, Inc. uses free cash flow to manage its operations. Suppose PepsiCo expects net cash inflow of $2.3 billion from operations. Assume PepsiCo plans to spend $1.9 billion to modernize its bottling plants. In this case, PepsiCo's free cash flow would be $0.4 billion ($2.3 billion − $1.9 billion). If a good investment opportunity comes along, PepsiCo should have $0.4 billion to invest in the other company. **Shell Oil Company** also uses free-cash-flow analysis. A large amount of free cash flow is preferable because it means that a lot of cash is available for new investments. The Making Managerial Decisions feature that follows shows some ways to use cash-flow and income data for investment and credit analysis.

MAKING MANAGERIAL DECISIONS

INVESTORS' AND CREDITORS' USE OF CASH-FLOW AND RELATED INFORMATION

Anne Gray is a private investor. Through years of experience she has devised some guidelines for evaluating both stock investments and bond investments. Gray uses a combination of accrual-accounting data and cash-flow information. Here are her decision guidelines for both investors and creditors.

INVESTORS

Questions	Factors to Consider*	Financial Statement Predictor/Decision Model*
1. How much in dividends can I expect to receive from an investment in stock?	Expected future net income	Income from continuing operations**
	Expected future cash balance	Net cash flows from (in order): • Operating activities • Investing activities • Financing activities
	Future dividend policy	Current and past dividend policy
2. Is the stock price likely to increase or decrease?	Expected future net income	Income from continuing operations**
	Expected future cash flows from operating activities	Income from continuing operations** Net cash flow from operating activities
3. What is the future stock price likely to be?	Expected future income from • continuing operations, *and* • net cash flow from operating activities	$\text{Expected future price of a share of stock} = \dfrac{\text{Expected future earnings per share**}}{\text{Investment capitalization rate}}$ or $\text{Expected future price of a share of stock} = \dfrac{\text{Net cash flow from operations per share}}{\text{Investment capitalization rate}}$

CREDITORS

Questions	Factors to Consider	Financial Statement Predictor
Can the company pay the interest and principal at the maturity of a loan?	Expected future net cash flow from operating activities	Income from continuing operations** Net cash flow from operating activities

*There are many other factors to consider in making these decisions. These are some of the more common.
**See Chapter 11.

Summary Problem

END-OF-CHAPTER

Granite Shoals Corporation reported the following comparative balance sheet and income statement for 20X6.

Granite Shoals Corporation
Balance Sheet
December 31, 20X6 and 20X5

	20X6	20X5
Cash	$ 19,000	$ 3,000
Accounts receivable	22,000	23,000
Inventories	34,000	31,000
Prepaid expenses	1,000	3,000
Equipment (net)	90,000	79,000
Intangible assets	9,000	9,000
	$175,000	$148,000
Accounts payable	$ 14,000	$ 9,000
Accrued liabilities	16,000	19,000
Income tax payable	14,000	12,000
Notes payable	45,000	50,000
Common stock	31,000	20,000
Retained earnings	64,000	40,000
Treasury stock	(9,000)	(2,000)
	$175,000	$148,000

Granite Shoals Corporation
Income Statement
Year Ended December 31, 20X6 and 20X5

	20X6	20X5
Sales revenue	$190,000	$165,000
Gain on sale of equipment	6,000	—
Total revenue and gains	196,000	165,000
Cost of goods sold	$ 85,000	$ 70,000
Depreciation expense	19,000	17,000
Other operating expenses	36,000	33,000
Total expenses	140,000	120,000
Income before income tax	56,000	45,000
Income tax expense	18,000	15,000
Net income	$ 38,000	$ 30,000

Assume that **Berkshire Hathaway** is considering buying Granite Shoals Corporation. Berkshire Hathaway requests the following cash-flow data for 20X6. There were no noncash investing and financing activities.

a. Collections from customers
b. Cash payments for inventory
c. Cash payments for operating expenses
d. Cash payment for income tax
e. Cash received from the sale of equipment. Granite Shoals paid $40,000 for new equipment during the year.
f. Issuance of common stock.
g. Issuance of notes payable. Granite Shoals paid off $20,000 during the year.
h. Cash dividends. There were no stock dividends.

Provide the requested data. Show your work.

Answer

a. Analyze Accounts Receivable (let X = Collections from customers):

Beginning	+	Sales	–	Collections	=	Ending
$23,000	+	$190,000	–	X	=	$22,000
				X		= $191,000

b. Analyze Inventory and Accounts Payable (let X = Purchases, and let Y = Payments for inventory):

Beginning inventory	+	Purchases	–	Ending inventory	=	Cost of Goods Sold
$31,000	+	X	–	$34,000	=	$85,000
		X				= $88,000

Beginning Accounts Payable	+	Purchases	–	Payments	=	Ending Accounts Payable
$9,000	+	$88,000	–	Y	=	$14,000
				Y		= $83,000

c. Start with Other Operating Expenses, and adjust for the changes in Prepaid Expenses and Accrued Liabilities:

Other Operating Expenses	+ Increase, or – Decrease in Prepaid Expenses	– Increase, or + Decrease in Accrued Liabilities	=	Payments for Operating Expenses
$36,000	– $2,000	+ $3,000	=	$37,000

d. Analyze Income Tax Payable (let X = Payment of income tax):

Beginning	+	Income Tax Expense	–	Payments	=	Ending
$12,000	+	$18,000	–	X	=	$14,000
				X		= $16,000

e. Analyze Equipment, Net (let X = Book value of equipment sold. Then combine with the gain or loss to compute cash received from the sale.)

Beginning	+	Acqusitions	–	Depreciation	–	Book Value Sold	=	Ending
$79,000	+	$40,000	–	$19,000	–	X	=	$90,000
						X		= $10,000

Cash received from sale	=	Book Value Sold	+	Gain	–	Loss on Sale
$16,000	=	$10,000	+	$6,000		

f. Analyze Common Stock (let X = issuance)

Beginning	+	Issuance	=	Ending
$20,000	+	X	=	$31,000
		X		= $11,000

g. Analyze Notes Payable (let X = issuance):

Beginning	+	Issuance	−	Payment	=	Ending
$50,000	+	X	−	$20,000	=	$45,000
		X				= $15,000

h. Analyze Retained Earnings (let X = dividends)

Beginning	+	Net Income	−	Dividends	=	Ending
$40,000	+	$38,000	−	X	=	$64,000
				X		= $14,000

REVIEW STATEMENT OF CASH FLOWS

Chapter Review Quiz

1. All of the following activities are reported on the statement of cash flows except:
   a. operating activities.
   b. marketing activities.
   c. investing activities.
   d. financing activities.

2. Activities that create revenues and expenses are
   a. operating activities.
   b. investing activities.
   c. financing activities.
   d. noncash investing and financing activities.

3. Activities affecting long-term assets are
   a. operating activities.
   b. financing activities.
   c. investing activities.
   d. marketing activities.

4. In 20X9, Lakeside Company borrowed $50,000, paid dividends of $12,000, issued 2,000 shares of stock for $30 per share, purchased land for $24,000, and received dividends of $6,000. Net income was $85,000. How much should be reported as net cash provided by financing activities?
   a. $98,000
   b. $80,000
   c. $110,000
   d. $104,000

5. Activities that obtain the cash needed to launch and sustain a company are
   a. operating activities
   b. financing activities.
   c. investing activities.
   d. marketing activities.

6. The exchange of stock for land would be reported as
   a. investing activities
   b. financing activities.
   c. Exchanges are not reported on the statement of cash flows.
   d. noncash investing and financing activities.

Use the following Kentucky Company information for questions 7–10.

Net income	$58,000	Increase in Accounts Payable	$ 7,000
Depreciation Expense	8,000	Decrease in Prepaid Expenses	1,000
Payment of Dividends	2,000	Acquisition of Equipment	24,000
Increase in Accounts Receivable	4,000	Sale of Treasury Stock	13,000
Collection of Notes Receivable	6,000	Payment of Long-term Debt	9,000
Loss on Sale of Land	12,000	Proceeds from Sale of Land	42,000
Decrease in Inventories	2,000		

7. Under the indirect method, net cash provided by operating activities would be:
   a. $72,000
   b. $76,000
   c. $84,000
   d. $86,000

8. Net cash provided by (used for) investing activities would be:
   a. $18,000
   b. $(12,000)
   c. $(6,000)
   d. $24,000

9. Net cash provided by (used for) financing activities would be:
   a. $4,000
   b. $2,000
   c. $(8,000)
   d. $(11,000)

10. The cost of land must have been
    a. $30,000
    b. $42,000
    c. $54,000
    d. Cannot be determined from the data given.

11. Lighthouse Industries began the year with $45,000 in accounts receivable and ended the year with $31,000 in accounts receivable. If sales for the year were $687,000, the cash collected from customers during the year amounted to:
    a. $701,000
    b. $672,000
    c. $733,000
    d. $655,000

12. Grafton Cheese Company made sales of $690,000 and had cost of goods sold of $390,000. Inventory increased by $15,000 and accounts payable increased by $9,000. Operating expenses were $190,000. How much was Grafton's net income for the year?
    a. $110,000
    b. $116,000
    c. $125,000
    d. $300,00

13. Use the Grafton Cheese Company data from question 12. How much cash did Grafton pay for inventory during the year?
    a. $384,000
    b. $390,000
    c. $396,000
    d. Cannot be determined from the data given.

Answers

1. b
2. a
3. c
4. a [$50,000 – $12,000 + (2,000 × $30) = $98,000]
5. b
6. d
7. c ($58,000 + $8,000 – $4,000 + $12,000 + $2,000 + $7,000 + $1,000 = $84,000)
8. d ($6,000 – $24,000 + $42,000 = $24,000)
9. b (–$2,000 + $13,000 – $9,000 = $2,000)
10. c ($12,000 + $42,000 = $54,000)
11. a [$687,000 + ($45,000 – $31,000) = $701,000]
12. a ($690,000 – $390,000 – $190,000 = $110,000)
13. c ($390,000 + $15,000 – $9,000 = $396,000)

Accounting Vocabulary

cash equivalents (p. 549)
cash flows (p. 548)
direct method (p. 551)
financing activities (p. 550)
free cash flow (p. 573)
indirect method (p. 551)
investing activities (p. 550)
operating activities (p. 550)
statement of cash flows (p. 548)

Assess Your Progress

Check Points

Purposes of the statement of cash flows (Obj. 1)

CP12-1 (p. 548) How does the statement of cash flows help investors and creditors perform each of the following functions?

a. Predict future cash flows.
b. Evaluate management decisions.

Evaluating operating cash flows—indirect method (Obj. 2)

CP12-2 (p. 555) Examine the **eBay** cash-flow statement on page 547. Suppose eBay's operating activities *used*, rather than *provided*, cash. Identify four things under the indirect method that could cause operating cash flows to be negative.

Reporting cash flows from operating activities—indirect method (Obj. 3)

CP12-3 (p. 556) Kleenex® Company began 20X6 with accounts receivable, inventory, and prepaid expenses totaling $65,000. At the end of the year the company had a total of $78,000 for these current assets. At the beginning of 20X6, Kleenex® owed current liabilities of $42,000, and at year end current liabilities totaled $40,000.

Net income for the year was $65,000. Included in net income were a $4,000 gain on the sale of land and depreciation expense of $9,000.

Show how Kleenex® should report cash flows from operating activities for 20X6. Kleenex® uses the *indirect* method. Use Exhibit 12-6 (page 554) as a guide.

Identifying items for reporting cash flows from operations—indirect method (Obj. 2)

CP12-4 (p. 556) Nutty Nuggets Corporation is preparing its statement of cash flows (indirect method) for the year ended September 30, 20X4. The company has provided the following list of items for you to consider in preparing the company's statement of cash flows. Identify each item as an operating activity—addition to net income (O+), or subtraction from net income (O–); an investing activity (I); a financing activity (F); or an activity that is not used to prepare the cash-flow statement by the indirect method (N). Place the appropriate symbol in the blank space.

____	a. Increase in accounts payable	____	h. Loss on sale of land
____	b. Sales revenue	____	i. Depreciation expense
____	c. Payment of dividends	____	j. Increase in inventory
____	d. Decrease in accrued liabilities	____	k. Decrease in prepaid expense
____	e. Issuance of common stock	____	l. Decrease in accounts receivable
____	f. Gain on sale of building	____	m. Purchase of equipment
____	g. Retained earnings	____	n. Collection of cash from customers

Computing operating cash flows—indirect method (Obj. 3)

CP12-5 (p. 556) (Check Point 12-6 is an alternate exercise.) Wohlgemuth, Inc. accountants have assembled the following data for the year ended June 30, 20X5.

Cost of goods sold	$100,000	Payment of dividends	$ 6,000
Other operating expenses	35,000	Proceeds from issuance	
Purchase of equipment	40,000	of common stock	20,000
Decrease in current liabilities	5,000	Sales revenue	203,000
Payment of note payable	30,000	Increase in current	
Proceeds from sale of land	60,000	assets other than cash	30,000
Depreciation expense	8,000	Purchase of treasury stock	5,000

Prepare the *operating* activities section of Wohlgemuth's statement of cash flows for the year ended June 30, 20X5. Wohlgemuth uses the *indirect* method for operating cash flows.

Preparing a statement of cash flows—indirect method (Obj. 3)

CP12-6 (p. 556) Use the data in Check Point 12-5 to prepare Wohlgemuth's statement of cash flows for the year ended June 30, 20X5. Wohlgemuth uses the *indirect* method for operating activities. Use Exhibit 12-7, page 556, as a guide, but you may stop after determining the net increase (or decrease) in cash.

Computing investing cash flows (Obj. 3)

CP12-7 (p. 558) Dover Elevator Company reported the following financial statements for 20X6:

Dover Elevator Company
Income Statement
Year Ended December 31, 20X6

(In thousands)	
Sales revenue	$710
Cost of goods sold	$340
Depreciation expense	60
Salary expense	50
Other expenses	150
Total expenses	600
Net income	$110

Dover Elevator Company
Comparative Balance Sheet
December 31, 20X6 and 20X5

(In thousands)

Assets	20X6	20X5	Liabilities	20X6	20X5
Current			Current		
Cash	$ 19	$ 16	Accounts payable	$ 47	$ 42
Accounts receivable	54	48	Salary payable	23	21
Inventory	80	84	Accrued liabilities	8	11
Prepaid expenses	3	2	Long-term notes payable	66	68
Long-term investments	75	90			
Plant assets, net	225	185	**Stockholders' Equity**		
			Common stock	40	37
			Retained earnings	272	246
Total	$456	$425	Total	$456	$425

Compute the following investing cash flows:

a. Acquisitions of plant assets (all were for cash). Dover sold no plant assets.
b. Proceeds from the sale of investments. Dover purchased no investments.

Computing financing cash flows (Obj. 3)

CP12-8 (p. 560) Use the Dover Elevator Company data in Check Point 12-7 to compute

a. New borrowing or payment of long-term notes payable. Dover had only one long-term note payable transaction during the year.
b. Issuance of common stock or retirement of common stock. Dover had only one common stock transaction during the year.
c. Payment of cash dividends (same as dividends declared).

Preparing a statement of cash flows—direct method (Obj. 4)

CP12-9 (p. 568) VISA Credit Cards, Inc., began 20X4 with cash of $44,000. During the year, VISA earned service revenue of $600,000 and collected $610,000 from customers. Expenses for the year totaled $420,000, of which VISA paid $410,000 in cash to suppliers and employees. VISA also paid $140,000 to purchase equipment and a cash dividend of $50,000 to its stockholders during 20X4.

Prepare the company's statement of cash flows for the year. Format operating activities by the direct method.

Computing operating cash flows—direct method (Obj. 4)

CP12-10 (p. 568) Check Point 12-11 is an alternate. **Austin-Healey Corporation** accountants have assembled the following data for the year ended June 30, 20X9.

Payment of dividends	$ 6,000	Cost of goods sold	$100,000
Proceeds from issuance of common stock	20,000	Payments to suppliers	87,000
Sales revenue	210,000	Purchase of equipment	40,000
Collections from customers	200,000	Payments to employees	70,000
Payment of income tax	10,000	Payment of note payable	30,000
Purchase of treasury stock	5,000	Proceeds from sale of land	60,000
		Depreciation expense	8,000

Prepare the *operating* activities section of Austin-Healey's statement of cash flows for the year ended June 30, 20X9. Austin-Healey uses the *direct* method for operating cash flows.

Preparing a statement of cash flows—direct method (Obj. 4)

CP12-11 (p. 568) Use the data in Check Point 12-10 to prepare Austin-Healey Corporation's statement of cash flows for the year ended June 30, 20X9. Austin-Healey uses the *direct* method for operating activities. Use Exhibit 12-13, page 566, as a guide, but you may stop after determining the net increase (or decrease) in cash.

Computing operating cash flows—direct method (Obj. 4)

CP12-12 (p. 571) Use the Dover Elevator Company data in Check Point 12-7 to compute the following:

a. Collections from customers **b.** Payments for inventory

Computing operating cash flows—direct method (Obj. 4)

CP12-13 (p. 572) Use the Dover Elevator Company data in Check Point 12-7 to compute the following:

a. Payments to employees **b.** Payments of other expenses

Exercises

PH Grade Assist

Most of the even-numbered exercises can be found within Prentice Hall Grade Assist (PHGA), an online homework and practice environment. Your instructor may ask you to complete these exercises using PHGA.

Identifying the purposes of the statement of cash flows (Obj. 1)

writing assignment ■

E12-1 **Triumph Corporation** has experienced an unbroken string of 10 years of growth in net income. Nevertheless, the company is facing bankruptcy. Creditors are calling all of Triumph's loans for immediate payment, and the cash is simply not available. It is clear that Triumph's top managers emphasized profits and gave too little attention to cash flows.

Required

Write a brief memo, in your own words, to explain to the managers of Triumph Corporation the purposes of the statement of cash flows.

Identifying activities for the statement of cash flows—indirect method (Obj. 2)

E12-2 MGA Corporation restores pianos and other keyboard musical instruments. Identify each of MGA's transactions as operating (O), investing (I), financing (F), noncash investing and financing (NIF), or a transaction that is not reported on the statement of cash flows (N). Indicate whether each item increases (+) or decreases (–) cash. The indirect method is used for operating activities.

____ **a.** Acquisition of equipment by issuance of note payable
____ **b.** Payment of long-term debt
____ **c.** Acquisition of building by cash payment
____ **d.** Accrual of salary expense
____ **e.** Purchase of long-term investment
____ **f.** Decrease in merchandise inventory
____ **g.** Increase in prepaid expenses
____ **h.** Cash sale of land
____ **i.** Decrease in accrued liabilities
____ **j.** Amortization of intangible assets
____ **k.** Issuance of long-term note payable to borrow cash
____ **l.** Depreciation of equipment
____ **m.** Purchase of treasury stock
____ **n.** Issuance of common stock for cash
____ **o.** Increase in accounts payable
____ **p.** Net income
____ **q.** Payment of cash dividend
____ **r.** Sale of long-term investment
____ **s.** Loss on sale of equipment

Classifying transactions for the statement of cash flows—indirect method (Obj. 2)

E12-3 Proxy Inc., performs investment-related services for **Merrill Lynch**, **Edward Jones**, and other brokerage companies. Indicate whether each of the following transactions records an operating activity, an investing activity, a financing activity, or a noncash investing and financing activity. The statement of cash flows is prepared by the *indirect* method.

a. Cash	81,000	
Common Stock		12,000
Capital in Excess of Par		69,000
b. Treasury Stock	13,000	
Cash		13,000
c. Cash	60,000	
Accounts Receivable	10,000	
Service Revenue		70,000
d. Salary Expense	22,000	
Cash		22,000
e. Land	87,000	
Cash		87,000
f. Depreciation Expense	9,000	
Accumulated Depreciation		9,000
g. Equipment	18,000	
Cash		18,000
h. Cash	7,200	
Long-Term Investment		7,200
i. Bonds Payable	45,000	
Cash		45,000
j. Building	164,000	
Note Payable, Long-Term		164,000
k. Loss on Disposal of Equipment	1,400	
Equipment Net		1,400
l. Dividends Payable	16,500	
Cash		16,500
m. Furniture and Fixtures	22,100	
Cash		22,100

Computing cash flows from operating activities—indirect method
(Obj. 3)

writing assignment ■

E12-4 The accounting records of Magic China Restaurant reveal the following:

Depreciation	$18,000	Net income	$22,000
Decrease in current liabilities	20,000	Collection of dividend revenue	7,000
Increase in current assets other than cash	27,000	Payment of interest	16,000
Payment of dividends	7,000	Sales revenue	9,000
Payment of income tax	13,000	Loss on sale of land	5,000
		Acquisition of land	37,000

Required

Compute cash flows from operating activities by the indirect method. Use the format of the operating activities section of Exhibit 12-7 (page 556). Also evaluate the operating cash flow of Magic China Restaurant. Give the reason for your evaluation.

Computing cash flows from operating activities—indirect method
(Obj. 3)

E12-5 The accounting records of Manitoba Company include these accounts:

Cash

Mar. 1	5,000		
Receipts	447,000	Payments	448,000
Mar. 31	4,000		

Accounts Receivable

Mar. 1	18,000		
Sales	443,000	Collections	447,000
Mar. 31	14,000		

Inventory

Mar. 1	19,000		
Purchases	337,000	Cost of sales	335,000
Mar. 31	21,000		

Equipment

Mar. 1	93,000		
Acquisition	6,000		
Mar. 31	99,000		

Accumulated Depreciation—Equipment

		Mar. 1	52,000
		Depreciation	3,000
		Mar. 31	55,000

Accounts Payable

		Mar. 1	14,000
Payments	332,000	Purchases	337,000
		Mar. 31	19,000

Accrued Liabilities

		Mar. 1	9,000
Payments	14,000	Expenses	11,000
		Mar. 31	6,000

Retained Earnings

		Mar. 1	64,000
Quarterly dividend	18,000	Net income	57,000
		Mar. 31	103,000

Compute Manitoba's net cash provided by (used for) operating activities during March. Use the indirect method. Does Manitoba have troubling collecting receivables or selling inventory? How can you tell?

E12-6 The income statement and additional data of Robinson & Company follow:

Preparing the statement of cash flows—indirect method (Obj. 3)

writing assignment ■

Robinson & Company Income Statement Year Ended December 31, 20X6		
Revenues:		
Sales revenue	$229,000	
Dividend revenue	8,000	$237,000
Expenses:		
Cost of goods sold	$103,000	
Salary Expense	45,000	
Depreciation expense	29,000	
Advertising expense	4,000	
Interest expense	2,000	
Income tax expense	9,000	192,000
Net income		$ 45,000

Additional data:

a. Acquisition of plant assets was $116,000. Of this amount, $101,000 was paid in cash and $15,000 by signing a note payable.
b. Proceeds from sale of land totaled $24,000.
c. Proceeds from issuance of common stock totaled $30,000.
d. Payment of long-term note payable was $15,000.
e. Payment of dividends was $11,000.
f. From the balance sheet:

	December 31, 20X6	December 31, 20X5
Current Assets:		
Cash	$34,000	$20,000
Accounts receivable	43,000	58,000
Inventory	83,000	77,000
Prepaid expenses	9,000	8,000
Current Liabilities		
Accounts payable	$35,000	$22,000
Accrued liabilities	13,000	21,000

Required

1. Prepare Robinson & Company's statement of cash flows for the year ended December 31, 20X6, using the indirect method.
2. Evaluate Robinson's cash flows for the year. In your evaluation, mention all three categories of cash flows and give the reason for your evaluation.

E12-7 Consider three independent cases for the cash flows of Mill Creek Golf Course. For each case, identify from the cash-flow statement how Mill Creek generated the cash to acquire new plant assets. Rank the three cases from the most healthy financially to the least healthy.

Interpreting a cash-flow statement—indirect method (Obj. 3)

	Case A	Case B	Case C
Cash flows from operating activities:			
Net income	$ 30,000	$ 30,000	$ 30,000
Depreciation and amortization	11,000	11,000	11,000
Increase in current assets	(19,000)	(7,000)	(1,000)
Decrease in current liabilities	(6,000)	(8,000)	0
	$ 16,000	$ 26,000	$ 40,000
Cash flows from investing activities:			
Acquisition of plant assets	$ (91,000)	$(91,000)	$ (91,000)
Sales of plant assets	97,000	4,000	8,000
	$ 6,000	$(87,000)	$(83,000)
Cash flows from financing activities:			
Issuance of stock	$ 16,000	$104,000	$ 50,000
Payment of debt	(21,000)	(29,000)	(9,000)
	$ (5,000)	$ 75,000	$ 41,000
Net increase (decrease) in cash	$ 17,000	$ 14,000	$ (2,000)

Computing investing and financing amounts for the statement of cash flows (Obj. 3)

E12-8 Compute the following items for the statement of cash flows:

a. Beginning and ending Plant Assets, Net, are $103,000 and $107,000, respectively. Depreciation for the period was $16,000, and purchases of new plant assets were $27,000. Plant assets were sold at a $1,000 loss. What were the cash proceeds of the sale?

b. Beginning and ending Retained Earnings are $45,000 and $73,000, respectively. Net income for the period was $62,000, and stock dividends were $8,000. How much were cash dividends?

Identifying activities for the statement of cash flows—direct method (Obj. 4)

E12-9 Identify each of the following transactions as operating (O), investing (I), financing (F), noncash investing and financing (NIF), or not reported on the statement of cash flows (N). Indicate whether each transaction increases (+) or decreases (–) cash. The direct method is used for operating activities.

____ **a.** Collection of account receivable
____ **b.** Issuance of long-term note payable to borrow cash
____ **c.** Depreciation of equipment
____ **d.** Purchase of treasury stock
____ **e.** Issuance of common stock for cash
____ **f.** Payment of account payable
____ **g.** Issuance of preferred stock for cash
____ **h.** Payment of cash dividend
____ **i.** Sale of long-term investment
____ **j.** Amortization of patent
____ **k.** Acquisition of equipment by issuance of note payable
____ **l.** Payment of long-term debt
____ **m.** Acquisition of building by payment of cash
____ **n.** Accrual of salary expense
____ **o.** Purchase of long-term investment
____ **p.** Payment of wages to employees
____ **q.** Collection of cash interest
____ **r.** Cash sale of land
____ **s.** Distribution of stock dividend

Classifying transactions for the statement of cash flows—direct method (Obj. 4)

E12-10 Indicate where, if at all, each of the following transactions would be reported on a statement of cash flows prepared by the *direct* method and the accompanying schedule of noncash investing and financing activities.

a. Building	164,000	
Cash		164,000
b. Cash	1,400	
Accounts Receivable		1,400
c. Dividends Payable	16,500	
Cash		16,500
d. Equipment	18,000	
Cash		18,000
e. Cash	7,200	
Long-Term Investment		7,200
f. Bonds Payable	45,000	
Cash		45,000

(continued)

g. Furniture and Fixtures	22,100	
Note Payable, Short-Term		22,100
h. Salary Expense	4,300	
Cash		4,300
i. Cash	81,000	
Common Stock		12,000
Capital in Excess of Par		69,000
j. Treasury Stock	13,000	
Cash		13,000
k. Retained Earnings	36,000	
Common Stock		36,000
l. Cash	2,000	
Interest Revenue		2,000
m. Land	87,700	
Cash		87,700
n. Accounts Payable	8,300	
Cash		8,300

E12-11 The accounting records of Royal Marquis Corporation reveal the following:

Computing cash flows from operating activities—direct method (Obj. 4)

writing assignment ■

Net income	$34,000	Payment of salaries and wages	$34,000
Payment of income tax	13,000	Depreciation	22,000
Collection of dividend revenue	7,000	Decrease in current liabilities	20,000
Payment of interest	16,000	Increase in current assets other than cash	27,000
Cash sales	31,000	Payment of dividends	7,000
Loss on sale of land	5,000	Collection of accounts receivable	93,000
Acquisition of land	37,000		
Payment of accounts payable	54,000		

Required

Compute cash flows from operating activities by the direct method. Use the format of the operating activities section of Exhibit 12-13 (page 566). Also evaluate Royal Marquis' operating cash flow. Give the reason for your evaluation.

E12-12 Selected accounts of Campbell Car Dealership show the following:

Identifying items for the statement of cash flows—direct method (Obj. 4)

Dividends Receivable

Beginning balance	**9,000**		
Dividend revenue	**40,000**	**Cash receipts of dividends**	**38,000**
Ending balance	**11,000**		

Land

Beginning balance	**90,000**		
Acquisitions	**127,000**	**Book value of land sold**	**109,000**
Ending balance	**108,000**		

Notes Payable

		Beginning balance	**273,000**
Payments	**69,000**	**Issuance of debt for cash**	**83,000**
		Ending balance	**287,000**

Required

For each account, identify the item or items that should appear on a statement of cash flows prepared by the direct method. State where to report the item.

Preparing the statement of cash flows—direct method (Obj. 4)

writing assignment ■

E12-13 The income statement and additional data of Echo Lawn Equipment Company follow:

Echo Lawn Equipment Company Income Statement Year Ended June 30, 20X6		
Revenues:		
Sales revenue	$229,000	
Dividend revenue	15,000	$244,000
Expenses:		
Cost of goods sold	$103,000	
Salary expense	45,000	
Depreciation expense	29,000	
Advertising expense	11,000	
Interest expense	2,000	
Income tax expense	9,000	199,000
Net income		$ 45,000

Additional data:

a. Collections from customers are $15,000 more than sales.
b. Payments to suppliers are $1,000 more than the sum of cost of goods sold plus advertising expense.
c. Payments to employees are $1,000 more than salary expense.
d. Dividend revenue, interest expense, and income tax expense equal their cash amounts.
e. Acquisition of plant assets is $116,000. Of this amount, $101,000 is paid in cash and $15,000 by signing a note payable.
f. Proceeds from sale of land total $24,000.
g. Proceeds from issuance of common stock total $30,000.
h. Payment of long-term note payable is $15,000.
i. Payment of dividends is $11,000.
j. Cash balance, June 30, 20X5, was $20,000.

Required

1. Prepare Echo's statement of cash flows and accompanying schedule of noncash investing and financing activities. Report operating activities by the *direct* method.
2. Evaluate Echo's cash flows for the year. In your evaluation, mention all three categories of cash flows and give the reason for your evaluation.

Computing amounts for the statement of cash flows—direct method (Obj. 4)

E12-14 Compute the following items for the statement of cash flows:

a. Beginning and ending Accounts Receivable are $22,000 and $32,000, respectively. Credit sales for the period total $81,000. How much are cash collections from customers?
b. Cost of goods sold is $90,000. Beginning Inventory was $25,000, and ending Inventory is $21,000. Beginning and ending Accounts Payable are $14,000 and $8,000, respectively. How much are cash payments for inventory?

Challenge Exercises

Computing cash-flow amounts (Obj. 3, 4)

E12-15 Walstar Company reported the following in its financial statements for the year ended August 31, 20X4 (in thousands):

	20X4	20X3
Income Statement		
Net sales	$24,623	$21,207
Cost of sales	18,048	15,466
Depreciation	269	230
Other operating expenses	4,883	4,248
Income tax expense	537	486
Net income	$ 886	$ 777
Balance Sheet		
Cash and equivalents	$ 17	$ 13
Accounts receivable	719	615
Inventory	3,482	2,831
Property and equipment, net	4,345	3,428
Accounts payable	1,547	1,364
Accrued liabilities	938	848
Income tax payable	224	194
Long-term liabilities	478	464
Common stock	676	446
Retained earnings	4,531	3,788

Determine the following cash receipts and payments for Walstar during 20X4:

a. Collections from customers
b. Payments for inventory
c. Payments for other operating expenses
d. Payment of income tax
e. Proceeds from issuance of common stock
f. Payment of cash dividends

Using the balance sheet and the cash-flow statement together (Obj. 3)

E12-16 Motor Speedway, Inc., reported the following at December 31, 20X6 (in thousands):

	20X6	20X5
From the comparative balance sheet:		
Property and equipment, net	$11,150	$9,590
Long-term debt	4,290	3,080
From the statement of cash flows:		
Depreciation	$2,350	
Capital expenditures	(4,130)	
Proceeds from dispositions of property and equipment	170	
Proceeds from issuance of long-term debt	1,190	
Repayment of long-term debt	(110)	
Issuance of common stock	383	

Determine the following items for Motor Speedway during 20X6:

1. Gain or loss on the sale of property and equipment
2. Amount of long-term debt issued for something other than cash

Practice Quiz

Test your understanding of the statement of cash flows by answering the following questions. Select the best choice from among the possible answers given.

PQ12-1 Making a loan to another company is reported on the statement of cash flows under

a. operating activities.
b. investing activities.
c. financing activities.
d. noncash investing and financing activities.

PQ12-2 The sale of equipment is reported on the statement of cash flows under

a. operating activities.
b. investing activities.
c. financing activities.
d. noncash investing and financing activities.

PQ12-3 Cash flows relating to treasury stock are reported on the statement of cash flows under

a. operating activities.
b. investing activities.
c. financing activities.
d. noncash investing and financing activities.

PQ12-4 Which of the following terms appears on a statement of cash flows—indirect method?

a. Depreciation expense
b. Payments to suppliers
c. Collections from customers
d. Cash receipt of interest revenue

PQ12-5 On an indirect method statement of cash flows, a decrease in a current liability would be:

a. included in payments to suppliers.
b. added to net income.
c. offset against increases in current assets.
d. deducted from net income.

PQ12-6 On an indirect method statement of cash flows, an increase in inventory would be:

a. reported in the investing activities section.
b. reported in the financing activities section.
c. added to net income in the operating activities section.
d. deducted from net income in the operating activities section.

PQ12-7 On an indirect method statement of cash flows, a gain on the sale of plant assets would be

a. ignored, since it did not generate any cash.
b. reported in the investing activities section.
c. added to net income in the operating activities section.
d. deducted from net income in the operating activities section.

PQ12-8 Earning cash dividends is a/an _______________ activity.

Paying cash dividends is a/an _______________ activity.

PQ12-9 Zee Company sold machinery with a cost of $20,000 and accumulated depreciation of $8,000 for an amount that resulted in a loss of $3,000. What amount should Zee Company report on the statement of cash flows as "proceeds from sale of plant assets"?

a. $9,000
b. $17,000
c. $15,000
d. Some other amount (fill in the blank)

PQ12-10 Write the formula to determine cash proceeds from selling used equipment.

Use the following data for questions 11–19. Baylor Corporation formats operating cash flows by the *indirect* method.

Baylor's Income Statement for 20X3

Sales revenue	$180,000	
Gain on sale of equipment	8,000	$188,000
Cost of goods sold	$110,000	
Depreciation	6,000	
Other operating expenses	25,000	141,000
Net income		$ 47,000

Baylor's Comparative Balance Sheet at the End of 20X3

	20X3	20X2		20X3	20X2
Cash	$ 4,000	$ 1,000	Accounts payable	$ 6,000	$ 7,000
Accounts receivable	7,000	11,000	Accrued liabilities	7,000	3,000
Inventory	10,000	9,000	Common stock	20,000	10,000
Plant and equipment, net	93,000	69,000	Retained earnings	81,000	70,000
	$114,000	$90,000		$114,000	$ 90,000

The book value of equipment sold during 20X3 was $20,000.

PQ12-11 How many items enter the computation of Baylor's net cash provided by operating activities?

a. Seven
b. Five
c. Three
d. Two

PQ12-12 How do Baylor's accrued liabilities affect the company's statement of cash flows for 20X3?

a. Increase in cash provided by operating activities.
b. Increase in cash provided by investing activities.
c. Increase in cash used by financing activities.
d. They don't because the accrued liabilities are not yet paid.

PQ12-13 How do accounts receivable affect Baylor's cash flows from investing activities for 20X3?

a. Increase in cash used by financing activities.
b. Increase in cash provided by investing activities.
c. They don't because accounts receivable result from operating activities.
d. Decrease in cash used by investing activities.

PQ12-14 Baylor's net cash provided by operating activities during 20X3 was:

a. $58,000
b. $51,000
c. $47,000
d. $3,000

PQ12-15 How many items enter the computation of Baylor's net cash flow from investing activities for 20X3?

a. Five
b. Seven
c. Two
d. Three

PQ12-16 The book value of equipment sold during 20X3 was $20,000. Baylor's net cash flow from investing activities for 20X3 was:

a. net cash provided of $28,000.
b. net cash used of $22,000.
c. net cash used of $28,000.
d. net cash used of $50,000.

PQ12-17 How many items enter the computation of Baylor's net cash flow from financing activities for 20X3?

a. Seven
b. Five
c. Three
d. Two

PQ12-18 Baylor's largest financing cash flow for 20X3 resulted from:

a. issuance of common stock.
b. payment of dividends.
c. sale of equipment.
d. purchase of equipment.

PQ12-19 Baylor's net cash flow from financing activities for 20X3 was:

a. net cash provided of $10,000.
b. net cash used of $26,000.
c. net cash used of $25,000.
d. net cash used of $20,000.

PQ12-20 Sales totaled $800,000, accounts receivable increased by $40,000, and accounts payable decreased by $35,000. How much cash did the company collect from customers?

a. $795,000
b. $800,000
c. $760,000
d. $840,000

PQ12-21 Income Tax Payable was $5,000 at the beginning of the year and $2,800 at the end. Income tax expense for the year totaled $59,100. What amount of cash was paid for income tax during the year?

a. $56,900
b. $59,100
c. $61,300
d. $61,900

Problems
(Group A)

 PH Grade Assist	Most of these A problems can be found within Prentice Hall Grade Assist (PHGA), an online homework and practice environment. Your instructor may ask you to complete these exercises using PHGA.

Using cash-flow information to evaluate performance (Obj.1, 2)

writing assignment ■

P12-1A Top managers of Internet Solutions, Inc., are reviewing company performance for 20X4. The income statement reports a 15% increase in net income, the fifth consecutive year with an income increase above 10%. The income statement includes a nonrecurring loss without which net income would have increased by 16%. The balance sheet shows modest increases in assets, liabilities, and stockholders' equity. The assets posting the largest increases are plant and equipment because the company is halfway through a 5-year expansion program. No other asset and no liabilities are increasing dramatically. A summarized version of the cash-flow statement reports the following:

Net cash provided by operating activities	$310,000
Net cash used for investing activities	(290,000)
Net cash provided by financing activities	70,000
Increase in cash during 20X4	$ 90,000

Required

Write a memo giving top managers of Internet Solutions your assessment of 20X4 operations and your outlook for the future. Focus on the information content of the cash-flow data.

Preparing an income statement, balance sheet, and statement of cash flows—indirect method (Obj. 2, 3)

P12-2A Dohn Corporation, a discounter of men's suits, was formed on January 1, 20X6, when Dohn issued its no-par common stock for $200,000. Early in January, Dohn made the following cash payments:

a. For store fixtures, $50,000
b. For inventory (1,000 men's suits), $120,000
c. For rent on a store building, $12,000

In February, Dohn purchased 2,000 men's suits on account from a Chinese company. Cost of this inventory was $160,000. Before year end, Dohn paid $140,000 of this debt. Dohn uses the FIFO method to account for inventory.

During 20X6, Dohn sold 2,800 units of inventory for $200 each. Before year end, Dohn collected 90% of this amount.

The store employs three people. The combined annual payroll is $90,000, of which Dohn owes $3,000 at year end. At the end of the year, Dohn paid income tax of $64,000.

Late in 20X6, Dohn declared and paid cash dividends of $40,000.

For store fixtures, Dohn uses the straight-line depreciation method, over 5 years, with zero residual value.

Required

1. Prepare Dohn Corporation's income statement for the year ended December 31, 20X6. Use the single-step format, with all revenues listed together and all expenses together.

2. Prepare Dohn's balance sheet at December 31, 20X6.
3. Prepare Dohn's statement of cash flows for the year ended December 31, 20X6. Format cash flows from operating activities by the indirect method.

Preparing the statement of cash flows—indirect method (Obj. 2, 3)

P12-3A Accountants for WWW.Smart, Inc. have assembled the following data for the year ended December 31, 20X4:

	December 31, 20X4	20X3
Current Accounts:		
Current assets:		
Cash and cash equivalents	$48,600	$34,800
Accounts receivable	70,100	73,700
Inventories	90,600	96,500
Prepaid expenses	3,200	2,100
Current liabilities:		
Accounts payable	$71,600	$67,500
Income tax payable	5,900	6,800
Accrued liabilities	28,300	23,200

Transaction Data for 20X4:

Stock dividends	$ 12,600	Payment of cash dividends	$48,300
Collection of loan	10,300	Issuance of long-term debt to borrow cash	71,000
Depreciation expense	29,200	Net income	50,500
Acquisition of equipment	69,000	Issuance of preferred stock for cash	36,200
Payment of long-term debt by issuing common stock	89,400	Sale of long-term investment	12,200
Acquisition of long-term investment	44,800	Amortization expense	1,100
Acquisition of building by issuing long-term note payable	118,000	Payment of long-term debt	47,800
		Gain on sale of investment	3,500

Required

Prepare WWW.Smart's statement of cash flows using the *indirect* method to report operating activities. Include an accompanying schedule of noncash investing and financing activities.

Preparing the statement of cash flows—indirect method (Obj. 2, 3)

writing assignment ■

■ spreadsheet

P12-4A The comparative balance sheet of CNA Leasing, Inc., at December 31, 20X5, reported the following:

	December 31, 20X5	20X4
Current Assets:		
Cash and cash equivalents	$ 8,400	$12,500
Accounts receivable	28,600	29,300
Inventories	51,600	53,000
Prepaid expenses	4,200	3,700
Current Liabilities:		
Accounts payable	$31,100	$28,000
Accrued liabilities	14,300	16,800
Income tax payable	11,000	14,300

CNA's transactions during 20X5 included the following:

Amortization expense	$ 5,000	Cash acquisition of building ...	$124,000
Payment of cash dividends	17,000	Net income	31,600
Cash acquisition of equipment .	55,000	Issuance of common stock	
Issuance of long-term note		for cash	105,600
payable to borrow cash	32,000	Stock dividend	13,000
Retirement of bonds payable		Sale of long-term investment ..	6,000
by issuing common stock ...	55,000	Depreciation expense	12,800

Required

1. Prepare the statement of cash flows of CNA Leasing, Inc., for the year ended December 31, 20X5. Use the *indirect* method to report cash flows from operating activities. Report noncash investing and financing activities in an accompanying schedule.
2. Evaluate CNA's cash flows for the year. Mention all three categories of cash flows and give the reason for your evaluation.

Preparing the statement of cash flows—indirect method (Obj. 2, 3)

writing assignment ■

■ spreadsheet

P12-5A The 20X8 comparative balance sheet and income statement of Genie Marketing, Inc., follows. Genie had no noncash investing and financing transactions during 20X8. During the year, there were no sales of land or equipment, no issuances of notes payable, no retirements of stock, and no treasury stock transactions.

Required

1. Prepare the 20X8 statement of cash flows, formatting operating activities by the indirect method.
2. How will what you learned in this problem help you evaluate an investment?

Genie Marketing, Inc.
Comparative Balance Sheet
December 31, 20X8 and 20X7

	20X8	20X7	Increase (Decrease)
Current assets:			
Cash and cash equivalents	$ 8,700	$ 15,600	$ (6,900)
Accounts receivable	46,500	43,100	3,400
Interest receivable	600	900	(300)
Inventories	94,300	89,900	4,400
Prepaid expenses	1,700	2,200	(500)
Plant assets:			
Land	35,100	10,000	25,100
Equipment, net	100,900	93,700	7,200
Total assets	$287,800	$255,400	$ 32,400
Current liabilities:			
Accounts payable	$ 16,400	$ 17,900	$ (1,500)
Interest payable	6,300	6,700	(400)
Salary payable	2,100	1,400	700
Other accrued liabilities	18,100	18,700	(600)
Income tax payable	6,300	3,800	2,500
Long-term liabilities:			
Notes payable	55,000	65,000	(10,000)
Stockholders' equity:			
Common stock, no-par	131,100	122,300	8,800
Retained earnings	52,500	19,600	32,900
Total liabilities and stockholders' equity	$287,800	$255,400	$ 32,400

Genie Marketing, Inc. Income Statement for 20X8		
Revenues:		
Sales revenue		$438,000
Interest revenue		11,700
Total revenues		449,700
Expenses:		
Cost of goods sold	$205,200	
Salary expense	76,400	
Depreciation expense	15,300	
Other operating expense	49,700	
Interest expense	24,600	
Income tax expense	16,900	
Total expenses		388,100
Net income		$ 61,600

Preparing the statement of cash flows—direct method (Obj. 2, 4)

writing assignment

P12-6A Data Solutions, Inc., accountants have developed the following data from the company's accounting records for the year ended July 31, 20X5:

a. Salary expense, $105,300
b. Cash payments to purchase plant assets, $181,000
c. Proceeds from issuance of short-term debt, $44,100
d. Payments of long-term debt, $18,800
e. Proceeds from sale of plant assets, $59,700, including $10,600 gain
f. Interest revenue, $12,100
g. Cash receipt of dividend revenue on stock investments, $2,700
h. Payments to suppliers, $673,300
i. Interest expense and payments, $37,800
j. Cost of goods sold, $481,100
k. Collection of interest revenue, $11,700
l. Acquisition of equipment by issuing short-term note payable, $35,500
m. Payments of salaries, $104,000
n. Credit sales, $608,100
o. Loan to another company, $35,000
p. Income tax expense and payments, $56,400
q. Depreciation expense, $27,700
r. Collections on accounts receivable, $681,100
s. Loan collections, $74,400
t. Proceeds from sale of investments, $34,700, including $3,800 loss
u. Payment of long-term debt by issuing preferred stock, $107,300
v. Amortization expense, $23,900
w. Cash sales, $146,000
x. Proceeds from issuance of common stock, $116,900
y. Payment of cash dividends, $50,500
z. Cash balance: July 31, 20X4—$53,800; July 31, 20X5—$68,300

I *Required*

1. Prepare Data Solutions' statement of cash flows for the year ended July 31, 20X5. Use the direct method for cash flows from operating activities. Follow the format of Exhibit 12-13, but do *not* show amounts in thousands. Include an accompanying schedule of noncash investing and financing activities.
2. Evaluate 20X5 in terms of cash flow. Give your reasons.

Preparing an income statement, balance sheet, and statement of cash flows—direct method (Obj. 2, 4)

P12-7A Use the Dohn Corporation data from Problem 12-2A.

I *Required*

1. Prepare Dohn Corporation's income statement for the year ended December 31, 20X6. Use the single-step format, with all the revenues listed together and all expenses together.
2. Prepare Dohn's balance sheet at December 31, 20X6.
3. Prepare Dohn's statement of cash flows for the year ended December 31, 20X6. Format cash flows from operating activities by using the direct method.

Preparing the statement of cash flows—direct method (Obj. 2, 4)

P12-8A Use the Genie Marketing, Inc., data from Problem 12-5A.

Required

1. Prepare the 20X8 statement of cash flows by using the direct method.
2. How will what you learned in this problem help you evaluate an investment?

writing assignment ■

■ spreadsheet

Preparing the statement of cash flows—direct and indirect methods (Obj. 3, 4)

P12-9A To prepare the statement of cash flows, accountants for Rolex Paper Company have summarized 20X8 activity in two accounts as follows:

Cash

Beginning balance	87,100	Payments of operating expenses	46,100
Issuance of common stock	34,600	Payment of long-term debt	78,900
Receipts of dividends	1,900	Purchase of treasury stock	10,400
Collection of loan	18,500	Payment of income tax	8,000
Sale of investments	9,900	Payments on accounts payable	101,600
Receipts of interest	12,200	Payments of dividends	1,800
Collections from customers	308,100	Payments of salaries and wages	67,500
Sale of treasury stock	26,200	Payments of interest	21,800
		Purchase of equipment	79,900
Ending balance	82,500		

Common Stock

		Beginning balance	103,500
		Issuance for cash	34,600
		Issuance to acquire land	62,100
		Issuance to retire long-term debt	21,100
		Ending balance	221,300

Required

1. Prepare Rolex's statement of cash flows for the year ended December 31, 20X8, using the *direct* method to report operating activities. Also prepare the accompanying schedule of noncash investing and financing activities. Rolex's 20X8 income statement and selected balance sheet data follow.
2. Prepare a supplementary schedule showing cash flows from operating activities by the *indirect* method.

Rolex Paper Company
Income Statement
Year Ended December 31, 20X8

Revenues and gains:		
Sales revenue		$291,800
Interest revenue		12,200
Dividend revenue		1,900
Gain on sale of investments		700
Total revenues and gains		306,600
Expenses:		
Cost of goods sold	$103,600	
Salary and wage expense	66,800	
Depreciation expense	20,900	
Other operating expense	44,700	
Interest expense	24,100	
Income tax expense	2,600	
Total expenses		262,700
Net income		$ 43,900

Rolex Paper Company Selected Balance Sheet Data	20X8 Increase (Decrease)
Current assets:	
Cash and cash equivalents	$ (4,600)
Accounts receivable	(16,300)
Inventories	5,700
Prepaid expenses	(1,900)
Loan receivable	(18,500)
Investments	(9,200)
Equipment, net	59,000
Land	62,100
Current liabilities:	
Accounts payable	$ 7,700
Interest payable	2,300
Salary payable	(700)
Other accrued liabilities	(3,300)
Income tax payable	(5,400)
Long-term debt	(100,000)
Common stock	117,800
Retained earnings	42,100
Treasury stock	(15,800)

P12-10A Heart O'Texas Optical Corporation's comparative balance sheet at September 30, 20X4 included the following balances:

Preparing the statement of cash flows—indirect and direct methods
(Obj. 3, 4)

Heart O'Texas Optical
Balance Sheet
September 30, 20X4 and 20X3

	20X4	20X3	Increase (Decrease)
Current assets:			
Cash	$ 11,700	$ 17,600	$ (5,900)
Accounts receivable	41,900	44,000	(2,100)
Interest receivable	4,100	2,800	1,300
Inventories	121,700	116,900	4,800
Prepaid expenses	8,600	9,300	(700)
Long-term investments	51,100	13,800	37,300
Equipment, net	131,900	92,100	39,800
Land	47,100	74,300	(27,200)
	$418,100	$370,800	$ 47,300
Current liabilities:			
Notes payable, short-term	$ 22,000	$ 0	$ 22,000
Accounts payable	61,800	70,300	(8,500)
Income tax payable	21,800	24,600	(2,800)
Accrued liabilities	17,900	29,100	(11,200)
Interest payable	4,500	3,200	1,300
Salary payable	1,500	1,100	400
Long-term note payable	123,000	121,400	1,600
Common stock	113,900	62,000	51,900
Retained earnings	51,700	59,100	(7,400)
	$418,100	$370,800	$ 47,300

Transaction data for the year ended September 30, 20X4:

a. Net income, $56,900
b. Depreciation expense on equipment, $8,500

c. Acquired long-term investments, $37,300
d. Sold land for $38,100, including $10,900 gain
e. Acquired equipment by issuing long-term note payable, $26,300
f. Paid long-term note payable, $24,700
g. Received cash of $51,900 for issuance of common stock
h. Paid cash dividends, $64,300
i. Acquired equipment by issuing short-term note payable, $22,000

Required

1. Prepare Heart O'Texas Optical's statement of cash flows for the year ended September 30, 20X4 using the *indirect* method to report operating activities. Also prepare the accompanying schedule of noncash investing and financing activities. All current accounts except short-term notes payable result from operating transactions.
2. Prepare a supplementary schedule showing cash flows from operations by using the *direct* method. The income statement reports the following: sales, $333,600; gain on sale of land, $10,900; interest revenue, $7,300; cost of goods sold, $161,500; salary expense, $63,400; other operating expenses, $29,600; income tax expense, $18,400; interest expense, $13,500; and depreciation expense, $8,500.

(Group B)

PH Grade Assist

Some of these B problems can be found within Prentice Hall Grade Assist (PHGA), an online homework and practice environment. Your instructor may ask you to complete these exercises using PHGA.

Using cash-flow data to evaluate performance (Obj. 1, 2)

writing assignment

P12-1B Top managers of Oasis Water, Inc., are reviewing company performance for 20X7. The income statement reports a 20% increase in net income over 20X6. However, most of the increase resulted from an extraordinary gain on insurance proceeds from storm damage to a building. The balance sheet shows a large increase in receivables. The cash-flow statement, in summarized form, reports the following:

Net cash used for operating activities	$(80,000)
Net cash provided by investing activities	40,000
Net cash provided by financing activities	50,000
Increase in cash during 20X7	$ 10,000

Required

Write a memo giving Oasis Water managers your assessment of 20X7 operations and your outlook for the future. Focus on the information content of the cash-flow data.

Preparing an income statement, balance sheet, and statement of cash flows—indirect method (Obj. 2, 3)

P12-2B Scott Corporation, a furniture store, was formed on January 1, 20X8, when Scott issued its no-par common stock for $300,000. Early in January, Scott made the following cash payments:

a. $150,000 for equipment
b. $120,000 for inventory (1,000 pieces of furniture)
c. $20,000 for 20X8 rent on a store building

In February, Scott purchased 2,000 units of furniture inventory on account from a Mexican company. Cost of this inventory was $260,000. Before year end, Scott paid $208,000 of this debt. Scott uses the FIFO method to account for inventory.

During 20X8, Scott sold 2,500 units of inventory for $200 each. Before year end, Scott collected 80% of this amount.

The store employs three people. The combined annual payroll is $95,000, of which Scott owes $4,000 at year end. At the end of the year, Scott paid income tax of $10,000.

Late in 20X8, Scott declared and paid cash dividends of $11,000.

For equipment, Scott uses the straight-line depreciation method, over 5 years, with zero residual value.

Required

1. Prepare Scott Corporation's income statement for the year ended December 31, 20X8. Use the single-step format, with all revenues listed together and all expenses together.
2. Prepare Scott's balance sheet at December 31, 20X8.
3. Prepare Scott's statement of cash flows for the year ended December 31, 20X8. Format cash flows from operating activities by using the indirect method.

Preparing the statement of cash flows—indirect method (Obj. 2, 3)

P12-3B Datex Corporation accountants have assembled the following data for the year ended December 31, 20X7.

	December 31, 20X7	20X6
Current Accounts:		
Current assets:		
Cash and cash equivalents	$50,700	$22,700
Accounts receivable	69,700	64,200
Inventories	88,600	83,000
Prepaid expenses	5,300	4,100
Current liabilities:		
Accounts payable	$57,200	$55,800
Income tax payable	18,600	16,700
Accrued liabilities	15,500	27,200

Transaction Data for 20X7:

Acquisition of land by issuing long-term note payable	$107,000	Purchase of treasury stock	$14,300
Stock dividends	31,800	Loss on sale of equipment	11,700
Collection of loan	8,700	Payment of cash dividends	18,300
Depreciation expense	21,800	Issuance of long-term note payable to borrow cash	34,400
Acquisition of building	125,300	Net income	57,100
Retirement of bonds payable by issuing common stock	65,000	Issuance of common stock for cash	41,200
Acquisition of long-term investment	31,600	Sale of equipment	58,000
		Amortization expense	5,300

Required

Prepare Datex Corporation's statement of cash flows using the *indirect* method to report operating activities. Include an accompanying schedule of noncash investing and financing activities.

Preparing the statement of cash flows—indirect method (Obj. 2, 3)

writing assignment ■

■ spreadsheet

P12-4B The comparative balance sheet of Southern Bell Company at March 31, 20X9, reported the following:

	March 31, 20X9	20X8
Current assets:		
Cash and cash equivalents	$19,900	$ 4,000
Accounts receivable	14,900	21,700
Inventories	63,200	60,600
Prepaid expenses	1,900	1,700
Current liabilities:		
Accounts payable	$30,300	$27,600
Accrued liabilities	10,700	11,100
Income tax payable	8,000	4,700

Southern Bell's transactions during the year ended March 31, 20X9, included the following:

Acquisition of land by issuing note payable	$76,000	Sale of long-term investment	$13,700
Amortization expense	2,000	Depreciation expense	15,300
Payment of cash dividend	30,000	Cash acquisition of building	47,000
Cash acquisition of equipment	78,700	Net income	70,000
Issuance of long-term note payable to borrow cash	50,000	Issuance of common stock for cash	11,000
		Stock dividend	18,000

Required

1. Prepare Southern Bell's statement of cash flows for the year ended March 31, 20X9, using the *indirect* method to report cash flows from operating activities. Report noncash investing and financing activities in an accompanying schedule.
2. Evaluate Southern Bell's cash flows for the year. Mention all three categories of cash flows and give the reason for your evaluation.

Preparing the statement of cash flows—indirect method (Obj. 2, 3)

■ **spreadsheet**

writing assignment ■

P12-5B The 20X5 comparative balance sheet and income statement of Town East Press follow. Town East had no noncash investing and financing transactions during 20X5. During the year, there were no sales of land or equipment, no issuance of notes payable, no retirements of stock, and no treasury stock transactions.

Required

1. Prepare the 20X5 statement of cash flows, formatting operating activities by using the indirect method.
2. How will what you learned in this problem help you evaluate an investment?

Town East Press
Comparative Balance Sheet

	December 31, 20X5	20X4	Increase (Decrease)
Current assets:			
Cash and cash equivalents	$ 10,500	$ 5,300	$ 5,200
Accounts receivable	25,300	26,900	(1,600)
Interest receivable	1,900	700	1,200
Inventories	83,600	87,200	(3,600)
Prepaid expenses	2,500	1,900	600
Plant assets:			
Land	89,000	60,000	29,000
Equipment, net	53,500	49,400	4,100
Total assets:	$266,300	$231,400	$34,900
Current liabilities:			
Accounts payable	$ 31,400	$ 28,800	$ 2,600
Interest payable	4,400	4,900	(500)
Salary payable	3,100	6,600	(3,500)
Other accrued liabilities	13,700	16,000	(2,300)
Income tax payable	8,900	7,700	1,200
Long-term liabilities:			
Notes payable	75,000	100,000	(25,000)
Stockholders' equity:			
Common stock, no-par	88,300	64,700	23,600
Retained earnings	41,500	2,700	38,800
Total liabilities and stockholders' equity	$266,300	$231,400	$34,900

Town East Press Income Statement for 20X5		
Revenues:		
Sales revenue		$213,000
Interest revenue		8,600
Total revenues		221,600
Expenses:		
Cost of goods sold	$70,600	
Salary expense	27,800	
Depreciation expense	4,000	
Other operating expense	10,500	
Interest expense	11,600	
Income tax expense	29,100	
Total expenses		153,600
Net income		$ 68,000

Preparing the statement of cash flows—direct method (Obj. 2, 4)

writing assignment ■

P12-6B Accountants for Triad Associates, Inc. have developed the following data from the company's accounting records for the year ended April 30, 20X5:

a. Credit sales, $583,900
b. Loan to another company, $12,500
c. Cash payments to acquire plant assets, $59,400
d. Cost of goods sold, $382,600
e. Proceeds from issuance of common stock, $8,000
f. Payment of cash dividends, $48,400
g. Collection of interest, $4,400
h. Acquisition of equipment by issuing short-term note payable, $16,400
i. Payments of salaries, $93,600
j. Proceeds from sale of plant assets, $22,400, including $6,800 loss
k. Collections on accounts receivable, $448,600
l. Interest revenue, $3,800
m. Cash receipt of dividend revenue, $4,100
n. Payments to suppliers, $368,500
o. Cash sales, $171,900
p. Depreciation expense, $59,900
q. Proceeds from issuance of short-term debt, $19,600
r. Payments of long-term debt, $50,000
s. Interest expense and payments, $13,300
t. Salary expense, $95,300
u. Loan collections, $12,800
v. Proceeds from sale of investments, $9,100, including $2,000 gain
w. Payment of short-term note payable by issuing long-term note payable, $63,000
x. Amortization expense, $2,900
y. Income tax expense and payments, $37,900
z. Cash balance: April 30, 20X4, $39,300; April 30, 20X5, $56,600

Required

1. Prepare Triad Associates' statement of cash flows for the year ended April 30, 20X5. Use the direct method for cash flows from operating activities. Follow the format of Exhibit 12-13, but do *not* show amounts in thousands. Include an accompanying schedule of noncash investing and financing activities.
2. Evaluate 20X5 from a cash-flow standpoint. Give your reasons.

Preparing an income statement, balance sheet, and statement of cash flows—direct method (Obj. 2, 4)

P12-7B Use the Scott Corporation data from Problem 12-2B.

Required

1. Prepare Scott Corporation's income statement for the year ended December 31, 20X8. Use the single-step format, with all revenues listed together and all expenses together.

2. Prepare Scott's balance sheet at December 31, 20X8.
3. Prepare Scott's statement of cash flows for the year ended December 31, 20X8. Format cash flows from operating activities by using the direct method.

Preparing the statement of cash flows—direct method (Obj. 2, 4)

writing assignment ■

P12-8B Use the Town East Press data from Problem 12-5B.

Required

1. Prepare the 20X5 statement of cash flows by using the direct method.
2. How will what you learned in this problem help you evaluate an investment?

Preparing the statement of cash flows—direct and indirect methods (Obj. 3, 4)

■ spreadsheet

P12-9B To prepare the statement of cash flows, accountants for Internet Guide, Inc., have summarized 20X8 activity in two accounts as follows:

Cash

Beginning balance	53,600	Payments on accounts payable	399,100
Collection of loan	13,000	Payments of dividends	27,200
Sale of investment	8,200	Payments of salaries and wages	143,800
Receipts of interest	12,600	Payments of interest	26,900
Collections from customers	673,700	Purchase of equipment	31,400
Issuance of common stock	47,300	Payments of operating expenses	34,300
Receipts of dividends	4,500	Payment of long-term debt	41,300
		Purchase of treasury stock	26,400
		Payment of income tax	18,900
Ending balance	63,600		

Common Stock

		Beginning balance	84,400
		Issuance for cash	47,300
		Issuance to acquire land	80,100
		Issuance to retire long-term debt	19,000
		Ending balance	230,800

Required

1. Prepare the statement of cash flows of Internet Guide, Inc., for the year ended December 31, 20X8, using the *direct* method to report operating activities. Also prepare the accompanying schedule of noncash investing and financing activities.
2. Use the following data from Internet Guide's 20X8 income statement and balance sheet to prepare a supplementary schedule of cash flows from operating activities by using the *indirect* method.

Internet Guide, Inc. Income Statement Year Ended December 31, 20X8		
Revenues:		
Sales revenue		$701,300
Interest revenue		12,600
Dividend revenue		4,500
Total revenues		718,400
Expenses and losses:		
Cost of goods sold	$402,600	
Salary and wage expense	150,800	
Depreciation expense	19,300	
Other operating expense	44,100	
Interest expense	28,800	
Income tax expense	16,200	
Loss on sale of investments	1,100	
Total expenses		662,900
Net income		$ 55,500

Internet Guide, Inc. Selected Balance Sheet Data	20X8 Increase (Decrease)
Current assets:	
Cash and cash equivalents	$ 10,000
Accounts receivable	27,600
Inventories	(11,800)
Prepaid expenses	600
Loan receivable	(13,000)
Long-term investments	(9,300)
Equipment, net	12,100
Land	80,100
Current liabilities:	
Accounts payable	$ (8,300)
Interest payable	1,900
Salary payable	7,000
Other accrued liabilities	10,400
Income tax payable	(2,700)
Long-term debt	(60,300)
Common stock, no-par	146,400
Retained earnings	28,300
Treasury stock	26,400

Preparing the statement of cash flows—indirect and direct methods (Obj. 3, 4)

P12-10B The comparative balance sheet of Safeco Defensive Driving, Inc., at June 30, 20X9, included the amounts given on the next page.

Transaction data for the year ended June 30, 20X9:

a. Net income, $56,200
b. Depreciation expense on equipment, $13,400
c. Purchased long-term investment, $4,900
d. Sold land for $46,900, including $6,700 loss
e. Acquired equipment by issuing long-term note payable, $14,300
f. Paid long-term note payable, $61,000
g. Received cash for issuance of common stock, $3,900
h. Paid cash dividends, $38,100
i. Paid short-term note payable by issuing common stock, $4,700

Required

1. Prepare the statement of cash flows of Safeco Defensive Driving, Inc., for the year ended June 30, 20X9, using the *indirect* method to report operating activities. Also prepare the accompanying schedule of noncash investing and financing activities. All current accounts except short-term notes payable result from operating transactions.
2. Prepare a supplementary schedule showing cash flows from operations by the *direct* method. The income statement reports the following: sales, $245,300; interest revenue, $10,600; cost of goods sold, $82,800; salary expense, $38,800; other operating expenses, $42,000; depreciation expense, $5,400; income tax expense, $9,900; loss on sale of land, $6,700; and interest expense, $6,100.

Safeco Defensive Driving, Inc.
Balance Sheet
June 30, 20X9 and 20X8

	20X9	20X8	Increase (Decrease)
Current assets:			
Cash	$ 24,500	$ 8,600	$ 15,900
Accounts receivable	45,900	48,300	(2,400)
Interest receivable	2,900	3,600	(700)
Inventories	68,600	60,200	8,400
Prepaid expenses	3,700	2,800	900
Long-term investment	10,100	5,200	4,900
Equipment, net	74,500	73,600	900
Land	42,400	96,000	(53,600)
	$272,600	$298,300	$(25,700)
Current liabilities:			
Notes payable, short-term	$ 13,400	$ 18,100	$ (4,700)
Accounts payable	42,400	40,300	2,100
Income tax payable	13,800	14,500	(700)
Accrued liabilities	8,200	9,700	(1,500)
Interest payable	3,700	2,900	800
Salary payable	900	2,600	(1,700)
Long-term note payable	47,400	94,100	(46,700)
Common stock	59,800	51,200	8,600
Retained earnings	83,000	64,900	18,100
	$272,600	$298,300	$(25,700)

APPLY YOUR KNOWLEDGE

Decision Cases

Preparing and using the statement of cash flows to evaluate operations (Obj. 3)

writing assignment ■

Case 1. The 20X6 comparative income statement and the 20X6 comparative balance sheet of Tennis, Tennis, Tennis!, Inc. have just been distributed at a meeting of the company's board of directors. The members of the board of directors raise a fundamental question: Why is the cash balance so low? This question is especially troublesome to the board members because 20X6 showed record profits. As the controller of the company, you must answer the question.

Tennis, Tennis, Tennis!, Inc.
Comparative Income Statement
Years Ended December 31, 20X6 and 20X5

(In thousands)	20X6	20X5
Revenues and gains:		
Sales revenue	$444	$310
Gain on sale of equipment (sale price, $33)	—	18
Totals	$444	$328
Expenses and losses:		
Cost of goods sold	$221	$162
Salary expense	48	28
Depreciation expense	46	22
Interest expense	13	20
Amortization expense on patent	11	11
Loss on sale of land (sale price, $61)	—	35
Total expenses and losses	339	278
Net income	$105	$ 50

Tennis, Tennis, Tennis!, Inc.
Comparative Balance Sheet
December 31, 20X6 and 20X5

(In thousands)	20X6	20X5
Assets:		
Cash	$ 25	$ 63
Accounts receivable, net	72	61
Inventories	194	181
Long-term investments	31	0
Property, plant and equipment	369	259
Accumulated depreciation	(244)	(198)
Patents	177	188
Totals	$624	$554
Liabilities and Owners' Equity		
Accounts payable	$ 63	$ 56
Accrued liabilities	12	17
Notes payable, long-term	179	264
Common stock, no par	149	61
Retained earnings	221	156
Totals	$624	$554

Required

1. Prepare a statement of cash flows for 20X6 in the format that best shows the relationship between net income and operating cash flow. The company sold no plant assets or long-term investments and issued no notes payable during 20X6. There were *no* noncash investing and financing transactions during the year. Show all amounts in thousands.
2. Answer the board members' question: Why is the cash balance so low? In explaining the business's cash flows, identify two significant cash receipts that occurred during 20X5 but not in 20X6. Also point out the two largest cash payments during 20X6.
3. Considering net income and the company's cash flows during 20X6, was it a good year or a bad year? Give your reasons.

Using cash-flow data to evaluate an investment (Obj. 1, 2)

writing assignment ■

Case 2. Carolina Technology, Inc., and Northwest Electric Power Corporation are asking you to recommend their stock to your clients. Because Carolina and Northwest earn about the same net income and have similar financial positions, your decision depends on their cash-flow statements, summarized as follows:

	Carolina		Northwest	
Net cash provided by operating activities:		$ 70,000		$ 30,000
Cash provided by (used for) investing activities:				
Purchase of plant assets	$(100,000)		$(20,000)	
Sale of plant assets	10,000	(90,000)	40,000	20,000
Cash provided by (used for) financing activities:				
Issuance of common stock		30,000		—
Paying off long-term debt		—		(40,000)
Net increase in cash		$ 10,000		$ 10,000

Based on their cash flows, which company looks better? Give your reasons.

Ethical Issue

writing assignment ■

Victoria British Auto Parts is having a bad year. Net income is only $37,000. Also, two important overseas customers are falling behind in their payments to Victoria, and Victoria's accounts receivable are ballooning. The company desperately needs a loan. The Victoria board of directors is considering ways to put the best face on the company's financial statements. Victoria's bank closely examines cash flow from operations. Daniel Peavey, Victoria's controller, suggests reclassifying as long-term the receivables from the slow-paying clients. He explains to the board that removing the $80,000 rise in accounts receivable from current assets will increase net cash provided by operations. This approach may help Victoria get the loan.

Required

1. Using only the amounts given, compute net cash provided by operations, both without and with the reclassification of the receivables. Which reporting makes Victoria look better?
2. Under what condition would the reclassification of the receivables be ethical? Unethical?

Focus on Financials: ■ YUM! Brands

Using the statement of cash flows (Obj. 1, 2, 3, 4)

writing assignment ■

Use **YUM! Brands, Inc.'s** statement of cash flows along with the company's other financial statements, all in Appendix A at the end of the book, to answer the following questions.

Required

1. By which method does YUM report cash flows from *operating* activities? How can you tell?
2. Suppose YUM reported net cash flows from operating activities by using the direct method. Compute these amounts for the year ended December 27, 2003 (ignore the statement of cash flows):
   a. Collections from customers, franchises, and licenses
   b. Payments for inventory (note 13 gives the Accounts Payable balance)
3. Prepare a T-account for Property, Plant, and Equipment. Net and show all activity in this account for 2003. Use the depreciation amount in note 11 and assume that YUM sold property, plant, and equipment with book value of $32 million.
4. Evaluate 2003 in terms of net income, total assets, stockholders' equity, cash flows, and overall results. Be specific.

Focus on Analysis: ■ Pier 1 Imports

Analyzing cash flows (Obj. 1, 2, 3, 4)

Refer to the Pier 1 Imports financial statements in Appendix B at the end of this book. Focus on 2004.

1. What is Pier 1's main source of cash? Is this good news or bad news to Pier 1 managers, stockholders, and creditors? What is Pier 1's main use of cash? Good news or bad news? Explain all answers in detail.
2. Explain in detail the three main reasons why net cash provided by operations differs from net income.
3. Did Pier 1 buy more fixed assets or sell more fixed assets during 2004? How can you tell?
4. Identify the sale price, the book value, and the gain or loss from selling fixed assets during 2004.
5. How much cash in total did Pier 1 return to stockholders during 2004?

Group Projects

Project 1. Each member of the group should obtain the annual report of a different company. Select companies in different industries. Evaluate each company's trend of cash flows for the most recent 2 years? In your evaluation of the companies' cash flows, you may use any other information that is publicly available—for example, the other financial statements (income statement, balance sheet, statement of stockholders' equity, and the related notes) and news stories from magazines and newspapers. Rank the companies' cash flows from best to worst and write a two-page report on your findings.

Project 2. Select a company and obtain its annual report, including all the financial statements. Focus on the statement of cash flows and, in particular, the cash flows from operating activities. Specify whether the company uses the direct method or the indirect method to report operating cash flows. As necessary, use the other financial statements (income statement, balance sheet, and statement of stockholders' equity) and the notes to prepare the company's cash flows from operating activities by using the *other* method.

spotlight

HOW WELL IS YUM! BRANDS DOING?

YUM! Brands, Inc.
Statements of Income (Adapted)
Years Ended December 31, 2003 and 2002

In millions	2003	2002
Revenues	$8,380	$7,757
Expenses:		
Food and paper (cost of goods sold)	2,300	2,109
Payroll and employee benefits	2,024	1,875
Occupancy and other operating expenses	2,013	1,806
General and administrative expenses	945	913
Interest expense	173	172
Other expense, net	39	24
Income before income taxes	886	858
Income tax expense	269	275
Net income	$ 617	$ 583

This book began with the financial statements of YUM! Brands, Inc., the company that owns Pizza Hut, Taco Bell, A&W, KFC, and Long John Silver restaurants. Throughout the book we have shown how to account for the operations, financial position, and cash flows of companies such as Pier 1 Imports, Best Buy, and General Electric. Only one aspect of the course remains: the overall analysis of financial statements.

We begin with the analysis of YUM! Brands' income statement. In 2003 YUM had revenues of $8,380 million, and the company earned net income of $617 million. These numbers look pretty good, but *how good* was the performance? We need to compare 2003 with prior years to see if YUM made progress during 2003. It could turn out that 2003 was worse than 2002. We also need to compare YUM to its competitors.

This chapter covers the basic tools of financial analysis. The first part of the chapter shows how to evaluate YUM! Brands from year to year and also how to compare different companies. For this comparison we use two leading fast-food chains, YUM! Brands and McDonald's. The second part of the chapter discusses the most widely used financial ratios. You have seen many of these ratios in earlier chapters—the current ratio in Chapter 3, days' sales in receivables in Chapter 5, and inventory turnover in Chapter 6.

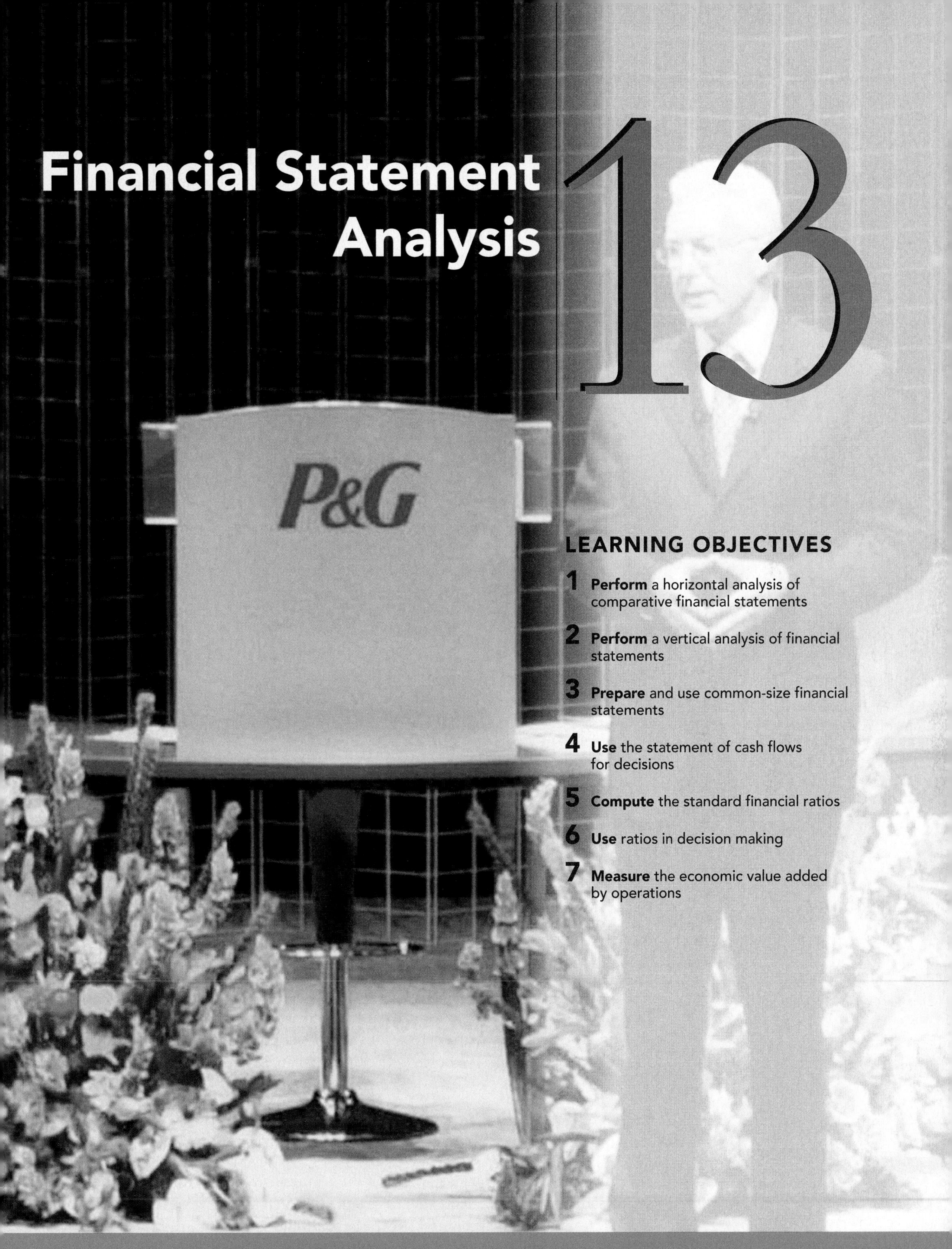

Financial Statement Analysis

13

LEARNING OBJECTIVES

1 **Perform** a horizontal analysis of comparative financial statements

2 **Perform** a vertical analysis of financial statements

3 **Prepare** and use common-size financial statements

4 **Use** the statement of cash flows for decisions

5 **Compute** the standard financial ratios

6 **Use** ratios in decision making

7 **Measure** the economic value added by operations

By studying all these ratios together

- You will get both the big picture and the tools of financial analysis.
- You will equip yourself to advance to the next level of a business education.
- You will build the foundation for a career in business.

Regardless of your chosen field—marketing, management, finance, entrepreneurship, or accounting—you will find these analytical tools useful as you move through your career.

Taking Action How Does an Investor Evaluate a Company?

Investors and creditors cannot evaluate a company by examining only 1 year's data. This is why most financial statements cover at least 2 periods, like the **YUM! Brands** income statement that begins this chapter. In fact, most financial analysis covers trends of 3, 5, or even 10 years. What is the goal of financial analysis? To predict the future.

The graphs in Exhibit 13-1 show some important data about YUM! Brands. The graphs depict YUM's 3-year trend of revenues and net income. How relevant are these facts for making decisions about YUM or its competitor McDonald's? They help managers, investors, and creditors chart the future.

EXHIBIT 13-1

Representative Financial Data of YUM! Brands, Inc.

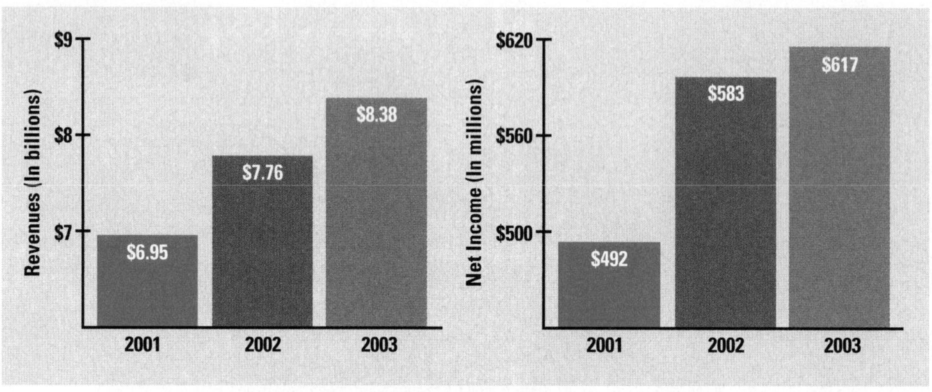

Both YUM's revenues and net income increased during 2002 and 2003. These are good signs. Consider what you would predict for YUM's revenues in 2004 and beyond. Based on the recent past, you would probably extend the revenue line upward. Normally growth in revenues increases profits too. Let's examine some financial analysis tools. We begin with horizontal analysis.

Horizontal Analysis

OBJECTIVE

1 **Perform** a horizontal analysis of comparative financial statements

Many decisions hinge on the trend of revenues, income, expenses, and so on. Have revenues increased from last year? By how much? We may find that sales have increased by $50,000. Considered alone this fact is not very helpful, but the *percentage change* in sales aids your understanding. It is more useful to know that sales have increased by 20% than to know that the increase is $50,000.

The study of percentage changes from year to year is called **horizontal analysis**. Computing a percentage change requires two steps:

1. Compute the dollar amount of the change from the base (earlier) period to the later period.
2. Divide the dollar amount of change by the base-period amount.

Horizontal analysis
Study of percentage changes in comparative financial statements.

Illustration: YUM! Brands

Horizontal analysis is illustrated for YUM! Brands as follows (dollars in millions):

			Increase (Decrease)	
	2003	2002	Amount	Percentage
Revenue	$8,380	$7,757	$623	8.0%

YUM's revenues increased by 8% during 2003, computed as follows:

STEP 1 Compute the dollar amount of change from 2002 to 2003:

2003		2002		INCREASE
$8,380	–	$7,757	=	$623

STEP 2 Divide the dollar amount of change by the base-period amount. This computes the percentage change for the period:

$$\text{Percentage change} = \frac{\text{Dollar amount of change}}{\text{Base-year amount}}$$

$$= \frac{\$623}{\$7,757} = 8.0\%$$

Exhibits 13-2 and 13-3 show detailed horizontal analysis for YUM! Brands. The income statements reveal that revenues increased by 8.0% during 2003. But net income on the bottom line grew by only 5.8%. Why the difference? YUM's expenses grew faster than revenues. For example, cost of goods sold increased 9.1%, and occupancy expenses (rent and depreciation) by 11.5%.

Check Point 13-1

■ **EXHIBIT 13-2**
Comparative Income Statement—Horizontal Analysis

YUM! Brands, Inc.
Statements of Income (Adapted)
Years Ended December 31, 2003 and 2002

			Increase (Decrease)	
Dollars in millions	**2003**	**2002**	**Amount**	**Percentage**
Revenues	$8,380	$7,757	$623	8.0%
Expenses:				
Food and paper (cost of goods sold)	2,300	2,109	191	9.1
Payroll and employee benefits	2,024	1,875	149	7.9
Occupancy and other operating expenses	2,013	1,806	207	11.5
General and administrative expenses	945	913	32	3.5
Interest expense	173	172	1	0.6
Other expense, net	39	24	15	62.5
Income before income taxes	886	858	28	3.3
Income tax expense	269	275	(6)	(2.2)
Net income	$ 617	$ 583	$ 34	5.8

■ **EXHIBIT 13-3**

Comparative Balance Sheet—Horizontal Analysis

YUM! Brands Inc.
Balance Sheet (Adapted)
December 31, 2003 and 2002

			Increase (Decrease)	
(Dollars in millions)	2003	2002	Amount	Percentage
Assets				
Current Assets				
Cash and cash equivalents	$192	$130	$62	47.7%
Short-term investments	15	27	(12)	(44.4)
Receivables, net	169	168	1	0.6
Inventories	67	63	4	6.3
Prepaid expenses and other	363	342	21	6.1
Total current assets	806	730	76	10.4
Property, plant, and equipment, net	3,280	3,037	243	8.0
Intangible assets	878	849	29	3.4
Other assets	656	784	(128)	(16.3)
Total assets	$5,620	$5,400	$220	4.1
Liabilities and Shareholders' Equity				
Current Liabilities				
Accounts payable and other current	$1,213	$1,166	$47	4.0%
Income tax payable	238	208	30	14.4
Short-term debt	10	146	(136)	(93.2)
Total current liabilities	1,461	1,520	(59)	(3.9)
Long-term debt	2,056	2,299	(243)	(10.6)
Other liabilities	983	987	(4)	(0.4)
Total liabilities	4,500	4,806	(306)	(6.4)
Shareholders' Equity				
Common stock	916	1,046	(130)	(12.4)
Retained earnings (accumulated deficit)	414	(203)	617	303.9
Accumulated other comprehensive (loss)	(210)	(249)	39	15.7
Total shareholders' equity	1,120	594	526	88.6
Total liabilities and shareholders' equity	$5,620	$5,400	$220	4.1

stop AND think. . .

Examine Exhibit 13-2. Which item had the largest percentage increase during 2003? Should this increase cause alarm? Explain your reasoning.

Answer:

Other expense had the largest percentage increase (62.5%). This increase would *not* cause alarm because the dollar amount of the expense is low. This illustrates the materiality concept, which says to give major consideration to big items and less attention to small (immaterial) items. In this case, other expense is immaterial to the analysis of YUM! Brands.

The comparative balance sheets in Exhibit 13-3 shows that total assets grew by 4.1% and total liabilities fell by 6.4%. Shareholders' equity increased by 88.6%. Retained earnings went from a deficit position to a positive balance. YUM! Brands' losses in its early years had produced the retained earnings deficit. The company's growth during 2003 is impressive.

Trend Percentages

Trend percentages are a form of horizontal analysis. Trends indicate the direction a business is taking. How have revenues changed over a 5-year period? What trend does net income show? These questions can be answered by trend percentages over a representative period, such as the most recent 5 years.

Trend percentages
A form of horizontal analysis that indicates the direction a business is taking.

Trend percentages are computed by selecting a base year whose amounts are set equal to 100%. The amount for each following year is stated as a percentage of the base amount. To compute a trend percentage, divide an item for a later year by the base-year amount.

$$\text{Trend \%} = \frac{\text{Any year \$}}{\text{Base year \$}}$$

YUM! Brands showed net income for the past 6 years as follows:

(In millions)	2003	2002	2001	2000	1999	Base 1998
Net income	$617	$583	$492	$413	$627	$445

We want trend percentages for the 5-year period 1999 to 2003. The base year is 1998. Trend percentages are computed by dividing each year's amount by the 1998 amount. The resulting trend percentages follow (1998 = 100%):

	2003	2002	2001	2000	1999	Base 1998
Net income	139%	131%	111%	93%	141%	100%

✔ Check Point 13-2

Net income skyrocketed in 1999, dipped in 2000, and began a steady climb in 2001.

You can perform a trend analysis on any item you consider important. Trend analysis is widely used for predicting the future.

Vertical Analysis

OBJECTIVE

2 **Perform** a vertical analysis of financial statements

Horizontal analysis highlights changes over time. However, no single technique gives a complete picture of a business.

Vertical analysis shows the relationship of a financial-statement item to its base, which is the 100% figure. All items on the statement are reported as a percentage of the base. For the income statement total revenue is usually the base. Suppose under normal conditions a company's net income is 8% of revenue. A drop to 6% may cause the company's stock price to fall.

Vertical analysis
Analysis of a financial statement that reveals the relationship of each statement item to a specified base, which is the 100% figure.

Illustration: YUM! Brands

Exhibit 13-4 shows the vertical analysis of YUM! Brands' income statement as a percentage of revenue. In this case,

$$\text{Vertical analysis \%} = \frac{\text{Each income statement item}}{\text{Total revenue}}$$

■ **EXHIBIT 13-4** Comparative Income Statement—Vertical Analysis

YUM! Brands, Inc.
Statements of Income (Adapted)
Years Ended December 31, 2003 and 2002

	2003		2002	
(Dollars in millions)	Amount	**Percentage of Total**	Amount	**Percentage of Total**
Revenues	$8,380	100.0%	$7,757	100.0%
Expenses:				
Food and paper (cost of goods sold)	2,300	27.4	2,109	27.2
Payroll and employee benefits	2,024	24.2	1,875	24.2
Occupancy and other operating expenses	2,013	24.0	1,806	23.3
General and administrative expenses	945	11.3	913	11.8
Interest expense	173	2.1	172	2.2
Other expense, net	39	0.4	24	0.3
Income before income taxes	886	10.6	858	11.0
Income tax expense	269	3.2	275	3.5
Net income	$ 617	7.4%	$ 583	7.5%

For YUM! Brands in 2003, the vertical-analysis percentage for cost of goods sold is 27.4% ($2,300/$8,380 = .274). Most of YUM's expenses kept their percentages intact from 2002. Net income's percentage of revenue (7.4%) is virtually unchanged from the year earlier.

Exhibit 13-5 shows the vertical analysis of YUM's balance sheet. The base amount (100%) is total assets.

Check Point 13-3

The vertical analysis of YUM! Brands' balance sheet reveals several things about the company's financial position at December 31, 2003:

- Current assets make up a small percentage of total assets (only 14.3%), and prepaid expenses are the largest current asset. It makes sense that inventory is a small percentage because food spoils quickly.
- Total liabilities make up 80.1% of YUM's total assets. This is a heavy debt load. However, YUM's trend is favorable because a year ago total liabilities were 89% of total assets. YUM's financial position improved during 2003.

■ Taking Action How Do We Compare One Company to Another?

OBJECTIVE

3 **Prepare** and use common-size financial statements

Common-size statement
A financial statement that reports only percentages (no dollar amounts).

The percentages in Exhibits 13-4 and 13-5 can be presented as a separate statement that reports only percentages (no dollar amounts). Such a statement is called a **common-size statement**. Envision these statements with only the percentages.

On a common-size income statement, each item is expressed as a percentage of the revenue amount. Total revenue is the *common size* to which we relate the other

■ **EXHIBIT 13-5** Comparative Balance Sheet—Vertical Analysis

YUM! Brands, Inc.
Balance Sheet (Adapted)
December 31, 2003 and 2002

	2003		2002	
(Dollars in millions)	Amount	Percentage of Total	Amount	Percentage of Total
Assets				
Current Assets				
Cash and cash equivalents	$ 192	3.4%	$ 130	2.4%
Short-term investments	15	0.3	27	0.5
Receivables, net	169	3.0	168	3.1
Inventories	67	1.2	63	1.2
Prepaid expenses and other	363	6.4	342	6.3
Total current assets	806	14.3	730	13.5
Property, plant, and equipment, net	3,280	58.4	3,037	56.3
Intangible assets	878	15.6	849	15.7
Other assets	656	11.7	784	14.5
Total assets	$5,620	100.0%	$5,400	100.0%
Liabilities and Shareholders' Equity				
Current Liabilities				
Accounts payable and other current	$1,213	21.6%	$1,166	21.6%
Income tax payable	238	4.2	208	3.8
Short-term debt	10	0.2	146	2.7
Total current liabilities	1,461	26.0	1,520	28.1
Long-term debt	2,056	36.6	2,299	42.6
Other liabilities	983	17.5	987	18.3
Total liabilities	4,500	80.1	4,806	89.0
Shareholders' Equity				
Common stock	916	16.3	1,046	19.4
Retained earnings (accumulated deficit)	414	7.4	(203)	(3.8)
Accumulated other comprehensive (loss)	(210)	(3.8)	(249)	(4.6)
Total shareholders' equity	1,120	19.9	594	11.0
Total liabilities and shareholders' equity	$5,620	100.0%	$5,400	100.0%

amounts. In the balance sheet, the common size is total assets. A common-size statement eases the comparison of different companies because their amounts are stated in percentages, and the dollar differences vanish.

Benchmarking

Benchmarking is the comparison of a company to a standard set by others, with a view toward improvement. Suppose you are a financial analyst for **Edward Jones Company**. You are considering an investment in the stock of a fast-food company, and you are choosing between YUM! Brands and McDonald's Corporation. A direct comparison of their financial statements is not meaningful because McDonald's is larger. However, you can convert the two companies' income statements to common size and compare the percentages.

Benchmarking
The comparison of a company to a standard set by other companies, with a view toward improvement.

stop AND think. . .

Calculate the common-size percentages for the following income statement:

Net sales	$150,000
Cost of goods sold	60,000
Gross profit	90,000
Operating expense	40,000
Operating income	50,000
Income tax expense	15,000
Net income	$ 35,000

Answer:

Net sales	100%	(= $150,000 ÷ $150,000)
Cost of goods sold	40	(= $ 60,000 ÷ $150,000)
Gross profit	60	(= $ 90,000 ÷ $150,000)
Operating expense	27	(= $ 40,000 ÷ $150,000)
Operating income	33	(= $ 50,000 ÷ $150,000)
Income tax expense	10	(= $ 15,000 ÷ $150,000)
Net income	23%	(= $ 35,000 ÷ $150,000)

Benchmarking Against a Key Competitor

Check Point 13-4

Exhibit 13-6 presents the common-size income statements of YUM! Brands and McDonald's. McDonald's serves as an excellent benchmark because it is the market leader. In this comparison, McDonald's comes out the winner. McDonald's seems to control expenses better than YUM! Brands. Net income is a higher percentage of revenue at The Golden Arches.

■ **EXHIBIT 13-6**

Common-Size Income Statement Compared with a Key Competitor

YUM! Brands, Inc.
Common-Size Income Statement for Comparison with Key Competitor
Year Ended During 2003

	YUM! Brands	McDonald's
Revenues	100.0%	100.0%
Cost of goods sold	27.4	25.2
Payroll expenses	24.2	19.9
Occupancy and other operating expenses	24.0	19.1
General and administrative expenses	11.3	10.7
Other expenses	5.7	16.5
Net income	7.4%	8.6%

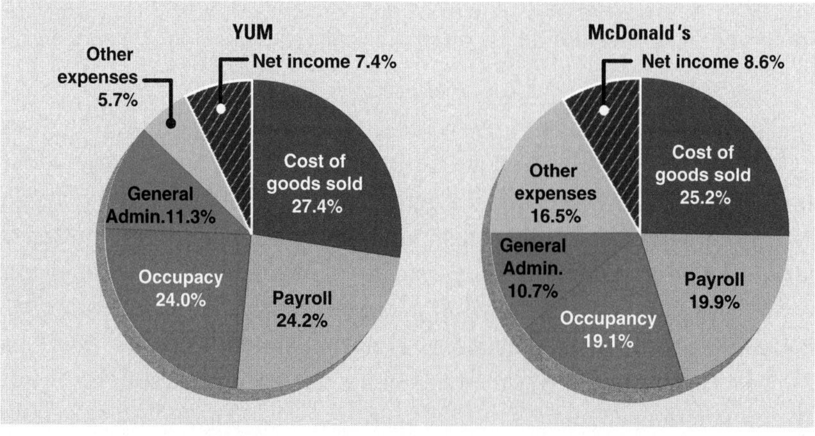

■ **Taking Action** Using the Statement of Cash Flows

OBJECTIVE

4 **Use** the statement of cash flows for decisions

This chapter has focused on the income statement and balance sheet. We may also perform horizontal and vertical analyses on the statement of cash flows. In Chapter 12, we showed how to prepare the statement. To continue our discussion of its role in decision making, let's use Exhibit 13-7 (p. 615), the statement of cash flows of **Unix Corporation**.

Analysts find the statement of cash flows more helpful for spotting weakness than for gauging success. Why? Because a *shortage* of cash can throw a company into bankruptcy, but lots of cash doesn't ensure success. The statement of cash flows in Exhibit 13-7 reveals the following:

■ **EXHIBIT 13-7**

Statement of Cash Flows

Unix Corporation
Statement of Cash Flows
Year Ended June 30, 2005

	Millions	
Operating activities:		
Net income		$ 35,000
Adjustments for noncash items:		
Depreciation	$14,000	
Net increase in current assets other than cash	(24,000)	
Net increase in current liabilities	8,000	(2,000)
Net cash provided by operating activities		33,000
Investing activities:		
Sale of property, plant, and equipment	$91,000	
Net cash provided by investing activities		91,000
Financing activities:		
Borrowing	$22,000	
Payment of long-term debt	(90,000)	
Purchase of treasury stock	(9,000)	
Payment of dividends	(23,000)	
Net cash used for financing activities		(100,000)
Increase (decrease) in cash		$ 24,000

- Unix's operations provide less cash than net income. Ordinarily, cash provided by operations exceeds net income because of the add-back of depreciation. The increases in current assets and current liabilities should cancel out over time, leaving depreciation to push cash flow above net income. For Unix Corporation, current assets increased far more than current liabilities during fiscal year 2005. This may be harmless, or it may signal difficulty in collecting receivables or selling inventory. Either event may cause trouble.
- The sale of plant assets is Unix's major source of cash. This may be a one-time situation. For example, Unix may be shifting from one line of business to another, and the company may be selling off old, unproductive assets. That may be okay. But if the sale of plant assets remains the major source of cash, Unix will face a cash shortage. A company cannot continue to sell off its plant assets, or it will go out of business.
- The only strength shown by the statement of cash flows is that Unix paid off more long-term debt than it did new borrowing. This will improve the debt ratio and Unix's credit standing.

Here are some cash-flow signs of a healthy company:

- Operations are the major source (not a use) of cash.
- Investing activities include more purchases than sales of long-term assets.
- Financing activities are not dominated by borrowing.

MID-CHAPTER Summary Problem

Perform a horizontal analysis and a vertical analysis of the comparative income statement of TRE Corporation, which makes metal detectors. State whether 20X6 was a good year or a bad year, and give your reasons.

TRE Corporation
Comparative Income Statement
Years Ended December 31, 20X6 and 20X5

	20X6	20X5
Total revenues	$275,000	$225,000
Expenses:		
Cost of products sold	194,000	165,000
Engineering, selling, and administrative expenses	54,000	48,000
Interest expense	5,000	5,000
Income tax expense	9,000	3,000
Other expense (income)	1,000	(1,000)
Total expenses	263,000	220,000
Net earnings	$ 12,000	$ 5,000

Answer

The horizontal analysis shows that total revenues increased 22.2%. This was greater than the 19.5% increase in total expenses, resulting in a 140% increase in net earnings.

TRE Corporation
Horizontal Analysis of Comparative Income Statement
Years Ended December 31, 20X6 and 20X5

			Increase (Decrease)	
	20X6	20X5	Amount	Percent
Total revenues	$275,000	$225,000	$50,000	22.2%
Expenses:				
Cost of products sold	194,000	165,000	29,000	17.6
Engineering, selling, and administrative expenses	54,000	48,000	6,000	12.5
Interest expense	5,000	5,000	—	—
Income tax expense	9,000	3,000	6,000	200.0
Other expense (income)	1,000	(1,000)	2,000	—*
Total expenses	263,000	220,000	43,000	19.5
Net earnings	$ 12,000	$ 5,000	$ 7,000	140.0%

*Percentage changes are typically not computed for shifts from a negative to a positive amount and vice versa.

The vertical analysis shows decreases in the percentages of net sales consumed by the cost of products sold (from 73.3% to 70.5%) and by the engineering, selling, and administrative expenses (from 21.3% to 19.6%). Because these two items are TRE's largest dollar expenses, their percentage decreases are quite important. The relative reduction in expenses raised 20X6 net earnings to 4.4% of sales, compared with 2.2% the preceding year. The overall analysis indicates that 20X6 was significantly better than 20X5.

TRE Corporation
Vertical Analysis of Comparative Income Statement
Years Ended December 31, 20X6 and 20X5

	20X6		20X5	
	Amount	Percent	Amount	Percent
Total revenues	$275,000	100.0%	$225,000	100.0%
Expenses:				
Cost of products sold	$194,000	70.5	$165,000	73.3
Engineering, selling and administrative expenses	54,000	19.6	48,000	21.3
Interest expense	5,000	1.8	5,000	2.2
Income tax expense	9,000	3.3	3,000	1.4**
Other expense (income)	1,000	0.4	(1,000)	(0.4)
Total expenses	263,000	95.6	220,000	97.8
Net earnings	$ 12,000	4.4%	$ 5,000	2.2%

**Number rounded up.

Using Ratios to Make Business Decisions

OBJECTIVE

5 **Compute** the standard financial ratios

Ratios are a major tool of financial analysis. A ratio expresses the relationship of one number to another. Suppose your balance sheet shows current assets of $100,000 and current liabilities of $50,000. The ratio of current assets to current liabilities is $100,000 to $50,000. We can express this ratio as 2 to 1, or 2:1. The current ratio is 2.0.

Many companies include ratios in a special section of their annual reports. RubberMate Corporation displays ratio data in the Summary section. Exhibit 13-8 shows data from that summary section. Investment services—**Moody's, Standard & Poor's, Risk Management Association**, and others—report these ratios.

■ **EXHIBIT 13-8**

Financial Summary of RubberMate Corporation (Dollar Amounts in Millions Except per-share Amounts)

Years Ended December 31	20X6	20X5	20X4
Operating Results			
Net earnings	$ 211	$ 164	$ 163
Per common share	$1.32	$1.02	$1.02
Percent of sales	10.8%	9.1%	9.8%
Return on average shareholders' equity	20.0%	17.5%	19.7%
Financial Position			
Current assets	$570	$477	$419
Current liabilities	$259	$223	$245
Working capital	$311	$254	$174
Current ratio	2.20	2.14	1.71

The ratios we discuss in this chapter may be classified as follows:

1. Ability to pay current liabilities
2. Ability to sell inventory and collect receivables
3. Ability to pay long-term debt
4. Profitability
5. Analyze stock as an investment

How much can a computer help in analyzing financial statements for investment purposes? Time yourself as you complete the problems in this chapter. Multiply your efforts by comparing 10 companies. Now rank these 10 companies on the basis of four or five ratios.

Measuring Ability to Pay Current Liabilities

Working capital
Current assets minus current liabilities; measures a business's ability to meet its short-term obligations with its current assets.

Working capital is defined as follows:

Working capital = Current assets − Current liabilities

Working capital measures the ability to pay current liabilities with current assets. In general, the larger the working capital, the better the ability to pay debts. Recall that capital is total assets minus total liabilities. Working capital is like a "current" version of total capital. Consider two companies with equal working capital:

	Company	
	A	B
Current assets	$100,000	$200,000
Current liabilities	50,000	150,000
Working capital	$ 50,000	$ 50,000

Both companies have working capital of $50,000, but A's working capital is only as large as its current liabilities. B's working capital is only one-third as large as current liabilities. Company A is in a better position because its working capital is a higher percentage of current liabilities. Two decision-making tools based on working-capital data are the *current ratio* and the *acid-test ratio*.

Current ratio
Current assets divided by current liabilities. Measures a company's ability to pay current liabilities with current assets.

Current Ratio. The most common ratio using current assets and current liabilities is the **current ratio**, which is current assets divided by current liabilities. The current ratio measures the ability to pay current liabilities with current assets. Exhibit 13-9 gives the income statement and balance sheet data of Palisades Furniture.

The current ratios of Palisades Furniture, Inc., at December 31, 20X5 and 20X4, follow, along with the average for the retail furniture industry:

Check Point 13-5

Formula	Palisades' Current Ratio 20X5	Palisades' Current Ratio 20X4	Industry Average
$\text{Current ratio} = \dfrac{\text{Current assets}}{\text{Current liabilities}}$	$\dfrac{\$262{,}000}{\$142{,}000} = 1.85$	$\dfrac{\$236{,}000}{\$126{,}000} = 1.87$	1.50

■ **EXHIBIT 13-9**

Comparative Financial Statements

Palisades Furniture, Inc.
Comparative Income Statement
Years Ended December 31, 20X5 and 20X4

	20X5	20X4
Net sales	$858,000	$803,000
Cost of goods sold	513,000	509,000
Gross profit	345,000	294,000
Operating expenses:		
Selling expenses	126,000	114,000
General expenses	118,000	123,000
Total operating expenses	244,000	237,000
Income from operations	101,000	57,000
Interest revenue	4,000	—
Interest expense	24,000	14,000
Income before income taxes	81,000	43,000
Income tax expense	33,000	17,000
Net income	$ 48,000	$ 26,000

Palisades Furniture, Inc.
Comparative Balance Sheet
December 31, 20X5 and 20X4

	20X5	20X4
Assets		
Current Assets:		
Cash	$ 29,000	$ 32,000
Accounts receivable, net	114,000	85,000
Inventories	113,000	111,000
Prepaid expenses	6,000	8,000
Total current assets	262,000	236,000
Long-term investments	18,000	9,000
Property, plant, and equipment, net	507,000	399,000
Total assets	$787,000	$644,000
Liabilities		
Current Liabilities:		
Notes payable	$ 42,000	$ 27,000
Accounts payable	73,000	68,000
Accrued liabilities	27,000	31,000
Total current liabilities	142,000	126,000
Long-term debt	289,000	198,000
Total liabilities	431,000	324,000
Stockholders' Equity		
Common stock, no par	186,000	186,000
Retained earnings	170,000	134,000
Total stockholders' equity	356,000	320,000
Total liabilities and stockholders' equity	$787,000	$644,000

The current ratio was virtually unchanged during 20X5. In general, a higher current ratio indicates a stronger financial position. The business has sufficient current assets to maintain its operations. Palisades Furniture's current ratio of 1.85 compares favorably with the current ratios of some well-known companies:

Company	Current Ratio
Hewlett-Packard Company	1.54
IHOP Corporation	2.80
The Boeing Company	0.94

Note: These figures show that ratio values vary widely from one industry to another.

What is an acceptable current ratio? The answer depends on the industry. The norm for companies in most industries is around 1.50, as reported by the Risk Management Association. Palisades Furniture's current ratio of 1.85 is better than average.

ACCOUNTING ALERT

The Limitations of Ratio Analysis

Business decisions are made in a world of uncertainty. As useful as ratios are, they aren't a cure-all. Consider a physician's use of a thermometer. A reading of 102.0° Fahrenheit tells a doctor something is wrong with the patient, but that doesn't indicate what the problem is or how to cure it.

In financial analysis, a sudden drop in the current ratio signals that *something* is wrong, but that doesn't identify the problem. A manager must analyze the figures to learn what caused the ratio to fall. A drop in current assets may mean a cash shortage or that sales are slow. The manager must evaluate all the ratios in the light of factors such as increased competition or a slowdown in the economy.

Legislation, international affairs, scandals, and other factors can turn profits into losses. To be useful, ratios should be analyzed over a period of years to consider all relevant factors. Any 1 year, or even any 2 years, may not represent the company's performance over the long term.

Acid-test ratio
Ratio of the sum of cash plus short-term investments plus net current receivables to total current liabilities. Tells whether the entity can pay all its current liabilities if they come due immediately. Also called the *quick ratio*.

Acid-Test Ratio. The **acid-test** (or *quick*) **ratio** tells us whether the entity could pass the acid test of paying all its current liabilities if they came due immediately. The acid-test ratio uses a narrower base to measure liquidity than the current ratio does.

To compute the acid-test ratio, we add cash, short-term investments, and net current receivables (accounts and notes, net of allowances) and divide by current liabilities. Inventory and prepaid expenses are excluded because they are less liquid. A business may be unable to convert inventory to cash immediately.

Palisades Furniture's acid-test ratios for 20X5 and 20X4 follow.

	Formula	Palisades' Acid-Test Ratio		Industry Average
		20X5	20X4	
Acid-test ratio	= (Cash + Short-term investments + Net current receivables) / Current liabilities	($29,000 + $0 + $114,000) / $142,000 = 1.01	($32,000 + $0 + $85,000) / $126,000 = 0.93	0.40

The company's acid-test ratio improved during 20X5 and is significantly better than the industry average. Compare Palisades' acid test ratio with the values of some leading companies.

Company	Acid-Test Ratio
YUM! Brands	.26
Motorola	1.32
Gap, Inc.	1.88

Check Point 13-6

An acid-test ratio of 0.90 to 1.00 is acceptable in most industries. How can a company such as YUM! Brands function with such a low acid-test ratio? YUM sells its food products very quickly and collects cash immediately. This points us to the next two ratios.

Measuring Ability to Sell Inventory and Collect Receivables

The ability to sell inventory and collect receivables is critical. In this section, we discuss three ratios that measure the ability to do this.

Inventory Turnover. Companies generally seek to sell their inventory as quickly as possible. The faster inventory sells, the sooner cash comes in.

Inventory turnover measures the number of times a company sells its average level of inventory during a year. A fast turnover indicates ease in selling inventory; a low turnover indicates difficulty. A value of 6 means that the company's average level of inventory has been sold six times during the year, and that's usually better than a turnover of 3 times. But too high a value can mean that the business is not keeping enough inventory on hand, which can lead to lost sales if the company can't fill orders. Therefore, a business strives for the most *profitable* rate of turnover, not necessarily the *highest* rate.

Inventory turnover
Ratio of cost of goods sold to average inventory. Indicates how rapidly inventory is sold.

To compute inventory turnover, divide cost of goods sold by the average inventory for the period. We use the cost of goods sold—*not sales*—in the computation because both cost of goods sold and inventory are stated *at cost*. Palisades Furniture's inventory turnover for 20X5 is

	Formula	*Palisades' Inventory Turnover*	Industry Average
Inventory turnover =	$\frac{\text{Cost of goods sold}}{\text{Average inventory}}$	$\frac{\$513{,}000}{\$112{,}000} = 4.6$	3.4

Cost of goods sold comes from the income statement (Exhibit 13-9). Average inventory is the average of beginning ($111,000) and ending inventory ($113,000). (See the balance sheet, Exhibit 13-9.) If inventory levels vary greatly from month to month, you should compute the average by adding the 12 monthly balances and dividing the sum by 12.

Inventory turnover varies widely with the nature of the business. For example, YUM! Brands has an inventory turnover ratio of 35 times per year because food spoils so quickly. **Pier 1 Imports**, on the other hand, turns over its furniture only around 3 times per year.

To evaluate inventory turnover, compare the ratio over time. A sharp decline suggests the need for corrective action.

Accounts receivable turnover Measures a company's ability to collect cash from credit customers. To compute accounts receivable turnover, divide net credit sales by average net accounts receivable.

Accounts Receivable Turnover. **Accounts receivable turnover** measures the ability to collect cash from customers. In general, the higher the ratio, the better. However, a receivable turnover that is too high may indicate that credit is too tight, and that may lose sales to good customers.

To compute accounts receivable turnover, divide net sales by average net accounts receivable. The ratio tells how many times during the year average receivables were turned into cash. Palisades Furniture's accounts receivable turnover ratio for 20X5 is

Formula	Palisades' Accounts Receivable Turnover	Industry Average
$\text{Accounts receivable turnover} = \dfrac{\text{Net sales}}{\text{Average net accounts receivable}}$	$\dfrac{\$858{,}000}{\$99{,}500} = 8.6$	51.0

Average net accounts receivable is figured by adding beginning ($85,000) and ending receivables ($114,000), then dividing by 2. If accounts receivable vary widely during the year, compute the average by using the 12 monthly balances.

Palisades' receivable turnover of 8.6 times per year is much slower than the industry average. Why the slow collection? Palisades is a hometown store that sells to local people who pay bills over a period of time. Many larger furniture stores sell their receivables to other companies called *factors*. This practice keeps receivables low and receivable turnover high. But companies that factor (sell) their receivables receive less than face value of the receivables. Palisades Furniture follows a different strategy.

Day's sales in receivables Ratio of average net accounts receivable to one day's sales. Indicates how many days' sales remain in Accounts Receivable awaiting collection. Also called the *collection period.*

Days' Sales in Receivables. Businesses must convert accounts receivable to cash. All else being equal, the lower the receivable balance, the better the cash flow.

The **days'-sales-in-receivables** ratio shows how many days' sales remain in Accounts Receivable. Compute the ratio by a two-step process:

1. Divide net sales by 365 days to figure average sales per day.
2. Divide average net receivables by average sales per day.

The data to compute this ratio for Palisades Furniture, Inc. are taken from the 20X5 income statement and the balance sheet (Exhibit 13-9):

Formula	Palisades' Days' Sales in Accounts Receivable	Industry Average
Days' Sales in Average Accounts Receivable:		
1. $\text{One day's sales} = \dfrac{\text{Net sales}}{365 \text{ days}}$	$\dfrac{\$858{,}000}{365 \text{ days}} = \$2{,}351$	
2. $\text{Days' sales in average accounts receivable} = \dfrac{\text{Average net accounts receivable}}{\text{One day's sales}}$	$\dfrac{\$99{,}500}{\$2{,}351} = 42 \text{ days}$	7 days

Check Point 13-7

Days' sales in average receivables can also be computed in a single step: $99,500/($858,000/365 days) = 42 days.

Palisades' collection period is much longer (worse) than industry average because Palisades collects its own receivables. Most furniture stores sell their receivables and carry lower receivables.

Measuring Ability to Pay Long-Term Debt

The ratios discussed so far relate to current assets and current liabilities. They measure the ability to sell inventory, collect receivables, and pay current bills. Two indicators of the ability to pay total liabilities are the *debt ratio* and the *times-interest-earned ratio*.

Debt Ratio. Suppose you are a bank loan officer and you have received $500,000 loan applications from two similar companies. The first firm already owes $600,000, and the second owes only $250,000. Which company gets the loan? Company 2, because it owes less.

This relationship between total liabilities and total assets is called the **debt ratio**. It tells us the proportion of assets financed with debt. A debt ratio of 1 reveals that debt has financed all the assets. A debt ratio of 0.50 means that debt finances half the assets. The higher the debt ratio, the greater the pressure to pay interest and principal. The lower the ratio, the lower the strain.

Debt ratio
Ratio of total liabilities to total assets. States the proportion of a company's assets that is financed with debt.

The debt ratios for Palisades Furniture follow.

Formula	Palisades' Debt Ratio 20X5	Palisades' Debt Ratio 20X4	Industry Average
Debt ratio = $\frac{\text{Total liabilities}}{\text{Total assets}}$	$\frac{\$431{,}000}{\$787{,}000} = 0.55$	$\frac{\$324{,}000}{\$644{,}000} = 0.50$	0.64

Risk Management Association reports that the average debt ratio for most companies ranges around 0.62, with relatively little variation from company to company. Palisades' 0.55 debt ratio indicates a fairly low-risk debt position compared with the retail furniture industry average of 0.64.

Times-Interest-Earned Ratio. Analysts use a second ratio—the **times-interest-earned ratio**—to relate income to interest expense. To compute the times-interest-earned ratio, divide income from operations (operating income) by interest expense. This ratio measures the number of times operating income can *cover* interest expense and is also called the *interest-coverage ratio*. A high ratio indicates ease in paying interest; a low value suggests difficulty.

Times-interest-earned ratio
Ratio of income from operations to interest expense. Measures the number of times that operating income can cover interest expense. Also called the *interest-coverage ratio*.

Palisades' times-interest-earned ratios are

Formula	Palisades' Times-Interest-Earned Ratio 20X5	Palisades' Times-Interest-Earned Ratio 20X4	Industry Average
Times-interest-earned ratio = $\frac{\text{Income from operations}}{\text{Interest expense}}$	$\frac{\$101{,}000}{\$24{,}000} = 4.21$	$\frac{\$57{,}000}{\$14{,}000} = 4.07$	2.80

The company's times-interest-earned ratio increased in 20X5. This is a favorable sign.

Check Point 13-8

Measuring Profitability

The fundamental goal of business is to earn a profit, and so the ratios that measure profitability are reported widely.

Rate of return on net sales
Ratio of net income to net sales. A measure of profitability. Also called *return on sales.*

Rate of Return on Sales. In business, *return* refers to profitability. Consider the **rate of return on net sales**, or simply *return on sales*. (The word *net* is usually omitted for convenience.) This ratio shows the percentage of each sales dollar earned as net income. The return-on-sales ratios for Palisades Furniture are

Formula	Palisades' Rate of Return on Sales		Industry Average
	20X5	20X4	
$\text{Rate of return on sales} = \dfrac{\text{Net income}}{\text{Net sales}}$	$\dfrac{\$48{,}000}{\$858{,}000} = 0.056$	$\dfrac{\$26{,}000}{\$803{,}000} = 0.032$	0.008

Companies strive for a high rate of return. The higher the percentage, the more sales dollars are providing profit. Palisades Furniture's return on sales is higher than the average furniture store. Compare Palisades' rate of return on sales to the rates of some leading companies:

Company	Rate of Return on Sales
The Boeing Company	0.014
PepsiCo., Inc.	0.132
Intel Corporation	0.187

Rate of return on total assets
Net income plus interest expense, divided by average total assets. This ratio measures a company's success in using its assets to earn income for the persons who finance the business. Also called *return on assets.*

Rate of Return on Total Assets. The **rate of return on total assets**, or simply *return on assets*, measures a company's success in using assets to earn a profit. Creditors have loaned money, and the interest they receive is their return on investment. Shareholders have bought the company's stock, and net income is their return. The sum of interest expense and net income is the return to the two groups that have financed the company. This sum is the numerator of the ratio. Average total assets is the denominator. The return-on-assets ratio for Palisades Furniture is

Formula	Palisades' 20X5 Rate of Return on Total Assets	Industry Average
$\text{Rate of return on assets} = \dfrac{\text{Net income} + \text{Interest expense}}{\text{Average total assets}}$	$\dfrac{\$48{,}000 + \$24{,}000}{\$715{,}500} = 0.101$	0.078

To compute average total assets, add the beginning and ending balances and divide by 2. Compare Palisades Furnitures' rate of return on assets to the rates of these leading companies:

Company	Rate of Return on Assets
McDonald's Corporation	0.075
Fossil, Inc.	0.128
Dell [Computer], Inc.	0.152

Rate of return on common stockholders' equity
Net income minus preferred dividends, divided by average common stockholders' equity. A measure of profitability. Also called *return on equity.*

Rate of Return on Common Stockholders' Equity. A popular measure of profitability is **rate of return on common stockholders' equity**, often shortened to *return on equity*. This ratio shows the relationship between net income and common stockholders' investment in the company—how much income is earned for every $1 invested.

To compute this ratio, first subtract preferred dividends from net income to measure income available to the common stockholders. Then divide income available to common by average common equity during the year. Common equity is total equity minus preferred equity. The 20X5 return on common equity for Palisades Furniture is

Formula	Palisades' 20X5 Rate of Return on Common Stockholders' Equity	Industry Average
Rate of return on common stockholders' equity = (Net income − Preferred dividends) / Average common stockholders' equity	($48,000 − $0) / $338,000 = 0.142	0.121

Average equity uses the beginning and ending balances [($356,000 + $320,000)/2 = $338,000].

Observe that Palisades' return on equity (0.142) is higher than its return on assets (0.101). This is a good sign. The difference results from borrowing at one rate—say, 8%—and investing the funds to earn a higher rate, such as the firm's 14.2% return on equity. This practice is called using *leverage*, or **trading on the equity**. The higher the debt ratio, the higher the leverage. Companies that finance operations with debt are said to *leverage* their positions.

Trading on the equity Earning more income on borrowed money than the related interest expense, thereby increasing the earnings for the owners of the business. Also called *leverage*.

For Palisades Furniture, leverage increases profitability. This is not always the case, because leverage can hurt profits. If revenues drop, debts still must be paid. Therefore, leverage is a double-edged sword. It increases profits during good times but compounds losses during bad times.

Palisades Furniture's rate of return on equity lags behind those of Fossil, Inc., and Dell computer.

Company	Rate of Return on Common Equity
McDonald's Corporation	0.132
Fossil, Inc.	0.179
Dell [Computer], Inc.	0.474

Check Point 13-9

Earnings per Share of Common Stock. *Earnings per share of common stock*, or simply **earnings per share (EPS)**, is the amount of net income earned for each share of outstanding *common* stock. EPS is the most widely quoted of all financial statistics. It's the only ratio that appears on the income statement.

Earnings per share (EPS) Amount of a company's net income earned for each share of its outstanding common stock.

Earnings per share is computed by dividing net income available to common stockholders by the number of common shares outstanding during the year. Preferred dividends are subtracted from net income because the preferred stockholders have a prior claim to their dividends. Palisades Furniture has no preferred stock and thus has no preferred dividends. The firm's EPS for 20X5 and 20X4 follows (Palisades has 10,000 shares of common stock outstanding).

Formula	Palisades' Earnings per Share 20X5	Palisades' Earnings per Share 20X4
Earnings per share of common stock = (Net income − Preferred dividends) / Number of shares of common stock outstanding	($48,000 − $0) / 10,000 = $4.80	($26,000 − $0) / 10,000 = $2.60

Palisades Furniture's EPS increased 85% during 20X5, and that's good news. Its stockholders should not expect such a significant boost every year. Most companies strive to increase EPS by 10% to 15% annually.

Analyzing Stock Investments

OBJECTIVE

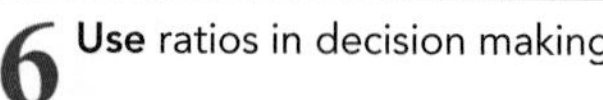

6 Use ratios in decision making

Investors buy stock to earn a return on their investment. This return consists of two parts: (1) gains (or losses) from selling the stock and (2) dividends.

Price/earnings ratio
Ratio of the market price of a share of common stock to the company's earnings per share. Measures the value that the stock market places on $1 of a company's earnings.

Price/Earnings Ratio. The **price/earnings ratio** is the ratio of common stock price to earnings per share. This ratio, abbreviated P/E, appears in *The Wall Street Journal* stock listings and online. It shows the market price of $1 of earnings.

Calculations for the P/E ratios of Palisades Furniture, Inc. follow. The market price of Palisades' common stock was $60 at the end of 20X5 and $35 at the end of 20X4. Stock prices can be obtained from a company's Web site, a financial publication, or a stockbroker.

Formula	Palisades' Price/Earnings Ratio 20X5	20X4
P/E ratio = $\frac{\text{Market price per share of common stock}}{\text{Earnings per share}}$	$\frac{\$60.00}{\$4.80} = 12.5$	$\frac{\$35.00}{\$2.60} = 13.5$

Check Point 13-10

Given Palisades Furniture's 20X5 P/E ratio of 12.5, we would say that the company's stock is selling at 12.5 times earnings. Each $1 of Palisades' earnings is worth $12.50 to the stock market.

Dividend yield
Ratio of dividends per share of stock to the stock's market price per share. Tells the percentage of a stock's market value that the company returns to stockholders as dividends.

Dividend Yield. **Dividend yield** is the ratio of dividends per share of stock to the stock's market price. This ratio measures the percentage of a stock's market value returned annually to the stockholders as dividends. *Preferred* stockholders pay special attention to this ratio because they invest primarily to receive dividends.

Palisades Furniture paid annual cash dividends of $1.20 per share in 20X5 and $1.00 in 20X4. The market prices of the company's common stock were $60 in 20X5 and $35 in 20X4. The firm's dividend yields on common stock are

Formula	Dividend Yield on Palisades' Common Stock 20X5	20X4
Dividend yield on common stock* = $\frac{\text{Dividend per share of common stock}}{\text{Market price per share of common stock}}$	$\frac{\$1.20}{\$60.00} = 0.020$	$\frac{\$1.00}{\$35.00} = 0.029$

*Dividend yields may also be calculated for preferred stock.

An investor who buys Palisades Furniture common stock for $60 can expect to receive around 2% of the investment annually in the form of cash dividends. Dividend yields vary widely, from 5% to 8% for older, established firms (such as **Procter & Gamble** and **General Motors**) down to the range of 0% to 3% for young, growth-oriented companies. **Dell Computer**, **Oracle**, and **eBay** pay no cash dividends.

Book Value per Share of Common Stock. **Book value per share of common stock** is simply common stockholders' equity divided by the number of shares of common stock outstanding. Common equity equals total equity less preferred equity. Palisades Furniture has no preferred stock outstanding. Calculations of its book value per share of common follow. Recall that 10,000 shares of common stock were outstanding.

Book value per share of common stock
Common stockholders' equity divided by the number of shares of common stock outstanding. The recorded amount for each share of common stock outstanding.

Formula		Book Value per Share of Palisades' Common Stock	
		20X5	20X4
Book value per share of common stock	$= \dfrac{\text{Total stockholders' equity} - \text{Preferred equity}}{\text{Number of shares of common stock outstanding}}$	$\dfrac{\$356{,}000 - \$0}{10{,}000} = \$35.60$	$\dfrac{\$320{,}000 - \$0}{10{,}000} = \$32.00$

Check Point 13-11

Check Point 13-12

Book value indicates the recorded accounting amount for each share of common stock outstanding. Many experts believe book value is not useful for investment analysis because it bears no relationship to market value and provides little information beyond what's reported on the balance sheet. But some investors base their investment decisions on book value. For example, some investors rank stocks by the ratio of market price to book value. The lower the ratio, the more attractive the stock. These investors are called "value" investors, as contrasted with "growth" investors, who focus more on trends in net income.

Other Measures

Economic Value Added (EVA®)

OBJECTIVE

7 **Measure** the economic value added by operations

The top managers of **Coca-Cola, Quaker Oats**, and other leading companies use **economic value added (EVA®)** to evaluate operating performance. EVA® combines accounting and finance to measure whether operations have increased stockholder wealth. EVA® can be computed as follows:

$$\text{EVA}^{\circledR} = \text{Net income} + \text{Interest expense} - \text{Capital charge}$$

where

$$\text{Capital charge} = \left(\begin{matrix}\text{(Beginning balances)} \\ \text{Notes payable} + \text{Current maturities of long-term debt} + \text{Long-term debt} + \text{Stockholders' equity}\end{matrix}\right) \times \text{Cost of capital}$$

Economic value added (EVA)
Used to evaluate a company's operating performance. EVA combines the concepts of accounting income and corporate finance to measure whether the company's operations have increased stockholder wealth. EVA = Net income + Interest expense − Capital charge.

All amounts for the EVA® computation, except the cost of capital, come from the financial statements. The **cost of capital** is a weighted average of the returns demanded by the company's stockholders and lenders. Cost of capital varies with the company's level of risk. For example, stockholders would demand a higher return from a start-up company than from YUM! Brands because the new company is untested and therefore more risky. Lenders would also charge the new company a higher interest rate because of its greater risk. Thus, the new company has a higher cost of capital than YUM! Brands.

Cost of capital
A weighted average of the returns demanded by the company's stockholders and lenders.

The cost of capital is a major topic in finance classes. In the following discussions we assume a value for the cost of capital (such as 10%, 12%, or 15%) to illustrate the computation of EVA®.

Capital charge
The amount that stockholders and lenders charge a company for the use of their money. Calculated as (Notes payable + Loans payable + Long-term debt + Stockholders' equity) × Cost of capital.

The idea behind EVA® is that the returns to the company's stockholders (net income) and to its creditors (interest expense) should exceed the company's capital charge. The **capital charge** is the amount that stockholders and lenders *charge* a company for the use of their money. A positive EVA® amount suggests an increase in stockholder wealth, and so the company's stock should remain attractive to investors. If EVA® is negative, stockholders will probably be unhappy with the company and sell its stock, resulting in a decrease in the stock's price. Different companies tailor the EVA® computation to meet their own needs.

Let's apply EVA® to YUM! Brands. The company's EVA® for 2003 can be computed as follows, assuming a 10% cost of capital (dollars in millions):

							(Beginning balances)				
YUM! Brand's EVA®	=	Net income	+	Interest expense	−	(Short-term borrowings	+	Long-term debt	+	Stockholders' equity)	× Cost of capital
	=	$617	+	$173	−	[($146	+	$2,299	+	$594)	× 0.10]
	=	$790			−			$3,039			× 0.10
	=	$790			−					$304	
	=				$486						

By this measure, YUM! Brands' operations added $486 million of value to its stockholders' wealth after meeting the company's capital charge. This performance is very strong.

Check Point 13-13

ACCOUNTING ALERT

Red Flags in Financial Statement Analysis

Recent accounting scandals have highlighted the importance of *red flags* in financial analysis. The following conditions may mean a company is very risky.

- **Earnings Problems.** Have income from continuing operations and net income decreased for several years in a row? Has income turned into a loss? This may be okay for a company in a cyclical industry, such as an airline or a home builder, but a company such as YUM! Brands may be unable to survive consecutive loss years.
- **Decreased Cash Flow.** Cash flow validates earnings. Is cash flow from operations consistently lower than net income? Are the sales of plant assets a major source of cash? If so, the company may be facing a cash shortage.
- **Too Much Debt.** How does the company's debt ratio compare to that of major competitors and to the industry average? If the debt ratio is much higher than average, the company may be unable to pay debts during tough times. As we saw earlier, YUM! Brands' debt ratio of 89% is very high. YUM's debt ratio needs to shrink over the next several years.
- **Inability to Collect Receivables.** Are days' sales in receivables growing faster than for other companies in the industry? A cash shortage may be looming. YUM's cash collections are very strong.

- **Buildup of Inventories.** Is inventory turnover slowing down? If so, the company may be unable to move products, or it may be overstating inventory as reported on the balance sheet. Recall from the cost-of-goods-sold model that one of the easiest ways to overstate net income is to overstate ending inventory. YUM! Brands has no problem here.
- **Trends of Sales, Inventory, and Receivables.** Sales, receivables, and inventory generally move together. Increased sales lead to higher receivables and require more inventory in order to meet demand. Strange movements among these items may spell trouble. YUM's relationships look normal.

Efficient Markets

Efficient capital market
A capital market in which market prices fully reflect all information available to the public.

An **efficient capital market** is one in which market prices fully reflect all information available to the public. Because stock prices reflect all publicly accessible data, it can be argued that the stock market is efficient. Market efficiency has implications for management action and for investor decisions. It means that managers cannot fool the market with accounting gimmicks. If the information is available, the market as a whole can set a "fair" price for the company's stock.

Suppose you are the president of Anacomp Corporation. Reported earnings per share are $4, and the stock price is $40—so the P/E ratio is 10. You believe Anacomp's stock is underpriced. To correct this situation, you are considering changing your depreciation method from accelerated to straight-line. The accounting change will increase earnings per share to $5. Will the stock price then rise to $50? Probably not; the company's stock price will probably remain at $40 because the market can understand the accounting change. After all, the company merely changed its method of computing depreciation. There is no effect on Anacomp's cash flows, and the company's economic position is unchanged: An efficient market interprets data in light of their true underlying meaning.

In an efficient market, the search for "underpriced" stock is fruitless unless the investor has relevant *private* information. But it is unlawful to invest on the basis of *inside* information. An appropriate strategy seeks to manage risk, diversify investments, and minimize transaction costs. Financial analysis helps mainly to identify the risks of various stocks and then to manage the risk.

The Making Managerial Decisions feature summarizes the most widely used ratios.

MAKING MANAGERIAL DECISIONS

USING RATIOS IN FINANCIAL STATEMENT ANALYSIS

Lane and Kay Collins operate a financial services firm. They manage other people's money and do most of their own financial-statement analysis. How do they measure companies' ability to pay bills, sell inventory, collect receivables, and so on? They use the standard ratios we have covered throughout this book.

(continued)

Ratio	Computation	Information Provided
Measuring ability to pay current liabilities:		
1. Current ratio	$\frac{\text{Current assets}}{\text{Current liabilities}}$	Measures ability to pay current liabilities with current assets
2. Acid-test (quick) ratio	$\frac{\text{Cash} + \text{Short-term investments} + \text{Net current receivables}}{\text{Current liabilities}}$	Shows ability to pay all current liabilities if they come due immediately
Measuring ability to sell inventory and collect receivables:		
3. Inventory turnover	$\frac{\text{Cost of goods sold}}{\text{Average inventory}}$	Indicates saleability of inventory—the number of times a company sells its average level of inventory during a year.
4. Accounts receivable turnover	$\frac{\text{Net credit sales}}{\text{Average net accounts receivable}}$	Measures ability to collect cash from credit customers
5. Days' sales in receivables	$\frac{\text{Average net accounts receivable}}{\text{One day's sales}}$	Shows how many days' sales remain in Accounts Receivable—how many days it takes to collect the average level of receivables.
Measuring ability to pay long-term debt:		
6. Debt ratio	$\frac{\text{Total liabilities}}{\text{Total assets}}$	Indicates percentage of assets financed with debt
7. Times-interest-earned ratio	$\frac{\text{Income from operations}}{\text{Interest expense}}$	Measures the number of times operating income can cover interest expense
Measuring profitability:		
8. Rate of return on net sales	$\frac{\text{Net income}}{\text{Net sales}}$	Shows the percentage of each sales dollar earned as net income
9. Rate of return on total assets	$\frac{\text{Net income} + \text{Interest expense}}{\text{Average total assets}}$	Measures how profitably a company uses its assets
10. Rate of return on common stockholders' equity	$\frac{\text{Net income} - \text{Preferred dividends}}{\text{Average common stockholders' equity}}$	Gauges how much income is earned with the money invested by the common shareholders
11. Earnings per share of common stock	$\frac{\text{Net income} - \text{Preferred dividends}}{\text{Number of shares of common stock outstanding}}$	Gives the amount of net income earned for each share of the company's common stock outstanding
Analyzing stock as an investment:		
12. Price/earnings ratio	$\frac{\text{Market price per share of common stock}}{\text{Earnings per share}}$	Indicates the market price of $1 of earnings
13. Dividend yield	$\frac{\text{Dividend per share of common (or preferred) stock}}{\text{Market price per share of common (or preferred) stock}}$	Shows the percentage of a stock's market value returned as dividends to stockholders each period
14. Book value per share of common stock	$\frac{\text{Total stockholders' equity} - \text{Preferred equity}}{\text{Number of shares of common stock outstanding}}$	Indicates the recorded accounting amount for each share of common stock outstanding

Summary Problem

END-OF-CHAPTER

The following financial data are adapted from the annual reports of Lampeer Corporation.

Lampeer Corporation
Five-Year Selected Financial Data
for Years Ended January 31, 2004, 2003, 2002 and 2001

Operating Results*	2004	2003	2002	2001
Net sales	$13,848	$13,673	$11,635	$9,054
Cost of goods sold and occupancy expenses excluding depreciation and amortization	9,704	8,599	6,775	5,318
Interest expense	109	75	45	46
Income from operations	338	1,445	1,817	1,333
Net earnings (net loss)	(8)	877	1,127	824
Cash dividends	76	75	76	77
Financial Position				
Merchandise inventory	1,677	1,904	1,462	1,056
Total assets	7,591	7,012	5,189	3,963
Current ratio	1.48:1	0.95:1	1.25:1	1.20:1
Stockholders' equity	3,010	2,928	2,630	1,574
Average number of shares of common stock outstanding (in thousands)	860	879	895	576

*Dollar amounts are in thousands.

Required

Compute the following ratios for 2002 through 2004, and evaluate Lampeer's operating results. Are operating results strong or weak? Did they improve or deteriorate during the 4-year period? Your analysis will reveal a clear trend.

1. Gross profit percentage*
2. Net income as a percentage of sales
3. Earnings per share
4. Inventory turnover
5. Times-interest-earned ratio
6. Rate of return on stockholders' equity

*Refer to chapter 6 if necessary.

Answer

	2004	2003	2002
1. Gross profit percentage	$\frac{\$13{,}848 - \$9{,}704}{\$13{,}848} = 29.9\%$	$\frac{\$13{,}673 - \$8{,}599}{\$13{,}673} = 37.1\%$	$\frac{\$11{,}635 - \$6{,}775}{\$11{,}635} = 41.8\%$
2. Net income as a percentage of sales	$\frac{\$(8)}{\$13{,}848} = (0.05\%)$	$\frac{\$877}{\$13{,}673} = 6.4\%$	$\frac{\$1{,}127}{\$11{,}635} = 9.7\%$
3. Earnings per share	$\frac{\$(8)}{860} = \$(0.01)$	$\frac{\$877}{879} = \$1.00$	$\frac{\$1{,}127}{895} = \$1.26$
4. Inventory turnover	$\frac{\$9{,}704}{(\$1{,}677 + \$1{,}904)/2} = 5.4$ times	$\frac{\$8{,}599}{(\$1{,}904 + \$1{,}462)/2} = 5.1$ times	$\frac{\$6{,}775}{(\$1{,}462 + \$1{,}056)/2} = 5.4$ times
5. Times-interest-earned ratio	$\frac{\$338}{\$109} = 3.1$ times	$\frac{\$1{,}455}{\$75} = 19.4$ times	$\frac{\$1{,}817}{\$45} = 40.4$ times
6. Rate of return on stockholders' equity	$\frac{\$(8)}{(\$3{,}010 + \$2{,}928)/2} = (0.3\%)$	$\frac{\$877}{(\$2{,}928 + \$2{,}630)/2} = 31.6\%$	$\frac{\$1{,}127}{(\$2{,}630 + \$1{,}574)/2} = 53.6\%$

Evaluation: During this period, Lampeer's operating results deteriorated on all these measures except inventory turnover. The gross profit percentage is down sharply, as are the times-interest-earned ratio and all the return measures. From these data it is clear that Lampeer could sell its merchandise, but not at the markups the company enjoyed in the past. The final result, in 20X4, was a net loss for the year.

REVIEW FINANCIAL STATEMENT ANALYSIS

Chapter Review Quiz

Analyze the **McDonald's Corporation** financial statements by answering the questions that follow.

McDonald's Corporation
Consolidated Statement of Income (Adapted)
Years Ended December 31, 2003, 2002 and 2001

In Millions, Except per Share Data	2003	2002	2001
Revenues			
Sales by Company-operated restaurants	$12,795.4	$11,499.6	$11,040.7
Revenues from franchised and affiliated restaurants	4,345.1	3,906.1	3,829.3
Total revenues	17,140.5	15,405.7	14,870.0
Operating Costs and Expenses			
Company-operated restaurant expenses			
Food & paper	4,314.8	3,917.4	3,802.1
Payroll & employee benefits	3,411.4	3,078.2	2,901.2
Occupancy & other operating expenses	3,279.8	2,911.0	2,750.4
Franchised restaurants—occupancy expenses	937.7	840.1	800.2
Selling, general & administrative expenses	1,833.0	1,712.8	1,661.7
Other operating expense, net	531.6	833.3	257.4
Total operating costs and expenses	14,308.3	13,292.8	12,173.0
Operating income	2,832.2	2,112.9	2,697.0
Interest expense	388.0	374.1	452.4
McDonald's Japan IPO gain			(137.1)
Nonoperating expense, net	97.8	76.7	52.0
Income before provision for income taxes and cumulative effect of accounting changes	2,346.4	1,662.1	2,329.7
Provision for income taxes	838.2	670.0	693.1
Income before cumulative effect of accounting changes	1,508.2	992.1	1,636.6
Cumulative effect of accounting changes, net of tax benefits of $9.4 and $17.6	(36.8)	(98.6)	
Net income	$ 1,471.4	$ 893.5	$ 1,636.6
Per common share–basic:			
Income before cumulative effect of accounting changes	$1.19	$0.78	$1.27
Cumulative effect of accounting changes	(0.03)	(0.08)	
Net income	$1.16	$0.70	$1.27
Dividends per common share	$0.40	$0.24	$0.23

McDonald's Corporation
Consolidated Balance Sheet
Years Ended December 31, 2003 and 2002

In Millions, Except per Share Data	2003	2002
Assets		
Current assets		
Cash and equivalents	$ 492.8	$ 330.4
Accounts and notes receivable	734.5	855.3
Inventories, at cost, not in excess of market	129.4	111.7
Prepaid expenses and other current assets	528.7	418.0
Total current assets	1,885.4	1,715.4
Other assets		
Investments in and advances to affiliates	1,089.6	1,037.7
Goodwill, net	1,665.1	1,558.5
Miscellaneous	960.3	1,075.5
Total other assets	3,715.0	3,671.7
Property and equipment		
Property and equipment, at cost	28,740.2	26,218.6
Accumulated depreciation and amortization	(8,815.5)	(7,635.2)
Net property and equipment	19,924.7	18,583.4
Total assets	$25,525.1	$23,970.5
Liabilities and Shareholders' Equity		
Current liabilities		
Accounts payable	$ 577.4	$ 635.8
Income taxes	71.5	16.3
Other taxes	222.0	191.8
Accrued interest	193.1	199.4
Accrued restructuring and restaurant closing costs	115.7	328.5
Accrued payroll and other liabilities	918.1	774.7
Current maturities of long-term debt	388.0	275.8
Total current liabilities	2,485.8	2,422.3
Long-term debt	9,342.5	9,703.6
Other long-term liabilities and minority interests	699.8	560.0
Deferred income taxes	1,015.1	1,003.7
Shareholders' equity		
Preferred stock, no par value; authorized—165.0 million shares; issued–none		
Common stock, $.01 par value; authorized—3.5 billion shares; issued—1,660.6 million shares	16.6	16.6
Additional paid-in capital	1,837.5	1,747.3
Unearned ESOP compensation	(90.5)	(98.4)
Retained earnings	20,172.3	19,204.4
Accumulated other comprehensive income (loss)	(635.5)	(1,601.3)
Common stock in treasury, at cost; 398.7 and 392.4 million shares	(9,318.5)	(8,987.7)
Total shareholders' equity	11,981.9	10,280.9
Total liabilities and shareholders' equity	$25,525.1	$23,970.5

See notes to consolidated financial statements.

1. Horizontal analysis of McDonald's income statement for 2003 would show which of the following for Selling, general, and administrative expenses?
   a. 0.107
   b. 0.143
   c. 1.144
   d. None of the above (fill in the blank).

2. Vertical Analysis of McDonald's income statement for 2003 would show which of the following for Selling, general, & administrative expenses?
   a. 0.107
   b. 0.143
   c. 1.144
   d. None of the above (fill in the blank).

3. Which item on McDonald's income statement has the most favorable trend during 2002–2003?
   a. Net income
   b. Total revenues
   c. Food and paper costs
   d. Payroll & employee benefits

4. On McDonald's common-size balance sheet, Goodwill would appear as
   a. up by 6.8%.
   b. 0.065.
   c. $1,665.1 million.
   d. 9.7% of total revenues.

5. A good benchmark for McDonald's Corporation would be
   a. Whataburger.
   b. Wendy's.
   c. Burger King.
   d. All of the above.

6. McDonald's inventory turnover for 2003 was
   a. 91 times.
   b. 62 times.
   c. 36 times.
   d. 21 times.

7. McDonald's Accounts and notes receivable must come from
   a. customers.
   b. the operators of franchised . restaurants
   c. government tax refunds.
   d. Employees who have borrowed money from the company.

8. McDonald's average collection period for accounts and notes receivables is
   a. 1 day.
   b. 2 days.
   c. 17 days.
   d. 30 days.

9. McDonald's total debt position looks
   a. risky.
   b. middle-ground.
   c. safe.
   d. Cannot tell from the financials.

10. McDonald's return on total revenues for 2003 was
    a. 5.9%
    b. 8.6%
    c. 13.2%
    d. $1.16.

11. McDonald's return on stockholders' equity for 2003 was
    a. 5.9%
    b. 8.6%
    c. 13.2%
    d. $11,981.9 million.

12. On June 30, 2004, McDonald's common stock sold for $26 per share. At that price, how much did investors say $1 of McDonald's net income was worth?
    a. $1.00
    b. $21.85
    c. $22.41
    d. $26.00

13. Use McDonald's financial statements and the data in question 12 to compute McDonald's dividend yield during 2003.
    a. 1.5%
    b. 2.2%
    c. 2.4%
    d. 3.1%

14. How much EVA® did McDonald's generate for investors during 2003? Assume the cost of capital was 8%.
    a. $973 million
    b. $239 million
    c. $1,471 million
    d. $1,859 million

Answers

1. d [1.070 = $1,833/$1,712.8 = 1.070]
2. a ($1,833/$17,140.5 = 0.107)
3. a (Net income: $1,471.4 – $893.5 = $577.9; $577.9/$893.5 = Increase of 64.7%)
4. b ($1,665.1/$25,525.1 = 0.065)
5. d
6. c $\left[\dfrac{\$4{,}314.8}{(\$129.4 + \$111.7)/2} = 35.8 \approx 36 \text{ times}\right]$
7. b
8. c $\left[\dfrac{(\$734.5 + \$855.3)/2}{\$17{,}140.5/365} = 16.9 \approx 17 \text{ days}\right]$
9. c (Debt ratio is ($25,525.1 – $11,981.9)/$25,525.1 = 0.53. This debt ratio is lower than the average for most companies, given in the chapter as 0.62.)
10. b ($1,471.4/$17,140.5 = 0.086)
11. c $\left[\dfrac{\$1{,}471.4}{(\$11{,}981.9 + \$10{,}280.9)/2} = 0.132\right]$
12. c ($26/$1.16 = 22.41)
13. a ($0.40/$26.00 = 0.015)
14. b ($1,471.4 + $388 – ($275.8 + $9,703.6 + $10,280.9) × 0.08 = $238.6)

Accounting Vocabulary

accounts receivable turnover (p. 622)
acid-test ratio (p. 620)
benchmarking (p. 613)
book value per share of common stock (p. 627)
capital charge (p. 628)
common-size statement (p. 612)
cost of capital (p. 627)
current ratio (p. 618)
days' sales in receivables (p. 622)
debt ratio (p. 623)
dividend yield (p. 626)
earnings per share (EPS) (p. 625)
economic value added (EVA)® (p. 627)
efficient capital market (p. 629)
horizontal analysis (p. 609)
inventory turnover (p. 621)
leverage (p. 625)
price/earnings ratio (p. 626)
quick ratio (p. 620)
rate of return on common stockholders' equity (p. 624)
rate of return on net sales (p. 624)
rate of return on total assets (p. 624)
return on equity (p. 624)
times-interest-earned ratio (p. 623)
trading on the equity (p. 625)
trend percentages (p. 611)
vertical analysis (p. 611)
working capital (p. 618)

Assess Your Progress

Check Points

Horizontal analysis of revenues and net income (Obj. 1)

writing assignment ■

CP13-1 (p. 609) Monaco Inc., reported the following amounts on its 2005 comparative income statement.

(In thousands)	2005	2004	2003
Revenues	$9,889	$9,095	$8,777
Total expenses	5,985	5,604	5,194

Perform a horizontal analysis of revenues and net income—both in dollar amounts and in percentages—for 2005 and 2004.

Required

Complete the following condensed balance sheet. Report amounts to the nearest million dollars.

Current assets		$?
Property, plant, and equipment	$?	
Less Accumulated depreciation	(?)	?
Total assets		$?
Current liabilities		$?
Long-term liabilities		?
Stockholders' equity		?
Total liabilities and stockholders' equity		$?

Using ratio data to reconstruct a leading company's income statement (Obj. 2, 3, 5)

E13-13 The following data (dollar amounts in millions) are from the financial statements of **McDonald's Corporation**:

Average stockholders' equity	$3,605
Interest expense	$ 413
Preferred stock	$ 0
Operating income as a percent of sales	24.04%
Rate of return on stockholders' equity	21.89%
Income tax rate	33.30%

Required

Complete the following condensed income statement. Report amounts to the nearest million dollars.

Sales	$?
Operating expense	?
Operating income	?
Interest expense	?
Pretax income	?
Income tax expense	?
Net income	$?

Practice Quiz

Use the **Dell [Computer] Inc.** *financial statements to answer the questions that follow.*

Dell Inc.
Consolidated Statements of Financial Position
(In millions)

	January 30, 2004	January 31, 2003
Assets		
Current assets:		
Cash and cash equivalents	$ 4,317	$ 4,232
Short-term investments	835	406
Accounts receivable, net	3,635	2,586
Inventories	327	306
Other	1,519	1,394
Total current assets	10,633	8,924
Property, plant, and equipment, net	1,517	913
Investments	6,770	5,267
Other noncurrent assets	391	366
Total assets	$19,311	$15,470

(continued)

	January 30, 2004	January 31, 2003
Liabilities and Stockholders' Equity		
Current liabilities:		
Accounts payable	$ 7,316	$ 5,989
Accrued and other	3,580	2,944
Total current liabilities	10,896	8,933
Long-term debt	505	506
Other noncurrent liabilities	1,630	1,158
Commitments and contingent liabilities (Note 7)	—	—
Total liabilities	13,031	10,597
Stockholders' equity:		
Preferred stock and capital in excess of $0.01 par value; shares issued and outstanding: none	—	—
Common stock and capital in excess of $0.01 par value; shares authorized: 7,000; shares issued: 2,721 and 2,681, respectively	6,823	6,018
Treasury stock, at cost; 165 and 102 shares, respectively	(6,539)	(4,539)
Retained earnings	6,131	3,486
Other comprehensive loss	(83)	(33)
Other	(52)	(59)
Total stockholders' equity	6,280	4,873
Total liabilities and stockholders' equity	$19,311	$15,470

Dell Inc.
Consolidated Statements of Income
(In millions, except per share amounts)

	Fiscal Year Ended		
	January 30, 2004	January 31, 2003	February 1, 2002
Net revenue	$41,444	$35,404	$31,168
Cost of revenue	33,892	29,055	25,661
Gross margin	7,552	6,349	5,507
Operating expenses:			
Selling, general, and administrative	3,544	3,050	2,784
Research, development, and engineering	464	455	452
Special charges	—	—	482
Total operating expenses	4,008	3,505	3,718
Operating income	3,544	2,844	1,789
Investment and other income (loss), net	180	183	(58)
Income before income taxes	3,724	3,027	1,731
Income tax provision	1,079	905	485
Net income	$ 2,645	$ 2,122	$ 1,246
Earnings per common share:			
Basic	$ 1.03	$ 0.82	$ 0.48

PQ13-1 During fiscal year 2004, Dell's total assets

a. increased by $3,841 million.
b. increased by 24.8%.
c. Both a and b.
d. increased by 19.9%

PQ13-2 Dell's current ratio at year end 2004 is closest to

a. 1.0.
b. 1.1.
c. 1.2.
d. 0.80.

PQ13-3 Dell's acid-test ratio at year end 2004 is closest to

a. $8,787 million.
b. $0.47.
c. 0.65.
d. 0.80.

PQ13-4 What is the largest single item included in Dell's debt ratio at January 30, 2004?

a. Cash and cash equivalents
b. Investments
c. Accounts payable
d. Common stock

PQ13-5 Using the earliest year available as the base year, the trend percentage for Dell's net revenue during fiscal year 2004 was

a. 117%.
b. 133%.
c. up by 17.1%.
d. up by $6,040 million.

PQ13-6 Dell's common-size income statement for fiscal year 2004 would report cost of revenue as

a. $33,892 million.
b. Up by 16.6%.
c. 132.1%.
d. 81.8%.

PQ13-7 Dell's days' sales in average receivables during fiscal year 2004 was

a. 27 days.
b. 32 days.
c. 22 days.
d. 114 days.

PQ13-8 Dell's rate of inventory turnover during fiscal year 2004 was

a. 129 times.
b. 107 times.
c. 54 times.
d. very slow.

PQ13-9 Assume that Dell's long-term debt bears interest at 6%. During the year ended December 31, 2004 Dell's times-interest-earned ratio was

a. 100 times.
b. 110 times.
c. 117 times.
d. 125 times.

PQ13-10 Dell's trend of return on sales is

a. stuck at 6%.
b. declining.
c. improving.
d. worrisome.

PQ13-11 How many shares of common stock did Dell have outstanding, on average, during fiscal year 2004? Hint: Compute earnings per share.

a. 2,721 million
b. 2,701 million
c. 2,645 million
d. 2,568 million

PQ13-12 Book value per share of Dell's common stock outstanding at January 30, 2004, was

a. $2.46.
b. $4.37.
c. $6,280.
d. $2.72.

Problems
(Group A)

Most of these A problems can be found within Prentice Hall Grade Assist (PHGA), an online homework and practice environment. Your instructor may ask you to complete these problems using PHGA.

Trend percentages, return on common equity, and comparison with the industry (Obj. 1, 5, 6)

P13-1A Net revenues, net income, and common stockholders' equity for xCel Corporation, a manufacturer of contact lenses, for a 4-year period follow.

(In thousands)	2008	2007	2006	2005
Net revenues	$781	$714	$641	$662
Net income	51	45	32	48
Ending common stockholders' equity	366	354	330	296

Required

1. Compute trend percentages for each item for 2006 through 2008. Use 2005 as the base year. Round to the nearest percent.
2. Compute the rate of return on common stockholders' equity for 2006 through 2008, rounding to three decimal places. In the contact lens industry, rates of 13% are average, rates above 16% are good, and rates above 20% are outstanding. xCel has no preferred stock outstanding.
3. How does xCel's return on common stockholders' equity compare with the industry?

Common-size statements, analysis of profitability, and comparison with the industry (Obj. 2, 3, 5, 6)

writing assignment ■

P13-2A Bose Stereo Shops has asked you to compare the company's profit performance and financial position with the average for the stereo industry. The proprietor has given you the company's income statement and balance sheet as well as the industry average data for retailers.

Bose Stereo Shops
Income Statement Compared with Industry Average
Year Ended December 31, 20X6

	Bose	Industry Average
Net sales	$781,000	100.0%
Cost of goods sold	497,000	65.8
Gross profit	284,000	34.2
Operating expenses	163,000	19.7
Operating income	121,000	14.5
Other expenses	6,000	0.4
Net income	$115,000	14.1%

Bose Stereo Shops
Balance Sheet Compared with Industry Average
December 31, 20X6

	Bose	Industry Average
Current assets	$350,000	70.9%
Fixed assets, net	74,000	23.6
Intangible assets, net	4,000	0.8
Other assets	22,000	4.7
Total	$450,000	100.0%
Current liabilities	$207,000	48.1%
Long-term liabilities	62,000	16.6
Stockholders' equity	181,000	35.3
Total	$450,000	100.0%

Required

1. Prepare a common-size income statement and balance sheet for Bose. The first column of each statement should present Bose's common-size statement, and the second column, the industry averages.
2. For the profitability analysis, compute Bose's (a) ratio of gross profit to net sales, (b) ratio of operating income to net sales, and (c) ratio of net income to net sales. Compare these figures with the industry averages. Is Bose's profit performance better or worse than the industry average?
3. For the analysis of financial position, compute Bose's (a) ratio of current assets to total assets, and (b) ratio of stockholders' equity to total assets. Compare these ratios with the industry averages. Is Bose's financial position better or worse than the industry averages?

Using the statement of cash flows for decision making (Obj. 4)

writing assignment ■

P13-3A You have been asked to evaluate two companies as possible investments. The two companies, America Roofing, Inc. and Imagine Time Software Corporation, are similar in size. Assume that all other available information has been analyzed, and the decision concerning which company's stock to purchase depends on their cash-flow data.

Required

Discuss the relative strengths and weaknesses of each company. Conclude your discussion by recommending one company's stock as an investment.

America Roofing, Inc.
Statement of Cash Flows
Years Ended September 30, 20X7 and 20X6

	20X7		20X6	
Operating activities:				
Net income		$17,000		$44,000
Adjustments for noncash items:				
Total		(14,000)		(4,000)
Net cash provided by operating activities		3,000		40,000
Investing activities:				
Purchase of property, plant, and equipment	$ (13,000)		$ (3,000)	
Sale of property, plant, and equipment	86,000		79,000	
Net cash provided by investing activities		73,000		76,000
Financing activities:				
Issuance of short-term notes payable	$ 43,000		$ 19,000	
Payment of short-term notes payable	(101,000)		(108,000)	
Net cash used for financing activities		(58,000)		(89,000)
Increase in cash		$18,000		$27,000
Cash balance at beginning of year		31,000		4,000
Cash balance at end of year		$49,000		$31,000

Imagine Time Software Corporation
Statement of Cash Flows
Years Ended September 30, 20X7 and 20X6

	20X7		20X6	
Operating activities:				
Net income		$89,000		$ 71,000
Adjustments for noncash items:				
Total		19,000		—
Net cash provided by operating activities		108,000		71,000
Investing activities:				
Purchase of property, plant, and equipment	$(121,000)		$(91,000)	
Net cash used for investing activities		(121,000)		(91,000)
Financing activities:				
Issuance of long-term notes payable	$46,000		$ 43,000	
Payment of short-term notes payable	(15,000)		(40,000)	
Payment of cash dividends	(12,000)		(9,000)	
Net cash provided by (used for) financing activities		19,000		(6,000)
Increase (decrease) in cash		$ 6,000		$(26,000)
Cash balance at beginning of year		54,000		80,000
Cash balance at end of year		$60,000		$ 54,000

P13-4A Financial statement data of Biz Mart Discount Center include the following items (dollars in thousands):

Effects of business transactions on selected ratios (Obj. 5, 6)

Cash	$ 22,000
Short-term investments	19,000
Accounts receivable, net	83,000
Inventories	141,000
Prepaid expenses	8,000
Total assets	657,000
Short-term notes payable	49,000
Accounts payable	103,000
Accrued liabilities	38,000
Long-term notes payable	160,000
Other long-term liabilities	31,000
Net income	71,000
Number of common shares outstanding	40,000

Required

1. Compute Biz Mart's current ratio, debt ratio, and earnings per share. Use the following format for your answer:

Requirement 1 Current ratio	Debt ratio	Earnings per share

2. Compute the three ratios after evaluating the effect of each transaction that follows. Consider each transaction *separately*.
   a. Purchased store supplies of $46,000 on account.
   b. Borrowed $125,000 on a long-term note payable.
   c. Issued 5,000 shares of common stock, receiving cash of $120,000.
   d. Paid short-term notes payable, $32,000.
   e. Received cash on account, $19,000.

   Format your answer as follows:

Requirement 2 Transaction (letter)	Current ratio	Debt ratio	Earnings per share

P13-5A Comparative financial statement data of i2 Networks, Inc. follow.

Using ratios to evaluate a stock investment (Obj. 5, 6)

writing assignment ■

i2 Networks, Inc.
Comparative Income Statement
Years Ended December 31, 20X9 and 20X8

	20X9	20X8
Net sales	$462,000	$427,000
Cost of goods sold	229,000	218,000
Gross profit	233,000	209,000
Operating expenses	136,000	134,000
Income from operations	97,000	75,000
Interest expense	11,000	12,000
Income before income tax	86,000	63,000
Income tax expense	30,000	27,000
Net income	$ 56,000	$ 36,000

i2 Networks, Inc.
Comparative Balance Sheet
December 31, 20X9 and 20X8

	20X9	20X8	20X7*
Current assets:			
Cash	$ 96,000	$ 97,000	
Current receivables, net	112,000	116,000	$103,000
Inventories	147,000	162,000	207,000
Prepaid expenses	16,000	7,000	
Total current assets	371,000	382,000	
Property, plant, and equipment, net	214,000	178,000	
Total assets	$585,000	$560,000	598,000
Total current liabilities	$206,000	$223,000	
Long-term liabilities	119,000	117,000	
Total liabilities	325,000	340,000	
Preferred stockholders' equity, 6%, $100 par	100,000	100,000	
Common stockholders' equity, no par	160,000	120,000	90,000
Total liabilities and stockholders' equity	$585,000	$560,000	

*Selected 20X7 amounts.

Other information:

1. Market price of i2 Networks' common stock: $53 at December 31, 20X9, and $32.50 at December 31, 20X8.
2. Common shares outstanding: 10,000 during 20X9 and 9,000 during 20X8.
3. All sales on credit.

Required

1. Compute the following ratios for 20X9 and 20X8:
   a. Current ratio
   b. Inventory turnover
   c. Times-interest-earned ratio
   d. Return on common stockholders' equity
   e. Earnings per share of common stock
   f. Price/earnings ratio
2. Decide (a) whether i2 Networks' financial position improved or deterioriated during 20X9 and (b) whether the investment attractiveness of its common stock appears to have increased or decreased.
3. How will what you learned in this problem help you evaluate an investment?

Using ratios to decide between two stock investments; measuring economic value added (Obj. 5, 6, 7)

writing assignment ■

P13-6A Assume that you are purchasing an investment and have decided to invest in a company in the air-conditioning/heating business. You have narrowed the choice to Caremark Laboratories and AmeriCorp, Inc., and have assembled the following data:

Select income statement data for current year:

	Caremark	AmeriCorp
Net sales (all on credit)	$371,000	$497,000
Cost of goods sold	209,000	258,000
Income from operations	79,000	138,000
Interest expense	—	19,000
Net income	48,000	72,000

Selected balance sheet data at *beginning* of current year:

	Caremark	AmeriCorp
Current receivables, net	$ 40,000	$ 48,000
Inventories	93,000	88,000
Total assets	259,000	270,000
Preferred stock, 5%, $100 par	—	20,000
Common stock, $1 par (10,000 shares)	10,000	
$2.50 par (5,000 shares)		12,500
Total stockholders' equity	118,000	126,000

Selected balance sheet and market price data at *end* of current year:

	Caremark	AmeriCorp
Current assets:		
Cash	$ 22,000	$ 19,000
Short-term investments	20,000	18,000
Current receivables, net	42,000	46,000
Inventories	87,000	100,000
Prepaid expenses	2,000	3,000
Total current assets	173,000	186,000
Total assets	265,000	328,000
Total current liabilities	108,000	98,000
Total liabilities	108,000*	131,000*
Preferred stock: 5%, $100 par		20,000
Common stock, $1 par (10,000 shares)	10,000	
$2.50 par (5,000 shares)		12,500
Total stockholders' equity	157,000	197,000
Market price per share of common stock	$ 51	$ 112

* Includes notes payable: Caremark $1,000 and AmeriCorp $86,000

Your strategy is to invest in companies that have low price/earnings ratios but appear to be in good shape financially. Assume that you have analyzed all other factors and that your decision depends on the results of ratio analysis.

Required

1. Compute the following ratios for both companies for the current year, and decide which company's stock better fits your investment strategy.
   a. Acid-test ratio
   b. Inventory turnover
   c. Days' sales in average receivables
   d. Debt ratio
   e. Times-interest-earned ratio
   f. Return on common stockholders' equity
   g. Earnings per share of common stock
   h. Price/earnings ratio
2. Compute each company's economic-value-added (EVA®) measure and determine whether their EVA®s confirm or alter your investment decision. Each company's cost of capital is 12%. Round all amounts to the nearest $1,000.

Analyzing a company based on its ratios (Obj. 6)

P13-7A Take the role of an investment analyst at **Goldman Sachs**. It is your job to recommend investments for your clients. The only information you have is the following ratio values for two companies in the pharmaceuticals industry.

Ratio	Pratt Corp.	Jacobs, Inc.
Days' sales in receivables	36	42
Inventory turnover	6	8
Gross profit percentage	49%	51%
Net income as a percent of sales	7.2%	8.3%
Times-interest-earned	16	9
Return on equity	32.3%	21.5%
Return on assets	12.1%	16.4%

Write a report to Goldman Sachs' investment committee. Recommend one company's stock over the others'. State the reasons for your recommendation.

(Group B)

PH Grade Assist

Some of these B problems can be found within Prentice Hall Grade Assist (PHGA), an online homework and practice environment. Your instructor may ask you to complete these exercises using PHGA.

Trend percentages, return on sales, and comparison with the industry (Obj. 1, 5, 6)

P13-1B Net sales, net income, and total assets for XT Communications, Inc., for a 4-year period follow:

(In thousands)	20X8	20X7	20X6	20X5
Net sales	$357	$313	$266	$281
Net income	29	21	11	18
Total assets	286	254	209	197

Required

1. Compute trend percentages for each item for 20X6 through 20X8. Use 20X5 as the base year and round to nearest percent.
2. Compute the rate of return on net sales for 20X6 through 20X8, rounding to three decimal places. In the telecommunications industry, rates above 5% are considered good, and rates above 7% are outstanding.
3. How does XT Communications' return on net sales compare with that of the industry?

Common-size statements, analysis of profitability, and comparison with the industry (Obj. 2, 3, 5, 6)

P13-2B Top managers of Escalade Technology Corporation have asked for your help in comparing the company's profit performance and financial position with the average for the cell phone industry. The accountant has given you the company's income statement and balance sheet and also the following data for the industry:

Escalade Technology Corporation
Income Statement Compared with Industry Average
Year Ended December 31, 20X5

	Escalade	Industry Average
Net sales	$957,000	100.0%
Cost of goods sold	652,000	65.9
Gross profit	305,000	34.1
Operating expenses	204,000	28.1
Operating income	101,000	6.0
Other expenses	13,000	0.4
Net income	$ 88,000	5.6%

Escalade Technology Corporation Balance Sheet Compared with Industry Average December 31, 20X5	Escalade	Industry Average
Current assets	$486,000	74.4%
Fixed assets, net	117,000	20.0
Intangible assets, net	24,000	0.6
Other assets	3,000	5.0
Total	$630,000	100.0%
Current liabilities	$246,000	45.6%
Long-term liabilities	136,000	19.0
Stockholders' equity	248,000	35.4
Total	$630,000	100.0%

Required

1. Prepare a common-size income statement and balance sheet for Escalade. The first column of each statement should present Escalade's common-size statement, and the second column should show the industry averages.
2. For the profitability analysis, compute Escalade's (a) ratio of gross profit to net sales, (b) ratio of operating income to net sales, and (c) ratio of net income to net sales. Compare these figures with the industry averages. Is Escalade's profit performance better or worse than the average for the industry?
3. For the analysis of financial position, compute Escalade's (a) ratios of current assets and current liabilities to total assets and (b) ratio of stockholders' equity to total assets. Compare these ratios with the industry averages. Is Escalade's financial position better or worse than the average for the industry?

writing assignment ■

Using the statement of cash flows for decision making (Obj. 4)

writing assignment ■

P13-3B You are evaluating two companies as possible investments. The two companies, similar in size, are commuter airlines that fly passengers from San Francisco to smaller cities in California. All other available information has been analyzed and your investment decision depends on cash flows.

Calair Corporation Statement of Cash Flows Years Ended November 30, 20X9 and 20X8	20X9		20X8	
Operating activities:				
Net income (net loss)		$(67,000)		$154,000
Adjustments for noncash items:				
Total		84,000		(23,000)
Net cash provided by operating activities		17,000		131,000
Investing activities:				
Purchase of property, plant, and equipment	$ (50,000)		$(91,000)	
Sale of long-term investments	52,000		4,000	
Net cash provided by (used for) investing activities		2,000		(87,000)
Financing activities:				
Issuance of short-term notes payable	$122,000		$143,000	
Payment of short-term notes payable	(179,000)		(134,000)	
Payment of cash dividends	(45,000)		(64,000)	
Net cash used for financing activities		(102,000)		(55,000)
Increase (decrease) in cash		$(83,000)		$ (11,000)
Cash balance at beginning of year		92,000		103,000
Cash balance at the end of year		$ 9,000		$ 92,000

San Fernando Airways, Inc.
Statement of Cash Flows
Years Ended November 30, 20X9 and 20X8

	20X9		20X8	
Operating activities:				
Net income		$184,000		$131,000
Adjustments for noncash items:				
Total		64,000		62,000
Net cash provided by operating activities		248,000		193,000
Investing activities:				
Purchase of property, plant, and equipment	$(303,000)		$(453,000)	
Sale of property, plant, and equipment	46,000		72,000	
Net cash used for investing activities		(257,000)		(381,000)
Financing activities:				
Issuance of long-term notes payable	$174,000		$118,000	
Payment of short-term notes payable	(66,000)		(18,000)	
Net cash provided by financing activities		108,000		100,000
Increase (decrease) in cash		$ 99,000		$ (88,000)
Cash balance at beginning of year		116,000		204,000
Cash balance at end of year		$215,000		$116,000

Required

Discuss the relative strengths and weaknesses of Calair and San Fernando Airways. Conclude your discussion by recommending one of the company's stocks as an investment.

Effects of business transactions on selected ratios (Obj. 5, 6)

P13-4B Financial statement data on Thunderbird Medical Supply include the following items:

Accounts payable	$ 96,000	Cash	$ 47,000
Accrued liabilities	50,000	Short-term investments	21,000
Long-term notes payable	146,000	Accounts receivable, net	102,000
Other long-term liabilities	78,000	Inventories	274,000
Net income	119,000	Prepaid expenses	15,000
Number of common		Total assets	933,000
shares outstanding	22,000	Short-term notes payable	72,000

Required

1. Compute Thunderbird's current ratio, debt ratio, and earnings per share. Use the following format for your answer:

Requirement 1 Current ratio	Debt ratio	Earnings per share

2. Compute the three ratios after evaluating the effect of each transaction that follows. Consider each transaction *separately*.
   a. Borrowed $27,000 on a long-term note payable.
   b. Issued 10,000 shares of common stock, receiving cash of $108,000.
   c. Paid short-term notes payable, $51,000.
   d. Purchased merchandise of $48,000 on account, debiting Inventory.
   e. Received cash on account, $6,000.

   Format your answer as follows:

Requirement 2 Transaction letter	Current ratio	Debt ratio	Earnings per share

Using ratios to evaluate a stock investment
(Obj. 5, 6)

writing assignment ■

P13-5B Comparative financial statement data of Advanced Automotive Company follow:

Advanced Automotive Company
Comparative Income Statement
Years Ended December 31, 20X6 and 20X5

	20X6	20X5
Net sales	$667,000	$599,000
Cost of goods sold	378,000	283,000
Gross profit	289,000	316,000
Operating expenses	129,000	147,000
Income from operations	160,000	169,000
Interest expense	57,000	41,000
Income before income tax	103,000	128,000
Income tax expense	34,000	53,000
Net income	$ 69,000	$ 75,000

Advanced Automotive Company
Comparative Balance Sheet
December 31, 20X6 and 20X5

	20X6	20X5	20X4*
Current assets:			
Cash	$ 37,000	$ 40,000	
Current receivables, net	208,000	151,000	$138,000
Inventories	352,000	286,000	184,000
Prepaid expenses	5,000	20,000	
Total current assets	602,000	497,000	
Property, plant, and equipment, net	287,000	276,000	
Total assets	$889,000	$773,000	707,000
Total current liabilities	$286,000	$267,000	
Long-term liabilities	245,000	235,000	
Total liabilities	531,000	502,000	
Preferred stockholders' equity, 4%, $20 par	50,000	50,000	
Common stockholders' equity, no par	308,000	221,000	148,000
Total liabilities and stockholders' equity	$889,000	$773,000	

*Selected 20X4 amounts.

Other information:

1. Market price of Advanced Automotive's common stock: $36.75 at December 31, 20X6, and $50.50 at December 31, 20X5.
2. Common shares outstanding: 15,000 during 20X6 and 14,000 during 20X5.
3. All sales on credit.

Required

1. Compute the following ratios for 20X6 and 20X5:
   a. Current ratio
   b. Inventory turnover
   c. Times-interest-earned ratio
   d. Return on assets
   e. Return on common stockholders' equity
   f. Earnings per share of common stock
   g. Price/earnings ratio
2. Decide whether (a) Advanced's financial position improved or deteriorated during 20X6 and (b) the investment attractiveness of its common stock appears to have increased or decreased.
3. How will what you learned in this problem help you evaluate an investment?

Using ratios to decide between two stock investments; measuring economic value added (Obj. 5, 6, 7)

writing assignment ■

P13-6B Assume that you are considering purchasing stock in a company in the music industry. You have narrowed the choice to Blues Inc. and Sonic Sound Corporation and have assembled the following data:

Selected income statement data for current year:

	Blues	Sonic
Net sales (all on credit)	$603,000	$519,000
Cost of goods sold	454,000	387,000
Income from operations	93,000	72,000
Interest expense	—	8,000
Net income	56,000	38,000

Selected balance sheet and market price data at *end* of current year:

	Blues	Sonic
Current assets:		
Cash	$ 25,000	$ 39,000
Short-term investments	6,000	13,000
Current receivables, net	189,000	164,000
Inventories	211,000	183,000
Prepaid expenses	19,000	15,000
Total current assets	450,000	414,000
Total assets	974,000	938,000
Total current liabilities	366,000	338,000
Total liabilities	667,000*	691,000*
Preferred stock, 4%, $100 par		25,000
Common stock, $1 par (150,000 shares)	150,000	
$5 par (20,000 shares)		100,000
Total stockholders' equity	307,000	247,000
Market price per share of common stock	$ 9	$ 47.50

*Includes notes and bonds payable: Blues $4,000, and Sonic $303,000

Selected balance sheet data at *beginning* of current year:

	Blues	Sonic
Current receivables, net	$142,000	$193,000
Inventories	209,000	197,000
Total assets	842,000	909,000
Preferred stock, 4%, $100 par		25,000
Common stock, $1 par (150,000 shares)	150,000	
$5 par (20,000 shares)		100,000
Total stockholders' equity	263,000	215,000

Your strategy is to invest in companies that have low price/earnings ratios but appear to be in good shape financially. Assume that you have analyzed all other factors and that your decision depends on the results of ratio analysis.

Required

1. Compute the following ratios for both companies for the current year and decide which company's stock better fits your investment strategy.
   - a. Acid-test ratio
   - b. Inventory turnover
   - c. Days' sales in average receivables
   - d. Debt ratio
   - e. Times-interest-earned ratio
   - f. Return on common stockholders' equity
   - g. Earnings per share of common stock
   - h. Price/earnings ratio

2. Compute each company's economic-value-added (EVA®) measure and determine whether their EVA®s confirm or alter your investment decision. Each company's cost of capital is 10%. Round all amounts to the nearest $1,000.

Analyzing a company based on its ratios (Obj. 6)

writing assignment ■

P13-7B Take the role of an investment analyst at **Edward Jones Company**. It is your job to recommend investments for your client. The only information you have are the following ratio values for two companies in the graphics software industry.

Ratio	GraphTech Inc.	Core Software Company
Days' sales in receivables	51	43
Inventory turnover	9	7
Gross profit percentage	62%	71%
Net income as a percent of sales	16%	14%
Times-interest-earned	12	18
Return on equity	29%	36%
Return on assets	19%	14%

Write a report to the Edward Jones investment committee. Recommend one company's stock over the other. State the reasons for your recommendation.

APPLY YOUR KNOWLEDGE

Decision Cases

Assessing the effects of transactions on a company (Obj. 5, 6)

Case 1. AOL Time Warner Inc. had a bad year in 20X1; the company suffered a $4.9 billion net loss. The loss pushed most of the return measures into the negative column and the current ratio dropped below 1.0. The company's debt ratio is still only 0.27. Assume top management of AOL Time Warner is pondering ways to improve the company's ratios. In particular, management is considering the following transactions:

1. Sell off the cable television segment of the business for $30 million (receiving half in cash and half in the form of a long-term note receivable). Book value of the cable television business is $27 million.
2. Borrow $100 million on long-term debt.
3. Purchase treasury stock for $500 million cash.
4. Write off one-fourth of goodwill carried on the books at $128 million.
5. Sell advertising at the normal gross profit of 60%. The advertisements run immediately.
6. Purchase trademarks from **NBC**, paying $20 million cash and signing a 1-year note payable for $80 million.

Required

1. Top management wants to know the effects of these transactions (increase, decrease, or no effect) on the following ratios of AOL Time Warner:
   a. Current ratio
   b. Debt ratio
   c. Times-interest-earned ratio (measured as [net income + interest expense]/interest expense)
   d. Return on equity
   e. Book value per share of common stock
2. Some of these transactions have an immediately positive effect on the company's financial condition. Some are definitely negative. Others have an effect that cannot be judged as clearly positive or negative. Evaluate each transaction's effect as positive, negative, or unclear.

Analyzing the effects of an accounting difference on the ratios (Obj. 5,6)

Case 2. Gap Inc. uses the first-in, first-out (FIFO) method to account for its inventory, and **Land's End** uses last-in, first-out (LIFO). Analyze the effect of this difference in accounting method on the two companies' ratio values. For each ratio discussed in this chapter, indicate which company will have the higher (and the lower) ratio value. Also identify those ratios that are unaffected by the FIFO/LIFO difference. Ignore the effects of income taxes, and assume inventory costs are increasing. Then, based on your analysis of the ratios, summarize your conclusions as to which company looks better overall.

Identifying action to cut losses and establish profitability (Obj. 2, 5, 6)

writing assignment ■

Case 3. Suppose you manage Outward Bound, Inc., a Vermont sporting goods store that lost money during the past year. To turn the business around, you must analyze the company and industry data for the current year to learn what is wrong. The company's data follow:

Outward Bound, Inc.
Common-Size Balance Sheet Data

	Outward Bound	Industry Average
Cash and short-term investments	3.0%	6.8%
Trade receivables, net	15.2	11.0
Inventory	64.2	60.5
Prepaid expenses	1.0	0.0
Total current assets	83.4%	78.3%
Fixed assets, net	12.6	15.2
Other assets	4.0	6.5
Total assets	100.0%	100.0%
Notes payable, short-term, 12%	17.1%	14.0%
Accounts payable	21.1	25.1
Accrued liabilities	7.8	7.9
Total current liabilities	46.0	47.0
Long-term debt, 11%	19.7	16.4
Total liabilities	65.7	63.4
Common stockholders' equity	34.3	36.6
Total liabilities and stockholders' equity	100.0%	100.0%

Outward Bound, Inc.
Common-Size Income Statement Data

	Outward Bound	Industry Average
Net sales	100.0%	100.0%
Cost of sales	(68.2)	(64.8)
Gross profit	31.8	35.2
Operating expense	(37.1)	(32.3)
Operating income (loss)	(5.3)	2.9
Interest expense	(5.8)	(1.3)
Other revenue	1.1	0.3
Income (loss) before income tax	(10.0)	1.9
Income tax (expense) saving	4.4	(0.8)
Net income (loss)	(5.6)%	1.1%

| *Required*

On the basis of your analysis of these figures, suggest four courses of action Outward Bound might take to reduce its losses and establish profitable operations. Give your reasons for each suggestion.

Ethical Issue

Turnberry Golf Corporation's long-term debt agreements make certain demands on the business. For example, Turnberry may not purchase treasury stock in excess of the balance of retained earnings. Also, long-term debt may not exceed stockholders' equity, and the current ratio may not fall below 1.50. If Turnberry fails to meet any of these requirements, the company's lenders have the authority to take over management of the company.

Changes in consumer demand have made it hard for Turnberry to attract customers. Current liabilities have mounted faster than current assets, causing the current ratio to fall to 1.47. Before releasing financial statements, Turnberry management is scrambling to improve the current ratio. The controller points out that an investment can be classified as either long-term or short-term, depending on management's intention. By deciding to convert an investment to cash within 1 year, Turnberry can classify the investment as short-term—a current asset. On the controller's recommendation, Turnberry's board of directors votes to reclassify long-term investments as short-term.

Required

writing assignment ■

1. What effect will reclassifying the investments have on the current ratio? Is Turnberry's financial position stronger as a result of reclassifying the investments?
2. Shortly after the financial statements are released, sales improve; so, too, does the current ratio. As a result, Turnberry management decides not to sell the investments it had reclassified as short term. Accordingly, the company reclassifies the investments as long term. Has management behaved unethically? Give the reasoning underlying your answer.

Focus on Financials: ■ YUM! Brands

Measuring profitability and analyzing stock as an investment (Obj. 1)

Use the financial statements and the data in **YUM! Brands** 5-year summary of selected financial data (Appendix A at the end of the book) to answer the following questions.

Required

writing assignment ■

1. Using 2000 as the base year, perform a trend analysis of YUM's total revenue, operating profit, net income, and net cash provided by operating activities for each year 2001 through 2003.
2. Evaluate YUM's operating performance record during 2001 through 2003. Comment on each item computed.

Focus on Analysis: ■ Pier 1 Imports

Analyzing trend data (Obj. 1)

Use the **Pier 1 Imports** financial statements in Appendix B at the end of this book to address the following questions. Study the financial highlights that precedes the financial statements.

During 2004, Pier 1's sales increased, but net income dropped. Ordinarily, sales increases bring higher profits but not for Pier 1 during 2004. A horizontal analysis of Pier 1's financial highlights through operating income, plus analysis of the number of Pier 1 stores worldwide, reveal why net income decreased during 2004. Perform these analyses for 2004, and then write a memo to explain for Pier 1 managers why net income decreased during 2004. Round all dollar amounts to the nearest $1 million.

Group Projects

writing assignment ■

Project 1. Select an industry you are interested in, and use the leading company in that industry as the benchmark. Then select two other companies in the same industry. For each category of ratios in the Making Managerial Decisions feature on pages 629 and 630, compute at least two ratios for all three companies. Write a two-page report that compares the two companies with the benchmark company.

Project 2. Select a company and obtain its financial statements. Convert the income statement and the balance sheet to common size and compare the company you selected to the industry average. **Risk Management Association's** *Annual Statement Studies*, **Dun & Bradstreet's** *Industry Norms & Key Business Ratios*, and **Prentice Hall's** *Almanac of Business and Industrial Financial Ratios* by Leo Troy, publish common-size statements for most industries.

Appendix A

YUM! BRANDS 2003 ANNUAL CUSTOMER MANIA REPORT

Power of Yum!

...not your ordinary restaurant company

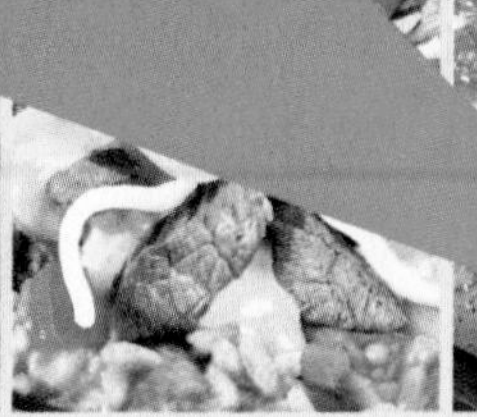
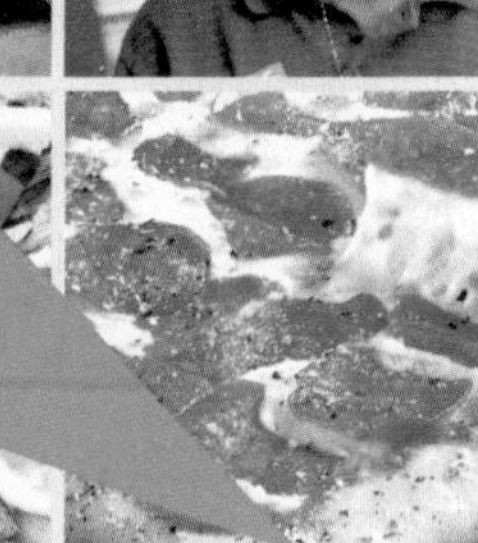

2. We are now the leading global developer of new restaurants. We've created the equivalent of a new division in China, which recently opened its 1,000th KFC and made $157MM in 2003.

We want to continue to add at least 1,000 new units outside the U.S., each year, and do it profitably.

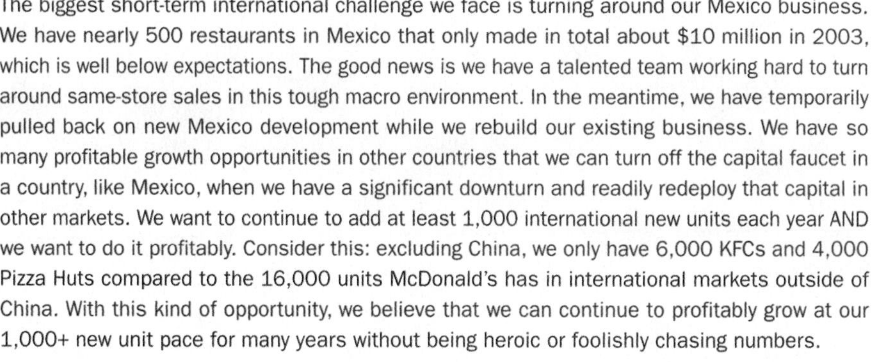

The biggest short-term international challenge we face is turning around our Mexico business. We have nearly 500 restaurants in Mexico that only made in total about $10 million in 2003, which is well below expectations. The good news is we have a talented team working hard to turn around same-store sales in this tough macro environment. In the meantime, we have temporarily pulled back on new Mexico development while we rebuild our existing business. We have so many profitable growth opportunities in other countries that we can turn off the capital faucet in a country, like Mexico, when we have a significant downturn and readily redeploy that capital in other markets. We want to continue to add at least 1,000 international new units each year AND we want to do it profitably. Consider this: excluding China, we only have 6,000 KFCs and 4,000 Pizza Huts compared to the 16,000 units McDonald's has in international markets outside of China. With this kind of opportunity, we believe that we can continue to profitably grow at our 1,000+ new unit pace for many years without being heroic or foolishly chasing numbers.

Top: Pizza Hut Korea President In-soo Cho serves up some of the new menu items in the world's first Pizza Hut Plus, which opened in Seoul during 2003.

Bottom: A new, 70-item menu highlights the world's first Pizza Hut Plus restaurant in Korea. In addition to the usual array of pizzas, the restaurant features a wide variety of appetizers, salads, pasta and beverages.

Our most significant longer term challenge is developing new markets ... getting to scale in Continental Europe, Brazil and India. This is tough sledding because building consumer awareness and acceptance takes time. It also takes time to build local operating capability. Our approach is to be patient and ever mindful of our overall profitability and returns. The promise is obvious.

Here are key measures for international: 15% operating profit growth per year, at least 7% system sales growth before foreign currency conversion, 1,000+ new units outside the U.S. and 20% return on invested capital.

In the U.S., Taco Bell is now the second most profitable QSR brand and just celebrated hitting the $1 million mark for average unit volumes. In 2003, company same-store sales were up 2% on top of 7% growth the previous year.

This result is coming from steadily improving operations and exceptional marketing. Taco Bell is now ranked #2 in *QSR Magazine*'s Annual Study for overall drive-thru service. And Taco Bell's "Think Outside the Bun" advertising campaign and strong new product pipeline is among the best in the industry.

Our biggest disappointment in the U.S. this year was negative 1% and negative 2% company same-store sales growth at Pizza Hut and KFC, respectively. However, 2003 was a year of steady progress at Pizza Hut as the brand showed positive same-store sales growth seven of the last eight periods in 2003. Most importantly, the Pizza Hut team laid a strong growth foundation for this year and beyond. The brand was repositioned to target the heart of the pizza category focusing on the family and the primary decision maker, Mom.

Yum! At-a-glance

29.

	U.S. Sales by Daypart	U.S. Sales by Distribution Channel
KFC	Dinner 59% · Lunch 34% · Snacks/Breakfast 7%	 Dine Out 80% · Dine In 20%
	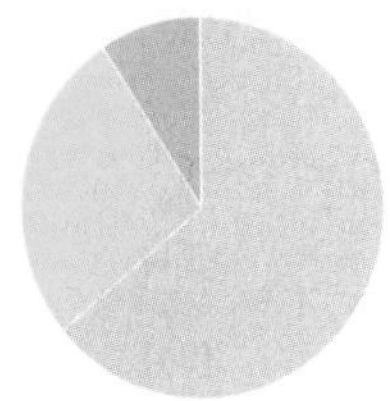 Dinner 64% · Lunch 27% · Snacks/Breakfast 9%	 Dine Out 72% · Dine In 28%
	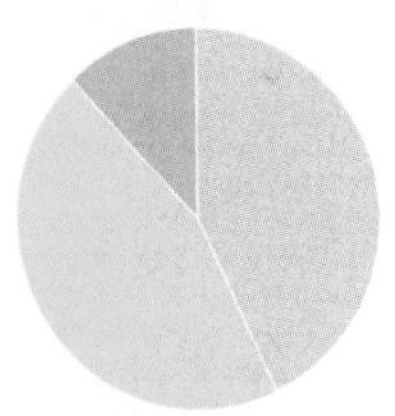 Dinner 43% · Lunch 45% · Snacks/Breakfast 12%	 Dine Out 73% · Dine In 27%
	 Dinner 54% · Lunch 40% · Snacks/Breakfast 6%	 Dine Out 58% · Dine In 42%
	 Dinner 27% · Lunch 49% · Snacks/Breakfast 24%	 Dine Out 43% · Dine In 57%

Source: Crest

48.

Consolidated Statements of Income

Fiscal years ended December 27, 2003, December 28, 2002 and December 29, 2001

(In millions, except per share data)	**2003**	2002	2001
Revenues			
Company sales	**$ 7,441**	$ 6,891	$ 6,138
Franchise and license fees	**939**	866	815
	8,380	7,757	6,953
Costs and Expenses, net			
Company restaurants			
Food and paper	**2,300**	2,109	1,908
Payroll and employee benefits	**2,024**	1,875	1,666
Occupancy and other operating expenses	**2,013**	1,806	1,658
	6,337	5,790	5,232
General and administrative expenses	**945**	913	796
Franchise and license expenses	**28**	49	59
Facility actions	**36**	32	1
Other (income) expense	**(41)**	(30)	(23)
Wrench litigation	**42**	—	—
AmeriServe and other charges (credits)	**(26)**	(27)	(3)
Total costs and expenses, net	**7,321**	6,727	6,062
Operating Profit	**1,059**	1,030	891
Interest expense, net	**173**	172	158
Income Before Income Taxes and Cumulative Effect of Accounting Change	**886**	858	733
Income tax provision	**268**	275	241
Income before Cumulative Effect of Accounting Change	**618**	583	492
Cumulative effect of accounting change, net of tax	**(1)**	—	—
Net Income	**$ 617**	$ 583	$ 492
Basic Earnings Per Common Share	**$ 2.10**	$ 1.97	$ 1.68
Diluted Earnings Per Common Share	**$ 2.02**	$ 1.88	$ 1.62

See accompanying Notes to Consolidated Financial Statements.

Consolidated Statements of Cash Flows

Fiscal years ended December 27, 2003, December 28, 2002 and December 29, 2001

(In millions)	2003	2002	2001
Cash Flows—Operating Activities			
Net income	$ 617	$ 583	$ 492
Adjustments to reconcile net income to net cash provided by operating activities:			
Cumulative effect of accounting change, net of tax	1	—	—
Depreciation and amortization	401	370	354
Facility actions	36	32	1
Wrench litigation	42	—	—
AmeriServe and other charges (credits)	(3)	—	(6)
Contributions to defined benefit pension plans	(132)	(26)	(48)
Other liabilities and deferred credits	17	(12)	37
Deferred income taxes	(23)	21	(72)
Other non-cash charges and credits, net	32	36	15
Changes in operating working capital, excluding effects of acquisitions and dispositions:			
Accounts and notes receivable	2	32	116
Inventories	(1)	11	(8)
Prepaid expenses and other current assets	—	19	(3)
Accounts payable and other current liabilities	(32)	(37)	(13)
Income taxes payable	96	59	(33)
Net change in operating working capital	65	84	59
Net Cash Provided by Operating Activities	1,053	1,088	832
Cash Flows—Investing Activities			
Capital spending	(663)	(760)	(636)
Proceeds from refranchising of restaurants	92	81	111
Acquisition of Yorkshire Global Restaurants, Inc.	—	(275)	—
Acquisition of restaurants from franchisees	(41)	(13)	(108)
Short-term investments	13	9	27
Sales of property, plant and equipment	46	58	57
Other, net	34	15	46
Net Cash Used in Investing Activities	(519)	(885)	(503)
Cash Flows—Financing Activities			
Proceeds from Senior Unsecured Notes	—	398	842
Revolving Credit Facility activity, by original maturity			
Three months or less, net	(153)	59	(943)
Proceeds from long-term debt	—	—	1
Repayments of long-term debt	(17)	(511)	(258)
Short-term borrowings-three months or less, net	(137)	(15)	58
Repurchase shares of common stock	(278)	(228)	(100)
Employee stock option proceeds	110	125	58
Other, net	—	(15)	(10)
Net Cash Used in Financing Activities	(475)	(187)	(352)
Effect of Exchange Rate on Cash and Cash Equivalents	3	4	—
Net Increase (Decrease) in Cash and Cash Equivalents	62	20	(23)
Cash and Cash Equivalents—Beginning of Year	130	110	133
Cash and Cash Equivalents—End of Year	$ 192	$ 130	$ 110

See accompanying Notes to Consolidated Financial Statements.

Total Sales (Dollars in millions)

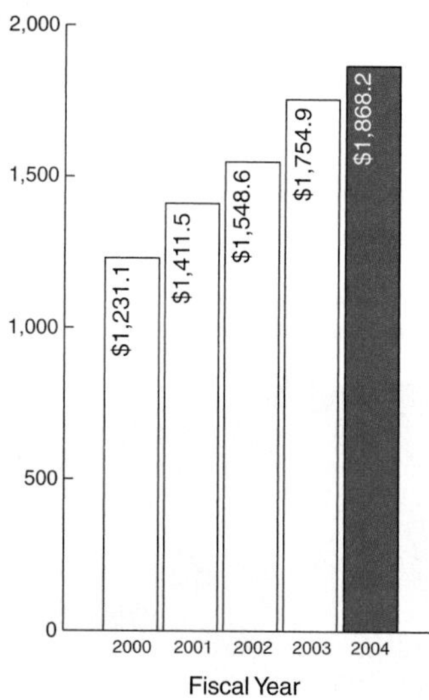

Stores Worldwide

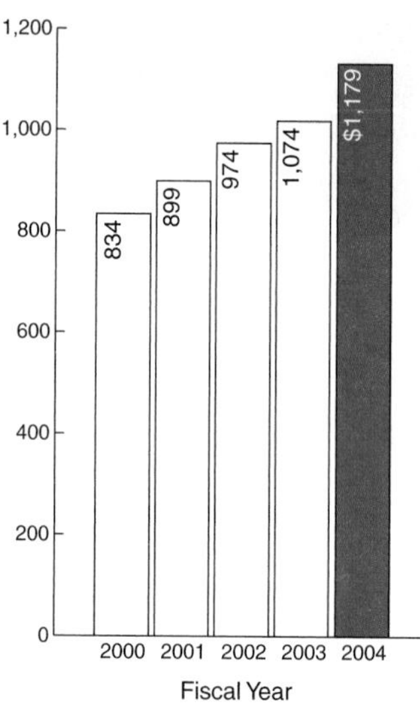

Financial Highlights

For the three years ended February 28, 2004

Pier 1 Imports, one of North America's largest specialty retailers of unique decorative home furnishings, gifts and related items, achieved record sales of almost $1.9 billion in fiscal 2004. Merchandise is directly imported from over 40 countries around the world and displayed in a visually appealing setting in stores throughout the United States, Canada, Puerto Rico, the United Kingdom and Mexico.

	2004	2003	2002
	($ in millions except per share amounts)		
For the year:			
Net sales	$1,868.2	$1,754.9	$1,548.6
Gross profit	781.6	753.4	649.8
Operating expenses	595.5	548.8	490.9
Operating income	186.2	204.7	158.8
Nonoperating (income) and expenses, net	(1.2)	(0.7)	(0.2)
Income before income taxes	187.3	205.4	159.0
Net income	$ 118.0	$ 129.4	$ 100.2
Basic earnings per share	$ 1.32	$ 1.39	$ 1.06
Diluted earnings per share	$ 1.29	$ 1.36	$ 1.04
Weighted average diluted shares outstanding (millions)	91.6	95.3	96.2
Increase (decrease) in comparable store sales[1]	(2.2%)	4.7%	4.5%
At year-end:			
Number of stores worldwide	1,179	1,074	974
Total retail square footage (thousands)	8,688	7,870	7,093

[1]Stores included in the comparable store sales calculation are those stores that were opened prior to the beginning of the preceding fiscal year and are still open, including qualifying relocated stores. For further explanation regarding the calculation of comparable store sales, see Management's Discussion and Analysis. For an explanation regarding the fluctuation in comparable store sales increases from year to year, refer to Management's Discussion and Analysis of Financial Condition and Results of Operations for those years.

Pier 1 Imports, Inc.
Report of Independent Auditors

To the Board of Directors of Pier 1 Imports, Inc.

We have audited the accompanying consolidated balance sheets of Pier 1 Imports. Inc. as of February 28, 2004 and March 1, 2003, and the related consolidated statements of operations, shareholders' equity and cash flows for each of three years in the period ended February 28, 2004. These financial statements are the responsibility of the Company's management. Our responsibility is to express an opinion of these financial statements based on our audits.

We conducted our audits in accordance with auditing standards generally accepted in the United States. Those standards require that we plan and perform the audit to obtain reasonable assurance about whether the financial statements are free of material misstatement. An audit includes examining, on a test basis, evidence supporting the amounts and disclosures in the financial statements. An audit also includes assessing the accounting principles used and significant estimates made by management, as well as evaluating the overall financial statement presentation. We believe that our audits provide a reasonable basis for our opinion.

In our opinion, the financial statements referred to above present fairly, in all material respects, the consolidated financial position of Pier 1 Imports, Inc. at February 28, 2004 and March 1, 2003, and the consolidated results of its operations and its cash flows for each of the three years in the period ended February 28, 2004, in conformity with accounting principles generally accepted in the United States.

Ernst + Young LLP

Ernest & Young, LLP
Fort Worth, Texas
March 24, 2004

Report of Management

To our shareholders:

Management is responsible for the preparation and the integrity of the accompanying consolidated financial statements and related notes, which have been prepared in accordance with accounting principles generally accepted in the United States and include amounts based upon our estimates and judgments, as required. The consolidated financial statements have been audited by Ernst & Young LLP, independent certified public accountants. The accompanying independent auditors' report expresses an independent professional opinion on the fairness of presentation of management's financial statements.

The Company maintains a system of internal controls over financial reporting. We believe this system provides reasonable assurance that transactions are executed in accordance with management authorization and that such transactions are properly recorded and reported in the financial statements, that assets are properly safeguarded and accounted for, and that records are maintained so as to permit preparation of financial statements in accordance with accounting principles generally accepted in the United States. The Company also has instituted policies and guidelines, which require employees to maintain a high level of ethical standards.

In addition, the Board of Directors exercises its oversight role with respect to the Company's internal control systems primarily through its Audit Committee. The Audit Committee consists solely of outside directors and meets periodically with management, the Company's internal auditors and the Company's independent auditors to review internal accounting, audit results, financial reporting, and accounting principles and practices. The Company's independent and internal auditors have full and free access to the Audit Committee with and without management's presence. Although no cost-effective internal control system will preclude all errors and irregularities, we believe our controls as of and for the year ended February 28, 2004 provide reasonable assurance that the consolidated financial statements are reliable.

Marvin J. Girouard
Chairman of the Board
and Chief Executive Officer

Charles H. Turner
Executive Vice President,
Chief Financial Officer and Treasurer

Pier 1 Imports, Inc.
Consolidated Statements of Operations

(In thousands except per share amounts)

	Year Ended		
	2004	2003	2002
Net sales	$1,868,243	$1,754,867	$1,548,556
Operating costs and expenses:			
Cost of sales (including buying and store occupancy costs)	1,086,623	1,001,462	898,795
Selling, general and administrative expenses	544,536	502,319	448,127
Depreciation and amortization	50,927	46,432	42,821
	1,682,086	1,550,213	1,389,743
Operating income	186,157	204,654	158,813
Nonoperating (income) and expenses:			
Interest and investment income	(2,851)	(3,047)	(2,484)
Interest expense	1,692	2,327	2,300
	(1,159)	(720)	(184)
Income before income taxes	187,316	205,374	158,997
Provision for income taxes	69,315	75,988	58,788
Net income	$ 118,001	$ 129,386	$ 100,209
Earnings per share:			
Basic	$ 1.32	$ 1.39	$ 1.06
Diluted	$ 1.29	$ 1.36	$ 1.04
Dividends declared per share	$ .30	$ .21	$ .16
Average shares outstanding during period:			
Basic	89,294	92,871	94,414
Diluted	91,624	95,305	96,185

The accompanying notes are an integral part of these financial statements.

Pier 1 Imports, Inc.
Consolidated Balance Sheets

(In thousands except share amount)

	2004	2003
Assets		
Current assets:		
Cash, including temporary investments of $208,984 and $225,882, respectively	$ 225,101	$ 242,114
Beneficial interest in securitized receivables	44,331	40,538
Other accounts receivable, net of allowance for doubtful accounts of $111 and $236, respectively	14,226	11,420
Inventories	373,870	333,350
Prepaid expenses and other current assets	40,623	36,179
Total current assets	698,151	663,601
Properties, net	290,420	254,503
Other noncurrent assets	63,602	54,632
	$1,052,173	$ 972,736
Liabilities and Shareholders' Equity		
Current liabilities:		
Notes payable	$ —	$ 393
Accounts payable	100,640	76,742
Gift cards, gift certificates and merchandise credits outstanding	46,118	37,924
Accrued income taxes payable	25,982	25,798
Other accrued liabilities	107,148	102,732
Total current liabilities	279,888	243,589
Long-term debt	19,000	25,000
Other noncurrent liabilities	69,654	60,211
Shareholders' equity:		
Common stock, $1.00 par, 500,000,000 shares authorized, 100,779,000 issued	100,779	100,779
Paid-in capital	145,384	144,247
Retained earnings	630,997	539,776
Cumulative other comprehensive income (loss)	1,667	(2,210)
Less—12,473,000 and 10,045,000 common shares in treasury, at cost, respectively	(195,196)	(138,656)
	683,631	643,936
Commitments and contingencies	—	—
	$1,052,173	$972,736

The accompanying notes are an integral part of these financial statements.

Pier 1 Imports, Inc.
Consolidated Statements of Cash Flows

(In thousands)

	Year Ended		
	2004	2003	2002
Cash Flow From Operating Activities:			
Net income	$118,001	$129,386	$100,209
Adjustments to reconcile to net cash provided by operating activities:			
Depreciation and amortization	64,606	57,934	51,504
Loss on disposal of fixed assets	143	980	247
Deferred compensation	8,264	5,043	5,059
Lease termination expense	3,258	395	—
Deferred income taxes	184	18,748	(2,238)
Tax benefit from options exercised by employees	4,897	6,867	628
Other	4,935	949	(2,564)
Change in cash from:			
Inventories	(40,520)	(57,917)	34,804
Other accounts receivable and other current assets	(16,927)	(14,362)	(8,213)
Accounts payable and accrued expenses	32,678	33,364	43,468
Accrued income taxes payable	184	(3,940)	21,952
Other noncurrent assets	(2,027)	(759)	(32)
Net cash provided by operating activities	177,676	176,688	244,824
Cash Flow from Investing Activities:			
Capital expenditures	(121,190)	(99,042)	(57,925)
Proceeds from disposition of properties	34,450	6,330	16,682
Net change in restricted cash	(8,752)	(500)	(500)
Beneficial interest in securitized receivables	(5,143)	4,082	30,783
Net cash used in investing activities	(100,635)	(89,130)	(10,960)
Cash Flow from Financing Activities:			
Cash dividends	(26,780)	(19,520)	(15,134)
Purchases of treasury stock	(76,009)	(78,474)	(44,137)
Proceeds from stock options exercised, stock purchase plan and other, net	15,125	17,305	13,463
Borrowings under long-term debt	—	—	712
Repayments of long-term debt and notes payable	(6,390)	(364)	—
Net cash used in financing activities	(94,054)	(81,053)	(45,096)
Change in cash and cash equivalents	(17,013)	6,505	188,768
Cash and cash equivalents at beginning of year	242,144	235,609	46,841
Cash and cash equivalents at end of year	$225,101	$242,114	$235,609
Supplemental cash flow information:			
Interest paid	$ 1,791	$ 2,065	$ 2,493
Income taxes paid	$ 63,788	$ 54,711	$ 35,951

The accompanying notes are an integral part of these financial statements.

Pier 1 Imports, Inc.
Consolidated Statements of Shareholders' Equity

(In thousands except per share amount)

	Common Stock				Cumulative Other			Total
	Outstanding Shares	Amount	Paid-in Capital	Retained Earnings	Comprehensive Income (Loss)	Treasury Stock	Unearned Compensation	Shareholders' Equity
Balance March 3,2001	96,141	$100,779	$139,424	$344,809	$ (3,115)	$ (49,933)	$ (85)	$531,879
Comprehensive income:								
Net income	—	—	—	100,209	—	—	—	100,209
Other comprehensive income:								
Currency translation adjustments	—	—	—	—	(1,587)	—	—	(1,587)
Comprehensive income								98,622
Purchases of treasury stock	(4,021)	—	—	—	—	(44,137)	—	(44,137)
Restricted stock amortization	—	—	—	—	—	—	85	85
Exercise of stock options, stock purchase plan and other	1,269	—	766	26	—	13,549	—	14,341
Cash dividends ($.16 per share)	—	—	—	(15,134)	—	—	—	(15,134)
Balance March 2, 2002	93,389	100,779	140,190	429,910	(4,702)	(80,521)	—	585,656
Comprehensive income:								
Net income	—	—	—	129,386	—	—	—	129,386
Other comprehensive income:								
Minimum pension liability adjustments, net of tax	—	—	—	—	(909)	—	—	(909)
Currency translation adjustments	—	—	—	—	3,401	—	—	3,401
Comprehensive income								131,878
Purchases of treasury stock	(4,397)	—	—	—	—	(78,474)	—	(78,474)
Exercise of stock options, stock purchase plan and other	1,693	—	4,057	—	—	20,339	—	24,396
Cash dividends ($.21 per share)	—	—	—	(19,520)	—	—	—	(19,520)
Balance, March1, 2003	90,685	100,779	144,247	539,776	(2,210)	(138,656)	—	643,936
Comprehensive income:								
Net income	—	—	—	118,001	—	—	—	118,001
Other comprehensive income:								
Minimum pension liability adjustments, net of tax	—	—	—	—	(1,033)	—	—	(1,033)
Currency translation adjustments	—	—	—	—	4,910	—	—	4,910
Comprehensive income								121,878
Purchases of treasury stock	(3,758)	—	—	—	—	(76,009)	—	(76,009)
Exercise of stock options, stock purchase plan and other	1,300	—	1,137	—	—	19,469	—	20,606
Cash dividends ($.30 per share)	—	—	—	(26,780)	—	—	—	(26,780)
Balance, February 28, 2004	88,227	$100,779	$145,384	$630,997	$ 1,667	$(195,196)	$ —	$683,631

The accompanying notes are an integral part of these financial statements.

Pier 1 Imports, Inc.
Notes to Consolidated Financial Statements (Excerpts)

Note 1: Summary of Significant Accounting Policies

Organization—Pier 1 Imports, Inc. is one of North America's largest specialty retailers of imported decorative home furnishings, gifts and related items, with retail stores located in the United States, Canada, Puerto Rico, the United Kingdom and Mexico. Concentrations of risk with respect to sourcing the Company's inventory purchases are limited due to the large number of vendors or suppliers and their geographic dispersion around the world. The Company sells merchandise imported from over 40 different countries, with 37% of its sales derived from merchandise produced in China, 11% derived from merchandise produced in Indonesia and 29% derived from merchandise produced in India, Thailand, Brazil, the Philippines, Italy and Mexico. The remaining 23% of sales was from merchandise produced in various Asian, European, Central American, South American and African countries or was obtained from U.S. manufacturers.

Inventories—Inventories are comprised of finished merchandise and are stated at the lower of average cost or market, cost being determined on a weighted average inventory method. Cost is calculated based upon the actual landed cost of an item at the time it is received in the Company's warehouse using actual vendor invoices and also includes the cost of warehousing and transporting product to the stores.

Properties, maintenance and repairs—Buildings, equipment, furniture and fixtures, and leasehold improvements are carried at cost less accumulated depreciation. Depreciation is computed using the straight-line method over estimated remaining useful lives of the assets, generally thirty years for buildings and three to ten years for equipment, furniture and fixtures. Depreciation of improvements to leased properties is based upon the shorter of the remaining lease term or the estimated useful lives of such assets. Depreciation costs were $49,572,000, $45,011,000 and $41,047,000 in fiscal 2004, 2003 and 2002, respectively.

Note 3: Properties

Properties are summarized as follows at February 28, 2004 and March 1, 2003 (in thousands):

	2004	2003
Land	$ 21,986	$ 27,284
Buildings	36,067	61,713
Equipment, furniture and fixtures	269,040	242,501
Leasehold improvements	212,447	201,099
Computer software	50,165	34,395
Projects in progress	63,650	12,268
	653,355	579,260
Less accumulated depreciation and amortization	362,935	324,757
Properties, net	$290,420	$254,503

Appendix C

Time Value of Money: Future Value and Present Value

The following discussion of future value lays the foundation for our explanation of present value in Chapter 8 but is not essential. For the valuation of long-term liabilities, some instructors may wish to begin on page 680.

The term *time value of money* refers to the fact that money earns interest over time. *Interest* is the cost of using money. To borrowers, interest is the expense of renting money. To lenders, interest is the revenue earned from lending. We must always recognize the interest we receive or pay. Otherwise, we overlook an important part of the transaction. Suppose you invest $4,545 in corporate bonds that pay 10% interest each year. After one year, the value of your investments has grown to $5,000. The difference between your original investment ($4,545) and the future value of the investment ($5,000) is the amount of interest revenue you will earn during the year ($455). If you ignored the interest, you would fail to account for the interest revenue you have earned. Interest becomes more important as the time period lengthens because the amount of interest depends on the span of time the money is invested.

Let's consider a second example, this time from the borrower's perspective. Suppose you purchase a machine for your business. The cash price of the machine is $8,000, but you cannot pay cash now. To finance the purchase, you sign an $8,000 note payable. The note requires you to pay the $8,000 plus 10% interest one year from the date of purchase. Is your cost of the machine $8,000, or is it $8,800 [$8,000 plus interest of $800 ($8,000 × .10)]? The cost is $8,000. The additional $800 is interest expense and not part of the cost of the machine.

Future Value

The main application of future value is the accumulated balance of an investment at a future date. In our first example above, the investment earned 10% per year. After one year, $4,545 grew to $5,000, as shown in Exhibit C-1.

■ **EXHIBIT C-1**

Future Value: An Example

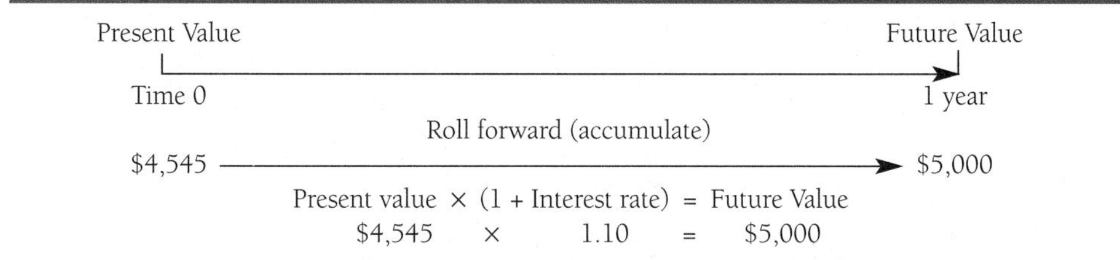

If the money were invested for five years, you would have to perform five such calculations. You would also have to consider the compound interest that your investment is earning. *Compound interest* is not only the interest you earn on your principal amount, but also the interest you receive on the interest you have already earned. Most business applications include compound interest. The following table shows the interest revenue earned on the original $4,545 investment each year for five years at 10%:

End of Year	Interest	Future Value
0	—	$4,545
1	$4,545 × 0.10 = $455	5,000
2	5,000 × 0.10 = 500	5,500
3	5,500 × 0.10 = 550	6,050
4	6,050 × 0.10 = 605	6,655
5	6,655 × 0.10 = 666	7,321

Earning 10%, a $4,545 investment grows to $5,000 at the end of one year, to $5,500 at the end of two years, and $7,321 at the end of five years. Throughout this appendix we round off to the nearest dollar.

Future-Value Tables

The process of computing a future value is called *accumulating* because the future value is *more* than the present value. Mathematical tables ease the computational burden. Exhibit C-2, Future Value of $1, gives the future value for a single sum (a present value), $1, invested to earn a particular interest rate for a specific number of periods. Future value depends on three factors: (1) the amount of the investment, (2) the length of time between investment and future accumulation, and (3) the interest rate. Future-value and present-value tables are based on $1 because unity (the value 1) is so easy to work with.

■ **EXHIBIT C-2**

Future Value of $1

Future Value of $1

Periods	4%	5%	6%	7%	8%	9%	10%	12%	14%	16%
1	1.040	1.050	1.060	1.070	1.080	1.090	1.100	1.120	1.140	1.160
2	1.082	1.103	1.124	1.145	1.166	1.188	1.210	1.254	1.300	1.346
3	1.125	1.158	1.191	1.225	1.260	1.295	1.331	1.405	1.482	1.561
4	1.170	1.216	1.262	1.311	1.360	1.412	1.464	1.574	1.689	1.811
5	1.217	1.276	1.338	1.403	1.469	1.539	1.611	1.762	1.925	2.100
6	1.265	1.340	1.419	1.501	1.587	1.677	1.772	1.974	2.195	2.436
7	1.316	1.407	1.504	1.606	1.714	1.828	1.949	2.211	2.502	2.826
8	1.369	1.477	1.594	1.718	1.851	1.993	2.144	2.476	2.853	3.278
9	1.423	1.551	1.689	1.838	1.999	2.172	2.358	2.773	3.252	3.803
10	1.480	1.629	1.791	1.967	2.159	2.367	2.594	3.106	3.707	4.411
11	1.539	1.710	1.898	2.105	2.332	2.580	2.853	3.479	4.226	5.117
12	1.601	1.796	2.012	2.252	2.518	2.813	3.138	3.896	4.818	5.936
13	1.665	1.886	2.133	2.410	2.720	3.066	3.452	4.363	5.492	6.886
14	1.732	1.980	2.261	2.579	2.937	3.342	3.798	4.887	6.261	7.988
15	1.801	2.079	2.397	2.759	3.172	3.642	4.177	5.474	7.138	9.266
16	1.873	2.183	2.540	2.952	3.426	3.970	4.595	6.130	8.137	10.748
17	1.948	2.292	2.693	3.159	3.700	4.328	5.054	6.866	9.276	12.468
18	2.026	2.407	2.854	3.380	3.996	4.717	5.560	7.690	10.575	14.463
19	2.107	2.527	3.026	3.617	4.316	5.142	6.116	8.613	12.056	16.777
20	2.191	2.653	3.207	3.870	4.661	5.604	6.728	9.646	13.743	19.461

In business applications, interest rates are always stated for the annual period of one year unless specified otherwise. In fact, an interest rate can be stated for any period, such as 3% per quarter or 5% for a six-month period. The length of the period is arbitrary. For example, an investment may promise a return (income) of 3%

per quarter for six months (two quarters). In that case, you would be working with 3% interest for two periods. It would be incorrect to use 6% for one period because the interest is 3% compounded quarterly, and that amount differs from 6% compounded semiannually. *Take care in studying future-value and present-value problems to align the interest rate with the appropriate number of periods.*

Let's see how a future-value table like the one in Exhibit C-2 is used. The future value of $1.00 invested at 8% for one year is $1.08 ($1.00 × 1.080, which appears at the junction of the 8% column and row 1 in the Periods column). The figure 1.080 includes both the principal (1.000) and the compound interest for one period (0.080).

Suppose you deposit $5,000 in a savings account that pays annual interest of 8%. The account balance at the end of one year will be $5,400. To compute the future value of $5,000 at 8% for one year, multiply $5,000 by 1.080 to get $5,400. Now suppose you invest in a 10-year, 8% certificate of deposit (CD). What will be the future value of the CD at maturity? To compute the future value of $5,000 at 8% for 10 periods, multiply $5,000 by 2.159 (from Exhibit C-2) to get $10,795. This future value of $10,795 indicates that $5,000, earning 8% interest compounded annually, grows to $10,795 at the end of 10 years. Using Exhibit C-2, you can find any present amount's future value at a particular future date. Future value is especially helpful for computing the amount of cash you will have on hand for some purpose in the future.

Future Value of an Annuity

In the preceding example, we made an investment of a single amount. Other investments, called *annuities*, include multiple investments of an equal periodic amount at fixed intervals over the duration of the investment. Consider a family investing for a child's education. The Dietrichs can invest $4,000 annually to accumulate a college fund for 15-year-old Helen. The investment can earn 7% annually until Helen turns 18—a three year investment. How much will be available for Helen on the date of the last investment? Exhibit C-3 shows the accumulation—a total future value of $12,860.

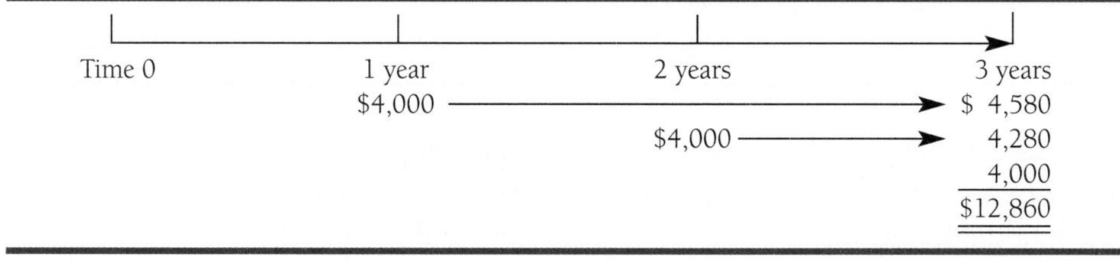

■ **EXHIBIT C-3**

Future Value of an Annuity

The first $4,000 invested by the Dietrichs grows to $4,580 over the investment period. The second amount grows to $4,280, and the third amount stays at $4,000 because it has no time to earn interest. The sum of the three future values ($4,580 + $4,280 + $4,000) is the future value of the annuity ($12,860), which can also be computed as follows:

End of Year	Annual Investment	Interest	Increase for the Year	Future Value of Annuity
0	—	—	—	0
1	$4,000	—	$4,000	$ 4,000
2	4,000	+ ($4,000 × 0.07 = $280) =	4,280	8,280
3	4,000	+ ($8,280 × 0.07 = $580) =	4,580	12,860

These computations are laborious. As with the Future Value of $1 (a lump sum), mathematical tables ease the strain of calculating annuities. Exhibit C-4, Future Value of Annuity of $1, gives the future value of a series of investments, each of equal amount, at regular intervals.

What is the future value of an annuity of three investments of $1 each that earn 7%? The answer, 3.215, can be found at the junction of the 7% column and row 3 in Exhibit C-4. This amount can be used to compute the future value of the investment for Helen's education, as follows:

Amount of each periodic investment	×	Future value of annuity of $1 (Exhibit C-4)	=	Future value of investment
$4,000	×	3.215	=	$12,860

■ **EXHIBIT C-4** Future Value of Annuity of $1

Future Value of Annuity of $1

Periods	4%	5%	6%	7%	8%	9%	10%	12%	14%	16%
1	1.000	1.000	1.000	1.000	1.000	1.000	1.000	1.000	1.000	1.000
2	2.040	2.050	2.060	2.070	2.080	2.090	2.100	2.120	2.140	2.160
3	3.122	3.153	3.184	3.215	3.246	3.278	3.310	3.374	3.440	3.506
4	4.246	4.310	4.375	4.440	4.506	4.573	4.641	4.779	4.921	5.066
5	5.416	5.526	5.637	5.751	5.867	5.985	6.105	6.353	6.610	6.877
6	6.633	6.802	6.975	7.153	7.336	7.523	7.716	8.115	8.536	8.977
7	7.898	8.142	8.394	8.654	8.923	9.200	9.487	10.089	10.730	11.414
8	9.214	9.549	9.897	10.260	10.637	11.028	11.436	12.300	13.233	14.240
9	10.583	11.027	11.491	11.978	12.488	13.021	13.579	14.776	16.085	17.519
10	12.006	12.578	13.181	13.816	14.487	15.193	15.937	17.549	19.337	21.321
11	13.486	14.207	14.972	15.784	16.645	17.560	18.531	20.655	23.045	25.733
12	15.026	15.917	16.870	17.888	18.977	20.141	21.384	24.133	27.271	30.850
13	16.627	17.713	18.882	20.141	21.495	22.953	24.523	28.029	32.089	36.786
14	18.292	19.599	21.015	22.550	24.215	26.019	27.975	32.393	37.581	43.672
15	20.024	21.579	23.276	25.129	27.152	29.361	31.772	37.280	43.842	51.660
16	21.825	23.657	25.673	27.888	30.324	33.003	35.950	42.753	50.980	60.925
17	23.698	25.840	28.213	30.840	33.750	36.974	40.545	48.884	59.118	71.673
18	25.645	28.132	30.906	33.999	37.450	41.301	45.599	55.750	68.394	84.141
19	27.671	30.539	33.760	37.379	41.446	46.018	51.159	63.440	78.969	98.603
20	29.778	33.066	36.786	40.995	45.762	51.160	57.275	72.052	91.025	115.380

This one-step calculation is much easier than computing the future value of each annual investment and then summing the individual future values. In this way, you can compute the future value of any investment consisting of equal periodic amounts at regular intervals. Businesses make periodic investments to accumulate funds for equipment replacement and other uses—an application of the future value of an annuity.

Present Value

Often a person knows a future amount and needs to know the related present value. Recall Exhibit C-1, in which present value and future value are on opposite ends of the same time line. Suppose an investment promises to pay you $5,000 at the *end* of one year. How much would you pay *now* to acquire this investment? You would be willing to pay the present value of the $5,000 future amount.

Like future value, present value depends on three factors: (1) the *amount of payment (or receipt)*, (2) the length of *time* between investment and future receipt (or payment), and (3) the *interest rate*. The process of computing a present value is called *discounting* because the present value is *less* than the future value.

In our investment example, the future receipt is \$5,000. The investment period is one year. Assume that you demand an annual interest rate of 10% on your investment. With all three factors specified, you can compute the present value of \$5,000 at 10% for one year:

$$\text{Present value} = \frac{\text{Future value}}{1 + \text{Interest rate}} = \frac{\$5{,}000}{1.10} = \$4{,}545$$

By turning the data around into a future-value problem, we can verify the present-value computation:

Amount invested (present value)	\$4,545
Expected earnings (\$4,545 × 0.10)	455
Amount to be received one year from now (future value)	\$5,000

This example illustrates that present value and future value are based on the same equation:

$$\text{Future value} = \text{Present value} \times (1 + \text{Interest rate})$$

$$\text{Present value} = \frac{\text{Future value}}{1 + \text{Interest rate}}$$

If the \$5,000 is to be received two years from now, you will pay only \$4,132 for the investment, as shown in Exhibit C-5. By turning the data around, we verify that \$4,132 accumulates to \$5,000 at 10% for two years:

Amount invested (present value)	\$4,132
Expected earnings for first year (\$4,132 × 0.10)	413
Value of investment after one year	4,545
Expected earnings for second year (\$4,545 × 0.10)	455
Amount to be received two years from now (future value)	\$5,000

You would pay \$4,132—the present value of \$5,000—to receive the \$5,000 future amount at the end of two years at 10% per year. The \$868 difference between the amount invested (\$4,132) and the amount to be received (\$5,000) is the return on the investment, the sum of the two interest receipts: \$413 + \$455 = \$868.

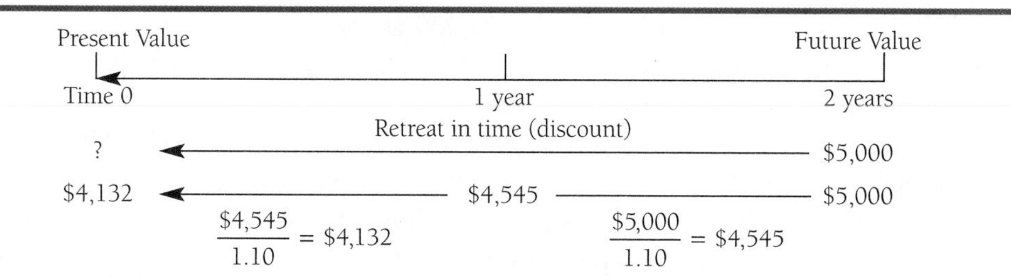

■ **EXHIBIT C-5**
Present Value: An Example

Present-Value Tables

We have shown the simple formula for computing present value. However, figuring present value "by hand" for investments spanning many years is time-consuming and presents too many opportunities for arithmetic errors. Present-value tables ease our work. Let's reexamine our examples of present value by using Exhibit C-6, Present Value of \$1, given at the top of the next page.

EXHIBIT C-6

Present Value of $1

Periods	4%	5%	6%	7%	8%	10%	12%	14%	16%
1	0.962	0.952	0.943	0.935	0.926	0.909	0.893	0.877	0.862
2	0.925	0.907	0.890	0.873	0.857	0.826	0.797	0.769	0.743
3	0.889	0.864	0.840	0.816	0.794	0.751	0.712	0.675	0.641
4	0.855	0.823	0.792	0.763	0.735	0.683	0.636	0.592	0.552
5	0.822	0.784	0.747	0.713	0.681	0.621	0.567	0.519	0.476
6	0.790	0.746	0.705	0.666	0.630	0.564	0.507	0.456	0.410
7	0.760	0.711	0.665	0.623	0.583	0.513	0.452	0.400	0.354
8	0.731	0.677	0.627	0.582	0.540	0.467	0.404	0.351	0.305
9	0.703	0.645	0.592	0.544	0.500	0.424	0.361	0.308	0.263
10	0.676	0.614	0.558	0.508	0.463	0.386	0.322	0.270	0.227
11	0.650	0.585	0.527	0.475	0.429	0.350	0.287	0.237	0.195
12	0.625	0.557	0.497	0.444	0.397	0.319	0.257	0.208	0.168
13	0.601	0.530	0.469	0.415	0.368	0.290	0.229	0.182	0.145
14	0.577	0.505	0.442	0.388	0.340	0.263	0.205	0.160	0.125
15	0.555	0.481	0.417	0.362	0.315	0.239	0.183	0.140	0.108
16	0.534	0.458	0.394	0.339	0.292	0.218	0.163	0.123	0.093
17	0.513	0.436	0.371	0.317	0.270	0.198	0.146	0.108	0.080
18	0.494	0.416	0.350	0.296	0.250	0.180	0.130	0.095	0.069
19	0.475	0.396	0.331	0.277	0.232	0.164	0.116	0.083	0.060
20	0.456	0.377	0.312	0.258	0.215	0.149	0.104	0.073	0.051

For the 10% investment for one year, we find the junction of the 10% column and row 1 in Exhibit C-6. The figure 0.909 is computed as follows: 1/1.10 = 0.909. This work has been done for us, and only the present values are given in the table. To figure the present value for $5,000, we multiply 0.909 by $5,000. The result is $4,545, which matches the result we obtained by hand.

For the two-year investment, we read down the 10% column and across row 2. We multiply 0.826 (computed as 0.909/1.10 = 0.826) by $5,000 and get $4,130, which confirms our earlier computation of $4,132 (the difference is due to rounding in the present-value table). Using the table, we can compute the present value of any single future amount.

Present Value of an Annuity

Return to the investment example on page 681. That investment provided the investor with only a single future receipt ($5,000 at the end of two years). *Annuity investments* provide multiple receipts of an equal amount at fixed intervals over the investment's duration.

Consider an investment that promises *annual* cash receipts of $10,000 to be received at the end of three years. Assume that you demand a 12% return on your investment. What is the investment's present value? That is, what would you pay today to acquire the investment? The investment spans three periods, and you would pay the sum of three present values. The computation is as follows:

Year	Annual Cash Receipt	Present Value of $1 at 12% (Exhibit C-6)	Present Value of Annual Cash Receipt
1	$10,000	0.893	$ 8,930
2	10,000	0.797	7,970
3	10,000	0.712	7,120
Total present value of investment			$24,020

The present value of this annuity is $24,020. By paying this amount today, you will receive $10,000 at the end of each of the three years while earning 12% on your investment.

This example illustrates repetitive computations of the three future amounts, a time-consuming process. One way to ease the computational burden is to add the three present values of $1 (0.893 + 0.797 + 0.712) and multiply their sum (2.402) by the annual cash receipt ($10,000) to obtain the present value of the annuity ($10,000 × 2.402 = $24,020).

An easier approach is to use a present-value-of-an-annuity table. Exhibit C-7 shows the present value of $1 to be received periodically for a given number of periods. The present value of a three-period annuity at 12% is 2.402 (the junction of row 3 and the 12% column). Thus, $10,000 received annually at the end of each of three years, discounted at 12%, is $24,020 ($10,000 × 2.402), which is the present value.

■ **EXHIBIT C-7**

Present Value of Annuity of $1

Present Value Annuity of $1

Periods	4%	5%	6%	7%	8%	10%	12%	14%	16%
1	0.962	0.952	0.943	0.935	0.926	0.909	0.893	0.877	0.862
2	1.886	1.859	1.833	1.808	1.783	1.736	1.690	1.647	1.605
3	2.775	2.723	2.673	2.624	2.577	2.487	2.402	2.322	2.246
4	3.630	3.546	3.465	3.387	3.312	3.170	3.037	2.914	2.798
5	4.452	4.329	4.212	4.100	3.993	3.791	3.605	3.433	3.274
6	5.242	5.076	4.917	4.767	4.623	4.355	4.111	3.889	3.685
7	6.002	5.786	5.582	5.389	5.206	4.868	4.564	4.288	4.039
8	6.733	6.463	6.210	5.971	5.747	5.335	4.968	4.639	4.344
9	7.435	7.108	6.802	6.515	6.247	5.759	5.328	4.946	4.608
10	8.111	7.722	7.360	7.024	6.710	6.145	5.650	5.216	4.833
11	8.760	8.306	7.887	7.499	7.139	6.495	5.938	5.453	5.029
12	9.385	8.863	8.384	7.943	7.536	6.814	6.194	5.660	5.197
13	9.986	9.394	8.853	8.358	7.904	7.103	6.424	5.842	5.342
14	10.563	9.899	9.295	8.745	8.244	7.367	6.628	6.002	5.468
15	11.118	10.380	9.712	9.108	8.559	7.606	6.811	6.142	5.575
16	11.652	10.838	10.106	9.447	8.851	7.824	6.974	6.265	5.669
17	12.166	11.274	10.477	9.763	9.122	8.022	7.120	6.373	5.749
18	12.659	11.690	10.828	10.059	9.372	8.201	7.250	6.467	5.818
19	13.134	12.085	11.158	10.336	9.604	8.365	7.366	6.550	5.877
20	13.590	12.462	11.470	10.594	9.818	8.514	7.469	6.623	5.929

Present Value of Bonds Payable

The present value of a bond—its market price—is the present value of the future principal amount at maturity plus the present value of the future stated interest payments. The principal is a *single amount* to be paid at maturity. The interest is an *annuity* because it occurs periodically.

Let's compute the present value of the 9% five-year bonds of **AMR Corporation** (discussed on page 377). The face value of the bonds is $100,000, and they pay 4½% stated (cash) interest semiannually (that is, twice a year).[1] At issuance, the market interest rate is expressed as 10% annually, but it is computed at 5% semiannually. Therefore, the effective interest rate for each of the 10 semiannual

[1]For a definition of stated interest rate, see page 374.

periods is 5%. We thus use 5% in computing the present value (PV) of the maturity and of the interest. The market price of these bonds is $96,149, as follows:

	Annual market interest rate ÷ 2	Number of semiannual interest payments	
PV of principal:	↓	↓	
$100,000 × PV of single amount at 5%		for 10 periods	
$100,000 × 0.614 (Exhibit C-6)			$61,400
PV of stated (cash) interest:			
$100,000 × 0.045 × PV of annuity at 5%		for 10 periods	
$4,500 × 7.722 (Exhibit C-7)			34,749
PV (market price) of bonds			$96,149

The market price of the AMR bonds shows a discount because the contract interest rate on the bonds (9%) is less than the market interest rate (10%). We discuss these bonds in more detail on pages 372–385.

Let's consider a premium price for the 9% AMR bonds. Assume that the market interest rate is 8% (rather than 10%) at issuance. The effective interest rate is thus 4% for each of the 10 semiannual periods:

	Annual market interest rate ÷ 2	Number of semiannual interest payments	
PV of principal:	↓	↓	
$100,000 × PV of single amount at 4%		for 10 periods	
$100,000 × 0.676 (Exhibit C-6)			$ 67,600
PV of contract (cash) interest:			
$100,000 × 0.045 × PV of annuity at 4%		for 10 periods	
$4,500 × 8.111 (Exhibit C-7)			36,500
PV (market price) of bonds			$104,100

We discuss accounting for these bonds on pages 375–378. It may be helpful for you to reread this section ("Present Value of Bonds Payable") after you've studied those pages.

Capital Leases

How does a lessee compute the cost of an asset acquired through a capital lease? (See page 388 for the definition of capital leases.) Consider that the lessee gets the use of the asset but does *not* pay for the leased asset in full at the beginning of the lease. A capital lease is therefore similar to an installment purchase of the leased asset. The lessee must record the leased asset at the present value of the lease liability. The time value of money must be weighed.

The cost of the asset to the lessee is the sum of any payment made at the beginning of the lease period plus the present value of the future lease payments. The lease payments are equal amounts occurring at regular intervals—that is, they are annuity payments.

Consider a 20-year building lease that requires 20 annual payments of $10,000 each, with the first payment due immediately. The interest rate in the lease is 10%, and the present value of the 19 future payments is $83,650 ($10,000

× PV of annuity at 10% for 19 periods, or 8.365 from Exhibit C-7). The lessee's cost of the building is $93,650 (the sum of the initial payment, $10,000, plus the present value of the future payments, $83,650). The lessee would base its accounting for the leased asset (and the related depreciation) and for the leased liability (and the related interest expense) on the cost of the building that we have just computed.

Appendix Problems

PC-1. For each situation, compute the required amount.

a. **Kellogg Corporation** is budgeting for the acquisition of land over the next several years. Kellogg can invest $100,000 today at 9%. How much cash will Kellogg have for land acquisitions at the end of 5 years? At the end of 6 years?
b. Davidson, Inc. is planning to invest $50,000 each year for 5 years. The company's investment adviser believes that Davidson can earn 6% interest without taking on too much risk. What will be the value of Davidson's investment on the date of the last deposit if Davidson can earn 6%? If Davidson can earn 8%?

PC-2. For each situation, compute the required amount.

a. **Intel, Inc.** operations are generating excess cash that will be invested in a special fund. During 20X2, Intel invests $5,643,341 in the fund for a planned advertising campaign on a new product to be released 6 years later, in 20X8. If Intel's investments can earn 10% each year, how much cash will the company have for the advertising campaign in 20X8?
b. Intel, Inc. will need $10 million to advertise a new type of chip in 20X8. How much must Intel invest in 20X2 to have the cash available for the advertising campaign? Intel's investments can earn 10% annually.
c. Explain the relationship between your answers to *a* and *b*.

PC-3. Determine the present value of the following notes and bonds:

1. Ten-year bonds payable with maturity value of $500,000 and stated interest rate of 12%, paid semiannually. The market rate of interest is 12% at issuance.
2. Same bonds payable as in number 2, but the market interest rate is 14%.
3. Same bonds payable as in number 2, but the market interest rate is 10%.

PC-4. On December 31, 20X1, when the market interest rate is 8%. Libby, Libby, & Short, a partnership, issues $400,000 of 10-year, 7.25% bonds payable. The bonds pay interest semiannually.

Required

1. Determine the present value of the bonds at issuance.
2. Assume that the bonds are issued at the price computed in Requirement 1. Prepare an effective-interest-method amortization table for the first 2 semiannual interest periods.
3. Using the amortization table prepared in Requirement 2, journalize issuance of the bonds and the first 2 interest payments and amortization of the bonds.

PC-5. St. Mere Eglise Children's Home needs a fleet of vans to transport the children to singing engagements throughout Normandy. **Renault** offers the vehicles for a single payment of 630,000 euros due at the end of 4 years. **Peugeot** prices a similar fleet of vans for 4 annual payments of 150,000 euros at the end of each year. The children's home could borrow the funds at 6%, so this is the appropriate interest rate. Which company should get the business, Renault or Peugeot? Base your decision on present value, and give your reason.

PC-6. American Family Association acquired equipment under a capital lease that requires 6 annual lease payments of $40,000. The first payment is due when the lease begins, on January 1, 20X6. Future payments are due on January 1 of each year of the lease term. The interest rate in the lease is 16%.

Required

Compute the association's cost of the equipment.

Answers

PC-1	a. 5 yrs. $153,900		
	6 yrs. $167,700		
	b. 6% $281,850		
	8% $293,350		
PC-2	a. $10,000,000		
	b. $5,640,000		
PC-3	1. $500,100	2. $446,820	3. $562,360
PC-4	1. $379,455	2. Bond	
	carry. amt. at 12-31-X2 $380,838		
PC-5	Renault PV € 498,960		
	Peugeot PV € 519,750		
PC-6	Cost $170,960		

Appendix D

Typical Charts of Accounts for Different Types of Businesses

A Simple Service Corporation

Assets	Liabilities	Stockholders' Equity
Cash	Accounts Payable	Common Stock
Accounts Receivable	Notes Payable, Short-Term	Retained Earnings
Allowance for Uncollectible Accounts	Salary Payable	Dividends
Notes Receivable, Short-Term	Wages Payable	**Revenues and Gains**
Interest Receivable	Payroll Taxes Payable	Service Revenue
Supplies	Employee Benefits Payable	Interest Revenue
Prepaid Rent	Interest Payable	Gain on Sale of Land (Furniture, Equipment, or Building)
Prepaid Insurance	Unearned Service Revenue	**Expenses and Losses**
Notes Receivable, Long-Term	Notes, Payable, Long-Term	Salary Expense
Land		Payroll Tax Expense
Furniture		Employee Benefits Expense
Accumulated Depreciation—Furniture		Rent Expense
Equipment		Insurance Expense
Accumulated Depreciation—Equipment		Supplies Expense
Building		Uncollectible Account Expense
Accumulated Depreciation—Building		Depreciation Expense—Furniture
		Depreciation Expense—Equipment
		Depreciation Expense—Building
		Property Tax Expense
		Interest Expense
		Miscellaneous Expense
		Loss on Sale (or Exchange) of Land (Furniture, Equipment, or Building)

Service Partnership

Same as service corporation, except for owners' equity

Owners' Equity

Partner 1, Capital
Partner 2, Capital
.
.
.
Partner *N*, Capital

Partner 1, Drawing
Partner 2, Drawing
.
.
.
Partner *N*, Drawing

A Complex Merchandising Corporation

Assets

Cash
Short-Term Investments
Accounts Receivable
Allowance for Uncollectible Accounts
Notes Receivable, Short-Term
Interest Receivable
Inventory
Supplies
Prepaid Rent
Prepaid Insurance
Notes Receivable, Long-Term
Investments in Subsidiaries
Investments in Stock (Available-for-Sale Securities)
Investments in Bonds (Held-to-Maturity Securities)
Other Receivables, Long-Term
Land
Land Improvements
Furniture and Fixtures
Accumulated Depreciation—Furniture and Fixtures
Equipment
Accumulated Depreciation—Equipment
Buildings
Accumulated Depreciation—Buildings
Organization Cost
Franchises
Patents
Leaseholds
Goodwill

Liabilities

Accounts Payable
Notes Payable, Short-Term
Current Portion of Bonds Payable
Salary Payable
Wages Payable
Payroll Taxes Payable
Employee Benefits Payable
Interest Payable
Income Tax Payable
Unearned Sales Revenue
Notes Payable, Long-Term
Bonds Payable
Lease Liability
Minority Interest

Stockholders' Equity

Preferred Stock
Paid-in Capital in Excess of Par—Preferred
Common Stock
Paid-in Capital in Excess of Par—Common
Paid-in Capital from Treasury Stock Transactions
Paid-in Capital from Retirement of Stock
Retained Earnings
Foreign Currency Translation Adjustment
Treasury Stock

Revenues and Gains

Sales Revenue
Interest Revenue
Dividend Revenue
Equity-Method Investment Revenue
Unrealized Holding Gain on Trading Investments
Gain on Sale of Investments
Gain on Sale of Land (Furniture and Fixtures, Equipment, or Buildings)
Discontinued Operations—Gain
Extraordinary Gains

Expenses and Losses

Cost of Goods Sold
Salary Expense
Wage Expense
Commission Expense
Payroll Tax Expense
Employee Benefits Expense
Rent Expense
Insurance Expense
Supplies Expense
Uncollectible Account Expense
Depreciation Expense—Land Improvements
Depreciation Expense—Furniture and Fixtures
Depreciation Expense—Equipment
Depreciation Expense—Buildings
Organization Expense
Amortization Expense—Franchises
Amortization Expense—Leasholds
Amortization Expense—Goodwill
Income Tax Expense
Unrealized Holding Loss on Trading Investments
Loss on Sale of Investments
Loss on Sale (or Exchange) of Land (Furniture and Fixtures, Equipment, or Buildings)
Discontinued Operations—Loss
Extraordinary Losses

A Manufacturing Corporation

Same as merchandising corporation, except for Assets

Assets

Inventories:
- Materials Inventory
- Work-in-Process Inventory
- Finished Goods Inventory

Factory Wages
Factory Overhead

Appendix E

Summary of Generally Accepted Accounting Principles (GAAP)

Every technical area has professional associations and regulatory bodies that govern the practice of the profession. Accounting is no exception. In the United States, generally accepted accounting principles (GAAP) are influenced most by the Financial Accounting Standards Board (FASB). The FASB has seven full-time members and a large staff. Its financial support comes from professional associations such as the American Institute of Certified Public Accountants (AICPA).

The FASB is an independent organization with no government or professional affiliation. The FASB's pronouncements, called *Statements of Financial Accounting Standards*, specify how to account for certain business transactions. Each new *Standard* becomes part of GAAP, the "accounting law of the land." In the same way that our laws draw authority from their acceptance by the people, GAAP depends on general acceptance by the business community. Throughout this book, we refer to GAAP as the proper way to do financial accounting.

The U.S. Congress has given the Securities and Exchange Commission (SEC), a government organization that regulates the trading of investments, ultimate responsibility for establishing accounting rules for companies that are owned by the general investing public. However, the SEC has delegated much of its rule-making power to the FASB. Exhibit E-1 outlines the flow of authority for developing GAAP.

■ **EXHIBIT E-1** Flow of Authority for Developing GAAP

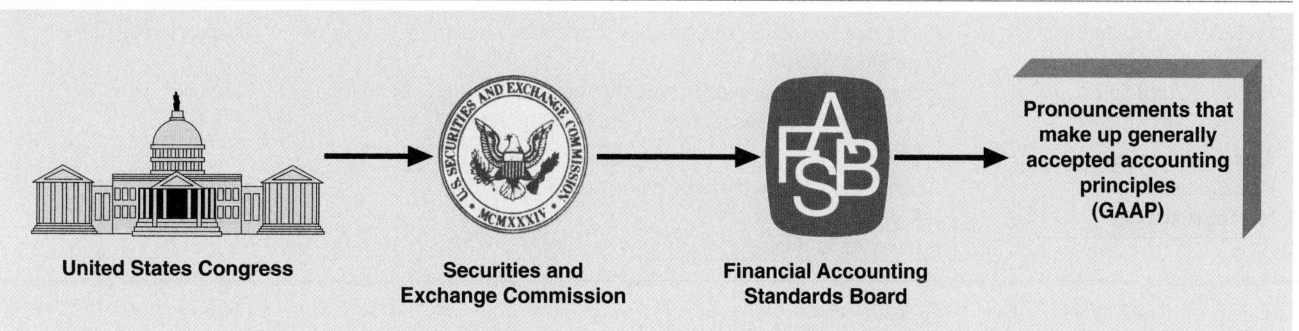

The Objective of Financial Reporting

The basic objective of financial reporting is to provide information that is useful in making investment and lending decisions. The FASB believes that accounting information can be useful in decision making only if it is *relevant, reliable, comparable*, and *consistent*.

Relevant information is useful in making predictions and for evaluating past performance—that is, the information has feedback value. For example, PepsiCo's disclosure of the profitability of each of its lines of business is relevant for investor evaluations of the company. To be relevant, information must be timely. *Reliable* information is free from significant error—that is, it has validity. Also, it is free from the bias of a particular viewpoint—that is, it is verifiable and neutral. *Comparable* and *consistent* information can be compared from period to period to help investors and creditors track the entity's progress through time. These characteristics combine to shape the concepts and principles that make up GAAP. Exhibit E-2 summarizes the concepts and principles that accounting has developed to provide useful information for decision making.

■ EXHIBIT E-2 Summary of Important Accounting Concepts, Principles, and Financial Statements

Concepts, Principles, and Financial Statements	Quick Summary	Text Reference
Concepts		
Entity concept	Accounting draws a boundary around each organization to be accounted for.	Chapter 1, page 14
Going-concern concept	Accountants assume the business will continue operating for the foreseeable future.	Chapter 1, page 15
Stable-monetary-unit concept	Accounting information is expressed primarily in monetary terms that ignore the effects of inflation.	Chapter 1, page 15
Time-period concept	Ensures that accounting information is reported at regular intervals.	Chapter 3, page 114
Conservatism concept	Accountants report items in the financial statements in a way that avoids overstating assets, owners' equity, and revenues and avoids understating liabilities and expenses.	Chapter 6, page 279
Materiality concept	Accountants perform strictly proper accounting only for items that are significant to the company's financial statements.	Chapter 6, page 279
Principles		
Reliability (objective) principle	Accounting records and statements are based on the most reliable data available.	Chapter 1, page 14
Cost principle	Assets and services, revenues and expenses are recorded at their actual historical cost.	Chapter 1, page 14
Revenue principle	Tells accountants when to record revenue (only after it has been earned) and the amount of revenue to record (the cash value of what has been received).	Chapter 3, page 115
Matching principle	Directs accountants to (1) identify and measure all expenses incurred during the period and (2) match the expenses against the revenues earned during the period. The goal is to measure net income.	Chapter 3, page 115
Consistency principle	Businesses should use the same accounting methods from period to period.	Chapter 6, page 278
Disclosure principle	A company's financial statements should report enough information for outsiders to make informed decisions about the company.	Chapter 6, page 278
Financial Statements		
Balance sheet	Assets = Liabilities + Owners' Equity at a point in time.	Chapter 1
Income statement	Revenues and gains – Expenses and losses = Net income or net loss for the period.	Chapters 1 and 11
Statement of cash flows	Cash receipts – Cash payments = Increase or decrease in cash during the period, grouped under operating, investing, and financing activities.	Chapters 1 and 12
Statement of retained earnings	Beginning retained earnings + Net income (or – Net loss) – Dividends = Ending retained earnings.	Chapters 1 and 11
Statement of stockholders' equity	Shows the reason for the change in each stockholders' equity account, including retained earnings.	Chapter 11
Financial statement notes	Provide information that cannot be reported conveniently on the face of the financial statements. The notes are an integral part of the statements.	Chapter 11

Appendix F

Check Figures*

Chapter 1

Check Points

CP1-1	NCF
CP1-2	NCF
CP1-3	NCF
CP1-4	NCF
CP1-5	NCF
CP1-6	NCF
CP1-7	NCF
CP1-8	NCF
CP1-9	2003 30.9%
CP1-10	RE, end. $295 mil.
CP1-11	Total assets $150,000
CP1-12	Cash bal., 12/31/06 $22,000
CP1-13	NCF

Exercises

E1-1	NCF
E1-2	NCF
E1-3	NCF
E1-4	Dell Total assets $19 bil.
E1-5	2. $410 mil.
E1-6	1. Net inc. $1 bil. 3. Net loss $2 bil.
E1-7	1. Total assets $588 mil. 2. SE $1.9 bil.
E1-8	NCF
E1-9	Total assets $388 bil.
E1-10	1. Net inc. $6 bil. 2. Dividends $3 bil.
E1-11	End. cash bal. $150 mil.
E1-12	RE 7/31/06 $5,500
E1-13	Total assets $43,700
E1-14	Net cash provided by oper. $9,500
E1-15	NCF
E1-16	NCF

Practice Quiz

PQ
1. d 2. a 3. b 4. b
5. d 6. a 7. b 8. c
9. d 10. c 11. d 12. d
13. b 14. a 15. c

Problems

P1	NCF
P1-2A	1. Net inc. $14 bil.
P1-3A	FedEx issuance of stock $1 bil. Coca-Cola exp. $15 bil.
P1-4A	1. Total assets $82,000
P1-5A	1. Total assets $164,000
P1-6A	1. Net inc. $108,000 2. RE, end. $48,000 3. Total assets $293,000
P1-7A	1. Cash, end. $445 mil.
P1-8A	1. b. $7,681 thou. g. $17,213 thou. m. $2,740 thou. s. $42,541 thou.
P1-1B	NCF
P1-2B	1. Net inc. $5.2 mil.
P1-3B	Best Buy issuance of stock $0.3 bil. Pier 1 exp. $1.4 bil.
P1-4B	1. Total assets $150,000
P1-5B	1. Total assets $164,000
P1-6B	1. Net inc. $58,000 2. RE, end. $127,000 3. Total assets $181,000
P1-7B	Cash, end. $2,477 mil.
P1-8B	1. b. $1,396 thou. g. $4,043 thou. m. $598 thou. s. $13,216 thou.

Cases

DC1	2. Net inc. $0 Total assets $55,000
DC2	NCF
FOF	3. Total resources $5,620 mil. Amount owed $4,500 mil. Stockholders owned $1,120 mil.
FOA	1. Total liab. $368 mil. Shareholders' equity $684 mil. 5. Net inc. $118 mil.

Chapter 2

Check Points

CP2-1	NCF
CP2-2	b. $3,000 d. $500 e. $5,800
CP2-3	Cash bal. $28,000
CP2-4	NCF
CP2-5	NCF
CP2-6	2. A/P bal. $1,500
CP2-7	3. Total assets $1,200
CP2-8	T/B total $35 mil.
CP2-9	3. $53,700 4. $5,800
CP2-10	NCF
CP2-11	NCF
CP2-12	Total debits = Total credits = $350,000

Exercises

E2-1	Total assets $360,000
E2-2	NCF
E2-3	NCF
E2-4	2. a. $55,800 d. $45,300 e. $ 5,300
E2-5	NCF
E2-6	1. $145 mil. 2. $41 mil. 3. Net inc. $4 mil.
E2-7	2. Cash $6,800 Net inc. $1,700
E2-8	3. Total assets $21,900 Total S/E $21,200
E2-9	Cash bal. $2,800
E2-10	1. T/B total $109,450 2. Net inc. $12,300
E2-11	T/B total $97,100
E2-12	Cash bal. $6,800
E2-13	1. T/B total $30,200 2. Net inc. $5,000
E2-14	4. T/B total $13,400
E2-15	a. Net inc. $19,300 b. Payments $87,800 c. Collections $47,000 d. Payments $17,500
E2-16	1. T/B out of balance by $3,300 3. a. $129,500
E2-17	NCF

Practice Quiz

PQ
1. a 2. d 3. d 4. b
5. c 6. b 7. a 8. d
9. a 10. c 11. a 12. a
13. b 14. a 15. c 16. c
17. d 18. b 19. b 20. b

Problems

P2-1A	NCF
P2-2A	2. Net inc. $7,240 4. Total assets $75,920
P2-3A	3. Cash bal. 44,610 A/P bal. $4,720
P2-4A	2. Total assets $35,100

*NCF = No check figure

P2-5A 2. Cash bal. $115,400
Total owed $130,900
P2-6A 3. T/B total $28,300
4. Total resources $24,470
Net inc. $1670
P2-7A 3. T/B total $165,300
4. Total assets $160,900
Net loss $700
P2-1B NCF
P2-2B 2. Net inc. $7,900
4. Total assets $26,850
P2-3B 3. Cash bal. $10,450
A/P bal. $4,000
P2-4B 2. Total assets $26,500
P2-5B 2. Cash bal. $24,000
Total owed $45,200
P2-6B 3. T/B total $37,600
4. Total resources $33,860
Net inc. $2,560
P2-7B 3. T/B total $83,200
4. Total assets $76,900
Net loss $1,400

Cases

DC1 Net inc. $20,000
Total assets $66,000
DC2 3. T/B total $44,550
4. Net inc. $9,000
FOF 3. Cash bal. $192 mil.
A/R bal. $169 mil.
5. Net inc. $617 mil.
FOA 3. Net sales increased by 20.6%
Net inc. increased by 18.0%

Chapter 3

Check Points

CP3-1 Net inc. $68 mil.
End. cash $158 mil.
CP3-2 NCF
CP3-3 NCF
CP3-4 a. Prepaid Rent bal. $2,500
b. Supplies bal. $500
CP3-5 3. $35,000
CP3-6 20X3 $2,400,000
20X4 $500,000
CP3-7 3. Interest Payable Oct. 31 $1,500
CP3-8 3. Interest Receivable Oct. 31 $1,500
CP3-9 NCF
CP3-10 Prepaid Rent at Apr. 30 $2,000
CP3-11 2. Income statement
Service rev. $7,400
CP3-12 Net inc. $1,757 thou.
Total assets $98,541 thou.
CP3-13 R/E bal. 8/31/X4 $3,088
CP3-14 2. Total assets $7,663 mil.
S/E $2,730 mil.
CP3-15 Current ratio 0.71
Debt ratio 0.55

Exercises

E3-1 NCF
E3-2 a. $88 mil.
E3-3 NCF
E3-4 NCF
E3-5 NCF
E3-6 2. Net inc. overstated by $17,900
E3-7 1. Payments for supplies $900
E3-8 NCF
E3-9 c. Debit Unearned
Rent Rev. $1,500
f. Book Value $48,000
E3-10 NCF
E3-11 Service Rev. bal. $5,850
Unearned Service Rev. bal. $250
E3-12 Net inc. $1,600
Total assets $19,800
E3-13 Sales rev. $20,946 mil.
Rent, insur. exp. $335 mil.
Other oper. exp. $4,226 mil.
E3-14 Hillcrest B/S: Unearned service rev. $3,500
E3-15 2. Income statement: Service rev. £420 mil.
E3-16 Net inc. $93 mil.
R/E bal. 12/31/X2 $1,578 mil.
E3-17 NCF
E3-18 1. Total assets $38,700
2. Current ratio 1.27
Debt ratio 0.27
E3-19 a. Current ratio 1.35
Debt ratio 0.48
E3-20 7. Net inc. $1,690
Total assets $11,790
E3-21 Current ratio 12/31/03 0.88
E3-22 a. Net inc. $108,600
b. Total assets $170,800
d. Total S/E $152,500

Practice Quiz

PQ1 1. b 2. b 3. d 4. c
5. a 6. b 7. c 8. a
9. d 10. a 11. b 12. c
13. b 14. Current ratio 2.00
Debt ratio 0.50 15. b
16. $5,750 17. a

Problems

P3-1A 1. $8.9 bil.
4. End. rec. $1.7 bil.
5. End. A/P and accrued exp. pay $0.9 bil.
P3-2A 2. Cash basis: loss $3,300
Accrual basis: inc. $1,700
P3-3A NCF
P3-4A c. Engineering Supplies Exp. $11,360
f. Insurance Exp. $2,200
P3-5A 2. Total assets $30,170
Total equity $9,260
Net inc. $25,120
P3-6A 1. Net inc. $57,370
Total assets $107,930
2. Debt ratio 0.61
P3-7A 2. Net inc. $9,200
Total assets $51,000
P3-8A 1. Total assets $59,000
2. Current ratio 1.30
Debt ratio 0.46
P3-9A 2. R/E bal. 12/31/X5 $16,800
P3-10A a. Current ratio 1.73
Debt ratio 0.61
P3-1B 1. $15.4 bil.
4. End rec. $1.5 bil.
5. End A/P and accrued exp. pay. $2.3 bil.
P3-2B 2. Cash basis: loss $1,300
Accrual basis: inc. $3,000
P3-3B NCF
P3-4B a. Insurance Exp. $2,850
d. Supplies Exp. $6,710
P3-5B 2. Total assets $68,670
Total equity $61,470
Net inc. $4,280
P3-6B 1. Net inc. $59,070
Total assets $46,970
2. Debt ratio 0.55
P3-7B 2. Net inc. $5,400
Total assets $52,400
P3-8B 1. Total assets $80,900
2. Current ratio 1.30
Debt ratio 0.33
P3-9B 2. R/E bal. 3/31/X3 $44,900
P3-10B a. Current ratio 3.31
Debt ratio 0.32

Cases

DC1 1. T/B out of balance by $800
2. T/B total $53,300
3. Current ratio 1.08
DC2 Net inc. $7,000
Total assets $24,000
DC3 1. Your price $210,000
2. Trotter's price $210,000
DC4 Total assets $56,270
FOF 5. 2003 ratios: Current 0.55
Debt 0.80
FOA NCF

Chapter 4

Check Points

CP4-1 NCF
CP4-2 NCF
CP4-3 Adj. bal. $1,980
CP4-4 NCF
CP4-5 NCF
CP4-6 NCF
CP4-7 NCF
CP4-8 NCF
CP4-9 Cash available to invest $37.1 mil.
CP4-10 New financing needed $3 mil.
CP4-11 NCF

Exercises

E4-1 NCF
E4-2 NCF
E4-3 NCF
E4-4 NCF
E4-5 NCF
E4-6 Adj. bal. $1,650
E4-7 Adj. bal. $2,979
E4-8 NCF
E4-9 NCF
E4-10 NCF
E4-11 1. Request $169.49
E4-12 Cash available to invest $255.2 mil.
E4-13 NCF
E4-14 NCF
E4-15 1. Cash available to invest $50 mil.
E4-16 8.42%

Practice Quiz

PQ 1. a 2. c 3. b 4. c 5. b 6. c 7. c 8. a 9. b 10. c 11. d 12. d

Problems

P4-1A NCF
P4-2A NCF
P4-3A 1. Adj. bal. $9,070
P4-4A 1. Adj. bal. $9,369.00
P4-5A NCF
P4-6A 1. Addnl. financing needed $7,428 mil.
P4-7A NCF
P4-1B NCF
P4-2B NCF
P4-3B 1. Adj. bal. $2,990
P4-4B 1. Adj. bal. $2,703.33
P4-5B NCF
P4-6B 1. Cash available to invest $1,186 mil.
P4-7B NCF

Cases

DC1 NCF
DC2 Cashier stole $300
FOF 1. Adj. bal. $192 mil.
FOA NCF

Chapter 5

Check Points

CP5-1 NCF
CP5-2 NCF
CP5-3 NCF
CP5-4 NCF
CP5-5 Accts. rec., net $81,000
CP5-6 NCF
CP5-7 3. $93,000
CP5-8 d. Uncollectible-acct. exp. $7,000
CP5-9 3. Accts. rec., net $65,000
CP5-10 b. Dr. Cash $103,000
CP5-11 3. $210,500
CP5-12 c. Dr. Cash $1,090
CP5-13 d. Interest rev. $15
CP5-14 1. 0.91 2. 35 days
CP5-15 2. Net loss $576 mil. 3. 1.48

Exercises

E5-1 3. Unrealized gain $30,000
E5-2 Unrealized gain $3,000
E5-3 2. Unrealized loss $2,000 in 20X3; Gain on sale $7,000 in 20X4
E5-4 NCF
E5-5 Accts. rec., net $84,100
E5-6 3. Accts. rec., net $30,400
E5-7 2. $32,300
E5-8 3. Accts. rec., net $255,600
E5-9 1. Ratio of write-offs to sales for 20X4 .0204
E5-10 Dec. 31 Interest rev. $656
E5-11 Interest rev: 20X8 $6,000 20X9 $2,000
E5-12 1. $500
E5-13 a. 1.03 b. 35 days
E5-14 1. 2 days
E5-15 Expected net income w/bank cards $138,200
E5-16 a. $351 mil. b. $35,400 mil. c. $34,729 mil.
E5-17 9%

Practice Quiz

PQ 1. c 2. d 3. c 4. b 5. $210,200 6. a 7. b 8. $7,000 9. c 10. d 11. b 12. d 13. Dr. Cash $6,280 14. d 15. a 16. a

Problems

P5-1A 3. Short-term investment $31,000 4. Unrealized gain $5,500
P5-2A NCF
P5-3A 5. Customers owed $561 mil. AOL expects to collect $464 mil.
P5-4A 3. Accts. rec., net 20X2 $278,200
P5-5A 2. Corrected ratios: Current 0.94 Acid-test 0.53 3. Net inc., corrected $48,000
P5-6A 2. Interest rec. at 12/31/X5 $616
P5-7A 1. 20X6 ratios: a. Current 1.42 b. Acid-test 0.60 c. Days' sales 25 days
P5-1B 3. Short-term investment $37,000 4. Unrealized loss $9,250
P5-2B NCF
P5-3B 5. Customers owed Nike $1,693 mil. Nike expects to collect $1,621 mil.
P5-4B 3. Accts. rec., net 20X4 $159,300
P5-5B 2. Corrected ratios: Current 1.17 Acid-test 0.45 3. Net inc., corrected $51,000
P5-6B Interest rec. at 12/31/X6 $666
P5-7B 1. 20X6 ratios: a. Current 1.35 b. Acid-test 0.78 c. Days' sales 21 days

Cases

DC1 Days' sales in rec. 20X6 81 days Est. cash collections 20X6 $1,578 thou.
DC2 Net inc. $142,000
DC3 Net inc.: 20X4 $68,500 20X5 $83,000
FOF 1. Gain on sale $1 mil. 2. Customers owed YUM! $210 mil. at 2002. 3. Collections $8,379 mil.
FOA 1. Customers owed Pier 1 $14,337 mil. at 2004. 2. % doubtful 2004 0.77

Chapter 6

Check Points

CP6-1 Invy. $24,000 Gross profit $28,000
CP6-2 Gross profit $80,000
CP6-3 NCF
CP6-4 NCF
CP6-5 COGS: a. $750; b. $720; c. $800
CP6-6 Net inc.: Avg. $2,060; FIFO $2,100; LIFO $2,000
CP6-7 Inc. tax exp.: Avg. $824; FIFO $840; LIFO $800
CP6-8 NCF
CP6-9 COGS $1,004 mil.
CP6-10 FIFO ratios: Gross profit % 46% Invy. turnover 2.3 times
CP6-11 Gross profit $757 mil.
CP6-12 1. Gross profit $5.6 mil. 2. Gross profit $3.2 mil.
CP6-13 1. and 2. $100,000
CP6-14 NCF

Exercises

E6-1 2. Gross profit $1,400 thou.
E6-2 3. Gross profit $5,700 End. invy. $1,410

E6-3 1. COGS: a. $2,830; b. $2,863; c. $2,800; d. $2,930
E6-4 LIFO tax advantage $46
E6-5 2. Net inc. $180
E6-6 1. Gross profit: FIFO $0.7 mil.; LIFO $1.6 mil.
E6-7 NCF
E6-8 NCF
E6-9 Gross profit $114,000
E6-10 Net inc., in sequence: $24,000; $19,800; $10,200; $6,000
E6-11 a. $1,055 mil.
c. $151,904 mil.
Coca-Cola net inc. $3,050 mil.
E6-12 Coca-Cola GP% 63.7%; Turnover 6.0 times
E6-13 GP% 29.8%
Turnover 5.3 times
E6-14 $7,320 mil.
E6-15 $64,000
E6-16 Net inc. 20X5 $36,000; 20X4 $51,000
E6-17 Gross profit $12,788 mil.
E6-18 NCF
E6-19 1. $151,000
2. $160,000
E6-20 20X7 ratios:
GP% 19.7%
Turnover 4.4 times

Practice Quiz

PQ 1. d 2. b 3. a 4. c
5. d 6. a 7. d 8. c
9. c 10. c 11. b 12. c
13. d 14. a 15. b 16. b
17. a

Problems

P6-1A 2. Invy. $1,200,000
3. Net inc. $834,000
P6-2A 2. Gross profit $1,292
3. $704
P6-3A 1. COGS: Avg. $57,533; FIFO $56,605; LIFO $58,589
P6-4A 1. Gross profit: Avg. $2,808; FIFO $2,945; LIFO $2,680
P6-5A NCF
P6-6A 1. Hershey GP% 41.5%; Turnover 4.1 times
P6-7A 1. $2,536,000
2. Gross profit $3,456,000
P6-8A 1. Purchase $766,000
2. Net inc. $150,000
P6-9A 1. Correct net inc.:
2007 $115 thou.
2006 $5 thou.;
2005 $130 thou.
P6-1B 2. Invy. $600,000
3. Net inc. $180,000
P6-2B 2. Gross profit $3,019
3. $2,027
P6-3B 1. COGS: Avg. $12,210; FIFO 11,911; LIFO $12,583
P6-4B 1. Gross profit: Avg. $60,106; FIFO $60,620; LIFO $59,635
P6-5B NCF
P6-6B 1. Company A GP% 21.5%
2. Turnover 7.3 times
P6-7B 1. $2,410,000
2. Gross profit $2,472,000
P6-8B 1. Purchase $769,000
2. Net inc. $150,000
P6-9B 1. Correct net inc.: 20X2 $-0-; 20X1 $3 bil.; 20X0 $-0-

Cases

DC1 1. Net inc. w/o year-end pur.: FIFO $249,000; LIFO $213,000
Net inc. w/year-end pur.:
FIFO $249,000; LIFO $189,750
DC2 NCF
FOF 3. $2,304 mil.
4. GP% 2003 69.1%
5. Turnover 35 times
FOA 1. c. Purchases $1,128 mil.
3. Payments $1,104 mil.
5. GP% 41.8%
Turnover 3.075 times

Chapter 7

Check Points

CP7-1 2. Book value $13,908 mil.
CP7-2 NCF
CP7-3 Building cost $56,250
CP7-4 Net inc. overstated
CP7-5 2. Book value: SL $17,200,000; UOP $17,900,000; DDB $12,000,000
CP7-6 a. $2,800,000; b. $3,500,000; c. $1,200,000
CP7-7 2. Save $2,080,000
CP7-8 a. €5,250,000; b. €3,500,000; c. €12,000,000
CP7-9 Depr. Exp. $15,000
CP7-10 1. a. Loss $15,000
b. Loss $4,760
CP7-11 3. Book value $29.0 bil.
CP7-12 1. $5,500,000
CP7-13 1. Net inc. $300,000
CP7-14 Net cash used by investing $82.0 mil.

Exercises

E7-1 Land $360,000
Land improve. $109,400
Building $1,280,000
E7-2 Gain on sale $7,470
E7-3 NCF
E7-4 2. Building, net $885,000
E7-5 NCF
E7-6 Depr. 20X6: SL $3,000; UOP $2,160; DDB $750
E7-7 I/S: Depr. exp.-building $10,500
B/S: Furn. & fixt., net $24,000
E7-8 2,000 hours
E7-9 Tax saved $6,600
E7-10 Depr. year 21 $45,000
E7-11 Depr. exp. $1,566
Loss on sale $2,854
E7-12 Cost of new truck $295,000
E7-13 c. Depletion Exp. $115,000
E7-14 2. Amortiz. Exp. $120,000
E7-15 1. $5 mil.
E7-16 NCF
E7-17 NCF
E7-18 NCF
E7-19 $38 mil.
E7-20 Expected net inc. $70.07 mil.
E7-21 Year 4 effects: 1. $-0-
2. Correct 3. €1.0 overstated

Practice Quiz

PQ 1. d 2. b 3. b 4. c
5. c 6. c 7. a 8. b
9. b 10. c 11. a 12. Gain $700
13. Book value $7,383
14. c 15. a

Problems

P7-1A 1. Land $683,250; Land improve. $136,400; Office bldg. $1,246,100
P7-2A 2. A/Depr.: Bldgs. $44,000; Security equip. $258,000
P7-3A Aug. 31 Gain on Sale $488,000
Dec. 31 Depr. Exp., Comm. Equip. $33,600 and $4,000
P7-4A NCF
P7-5A 3. Cash-flow advantage of DDB $5,733
P7-6A 1. Book value $608 mil.
P7-7A Part 1. 2. Goodwill $285,000
Part 2. 2. Net inc. $39,830
P7-8A 1. Gain on Sale $0.6 bil.
2. PPE, net $11.2 bil.
P7-1B 1. Land $202,100; Land improve. $89,050; Sales bldg. $986,150
P7-2B 2. A/Depr.: Bldgs. $46,000; Equip. $398,000
P7-3B July 3 Gain on Sale $205,750
Dec. 31 Depr. Exp.: Motor Car. Equip. $61,200; Bldgs. $625
P7-4B NCF
P7-5B 3. Cash-flow advantage of DDB $18,200
P7-6B 1. Book value $116 mil.
P7-7B Part 1. 2. Goodwill $3,200,000
Part 2. 2. Net inc. $509,425
P7-8B 1. Gain on sale $0.1 bil.
2. PPE, net $3.8 bil.

Cases

DC1 1. Net inc.: 360 $116,350; Beepers $91,650
DC2 NCF
FOF NCF
FOA 1. Book value of assets sold $34 mil.
4. % of assets used up at year end 2004 55.6%

Chapter 8

Check Points

CP8-1 3/31/X6 Debits include Internet Expense $200
CP8-2 2. Interest expense $200
CP8-3 2. End. bal. $10,000
CP8-4 NCF
CP8-5 NCF
CP8-6 a. $97,500
b. $410,500
CP8-7 NCF
CP8-8 12/31/00 Interest Expense $163
CP8-9 Bond carrying amt. 7/31/X9 $441,509
CP8-10 3. Interest expense 1/31/X9 $19,668
CP8-11 3. $162.50
4. $167.50
CP8-12 b. Interest Expense $173
CP8-13 EPS-Plan A $2.39
Plan B $1.73
CP8-14 Times-int.-earned ratio 0.64
CP8-15 Total current liab. $84,000; Bonds pay., net $344,000

Exercises

E8-1 2. Warranty exp. $12,000
Est. Warranty pay., $11,000
E8-2 Unearned subscription rev. balance $225
E8-3 NCF
E8-4 1. $4,000
2. $108,000
3. Int. exp. 20X7 $4,000
E8-5 Income tax pay. $288
Income tax exp. $296
E8-6 2. Debt ratio 0.49
E8-7 NCF
E8-8 Pay $2.2 bil. of current liabil.
E8-9 Total current liab. $99,150
E8-10 12/31 Interest Exp. $30,000
E8-11 3. Total interest exp. $353,200,000
E8-12 12/31/X7 1. Bond carry. amt. $374,509
2. Interest Exp. $14,943
E8-13 1. 1/1/10 Bond carry. amt. $330,681
2. 12/31/08 Interest Exp. $11,616
E8-14 12/31/X8 Bond carry. amt. $593,836
E8-15 1. $396,400
2. Credit Common Stock $16,000 and PIC in Excess of Par $380,400
E8-16 Daimler current ratio 0.92; debt ratio 0.81; times-int.-earned ratio 6.2
E8-17 1. EPS-Plan A $8.28
Plan B $4.26
E8-18 3. Debt ratio after: 0.64
E8-19 5. Bond carry amt. 3/15/04 $197,311

Practice Quiz

PQ 1. b 2. a 3. d 4. c
5. b 6. c 7. c 8. a
9. e 10. d 11. c 12. a
13. NCF 14. NCF 15. e 16. b
17. d 18. b 19. a 20. c

Problems

P8-1A b. Unearned rent rev. $3,600
d. Est. warranty pay. $14,100
P8-2A 12/31/X8 Warranty Exp. $19,500
Interest Exp. $15,000
P8-3A 2. Interest pay. $40,000
Bonds pay. $2,000,000
P8-4A 4. Interest pay. $7,750
Notes pay., net $305,500
P8-5A 2. Bonds pay., net $476,000
P8-6A 2. Bond carry. amt. 9/30/Yr. 4 $124,423
P8-7A 1. Bond carry. amt. 12/31/X3 $314,688
3. Convertible bonds pay., net $104,896
P8-8A NCF
P8-9A 1. Total current liab. $66,200
Total long-term liab. $694,000
3. Times-int.-earned ratio 1.5
P8-1B d. Note pay. due in 1 yr. $20,000
Interest pay. $6,000
e. Est. warranty pay. $14,300
P8-2B 12/31/X5 Warranty Exp. $2,900
Interest Exp. $6,000
P8-3B 2. Interest pay. $17,500
Bonds pay. $3,000,000
P8-4B 4. Interest pay. $14,167
Bonds pay., net $485,625
P8-5B 2. Bonds pay., net $973,000
P8-6B 2. Bond carry. amt. 9/30/Yr. 4 $123,639
P8-7B 1. Bond carry. amt. 12/31/X9 $474,920
3. Convertible bonds pay., net $94,984
P8-8B NCF
P8-9B 1. Total current liab. $123,000
Total long-term liab. $787,000
3. Times-int.-earned ratio 5.5

Cases

DC1 1. EPS-Plan A $3.22;
Plan B $3.09; Plan C $3.03
DC2 1. Ratios after: debt 0.93
times-int.-earned 1.3
FOF 4. Debt ratio 0.80
FOA 1. Debt ratio 0.35
3. Est. interest rate 6.7%

Chapter 9

Check Points

CP9-1 NCF
CP9-2 NCF
CP9-3 NCF
CP9-4 1. Total increase in PIC $829,055
CP9-5 NCF
CP9-6 Total SE $1,077 mil.
CP9-7 a. $294 mil.
b. $2,613 mil.
c. $3,690 mil.
CP9-8 Overall, SE decreased by $21 mil.
CP9-9 NCF
CP9-10 RE increased by $46,000
CP9-11 4. Preferred $450,000
Common $200,000
CP9-12 Credit PIC in X/S of Par $31,500
CP9-13 Book value per share $63.46
CP9-14 NCF
CP9-15 ROA 10.4%
ROE 64.4%
CP9-16 Net cash provided $160 mil.

Exercises

E9-1 NCF
E9-2 2. Total SE $34,000
E9-3 Total SE $198,000
E9-4 Total PIC $1,470,000
E9-5 Total SE $371 mil.
E9-6 Overall effect on SE $53,300
E9-7 NCF
E9-8 Total SE $13,570 mil.
E9-9 3. 379 mil.
4. $51
5. Dividends $406 mil.
E9-10 20X4: Preferred $10,800
Common $89,200
E9-11 2. Total SE $6,491 mil.
E9-12 c. Decrease SE by $8,500
d. Increase SE by $3,000
E9-13 Total SE $1,584 mil.
E9-14 1. $8.20 2. $8.12
E9-15 ROA .136 ROE .328
E9-16 ROA .062 ROE .100
E9-17 NCF

E9-18 NCF
E9-19 NCF
E9-20 12/31/X6 Total SE $72 mil.

Practice Quiz

PQ 1. b 2. a 3. d 4. c 5. a 6. b 7. a 8. c 9. b 10. a 11. b 12. d 13. e 14. b 15. d 16. b 17. d 18. b 19. a 20. d 21. b 22. d

Problems

P9-1A NCF
P9-2A 2. Total SE $298,800
P9-3A Total SE $755,000
P9-4A NCF
P9-5A Total SE $6,180,000
P9-6A 4. $22,500,000
P9-7A 2. Total SE $80,300
P9-8A NCF
P9-9A 1. Total assets $535,000
Total SE $477,000
2. ROA .096 ROE .084
P9-10A 2. Net increase in liab. $593.9 mil.
Net decrease in SE $565.5 mil.
P9-1B NCF
P9-2B 2. Total SE $308,000
P9-3B Total SE $429,000
P9-4B NCF
P9-5B Total SE $2,341,000
P9-6B 4. $212,080
P9-7B 2. Total SE $99,010
P9-8B NCF
P9-9B 1. Total assets $486,000
Total SE $348,000
2. ROA .083 ROE .113
P9-10B 2. Net decrease in liab. $249 mil.
Net increase in SE $1,084 mil.

Cases

DC1 3. Debt ratio: As reported 0.82
Adjusted 0.87
DC2 3. Total SE: Plan 1 $371,000
Plan 2 $386,000
DC3 NCF
FOF 5. ROE 72.0% ROA 14.3%
FOA 1. Avg. price paid for T/S $20.23
Avg. price rec'd. for T/S $15.85

Chapter 10

Check Points

CP10-1 1. 12/31/X8 Unrealized Loss $530
CP10-2 1. Gain on Sale $525
CP10-3 3. LT Investment balance $230 mil.
CP10-4 Gain on sale $25 mil.
CP10-5 NCF
CP10-6 NCF
CP10-7 2. Cash interest $350,000
4. Interest rev. $340,000
CP10-8 NCF
CP10-9 May 10 FC Transaction Gain $3,000
CP10-10 Sept. 29 FC Transaction Loss $200
CP10-11 NCF
CP10-12 NCF

Exercises

E10-1 d. Gain on Sale $400
E10-2 2. Unrealized Loss $38,750
E10-3 End. bal. $2,455,000
E10-4 Gain on sale $245,000
E10-5 2. LT investment, at equity bal. $436,000
E10-6 2. Total SE $321,000
E10-7 3. LT investment $19,490
E10-8 1. Dec. 16 FC Transaction Gain $80
E10-9 FC translation adj. $21,000
E10-10 Net cash used for investing $(3,996)
E10-11 NCF
E10-12 3. a. LT investment, at equity $755 mil.
E10-13 3. Accum. other comp. (loss) at 12/31/X3 $(40) mil.

Practice Quiz

PQ 1. b 2. c 3. NCF 4. a 5. d 6. d 7. b 8. a 9. c 10. c 11. b 12. d

Problems

P10-1A 2. LT invest., at equity $716,300
Unrealized (loss) $(1,800)
Equity-method invest. rev. $87,500
P10-2A 2. LT Invest. in Affiliates bal. $783,000
P10-3A 1. 0.824 3. 0.891
P10-4A 1. Consolidated total $1,146,000
P10-5A 2. LT invest. in bonds $464,314
Interest rev. $31,814
P10-6A 1. July 21 FC Transaction Gain $3,000
Aug. 17 FC Transaction Loss $7,000
P10-7A 1. FC translation adj. $(83,000)
P10-8A NCF
P10-1B 2. LT invest., at equity $643,300
Unrealized (loss) $(3,400)
Equity-method invest. rev. $178,500
P10-2B 2. LT Invest. in UPS bal. $384,000
P10-3B 1. 0.727 3. 0.900
P10-4B 1. Consolidated total $1,033,000
P10-5B 2. LT invest. in bonds $614,250
Interest rev. $26,250
P10-6B 1. Feb. 22 FC Transaction Gain $2,460
Mar. 24 FC Transaction Loss $3,000
P10-7B 1. FC translation adj. $364,000
P10-8B NCF

Cases

DC1 NCF
DC2 2. Gain on sale $6,200
3. Gain on sale $80,000
FOF NCF
FOA NCF

Chapter 11

Check Points

CP11-1 NCF
CP11-2 NCF
CP11-3 Net inc. $39,000
CP11-4 Est. value of one share $33.67
CP11-5 EPS for net inc. $3.40
CP11-6 NCF
CP11-7 Comp. inc. $40,000
CP11-8 2. Net inc. $72,000
Deferred tax liab. $12,000
CP11-9 RE 12/31/X7 $475,000
CP11-10 1. $85,000
3. Sold T/S for $11,000

Exercises

E11-1 Net inc. $1,470 mil.
E11-2 1. Net inc. $4,000 thou.
2. Est. value of one share $37.50
E11-3 NCF
E11-4 3.8%
E11-5 EPS $5.31
E11-6 EPS for net inc. $0.69
E11-7 Net inc. $240,000
Deferred tax liab. $20,000
E11-8 2. $324,000
3. $56,000
E11-9 RE 12/31/X5 $362 mil.
E11-10 Total SE 12/31/X5 $1,800,000
E11-11 1. Total SE 12/31/X7 $6,660 thou.
2. 51.2%
4. $44 per share
E11-12 NCF

Practice

PQ 1. d 2. b 3. a 4. b 5. a 6. a 7. c 8. c 9. d 10. c 11. b 12. a 13. d 14. d

Problems

P11-1A 1. Net inc. $35,000
EPS for net inc. $1.04

P11-2A RE 9/30/X3 $102,000
P11-3A Est. value of stock $762,500
Current mkt. value $810,000
P11-4A 1. EPS for net inc. $1.54
2. Est. value at 12% $9.17
P11-5A Comp. inc. £91,200
EPS for net inc. £1.70
P11-6A 1. Taxable inc. $185,000
3. Net inc. $130,000
P11-7A 1. $560 mil.
2. $1.30 per share
3. $4.90 per share
4. Increase in SE $28 mil.
5. 5%
P11-1B 1. Net inc. $73,800
EPS for net inc. $3.39
P11-2B RE 12/31/X3 $95,800
P11-3B Est. value of stock $800,000
Current mkt. value $840,000
P11-4B 1. EPS for net inc. $3.07
2. Est. value at 9% $32.33
P11-5B Comp. inc. $55,200
EPS for net inc. $2.88
P11-6B 1. Taxable inc. $120,000
3. Net inc. $84,500
P11-7B 1. £800 mil.
2. £1.40 per share
3. £10.60 per share
4. Increase in S/E £33,000,000
5. 10%

Cases

DC1 EPS for prediction $2.75
DC2 NCF
FOF 3. Est. value at 6% $35.00
FOA 2. Est. value at 6% $22.00

Chapter 12

Check Points

CP12-1 NCF
CP12-2 NCF
CP12-3 Net cash, oper. $55,000
CP12-4 NCF
CP12-5 Net cash, oper. $33,000
CP12-6 Net cash, oper. $33,000
Net increase in cash $32,000
CP12-7 a. $100,000 b. $15,000
CP12-8 a. Payment $2,000
b. Dividends $84,000
CP12-9 Net cash, oper. $200,000
Cash bal., end. $54,000
CP12-10 Net cash, oper. $33,000
CP12-11 Net cash, oper. $33,000
Net increase in cash $32,000
CP12-12 a. $704,000
b. $331,000
CP12-13 a. $48,000
b. $154,000

Exercises

E12-1 NCF
E12-2 NCF
E12-3 NCF
E12-4 Net cash, oper. $(2,000)
E12-5 Net cash, oper. $64,000
E12-6 1. Net cash, oper. $87,000
Net cash, finan. $4,000
E12-7 NCF
E12-8 a. $6,000 b. $26,000
E12-9 NCF
E12-10 NCF
E12-11 Net cash, oper. $14,000
E12-12 NCF
E12-13 1. Net cash, oper. $87,000
Net cash, finan. $4,000
E12-14 a. $71,000 b. $92,000
E12-15 All in thousands:
a. $24,519 b. $18,516
c. $4,793 d. $507
e. $230 f. $143
E12-16 1. Loss $50 thou.
Debt issued $130 thou.

Practice Quiz

PQ 1. b 2. b 3. c 4. a
5. d 6. d 7. d 8. NCF
9. a 10. NCF 11. a
12. a 13. c 14. b 15. c
16. b 17. d. 18. b 19. b
20. c 21. c

Problems

P12-1A NCF
P12-2A 1. Net inc. $120,000
2. Total assets $303,000
3. Net cash, oper. $81,000
P12-3A Net cash, oper. $94,000
Net cash, invest. $(91,300)
Net cash, finan. $11,100
Noncash invest. & finan. $207,400
P12-4A 1. Net cash, oper. $48,300
Net cash, invest. $(173,000)
Net cash, finan. 120,600
P12-5A 1. Net cash, oper. $70,600
Net cash, invest. $(47,600)
Net cash, finan. $(29,900)
P12-6A 1. Net cash, oper. $(30,000)
Net cash, invest. $(47,200)
Net cash, finan. $91,700
Noncash invest. & finan. $142,800
P12-7A 1. Net inc. $120,000
2. Total assets $303,000
3. Net cash, oper. $81,000
P12-8A 1. Net cash, oper. $70,600
Net cash, invest. $(47,600)
Net cash, finan. $(29,900)
P12-9A 1. Net cash, oper. $77,200
Net cash, invest. $(51,500)
Net cash, finan. $(30,300)
Noncash invest. & finan. $83,200
P12-10A 1. Net cash, oper. $30,400
Net cash, invest. $800
Net cash, finan. $(37,100)
Noncash invest. & finan. $48,300
P12-1B NCF
P12-2B 1. Net inc. $30,000
2. Total assets $375,000
3. Net cash, oper. $(49,000)
P12-3B 1. Net cash, oper. $75,200
Net cash, invest. $(90,200)
Net cash, finan. $43,000
Noncash invest. & finan. $172,000
P12-4B 1. Net cash, oper. $96,900
Net cash, invest. $(112,000)
Net cash, finan. $31,000
P12-5B 1. Net cash, oper. $72,900
Net cash, invest. $(37,100)
Net cash, finan. $(30,600)
P12-6B 1. Net cash, oper. $115,700
Net cash, invest. $(27,600)
Net cash, finan. $(70,800)
Noncash invest. & finan. $79,400
P12-7B 1. Net inc. $30,000
2. Total assets $375,000
3. Net cash, oper. $(49,000)
P12-8B 1. Net cash, oper. $72,900
Net cash, invest. $(37,100)
Net cash, finan. $(30,600)
P12-9B 1. Net cash, oper. $67,800
Net cash, invest. $(10,200)
Net cash, finan. $(47,600)
Noncash invest. & finan. $99,100
P12-10B 1. Net cash, oper. $69,100
Net cash, invest. $42,000
Net cash, finan. $(95,200)
Noncash invest. & finan. $19,000

Cases

DC1 Net cash, oper. $140 thou.
Net cash, invest. $(141) thou.
Net cash, finan. $(37) thou.
DC2 NCF
FOF 2. a. $8,379 mil. b. $2,282 mil.
FOA 3. Book value sold $34,593 thou.
5. Returned to stockholders $102,789 thou.

Chapter 13

Check Points

CP13-1 Rev. increase 2004 3.6%
CP13-2 1. 2004 Sales trend 100%
CP13-3 1. 20X2 Cash 3.7%
PPE 64.0%
CP13-4 Net inc. %: Home Depot 4.8%; Nike 6.2%
CP13-5 20X4 Current ratio 2.71

CP13-6 1. 2002 Acid-test ratio 0.21
CP13-7 a. 35 times b. 7.3 days
CP13-8 1. 0.801 2. 6.1 times
CP13-9 a. 7.4% b. 14.3% c. 72.0
CP13-10 1. EPS $6.08 P/E 20 times
CP13-11 a. $4,264 thou.
d. $698 thou.
CP13-12 a. $631 thou.
e. $857 thou.
CP13-13 1. $404 thou.

Exercises

E13-1 2007 W/C (decrease) (5.0)%
E13-2 Net inc. increased by 52.9%
E13-3 Yr. 5 net inc. trend 147%
E13-4 Current assets 13.0%
Total liabil. 48.1%
E13-5 2005 Net inc. 13.7%
E13-6 NCF
E13-7 b. 0.70 c. 4.01 e. 55
E13-8 20X6 ratios: a. 1.56
b. 0.69 c. 0.59 d. 3.44
E13-9 20X6 ratios: a. 0.103
b. 0.137 c. 0.162 d. $0.60
E13-10 20X7 ratios: a. 15
b. 0.013 c. $4.75
E13-11 2. Intel EVA $1,800 mil.
E13-12 Total assets $19,565 mil.
Current liab. $6,752 mil.
E13-13 Sales $6,639 mil.
Net inc. $789 mil.

Practice Quiz

PQ 1. c 2. a 3. d 4. c
5. b 6. d 7. a 8. b
9. c 10. c 11. d 12. a

Problems

P13-1A 1. 2008 Net rev. trend 118%
2. 2008 ROE 0.142
P13-2A 1. Bose GP% 36.4%; net inc. 14.7%; current assets 77.8%; SE 40.2%
P13-3A NCF
P13-4A 2. c. Current ratio 2.07; Debt ratio 0.49; EPS $1.58
P13-5A 1. 20X9 ratios: a. 1.80
b. 1.48 d. 0.357 f. 10.6
P13-6A 1. AmeriCorp ratios: a. 0.85
b. 2.74 c. 35 f. 0.502
h. 7.9
P13-7A NCF
P13-1B 1. 20X8 Net sales trend 127%
2. 20X8 Ret. on sales 0.081
P13-2B 1. Escalade GP 31.9%; net inc. 9.2%; current assets 77.1%; SE 39.4%
P13-3B NCF
P13-4B 2. b. Current ratio 2.60; Debt ratio 0.42; EPS $3.72
P13-5B 1. 20X5 ratios: b. 1.20
d. 0.157 e. 0.396 g. 9.7
P13-6B 1. Sonic Sound ratios: a. 0.64
b. 2.04 c. 126 f. 0.180
h. 25.7
P13-7B NCF

Cases

DC1 NCF
DC2 NCF
DC3 NCF
FOF 1. 2003 Total rev. trend 118%
Net cash-oper. trend 214%
FOA Net sales increase 6.4%
Oper. inc. decrease (9.3)%

Glossary

Accelerated depreciation method. A depreciation method that writes off a relatively larger amount of the asset's cost nearer the start of its useful life than the straight-line method does (*p. 324*).

Account. The record of the changes that have occurred in a particular asset, liability, or stockholders' equity during a period. The basic summary device of accounting (*p. 50*).

Account format. A balance-sheet format that lists assets on the left and liabilities and stockholders' equity on the right (*p. 133*).

Account payable. A liability backed by the general reputation and credit standing of the debtor (*p. 13*).

Accounting. The information system that measures business activities, processes that information into reports and financial statements, and communicates the results to decision makers (*p. 5*).

Accounting equation. The most basic tool of accounting: Assets = Liabilities + Owners' Equity (*p. 12*).

Accounts receivable turnover. Measures a company's ability to collect cash from credit customers. To compute accounts receivable turnover, divide net credit sales by average net accounts receivable (*p. 622*).

Accrual. An expense or a revenue that occurs before the business pays or receives cash. An accrual is the opposite of a deferral (*p. 112*).

Accrual accounting. Accounting that records the impact of a business event as it occurs, regardless of whether the transaction affected cash (*p. 106*).

Accrued expense. An expense incurred but not yet paid in cash. Also *called accrued liability* (*pp. 117, 366*).

Accrued liability. A liability for an expense that has not yet been paid by the company. Another name for accrued expense. Also called *accrued expense* (*p. 52*).

Accrued revenue. A revenue that has been earned but not yet received in cash (*p. 119*).

Accumulated depreciation. The cumulative sum of all depreciation expense from the date of acquiring a plant asset (*p. 116*).

Acid-test ratio. Ratio of the sum of cash plus short-term investments plus net current receivables to total current liabilities. Tells whether the entity can pay all its current liabilities if they come due immediately. Also called the *quick ratio* (*pp. 236, 620*).

Adjusted trial balance. A list of all the ledger accounts with their adjusted balances (*p. 123*).

Adverse opinion. An audit opinion stating that the financial statements are unreliable (*p. 525*).

Aging-of-accounts receivable. A way to estimate bad debts by analyzing individual accounts receivable according to the length of time they have been receivable from the customer. Also called the *balance-sheet approach* (*p. 228*).

Allowance for doubtful accounts. Also called *allowance for uncollectible accounts* (*p. 226*).

Allowance for uncollectible accounts. A contra account, related to accounts receivable, that holds the estimated amount of collection losses. Also called *allowance for doubtful accounts* (*p. 226*).

Allowance method. A method of recording collection losses based on estimates of how much money the business will not collect from its customers (*p. 226*).

Amortization. The systematic reduction of a lump-sum amount. Expense that applies to intangible assets in the same way depreciation applies to plant assets and depletion applies to natural resources (*p. 334*).

Asset. An economic resource that is expected to be of benefit in the future (*p. 12*).

Audit. A periodic examination of a company's financial statements and the accounting systems, controls, and records that produce them (*p. 176*).

Available-for-sale investments. All investments not classified as held-to-maturity or trading securities (*p. 471*).

Average cost method. Inventory costing method based on the average cost of inventory during the period. Average cost is determined by dividing the cost of goods available by the number of units available. Also called the *weighted average method* (*p. 268*).

Balance sheet. List of an entity's assets, liabilities, and owners' equity as of a specific date. Also called the *statement of financial position* (*p. 18*).

Balance-sheet approach. Also called *aging-of-accounts receivable* (*p. 228*).

Bank collection. Collection of money by the bank on behalf of a depositor (*p. 184*).

Bank reconciliation. A document explaining the reasons for the difference between a depositor's records and the bank's records about the depositor's (*p. 183*).

Bank statement. Document showing the beginning and ending balances of a particular bank account listing the month's transactions that affected the account (*p. 182*).

Benchmarking. The comparison of a company to a standard set by other companies, with a view toward improvement (*p. 613*).

Board of directors. Group elected by the stockholders to set policy for a corporation and to appoint its officers (*p. 9, 419*).

Bonds payable. Groups of notes payable (bonds) issued to multiple lenders called bondholders (*p. 372*).

Book value (of a plant asset). The asset's cost minus accumulated depreciation (*p. 116*).

Book value (of a stock). Amount of owners' equity on the company's books for each share of its stock (*p. 436*).

Book value per share of common stock. Common stockholders' equity divided by the number of shares of common stock outstanding. The recorded amount for each share of common stock outstanding (*p. 627*).

Brand name. See *trademark, trade name* (*p. 335*).

Budget. A quantitative expression of a plan that helps managers coordinate the entity's activities (*p. 191*).

Bylaws. Constitution for governing a corporation (*p. 419*).

Callable bonds. Bonds that the issuer may call (pay off) at a specified price whenever the issuer wants (*p. 383*).

Capital. Another name for the *owners' equity* of a business (*p. 12*).

Capital charge. The amount that stockholders and lenders charge a company for the use of their money. Calculated as (Notes payable + Loans payable + Long-term debt + Stockholders' equity) x Cost of capital (*p. 628*).

Capital expenditure. Expenditure that increases an asset's capacity or efficiency or extends its useful life. Capital expenditures are debited to an asset account (*p. 319*).

Capital lease. Lease agreement that meets any one of four criteria: (1) The lease transfers title of the leased asset to the lessee. (2) The lease contains a bargain purchase option. (3) The lease term is 75% or more of the estimated useful life of the leased asset. (4) The present value of the lease payments is 90% or more of the market value of the leased asset (*p. 388*).

Cash. Money and any medium of exchange that a bank accepts at face value (*pp. 12, 51*).

Cash equivalents. Highly liquid short-term investments that can be converted into cash immediately (*p. 549*).

Cash flows. Cash receipts and cash payments (disbursements) (*p. 548*).

Cash-basis accounting. Accounting that records only transactions in which cash is received or paid (*p. 106*).

Chairperson. Elected by a corporation's board of directors, usually the most powerful person in the corporation (*p. 419*).

Chart of accounts. List of all a company's accounts and their account numbers (*p. 72*).

Check. Document instructing a bank to pay the designated person or business the specified amount of money (*p. 182*).

Classified balance sheet. A balance sheet that shows current assets separate from long-term assets, and current liabilities separate from long-term liabilities (*p. 132*).

Clean opinion. See *unqualified (clean) opinion* (*p. 524*).

Closing entries. Entries that transfer the revenue, expense, and dividends balances from these respective accounts to the Retained Earnings account (*p. 130*).

Closing the books. The process of preparing the accounts to begin recording the next period's transactions. Closing the accounts consists of journalizing and posting the closing entries to set the balances of the revenue, expense, and dividends accounts to zero. Also called *closing the accounts* (*p. 130*).

Common stock. The most basic form of capital stock. (*pp. 13, 421*).

Common-size statement. A financial statement that reports only percentages (no dollar amounts) (*p. 612*).

Comprehensive income. A company's change in total stockholder's equity from all sources other than from the owners of the business (*p. 518*).

Conservatism. The accounting concept by which the least favorable figures are presented in the financial statements (*p. 275*).

Consistency principle. A business must use the same accounting methods and procedures from period to period (*p. 274*).

Consolidated statements. Financial statements of the parent company plus those of majority-owned subsidiaries as if the combination were a single legal entity (*p. 478*).

Contra account. An account that always has a companion account and whose normal balance is opposite that of the companion account (*p. 116*).

Contributed capital. See *paid-in capital* (*pp. 13, 420*).

Controller. The chief accounting officer of a business (*p. 175*).

Controlling (majority) interest. Ownership of more than 50% of an investee company's voting stock (*p. 478*).

Convertible bonds (or notes). Bonds (or notes) that may be converted into the issuing company's common stock at the investor's option (*p. 384*).

Copyright. Exclusive right to reproduce and sell a book, musical composition, film, other work of art, or computer program. Issued by the federal government, copyrights extend 70 years beyond the author's life (*p. 335*).

Corporation. A business owned by stockholders. A corporation is a legal entity, an "artificial person" in the eyes of the law (*p. 9*).

Cost of capital. A weighted average of the returns demanded by the company's stockholders and lenders (*p. 627*).

Cost of goods sold. Cost of the inventory the business has sold to customers (*p. 262*).

Cost principle. Principle that states that assets and services should be recorded at their actual cost (*p. 11*).

Cost-of-goods-sold model. Formula that brings together all the inventory data for the entire accounting period: Beginning inventory + Purchases = Goods available. Then, Goods available - Ending inventory = Cost of goods sold (*p. 278*).

Credit. The right side of an account (*p. 63*).

Creditor. The party to whom money is owed (*p. 218*).

Cumulative preferred stock. Preferred stock whose owners must receive all dividends in arrears before the corporation can pay dividends to the common stockholders (*p. 433*).

Current asset. An asset that is expected to be converted to cash, sold, or consumed during the next 12 months, or within the business's normal operating cycle if longer than a year (*pp. 18, 132*).

Current installment of long-term debt. The amount of the principal that is payable within one year (*p. 366*).

Current liability. A debt due to be paid within one year or within the entity's operating cycle if the cycle is longer than a year (*pp. 19, 132*).

Current ratio. Current assets divided by current liabilities. Measures a company's ability to pay current liabilities with current assets (*pp. 134, 618*).

Day's sales in receivables. Ratio of average net accounts receivable to one day's sales. Indicates how many days' sales remain in Accounts Receivable awaiting collection. Also called the collection period (*pp. 235, 622*).

Debentures. Unsecured bonds—bonds backed only by the good faith of the borrower (*p. 373*).

Debit. The left side of an account (*p. 63*).

Debt instrument. A receivable or a payable, usually some form of note (*p. 218*).

Debt ratio. Ratio of total liabilities to total assets. States the proportion of a company's assets that is financed with debt (*pp. 135, 623*).

Debtor. The party who owes money (*p. 218*).

Deferral. An adjustment for which the business paid or received cash in advance. Examples include prepaid rent, prepaid insurance, and supplies (*p. 112*).

Deficit. Debit balance in the Retained Earnings account (*p. 421*).

Depletion expense. That portion of a natural resource's cost that is used up in a particular period. Depletion expense is computed in the same way as units-of-production depreciation (*p. 334*).

Deposit in transit. A deposit recorded by the company but not yet by its bank (*p. 184*).

Depreciable cost. The cost of a plant asset minus its estimated residual value (*p. 322*).

Depreciation. Expense associated with spreading (allocating) the cost of a plant asset over its useful life (*p. 112*).

Direct method. Format of the operating activities section of the statement of cash flows; lists the major categories of operating cash receipts (collections from customers and receipts of interest and dividends) and cash disbursements (payments to suppliers, to employees, for interest and income taxes) (*p. 551*).

Direct write-off method. A method of accounting for bad debts in which the company waits until a customer's account receivable proves uncollectible and then debits Uncollectible-Account Expense and credits the customer's Account Receivable (*p. 230*).

Disclaimer. An audit opinion stating that the auditor was unable to reach a professional opinion regarding the quality of the financial statements (*p. 525*).

Disclosure principle. A business's financial statements must report enough information for outsiders to make knowledgeable decisions about the business. The company should report relevant, reliable, and comparable information about its economic affairs (*p. 275*).

Discount (on a bond). Excess of a bond's face (par value) over its issue price (*p. 373*).

Dividend.. Distribution (usually cash) by a corporation to its stockholders (*pp. 14, 432*).

Dividend yield. Ratio of dividends per share of stock to the stock's market price per share. Tells the percentage of a stock's market value that the company returns to stockholders as dividends (*p. 626*).

Double taxation. Corporations pay income taxes on corporate income. Then, the stockholders pay personal income tax on the cash dividends that they receive from corporations (*p. 419*).

Double-declining-balance (DDB) method. An accelerated depreciation method that computes annual depreciation by multiplying the asset's decreasing book value by a constant percentage, which is 2 times the straight-line rate (*p. 324*).

Earnings per share (EPS). Amount of a company's net income earned for each share of its outstanding common stock (*pp. 385, 517, 625*).

Economic value added (EVA). Used to evaluate a company's operating performance. EVA combines the concepts of accounting income and corporate finance to measure whether the company's operations have increased stockholder wealth. EVA = Net income + Interest expense - Capital charge (*p. 627*).

Efficient capital market. A capital market in which market prices fully reflect all information available to the public (*p. 629*).

Electronic fund transfer (EFT). System that transfers cash by electronic communication rather than by paper documents (*p. 182*).

Entity. An organization or a section of an organization that, for accounting purposes, stands apart from other organizations and individuals as a separate economic unit (*p. 10*).

Equity method. The method used to account for investments in which the investor has 20–50% of the investee's voting stock and can significantly influence the decisions of the investee (*p. 475*).

Equity security. Stock certificate that represents the investor's ownership in a corporation (*p. 218*).

Estimated residual value. Expected cash value of an asset at the end of its useful life. Also called *residual value*, *scrap value*, or *salvage value* (*p. 321*).

Estimated useful life. Length of a service that a business expects to get from an asset. May be expressed in years, units of output, miles, or other measures (*p. 321*).

Expense. Decrease in retained earnings that results from operations; the cost of doing business; opposite of revenues (*p. 13*).

Extraordinary gains and losses. Also called *extraordinary items*, these gains and losses are both unusual for the company and infrequent (*p. 515*).

Extraordinary items. See *extraordinary gains and losses* (*p. 515*).

FIFO (first-in, first out) method. Inventory costing methods by which the first costs into inventory are the first costs out to cost of goods sold. Ending inventory is based on the costs of the most recent purchases (*p. 267*).

Financial accounting. The branch of accounting that provides information to people outside the firm (*p. 6*).

Financial statements. Business documents that report financial information about a business entity to decision makers (*p. 5*).

Financing activities. Activities that obtain from investors and creditors the cash needed to launch and sustain the business; a section of the statement of cash flows (*pp. 20, 550*).

Fixed assets. See *property, plant, and equipment* (*p. 12*).

Foreign-currency exchange rate. The measure of one country's currency against another country's currency (*p. 485*).

Foreign-currency translation adjustment. The balancing figure that brings the dollar amount of the total liabilities and stockholders' equity of the foreign subsidiary into agreement with the dollar amount of its total assets (*p. 488*).

Franchises and licenses. Privileges granted by a private business or a government to sell a product or service in accordance with specified conditions (*p. 336*).

Free cash flow. The amount of cash available from operations after paying for planned investments in plant, equipment, and other long-term assets (*p. 573*).

Generally accepted accounting principles (GAAP). Accounting guidelines, formulated by the Financial Accounting Standards Board, that govern how accounting is practical (*p. 9*).

Going-concern concept. Holds that the entity will remain in operation for the foreseeable future (*p. 11*).

Goodwill. Excess of the cost of an acquired company over the sum of the market values of its net assets (assets minus liabilities) (*p. 336*).

Gross margin method. See *gross profit method* (*p. 279*).

Gross margin percentage. See *gross profit percentage* (*p. 276*).

Gross margin. See *gross profit* (*p. 263*).

Gross profit. Sales revenue minus cost of goods sold. Also called *gross margin* (*p. 263*).

Gross profit method. A way to estimate inventory based on a rearrangement of the cost-of-goods-sold model: Beginning inventory + net purchases = Goods available - Cost of goods sold = Ending inventory. Also called the *gross margin method* (*p. 279*).

Gross profit percentage. Gross profit divided by net sales revenue. Also called the *gross margin percentage* (*p. 276*).

Hedging. To protect oneself from losing money in one transaction by engaging in a counterbalancing transaction (*p. 488*).

Held-to-maturity investments. Bonds and notes that an investor intends to hold until maturity (*p. 481*).

Horizontal analysis. Study of percentage changes in comparative financial statements (*p. 609*).

Imprest system. A way to account for petty cash by maintaining a constant balance in the petty cash account, supported by the fund (cash plus payment tickets) totaling the same amount (*p. 191*).

Income statement. A financial statement listing an entity's revenues, expenses, and net income or net loss for a specific period. Also called the *statement of operations* (*p. 16*).

Indirect method. Format of the operating activities section of the statement of cash flows; starts with net income and reconciles to cash flows from operating activities. (*p. 551*).

Intangible asset. An asset with no physical form, a special right to current and expected future benefits (*p. 316*).

Interest. The borrower's cost of renting money from a lender. Interest is revenue for the lender and expense for the borrower (*p. 232*).

Interest-coverage ratio. See *times-interest-earned ratio* (*p. 623*).

Internal control. Organizational plan and related measures adopted by an entity to safeguard assets, encourage adherence to company policies, promote operational efficiency, and ensure accurate and reliable accounting records (*p. 174*).

Inventory. The merchandise that a company sells to customers (*p. 262*).

Inventory turnover. Ratio of cost of goods sold to average inventory. Indicates how rapidly inventory is sold (*pp. 278, 621*).

Investing activities. Activities that increase or decrease the long-term assets available to the business; a section of the statement of cash flows (*pp. 20, 550*).

Investment capitalization rate. An earnings rate used to estimate the value of an investment in stock (*p. 514*).

Journal. The chronological accounting record of an entity's transactions (*p. 65*).

Lease. Rental agreement in which the tenant (lessee) agrees to make rent payments to the property owner (lessor) in exchange for the use of the asset (*p. 387*).

Ledger. The book of accounts and their balances (*p. 66*).

Legal capital. Minimum amount of stockholders' equity that a corporation must maintain for the protection of creditors. For corporation's with par-value stock, legal capital is the par value of the stock issued (*p. 422*).

Lessee. Tenant in a lease agreement (*p. 387*).

Lessor. Property owner in a lease agreement (*p. 387*).

Leverage. See *trading on the equity* (*pp. 385, 625*).

Liability. An economic obligation (a debt) payable to an individual or an organization outside the business (*p. 12*).

LIFO (last-in, first-out) method. Inventory costing method by which the last costs into inventory are the first costs out to cost of goods sold. This method leaves the oldest costs—those of beginning inventory and the earliest purchases of the period—in ending inventory (*p. 267*).

Limited liability. No personal obligation of a stockholder for corporation debts. A stockholder can lose no more on an investment in a corporation's stock than the cost of the investment (*pp. 132, 418*).

Liquidity. Measure of how quickly an item can be converted to cash (*p. 132*).

Long-term asset. An asset that is not a current asset (*p. 132*).

Long-term debt. A liability that falls due beyond one year from the date of the financial statements (*p. 13*).

Long-term investment. Any investment that does not meet the criteria of a short-term investment; any investment that the investor expects to hold longer than a year or that is not readily marketable (*p. 470*).

Long-term liability. A liability that is not a current liability (*p. 132*).

Lower-of-cost-or-market (LCM) rule. Requires that an asset be reported in the financial statements at whichever is lower—its historical cost or its market value (current replacement cost for inventory) (*p. 275*).

Management accounting. The branch of accounting that generates information for the internal decision makers of a business, such as top executives (*p. 6*).

Market interest rate. Interest rate that investors demand for loaning their money. Also called *effective interest rate* (*p. 374*).

Market value (of a stock). Price for which a person could buy or sell a share of stock (*p. 435*).

Marketable securities. See *short-term investment* (*pp. 218, 470*).

Matching principle. The basis for recording expenses. Directs accountants to identify all expenses incurred during the period, to measure the expenses, and to match them against the revenues earned during that same period (*p. 109*).

Maturity. The date on which a debt instrument must be paid (*p. 218*).

Merchandise inventory. The merchandise that a company sells to customers (*p. 12*).

Minority interest. A subsidiary company's equity that is held by stockholders other than the parent company (*p. 480*).

Modified Accelerated Cost Recovery System (MACRS). A special depreciation method used only for income tax purposes. Assets are grouped into classes, and for a given class depreciation is computed by the double-declining-balance method, the 150%-declining balance method, or, for most real estate, the straight-line method (*p. 329*).

Multi-step income statement. An income statement that contains subtotals to highlight important relationships between revenues and expenses (*p. 134*).

Net earnings. See *net income* (*p. 13*).

Net income. Excess of total revenues over total expenses. Also called *net earnings* or *net profit* (*p. 13*).

Net loss. Excess of total expenses over total revenues (*p. 14*).

Nonsufficient funds (NSF) check. A "hot" check, one for which the payer's bank account has insufficient money to pay the check. NSF checks are cash receipts that turn out to be worthless (*p. 184*).

Note payable. A liability evidenced by a written promise to make a future payment (*p. 13*).

Objectivity principle. See *reliability principle* (*p. 10*).

Operating activities. Activities that create revenue or expense in the entity's major line of business; a section of the statement of cash flows. Operating activities affect the income statement (*pp. 20, 550*).

Operating cycle. Time span during which cash is paid for goods and services that are sold to customers who pay the business in cash (*p. 132*).

Operating lease. Usually a short-term or cancelable rental agreement (*p. 387*).

Outstanding check. A check issued by the company and recorded on its books but not yet paid by its bank (*p. 184*).

Outstanding stock. Stock in the hands of stockholders (*p. 421*).

Owners' equity. The claim of the owners of a business to the assets of the business. Also called *capital, stockholders' equity,* or *net assets* (*p. 12*).

Paid-in capital. The amount of stockholders' equity that stockholders have contributed to the corporation. Also called *contributed capital* (*pp. 13, 420*).

Par value. Arbitrary amount assigned by a company to a share of its stock (*p. 422*).

Parent company. An investor company that owns more than 50% of the voting stock of a subsidiary company (*p. 478*).

Partnership. An association of two or more persons who co-own a business for profit (*p. 8*).

Patent. A federal government grant giving the holder the exclusive right for 20 years to produce and sell an invention (*p. 33*).

Payroll. Employee compensation, a major expense of many businesses (*p. 366*).

Pension. Employee compensation that will be received during retirement (*p. 389*).

Percent-of-sales-method. Computes uncollectible-account expense as a percentage of net sales. Also called the *income statement approach* because it focuses on the amount of expense to be reported on the income statement (*p. 227*).

Periodic inventory system. An inventory system in which the business does not keep a continuous record of the inventory on hand. Instead, at the end of the period, the business makes a physical count of the inventory on hand and applies the appropriate unit costs to determine the cost of the ending inventory (*p. 264*).

Permanent account. Asset, liability, and stockholders' equity accounts that are not closed at the end of the period (*p. 130*).

Perpetual inventory system. An inventory system in which the business keeps a continuous record for each inventory item to show the inventory on hand at all times (*p. 264*).

Petty cash. Fund containing a small amount of cash that is used to pay minor amounts (*p. 190*).

Plant assets. Long-lived assets, such as land, buildings, and equipment, used in the operation of the business. Also called *fixed assets* (*pp. 12, 115, 316*).

Posting. Copying amounts from the journal to the ledger (*p. 66*).

Preferred stock. Stock that gives its owners certain advantages, such as the priority to receive dividends before the common stockholders and the priority to receive assets before the common stockholders if the corporation liquidates (*p. 421*).

Premium (on a bond). Excess of a bond's issue price over its face (par) value (*p. 373*).

Prepaid expense. A category of miscellaneous assets that typically expire or get used up in the near future. Examples include prepaid rent, prepaid insurance, and supplies (*p. 51, 113*).

Present value. Amount a person would invest now to receive a greater amount at a future date (*p. 374*).

President. Chief operating officer in charge of managing the day-to-day operations of a corporation (*p. 419*).

Pretax accounting income. Income before tax on the income statement (*p. 520*).

Price/earnings ratio. Ratio of the market price of a share of common stock to the company's earnings per share. Measures the value that the stock market places on $1 of a company's earnings (*p. 626*).

Principal. The amount borrowed by a debtor and lent by a creditor (*p. 232*).

Prior-period adjustment. A correction to beginning balance of retained earnings for an error of an earlier period (*p. 521*).

Property, plant, and equipment. Long-lived assets, such as land, buildings, and equipment, used in the operation of the business. Also called *plant assets* or *fixed assets* (*p. 12*).

Proprietorship. A business with a single owner (*p. 8*).

Purchase allowance. A decrease in the cost of purchases because the seller has granted the buyer a subtraction (an allowance) from the amount owed (*p. 265*).

Purchase discount. A decrease in the cost of purchases earned by making an early payment to the vendor (*p. 266*).

Purchase return. A decrease in the cost of purchases because the buyer returned the goods to the seller (*p. 265*).

Qualified opinion. An audit opinion stating that the financial statements are reliable, except for one or more items for which the opinion is said to be qualified (*p. 524*).

Quick ratio. See *acid-test ratio* (*p. 236*).

Rate of return on common stockholders' equity. Net income minus preferred dividends, divided by average common stockholders' equity. A measure of profitability. Also called *return on equity* (*pp. 438, 624*).

Rate of return on net sales. Ratio of net income to net sales. A measure of profitability. Also called *return on sales* (*p. 624*).

Rate of return on total assets. Net income plus interest expense, divided by average total assets. This ratio measures a company's success in using its assets to earn income for the persons who finance the business. Also called *return on assets* (*p. 437*).

Receivables. Monetary claims against a business or an individual, acquired mainly by selling goods or services and by lending money (*p. 223*).

Reliability principle. The accounting principle that ensures that accounting records and statements are based on the most reliable data available. Also called the *objectivity principle* (*p. 10*).

Report format. A balance-sheet format that lists assets at the top, followed by liabilities and stockholders' equity below (*p. 133*).

Retained earnings. The amount of stockholders' equity that the corporation has earned through profitable operation and has not given back to stockholders (*pp. 13, 420*).

Return on assets. See *rate of return on total assets* (*pp. 437, 624*).

Return on equity. See *rate of return on common stockholders' equity* (*pp. 438, 624*).

Revenue. Increase in retained earnings from delivering goods or services to customers or clients (*p. 13*).

Revenue principle. The basis for recording revenues; tells accountants when to record revenue and the amount of revenue to record (*p. 109*).

Segment of the business. An identifiable part of a company (*p. 515*).

Serial bonds. Bonds that mature in installments over a period of time (*p. 373*).

Shareholder. Another name for a *stockholder* (*p. 9*).

Short-term investment. Investment that a company plans to hold for 1 year or less. Also called *marketable securities* (*pp. 218, 470*).

Short-term note payable. Note payable due within one-year (*p. 364*).

Single-step income statement. An income statement that lists all the revenues together under a heading such as Revenues or Revenues and Gains. Expenses appear in a separate category called Expenses, Costs or perhaps Expenses and Losses (*p. 133*).

Specific-unit-cost method. Inventory cost method based on the specific cost of particular units of inventory (*p. 268*).

Stable-monetary-unit concept. The basis for ignoring the effect of inflation in the accounting records, based on the assumption that the dollar's purchasing power is relatively stable (*p. 11*).

Stated interest rate. Interest rate that determines the amount of cash interest the borrower pays and the investor receives each year (*p. 374*).

Stated value. An arbitrary amount assigned to no-par stock; similar to par value (*p. 422*).

Statement of cash flows. Reports cash receipts and cash payments classified according to the entity's major activities: operating, investing, and financing (*p. 21, 548*).

Statement of financial position. See *balance sheet* (*p. 18*).

Statement of operations. See *balance sheet* (*p. 18*).

Statement of retained earnings. Summary of the changes in the retained earnings of a corporation during a specific period (*p. 17*).

Statement of stockholders' equity. Reports the changes in all categories of stockholders' equity during the period (*p. 522*).

Stock. Shares into which the owners' equity of a corporation is divided (*pp. 9, 421*).

Stock dividend. A proportional distribution by a corporation of its own stock to its stockholders (*p. 433*).

Stock split. An increase in the number of authorized, issued, and outstanding shares of stock coupled with a proportionate reduction in the stock's par value (*p. 435*).

Stockholder. A person who owns stock in a corporation. Also called a *shareholder* (*pp. 9, 418*).

Stockholders' equity. The stockholders' ownership interest in the assets of a corporation (*pp. 13, 420*).

Straight-line (SL) method. Depreciation method in which an equal amount of depreciation expense is assigned to each year of asset use (*p. 322*).

Strong currency. A currency whose exchange rate is rising relative to other nations' currencies (*p. 485*).

Subsidiary company. An investee company in which a parent company owns more than 50% of the voting stock (*p. 478*).

Taxable income. The basis for computing the amount of tax to pay the government (*p. 520*).

Temporary account. The revenue and expense accounts that relate to a limited period and are closed at the end of the period are temporary accounts. For a corporation, the Dividends account is also temporary (*p. 130*).

Term. The length of time from inception to maturity (*p. 218*).

Term bonds. Bonds that all mature at the same time for a particular issue (*p. 373*).

Time-period concept. Ensures that accounting information is reported at regular intervals (*p. 108*).

Times-interest-earned ratio. Ratio of income from operations to interest expense. Measures the number of times that operating income can cover interest expense. Also called the *interest-coverage ratio* (*p. 623*).

Trademark, trade name. A distinctive identification of a product or service. Also called a *brand name* (*p. 335*).

Trading investments. Stock investments that are to be sold in the near future with the intent of generating profits on the sale (*p. 219*).

Trading on the equity. Earning more income on borrowed money than the related interest expense, thereby increasing the earnings for the owners of the business. Also called *leverage* (*p. 385*).

Transaction. Any event that has a financial impact on the business and can be measured reliably (*p. 50*).

Treasury stock. A corporation's own stock that it has issued and later reacquired (*p. 429*).

Trend percentages. A form of horizontal analysis that indicates the direction a business is taking (*p. 611*).

Trial balance. A list of all the ledger accounts with their balances (*p. 71*).

Uncollectible-account expense. Cost to the seller of extending credit. Arises from the failure to collect from credit customers. Also called doubtful-account expense or bad-debt expense (*p. 226*).

Underwriter. Organization that purchases the bonds from an issuing company and resells them to its clients or sells the bonds for a commission, agreeing to buy all unsold bonds (*p. 373*).

Unearned revenue. A liability created when a business collects cash from customers in advance of earning the revenue. The obligation is to provide a product or a service in the future (*p. 119*).

Units-of-production (UOP) method. Depreciation method by which a fixed amount of depreciation is assigned to each unit of output produced by the plant asset (*p. 323*).

Unqualified (clean) opinion. An audit opinion stating that the financial statements are reliable (*p. 524*).

Vertical analysis. Analysis of a financial statement that reveals the relationship of each statement item to a specified base, which is the 100% figure (*p. 611*).

Weak currency. A currency whose exchange rate is falling relative to that of other nations (*p. 485*).

Working capital. Current assets minus current liabilities; measures a business's ability to meet its short-term obligations with its current assets (*p. 618*).

Company Index

Real company names are in bold type,

V

W

X

Y

Z